Portrait
miniature by
Nicholas
Hilliard

'Young Man
among Roses'

THE STORY
THAT
THE
SONNETS
TELL

A.D. WRAIGHT

ADAM HART (Publishers) Ltd
LONDON U.K.

By the same author
in collaboration with Virginia F. Stern
IN SEARCH OF CHRISTOPHER MARLOWE
First published 1965, London and NY
Reissued paperback February 1993

CHRISTOPHER MARLOWE AND EDWARD ALLEYN
A.D. Wraight
First Published October 1993

First Published in 1994 by
ADAM HART (Publishers) Ltd
London SE27 9HG
England

A Catalogue Record of this title
is held at the British Library

Hardback ISBN 1 897763 01 8
Paperback ISBN 1 897763 05 0

Typeset by Remus Print Services, London SE23 3TY England
Printed and bound by The Cromwell Press
Broughton Gifford, Melksham, Wiltshire England

IN MEMORIAM

To the Great 'Sherlock Holmes'
of the Elizabethan Era

J. LESLIE HOTSON

We are all aware. . . of an ever-present danger: nothing is easier in any kind of investigation than to overlook a vital piece of evidence staring us in the face. For if that piece of evidence does not seem to corroborate or to fall in with our already-settled ideas, our minds either simply ignore it, or else wrest it by 'interpretation' to make it mean what we think it ought to mean. Such behaviour is certainly human, but it blocks the road to knowledge.

J. Leslie Hotson
The First Night of Twelfth Night
(1964)

CONTENTS

PART ONE

PART TWO

PART THREE
THE BOOK OF THE SONNETS   425

ILLUSTRATIONS

PROLOGUE

IN THIS BOOK you are invited to embark on a literary Odyssey through the *Sonnets* of Shakespeare to discover the vibrant Poet behind the accretion of traditional mythos that has clothed his genius in a garment of mediocrity. Our aim is to reach the essential, living breathing man whose heart beats in these autobiographical poems, and to unlock their centuries-old secret, which has been aptly named 'The Riddle of the Sonnets'.

The quest is one that has defied all previous attempts. Although research on Shakespeare's life has been more intense and more universally pursued than on any other historical figure, nothing has been discovered to date establishing unequivocally a single event, or person addressed in the book called SHAKE-SPEARES SONNETS, published by T. Thorpe in 1609. Nevertheless, by general consensus of informed, scholarly opinion, his sonnets are held to represent Shakespeare's sole autobiographical testimony. The editor of the Penguin edition of the *Sonnets*, G.B. Harrison, has described them as

> 'personal and intimate poems written to individuals, which would tell much of Shakespeare's life if only some facts about them could be indisputably established.'[1]

That is what is offered here in what may be claimed as a 'break-through' in Shakespearean research. My *modus operandi* has been to take the Sonnets *literally* as my guide – a method adopted with singular success by Dr. Leslie Hotson in his *Shakespeare's Sonnets Dated* (1949) to elucidate the meaning of three sonnets which had previously defied explanation: *Sonnets 107, 123* and *124*. The application of this method to the entire sonnet-sequence, uninhibited by preconceptions as to where it might lead, has produced the astonishing results presented in this book.

For striking corroboration that the Poet's Word, taken literally, can be trusted to lead to historical discovery, a precedent has been set by two researchers in pursuit of the historical truth about the War of Troy. First, the nineteenth century German business-tycoon-turned-amateur-archaeologist, Heinrich Schliemann, took the epic poems of Homer as his sole guide to excavate the place which he believed, according to Homer's description, to have been the site of 'windy Troy'. His quest was laughed at by the academics as the mad scheme of a crazy romantic who believed that Homer – a poet – spoke the literal truth. In the face of their derision, Schliemann believed that archaeological excavation would prove his case. He had taught himself both modern and ancient Greek so that he could read Homer in the original, and, knowing large tracts of Homer's poems by heart, he set out to prove that the Poet's Word spoke the historical truth. There is no need for me here to describe the thrilling discovery of what proved to be one of the richest archaeological finds ever made, which has been so memorably told in Leonard Cottrell's book, *The Bull of Minos* (1953).

It matters little now that Schliemann erroneously believed that the golden death-mask he found at Mycenae and called 'the Face of Agamemnon' was later proved to be of an even earlier date than the Trojan War was then calculated; nor is it of exclusive significance that Schliemann's work has since been superseded by the immense research of the classical scholar Iman Wilkens, the Dutchman whose revolutionary relocation of Homer's world to Western Europe is presented in his fascinating book, *Where Troy Once Stood* (1990). Man's discoveries advance in ways that are often tortuous and uneven, outdating what had been accepted to make a new leap in the unravelling of scientific knowledge about our world and universe, or rolling back the mists of time. This does not invalidate the process of our progress. Wilkens, like Schliemann, relied on the detailed descriptions given by Homer, but in a far wider sense, not merely of Troy, but of the topography of the entire setting of the *Iliad* and the *Odyssey*, which does not fit the Aegean, but is precisely found in Western Europe where it is supported by the profusion of etomological remains of Homer's ancient place-names. These names were only long after the Trojan War transferred by the migration of Western European tribes to Greece, just as their familiar place-names have migrated with the peoples who crossed the Atlantic to settle in the New World or travelled south to Australia. Both Wilkens and Schliemann took Homer's poetry literally as their trusted guide to produce exciting results shedding light on different aspects of the ancient Homeric epic; both open to debate and controversy, but each contributing something inspiring and historically important for us to consider.

Both these seekers after the historical truth of Homer's epic story trusted the inherent historicity of the Poet's Word to make their amazing discoveries. Schliemann added to the history of archaeology one of its richest, most exciting and romantic chapters by believing that Homer, though a poet, was describing *real* historical events. Wilkens consolidated this by trusting the Poet's Word as an accurate description of the topography of his familiar world to establish the real site of Priam's Troy and to trace the homelands of the Achaean warriors who made common cause to attack it; and by dauntlessly sailing in the wake of Odysseus he uncovered the heartland of the Celtic mystery cult from which the Greek pantheon derived. These Homeric explorers have added a new criterion of judgement in historical research by taking the Poet's Word as their reliable guide to discovery.

I purpose to do the same. When our Poet writes of his 'outcast state' and of 'large lengths of miles' that separate him from his friends, and exhorts the recipient of his sonnets, 'Do not so much as my poor name rehearse', I take it that he means exactly what he says, and is not merely indulging in poetic rhetoric. This is not to say that he makes no use of poetic conventions, or employs none of the artifices of his art.

The hyperbole of poetic imagery of the time abounds in the flattering and evocative use of language in praise of a patron, which rarely means literally what it says. It is for us to ponder when the Poet is to be taken literally, and when he is embellishing his poems to enhance their beauty and their emotive power in an imaginative, a-literal use of words, without losing our way and mistrusting him when he is telling us the literal truth.

The genius of men like Schliemann and Wilkens lies in that they did not allow their minds to be misled by the element of fairytale and imagination in poetry, so that the historical facts embedded in Homer's epics were not obscured. They saw clearly what others did not see. With them I place Leslie Hotson, who also attuned his ear to the Poet's Word, applying this method in the light of what the Elizabethan language really meant, to discover the identities of 'Mr.W.H.' and the Dark Lady. I have only had to adjust his sights, which are bound by his orthodox academic preconceptions, in order to focus them to reveal the true sonnet-story, which presents a seamless and coherent account of our poet-dramatist's life with clearly recognisable persons and events.

This is an historic record as is any diary. It is this precision and certitude of factual historic evidence matching these poems that alone led me on to research ever further as the story unfolded. Testing every poem in the entire sonnet-sequence with the relevant facts, step by step, the chronological confusion as presented in Thorpe's cryptic edition gradually gave way to the correct chronological sequence of the poems to reveal the moving autobiographical story that has lain for so long obscured and misunderstood in the 'Riddle of the Sonnets', a story that is as amazing as it is inspiring.

In essence, this is an historical detective story which is as great a drama as any play that Shakespeare wrote. It poses the solving of several historical conundrums besides the solution of the cryptic dedication of the *Sonnets* to the mysterious 'Mr.W.H.' and boldly delves into the problems raised by those puzzling, dark sonnets that speak insistently of disgrace, anonymity, exile and personal hurt, for which orthodoxy can offer no explanation. It asks hitherto unasked, potentially revealing questions, almost all of which have been answered with gratifying certitude. The reader is invited to test these personally, sonnet by sonnet.

This revolutionary thesis is not an end, but a new beginning, presaging a surge of eager research on Shakespeare to follow up the many clues here uncovered. Others will predictably follow to fill in the extraordinary life story and the vibrant portrait that has emerged of a charismatic personality, whose genius is illuminated by rare qualities of humanity, highest intelligence, broad-mindedness, understanding, wit, humour and heroism. This is a man who is rightly honoured universally as the creator of the greatest dramatic works about the human condition, which, written in the English language, yet speak across the boundaries of race, language and creed to all humanity in many translations, and once we really know him and understand his message his power to move us will increase. He is too great a man to remain forever the 'sacred cow' of academic and commercial self-interest. His true spirit, once discovered, will be liberated. It is for the reader to judge whether this has been achieved.

Acknowledgements and Apologies

My enormous indebtedness to Dr. Leslie Hotson is expressed in my dedication of this book to him. It remains for me to add here my gratitude to his widow, Mary Peabody Hotson, in her own right a consummate artiste of Elizabethan songs and music with which she has delighted many audiences in performances of sheer enchantment, for her kind acceptance on behalf of Leslie Hotson of this dedication at a time when he was in hospital after suffering a fall on his boat which he was still sailing at the age of 93. His recent death at the age of 95 is a grievous loss.

I wish also to acknowledge my gratitude to the late Dr. C.B. Williams for permission to include his article, 'A Note on an Early Study of Literary Style', which was kindly granted by the owner of the copyright, Mr. James Griffin, who wrote to say that as he had known Dr. Williams personally he was 'quite certain that this lovely man would have been delighted to grant his permission too had he been here.'

My sincere thanks are due to many friends who have helped and supported me in this long task. I am especially grateful to Prospero for his trouble in researching and providing copies of the articles on Dr. Mendenhall's work mentioned above, and for his unfailing interest and enthusiasm; to my true friend Olivia for drawing my attention to Donald W.Foster's paper on the *Sonnets*, and for not stinting her critical comments that sharpened my own critical faculties; to Tybalt for ruthlessly eradicating the 'But' from my manuscript as a beginning to sentences (there are a few left as mementos); to my beloved Beatrice and Benedick for being so incisively critical, yet supportive and appraising from beginning to end; to Orlando and Rosalind for their valuable assistance in the early editing of my text with such care and ever generous support and interest; and latterly, in its revised form, to the faithful Gonzalo for picking up some important errata in my manuscript, adding comments from his fund of erudition; above all, to my dear Coriolanus, who was so fortuitously here on his sabbatical year and, with his lovely wife Virgilia, gave me enthusiastic encouragement and provided his invaluable practical expertise in critically editing the first draft of the book, bringing to bear a sceptical, scientifically trained mind. I want also to thank the lovely Titania and her Oberon, who with their charming fairy family have sustained me with their keen interest over the many years for what seemed never-ending research in the Elizabethan period for which we share a passion, providing a sounding board for my interpretations and findings. Last, but certainly not least, I thank my loyal Hermione, and her family, without whom this book might never have been launched; next to herself, Perdita, who has happily found her Florizel; and that temerarious, volatile spirit, Mercutio, who spurred me on to accept this daunting challenge, heedless of obstacles that would have to be overcome.

I wish to offer two sincere apologies. Firstly, to express my deep regret that I have not been able to avoid severely criticising the last work of the late Dr. William Urry, most lovable of men and deeply mourned. Had he been able to read my thesis before his last fatal illness, I am convinced he would have revised his opinion to concur with mine. Secondly, to Professor Samuel Schoenbaum, whose wit and learning I reverence, for my failure to heed his worldly-wise admonition, waggishly given by our mutual, late lamented friend, Puck, 'Not to rock the boat'. I fear that my apostasy may have wrecked the leaky vessel! But he need not really worry. Of all mortals who have ever lived, Shakespeare is truly, gloriously and jubilantly immortal.

October 1994   A.D.W.

PART ONE

THE PRESENTATION OF
THE ARGUMENT

SHAKE-SPEARES

SONNETS.

Neuer before Imprinted.

AT LONDON
By *G. Eld* for *T. T.* and are
to be solde by *william Aspley.*
1609. Q 4

Title page of Thorpe's edition of
The Sonnets 1609

I

SHAKE-SPEARES SONNETS
Neuer before Imprinted

'With this key Shakespeare unlocked his heart'
William Wordsworth

SHAKESPEARE'S *SONNETS* are his sole autobiographical legacy to us, and as such they hold a unique place in our literature deserving of the most dedicated and intensive study we can give them. This has certainly not been wanting. Yet the galaxy of profound scholars who have attempted to penetrate the mysteries of these 154 beautiful poems have between them been unable to elucidate answers that are acceptable or enlightening with regard to the Poet's life. As Edward Hubler, in the appropriately titled collection of critical, interpretative essays, *The Riddle of Shakespeare's Sonnets*, has remarked:

> 'With the possible exception of *Hamlet,* no work of Shakespeare's
> has called forth more commentary and controversy than his sonnets,
> and on no other work has more nonsense been written.' [1]

This collection of intimate, personal poems was not published until 1609, only some two years before William Shakespeare disappeared from the London scene and total silence descended on his creative genius until his death at the age of fifty-two in 1616.

From the first, the appearance of the *Sonnets*, with their tantalizingly cryptic dedication signed 'T.T.' by their publisher, Thomas Thorpe, must have raised speculation, and after nearly four centuries many seemingly unanswerable questions still hover unresolved around the poems. To whom were they addressed and dedicated? To what events in the life of the author do they refer? When precisely, or even approximately, were they written? Whose hand was behind their arrangement – the author's or the publisher's? Why did Shakespeare, apparently never averse to any transaction that would financially benefit him, defer publication of his sonnet series until many years after the Elizabethan sonneteering vogue had spent itself? So that, whereas all other sonnet sequences went into many editions, his only made one very limited edition, never to be reprinted for over thirty years? Was their publication, in fact, suppressed?

To date not a single one of these questions has been satisfactorily answered, although theories abound.

On 20th May 1609 'a Booke called Shakespeare's sonnettes' had been entered in the Stationers' Register establishing the copyright to Thomas Thorpe for publication. A rare and fascinating piece of personal documentation has high-lighted for us the appearance of Thorpe's slim quarto volume on the book-seller's stall. On the back of a letter dated 19th June 1609, the famous Elizabethan actor, Edward Alleyn, recorded the items of a shopping list in which he noted his purchase of 'a book Shaksper Sonetts – 5d.' [2] They must have been just off the press.

What did Alleyn make of these poems? one wonders. The cryptic dedication 'TO.THE.ONLIE.BEGETTER...Mr.W.H.' may not have mystified him, for Edward Alleyn had a wide knowledge of dealings in the theatrical world of his day. He probably had a good idea who 'Mr.W.H.' was, or was not, and he may have noted with a wry smile that the 'well-wishing adventurer . . T.T.' was tak-ing a risk in publishing these revealing personal poems. Thomas Thorpe's ini-tials at the end of the dedication, instead of the author's, suggests that he was publishing this collection of poems without their author's sanction, and most editors of the *Sonnets* take the view that the curious wording of the dedication is Thorpe's invention, since he signed it.

Copyright (or what stood for it in those days, for it did not exist in the form we now know it) was the arena for profits to the first claimant to make his entry in the Stationers' Register, and many of the publishers and printers were none too scrupulous how this was achieved. Publishers frequently transgressed authorial rights, ascribing poems, plays and writings to the wrong authors in a chaotic scramble to bring out publications which would turn a pretty penny for them; much work being also published anonymously. By the late 1590's the, by then, famous name of *William Shakespeare* was freely used to promote the sale of publications of plays and poems not from his pen at all. Thus the collection of poems called *The Passionate Pilgrim* 'By W. Shakespeare', brought out in 1599 by the printer William Jaggard, was actually a miscellany of twenty poems by no less than five different poets, plus nine unidentified poems, together with three poems taken from *Love's Labour's Lost*, and two sonnets (numbers *138* and *144* from the Dark Lady group) by Shakespeare.

Despite these flagrant misappropriations, *The Passionate Pilgrim* went tri-umphantly into three editions under the name 'W. Shakespeare'. The third edi-tion in 1612 drew an angry complaint from Thomas Heywood, for Jaggard had been bold enough to augment his piratical miscellany with two more literary thefts; this time from Heywood's *Troia Britannica* – his two love letters between Helen of Troy and Paris – which had evidently taken Jaggard's fancy.

Heywood, less tolerant than Shakespeare, protested against 'the manifest injury done me in that work' (Jaggard's piracy), adding: 'the Author I know much offended with Mr. Jaggard that (altogether unknown to him) presumed to make so bold with him name'[3] . Jaggard need not have worried, however; although Shakespeare's name was continually used, apparently without his authority, he has never gone on record in his own person as having complained about this misuse, though prone to be litigious in matters touching his property. Was he perhaps getting a rake-off on the works to which he was so generously and uncomplainingly 'lending' his famous name? The freedom with which it was used by publishers almost suggests a tacit business arrangement.

How Thomas Thorpe acquired the manuscript of the *Sonnets* we do not know, but among the publishing fraternity T.T. was a sly one. In 1600 he had boasted gleefully to his fellow publisher, Edward Blount, of his acquisition of Marlowe's translation of the First Book of Lucan's *Pharsalia*, which had once been in Blount's copyright. T.T. enjoyed a bit of one-up-manship. How he managed to lay his hands on this latest prize is something we would all give a great deal to know, for the *Sonnets* comprise a truly remarkable collection of poems which is almost a personal confessional of the most acclaimed poet-dramatist of his day, and all our days. Additionally, Thorpe had acquired the manuscript of a poem of somewhat maudlin weepiness entitled *A Lover's Complaint* about a lovelorn, abandoned maiden, which some critics have expressed difficulty in ascribing to Shakespeare. Thorpe, of course, found no such difficulty, and the two works are printed together under the best selling name, William Shakespeare.

Several distinguished scholars doubt whether Thorpe had been given these poems by Shakespeare himself for publication, or whether he had, in fact, appropriated them without their author's knowledge. Samuel Schoenbaum, most objective of all Shakespearean authorities, comments: 'All the signs point to an unauthorized publication: unauthorized, that is, by the writer, not the Stationers' Hall.'[4] The fact that the *Sonnets* had never been published during the high season of the sonneteering fashion suggests that in their author's eyes they were private papers and not for public consumption.

After 1598 the publication of sonnet sequences abruptly ceased as the sonneteering vogue, which had become all the rage with the posthumous publication of Sir Philip Sidney's *Astrophel* and *Stella*, petered out. The popular imagination had been caught by the unconsummated love story of Sidney's sonnet series, which may also have gained glamour from his tragic death from wounds sustained in the Battle of Zutphen. This much admired Elizabethan soldier-poet and scholar, whose love for the Lady Penelope Devereux, the young sister of the Earl of Essex, had been thwarted by her marriage to the wealthy but hated Lord Rich, was later married himself, and happily, to Frances Walsingham, daughter of Queen Elizabeth's Secretary of State, Sir Francis Walsingham; but it was generally recognized that his early love for Penelope had been the inspiration for his *Astrophel* and *Stella* left in manuscript. Following the publication of this sonnet sequence in 1591, every scribbling poet had tried his hand at emulating Sidney's superb achievement in the genre, and sonneteering an imaginary lady, or eulogizing a flesh and blood patroness disguised under another name in idealized form, became the most popular poetic pastime. No less than twenty sonnet sequences were published in quick succession within a space of some six years, the most popular going into several editions.

If Shakespeare wrote his sonnets during this period, or even earlier as an innovator rather than a slavish follower of fashion, as has been posited by Dr.

Leslie Hotson in his *Mr. W.H.*, it is extraordinary that they were not published at this golden time. They were only handed round among his 'private friends' in manuscript, according to Francis Meres, a literary schoolmaster who wrote a critique and commentary on contemporary ideas and people entitled *Palladis Tamia* in 1598, in which he included a section reviewing the English poets in comparison with the classical authors. Of Shakespeare he wrote:

> 'As the soule of *Euphorbus* was thought to liue in *Pythagoras:* so the sweete wittie soule of *Ouid* liues in mellifluous & hony-tongued *Shakespeare*, witnes his *Venus* and *Adonis,* his *Lucrece,* his sugred Sonnets among his priuate friends, &c.' [5]

In some respects Meres was a purveyor of unreliable gossip rather than an authority, and he may not have seen any of these sonnets personally. However, this sounds like honest reportage, though it could not be taken to refer to the entire sequence many of which are anything but 'sugred'.

Thorpe's 1609 quarto was the first and only complete publication of Shakespeare's sonnet sequence in his lifetime. Even this single edition was soon suppressed, if we may judge from the total absence of contemporary reference to the content of this remarkable autobiographical collection of poems, which one would have expected to cause at least a ripple of comment in literary circles.

Not until thirty years later did John Benson bring out his edition of *Poems: Written by Wil. Shakespeare, Gent.* (1640) in which he published 146 of the Sonnets, but interspersed them with 17 miscellaneous poems from several anonymous authors, all purporting to be by Shakespeare. The sonnets he presented in his own arrangement, mainly in groups of two, three or more printed continuously as one long poem under a subject heading: 'Injurious Time', 'Love's cruelty', 'Constant affection', and so on. Where he feels this is appropriate to the sonnet group he has chosen, he implies in his heading that the loved one addressed is a woman, and not a man: '. . flattery of her beautie', 'Vpon the receit of a Table Booke from his Mistris', and the headings generally obscure the original sonnet arrangement which makes it clear that many of these are addressed to his Friend and Patron.

Benson is another publisher in the tradition of Jaggard. Not only does he include Heywood's 'Amorous Epistle of Paris to Hellen' and 'Helen's Reply', but he appends five long poems on Greek mythological themes not known to be from Shakespeare's pen, although 'A Lover's Complaint' and Shakespeare's contribution of two poems from The *Phoenix and the Turtle* are here, as is also a poem from *As You Like It.* He ends his collection with a few poems 'By Other Gentlemen', including two versions of Marlowe's ubiquitous 'Come live with me', plus 'The Nymph's Reply' attributed to Raleigh (though not by Benson). He prefaces and ends his book with a selection of memorial verses to Shakespeare from Leonard Digges, W.B., and I.M., and an anonymous contributor; with one written, it would appear, specially for this publication by John Warren – all this in obvious imitation of the First Folio, one edition also having a copy of the portrait engraving originally by Droeshout, here rendered even less successfully by W.M. (William Marshall). Nevertheless, an interesting little volume, which attests the fame and adulation which Shakespeare's name and work had already attained in the period just before the Civil War, which was to all intents and purposes to close the theatres for the public performance of plays for the duration of the Puritan Protectorate. Benson's edition dispenses with 'Mr. W.H.' entirely and, as a final improving touch, the good man felt constrained to alter masculine pronouns to feminine in *Sonnet 101* so that the poet's 'truant Muse' is serenading his mistress. In foisting this dressed up version of the *Sonnets* on the public, Benson recommended them to his readers with a suitably sleight-of-hand flourish:

> '. . you shall finde them Seren, cleare and elegantly plaine, such gentle straines as shall recreate and not perplexe your braine, no intricate or cloudy stuffe to puzzell intellect, but perfect eloquence . .' [6]

This comforting commendation reads curiously to us who must perforce acknowledge that to later generations the sonnets have remained intractably just this very 'intricate, cloudy stuff' which has puzzled the intellect of even the most erudite scholars. So thick, indeed, is the mystery surrounding them that one writer, Logan Pearsall Smith, has seen fit to issue a dark warning to the would-be historical detective against entering what he calls this 'Wandering Wood', this 'Error's Den', 'the Serbonian Sonnet-bog in which whole armies have been sunk'[7]. When one reads the results of the vast literary effort that has been expended in vainly attempting to explain the meaning and historical background of the sonnets in relation to what little is known of Shakespeare's life, these words are seen to be no exaggeration.

And yet, despite the inherent difficulties in finding any basis of fact for the major themes of the sonnets, the overwhelming consensus of considered and informed opinion among scholars is that the content of the sonnets is autobiographical. In this respect, they are unique among Elizabethan sonnet sequences. Other sonneteers did not bare their souls, were not so self-revealing, and did not address their poems to real people in their lives to the same degree as Shakespeare; rather they embraced the sonnet form eagerly as a poetic artefact whereby to enhance their literary reputations. 'Sonneteering was a polite accomplishment', writes C.L. Barber in his *Essay* on the Sonnets prefacing the Laurel edition of *The Sonnets of Shakespeare*, and he points out:

> Shakespeare makes game of the fashion in *Love's Labour's Lost,* where the elegant young lords 'turn sonnet' when they turn from study to courting: they compose sonnets, recite them, talk them, and finally forswear them as part and parcel of 'spruce affectation'. [8]

Even Sidney's *Astrophel and Stella,* though inspired by his first love and embodying real experiences, is transmuted to a poetic exercise, and the poems in this sequence, whilst beautiful and sometimes moving, lack the sense of intimacy felt in Shakespeare's sonnets. These are also unusual in that the beloved person to whom they are mainly addressed is a man, and despite the mystery surrounding his identity we cannot doubt that he was a real man, not a figment of the poet's imagination. Dr. Leslie Hotson, doyen of Shakespearean scholars, whose highly original researches on Shakespeare, and especially on the sonnets, have largely provided the guide-lines and basis for my thesis, states his conviction on this matter:

> I am one of those who believes that identifying Shakespeare's Friend could not fail to throw a flood of light upon important matters both of meaning and of poetic quality, as well as upon the poet's life and work.' [9]

The essentially autobiographical nature of Shakespeare's *Sonnets* is testified repeatedly and with conviction by the most authoritative among Shakespearean critics.

'What is astonishing about the sonnets, especially when one remembers the age in which they are written, is the impression they make of naked autobiographical confession.'
W.H. Auden: *Introduction: The Sonnets,* Signet Classic Shakespeare edition. [10]

'A theory which can be rejected is the one taken up from time to time by defenders of Shakespeare's good name: that the narrative of a poet who loves a young man with whom he shares a mistress, and who is jealous both of friend and mistress, is fiction. This cannot be so: there are too many glancing references to people and events that must have existed. We feel sure that these are real . . The story has every appearance of bitter, frustrating, unrewarding truth, out of which an extraordinary blossoming and harvest have been wrung.'
Stephen Spender: *The Alike and the Other: The Riddle of Shakespeare's Sonnets.* [11]

'Shakespeare's Sonnets can be read biographically despite all the difficulties and confusions inherent in such an approach. There is, indeed, much in them too specific to be explained away by any general reading.'
Leslie A. Fielder: *Some Contexts of Shakespeare's Sonnets: The Riddle of Shakespeare's Sonnets.* [12]

'The sonnets not only include some of the most beautiful poems ever written, but ... they are the only poems we have which Shakespeare wrote out of his own

life, in his own person – a remarkable, indeed astonishing collection. People often wish that a diary or correspondence might turn up from which we could learn about Shakespeare: in the sonnets we have, by a fluke, something of this kind.'
C.L. Barber: *An Essay on the Sonnets:* The Laurel edition of *The Sonnets of Shakespeare.* [13]

'Shakespeare's Sonnets are the most disputed of all collections of poetry in the English language. This is not surprising, for they are personal and intimate poems written to individuals, which would tell much of Shakespeare's life if only some facts about them could be indisputably established.'
G.B. Harrison: *Introduction:* Penguin edition of *The Sonnets and A Lover's Complaint.* [14]

'The position generally held today is that Shakespeare's sonnets are basically autobiographical though they may employ at times the language of convention and share in the artifice which is inseparable from art.'
G.P.V. Akrigg: *Shakespeare & the Earl of Southampton.* [15]

'No one can understand Shakespeare who does not hold that his sonnets are autobiographical, and that they explain the depths of the soul of the Shakespeare who wrote the plays.'
F.J. Furnivall: *The Leopold Shakespeare.* [16]

It is 'inconceivable that such intensity of passion as [the Sonnets] reveal . . should spring from no solid basis of fact.'
Frederick S. Boas: *Shakespeare and His Predecessors.* [17]

To say that the Sonnets do not express Shakespeare's feelings in his own person is 'as much as to say that they are not sincere. And every lover of poetry who has once read the Sonnets knows this to be untrue.'
Walter Raleigh: *Shakespeare.* [18]

The Sonnets represent 'substantially a real story of Shakespeare himself and of certain other persons.'
A.C. Bradley: *Oxford Lectures.* [19]

The dawning of the nineteenth century first brought the tentative recognition that in Shakespeare's *Sonnets* we have what may be regarded as a record of his life, private thoughts and feelings, which idea was mooted by Edmund Malone in editing the works of Shakespeare and was shortly taken up by the German Shakespearean scholar, A.W. Schlegel, who was positive on this point.

'These Sonnets paint most unequivocally the actual situation and sentiments of the poet; they make us acquainted with the passions of the man; they even contain remarkable confessions of his youthful errors.' [20]

Wordsworth was completely won over and canvassed this idea with conviction among poets, writers and scholars. It became the battleground of hotly contested interpretations, some still clinging to the belief that the poems represent mere poetic imagination and cannot be related to real life.

James Winny in his thesis *The Master-Mistress: A Study of Shakespeare's Sonnets* (1968) has commented, 'the notion that the Sonnets are to be read as a journal of their author's private affairs becomes very difficult to discredit.' [21] Even the great E.K.Chambers 'concedes that the order of the Sonnets is "an autobiographical one, following the ups and downs of an emotional relationship" '. [22] While to J. Dover Wilson 'the literal truth of the Sonnets is self-evident,' [23] but he sees in the poems a dialogue in which the Friend also contributes some sonnets to the sequence, and he fancifully suggests that it was Shakespeare's mistress, the Dark Lady, who surreptitiously sold the poems to the printer – a strange idea, since they are for the most part so devastatingly unflattering to her! Such wild fancies, beating off down side-tracks without any substantiating evidence to support them, only lead us away from the real sonnet-story, which is there, waiting to be discovered, and which demands that we keep unswervingly to that path indicated by the poet's words, which this thesis follows through to the end.

Those who profess to love Shakespeare should also trust his words to lead us to the truth about his life, for in these poems he has indeed 'unlocked his heart'. The very private nature of the poems, many of which are written in the form of poetic letters to his patron, sets them apart from the general sonneteering convention which was a public art form aiming to please the public whilst ostensibly addressed to and wooing a lady, who is also sometimes the poet's patroness. C.L. Barber emphasizes that, in contrast, 'Many of Shakespeare's sonnets are drastic (and unparalleled) exceptions to this rule: they refer to complicated and very private relations.' [24]

This, I suggest, sufficiently explains why they were not entered for publication along with other sonnet sequences in their hey-day of the 1590's.

I agree with Dr. Hotson in his belief that the sonnets had their inception in the earliest period of the Elizabethan sonneteering vogue. They were trend setters, not fashion followers. But thereafter Shakespeare adopted the sonnet form as his very own personal medium and continued to use it to express his innermost thoughts and feelings in circumstances of his life when he desperately needed such an outlet. Once we have discovered what these circumstances were, a great light of understanding is shed on the torment of soul which underlies the most poignant of these intensely personal poems.

It is here in the dark regions of the sonnets that the heart of the mystery lies, and any theory concerning the historical facts embodied in the sonnet-story must come up with a satisfactory explanation of the circumstances that gave rise to the anguish experienced by the Poet. This is precisely where all attempts to explain the background of the sonnets have foundered.

The reader is invited to follow the path mapped out by the themes of the sonnets to discover what was this tragic circumstance that affected the Poet, and who were the persons addressed, often very intimately, in his poems.

II

THE POET'S WORD

POETRY is by virtue of its imaginative and fanciful aspect permitted to be somewhat obscure, where in prose this would be considered a grave fault. But the best poetry is never too obscure, or it would not survive in the readers' appreciation. Poetry, as all art, must communicate or it becomes sterile.

The sonnets of Shakespeare were, above all, written to communicate, and they do this so effectively that even while we are lacking knowledge of their background, as to what events are referred to, or what men friends or mistresses are addressed, we still are moved by them for they communicate powerfully even through the fog of our unknowing. This makes them a very effective guide to the discovery of the story they tell once we have read the clues aright, for a story of some significance there must be. No author or his publisher would have gone to such lengths to create a cryptic dedication if there was nothing to hide!

It is the discovery of this coherent story that is the quest that we are relentlessly pursuing.

The first essential step in this investigation was to dismantle the entire 154 sonnet-sequence as presented in Thorpe's edition, and to reassemble the poems grouped into their themes, or subjects, as described by the Poet. A matter involving some subtlety of understanding and much close critical rereading of the poems, but once perceived it became surprisingly clear and absolutely definite, unravelling in a marvellous way in which every step corroborated what had gone before, so that from tentative beginnings grew confidence, and eventually certainty.

If we agree that the sonnets do represent an autobiographical record, we must seek some sufficient and satisfactory explanation for the most important events in the Poet's life. In that case, what was this journey that he made which wrung from him the cry:

'My grief lies onward and my joy behind'?

Assuredly it was not a trip into the country away from London for a spell which caused him such devastating anguish, but a journey of some length of both distance and duration.

How heavy do I journey on the way,
When what I seek (my weary travel's end)
Doth teach that ease and that repose to say,
Thus far the miles are measur'd from thy friend.
The beast that bears me, tired with my woe,
Plods dully on, to bear that weight in me,
As if by some instinct the wretch did know
His rider lov'd not speed being made from thee.
The bloody spur cannot provoke him on,
That sometimes anger thrusts into his hide,
Which heavily he answers with a groan,
More sharp to me than spurring to his side;
    For that same groan doth put this in my mind:
    My grief lies onward and my joy behind.

Sonnet 50

When we apply ourselves to a detailed and unprejudiced analysis of the major themes of the Sonnets, we are struck by the inescapable fact that by far the largest group of all deals with the theme of a journey that was undertaken in great heaviness of heart, and that represented a period of cruel separation from his former life and friends, a journey into what can only be likened to a state of exile. It is amazing, but there is no other way to describe this major event in the Poet's life.

When in disgrace with Fortune and men's eyes,
I all alone beweep my outcast state,
And trouble deaf Heaven with my bootless cries,
And look upon myself and curse my fate,
Wishing me like to one more rich in hope,
Featur'd like him, like him with friends possess'd,
Desiring this man's art, and that man's scope,
With what I most enjoy contented least;
Yet in these thoughts myself almost despising,
Haply I think on thee, and then my state
(Like to the lark at break of day arising)
From sullen earth sings hymns at Heaven's gate,
    For thy sweet love remember'd such wealth brings,
    That then I scorn to change my state with kings.

Sonnet 29

The suggestion that he is in disgrace with 'men's eyes', implying that he must not now be seen publicly, is an image that recurs in many different forms in these sonnets that tell of some nameless tragedy involving a far journey and enforced absence. This group of sonnets contains many that are in the form of

11

letter-poems to his Friend and Patron from whom he is separated by 'large lengths of miles'. There can be no doubt that this was a major event in the Poet's life, for the Sonnets of Exile, as I have called them, comprise a dominant theme in the sonnet-story, numbering thirty-six sonnets in all. These are deliberately interspersed with small groups of unrelated sonnets which deceptively distract attention from this tragic theme in which the Poet speaks also of his painful and enforced anonymity. If we add to this group those sonnets on the theme of his Vilification and Disgrace, we arrive at a total of forty sonnets in this dark group, the largest in the entire series of one hundred and fifty-four poems. Its very size suggests the importance of this theme, which undoubtedly reflects events in the Poet's life.

Nowhere in the life of William Shakespeare do we know of a journey which can be described even remotely as a journey into exile; nor is there any question of his anonymity, or of vilification of his famous name, or serious disgrace that is applicable to the steadily well-to-do Stratford property-owning actor whom we know from the records as William Shakespeare, who aspired to a status of considerable respectability by acquiring a family coat-of-arms. The total failure of the efforts of erudite Shakespearean scholars to solve any part of the story told by the sonnets is no longer surprising once we realize that we have been playing with the wrong pieces to fit into this jigsaw.

Generations of scholars have attempted to fit this square peg into the round hole without success. Those wiser have contented themselves with the acceptance of the insoluble mystery of the sonnets, rejoicing in their beauty and finding their mystery infinitely more appealing than that peg in its uncomfortable hole. One almost hesitates to destroy it, for the haunting mystery lends its own enchantment, and for more than twenty years I have been tempted to leave it there. But nagging conscience to fulfil an obligation to pursue a suspected historical truth and put it to the ultimate test has finally won commitment. Dr. Hotson had begun to unravel the thread of the sonnet-story. Taking up his thread, I propose to follow through wherever it may lead, hopeful of a little Hotsonian serendipity, using his method of familiar acquaintance with things Elizabethan to test each premise, and flinging a net as wide as possible to dredge evidence from the historical context, always in faithful adherence to the Poet's Word. The voice of the sonnets has been listened to attentively, and whatever did not fit when tested in the light of the words of the poems has been rejected as misleading.

Such a literary-historical quest can only bear the ultimate fruit of truth if total objectivity prevails, unaffected by the constant weight of academic opinion that exerts a powerful pressure on scholars to think along the hallowed lines prescribed by orthodoxy. Dr. Hotson as a committed orthodox Shakespearean scholar had thereby limited himself to a prescribed conclusion, and was doomed to fail to find the true quarry, though he has laid the invaluable trail.

We are often told that the Elizabethan writers are obscure. This is not really true. It is we who are prevented from understanding them by our twentieth century conception of the Elizabethans whose use of language reflects a way of life and customs different from ours. When sufficiently wide research is done to illuminate the text we are aiming to decipher, it is almost invariably possible to penetrate the initial obscurity. This is the method Dr. Hotson has taught us, taking Shakespeare at his word – literally – as impressively demonstrated in his *Shakespeare's Sonnets Dated* (1949).

No doubt some will make the poetic use of imagery in the sonnets their pre-text for claiming that one cannot really hope to explain these poems in terms of actual happenings. Whilst readily conceding that it is of the very essence of the poetic idiom that imagery may at times be used to create a degree of obscurity in order to heighten the emotional or sensory climate, or to pose an intellectual challenge, such poetic obscurantism is rarely encountered in these sonnets. *They were written to communicate.*

> To thee I send this written ambassage
> To witness duty, not to show my wit.
>
> *Sonnet 26.*

> O learn to read what silent love hath writ,
> To hear with eyes belongs to love's fine wit.
>
> *Sonnet 23.*

In those sonnets which are teasingly ambiguous, the favourite ploy of *double entendre* is sometimes present, for these are witty poems. But the perceptive reader will find no difficulty in discriminating between poetic imagery and fact, once we have some facts to relate to. These have been entirely absent from the story when seen as a record of Shakespeare's life, so that we have felt lost. But fiction holds no place here. The story that is told is true. It really happened.

It is the ring of truth to which we must attune our ears. The question to ask is only: What is the Poet really saying? Not just of this sonnet or that which suits our book, but of all of them. A selective approach cannot suffice. Dr. Hotson, having taught us how to read the Poet's Word literally, has not escaped the very pitfalls against which he himself has warned us. In his delight, believing that he had discovered the identity of *Mr. W.H.* (the title of his thesis published in 1964), he waxes over-enthusiastic in embracing his new-found candidate, Master William Hatcliffe, as the patron of the *entire* sonnet-sequence, although many of the sonnets do not fit him at all, any more than they fit William Shakespeare as the sonneteer whom he sees as Hatcliffe's poet. Accordingly, Hotson's William Hatcliffe has not found much acceptance in academic circles, despite being an attractive candidate.

But it is not enough to tear down Dr. Hotson's palace of dreams. It is necessary to put something in its place, and to look very carefully at what we are discarding before we discard it. I had been on the brink of dismissing William Hatcliffe, when I looked again at those poems that seem to apply to him, to compare and scrutinize. And *there was the revelation of his presence* – which became so vital a clue to deciphering the rest. That second look, like a second opinion that is so rightly valued, has been a factor of basic importance for this thesis.

Where other scholars have been content to concentrate on re-interpreting familiar texts, challenging the opinions of their colleagues with variants in the same old fields, Hotson has gone out to dig in the largely unexplored mines of recondite literary archives, and from their dust he has produced pure gold. My function has been to sift the gold from the dross of the orthodox preconceptions in which this treasure has been partly submerged. By his adventurous detective work Hotson has made a remarkable discovery which has opened the way to disclosure of deeply hidden evidence that is destined to change our ideas about Shakespeare. And, like Schliemann, Hotson has pioneered a new method – taking the Poet at his Word, which, in his case, has been subject to the limitations of an erroneous orthodox Shakespearean philosophy blocking the way to total success, only just missing the mark. Other critics, baffled by the fact that not one of the sonnets can be seen to apply to what is known about William Shakespeare's life as revealed by two centuries of intensive research, have tended to throw in the sponge, defeated by what appears to be deliberate ambiguity on the part of the Poet.

In a recent paper entitled *Master W.H., R.I.P.* Donald W. Foster has expressed the dilemma of a scholar's exasperation on this point. Referring to Kenneth Muir's 'curiously ambivalent treatise' on the sonnets in which Muir has sought his solution by asserting that the poems are *not* autobiography, but in his treatment of various sonnets 'seems to assume that, in fact, they are' autobiographical, Foster comments:

> 'Muir is at cross-purposes with himself on every page. . .
> Approaching the sonnets with his head full of Stephen Booth and
> his heart full of Leslie Hotson, Muir ends in a muddle.
> 'Nor is Muir alone in this respect. I think it difficult, perhaps
> impossible, for anyone to read the sonnets without experiencing
> something of the same ambivalence.' [1]

This is the penalty exacted for denying the autobiographical content of the sonnets which – there is no getting away from it – *were written to communicate*. Many, as has been noted, are indeed verse-letters.

> But if the while I think on thee (dear friend)
> All losses are restor'd, and sorrows end.

> *Sonnet 30*

Foster expands on this quality of intransigent ambiguity in the *Sonnets,* as he sees them:

> 'The sonnets are in large measure defined for us by their very ambiguity. If we were someday to discover the 'facts' concerning Shakespeare's relationship with the persons alluded to in this work, what we have always known as Shakespeare's Sonnets would, in a sense, cease to exist, to be replaced by another book of the same title.
> 'Such an event is not likely. After nearly two hundred years of speculation and scholarship, we have made remarkably little progress toward uncovering the 'true story' behind Shakespeare's Sonnets, if indeed there is a story to be uncovered. The poems tease us with what appear to be references to real persons, persons who knew the man, Shakespeare, much better than we. Yet we still have no plausible candidates for the role of the dark lady (or ladies), or of the rival poet (or poets) or of the speaker's young friend (or friends).' [2]

Defeated by 'Mr. W.H.' and by the content of the sonnets themselves, Foster falls back onto the last resort of the baffled scholar: 'That 'W.H.' is simply a misprint.' [3] It is the handy hypothesis that begs every question and answers none. Foster concedes finally that knowledge is not 'altogether inaccessible to us, if by "knowledge" we mean a hypothesis with enough supporting evidence to convince most readers.' [4] It is this and more that is offered here.

This thesis affirms that the sonnets are indeed autobiography, and that clearly recognizable people, facts and events were contributory to this real-life poetic collection. Like Homer, Shakespeare tells the historical truth. As a result it may be that the sonnets will suffer a sea-change, losing their mystery and the tantalizing ambiguity that contribute to the spell they weave, but our gain will be commensurately immense. For from this new knowledge perceived in the light of his sonnets the Spear-shaker emerges, not as a lesser figure, but as a greater than even those who best love him have suspected, and certainly an immeasurably more exciting personality – a self-conscious and original genius, who is, at one and the same time, a colossus bestriding the Elizabethan world from court to commoner's home, and a real man; a complex personality, imperfect, erring, and hence more human, more pitiable in his suffering, and more understandable to us. From the rash errors of his early life a dire lesson was learnt, which chastened him and bore immortal fruit. The sonnets shed light on that shattered and resuscitated life in the real historical context that gives coherence to the story they tell.

The scope for radical research opened up will inevitably further confirm this thesis, for it is based on the bed-rock of the Poet's autobiographical writings, which for the first time make complete sense, speaking to us without ambiguity.

We have been 'the fools of Time' till now, but 'reckoning Time', so often seen by the Poet as the cruel thief of life and beauty, has finally brought a benediction in the revelation of historical truth to a generation that, hopefully, is willing to change preconceived ideas and ready to receive what has for so long lain in necessary and protective obscurity.

The Poet's Word is more powerful than the scholar's tome, as our Poet well knew when he wrote what was really his own epitaph rather than his Patron's.

Or I shall live your epitaph to make,
Or you survive when I in earth am rotten,
From hence your memory death cannot take,
Although in me each part will be forgotten.
Your name from hence immortal life shall have,
Though I, once gone, to all the world must die.
The earth can yield me but a common grave,
When you entombed in men's eyes shall lie.
Your monument shall be my gentle verse,
Which eyes not yet created shall o'er-read,
And tongues to be your being shall rehearse,
When all the breathers of this world are dead,
   You still shall live (such virtue hath my pen)
   Where breath most breathes, even in the mouths
                        of men.

Sonnet 81.

III

Dr. Hotson's 'Mr. W.H.'

ALL THE WORLD loves a puzzle, and cryptograms and acrostics were popular diversions of the Elizabethans. The dedication of the *Sonnets* seems deliberately to present such a puzzle to our eyes centred around the mysterious 'Mr.W.H.' which has become a challenge to our ingenuity to decipher and solve.

If the sophistication with which this particular conundrum has been devised has for so long defied solution, it has not been for lack of trying. Donald W. Foster attempted to wipe the slate clean by doing away with 'Mr.W.H.' altogether as a printer's error for 'Mr.W.SH.' (W. Shakespeare), claiming that the dedication is perfectly straightforward. [1] There *is* no puzzle! This spoilsport academic theorizing would nullify the thesis of the redoubtable Dr. Hotson, whose bold claim to have discovered the real 'Mr.W.H.' at last is the only puzzle-solving exercise to date worthy of consideration. Fortunately, not only is the conundrum more fun, it can also be tested, whereas an error remains conjecture.

Dr. Hotson's sceptical critics have not been won over, but I hope to show that he has made a vital contribution to solving the mystery surrounding the Sonnets, if not wholly as he claims, nor in quite the way he expected, for 'Mr.W.H.' is himself only an enticing mirage designed to deflect the would-be conundrum-solver from pursuit of the real Patron by lulling him into the complacent belief that the goal is reached. The dedication with its declared dedicatee is a measure of the sophistication and subtlety employed that has ensured its remarkable success. When Dr. Hotson penetrated the puzzle of 'Mr.W.H.' he interpreted it as pointing to the Patron – 'the Onlie Begetter' – of the entire sonnet-sequence, but he had only breached the first layer of the Poet's protective cover for the true Patron. The second and deeper layer is the investigation pursued in this thesis. But first we must take a critical look at Hotson's 'Mr.W.H.' for he is indeed part of the total picture, and a very fascinating one too.

In 1964, with the publication of his *Mr. W.H.* Dr.Hotson triumphantly claimed to have discovered the identity of Shakespeare's Friend. By an elaborate system of re-alignment of the printed lay-out of the dedication with its curious full-stops he uncovered the hidden name of 'Mr.W.H.' as one William Hatcliffe, a young gentleman of Gray's Inn, exceedingly handsome, personable and well-born, hailing from Lincolnshire, who was accorded the rare honour to be elected their 'Prince of Purpoole' by the law students of Gray's Inn for the celebration of the Grayans' Christmas festivities in 1587. [2] This exceedingly beautiful young man, then aged nineteen years, seemed ideally to fit the role of the 'lovely Boy' of the Sonnets, whom Shakespeare hymned with praise, offering him loyalty and love as his courtly sonneteer, and even addressing him 'my sovereign' (*Sonnet 57*). This seemed to clinch it.

Having been chosen as the Christmas Prince of the Grayans, young William Hatcliffe was set up with the lavish splendour of a real court, with retinues of servants, and courtiers, banquets and music and dancing, dramatic entertainments, fine orations and poetics, in replication of all the trappings of royalty. It was play-acting carried off at a high level in the exuberant spirit of youth with total commitment to fun and fantastic invention. It is indeed a delightful and appealing picture to which we shall return in some detail later.

In solving cryptograms it is often an essential first step to 'square' the text to be deciphered. Hotson has accordingly re-aligned the Dedication in a rectangular tabular format. Noting the blank space or 'white' following the cryptic name 'Mr.W.H.' he takes this as the clue to begin on *line 3* of the Dedication.

> TO.THE.ONLIE.BEGETTER.OF.
> THESE.INSVING.SONNETS
> M^r.W.H. ALL.HAPPINESSE.
> AND.THAT.ETERNITIE.
> PROMISED.
> BY.
> OVR. EVER-LIVING.POET.
> WISHETH.
> THE.WELL-WISHING.
> ADVENTVRER.IN.
> SETTING.
> FORTH.
>
> T.T.

	1	2	3	4	5	6	7	8	9	10	11	12	13	14	15	16	17	18	19	20	21	22
LINE *No.3*	M	r	.	W	.	H	.	A	L	L	.	H	A	P	P	I	N	E	S	S	E	.
No.4	A	N	D	.	T	H	A	T	.	E	T	E	R	N	I	T	I	E	.			
No.5	P	R	O	M	I	S	E	D	.													
No.6	B	Y	.																			
No.7	O	V	R	.	E	V	E	R	-	L	I	V	I	N	G	P	O	E	T	. ³		

The numerical clue is 3 + 4 = 7: these lines alone are significant for deciphering the cryptogram, such number relationships being present in all cryptograms, as is made abundantly clear in the numerous books on the subject published in Elizabethan times.

The rather unusual word 'EVER-LIVING' to describe the Poet supplies Dr. Hotson with his hidden name 'HATLIV' for Hatlif or Hatliffe, as William Hatcliffe's name was often written. I suggest that this has a special significance for the Poet of the Sonnets also for in such dedications it is usually the Patron on whom eternal life is conferred by the Poet's works. Here, however, it is the Poet himself who is 'EVER-LIVING'. Thorpe was, in effect, giving the game away, as will be substantiated when we come to identify the Poet. This may have been a main reason why Thorpe's edition of the *Sonnets* was, perhaps, suppressed, for their publication was seen to be dangerous, because too revealing, not of Hatcliffe, but of the Poet. However, here it is Master Hatcliffe whom we are considering for his eligibility as 'Mr.W.H.'

In resolving the riddle of the name 'Mr.W.H.' Dr. Hotson takes his clue for the start of his 'reading' from the only blank space or 'white' in the entire layout of the printed type which is all in capitals with full-stops after every word. This appeared to be significant to Hotson. Working from this point, by re-aligning the lettering from its original format in the shape of three triangular slabs of print, he extracted the name 'HATLIV' from the text. The Elizabethans varied the spelling of names as much as their fanciful spelling of all words, so that Hatliv would readily have been accepted as a variant form of Hatcliffe, which might be written Hatliff or Hatlyffe, omitting the 'c'. Dr Hotson's solution is therefore seen to be both ingenious and plausible. Regrettably he then goes on to mar it by overstating his case. [4]

Dr Hotson has clearly fallen in love with his theory, and he leaves no literary leaf unturned in his effort to amass the corroborative evidence he needs to bolster up his identification of the young 'shadow Prince' as 'The Onlie Begetter' to whom the *Sonnets* are dedicated. The mountain of contemporary literary references with which he impressively supports the concept of 'royalty' leaves the reader dazzled as this erudite guide leads us through the maze of Elizabethan ideology and classical allusion in which Dr Hotson is so delightfully versed. Yet when one comes back to the sonnets themselves, one is left disappointed and increasingly doubtful that this is the true, final answer to the mystery, for his thesis in no way explains the tragic autobiographical themes of the sonnet-story. Will Hatcliffe does not really fit the whole picture. And where in 1587-8 was there any sign of William Shakespeare making his mark in London?

It was a popular sonneteering convention to address the patroness of a sonnet series with extravagant flattery as 'princess', but Hotson posits that Shakespeare's use of royal terms in relation to his patron is so frequent that it transcends this convention and substantiates his theory, that these poems are addressing a young man who is actually playing his part as a Christmas Prince. Careful perusal of the sonnets to find references to the putative royalty of his admired Friend, however, reveals only six sonnets that answer this claim; only three in which he is so addressed directly, *Sonnets 57, 63* and *64*. In other sonnets the use of royal terminology is not applicable to the Patron, and is sometimes used to denote the Poet himself, as when referring to flattery as 'the monarch's plague' in *Sonnet 114:*

> Oh, 'tis the first, 'tis flattery in my seeing,
> And my great mind most kingly drinks it up.

19

Our Poet delights in kingly imagery, and at times he descants on himself as having, or lacking the riches of a king. It is a characteristic trait that the touching humility he so often expresses is ever and again counterpoised with the use of kingly imagery as applied to himself. This is the concept of Ovid, that a poet was a veritable 'king' among men.

> Verse is immortal, and shall ne'er decay
> To verse let kings give place, and kingly shows.

Ovid's Amores Book I, Elegy XV. ^{5.}

Shakespeare, it is generally held, was steeped in Ovid, and the Ovidian love of royal imagery pervades the sonnets.

Dr Hotson's promotion of William Hatcliffe as 'Mr.W.H.' is beset with unanswered questions, and has found little favour in academic circles. Nevertheless, in leading us to consider his 'royal' person as the 'lovely Boy' of the Sonnets, the Grayan 'Prince' whose royal debut was at the Christmas season of 1587-8, Dr Hotson has uncovered the first layer of the Sonnets' secret – and that is no mean achievement! His thesis has been the only brave and original essay at cracking Thorpe's cryptic dedication, and he has come nearer the mark than his critics have been prepared to concede, missing by a hair's breadth the vital target of identification which reveals the human drama of this remarkable sonnet-story. Hotson's contribution is of the utmost importance to the final solution. The identification of the 'lovely Boy' is an essential step without which the true Patron cannot be satisfactorily extricated from the tangled web of the sonnet-sequence. Hotson has put the thread of unravelling into our hands.

The identification of 'Mr.W.H.' has high-lighted an important and often debated question. Was the order of the *Sonnets* Thorpe's or was it the Poet's? Without doubt we can now say it was the Poet's. For the purpose of the order of the sonnet-sequence is to confuse and mislead the reader, as much as the cryptic dedication is designed to do. How is this achieved? Aesthetically, the order of the sonnets is delightful, for to read all the poems on one theme one after the other would be too much for pleasure; nor would they have been written in that kind of concentration. It was in placing the sonnets into their theme groups that a most fascinating aspect emerged. Only the first seventeen sonnets, addressed to a young nobleman, appealing to him to marry and beget heirs to his line, is presented in an entirely unbroken group. This sets them apart. The twenty-five sonnets to the Dark Lady, and the fourteen on the Rival Poet, are each interrupted once only by a sonnet having no obvious relevance to that group; whereas the group relating to a far journey – the Sonnets of Exile – is broken up repeatedly by sonnets, singly or in small groups, which have no relevance to this theme at all; these are taken mainly from the group addressed to the 'lovely Boy'. A very scattered and confused order is deliberately created – and the vital information it conceals is that the 'lovely Boy' and the Patron are *not the same man*.

20

There has been a carefully orchestrated confusion of identity between the true Patron and the 'lovely Boy' whose fair outside is not matched by his dubious character, which has given to the Patron an apparently two-faced image that has baffled critics. The aim has been to throw us off the scent of the true Patron, which has been cleverly achieved by the skilful muddling of the two sonnet groups addressing these two men in such a subtle way that it seems as though they are one. Once we realise that two different young men are addressed all begins to fall into place.

This deliberate arrangement of the order of the sonnets to mislead the reader is undoubtedly the Poet's own, for it is presented with great sophistication. It is the extraordinary skill with which this web of poetry is woven that has enabled their secret to be kept so completely and so long – aided by the artifice of the dedication which predisposes us to the assumption that the poems are written to one sole patron, 'THE.ONLIE.BEGETTER.'

Dr Hotson's superstructure of argumentation is built upon his identification of 'Mr.W.H.' based on his ingenious and well calculated manipulation of the printed format of the dedication to reveal the name of Shakespeare's Friend as 'Mr.W.HATLIV', yielding the only solution to make sense to date. This is just the sort of clever 'red herring' T.T. intended, hoping that some expert puzzle-solver would discover 'Mr.W.H.' and satisfy his curiosity, accepting him as the sole patron, so drawing us off the scent of the real Patron, whose identity has been masked so effectively that even Dr Hotson did not suspect his existence.

When the *Sonnets* were published in 1609 memories of William Hatcliffe's brief reign of splendour were twenty-two years distant, so that the connection was sufficiently removed to give some mystery and would not have been too obvious to qualify as a sophisticated Elizabethan cryptogram, cleverly devised – probably by T.T. – in order to mislead and supply the right 'wrong' answer. This was essential in publishing these autobiographical poems, for concealment of their secret was vital for the protection of both Poet and Patron for cogent reasons. There is evidence that T.T. must have known that the true story of the Sonnets was dynamite! [6]

❖   ❖   ❖

We are now on the right track, for Hotson has placed the vital thread in our hands. But we must turn elsewhere to fill in the portrait of the elusive Patron, or patrons – and of the Poet himself.

In arriving at a true portrait of the genius whose poetic diary we are considering, a very important contribution has been made by the extensive, analytical work of those critics whose sensitive and finely judged reading of the Sonnets has led them to eschew conjectural theorizing, and confine their valuable interpretative work to analyzing the poems without the urge to delve into their nebulous historical background. Within the limitations imposed by an almost total lack of reliable historical knowledge, this approach has yielded a harvest of profound perceptive appreciation of what the Poet is telling us about himself, his character, feelings, attitudes and aspirations. Such penetrating interpretative essays as Stephen Spender's, Edward Hubler's, C.L. Barber's, W.H. Auden's, Northrop Frye's have proved especially relevant when tested against the eventual historical truth, each contribution augmenting the portrait of the sonneteer of the Sonnets with finely etched lines. It is significant that the most sensitive and sympathetic critics have sensed that those emotionally charged poems of the dark sonnet-themes were born out of an experience of singular and extraordinary circumstances. If this is so, we would be justified in expecting the sonnet-story to be a commensurately extraordinary one.

It is only when we realise that it has been due to the remarkable, indeed, the incredible success of the concealment of both the true Patron and the Poet, whose personal history is highlighted only in his Sonnets, and which has induced a myopic obsession with the name so carefully and deliberately presented to our view in T.T.'s curious inscription – SHAKE-SPEARES SONNETS – that we are no longer surprised at our total failure to penetrate the curtain and draw the right conclusions. The name Shakespeare was frequently hyphenated by printers.

If this is a pen-name for someone else, it sufficiently explains why his autobiographical writings in no way reflect the life of another man of the same name – the man born William Shakespeare of Stratford-upon-Avon. True, there are those who have long sensed that there was a basic error of identification in attributing the great works to the actor; and other candidates, mostly too ridiculous and too numerous to contemplate (there are over sixty to date!) have been presented. But no theory has as yet been advanced whose consistency has been entirely accredited through the Sonnets, and which has tested its relevance in every point to these poems. Attempts to relate the Sonnets to the lives of Sir Francis Bacon or the Earl of Oxford, two main contenders for the Shakespearean crown, have proved disastrous to these theories. They do not fit the jigsaw any more aptly than our worthy William Shakespeare, despite some weird and wonderful wresting of the sense of the words and curious contortions of facts, dates and fancies in vain attempts to 'interpret' some of the sonnets to suit their man.

Thereis only one who fits this scenario throughout the entire sweep of the autobiographical tale told, and *the Sonnets fit him as the glove fits the hand for which it was made.* This degree of accuracy and truth is essential if we are to be sure that we have found the man who has waited behind the curtain for nearly four hundred years.

IV

THE BROKEN LINK

O let my books be then the eloquence
And dumb presagers of my speaking breast.

Sonnet 23

SHAKESPEARE'S works today span the world. The plays are performed in all the major languages, and there is no writer who has such a universal appeal. Yet his autobiographical poems have *not revealed a single fact* about this great writer's life, and what we know from documentary records seems to have no relevance to his sonnets. There is still no agreement about who 'Mr.W.H.' might be – even Dr Hotson's meticulously researched evidence is not widely accepted. The slim volume published by Thorpe constitutes an enigma, a riddle guarding its secret as jealously as the Sphinx – though the poems cry out to be understood!

Was there ever a more strange case in all autobiographical writing?

And yet, in a sense, we know a great deal about Shakespeare as author of the plays and poems, for every writer reveals something of his personality in his writings, and no author has been so assiduously studied as Shakespeare. Years of dedicated study of his writings has produced a vast body of interpretative literature on every aspect of his works which has elucidated for us what kind of man he was. One of his most ardent admirers, the American poet and essayist, Ralph Waldo Emerson, expressed it well:

> 'Who ever read the volume of the 'Sonnets' without finding that the poet had there revealed, under masks that are no masks to the intelligent, the lore of friendship and of love; the confusion of sentiments in the most susceptible, and, at the same time, the most intellectual of men? or what trait of his private mind has he hidden in his dramas? One can discern in his ample pictures of the gentleman and the king, what forms and humanities pleased him; his delight in troops of friends, in large hospitality, in cheerful giving. Let Timon, let Warwick, let Antonio the merchant answer for his great heart. So far from Shakespeare's being the least known, he is the one person in all modern history known to us. What point of morals, of manners, of economy, of philosophy, of religion, of taste, of the conduct of life, has he not settled? What mystery has he not signified his knowledge of? What office or function or district of man's work has he not remembered?' [1]

It's a tall order for the country lad from Stratford to encompass, who never saw the inside of a university. But by some miracle he managed to write the marvellous works which drew such rhapsodic eulogies from the great minds of men in America as well as in Germany, where Goethe exclaimed on discovering Shakespeare for the first time: 'I stood as one blind from birth, upon whom a miraculous hand bestows sight in an instant. I saw, I felt, in the most vivid manner, that my existence had been infinitely expanded.' [2]

The nineteenth-century Scottish historian, Thomas Carlyle, an outstanding scholar and critic, deeply versed in the Shakespearean canon, states as his considered opinion that, 'Shakespeare is the chief of all poets, hitherto; the greatest intellect who, in our recorded world, has left record of himself in the way of literature. On the whole I know not such power of vision, faculty of thought, if we take all the characters of it, in any other man.' For Carlyle, Shakespeare is an even greater mind than Dante: 'If I say, therefore, that Shakespeare is the greatest intellect, I have said all about him.' [3]

Samuel Taylor Coleridge is equally overwhelmed. 'That such a mind involved itself in a human form is a problem indeed which my feeble powers may witness with admiration, but cannot explain. My words are indeed feeble when I speak of that myriad-minded man, whom all artists feel above all praise.' [4] Robert Ingersoll adds his laurel wreath of adulation: 'Shakespeare was an intellectual ocean whose waves touched all the shores of thought.' [5]

Such was the impact that the contemplation of Shakespeare's genius, and especially his intellectual stature, engendered, swelling to a flood-tide of bardolatry in the nineteenth century. It is astonishing, then, that this great light seems to have been hidden under a bushel, for the boy William Shakespeare's astounding intellectual gifts (which no teacher could have failed to notice) were never remarked upon by his Stratford Grammar School master, who, one would have thought, would have mentioned the lad's exceptional brightness to his father; and with such advice as he could give it should have been possible to find a patron among the local gentry, or send him as a poor sizar to the university, as happened to Robert Greene, who was a saddler's son, and innumerable others who were the most intelligent youngsters of the humble artisan class. Nor is there, surprisingly, the slightest evidence of this remarkable intellect in his later years from what we can glean of William Shakespeare's recorded life, activities, friendships and interests. The man, the player, seems to inhabit a different sphere from the poet and dramatist. Emerson, whose admiration for the Bard of Avon was unbounded, after much deep thought on all things Shakespearean, permitted himself some troubled musings on the polarized existence of his idol.

'As long as the question is of talent and mental power, the world of men has not his equal to show. But when the question is of life, and its materials, and its auxiliaries, how does he profit me? . . The Egyptian verdict of the Shakespeare societies comes to mind, that he was a jovial actor and manager. I cannot marry this fact to his verse. Other admirable men have lives in some sort of keeping with their thought, but this man in wide contrast. Had he been less, had he reached only the common measure of great authors, of Bacon, Milton, Tasso, Cervantes, we might leave the fact in the twilight of human fate; but that this man of men, he who gave to the science of mind a new and larger subject than had ever existed, and planted the standard of humanity some furlongs forward into chaos, that he should not be wise for himself, it must even go into the world's history, that the best poet led an obscure and profane life, using his genius for the public amusement.' [6.]

Indeed a curious dichotomy is presented to our view. On the one hand, the divine works, on the other, the mundane life. In order to patch this discrepancy, the biographers and critics of Shakespeare have no alternative but to argue from the internal evidence in the dramatic works and poems back to the man, to imbue him with the characteristics of genius and mental brilliance which are otherwise not apparent, in order to fit him for his part as the great Shakespeare, and so to gloss over the inconsistencies that they no longer glare at us. They cease to matter. Genius is a phenomenon, so why try to explain it? So runs the argument. But even the wit, the humour and the stylistic sparkle of his greatest twentieth-century biographer, Samuel Schoenbaum, in his *William Shakespeare: A Documentary Life* (1975) have been unable to conceal from us that the subject of this monumental tribute is really a monumental bore. From this large and lavishly illustrated, beautifully presented book it is the little provincial town of Stratford-upon-Avon which emerges as of more lively interest than her illustrious son, and this padding out of his background is the best that can be done to bolster up his undistinguished image.

Making so much of what little we have may be acceptable to some, but – *pace* Schoenbaum – for an increasing number the veneer is wearing thinner and thinner as we seek in vain for some sign of the passionate poet inside this litigious actor-cum-businessman. Professor Schoenbaum's researches detailing the persistent progress of his steady rise to affluence from 1594 onwards, are revealing of a man with his heart set on a worldly goal. From the cunning evasion of modest rate payments as a householder in London's Bishopsgate and the Liberty of the Clink, where he successively dwelt, which he seems to have got away with from 1596 to 1600; [7] to the purchase of a fine mansion in Stratford, New Place, the second largest residence in the town, with a sixty-foot frontage and spacious grounds, comprising two gardens and two orchards with two barns, which he acquired in 1597; adding to this in May 1602 a further 107 acres of arable land in Old Stratford; and finally, in July 1605, he invested £440 in a half-interest for a lease of thirty-one years on tithes of corn, grain, blade and hay in three nearby hamlets, together with small tithes of Stratford parish which yielded him £60 per annum income; [8] a comfortable propertied man within four years of the first appearance of his name on the publication of *Venus and Adonis* in the summer of 1593, and the first official listing of his name as a member of the Lord Chamberlain's Men for their performance at Court in December 1594, represents a rapid consolidation in terms of material gain.

Ever litigious, we find Shakespeare pursuing the reclamation of debts from his Stratford-upon-Avon neighbours (of 35s. 10d. and £6 respectively)[9] through the Court of Records which dealt in suits for sums under £30. All this adds up to a nature with a keen eye to worldly interest. And there is, of course, nothing wrong in this. The question is only, how does this fadge with the poet whose sonnets speak to us of a nature whose highest ambition is the celebration of Love and Beauty in immortal poetry?

> As a decrepit father takes delight
> To see his active child do deeds of youth,
> So I, made lame by Fortune's dearest spite,
> Take all my comfort of thy worth and truth.
> For whether beauty, birth or wealth, or wit,
> Or any of these all, or all, or more,
> Entitled in their parts do crowned sit,
> I make my love engrafted to this store.
> So then I am not lame, poor, nor despis'd,
> Whilst that this shadow doth such substance give,
> That I in thy abundance am suffic'd,
> And by a part of all thy glory live.
> Look what is best, that best I wish in thee.
> This wish I have, then ten times happy me.

Sonnet 37

When we compare the moving utterances of his autobiographical poems with the records of the man, William Shakespeare, the incongruity is so striking as to arouse profound doubt and disbelief. It is no use pretending that the learned scholars who have spent their lives studying and writing about Shakespeare are unaware of this. There is even a tacit admission of the realization that something is amiss in the choice of the portraits of Shakespeare chosen to represent the poet-dramatist. Brushing aside the numerous portraits purporting to be of Shakespeare, which all bear some resemblance to the Droeshout engraving (all of them suspect, having doubtful pedigrees) Samuel Schoenbaum has opted to adorn the cover of his great book with a wholly unauthentic and fanciful eighteenth century miniature by George Vertue. Whilst Dover Wilson, in seeking a portrait to express his sensitive assessment of the poet-dramatist in *The Essential Shakespeare*, has with unerring prescience, chosen the totally unauthentic, but beautiful and genuinely Elizabethan 'Grafton' Portrait of a young man who happens to be Shakespeare's exact contemporary, 'AETATIS SVAE 24 1588',

26

because to him the unnamed sitter looks like a poet. He confesses:

> 'Of course, the picture has been claimed as a genuine Shakespeare portrait. The temptation so to claim it is almost irresistible; and for my part, since I first had it brought to my notice in 1914, the temptation has grown stronger every time I have looked at it.' [10]

Anyone who is concerned with Shakespearean study may indulge in a little romancing. But here, interestingly, we have an implicit self-confession on the part of two of our very finest Shakespearean authorities that they are not quite comfortable with the identification of the man from Stratford as author of the sublime works. As indeed who with intelligence can be? The bare facts from which this illustrious poet-dramatist emerged in his thirtieth year with the publication of *Venus and Adonis*, audaciously dedicated to a peer of the realm, the young Earl of Southampton no less, are in such stark contrast to his sudden leap to fame as to merit incredulity. This incredulity has been voiced even by such a great Shakespearean scholar as Dover Wilson. Let us consider the facts.

WILLIAM SHAKESPEARE was born in 1564, christened the son of John Shakespeare of Stratford-upon-Avon, a glover by trade, in the parish church of Holy Trinity on 26th April. Married at the age of eighteen to Anne Hathaway, aged twenty-six, their first child, a daughter, Susanna, born six months later; and in 1585, when he was aged twenty-one, twins were born, Hamnet and Judith. And thereafter a blank, until he arrived eight years later, without any preparation for this great leap into fame, the complete and self-assured poet, who is equally the superb and practised dramatist, out-shining all his contemporaries whose plays had been performed on the London stage; chief of whom was Christopher Marlowe – and his development we can trace precisely. But where Shakespeare learnt his amazing expertise we do not know. We are left guessing. No wonder Dover Wilson is prompted to exclaim:

> 'Surely there is no more dramatic entry in the whole of history than this of history's greatest dramatist.' [11]

No records exist to testify to William Shakespeare's schooling, but it is assumed that he would have attended Stratford's grammar school and there learnt literacy and that 'little Latin and less Greek' of which Ben Jonson writes in the First Folio. This, however, does not satisfy Dover Wilson. Commenting on that brilliant comedy *Love's Labour's Lost* he puts it frankly:

> 'To credit that amazing piece of virtuosity . . to one whose education was nothing more than what a grammar school and residence in a little provincial borough could provide is to invite one either to believe in miracles or to disbelieve in "the man of Stratford".' [12]

Having faced the issue and come so near the brink, he retreats, as all sound orthodox scholars must, and takes refuge in hypothesizing. Ingeniously, Dover Wilson suggests that it was not the Stratford grammar school that young William Shakespeare attended, but that his father, John Shakespeare, who is suspected of being an adherent of the Old Faith, took steps to send his son to the home of a Catholic nobleman, there to serve as a singing-boy and receive his education in the lord's household. It would at least partly solve the problem, if provable, though a university education to follow is needed to meet the evidence of the plays. But which Catholic nobleman? What evidence of a Catholic education is there in the plays? None. Education fashions the man, and none more so than the writer. Shakespeare's writings reveal him to be deeply versed in the Protestant Bible. Dover Wilson's solution remains a happy hypothesis without an iota of foundation, but the fact that he seeks it shows that it is necessary to fulfil the conditions for bringing the actor from Stratford-upon-Avon into focus as author of the immortal works.

William Shakespeare was, on the evidence, no infant prodigy, for no one remarked on his youthful precocity. If he received his education in Stratford, then where did he manage to supplement this modest learning? For Shakespeare's great erudition and wide knowledge and experience of all branches of human endeavour in the Elizabethan world are the hallmark of his literary works. Books were expensive and not readily come by in little Stratford. In recognition of their value, Ben Jonson received a grant of £20 a year from the Earl of Pembroke for the purchase of books. We know of no such bequest to Shakespeare, and two hundred years of intensive research has failed to discover any links with a source at which he could have drunk so deeply of those springs that were to influence his Muse.

If he had this great poetic inspiration in him, what was he doing living his humble life, begetting children, apparently not possessing a library (for his will lists not as single book) until he reached the ripe age of twenty-nine? Why was his Muse silent during the vibrant years of his early manhood, only to emerge suddenly with the publication of *Venus and Adonis*? This has been described as 'an extraordinary poem' for a man of basic education from an unexceptional, provincial small town background to have produced as the 'first heir' of his invention. It is a 'scholarly, courtly poem, saturated with Ovid', [13] and revealing the influence of Virgil, which reflects experience of life at the Court and its fashionable elegancies – an experience that is in sharpest contrast to everything that we can discover about William Shakespeare's life.

From the time when the twins were born to William and Anne Shakespeare in the February of 1585 until the sudden appearance in the summer of 1593 of his name, 'William Shakespeare', appended as signature to the dedication of *Venus and Adonis* where it has all the semblance of a carefully presented *nom de plume* being introduced to the world, there is only one piece of documentary evidence relating to him. This is the Bill of Complaint, *Shakespeare v. Lambert*, dated 1588, in which he is named 'Willielmo Shackespere filio' together with his father, John Shakespeare, and his mother, Mary, in a family dispute over some land that had been mortgaged to Mary's brother-in-law, Edmund Lambert, for a sum of £40 ready money. [14]

The complications of this protracted law suit need not concern us here, but it testifies that William Shakespeare was still around in Stratford in 1588, Armada year, during what are termed his 'lost years'.

As every historian knows, negative evidence regarding the existence of any records to establish Shakespeare's presence in Stratford is very doubtful grounds for assuming, as Shakespearean scholars do, that he was no longer there but had left home to begin his career as an actor-playwright. This is, again, to argue from the plays back to the man as the great actor-dramatist, but all the scouring of the records of the actors' companies of the time has failed to discover his name with any of them before the Christmas season of 1594–5. Up till that time all is a blank.

This disturbing blank has naturally received intense attention, fleshing out the total lack of evidence with hypotheses as to how William Shakespeare of Stratford-upon-Avon developed into the superlative dramatist who was hailed by Ben Jonson in the First Folio as 'Soul of the Age!' A theory, first advanced by E.K. Chambers, that he might have been the William Shakeshafte who was one of the servants named in the will of Alexander Hoghton of Lea in Lancashire, dated 3rd August 1581, when William Shakespeare would have been aged seventeen, has since been hopefully pursued by Douglas Hamer in 'Was William Shakespeare, William Shakeshafte?' (R.E.S. 1970, XXI, 41–8). Hamer's research has shown that Shakeshafte was a common family name in this part of Lancashire, and that William was a favourite name among the local Shakeshaftes listed in the Preston Burgess Rolls, Preston being near to Hoghton's manor in Lea. He also concluded that the William Shakeshafte of Hoghton's will was probably aged thirty to forty years in 1581 since he was bequeathed an annuity of 40s. in a list of ten especially favoured servants who each received annuities ranging from £3 6s. 8d. down to 13s. 4d. in addition to the year's wages that their master willed to all his household. Among these favoured ten only the age of Thomas Coston has been traced; he was twenty-nine years old in 1581, and he received 20s. It seems highly unlikely that a mere lad of seventeen with no wife or children to maintain would have been willed twice that amount to be paid 'for & during their natural lives' to these special servants. Henry Bond, aged 55, and Thomas Barton, aged 44, did not receive any annuity but only their year's wages. [15] The variation in the name from Shakespeare to Shakeshafte is not in itself an obstacle, for Elizabethan practice was elastic on this point. Marlowe signed his name Marley, and was also known as Marlin, and Henslowe, of the famous theatrical Diary, called himself Hinchlowe. The main point of interest was that Hoghton kept a troupe of players, and William Shakeshafte may have served him in this capacity – as a player. But here the possible connection ends, for Douglas Hamer points out that the Lancashire William Shakeshafte turns up in the service of Sir Thomas

Hesketh in 1597 as a player (?) still named Shakeshafte; whereas William Shakespeare was then with the Lord Chamberlain's Men. In 1582 he married in Stratford and was still there in 1585 when the twins were born, and is named in the Lambert case in 1588. Hamer therefore concludes that William Shakeshafte and William Shakespeare are two different people.

This conclusion does not satisfy E.A.J. Honigmann, however, who has taken up the challenge in his *Shakespeare: the 'lost' years* (1985) in which he claims that Hamer's case 'collapses'. He dismisses Hamer's solid evidence of the Lancashire Shakeshaftes and the incompatibility of age and dates and size of annuity, and replaces it with his theory of Shakespeare-Shakeshafte which he bases on John Aubrey's tale of Shakespeare's alleged youthful spell as a country schoolmaster. Aubrey is the least reliable of the early sources of biographical stories about Shakespeare, described by Anthony à Wood as 'magotie-pated' and 'exceedingly credulous'. Anthony à Wood had engaged Aubrey, who was then very impoverished, to gather information for his antiquarian research, but he soon found him a hopelessly unreliable investigator who stuffed his letters with 'follies and misinformation' which Wood rejected. [16] We do not know how Aubrey obtained his information, but doubtless a bit of palm-greasing was part of his method. He had the schoolmastering story from an aged actor, William Beeston, whose father, Christopher Beeston, had once been one of the 'principall Comœdians' of the Lord Chamberlain's company in 1598, but in 1602 had moved to the Earl of Worcester's Men. His son William died in 1682, so probably was born after his father had joined Worcester's Men. (His date of birth is not known.) Regarding his informant Beeston, Aubrey writes in his notes under '*W. Shakespeare*': 'quaere [query] Mr. Beeston, who knowes most of him from Mr. Lacy'. [17] So even Beeston's information was second-hand! Honigmann mentions none of these documented data, but, ignoring Anthony à Wood, he claims William Beeston as 'an excellent witness who was in a position to know the truth when he asserts that Shakespeare was in his younger years a schoolmaster in the country'.[18] If so, why was this most important piece of information never divulged to Thomas Betterton, who made a personal fact-finding pilgrimage to Stratford-upon-Avon to speak to the natives, who told him quite a different story about Shakespeare's early life and education? According to Betterton, Shakespeare had had only a brief grammar school education which would hardly have fitted him to become a schoolmaster. Betterton gives correct data on his father's trade, but Aubrey informs us that he was a butcher! So much for Professor Honigmann's 'excellent witness' reported by Aubrey.

On this dubious foundation, Honigmann constructs a tenuous hypothesis that Shakespeare, at the age of sixteen, was recommended to Hoghton's establishment as a young schoolmaster to teach children of his household (Hoghton himself had no children), but then gravitated swiftly to become a player instead of fulfilling his schoolmaster's job, and that he was the William Shakeshafte named so generously in his will, although he had only *recently* entered

Hoghton's service. Honigmann's 'reconstruction of events' is pure hypothesis based on the unreliable gossip of Aubrey, but it has nevertheless won acceptance in the academic traditions of Shakespearean orthodoxy. Honigmann claims that Hamer's evidence 'collapses', which is impossible since it is firmly founded on *documentary evidence*, whereas Honigmann's case is myth-based conjecture that flies in the face of both Hamer's well researched evidence and Betterton's more reliable reportage. [19] Both these are brushed aside in order to bolster the image of the Stratford Shakespeare, for whom historical truth is freely sacrificed.

The academics who rule our universities, of whom Professor Honigmann is one, are the sole arbiters of what is accepted as 'evidence' concerning Shakespeare. The criterion is simply: Does it fit in with received Shakespearean dogma? If so, it is 'in', no matter how tenuous the evidence. If it does not fit (e.g. Hotson's identification of 'Mr.W.H.' and the Dark Lady and even his remarkable research in *The First Night of Twelfth Night*) then it is passed over in silence, the evidence not cited in books on Shakespeare. This has been the fate of Dr. Allison Gaw's brilliant thesis on *The Origin and Development of I Henry VI: In Relation to Shakespeare, Marlowe, Peele and Greene* (1926) which represents the most thorough research that has ever been conducted on this play; but its inherent revolutionary implications for the orthodox view of Shakespeare inevitably meant that it would be relegated to oblivion by the *status quo*. Similarly, F.C. Tucker Brooke's definitive research in *The Authorship of the Second and Third Parts of 'King Henry VI'* (1921) has been buried in impenetrable silence after it was first subjected to a spurious debunking by Peter Alexander in his feigned refutation of the redoubtable Tucker Brooke's findings, which were fully supported by Marlowe's great biographer John Bakeless in 1942 attributing both these plays to Marlowe, written by him for the Pembroke Players for whom he wrote his *Edward the Second*. Bakeless has also been an embarrassment to the orthodox Shakespearean scholars. Both the foregoing outstanding pieces of research by Gaw and Tucker Brooke have been reviewed in detail in my *Christopher Marlowe and Edward Alleyn* (1993). As a result Tucker Brooke's findings have been completely validated; and a thorough reassessment of Gaw's long neglected research shows the vital importance of his work to our proper understanding of the theatrical history of this period in which Marlowe's partnership with Edward Alleyn was a dominant influence.

My research on Edward Alleyn has also thrown new light on the person lampooned as 'Shake-scene' in 1592, who is believed to be Shakespeare – an identification that is of crucial importance to the study of Shakespeare. If he really were William Shakespeare, as has been assumed, this would happily resolve the problem of his 'lost years', establishing his presence in London in 1592 as a practising actor-playwright. So who was he?

'Shake-scene' was scurrilously attacked by the dying, poverty-stricken Robert Greene in his *Groatsworth of Wit* in September 1592, to which he appended a Letter to his fellow dramatists: Marlowe, addressing him as 'Thou famous gracer of Tragedians', Peele, and Nashe, begging them to write no more for the actors who profiteered from their works, and denouncing one he cant-ingly described as a 'Shake-scene' who was cruel-hearted. The identification with Shakespeare was for years the subject of endless dispute among Shakespearean scholars when first made in 1766 by Thomas Tyrwhitt, splitting opinion into opposing camps as to why Greene was attacking Shakespeare as 'Shake-scene', for there is no evidence that the two men ever knew each other. At the height of the heated debate in 1928 J.S. Smart declared in exasperation: 'This passage from Greene has had such a devastating effect on Shakespearean study that we cannot but wish it had never been written, or never discovered.' [20] In a recent paper (1985) D. Allen Carroll, surveying the two-hundred-year-old debate on 'Shake-scene', comments:

> 'It is the first text after the plays themselves to command our atten-tion. And yet its special kind of vitality is so unsettled and compli-cated that we have not been able to agree as to its meaning or meanings. We turn to it again and again, and consequently have produced a small literature on the subject.' [21]

Clearly then, Shakespearean scholars themselves realise that the identifica-tion is extremely dubious. Nevertheless, orthodoxy clings to it with the tenac-ity of desperation because it is the *only* contemporary reference that can remotely be made to apply to Shakespeare's 'lost years'. Greene's 'Shake-scene' has become the linch-pin of the orthodox case for William Shakespeare of Stratford-upon-Avon as the author of the plays. But, alas for the Stratfordian case, this identification has been demolished by my research on Edward Alleyn. I give a brief resumé of these findings below.

GREENE'S GROATSWORTH OF WIT AND 'SHAKE-SCENE'

The whole episode of Greene's *Groatsworth of Wit* was a turbulent passage in Elizabethan London's literary, theatrical world, and proves most revealing – though not of Shakespeare. With his last breath Greene gave posterity the frank confessions of his profligate life, with much breast-beating public repentance. His autobiographical allegory, entitled *Greenes Groatsworth of Wit* is an extremely clever piece of writing, and most entertaining! It is essen-tial reading for anyone wishing to understand the gist of his Letter, which bears a direct relationship to his *Groatsworth* story, and is a bitter invective against the 'Apes' and 'Puppets' who lived off the backs of the dramatists whose plays, once sold to the players' company, became their copyright. It was an injustice that rankled with Greene. It was against this that he railed in impotent rage as he lay sick and dying of dropsy and the pox, with not even

32

the money to buy the medicines to alleviate his pain. Bitterly he blames the exploitation of his talents by one great actor in particular whom he described as being 'in his owne conceit the onely Shake-scene in a countrey', and gave him the canting name of *Johannes fac totum* by which to identify him satirically to his readers. Shakespearean scholars have ignored these clues so carefully left by Greene, who had a business relationship with the actor-manager Alleyn from the start of his career as a dramatist, which is documented in contemporary sources, in the Alleyn Papers and in Greene's autobiographical writings. Edward Alleyn acted as banker and money-lender to the impecunious dramatists he employed to write for his company, of whom Greene was one who was perennially in debt – and he charged interest, of which there is documentary evidence. [22.] Greene's *Groatsworth* makes a special point of attacking 'Usury'. His bitter diatribe blames the hard-hearted actors for his poverty and misery, and he aims his barbed satire at one great actor especially who epitomizes extreme cruelty 'with his Tygers hart wrapt in a Players hyde' – parodying a well-known line from a recent play, *The True Tragedy of Richard Duke of York*. This was the original publication – a truncated 'bad quarto' of *3 Henry VI* as it appears in the First Folio, and attributed to Marlowe by Tucker Brooke and Bakeless and Allison Gaw, among a host of other scholars. When Greene quoted this line it had no connection with Shakespeare or the First Folio, but the source is certainly the same play in which the quoted and parodied line appears.

Shakespearean orthodox scholars ignore the fact that the tiger was an Elizabethan symbol of cruelty and deceit, which Greene employs in order to libel the hated actor against whom he is pitifully railing, recalling the scene from the play in which this line is spoken by Richard, Duke of York, when Queen Margaret, the 'She-wolf of France', hands him a napkin soaked in the blood of his dead son:

> Oh Tygers hart wrapt in a womans hide!
> How couldst thou draine the life bloud of the childe,
> To bid the father wipe his eies withall,
> And yet be seene to beare a womans face? [23.]

As Ivor Brown has commented: 'The passage must have been powerfully delivered in the theatre and left its mark in the memory of audiences. Otherwise there would have been no point in pulling out the first line quoted, altering one word, and so talking of 'Shake-scene's' possession of a 'tyger's hart wrapt in a player's hide'. Nor would there have been any point in the taunt if Shakespeare had not been known as an actor.' [24.] Precisely. And in 1592 Shakespeare was not known as an actor, nor was he a money-lending actor-manager who employed Greene. Alleyn was all these things. But that is not all in this identification kit.

Greenes.

Sweet boy, might I aduise thee, be aduisde, and get not many enemies by bitter wordes : inueigh against vaine men, for thou canst do it, no man better, no man so well : thou hast a libertie to reprooue all, and name none; for one being spoken to, all are offended; none being blamed no man is iniured. Stop shallow water still running, it will rage, or tread on a worme and it will turne : then blame not Schollers vexed with sharpe lines, if they reproue thy too much liberty of reprofe.

And thou no lesse deseruing than the other two, in some things rarer, in nothing inferiour ; driuen (as my selfe) to extreme shifts, a litle haue I to say to thee: and were it not an idolatrous oth, I would sweare by sweet S. George, thou art vnworthy better hap, sith thou dependest on so meane a stay . Base minded men all three of you, if by my miserie you be not warnd: for vnto none of you (like mee) sought those burres to cleaue : those Puppets (I meane) that spake from our mouths, those Anticks garnisht in our colours. Is it not strange, that I, to whom they all haue beene beholding: is it not like that you, to whome they all haue beene beholding, shall (were yee in that case as I am now) bee both at once of them forsaken ? Yes trust them not : for there is an vpstart Crow, beautified with our feathers, that with his Tygers hart wrapt in a Players hyde, supposes he is as well able to bombast out a blanke verse as the best of you : and beeing an absolute Iohannes fac totum, is in his owne conceit the onely Shake-scene in a countrey. O that I might intreat your rare wits to be imploied in more profitable courses : & let those Apes imitate your past excellence, and neuer more acquaint them with your admired inuentions . I knowe the best husband of
you

Greene's *Groatsworth of Wit* Letter, 1592

As can be seen in the *Groatsworth* text in facsimile opposite, Greene used the term 'Shake-scene' as a descriptive common noun for a great actor who 'shakes a stage' and not as a homophonous name for a man called Shakespeare (or Shakeshaft, or Shake-anything) for the Elizabethan printer only capitalized the word, just as he capitalized most of the other common nouns in the passage, but he did not *italicize* 'Shake-scene' as he did all the proper nouns, such as *Robert Greene, Caine, Judas,* and *Johannes fac totum,* as was the invariable practice in printing at the time. *Johannes fac totum* is the actual name that Greene chose for his hated actor, which precisely satirized Edward Alleyn to his readers. Alleyn was just such a versatile Jack-of-all-trades with several strings to his bow. He was the greatest actor of his day, at twenty-six without rival and king of the stage; he was a fine musician, a successful theatre-manager, a property owner and landlord, a banker and money-lender; and (most galling to Greene) a successful, if minor, playwright who wrote what Greene considered to be mediocre plays in blank verse in excruciatingly bad English!

We have evidence in the theatrical *Diary* kept by Alleyn's father-in-law, Philip Henslowe, preserved among the Alleyn Papers, of a copious playwriting activity among the actors of the Lord Admiral's Men, who seem to have been a crew of scribbling actors, foremost of whom was Edward Alleyn himself. There are recorded numerous acquittances for the sale of plays to the company by the known dramatists of the day, such as Heywood, Dekker, Munday, Houghton, Chettle, and also a number of the actors of the Lord Admiral's, with no less than ten plays sold by Edward Alleyn, for which no other author is known. Since the play *Tambercam* is certainly by Alleyn, and is so acknowledged by the *Dictionary of National Biography*, there is no reason to doubt that the others he sold were all his own works, for this was an ambitious young man who would not have stopped at one successful play. Most of these were lost when Alleyn's theatre, the Fortune, was burnt to the ground in 1621 with all their play-scripts and properties. On external and internal evidence I have identified two plays by Alleyn that survived because they are in print. [25] These are heavily alliterative in style and use instances of a 'Dogberry-like' vocabulary that would merit the scorn poured on Alleyn's works by Greene, who was a Master of Arts twice over, whereas Alleyn was self-educated. However, the blank verse metre did not present difficulty, for had he not learnt the great roles of Marlowe by heart?

Alleyn's playwriting activity puts a completely different complexion on the passage in Greene's *Groatsworth* Letter, and removes forever the dubious credibility for fastening this unedifying quarrel onto William Shakespeare. Alleyn fits the bill in every punctilio, for he is also identifiable as the 'Player' featured in Greene's autobiographical *Groatsworth* story, who boasts that he wrote 'Morrals' (the old-fashioned genre of morality plays) for his 'Puppets', and who employed the hero of this tale, 'Roberto' (*alias* Robert Greene, as he expressly tells us) as his 'Arch-plaimaking poet' to whom the tiger-hearted 'Player' of the Letter is organically related. The 'Player' and 'Shake-scene' are one and the same man, a great actor to whom Greene was tied by his financial dependence. Greene's lampoon is very skilfully devised to make the identification of both 'Players' unmistakable, as *'Johannes fac totum* - Shakescene' of his libellous Letter, and as the character in the story who becomes his employer. He lards his whole *Groatsworth* story and Letter with identification tags which his readers would not fail to pick up, especially when read as cross-references. It was a game at which the Elizabethans were adept.

In treating Greene's notorious *Groatsworth* Letter in isolation, without reference to his autobiographical-allegorical tale to which it is appended, scholars have laid themselves open to being misled into the wishfulfilment that he could have been referring to William Shakespeare as 'Shake-scene'. This fallacious assumption has proved a major tragedy for Shakespearean scholars, diverting much fruitless effort into research that has proved a dead end.

This spurious identification is finally corrected by Edward Alleyn's authentic eligibility as *Johannes fac totum*. We can now write: 'Shake-scene' R.I.P.

Which brings us back to the unresolved problem: What was Shakespeare doing, and how did he become the superlative dramatist of the First Folio? If there is a frustrating lack of reliable evidence to cover Shakespeare's 'lost years', there is no dearth of mythos to fill the gap. We shall now examine the credibility of the evidence presented by the numerous, unedifying, traditional stories about William Shakespeare that have been assiduously garnered by ardent admirers.

V

THE SHAKESPEARE MYTHOS

IN THE RECORDS of human achievement William Shakespeare is peculiarly unique. There is no man of genius around whom such an accretion of hypothesis and mythos has formed, protecting and encapsulating his person from its historic, dim obscurity which, when placed in the context of factual documentary evidence, breathes only an air of mediocrity. This mythos about William Shakespeare of Stratford-upon-Avon consists of traditional tales based on local Stratford gossip recorded by antiquarians and others, who, knowing and revering Shakespeare's works, wished to learn more about the author himself. One of the most dedicated seekers after knowledge about Shakespeare was the actor, Thomas Betterton, who was famous for his performance of Hamlet during the Restoration.

Betterton made a special journey to Warwickshire in about 1690 'to gather up what remains he could of a name for which he had so great a value.'[1] He then passed on the information he gleaned to the poet, Nicholas Rowe, who brought out the first critical edition of Shakespeare's plays in 1709, prefaced with a formal biography incorporating what Betterton's informants had told him. This amounted to confirmation that Shakespeare had indeed had very little education. He learnt that William had attended 'a Free-School', such education being provided by Stratford's only grammar school, 'where 'tis probable he had acquir'd that little *Latin* he was Master of, but the narrowness of his circumstances, and the want of his assistance at home, forc'd his Father to withdraw him from thence, and unhappily prevented his further proficiency in that language.'[2] His schooling, then, was brief according to Stratfordian memory *circa* 1690.

Numerous anecdotes circulated from such late seventeenth century sources, all more or less unreliable. These proliferated from the 'magotie-pated' and 'exceedingly credulous' John Aubrey, whose tall stories were rejected by the antiquary Anthony à Wood, but eventually published posthumously as *Brief Lives*; and from the dramatist and theatrical impresario William Davenant (for whom Aubrey claimed Shakespeare as his illegitimate son) who copiously rewrote and revamped the great works for the theatrical tastes of the Restoration; from the Reverend John Ward, vicar of Stratford-upon-Avon from 1662, who, although on the spot, fell for some fanciful tales; and from sundry visitors to Stratford down the years who added to the store. All these traditional tales, the earliest dating from 1662, do absolutely nothing to enhance the image of William Shakespeare as the credible author of the works bearing his name.

Pope's version of the story that Davenant was Shakespeare's natural son, conceived when he stayed at the Davenant's inn in Oxford on his journeys to and from Stratford and London, derives from George Steevens' *Additional Anecdotes* in his edition of Shakespeare's plays in 1766, which are based on the eighteenth century antiquarian William Oldys's *Life of Shakespeare*, which is lost. The story originated from Aubrey, is not in Wood's *Athenae Oxonienses* and is unconfirmed by Rowe, *viz*. Betterton, who was a member of Davenant's company, which argues that it was spurious.

In sorting out myth from fact, it is Betterton who is our most reliable informant. He had assiduously questioned the inhabitants of Stratford-upon-Avon himself, and some of his data has proved verifiable and correct in the historical context; for instance, that John Shakespeare was in financial straits, whereas Aubrey's 'facts' have proved to be palpably inaccurate in all verifiable instances. It is from Betterton, himself a really great actor, that we learn that 'the top of his [Shakespeare's] performance was the Ghost in his own *Hamlet',* and also the deer stealing incident, when he poached venison from the lands of Sir Thomas Lucy, and to escape the law was 'oblig'd to leave his Business and Family' in *Warwickshire,* for some time, and shelter himself in *London'.* [3] No date for this departure is offered, so we are none the wiser; but it is stated by Betterton that until this 'Misfortune' Shakespeare had been living 'In this kind of Settlement', meaning 'his Business and Family' continually 'for some time'. There is no hint of any interlude as a country schoolmaster as Aubrey claims, nor can we deduce that he had begun acting in Lancashire as Honigmann believes.

Rowe, quoting Betterton, takes up the story from the time of the deer stealing incident:

> 'It is at this Time, and upon this Accident, that he is said to have made his first Acquaintance in the Play-house. He was receiv'd into the Company then in being, at first in a very mean Rank; but his admirable Wit, and the natural Turn of it to the Stage, soon distinguished him, if not as an extraordinary Actor, yet as an excellent Writer. His Name is Printed, before some old Plays, but without any particular Account of what sort of Parts he us'd to play, and tho' I have inquir'd, I could never meet with any further Account of him in this way, [here we are told of his performance as the ghost in *Hamlet,* and we note that Betterton had made the most earnest enquiries]. I should have been much more pleas'd, to have learn'd from some certain Authority, which was the first Play he wrote; it would be without doubt a pleasure to any Man, curious in Things of this Kind, to see and know what was the first Essay of a Fancy like *Shakespear's.* Perhaps we are not to look for his Beginnings, like those of other Authors, among their least perfect Writings; Art had so little, and Nature so large a Share in what he

did that, for ought I know, the Performances of his Youth, as they were the most vigorous, and had the most fire and strength of Imagination in 'em, were the best.' [4]

On the authority of Betterton, then, it seems that Shakespeare was, from the start, mainly of value to his company as a writer, not as an actor. The implication is that his position in the company was that of their play-broker, the provider of play-scripts, whether his own compositions or by other dramatists from whom they were purchased, as was the practice of the time for which Henslowe's *Diary* gives ample evidence. [5] The tantalizing question that hovers is: Were the superlative 'Shakespeare' plays his own compositions or were they supplied to him in his capacity of play-broker acting in this instance as the 'front man' cover for another? This is the problem we shall be addressing in detail in Chapter 22.

Rowe prints one story of doubtful origin of which he writes apologetically: 'If I had not been assur'd that the Story was handed down by Sir *William D'Avenant* . . I should not have ventur'd to have inserted, that my Lord *Southampton* at one time, gave him [Shakespeare] a thousand Pounds, to enable him to go through with a Purchase which he heard he had a mind to . .' [6] Now here is a tradition to be looked into more closely. Rowe was born in 1674, six years after Davenant's death in 1668 at which date Betterton, aged 23 years, was an actor in Davenant's company, but whether the story stems from Betterton is not clear. The sum of a thousand pounds is incredible, for the Earl of Southampton was a Ward of Court until he was aged 21 in 1595, when he was forced to pay five thousand pounds in breach of promise to Burghley's granddaughter, Elizabeth de Vere. He remained in dire financial straits for all his younger years, suffered imprisonment for his part in the Essex rebellion, and only gained stability in his affairs after the accession of King James, *by which time Shakespeare was comfortably off and had completed his purchase of New Place.* But we note that the giving of money from some other source is involved, and certainly William Shakespeare gained affluence above most of his fellow actors, but whence this flowed into his pockets we have no reliable evidence at all.

The deer stealing incidents were embellished by the Reverend Richard Davies, at one time rector of the Cotswold village of Sapperton, by whom the story was first written down at some time between 1688 and 1708, and he asserts that Sir Thomas Lucy had Shakespeare 'oft whipt & sometimes Imprisoned & at last made Him fly his Native Country', [7] but to date no legal records supporting these claims have turned up; or has such evidence not been zealously sought after? The stories are a hotch-potch of half-remembered gossip and local invention. Aubrey claims he was a butcher's son who 'kill'd a Calfe . . in a high style' and would 'make a Speech'. [8] A Mr Dowdall visiting Stratford in 1693 was also told by the clerk of Stratford parish church that Shakespeare had been 'bound apprentice to a butcher, that he ran from his master to London and was received into the playhouse as a serviture'. [9] Rowe more accurately described Shakespeare's father as 'a considerable Dealer in Wool', [10] who had a large family of ten children of whom William was the eldest, and with so many mouths to feed they were kept poor. In fact, William was the Shakespeares' third child, but eldest son, and their offspring numbered eight. But modern research has established that whilst his father was a glover, he also dealt in wool as a side-line. He owned rented property, and played a part in the municipal affairs of Stratford, eventually rising to the respectable position of alderman. In 1567 he was elected to the office of bailiff of the town, when William was aged three. He has left no single autograph, and was probably illiterate. In the late 1570's he fell on hard times and was unable to pay his debts. In the 1580's his financial troubles increased, and Stratford at this time was not thriving, for by the turn of the century 'the poor of Stratford numbered over 700, young and old: approximately half the population'. [11] The last decade of the century saw the little town in decline, and in 1594 and 1595 raging fires swept it, but spared the Shakespeares' house in Henley Street. William Shakespeare's fortunes were soon to look up – dramatically.

In 1662, the Reverend John Ward entered upon his living as vicar of Stratford, when in February of that year Shakespeare's daughter Judith was buried. The entries in Ward's notebook are the earliest recorded of traditional tales, and we hear again of Shakespeare's reputed affluence: 'I have heard y^t Mr Shakespeare was a natural wit, without any art at all; hee frequented ye plays all his younger time, but in his elder days lived at Stratford: and supplied ye stage with 2 plays every year, and for y^t had an allowance so large, y^t hee spent att ye Rate of a 1,000 ^{li} a year, as I have heard.' He reminds himself 'to peruse Shakespears plays, and bee versd in them, y^t I may not bee ignorant in y^t matter.' Perhaps he quoted them in his sermons? He adds: 'Shakespeare, Drayton, and Ben Jhonson, had a merry meeting, and itt seems drank too hard, for Shakespear died of a feavour there contracted.' [12]

If there were any truth at all in this, how very strange that neither Ben Jonson nor Michael Drayton, both great poets, contributed not a word, no poem, no elegy, no encomium upon the death of the greatest of them all, Shakespeare, which had followed so soon after their 'merry meeting'. It was unheard of for a poet of any repute to die unsung by his fellow poets. When Ben Jonson died in 1637 there was such a crowd of poets who hastened to pay tribute to him that a collection of elegies, in both English and Latin, was published the following year under the title *Jonsonus Virbius*. He was buried with all honour in Westminster Abbey, his tombstone inscribed: 'O rare Ben Jonson'.

Francis Beaumont died in the same year as Shakespeare, 1616, and was also laid to rest in Westminster Abbey with many elegiac verses to his memory. Michael Drayton, also hailing from Warwickshire, died in 1631 and was buried in Westminster Abbey his memory honoured by all his fellow poets, his monument erected by the Countess of Dorset with an inscription attributed to Ben Jonson. John Fletcher died in 1625, and was buried in St. Saviour's, now

Southwark Cathedral, joined in the same grave by his friend Philip Massinger in 1640, both remembered with many tributes by their poet friends. George Chapman died in 1634, and was buried in St Giles', the parish church of St Giles-in-the-Fields, duly honoured in verse by his friends, his monument designed by Inigo Jones. Edmund Spenser died in 1599, deeply mourned and laid in Westminster Abbey near Chaucer, his funeral expenses borne by the Earl of Essex. His monument was erected twenty years later by the Lady Anne Clifford naming him 'THE PRINCE OF POETS IN HIS TYME'.

In stark contrast, Shakespeare was left to be interred by the members of his family at Stratford, totally unremembered and unremarked by a single poet or writer of the time. The Earl of Southampton was still living, highly favoured by King James, now affluent, his title and lands all restored, but he too totally ignored the death of one who was allegedly *his* poet, to whom he had given large presents of money in his lifetime, we are told. No explanation for this strange silence is offered by orthodox Shakespearean scholars. The matter is not even discussed. It is simply ignored even by Southampton's biographers.

The doggerel verse inscription carved on a 'plain free stone' over his grave, placed there at his burial, was reputedly Shakespeare's own composition:

> GOOD FRIEND FOR JESUS SAKE FORBEARE,
> TO DIGG THE DUST ENCLOASED HEARE:
> BLESTE BE $\overset{E}{Y}$ MAN $\overset{T}{Y}$ SPARES THES STONES,
> AND CURST BE HE $\overset{T}{Y}$ MOVES MY BONES

This is seen as a warning to the church sexton not to disinter him and remove his remains to the nearby charnel-house, a practice used to make room for further burials. The monument later erected to William Shakespeare in Stratford's Holy Trinity Church also has a most curious history. The full story is told in the sequel to this book which presents new research on the First Folio.

Not until seven years later when the First Folio was brought out was any public recognition accorded to the immortal Shakespeare. Beaumont and Fletcher were similarly posthumously honoured with the publication of the first folio of their plays in 1647, but they had *also* been remembered in elegiac verse at their deaths. Ben Jonson saw his folio of works to the press in his lifetime. No shadow of doubt attaches to him: 'Contemporary literature of every description – from Clarendon to Milton, and from Milton to Herrick – abounds with testimonies together proving his position to have been unrivalled among the men of letters of his times.' [13] Ben Jonson was 'Father Ben' to the younger generation of poets, who adulated him, calling themselves his sons 'of the tribe of Ben'. In later life he held court in the Apollo Room of the Devil's Tavern, relishing the convivial company of his large circle of literary friends. Shakespeare, by contrast, had no literary friends.

There is an abundance of real evidence giving us a vivid picture of Ben

Jonson as man and writer – a credible human being of genius. But his name is dragged into some of the traditional yarns about Shakespeare, presumably in order to colour them with a semblance of truth, which have nothing to do with the genuine evidence of Ben Jonson and his friendships, which are all in the literary world of his day, including the cultured literary nobility. Placed against this genuine evidence of social intercourse with his real friends, the stories of Ben's supposed friendship with William Shakespeare (whom he certainly knew well, but never befriended) are obviously spurious. The antiquary Thomas Fuller, in his *Worthies of England*, (1662) which contains a chapter devoted to 'Worthies of Warwickshire', gives free rein to his imagination in depicting supposed 'wit-combats betwixt him [Shakespeare] and Ben Johnson, which two I behold like a Spanish great galleon and an English man-of-war; Master Johnson (like the former) was built far higher in learning; solid, but slow in his performances. Shake-spear with the English man-of-war, lesser in bulk, but lighter in sailing, could turn with all tides, tack about and take advantage of all winds, by the quickness of his wit and invention.' [14] Fuller was aged eight when Shakespeare died.

These fanciful tales of wit-combats between Shakespeare and his very good 'friend' Ben Jonson with whom he indulged in merry drinking bouts (but who did not bother to acknowledge his death), and the repeated mythos about unedifying doggerel verses composed by Shakespeare, to which Jonson allegedly sometimes contributed an extempore couplet or verse, are evidence of persistent attempts to infuse some literary, poetic element into these traditional stories. It is as though a confused sense of the greatness of a poet-dramatist called William Shakespeare had slowly penetrated the consciousness of the Stratford inhabitants; and when eager seekers after knowledge about this native genius arrived to question them long after he was dead, the locals did their best to marry the great writer with their recollection of this prosperous Stratford citizen, and a curiously garbled collection of stories emerged which became established tradition. In a small town gossip soon circulates – and there was, of course, the monument, which is not quite all it seems as we shall see in the comprehensive investigation that is included in the sequel to this book.

❖   ❖   ❖

When Shakespeare died he left a detailed will in which he made careful allocation of bequests of money to his former fellow actors, Burbage, Heminge and Condell for the purchase of memorial 'ringes'. Not a single *literary* figure is mentioned, not even Ben Jonson! Obviously he had no literary friends at all. Is that not strange? No books or manuscripts are mentioned, very valuable items in those days, especially to a writer. We can compare Shakespeare's will with that of his son-in-law, the physician Dr. John Hall, married to his favourite daughter, Susanna, to whom Shakespeare left the bulk of his estate. Hall specifically mentions his 'study of books' and his 'manuscripts' with solicitous care in his nuncupative (orally declared) will in 1635. Schoenbaum suggests that Shakespeare did not mention these because: 'Books might have been separately itemized in the inventory post-mortem, but this has not come down. In any event, they would form part of the goods inherited by the Halls, and perhaps thus found a place on the doctor's shelves alongside his medical treatises.' [15] 'Perhaps' is a useful word. Scholars take comfort from the fact that some other writers have failed to mention books in their wills – although this is not the case with Bacon, as is sometimes falsely alleged. This negative evidence leaves the question open. Nevertheless, it is sufficiently demonstrated that the evidence of the will, with its bequests to fellow actors and Stratford friends and his family is wholly compatible with the image of the Stratford Shakespeare of the traditional tales, some of which derive from times within living memory of this prominent citizen of that little town.

What is significant is that William Shakespeare of Stratford himself never made any claim to the authorship of the plays presented to the world in his name. Any printer was free to use his famous name on the title pages of works, irrespective of their authenticity. He never complained. The sole instance that is recorded of Shakespeare having *allegedly* objected to these piratical practices was reported second-hand to the printer Jaggard by Thomas Heywood, who was lodging a severe complaint on his own account over Jaggard's theft of two of his own poems – but Shakespeare, whose name was being misused, referred to by Heywood as 'the Author' (not by name) who was 'much offended', [16] here only spoke *through* Heywood, and did not bother to complain in his own person, although this was the third edition of that piratical work! Jaggard thereupon did take note by removing the offending title-page bearing the legend 'By W. Shakespeare', and the whole miscellany was anonymously presented. Anonymous publication and casual authorial ascription were so commonly practised that *the ideal conditions were created in which a pseudonymous author could remain obscured.*

The reader is by now perceiving my drift. We are on the track of a pseudonymous author named William Shakespeare, about whose identity there was some confusion even in his own day, for many plays and poems were falsely ascribed to him in publications using his name. There was also an actor named William Shakespeare, hailing from Stratford-upon-Avon – whose name was spelt in the usual whimsical variants current in Elizabethan practice: Shakespere, Shaxsper, Shakyspere, Shakspear, but this need not concern us for it was normal in those days. They all refer to the same man without question. And that is not the point. The actor was a real man, and he performed a vitally important function in this history.

It is also evident that the pseudonymous writer William Shakespeare, whose name was often deliberately printed as Shake-speare, with the intent, I believe, to indicate its identification as a *nom de plume*, and the actor of that name were, over the years, in some degree associated, until finally, with the publication of the First Folio seven years after the Stratford actor's death, they were *deliberately* fused and publicly identified as the same, yet *in a cryptographic manner* as subsequent investigation of the First Folio will demonstrate.

We have already noted evidence that the actor Shakespeare and Ben Jonson were not dear friends – they are so presented only in the traditional stories. No evidence in their real lives supports this: in fact, it is contradicted by all the evidence. Yet they knew each other well, for both belonged for many years to the same leading company of actors, and William Shakespeare, the player, is listed in the cast of Jonson's *Every Man in his Humour*, acted in 1598, and *Sejanus* in 1603; but Jonson's attitude to Shakespeare is one of the puzzles to be solved.

Ben Jonson is a key figure in this inquiry. His controversial testimony concerning Shakespeare is fully covered in the sequel to this book, but it is relevant to refer to it briefly here. In his book *Timber or Discoveries, made upon Men and Matter*, in 1641, which is a collection of his literary commentaries and thoughts 'flowing out of his Daily Readings', Jonson passes censure on the poets of his day in general. His criticism is sometimes trenchant. He singles out Shakespeare and Bacon for individual appraisal, devoting about a page of his little book to each of these greatest men and writers of his time. Of Shakespeare, after censuring him for what he considers the prolixity of his style, he adds: 'I loved the man, and do honour his memory (this side of idolatry) as much as any.' [17] Is this, then, the actor whose funeral obsequys he ignored? And of whom we have not a single valid, genuine piece of evidence testifying that Ben loved him in real life? Nothing – except the spurious traditional tales that proliferated in the absence of credible consistent documentary evidence. The relationship of Ben Jonson with the Stratford actor is strangely blank, whereas his friendships and quarrels with other dramatists are without question; and into this lacuna the traditional tales have expanded to swamp the historical picture.

The spate of legend and mythos which surrounds Shakespeare is without parallel. The stories have become increasingly extravagant and exaggerated as his figure receded into the dimness of the past. They burgeoned throughout the eighteenth century, and in the nineteenth century, when Bardolatry acquired the zeal of a religion, they emerged dressed in such glittering fancy as to proclaim them blatantly spurious. Invention ran riot, casting historicity to the winds.

One story tells how Queen Elizabeth herself attended the Globe to see Shakespeare act – he has by now blossomed into a superb actor as well as a great dramatist!

This gem is taken from Richard Ryan's collection of *Dramatic Table Talk; or Scenes, Situations & Adventures, Serious & Comic in Theatrical History & Biography* published in 1852, and doubtless lapped up by the Victorian readers avid for any stories about their favourite theatrical personalities. It is pure fantasy.

'It is well known that Queen Elizabeth was a great admirer of the immortal Shakespeare, and used frequently (as was the custom with persons of great rank in those days) to appear upon the stage before the audience, or to sit delighted behind the scenes, when the plays of our bard were performed. One evening, when Shakespeare himself was personating the part of a King, the audience knew of her Majesty being in the house. She crossed the stage when he was performing, and, on receiving the accustomed greeting from the audience, moved politely to the poet, but he did not notice it! When behind the scenes, she caught his eye, and moved again, but still he would not throw off his character, to notice her: this made her Majesty think of some means by which she might know, whether he would depart, or not, from the dignity of his character, while on the stage. Accordingly, as he was about to make his exit, she stepped before him, dropped her glove, and re-crossed the stage, which Shakespeare noticing, took up, with these words, immediately after finishing his speech, and so aptly were they delivered, that they seemed to belong to it:

> 'And though now bent on this high embassy,
> Yet *stoop* we to take up our *Cousin's* glove!'

'He then walked off the stage, and presented the glove to the Queen, who was greatly pleased with his behaviour, and complimented him upon the propriety of it.'

Whoever concocted this one is following the tradition of extempore composition of verses that is found in some of the spurious tales about Jonson and Shakespeare. Queen Elizabeth, of course, never attended the public theatres! The players came to her at the Court.

In the nineteenth century an over-zealous Bardolatry went to ridiculous lengths in the creation of fictions to amuse those ignorant and credulous readers, who were the stage-struck fans of Victorian England. The Shakespeare myths could fill a book and there are endless variant versions of the same stories inspired by a desire to know more about the man who wrote the great dramatic works than is afforded by the recorded history, which is so excessively dull as to engender romanticizing.

As a dramatist Shakespeare stands in a class apart, even when seen in the context of the talented poet-dramatists of his own day. Yet he chose, apparently, to clothe his genius in the person of a mundane actor about whom nothing of interest is known, who had no intellectual or cultured friends to cluster at his graveside; and no matter how we try, no one has succeeded in discovering any

attributes that make the actor William Shakespeare, who spent his entire professional life cloistered always with the one actors' company, appear as the
credible personification of the superlative dramatic poet,

Shake-speare.

That this form of the name was widely known by his contemporaries to be a
nom de plume is demonstrated repeatedly by the way it was used in print.

Here, for instance, John Webster, in his preface 'To the Reader' when his
play *The White Devil* was published in 1612, includes a warm commendation
of the work of his fellow dramatists:

> 'I have ever truly cherisht my good opinion of other mens worthy
> labours; especially of that full and heightned stile of Maister *Chapman,*
> the labor'd and understanding workes of Maister *Johnson,* the no lesse
> worthy composures of both worthily excellent Maister *Beaumont,* &
> Maister *Fletcher,* and lastly (without wrong last to be named) the right
> happy and copious industry of M. *Shake-speare,* M. *Decker,* & M.
> *Heywood;* wishing what I write may be read by their light ..' [18]

The other dramatists do not have their names hyphenated – we never see
them printed Chap-man or Hey-wood or Beau-mont. Whereas we frequently
encounter Shake-speare. Why is this? It is a question orthodoxy never asks, but
there must be a reason for this constantly repeated form of the name. It is strikingly presented in Heywood's poem *The Hierarchie of the Blessed Angells*, in
1634, in which he lists the poets of his day with their familiarly used abbrevi-
ated Christian names:

> *Marlo,* renown'd for his rare art and wit,
> Could ne'er attaine beyond the name of *Kit;*
> Although his *Hero and Leander* did
> Merit addition rather. Famous *Kid*
> Was called but *Tom. Tom Watson,* though he wrote
> Able to make *Apollo's* selfe to dote
> Upon his Muse; for all that he could strive,
> Yet never could at his full name arrive.
> *Tom Nash* (in his time of no small esteeme)
> Could not a second syllable redeeme.
> Excellent *Bewmont,* in the formost ranke
> Of the rar'st Wits, was never more than *Franck.*
> Mellifluous *Shake-speare,* whose inchanting Quill
> Commanded Mirth or Passion, was but *Will.*
> And famous *Johnson,* though his learned Pen
> Be dipt in *Castaly,* is still but *Ben.*
> *Fletcher* and *Webster,* of that learned packe
> None of the mean'st, yet neither was but *Jacke.*

Deckers but *Tom;* nor *May* nor *Middleton,*
But hee's now but *Jacke Foord,* that once were *John.* [19]

Not one of these names in hyphenated, excepting Shake-speare. Numerous similar examples could be cited, and the practice continued for decades after the actor's death, always with reference to his literary work. As late as 1656 the anonymous play *The Hectors: or the False Challenge* printed the name in this hyphenated form along with the characters Know-well and Mrs Love-wit in this style for obvious reasons:

> *Mrs Love-wit.* Some times your wife may read a piece
> of *Shake-spear, Suckling* and *Ben Jonson,*
> if you can understand him. [20]

This is more than mere fashion. The hyphenated name has, I suggest, a special significance in literature denoting contemporary knowledge that it represented a *nom de plume*; but this knowledge was held by tacit agreement as an open secret amongst the circle of poets, writers and cultured people, the *'literati'* of England, one might call them, some of whom, as may be deduced from the evidence, must also have known who this concealed author was, and were party to assisting him in the maintenance of his secret identity. From the late 1590's onwards the name Shake-speare became increasingly current, although also sometimes printed Shakespeare. Its original introduction with *Venus and Adonis* was simply 'William Shakespeare'.

Such a tacit agreement recognizing the *nom de plume*, yet never divulging the real identity of the pseudonymous writer, should not prove too difficult for orthodox Shakespearean scholars to accept as feasible, for orthodoxy has for decades practised a similar collusion; observing a tacit agreement not to ask any awkward questions about Shakespeare of Stratford, and carefully papering over the cracks that reveal his lack of education, his low level of life amongst the actors who were his friends, Burbage, Heminge, Condell, and his Stratford cronies – good people, doubtless, but hardly offering the intellectual stimulus his writings so amply reflect; and his main interest in property acquisition and material gain which squares not at all with the Poet of the Sonnets.

This is further reinforced by the documentary evidence identifying William Shakespeare merely as an actor, associating him with his fellow players without any hint of the admiration for his genius so ardently expressed in comments from the literary men of his day for the famous poet, 'mellifluous Shakespeare'. The discrepancy is striking. When the actor Augustine Phillips died in 1605 he named Shakespeare in his will:

> 'Item. I give and bequeath to my fellow William Shakespeare a thirty shillings piece in gold.' [21]

Perhaps the most significant of these pieces of documentary evidence under-lying the separate identities of the two William Shakespeares, the humble actor and the great poet-dramatist, is that presented by the Burbages, Cuthbert Burbage and Winifred, widow of Cuthbert's brother, the great actor Richard Burbage. In 1635 these two were presenting a petition to Philip, Earl of Pembroke and Montgomery, the surviving brother of the 'Incomparable Paire' to whom the First Folio is dedicated, appealing to him for recognition of their rights and interests in the Globe theatre, then in jeopardy, which had been built at their expense. Referring to the past history of their theatre, and to those play-ers and profit-sharers with them, the petition states:

> 'To ourselves we joined those deserving men, Shakspere, Heminge, Condall, Phillips, and others, partners in the profits' [22]

They also refer to their other theatrical venture, the Blackfriars theatre, for-merly leased for the performances of the Children of the Chapel, which the Burbages reclaimed for the use of their own company in 1608, when they 'placed men players, which were Heminge, Condall, Shakespeare, etc.'[23]

Here is how Shakespeare's fellow actors saw him; he was one of those 'deserving men' of the Globe, and a man player at the Blackfriars, not the author of their most outstanding dramatic works, constantly performed. And, more significantly, *this* is how they presented him to the Earl of Pembroke who was patron of the dramatic literature of this genius, whose First Folio was ded-icated to him.

This documentary reference to Shakespeare is omitted from Schoenbaum's great, comprehensive, definitive biography of William Shakespeare of Stratford-Upon-Avon. One cannot help wondering what prompted this over-sight.

It is perhaps also significant that in 1602, when a dispute arose in the College of Arms over the granting of heraldic arms somewhat freely to applicants con-sidered to be too base-born for such honours, a list of cases for complaint was drawn up, in which Shakespeare's arms appear. Under a drawing of his armor-ial shield and crest is written:

> 'Shakespear y[e] Player
> by garter' [24]

Schoenbaum suggests that this association with his profession is here intended pejoratively to emphasise the reason for the complaint. Be that as it may, the York Herald, Ralph Brooke, who drew up this list, evidently did not associate William Shakespeare, the player, with the famous poet who wrote *Venus and Adonis* and *Lucrece,* dedicated to the Earl of Southampton who, we are told, highly favoured the poet. A poet, if not a player, could certainly com-mand respect. Heralds were drawn from the educated classes, and it seems strange that, in the small world of the Elizabethan Court, Brooke was totally unaware that this applicant for arms was one of the most famous poets of the day. Or did Brooke know more than we do?

THE SHAKESPEAREAN AUTHORSHIP PROBLEM

The rumblings of inevitable doubts concerning the attribution of the authorship of the superb works to the actor, William Shakespeare, erupted in the emergence of the 'Baconian' theory in the mid-nineteenth century when Bardolatry was at its height. It was, in a sense, a by-product of that zealous adulation of the Bard, which threw into sharper relief the inadequacy of the man from Stratford to measure up to his elevated image. 'Baconians' were soon locked in battle with the orthodox Shakespearean school and echoes of the furore travelled across the Atlantic, where Henry James' attentive ear caught them. In August 1903 Henry James wrote a letter to a friend in which he confessed:

> 'I am "sort of" haunted by the conviction that the divine William is the biggest and most successful fraud ever practised on a patient world. The more I turn him round and round the more he so affects me. But that is all – I am not pretending to treat the question or carry it further. It bristles with difficulties, and I can only express my general sense by saying that I find it *almost* as impossible to conceive that Bacon wrote the plays as to conceive that the man from Stratford, as we know the man from Stratford, did.' [25]

It was another sceptic, who was also not a 'Baconian', nor proffering an alternative authorship theory, who grasped this nettle danger, bristling with difficulties as it is, and tackled the problem with great erudition that shook the orthodox school out of its complacency. This was George Greenwood who is also known as Sir Granville Greenwood, an eminent barrister-at-law and member of Parliament, who presented the case against William Shakespeare of Stratford, with all the urbanity, intelligence and logical exposition of the practised lawyer, to devastating effect in his book *The Shakespeare Problem Restated* in 1908.

This publication drew upon his head the baleful ire of Shakespearean scholars, who attacked him with so many blows below the belt that Greenwood found it necessary to write a second book to reply to the falsehoods of his accusers, *Is There a Shakespeare Problem?*, which appeared in 1916. He followed this with *Ben Jonson and Shakespeare* in 1921. These works remain classics in the battle over the authorship question, which refuses to lie down, every now and again rising to disturb the surface of complacent acceptance of the *status quo*. It is an emotive question Greenwood asks, for precisely what

49

orthodoxy does not permit is the asking of questions.

Greenwood's summing up is pertinent: 'My last comment on the life of William Shakespere of Stratford shall be this. Meagre as our knowledge of it is, it is yet too much. Mr. Lee's claim [this is Sir Sidney Lee, the great Shakespearean biographer] that we have "a mass of biographical detail which far exceeds that of any poet contemporary with Shakespeare" is indeed sufficiently ridiculous, but it would be far better for the Stratfordian theory if we had no biographical detail at all. If we knew nothing we might imagine anything. What we do know is fatal to the case. It gives rise to the strongest possible presumption against the identity of Shakspere the player with Shakespeare the poet.' [26]

Greenwood suggests that the actor Shakespeare was accepted by his fellows as the broker for the 'Shakespearean' plays, the middle-man dealer who bought them for the company from his source of supply, hence to them they were 'Shakespeare's plays' [27] This brokerage was normal practice, as already discussed. A leading actor would make the purchase of plays to add to the stock of play-scripts, which belonged to the company and after the completed transaction they were usually held jointly, together with their properties, and perhaps their musical instruments, in the name of those members who were share-holders or 'house-keepers' and not 'hired men'. Greenwood's theory is both feasible and practical, and reflects the known theatrical practices of the time. It does not explain the whole of this complex situation but it is, I believe, an essential part of it.

The evidence so far has presented a reasoned basis for the theory that the name William Shakespeare was a well-known *nom de plume*. There are many famous examples in literary history, and it is always the *nom de plume* which survives as immortal and seems to acquire an identity of its own. No one today remembers that Voltaire was really Francois-Marie Arouet, or that Mark Twain was born Samuel Langhorne Clemens. Lewis Carroll conceals the Oxford don, Charles Dodgson; André Maurois was Emile Herzog in real life; George Eliot was the disguise for Mary Ann Evans, and George Sand was born Amandine Aurore Lucie Dupin, who became Baronne Dudevant by marriage, and wrote her novels as a plea for feminine independence. These writers chose to cloak themselves in pseudonyms for reasons partly or wholly of protection for their professional or social status, or for political, philosophical or religious ideas they wanted to be free to express. The *nom de plume* William Shakespeare as Shake-speare came to have a special connotation: *to shake a spear at ignorance* – an easy adaptation from the name of the living man with whom a deal was struck, as will be established, to use his name as a protective device for the hidden author and his friends in circumstances of great danger.

Who was he, this man behind the *nom de plume* 'William Shakespeare'?

This question Greenwood left in abeyance awaiting the candidate who would eventually claim the seat of honour, all conditions fulfilled. But Greenwood's thesis is not negative, for he paved the way by asking the pertinent questions and stating the case.

> 'What I submit is, that this traditional Shakspere, taking him as a
> whole, does not in any way fulfil the conditions necessary for the
> sublime poet, the profound philosopher, the universal teacher, the
> creator of Hamlet and Lear and Prospero, the cultured courtier, the
> erudite lawyer, in short, the all in all that the greatest critics have
> recognized in Shakespeare, as revealed to them by the immortal
> works themselves.' [28]

It is difficult enough to accept him as the author of the plays, yet orthodoxy
has managed it by blind loyalty to the Stratford actor, recreating him in the
image of the dramatist by arguing back from the plays to the man. He is almost
a symbol rather than a man – a super-human being who is the very essence of
human genius, who transcended his mundane background by sheer force of his
imagination, to roam in Illyria, to recreate English history, and to breathe powerful dramatic life into human scenes ranging from the tavern to the throne
room, and all of it informed with scholarly erudition in every field he touches.
Who knows what arduous reading he did to acquire all this specialist knowledge? He was, above all else, a born poet to whom the music of language was
a part of his being, and such a poet begins to practise his art early in life. He
could not suddenly emerge in his thirtieth year as the author of *Venus and
Adonis.*

If it is difficult to see the Stratford actor as the author of the plays, it is
impossible to do so in relation to the sonnets. These remarkable poems, it is
widely agreed, represent his autobiographical writings, and to the puzzlement
and frustration of orthodox Shakespearean scholars, there is no link at all
between the sonnets and Shakespeare of Stratford. But no one asks, Why?

It is this forbidden question that I have the temerity to ask here. I hope I shall
be forgiven, when the dust has settled. It is, after all, the *nom de plume* William
Shakespeare which personifies his spirit. Stratford-upon-Avon need have no
worries. It will always survive as the seat of the 'Divine William', and even if
he does turn out to be the biggest fraud his continued success is assured, for he
is irretrievably linked with the greatest poet-dramatist in our language, who
lives immortally in his *nom de plume*, William Shakespeare.

The Presentation of the Argument thus concluded will seem heavy with mystery to some who have grown accustomed to thinking of their Shakespeare as that country-bred, natural genius, who could read sermons from stones, and without more than a basic education nevertheless achieved universal acclaim as the greatest poet-dramatist the world has known; deeply-read in the classics, in philosophy and the highest reaches of the knowledge of his time, as familiar with the manners of the court as he was with those of the tavern – as testified by his canon of works; but his life simple, clear and uncontroversial, himself a child of nature, a blessed and unexplained phenomenon of human genius.

In fact, controversy has divided scholars and informed, intelligent laymen and women as far back as the beginning of Shakespearean study, and the 'Riddle of the Sonnets' has been at the centre of the argument and speculation wherever these poems have been read. The mystery is right here – in these poems. They are both the mystery and the solution.

We are now launched on a voyage of discovery to find the true author, if he is to be found, who is concealed behind the famous *nom de plume*, 'William Shakespeare', tracking him down through the entire sequence of his acknowledged autobiographical writings, his *Sonnets,* through separating these poems into *their themes* in which each individual poem must appear plainly relevant to the life of the author – a style and mode of procedure that has not been attempted before in precisely this manner.

THE REVELATION

VI

THE RIDDLE OF THE SONNETS ANSWERED

THE DISTURBING BLANK of William Shakespeare's early manhood culminates in his sudden emergence in 1593 – a significant date to note – with the publication of *Venus and Adonis* revealing him as the consummate poet. Immediately we are presented with a paradox – the common player of no known experience bursts onto the scene as this highly educated, courtly writer. A deal of scholarly guesswork has endeavoured to supply a framework in which we may discern the developing dramatic poet, using tenuous arguments drawn from the plays to flesh out the image of the man who is the genius of the First Folio. This is accepted as a valid and proper procedure.

Orthodox scholarship has thus set the precedent. I propose to adopt the orthodox approach applying this to the acknowledged autobiographical evidence in the Sonnets, matching this meticulously to argue from what is clearly stated in these poems to flesh out the man, the Poet who wrote them, whose life must reflect *precisely* what the poems tell us in order to identify the author as the pseudonymous poet-dramatist Shake-speare. What we are seeking is a close and clearly identifiable correlation in the Poet's life with the main themes of the sonnet-sequence which is acknowledged as his autobiographical testimony. Following these main themes which are derived from the Sonnets, as can be verified by simply reading the poems, the criteria to be met are readily identifiable.

1. The Theme of the Poet's Anonymity

One of the strangest and most puzzling themes of the Sonnets is their recurring reference to the Poet's *anonymity*. Whoever he was, he must, therefore, have had *a compelling reason in his life for concealing his identity*. A concealment which it was not intended should ever be disclosed.

> No longer mourn for me when I am dead,
> Than you shall hear the surly sullen bell
> Give warning to the world that I am fled
> From this vile world with vilest worms to dwell;
> Nay, if you read this line, remember not
> The hand that writ it, for I love you so,
> That I in your sweet thoughts would be forgot,
> If thinking on me then should make you woe.
> O if (I say) you look upon this verse,
> When I (perhaps) compounded am with clay,

Do not so much as my poor name rehearse,
But let your love even with my life decay,
   Lest the wise world should look into your moan,
   And mock you with me after I am gone.

Sonnet 71

My name be buried where my body is,
And live no more to shame nor me, nor you;

Sonnet 72

Though I, once gone, to all the world must die.

Sonnet 81

2. The Maintenance of his Anonymity for 400 Years.

He must have had the able *assistance of others* in maintaining his anonymity
to the grave and beyond, for this is what was achieved with astonishing and
total success. It was clearly planned and intended.

3. The Identification of the Patron Who was a True Friend.

He must already have gained a *Patron of sufficient social standing* to be
addressed both as 'Lord' and 'dear friend'. The central theme is that of truest,
undying friendship, which is movingly expressed in the Sonnets. His true
friend was somehow involved in the tragedy that overwhelmed the Poet in
which this influential man was able to comfort and succour him.

Lord of my love, to whom in vassalage
Thy merit hath my duty strongly knit;
To thee I send this written ambassage
To witness duty, not to show my wit;
Duty so great, which wit so poor as mine
May make seem bare, in wanting words to show it,
But that I hope some good conceit of thine
In thy soul's thought (all naked) will bestow it;
Till whatsoever star that guides my moving,
Points on me graciously with fair aspect,
And puts apparel on my tattered loving,
To show me worthy of thy sweet respect.
   Then may I dare to boast how I do love thee,
   Till then, not show my head where thou mayst prove me.

Sonnet 26

Let me confess that we two must be twain,
Although our undivided loves are one,
So shall those blots that do with me remain,
Without thy help, by me be borne alone.
In our loves there is but one respect,
Though in our lives a separable spite,
Which though it alter not love's sole effect,
Yet doth it steal sweet hours from love's delight.
I may not ever more acknowledge thee,
Lest my bewailed guilt should do thee shame,
Nor thou with public kindness honour me,
Unless thou take that honour from thy name.
    But do not so: I love thee in such sort,
    As thou being mine, mine is thy good report.

Sonnet 36

4. A major Theme is a Journey into Exile.

He must have experienced *a distant journey* in which he felt lonely and afflicted – a journey which can only be likened to a journey into exile. The Sonnets of Exile, as I have termed them, when extracted from the whole sonnet-sequence form the largest group on any major theme in the entire book. This is broken up by small groups, or single sonnets that are unrelated to the theme of exile. This deliberately broken method of presentation has skilfully obscured the length and duration of this journey which cut him off from his friends and former life. Once the strands of the themes are sorted out, the fact emerges that this event was of the gravest, indeed of cataclysmic importance in the Poet's life. It represented a turning point from which there was no going back, and he had to accept his tragic fate. I have already quoted *Sonnet 50* (How heavy do I journey on the way) and *Sonnet 29* (When in disgrace with Fortune and men's eyes) from this group. Here are two more:

Weary with toil, I haste me to my bed,
The dear repose for limbs with travel tired,
But then begins a journey in my head
To work my mind, when body's work's expired;
For then my thoughts (from far where I abide)
Intend a zealous pilgrimage to thee,
And keep my drooping eyelids open wide,
Looking on darkness which the blind do see:
Save that my soul's imaginary sight
Presents thy shadow to my sightless view,
Which like a jewel (hung in ghastly night)
Makes black night beauteous, and her old face new.

Lo, thus by day my limbs, by night my mind,
For thee, and for myself, no quiet find.

In the next sonnet he bemoans the loss of 'vanish'd sights' and 'precious friends hid in death's dateless night', but it is not his friends who are dead, it is the Poet himself who is 'dead' to the world, and is now in exile.

When to the sessions of sweet silent thought,
I summon up remembrance of things past,
I sigh the lack of many a thing I sought,
And with old woes new wail my dear times' waste:
Then can I drown an eye (unus'd to flow)
For precious friends hid in death's dateless night,
And weep afresh love's long-since cancell'd woe,
And moan th' expense of many a vanish'd sight.
Then can I grieve at grievances foregone,
And heavily from woe to woe tell o'er
The sad account of fore-bemoaned moan,
Which I new pay, as if not paid before.
    But if the while I think on thee (dear friend)
    All losses are restor'd, and sorrows end.

Sonnet 30

5. The Theme of Disgrace and Scandal attached to his Name

His name and reputation must have suffered *unmerited disgrace and scandal* which he felt powerless to refute, though he was innocent. Four sonnets are entirely devoted to this theme, but the echoes of 'this disgrace' are never far absent from many in the group of Exile. These wounds have scars which have never fully healed. The bitterness in some of these lines is sheer gall.

'Tis better to be vile than vile esteemed,
When not to be, receives reproof of being,

Sonnet 121

Your love and pity doth th' impression fill
Which vulgar scandal stamp'd upon my brow,
For what care I who calls me well or ill,
So you o'er-green my bad, my good allow?
You are my All the world, and I must strive
To know my shames and praises from your tongue;
None else to me, nor I to none alive,

That my steel'd sense or changes right or wrong.
In so profound abysm I throw all care
Of others' voices, that my adder's sense
To critic and flatterer stopped are.
Mark how with my neglect I do dispense:
   You are so strongly in my purpose bred,
   That all the world besides me thinks y'are dead. *

Sonnet 112

* 'y'are dead' follows Thorpe's edition. This line has had some nonsensical alterations by some editors. It is discussed later.

6. Identification of the Rival Poet in Relation to the True Patron.

He must be seen to stand in a *triangular relationship of appropriate significance with the Patron and the Rival* Poet to account for the searing jealousy expressed in the Sonnets of the Rival Poet, which form a group of fourteen poems, followed by four sonnets of reconciliation which are clearly relevant to this episode. This group of sonnets has the strongest possible bearing not only on the correct identification of the Rival Poet, but also on the identification of the Patron. Both must fit precisely into the picture and the context to justify the strength of the emotional reaction aroused in the Poet. This group has had more nonsense written about it probably than all the rest of the sonnets put together.

7. Identification of the Poet Himself in Relation to Sonnets 73 and 74.

His life must bear a genuine and unforced, *readily corroborated relevance to the two purely autobiographical sonnets,* placed (I believe calculatedly) at the heart of the entire sequence of one hundred and fifty-four sonnets - *Sonnets 73 and 74.* This central sonnet-pair is crucial to this thesis, and we can confidently turn to them again and again for corroboration that we are indeed on the right track. The italicized lines reveal the identity of the Poet of the Sonnets with perfect precision.

That time of year thou mayst in me behold
When yellow leaves, or none, or few do hang
Upon those boughs which shake against the cold,
Bare ruin'd choirs, where late the sweet birds sang.
In me thou seest the twilight of such day
As after sunset fadeth in the West,
Which by and by black night doth take away,
Death's second self that seals up all in rest.
In me thou seest the glowing of such fire

That on the ashes of his youth doth lie,
As the death-bed, whereon it must expire,
Consum'd with that which it was nourish'd by.
 This thou perceiv'st, which makes thy love more strong
 To love that well, which thou must leave ere long.

Sonnet 73

But be contented, when that fell *arrest*
Without all *bail* shall carry me away,
My life hath in this line some interest,
Which for memorial still with thee shall stay.
When thou reviewest this, thou dost review
The very part was consecrate to thee.
The earth can have but earth, which is his due;
My spirit is thine, the better part of me.
So then thou hast but lost the dregs of life,
The prey of worms, *my body being dead,*
The coward conquest of a wretch's knife,
Too base of thee to be remembered.
 The worth of that, is that which it contains,
 And that is this, and this with thee remains.

Sonnet 74

8. Identification of the Poet whose glorious Career had been suddenly Eclipsed.

He must already have made his mark as *a poet-dramatist of established fame,* who had a body of dramatic works to his credit as the basis of the experience from which the flood of mature dramas of the Shakespearean canon flowed. The sonnets tell us that his former pre-eminence of 'triumphant splendour' had suffered a sudden eclipse.

Full many a glorious morning have I seen
Flatter the mountain tops with sovereign eye,
Kissing with golden face the meadows green,
Gilding pale streams with heavenly alchemy;
Anon permit the basest clouds to ride
With ugly rack on his celestial face,
And from the forlorn world his visage hide,
Stealing unseen to west with this disgrace.
Even so my sun one early morn did shine
With all triumphant splendour on my brow;
But out alack, he was but one hour mine,

> *The region cloud hath mask'd him from me now.*
> Yet him for this, my love no whit disdaineth;
> Suns of the world may stain when heaven's sun staineth.

Sonnet 33

9. Identification of the Poet as a Man of outstanding Intellect.

Shakespeare has been hailed as the *greatest intellect,* a man of outstanding erudition. Evidence of these attributes in the life and person of the Poet of the Sonnets is an essential prerequisite for correct identification of the author. The Poet reveals himself in these poems as a man of deep and passionate feelings and acute sensibility, of exceptional intelligence and wit, of philosophic insight and human understanding of a rare degree. These qualities permeate the works of Shakespeare. It is the demonstrable lack of them in the actor from Stratford-upon-Avon which has prompted dissatisfaction with the complacent acceptance of this lack-lustre person as the author of the great works bearing his name.

These nine points based on his autobiographical Sonnets, identifying the Patron and events in this story, are the minimum requirement that must be met to qualify any candidate as the Poet of the Sonnets. William Shakespeare cannot meet any of them, even though these poems are acknowledged to represent his intimate poetic 'diary'. Strenuous attempts to fit the Sonnets to the lives of Francis Bacon and the Earl of Oxford have proved futile. The rock on which all these alleged authors founder is Shakespeare's autobiographical touchstone, the *Sonnets,* cryptically published in 1609. The present thesis, unlike other sonnet theories, is not concerned with a piece-meal approach, with individual sonnets that may, perhaps, be read as applying to some identifiable event or person, but with the *entire sonnet-sequence,* which must yield sufficiently precise information matching the Poet's life to fit the demanding criterion of historical veracity as expressed in these autobiographical poems.

These precise criteria are met by only one candidate whose life measures up to this challenge in every detail with a verisimilitude that is truly marvellous, every sonnet revealing, in its most literal and unequivocal sense, that he is their author. He is the great innovating genius who created what is now known as 'Shakespearean' blank verse, the acknowledged forerunner of Shakespeare, named the 'Morning Star' of the Elizabethan era of poetic drama, Christopher Marlowe.

When I first encountered the Marlowe theory it at once struck me as having a disturbing relevance to the Sonnets, which had long been my favourite reading. It also struck me as being too good to be true. I felt there must be a flaw, for at this time I was a good, orthodox Shakespearean committed to belief in the actor from Stratford-upon-Avon as the author of the great works in his name. So I spent six months in research determined to *disprove* this seductive theory – to no avail. It was a salutary exercise! For I uncovered the forbidden mare's nest of irreconcilable facts concerning William Shakespeare of Stratford-upon-Avon that has spawned 64 theories about alternative authorship. I read George Greenwood, who so courageously asked the unaskable questions, and Henry James who expressed inexpressible doubts. I examined theories promoting Bacon and the Earl of Oxford as the 'real' Shakespeare, and found that their initial element of plausibility was bolstered by sophistical arguments that rely on twisting or ignoring proven historical evidence, which no *bona fide* historian can accept. Historical data is picked over selectively to suit the authorship theorist's case, and a blind eye is turned to anything that does not fit the new contender aiming to snatch the crown from William Shakespeare of Stratford-upon-Avon as the author of the great dramatic, poetic works. The Marlowe theory alone refused to lie down. As I proceeded, testing every piece of historical evidence for validity, the nagging suspicion grew that it was not my orthodox belief in Shakespeare of Stratford that would survive this investigation, but this theory which nothing could unseat: only further evidence, if it could be found, would eventually seal it as the historical truth, for here was a candidate whose life and achievements, and tragic history, provide an undeniable correlation with the story of the Sonnets which could not be explained away.

The Marlowe theory is based on five established historical facts, requiring no research. They are beyond dispute. It is unique among Shakespearean authorship theories in being based on fact and not hypothesis up to the time of Marlowe's tragic murder. Only after this does hypothesis begin as an attempt to answer the questions raised by the facts. These five facts are:

1. Christopher Marlowe was in deep trouble in 1593, when a witch-hunt against Raleigh's circle of free-thinkers, stigmatized as 'Atheists' was instigated beginning with an attack on Marlowe. This witch-hunt continued after his death into 1594 when Raleigh's friends at Cerne Abbas were investigated, but it petered out, it is not known exactly why.

2. All four men present at Deptford on 30th May were closely connected with Marlowe's friend and patron, Thomas Walsingham, who had been the right-hand man in the espionage service of his cousin, Sir Francis Walsingham. His connections with Raleigh's circle are also close and point to his membership of this circle of free-thinkers, all of whom had an interest in extricating Marlowe from the clutches of the Court of Star Chamber which employed tor-

ture to obtain confessions, hence they might themselves become implicated if he came to trial.

3. Marlowe's murder at the eleventh hour, on what would have been the last day of his freedom on bail for the informer's lethal report indicting him of criminal Atheism was already delivered, conveniently removed him from danger of trial or torture. This fact supplies an undeniable motive for murdering him as a means of escape from imminent re-arrest, or, alternatively, for *faking* his murder.

4. At the time of his death, Marlowe was the pre-eminent poet-dramatist of his day. While still at the university he began creating what is known as Shakespearean blank verse drama. His pervasive influence on the style and dramatic construction of the plays of Shakespeare presaged a great future had he lived.

5. The first documented evidence of Shakespeare as a new poet is the appearance of his name 'William Shakespeare' subscribed to the dedication to the earl of Southampton of *Venus and Adonis* as 'the first heir of my invention', which is known to have been in print on 12th June 1593, but not before – i.e. *twelve days after Marlowe's death.* It had already been entered in the Stationers' Register on 18th April, without mention of the name of any author, so that it is likely to have been about to be published at the time of Marlowe's trouble. Before 12th June the only documented evidence of Shakespeare is that establishing his humble existence at Stratford-upon-Avon. His first appearance as an actor with the Lord Chamberlain's Men is not until 15th March 1595 referring to performances by this company during Christmas 1594-5, eighteen months after Marlowe's death. All the large claims made for Shakespeare's activity as a writer before 1593 and as an actor before 1595 are hypothetical, and unsupported by sound evidence. This fact poses unanswered questions.

❖ ❖ ❖ ❖

The Marlowe theory is associated with the name of the American journalist, Calvin Hoffman, whose book, *The Murder of the Man Who Was Shakespeare,* was published in 1955; reduced from a 700-page manuscript full of purple passages, it was edited by the publisher to a compact detective-novel popular read which made quite a stir. Written in sensationalist, journalistic, highly-coloured language, Hoffman cast himself 'as an unofficial detective in a murder mystery that rivals any Sir Arthur Conan Doyle ever wrote. I uncovered a real-life "thriller" complete with murder, brawls, and normal and abnormal sexuality. A violent crimson-coloured pattern unfolded itself, with England as the background and the splendidly barbaric Elizabethan era as the setting.'

Romanticizing his portrayal of himself in the self-appointed role of researcher, he writes: 'I roamed through graveyards, I crawled into dusty tombs, I shivered in the dampness of veritable archives, and in the musty atmosphere of libraries whose book-lined shelves had remained undisturbed for centuries.' [1]

Hoffman, it will be appreciated, was no historian! And he wrote to sensationalize. His approach to his subject was emotional, fuelled by passionate conviction and informed by such historical data as he gleaned from the research of others which he appropriated as his by right without acknowledgement. He had a cavalier contempt for those he considered the pedants of the academic world who refused to regard him seriously on the basis of such evidence as he presented. What he lacked in scholarship, however, he made up in indefatigable promotion of his ideas and journalistic flair for capturing the attention of the media. His abortive attempt in 1956 to open the tomb of Marlowe's patron, Sir Thomas Walsingham, in St Nicholas's Church at Chislehurst in Kent, made the headlines. Hoffman was convinced he would there find the manuscripts of the Folio plays preserved for posterity proving that Marlowe had written them; but it was a shot in the dark in more ways than one. He had failed to inform himself of the nature of these stone sarcophagae which never contain the body but are merely memorial monuments. This one was packed with sand. A small hole was drilled in the floor enabling him to peep into the vault below, revealing sight of the lead-lapped bodies, but no sign of any box containing manuscripts.

Nothing daunted, if disappointed, Hoffman insisted that he had already proved his theory and that further research to substantiate it was not essential. He maintained that it was only the vested interest of the academics in Shakespeare of Stratford as author of the great works that prevented universal acceptance of *his* theory, of which he was excessively possessive, threatening legal action as an infringement of copyright if anyone dared to write about it without his permission, let alone acknowledgement. Hoffman's case rested mainly on the copious parallelisms in the plays of Marlowe and Shakespeare, many of which had already been researched by such scholars as Tucker Brooke and Bakeless, to which Hoffman added. These parallelisms he claimed were proof that the plays were all written by the same hand, citing in support the suspicious circumstances of Marlowe's murder in 1593 shortly before the emergence of the name 'William Shakespeare' with the publication of *Venus and Adonis*. Unfortunately, he sought to bolster this with fanciful ideas which were clearly erroneous and based on slight knowledge of Elizabethan history; such as that George Chapman's completion in 1598 of Marlowe's *Hero and Leander* represented, not Chapman's work, but Marlowe's own, written 'from beyond the grave' using Chapman's name as his pseudonym – an untenable hypothesis, but to Hoffman 'proof positive' that Marlowe was still alive. He contended that the dedication of the *Sonnets* to 'Mr.W.H.' connoted Mr. Walsing-Ham, which, as I shall show, is a simplistic solution that totally misunderstands

Thorpe's sophisticated conundrum. Eventually, Hoffman was persuaded by his wife Rose that only further research would convince the world of his theory, and together they funded the Calvin and Rose G. Hoffman Memorial Competition encouraging research to this end, administered by the King's School.

Although Hoffman added no original research of his own, it may be fairly claimed that he assembled the evidence and put the Marlowe theory 'on the map', lecturing extensively in America and gaining a following. But he was by no means the first in the field to propose Marlowe as the author of Shakespeare, hence surviving his 'death' in 1593.

Several writers have proposed Marlowe as the hidden Shakespeare, but only Archibald Webster in his long article 'Was Marlowe the Man?' *(National Review*, 82: 81–86 S. 1923) succinctly stated the case for Marlowe with sustained logic (whom Hoffman barely mentions, whereas Bakeless gives a proper account on page 216, Volume II of his great biography of Marlowe in 1942). Webster credibly claimed that Marlowe survived and that he subsequently wrote his greatest dramatic works under the *nom de plume* William Shakespeare, citing the Sonnets as evidence supporting his hypothesis.

Two years later, in 1925, Dr Hotson made his startling discovery of the inquisition on Marlowe's death, which he tracked down in the archives of the Public Records Office in a classic example of his remarkable detective skills in action. Without the discovery of this vitally important document the present thesis proposing Marlowe as the Poet of the Sonnets could not have been formulated with any foundation of evidence concerning his untimely death, for what Hotson uncovered was the coroner's inquisition, an official legal document, revealing a story so extraordinary for its air of skulduggery as to stretch credulity to the limit. There is inherent the strongest circumstantial evidence that the whole affair was a cleverly devised plot.

Some eminent scholars have expressed their doubts about the truthfulness of the official account of what transpired at Deptford, but after tossing the unanswered questions to and fro, the world of academia, well furnished with weighty Shakespearean scholars (with a heavily vested interest in maintaining the *status quo*, to which these questions pose an unwelcome likelihood of destabilization) has, predictably, opted to accept *verbatim* the demonstrably suspect story rehearsed in the inquisition as representing the true facts of the murder of Christopher Marlowe, England's premier poet-dramatist and the creator of 'Shakespearean' drama.

Briefly to put the case. Marlowe's prestigious education by scholarship to the King's School in Canterbury and then to Cambridge University, was intended to fit the shoemaker's son for a career in the Anglican church. However, he abandoned this path to enter the service of the Queen's two chief ministers of state, Lord Burghley and Sir Francis Walsingham, as a secret agent. He soon found high-born patronage and friends in the Elizabethan Court, becoming a member of Sir Walter Raleigh's esoteric circle of advanced thinkers. Early in 1593 Archbishop Whitgift instigated a witch-hunt to stamp out this circle of free-thinkers, whose scientific speculations were termed criminal Atheism, and it was in this connection that Marlowe was being hounded by the informer set on his track by the Court of Star Chamber, which alone had powers to extract confessions by torture. Marlowe was arrested, but granted bail, and on the last day of his bail he was murdered in dubious circumstances which have never been thoroughly investigated or satisfactorily explained.

The discovery of the inquisition enables us to deduce what might have happened, and to ask the leading question: If Marlowe's murder had been engineered to enable him to escape the fate that was closing in on him as the victim of the dreaded Star Chamber by means of faking his death, and he were *still alive* after 1593 – what then? Webster seemingly remained silent upon Hotson's discovery of the inquisition with its questionable evidence, leaving Hoffman eventually to raise this bogey to affright Shakespearean orthodoxy.

Hoffman's detective-style book, has proved scandalous to Marlowe's reputation and typifies the way in which he is now seen, for he had a scant understanding of the Elizabethan age and its mores and language in which the words 'love' and 'lover' are used between friends without any sexual connotation. Beginning with Hoffman, whose book in its semi-fictionalized approach depicted Marlowe and his patron as homosexual lovers, the fashion was set to present Marlowe in an increasingly sensational and lurid light. Scholars have been quick to follow suit, exaggerating this spurious portrait of a brilliant dramatist who was stigmatized in his own day as an 'Atheist', (as were all free-thinkers) not only an alleged blasphemer of Holy Scripture, but a man given to violence (as seen in his death when he was stabbed as a result of a petty quarrel about paying a bill) and allegedly a homosexual. This latter stigmatization derives *solely from the informer's dossier* and nowhere else in any contemporary source. *Sexual depravity was a favourite indictment of the informer.* This document is as much to be believed as the records of the KGB or the Gestapo. On evidence unexamined by other scholars I have shown conclusively that these allegations are false. They are typical sixteenth century libels drawn from the informers' arsenal for nailing their victim. These have over the past half century become woven into a constantly repeated sensational folklore about Marlowe as an 'Elizabethan Roaring Boy'. This distorted image has increasingly dominated academic thinking on him, which has culminated in Charles Nicholl's widely publicised defamatory book, published on the eve of the quatercentenary of Marlowe's death, *The Reckoning: The Murder of Christopher Marlowe* (1992). [2] In a 'Riposte' I have answered his unproven hypothesis which is based, not on evidence, but on personal prejudice and artful insinuation drawn from Nicholl's research in the espionage records relating to others employed in Walsingham's espionage network. There were indeed rogues amongst these spies operating in a dangerous profession, with whom

Nicholl equates Marlowe, each mention of his name spattered with pejoratives. Marlowe differed from the basest of them as an eagle differs from tadpoles, to use Swinburne's analogy. He was in a different class as poet and man and agent.

This distorted image of Marlowe is based solely on the words of his enemies, bolstered by a highly suspect judicial report in the coroner's inquisition on his murder, which no modern court of law would accept. It *totally ignores* the testimony of his friends. The evidence is examined in the chapter 'The Poet Vilified and Vindicated' in which it is conclusively demonstrated that not one of these defamatory allegations concerning Marlowe's character is true. That he was most unjustly libelled in his own day is the bitter heart-cry we hear repeatedly in the Sonnets.

> 'Tis better to be vile than vile esteemed,
> When not to be, receives reproach of being.

Sonnet 121

In presenting Christopher Marlowe as the Poet of the Sonnets – hence as Shakespeare – it falls to my hand to exonerate him from the plethora of cruel and unjust calumny that he has borne for so long, adding a weighty chapter to this book, for which I crave the reader's indulgence. However, through such detailed investigation we come to know him better, and that is invaluable compensation.

VII

THE POET IDENTIFIES HIMSELF

Why write I still all one, ever the same,
And keep invention in a noted weed,
That every word doth almost tell my name,
Showing their birth, and where they did proceed?

Sonnet 76

IN CHRISTOPHER MARLOWE we have an established poet-dramatist of genius who is the very prototype of Shakespeare in the style and content of his versification in the blank verse medium, which Marlowe first developed to near perfection; and in his dramatic technique; even in the words and imagery which he typically uses. The likeness of Shakespeare's style to Marlowe's is most marked in the early works, but there it is so marked as to have provoked serious debate as to how much of these similarities can be attributed to influence of the one on the other. Collaboration has been suggested, but there is no evidence that these twin stars ever knew each other.

The early works showing affinity with Marlowe's to an inexplicable degree are *Titus Andronicus, Richard III, Richard II,* and the *Henry VI* trilogy. The latter has been called the 'Achilles heel' of the Shakespearean authorship; some eminent scholars having given the *Henry VI* plays outright to Marlowe in origin. The array of great Shakespearean scholars who have expressed suspicions that there is not merely an influence, but a hand attributable to Marlowe in some or all of these six early plays includes Edmund Malone, Richard Farmer, Henry Hallam, Alexander Dyce, Richard Grant White, F.G. Fleay, A.W. Verity, J.Q. Adams, Edward Dowden, Felix Schelling, A.H. Thorndike, E.H.C. Oliphant, A.C. Swinburne, Jane Lee, Sir Sidney Lee, A.W. Ward, George Chalmers, C.F. Tucker Brooke, Allison Gaw, and John Bakeless. Not all agree on the extent of the attribution, but Marlowe's hand is inescapably seen to be present to a degree beyond mere influence.

Dr. Bakeless has put it succinctly:

'That Shakespeare knew Marlowe's works in plain enough. Several of their characters can be paired off, one against the other, Shakespeare having obviously borrowed from Marlowe, since he had barely begun to write for the stage at the time of Marlowe's murder. Thus Barabas and Shylock; Abigail and Jessica; Edward II and Richard II, Kent in *Edward the Second* and Kent in *King*

Lear; Young Mortimer and Hotspur; the Duke of Guise and Aaron; the murderers of the two little princes and the murderers of Edward II show many points of close resemblance. If Marlowe had never conceived these characters as he did, Shakespeare's characters would have been quite other than they are.' [1]

Evidence of Shakespeare's stylistic resemblance to Marlowe is seen in the numerous parallelisms that have been culled from the works of Marlowe and Shakespeare, which emphatically underline the enormous debt Shakespeare owed to Marlowe. But let us hear Bakeless out:

'The abundance of Shakespeare's quotations, echoes, and allusions is especially important because he lets his other literary contemporaries severely alone. At the very least, this shows a relationship of some kind between the two dramatists.' [2]

What that relationship was no one knows. Bakeless confesses he has spent 'years of speculation on this subject', and he proposes four alternative answers to explain the closeness of the relationship in those plays in the Shakespearean canon that 'reveal definite traces of Marlowe which can hardly be due to mere imitation.' He proceeds to postulate: 'The first and obvious suggestion is that Shakespeare wrote, as most young writers do, under the powerful influence of the foremost author of the moment.' He goes on, 'The second is that the two writers collaborated', but this was not Marlowe's habit, nor Shakespeare's. He then courageously puts forward the alternative which makes most Shakespearean scholars blench:

'The third is that Marlowe actually wrote the plays in question and that their attribution to Shakespeare is entirely erroneous'.

Historical evidence for this is not pursued, and he continues his speculation: 'Still a fourth view . . is that Shakespeare used as sources early Marlowe plays, which were already forgotten . . and that in reworking them he had intelligence and literary feeling sufficient to let the more magnificently sonorous passages stand unchanged.' [3]

It would seem to be an insuperable problem. Dr. Bakeless faces it squarely and honestly, but to most orthodox Shakespeareans the subject is painful. Marlowe's genius has become an embarrassment. The trend in recent scholarly studies is to shift away from the free discussion of the problem as boldly stated by Bakeless. Instead scholars tend to ignore Marlowe's influence altogether as their best way out of this coil. It is understandable. No one wants to admit that Shakespeare imitated Marlowe, particularly when the latter's striking originality so clearly proclaims his genius – for the distinguishing, indeed the quintessential benediction of genius is individuality. Whatever it touches genius does not imitate but transmutes to itself.

Dr Bakeless in his classic two-volume biography of Marlowe begins his chapter on 'Marlowe and Shakespeare' with the words: 'The exact relationship between the work of Marlowe and the work of Shakespeare will remain in doubt for ever.' For ever is a long time, and I hope that this thesis will be seen to resolve the problem in the only way that is coherent and enlightening. For if only we can come to accept as fact that Marlowe escaped the fateful end that was prepared for him, and adopted 'William Shakespeare' as a most skilfully conceived and maintained *nom de plume* with a well adapted front man to bear it out, the problem of Shakespeare's enormous debt to Marlowe's work disappears. The tremendous sweep of development of this genius's achievements from the works of Marlowe through the entire range of the Shakespearean canon as the writings of one man becomes the logical explanation. It is the only explanation consistent with genius.

For so sensitive a poet-dramatist as was Marlowe the traumatic experience of his eclipse inevitably had effect on his art. There is clear evidence that his development was already on the brink of its great leap forward into maturity, and in noting some subtle differences in his dramatic work after 1593, we are aware also of those *similarities* which are part of the essential being from whose mind and spirit his creative work emanates. They are the identifying ticks of individuality. The tragic events of 1593 proved the watershed in the Poet's life, and this alone accounts for the 'difference' in the work of Marlowe's youth and his maturity. It is the only explanation that such genius allows. Such men do not imitate others, not even in this age when plagiarism was commonly indulged in, though nevertheless resented. Marlowe did not imitate others – he was the greatest trend-setter of his day, whom everyone else imitated, as a study of the period amply confirms.

An assessment of Marlowe's achievement as the great innovating genius of his time is appropriate. We begin again with Bakeless:

'Marlowe died in his immaturity, still an experimenter . . He used a form once – and dropped it. He did not produce a series of classical plays, all in the same style, like Lyly, who preceded him; nor pour out comedy upon comedy, history upon history, tragedy upon tragedy, like his pupil from Stratford, who succeeded him. . . Marlowe's reputation rests wholly on the work of his 'prentice hand. He lived to do no other; and what he did, he did almost without models . . Nothing sets the sheer genius of the man so far beyond cavil or dispute as the way in which his plays, one by one, – each in its own separate and unrepeated genre – are caught up and the formula of each developed by other hands.' [4.]

John Bakeless: *The Tragicall History of Christopher Marlowe,* 1942.

' "If ever there was a born poet, Marlowe was one", declared a later and lesser poet, Leigh Hunt. What was even more to the purpose, in a period which already boasted its Sidney and Spenser, but had still to achieve pre-eminence

in dramatic poetry, Marlowe was a born playwright.' [5]
Harry Levin: *The Overreacher,* 1954.

'Marlowe introduced other innovations: the occasional use of shorter or longer lines, the frequency of feminine endings, the variable place of the *caesura* and above all the displacement of the accents . . his ease and aesthetic sense in handling blank verse, and the purity and clarity as well as the essential musical quality of his verse, which defies analysis to a great extent . . [and] that magical quality which recurs only in Shakespeare and Keats .' [6]
Michel Poirier: *Christopher Marlowe,* 1951.

'In all literature there are few figures more attractive, and few more exalted, than this of the young poet who swept from the English stage the tatters of barbarism, and habited Tragedy in stately robes; who was the first to conceive largely and exhibit souls struggling in the bonds of circumstance.' [7]
A.H. Bullen: *The English Dramatists,* 1885.

'Marlowe is the greatest discoverer, the most daring pioneer, in all our poetic literature. Before Marlowe there was no genuine blank verse and genuine tragedy in our language. After his arrival the way was prepared, the path made straight for Shakespeare.' [And comparing Marlowe with his contemporaries, Greene, Peele and Lodge] 'Marlowe differs from such people, not in degree, but in kind; not as an eagle differs from wrens and tit-mice, but as an eagle differs from frogs and tadpoles . . He first, and he alone, gave wings to English poetry; he first brought into its serene and radiant atmosphere the new strange element of sublimity . . . Among all English poets he was the first full-grown man.' Only young and immature by comparison with 'such disciples and successors as Shakespeare and Milton; but the first born among us of their kind.' [8]
Algernon Charles Swinburne: *Letters on the Elizabethan Dramatists,* 1914

'There is perhaps no figure among the great Elizabethans whom it is so difficult to approach without a sympathetic bias. He comes trailing the clouds of glory of the pioneer, of the herald of the full dramatic day. His is the magnetic appeal of genius cut down in its prime, with its rich achievement, and with an even richer promise unfulfilled.' [9]
F. Boas: *Marlowe and his Circle,* 1929.

'If Marlowe had lived longer and accomplished the work that lay clearly before him, he would have stood beside Shakespeare.' [10]
Edward Dowden: *The Tragedies of William Shakespeare,* 1912.

'Without Marlowe there would never have been the William Shakespeare we know.' [11]
Thomas Marc Parrott: *William Shakespeare: A Handbook,* 1934

70

In other words, there is absolutely no doubt that he qualifies for the position of author of the works of Shakespeare most fully and eminently, for he had prepared that niche with his own hand. Marlowe's eligibility has been given the unwitting support of an imposing body of authoritative critics.

❖　❖　❖　❖

VIII

The Sonnet Story Tested

THE HYPOTHESIS that Christopher Marlowe is the author behind the name William Shakespeare must now be put to the test by comparing his life, and what can reasonably be deduced from the available evidence regarding his later circumstances if he had in fact survived his 'death' at Deptford, with the nine points that must be met to fulfil the requirements of the sonnet-story as outlined. Where hypothesis is presented as historical fact at this stage, it will later be validated, and I ask the reader's indulgence in using this form of procedure here.

1. The Poet's Anonymity

Christopher Marlowe alone had *a cogent and compelling reason for conceal-ment of his identity,* for he was a wanted man, fleeing from persecution by Church and State. His fellow dramatist, Thomas Kyd, had been arrested and under torture had incriminated Marlowe as the owner of a heretical treatise which was found amongst Kyd's papers when his room was searched by the officers of the law. Heresy and Atheism were punishable by burning at the stake. Following Kyd's arrest, informers were set on Marlowe's tracks, and their indictment, no matter how false, would be 'proved' under torture. It was to escape the fatal coils of the powerful Star Chamber that were closing in on him that Marlowe's Patron staged his faked 'death'. Thereafter total conceal-ment and anonymity were essential to protect the Poet from the law. This was the vital reason behind the extraordinary web of secrecy which was woven around the true identity of the writer, William Shakespeare.

2. Aid in Concealment

Anonymity was the cloak adopted to protect Marlowe and those who had engineered his flight. Nothing must be allowed to leak out. *Aid in maintain-ing this* was provided by his great contemporary, Sir Francis Bacon, around whose figure an element of mystery clings linking him with the works of Shake-speare by his suspected hand in the publication of the First Folio. But those who have adduced the well-known 'Baconian' theory of his authorship of the Shakespearean canon have mistaken the smoke for the fire. This brilliant and far-sighted Elizabethan dedicated his life to the 'Advancement of Learning' to promote the scientific knowledge which was pursued by the free-thinkers in secret. Parallel studies were pursued by Bacon and by Raleigh's circle, but it was Bacon who shrewdly foresaw the need for protection against just such persecution as Marlowe had attracted, and he bent his resourceful mind to the task of providing an umbrella organisation for the writing and publication of works disseminating the new-born scientific philosophy, and for preparing men's minds for a more tolerant world. It was Bacon's society, the Freemasons, who acted to protect the stricken poet, by providing a cover of anonymity – total anonymity – behind which he was concealed. The evidence for this Masonic involvement is irrefutable, establishing that the First Folio was a Masonic publication. This is the subject of the sequel to the present book.

3. Noble Patronage

Marlowe had already gained *the patronage and friendship of Thomas Walsingham,* the scion of a distinguished family, at whose moated manor house at Chislehurst in Kent he was arrested on the charge of 'Atheism'. But he was not dragged off to prison to be stretched on the rack as had been the fate of his fellow dramatist Thomas Kyd, but was granted bail and commanded to report daily to their Lordships 'until he shall be licensed to the contrary.' The following nine days' respite enabled his patron to devise and organize the 'murder' plot that enabled Marlowe to escape, as postulated by this hypothesis. Many sonnets are a moving record of the Poet's undying gratitude to his Patron for the faithful friendship he extended to his Poet in his adversity. The Poet's dependence on his Patron beyond the normal ties of patronage, arising from his involvement personally in the Poet's tragedy, underlies the tenor of these poems and gives them their especially sincere, intimate quality. Theirs was such a sacred friendship as had been tested 'even to the edge of doom'.

> Let me not to the marriage of true minds
> Admit impediments. Love is not love
> Which alters when it alteration finds,
> Or bends with the remover to remove.
> O no, it is an ever-fixed mark
> That looks on tempest and is never shaken;
> It is the star to every wand'ring bark,
> Whose worth's unknown, although his height be taken.
> Love's not Time's fool, though rosy lips and cheeks
> Within his bending sickle's compass come;
> Love alters not with his brief hours and weeks,
> But bears it out even to the edge of doom.
>   If this be error and upon me proved,
>   I never writ, nor no man ever loved.
>   *Sonnet 116*

The journey into exile which forms such a significant part of the sonnet-story, necessarily followed on Marlowe's escape from his persecutors. His 'murder' was enacted at the eleventh hour when the indictment prepared by the informer Richard Baines *had already been delivered* and was about to receive official attention. By hypothesis the scenario is as follows.

The 'murder' plot was organized by his patron, Thomas Walsingham, who had for years worked closely with his cousin, Sir Francis Walsingham, in the espionage service. The venue chosen was Deptford, then a port with regular shipping to the Continent, whither the master-spy Robert Poley could sail direct from his assignment at The Hague in order to be present as a witness to the planned 'murder' to testify, and ensure that Walsingham's servant, Ingram Frizer, who was to do the deed, would be acquitted on the plea of self-defence. Frizer (the murderer) and Poley (the expert smooth-talking spy) were joined by another spy well known to Walsingham, called Nicholas Skeres. These three, with Marlowe, met at a house in Deptford where rooms were to let, and meals were provided. They spent the entire day there apparently in deep consultation, which ended after their supper with a violent quarrel over payment of the bill(!) in which Marlowe was 'killed' by Frizer's dagger.

To make his escape Marlowe would take ship from Deptford Strand to commence that traumatic journey away from friends and home to face the long period of exile which is a main theme in the *Sonnets*.

In presenting this admittedly strange tale as the truth there are several strongly supportive strands of argument and circumstantial evidence which seal this as the only feasible conclusion.

(i) The Coroner's Inquisition, which no modern court of law would accept as representing the true facts. (Described in Chapter 10).

(ii) The air of collusion which hangs over the coming together of four such characters *all of whom have connections with Thomas Walsingham*, and who spent all day together, discussing 'in quiet sort' some weighty matters as they walked in Dame Eleanor Bull's garden, the landlady in question. The choice of venue at Deptford adds its question mark.

(iii) Marlowe's influential friends in high places who would have had ready access to Privy Council affairs, and would have been able to anticipate his re-arrest – which, in the event, they only just managed to do in the nick of time.

(iv) Marlowe's high intelligence and poetic genius were as apparent to his contemporaries as they are to us today, so that protection of such a brilliant man, whom his friends knew to be falsely accused, must have been felt imperative the more so since, as free-thinkers themselves, they were *also* protecting their own skins!

(v) It is in the *Sonnets* that we find remarkable confirmation that this story is not just a melodramatic invention, but is the historical truth which explains the enigma of Marlowe's 'murder' and throws light on what has hitherto been obscure in the sonnet-story, making it *for the first time coherent and understandable to us*. At the same time it fully resolves the problem of the relationship between Marlowe and Shakespeare that has for so long puzzled scholars, and answers all the related questions with total satisfaction. Every piece of this jigsaw fits perfectly.

5. *Vilification of his Name*

After Marlowe's murder became public news, and doubtless engendered a great deal of gossip, the Puritan *castigation of his reputation* as a 'vile Atheist' and a lewd writer of plays whose fatal end they proclaimed in their pamphlets as the just retribution of God's vengeance on his heretical views, grew in virulence and gossipy embellishment distorting the events of his reported death. Of no man can it be more truly said that his good name has been blasted down the ages, even to our own day. Below is a choice example taken from Edmund Rudierde's *The Thunderbolt of Gods Wrath against Hard-Harted and stiff-necked sinners,* 1618, which repeats the tale told by earlier moralists.

> 'We read of one *Marlin,* '[by this he was also known] 'a Cambridge Scholler who was a Poet, and a filthy Play-maker, this wretch accounted that meeke seruant of God *Moses* to be but a Coniurer, and our sweete Sauiour but a seducer and a deceiuer of the people. But harken yee braine-sicke and prophane Poets and Players, that bewitch idle eares with foolish vanities: what fell vpon this prophane wretch, hauing a quarrell against one whom he met in a streete in London, and would haue stabd him; But the partie perceiuing his villany preuented him with catching his hand, and turning his owne dagger into his braines, and so blaspheming and cursing, he yeelded vp his stinking breath: marke this yee Players that liue by making fooles laugh at sinne and wickednesse.'

In *Sonnets 110, 111, 112, 121,* the Sonnets of Vilification as I have called them, we hear the Poet's bitter outcry against these slanders and libels, which proliferated over the years.

6. *The Rival Poet*

In the intimate relationship of Thomas Walsingham as the Patron of *both* Christopher Marlowe and George Chapman, the two foremost poets of the circle of free thinkers led by Raleigh, known as the 'School of Night', we have the only significant *triangular relationship of one patron and two poets* that Elizabethan history affords. The identification of George Chapman as the *Rival Poet of the Sonnets* has been cogently argued by orthodox Shakespearean scholars basing this on the descriptive clues in *Sonnets 80* and *86,* which fit Chapman exactly. Since there is no evidence linking William Shakespeare and Chapman as rivals for the hypothetical patronage of the Earl of Southampton, or any of the other alleged patrons of Shakespeare (his 'Mr.W.H.') scholars have scoured the period for other 'Rival Poets', all equally unconvincing, but to date no alternative candidate to George Chapman has been generally agreed. Chapman's close relationship with both Marlowe and his patron, Thomas Walsingham, on the other hand, are well established, and the reason for the intense jealousy evoked in the sonnets is not far to seek.

When Marlowe was arrested in 1593 at the home of his Patron, he left behind the unfinished manuscript of his narrative poem *Hero and Leander,* a work that is acclaimed as a masterpiece among Elizabethan poems. George Chapman undertook to complete this poem in 1598 to present as his epithalamium on the marriage of the Lady Audrey Shelton to their Patron, now Sir Thomas Walsingham, newly knighted by the Queen. Marlowe's beautiful incomplete fragment was bound elegantly together with Chapman's completion in the same book, with a dedication to Sir Thomas Walsingham written by his friend, the publisher Edward Blount, so that both parts came out as their wedding offering to Walsingham and his Lady. Here we have the perfect triangular relationship of *one patron with his two poets in rivalry at the time of his marriage,* for which Shakespearean scholars have sought in vain in relation to William Shakespeare. In the circumstances of the Marlowe-Walsingham-Chapman triangle a more potent breeding ground for intense jealousy over the completion of his poetic masterpiece by another hand can hardly be imagined. Both the Rival Poet and the cause of the searing jealousy are identified precisely.

7. Two Sonnets of Identification

The central pair of *autobiographical Sonnets, 73* and *74,* are the touchstones which reveal unequivocally that their author is Christopher Marlowe and can be none other, for they fit him in every detail. *Sonnet 73,* written in his late years, looks back on his youth, beginning with his Canterbury childhood when he often played amid the 'ruin'd choirs' of St. Augustine's Abbey very near to his home, recalling his choirboy days; then remembering his portrait, painted when he was aged twenty-one, to commemorate a very important event in his life – *his entry into the Queen's service as her special agent,* and presented to the Master of Corpus Christi, Cambridge, where it hangs today. That is, I believe, the true interpretation of this sonnet, which is clearly indicated to us by the Poet's words. His personal motto which is inscribed on the Corpus Christi portrait, QUOD ME NUTRIT ME DESTRUIT, is rendered in English in this sonnet: *'Consum'd with that which it was nourish'd by'.* It is impossible to deny the relevance to Marlowe's life when we consider what this contemplative sonnet is telling us as the Poet looks back over the past from the viewpoint of his declining years.

That time of year thou mayst in me behold
When yellow leaves, or none, or few do hang
Upon those boughs which shake against the cold,
Bare ruin'd choirs, where late the sweet birds sang.
In me thou seest the twilight of such day
As after sunset fadeth in the West,
Which by and by black night doth take away,
Death's second self that seals up all in rest.
In me thou seest the glowing of such fire
That on the ashes of his youth doth lie,
As the death-bed, whereon it must expire,
Consum'd with that which it was nourish'd by. *
   This thou perceiv'st, which makes thy love more strong
   To love that well, which thou must leave ere long.

Sonnet 73

* Marlowe's motto: QUOD ME NUTRIT ME DESTRUIT

Sonnet 74 recalls the very circumstances of his 'death' in 1593; his *'arrest'*, his *'bail'*, and his 'murder' by *'a wretch's knife'*. The phrase 'Without all bail' connotes actual death, which is final, implying that the 'arrest' and 'bail' with which the poem opens reflect incidents in his life which were not final, in the event. According to the story told at the inquest, Frizer had stabbed Marlowe with his dagger over the right eye, disfiguring his face and thus creating a useful disguise for the corpse. Note that he speaks of *'my* body', *'my* spirit', *'my* life' – not *his* body, so that unless we 'do a Benson' on this sonnet and alter the pronouns to suit our ideas of what we think the Poet ought to be telling us, there is no escape from the essentially autobiographical content of this crucially relevant sonnet. Scholars have suggested that this is Shakespeare recollecting the death of his 'friend' Marlowe, but such an interpretation is impossible. The content and sequence of facts presented fit Marlowe's tragic Deptford incident precisely.

But be contented, when that fell *arrest*
Without all *bail* shall carry me away,
My life hath in this line some interest,
Which for memorial still with thee shall stay.
When thou reviewest this, thou dost review
The very part was consecrate to thee.
The earth can have but earth, which is his due;
My spirit is thine, the better part of me.
So then thou hast but lost the dregs of life,
The prey of worms, *my body being dead,*
The coward conquest of a wretch's knife,
Too base of thee to be remembered.

The worth of that, is that which it contains,
And that is this, and this with thee remains.

Sonnet 74

8. A Poet-Dramatist of Established Fame

Christopher Marlowe was without question *the pre-eminent dramatic poet of Elizabethan England at the time of his tragic eclipse.* Tennyson has called him the 'Morning Star' of that great outburst of dramatic activity in blank verse – the idiom which Marlowe refined and fashioned to make it the instrument for his own use, which all others then imitated and which Shakespeare would first have had to create if Marlowe's hand had not already done so. Robert Greene addressed Marlowe as 'Thou famous gracer of Tragedians' in 1592. From the appearance of *Tamburlaine*, Greene together with Nashe made envious satirical canting comments on him and his works, and they were not doing this to lampoon a nonentity but one who was foremost in the minds of their readers.

Full many a glorious morning have I seen,
Flatter the mountain-tops with sovereign eye,
Kissing with golden face the meadows green,
Gilding pale streams with heavenly alchemy;
Anon permit the basest clouds to ride
With ugly rack on his celestial face,
And from the forlorn world his visage hide,
Stealing unseen to west with this disgrace,
Even so my sun one early morn did shine
With all triumphant splendour on my brow;
But out alack, he was but one hour mine,
The region cloud hath mask'd him from me now.
    Yet him for this, my love no whit disdaineth:
    Suns of the world may stain, when heaven's sun staineth.

Sonnet 33

9. A Man of Great Intellect

Christopher Marlowe was *one of the intelligentsia of his day.*

He was accepted as the peer of the courageous circle of advanced thinkers led by Sir Walter Raleigh and the Earl of Northumberland in their esoteric club, the 'School of Night', who comprised the 'heroical spirits' of this 'little academy', who were all stigmatized unjustly as 'Atheists' because they dared to discuss and examine all subjects scientifically and critically. Unlike William Shakespeare, he was not content to spend his days in the company of the 'taffeta fools', as Nashe named the actors. Shakespeare had no intellectual friends, so far as we can ascertain, as did Marlowe, and as did Ben Jonson, who was granted an honorary M.A. by the University of Oxford in recognition of his great erudition, though he never attended any university but was educated at Westminster Grammar School. Strange to say, such acknowledgement of the outstanding intellectual gifts apparent in his plays never came to William Shakespeare.

Christopher Marlowe's closest friends were of the Elizabethan intelligentsia, all members of Raleigh's circle. Chief of these was the brilliant mathematician and astronomer, Thomas Hariot, considered the greatest scientific brain before Isaac Newton; and with him the philosopher, mathematician and alchemist, Walter Warner. Of poets in this circle, Matthew Roydon, who had a high reputation among his contemporaries, but whose works were left in manuscript and have not survived, and George Chapman, were among his best friends. He became a close friend of the Latin poet, and musician and dramatist, famous for his scintillating wit, Thomas Watson, who numbered William Byrd among his friends, and was on intimate terms with his patron, Sir Francis Walsingham, (who was Marlowe's employer in espionage) and with his young cousin, Thomas Walsingham, who became Marlowe's patron and dear friend. The Walsinghams were a wealthy, cultured family with interests in poetry, music, literature and drama, painting, philosophy and world exploration. Thomas Walsingham was very probably a co-member of the 'School of Night', as may be deduced from his patronage of, and personal friendship with *both* Marlowe and Chapman, the two foremost poets of the Raleigh 'academy' – Spenser being away in Ireland at that time. Marlowe doubtless also knew Spenser, and Michael Drayton. Amongst the dramatists of the so-called 'University Wits' of London, the merry spark George Peele seems to have been a good friend; whereas Robert Greene stood in a relationship of envious professional rivalry, whilst the sharp-witted young satirist, Thomas Nashe, seems to have been on genuinely friendly terms despite his squibs of satire directed at Marlowe, which the latter took in good part.

Sir Walter Raleigh, and the young Earl of Northumberland, together with Ferdinando Stanley, Lord Strange, later Earl of Derby, were the leading lights of an 'academy' of intellectuals, and Marlowe claimed a good acquaintance with all three of them.[1]

The catalogue of Marlowe's friendships is distinguished, to say the least.

Here, then, we have a portrait of a man whose high intelligence shines through his interests, his friendships, and his achievements from childhood when his gifts won him the award of two rare scholarships to a privileged education for a boy of humble origin. Such intelligence, which catapulted him into the society of high-born young men from a tender age, and aroused the envy of some in his own class, evidently engendered in him that mordant wit which was his armature against the wounds likely to be inflicted by the envious world on such a sensitive, eager, receptive nature as his.

If life was rich in opportunities beyond those for most of his class, it was also not easy for the fledgling genius. The Sonnets are proof, if proof we needed, that the picture presented to us by devout Shakespeareans, of the 'gentle Shakespeare' pursuing the creation of his immortal works in unruffled calm to build his position of success and affluence, is false. The Poet was indeed of a most sensitive and gentle nature, as his Sonnets testify and the affectionate testimonials of his friends confirm; but there was also a deep vein of passion in this immensely complex personality, and the more he suffered, was misunderstood and maligned, and fell into the error of proselytizing to dispel contemporary ignorance – and paid a heavy price.

Our search for the Poet of the Sonnets inevitably leads us to perceive 'as in a glass darkly' the hidden identity of the 'dead shepherd', Christopher Marlowe. For the first time we gain insight into what happened to the Poet, and what caused the deep suffering 'out of which an extraordinary blossoming and harvest have been wrung', [2] as Stephen Spender has so movingly and perceptively noted.

❖   ❖   ❖

A brief survey of the recorded history of the life of the genius whom George Peele named 'the Muses darling' is here appropriate.

IX

THE MUSE'S DARLING

CHRISTOPHER MARLOWE was born just two months before William Shakespeare, in the ancient and important city of Canterbury, seat of the Primate of the Church of England, who ranked second in authority only to the sovereign. His father, the shoemaker John Marlowe, became a freeman of the city the year his son was born, probably in the house in St. George's Street near to the precincts of the great Cathedral where his father plied his trade in the front room facing the street. Christopher was christened on 26th February 1563/4 in the parish church of St. George the Martyr near his home, whose great waking bell clanged at four o'clock every morning to arouse the sleepy citizens of this ancient, walled city to commence their day. *

Canterbury was then, as it still is now, an especially beautiful city, dominated by its lovely Cathedral, and watered by the River Stour which divides and partly encircles the city. In deference to its importance the main streets were paved with Folkstone stone and pitched boulders, so John Marlowe's customers walked dry-shod where most Elizabethan towns and villages offered trodden earth roads under-foot. Canterbury lay on the main highway between London and Dover, and an endless stream of travellers passed through the massive Westgate, chief of the city's six gates, to swell the three to four thousand inhabitants, who included various immigrant communities of whom the French-speaking Huguenots was the largest, but there were also Welsh-speaking Welsh families, and pockets of Dutch, German, Italian and even Spanish settlers. [1]

Catering for travellers in its numerous inns and hostelries, and the weaving and dyeing of cloth and spinning of yarns introduced by the Huguenots, were two of Canterbury's most thriving and expanding industries; and there were weekly and annual fairs, while the law courts were kept constantly busy dealing with the litigation that its squabbling citizens indulged in. Among these, John Marlowe, a literate fellow, acted as bondsman for couples seeking wedlock, as a side-line to his shoemaking, and dabbled on the fringes of the law as jury-man, deponent or witness when not himself the plaintiff or defendant. He became sidesman, churchwarden and parish clerk by turns, and eventually held minor office in the shoemakers' guild, suggesting a genial, gregarious man who enjoyed being in the hub of community life. The occasional battle with his apprentices, and snatches of bawdy gossip recounted from legal cases he attended must have made a lively home-life in the Marlowe household,

* Foot-note: St. George's church was destroyed by bombs on the night of May 31st–1st June 1942. Only the tower remains as a memorial.

presided over by a loving mother, six of whose nine children survived; Christopher, the eldest son but second born, had four younger sisters and eventually was joined by the much younger Thomas, who became a chorister in the Cathedral like Christopher.

Canterbury's great tradition of learning survived in her choir school, refounded in 1541 and renamed the King's School by Henry VIII following his destruction of the ancient Abbey of St. Augustine, which had previously administered the school.

Henry's reformation placed it under the authority of the Dean and Chapter of the Cathedral with provision for scholarships for 'fifty poor boys, both destitute of the help of friends and endowed (so far as may be) with minds apt for learning, who shall be called scholars of the grammar school, and shall be sustained out of the funds of our church'. [2] This was a euphemism, for it was the sons of the Kentish gentry who were largely the beneficiaries of the church's bounty, although Archbishop Cranmer's words impart a note of admonition: 'if the Gentleman's Son be apt to Learning, let him be admitted; if not apt, let the Poor Man's child apt enter his Room.' [3]

Clearly the policy was to cream off the cleverest boys of the Kent population irrespective of class, though this inevitably included a preponderance of the advantaged children, and about two-thirds came from outside Canterbury and were boarders at the school. Besides the sons of distinguished landed and propertied Kentish families, the next largest group were sons of the local clergy; a couple were sons of 'yeomen' from Dover and the Maidstone area; one was the son of a local builder and decorator, another of a Canterbury butcher, [4] and with these was admitted to a scholarship in the Michaelmas term of 1578 the shoemaker's son, Christopher Marlowe.

He was then only a few months within the statutory age limit of admission which was between nine and fifteen years, but the implication of his late admission is that he was already a chorister in the Cathedral, probably having been so from the age of nine years at which time choir-boys are normally recruited to the choir schools, and had been a fee-paying commoner at the King's School hopefully awaiting a vacancy for a scholarship, for a number of these fee-paying commoners were educated along with the scholars. Patronage by the charitable Kentish knight, Sir Roger Manwood, has been suggested as very likely in helping to defray the costs of his pre-scholarship education at the school up to this point. [5] Such charitable assistance for educational purposes was extremely popular in Elizabethan times for intelligent and promising youngsters worthy of help, or for the founding of the many excellent grammar schools which came into being during the sixteenth century. All those 'poor' boys admitted to the King's School would by definition of the Statutes have been picked out for their intelligence, and far from being 'destitute of the help of friends' would probably have received initial help from some benevolent well-wisher. [6] The intention behind the church's educational policy was to fill the crying need for well educated Anglican clergy, for want of whom many incumbencies were left vacant.

The glorious Choir of Canterbury Cathedral, built by the French master-builder William of Sens and completed by William the Englishman during the last three decades of the thirteenth century. Here Christopher Marlowe sang daily as a King's chorister probably from the age of nine years.

It is likely that Christopher Marlowe was selected to receive this privileged status as a King's scholar in time before his fifteenth birthday with a view to preparing him for a career in the Anglican church, for his scholarship to the King's School now made him eligible for the next step up the ladder, which was shortly to be granted to him – a scholarship to Corpus Christi College, Cambridge, where he was to continue his studies for six and a half years under Archbishop Parker's munificent bequest, to emerge with the coveted title of Master of Arts, ostensibly to proceed to holy orders. He would doubtless have made a brilliant churchman – if controversial!

But he was destined to follow his dramatic Muse instead, for the seed of his future development as a great poet-dramatist had long since been sown in the fertile soil of Canterbury.

Education at the King's School was rigorous. Emphasis was on the classical languages, religion, history (basic maths) and, of course, music. It was both formal and creative, for beside studious translation of classical authors there was encouragement to write Latin poetry. Music and drama featured on an unusually lavish scale. We learn of the performance of plays in Latin – tragedies, comedies and interludes. Through weekly testing of all the boys there was close personal contact with the scholarly mind of Dr John Gresshop, the headmaster, who possessed what was then rated as an enormous, private library of over three hundred and fifty books, to which this ardent bibliophile may sometimes have given access for his most promising pupils; and if he had been so inclined to open his treasures to young minds, we cannot doubt that Christopher Marlowe would have been favoured, for this library contained several volumes on history and the classical authors which influenced his dramatic works, as well as his thought. [7.]

The long school day began at 6 a.m. with prayers and a psalm, and ended at 5 p.m. with prayers, a psalm or a litany, and from 6–7 p.m. there was 'prep' to do in which the abler pupils helped those who were lagging behind. The boys were supposed to speak only Latin, even when at play scampering about in their long gowns (a new one every Christmas). A welcome break in their day was attendance at High Mass in the Cathedral every morning when they exercised their lungs in singing.

The sense of its great historic past that pervades Canterbury combined with the excellence of his education to exert a powerful influence on the boy Marlowe. The impact of the sheer beauty of the Cathedral on anyone entering its soaring choir for the first time can be a breath-taking experience. These were the crucial factors in shaping this highly intelligent and sensitive young-ster into the future poet-dramatist of his maturity. The genius who created Shakespearean blank verse was nurtured in an environment of extraordinary richness and stimulation, mentally, visually and aurally. Marlowe's early dramatic works reflect his choirboy experience in the great Cathedral. Doubtless he heard tales of the jewel-rich shrine of St. Thomas à Becket, in which 'gold was the meanest thing'. The Saint's shrine had been the magnet drawing an endless stream of pilgrims who came to gape at the priceless jewels, to pray, and to hope for miraculous cures for the sick, until Henry VIII dismantled the marvellous treasure-house and appropriated its riches as part of his policy of iconoclasm, demoting the power of Rome.

Canterbury particularly suffered as the seat of the Primate of England, formerly the direct representative of the Pope; but by degrees, and not without opposition, the city was brought into the Anglican fold. Evidence of this iconoclasm was all around the boy, Marlowe. His childhood memories of the ruins of the once powerful Abbey of St Augustine which lay just without St George's Gate only a few minutes from his home, where he must often have played among the piles of great stones, were indelibly printed on his mind and soul, for he recollects those 'bare ruin'd choirs' in his most autobiographical *Sonnet 73*. Iconoclasm recurs in play after play, as though he were writing this out of his system, testifying to the intensity of feeling with which the boy reacted to his environment. [*]

Surrounding the city's ancient flint-stone walls were fields where cows and sheep grazed among the flowery meadows of this fertile 'Garden of England' in which Henry VIII ordered the extensive planting of apple orchards, happily recollected by Marlowe when he wrote of 'the orchards and the primrose lanes' and the woodlands in their 'goodly green'. [9]

City and country in Elizabethan times were closely allied, and for young Christopher Marlowe easy access to the sea was another formative element in his life. The coast at its nearest point due east is but ten miles away, in those days considered an easy walk across the Downs, and Dover with its important harbour and the excitement of the ships must have been a memorable experience for there lived his maternal grandparents, the Arthurs of yeoman stock. The 'Shakespeare Cliffs' are justly famous for their vivid description in *King Lear*, and into his *Jew of Malta* he sailed a ship that rode in Dover harbour during his boyhood, 'The Flying Dragon'. This play, despite its exotic subject, is full of Canterbury recollections. It features the Abbey of St Augustine and the passage called 'The Dark Entry' leading to the King's School from the Cathedral cloisters.

The Jew's enraptured recounting of his jewels opens the play on a theme that the oft retelling of the riches of the famous shrine of St Thomas à Becket would have vividly prefigured in his imagination:

> Bags of fiery opals, sapphires, amethysts,
> Jacinths, hard topaz, grass-green emeralds,
> Beauteous rubies, sparkling diamonds,
> And seld-seen costly stones of so great price,
> As one of them, indifferently rated,
> And of a carat of this quantity,
> May serve, in peril of calamity,
> To ransom great kings from captivity.

> *The Jew of Malta* Act I, 11.25–32

Houses heaped with 'pearl like pebble stones', and coffers 'cramm'd full' with coin; talk of 'Arabians, who so richly pay/ The things they traffic for with wedge of gold', whereas 'paltry silverlings' are accounted mere 'trash!' – and his delight over 'Infinite riches in a little room'. It is not hard to see why the composition of a play about a fabulously wealthy Jew appealed to Marlowe. This opulent vein he exploited first in *Tamburlaine the Great,* a play that simply glitters with gold!

The most abiding influence of his Canterbury childhood was his love of history, which remained the greatest inspiration of his dramatic work. Present history in the making, as well as the past, enveloped his most impressionable years, for when he was nine years old Queen Elizabeth came to Canterbury on her progress to stay with Archbishop Parker and to celebrate her fortieth birthday there in September 1573. For a fortnight she resided with her retinue of servants and courtiers in the Palace of St Augustine, once part of the now demolished Abbey which Henry VIII had retained for his use, which stood within a stone's throw of the Marlowe's house. Christopher must have gazed on the Queen often during those exciting two weeks, for it was the Queen's pleasure to let herself be seen by her people, and she would sometimes stop to apeak with them. As a chorister, which he most probably was at this age, he would have sung to her at the services in the Cathedral, where the beauty of the music had been rapturously extolled by the French Ambassador on this visit, who was moved to exclaim: 'O God, I think no Prince beside, in all Europe, ever heard the like; no, not our holy father, the Pope himself.' [10]

The glorious music in the Cathedral was an important part of that 'splendid and solemn' entertainment for which the Queen especially warmly thanked Archbishop Parker on her departure. [11]

This was the tradition in which the young lad destined to become the innovator of Shakespearean drama was nurtured. His poetic gift owed much of its typical lyrical quality to the musical content of his education, a historical connection of immense significance in his development. The essentially musical sonority of the blank verse that Marlowe developed is repeatedly remarked on by literary critics. Michel Poirier described it as that 'magical quality .. which recurs only in Shakespeare and Keats'. [12] Marlowe's contemporaries hearing the aspiring verse of his first masterpiece *Tamburlaine the Great* were intoxicated by this thrilling new speech-music, which even we who are familiar with the mature tones of Shakespearean blank verse are not unaffected by. The revivals of *Tamburlaine* in modern times have been ecstatically received, so appealing is the youthful passion that rings in the 'high astounding terms' of this great work.

The last three endowments that Archbishop Parker made before he died in 1575, when Christopher was aged eleven, included one that was especially created for a boy who was a King's scholar and a native of Canterbury. It might have been tailor-made for young Christopher Marlowe, for the requirements of the scholarship stipulate that the candidate must not only be well schooled in

Latin grammar, but be able to compose a Latin verse, and, on sight-reading, he must 'solf and sing plaine song'. [13.] This emphasis on scholastic and poetic and musical ability reflects Canterbury's ancient cultural tradition. Having been awarded this second scholarship, Marlowe proceeded to Corpus Christi College, Cambridge, as Archbishop Parker's scholar destined for a career in the church, arriving there just before Christmas 1580. He would be seventeen the following February. Most freshmen at the universities matriculated at fourteen or fifteen, some even younger; in that age children were expected to mature early.

At Cambridge he found himself in a yet more exclusive and privileged environment in which learning's golden gifts were increasingly being sought by the rising gentrified class as well as by the nobility for their sons. The Queen surrounded herself at Court with well-educated men. She did not suffer fools gladly! So the colleges were over subscribed. Corpus Christi was bursting at the seams with its over ninety members. Marlowe's chamber was a newly-converted store-room on the ground floor of the Old Court which he shared with two other students. The generosity of Archbishop Parker's bequest provided for his scholars as 'pensioners', and not at the lowest level of 'sizars' who carried out menial tasks for the wealthy, well-born students in the privileged class of 'fellow commoners'. His bursary was £3. 6s. 8d. per annum, and he also received a stipend of one shilling a week when in residence. His barber, who saw to it that his hair was kept short or 'polled', and his laundry were provided free. As a King's scholar he was used to wearing an ankle-length gown of woollen cloth woven by the Huguenots; at Cambridge the regulation garment was a similar gown of a 'sad colour', black or London brown, with a hood. The scholars were expected to remain in residence throughout the vacations to pursue their studies on their own, with entitlement to four weeks' stipendless leave in the summer vacation; for other absences, illness excepted, official sanction was required, although lengthy and apparently unauthorized leave was commonly indulged in. [14.] Marlowe seems to have been a model student for his first four years, almost continuously in residence, apparently studying diligently for his Bachelor of Arts degree, but also writing poetry and plays.

His first major dramatic work was probably written at 17, the lost play, *The True History of George Scanderbeg,* about a heroic Christian Prince of Albania who mightily fought the Turks, driving the infidels out of his land and restoring it to Christianity. Scanderbeg had an extraordinary and dramatic life and seems to have been a hero-figure of the adolescent Marlowe. His courage, chivalry and warlike prowess were legendary, reminiscent of Roland, and after his death he was sainted. He adored his wife and taught his soldiers to respect all women, forbidding rape of their enemies and hating all vice, especially 'the sin of Gomorrah'. [15.] This tells us much about the young Marlowe, who was committed to taking holy orders at this time. The choice of the history of George Scanderbeg may have been suggested to the budding dramatist by Gabriel Harvey, who refers to Marlowe twice by this suggestive sobriquet in his poem 'Gorgon'.

Inspired by his classical studies, his next play, as I believe, was *Dido Queen of Carthage,* based on Virgil's *Aeneid* – a play full of lyricism with all the youthful charm of an early work from the hand of a genius. He also set himself to translate from the Latin the First Book of Lucan's *Pharsalia,* in blank verse, a great epic poem relating to the civil war between Caesar and Pompey; and, by contrast, Ovid's *Amores,* a collection of erotic love poems to his mistress, in rhyming couplets; both self-set exercises in conscious preparation for the formulation of his very individual style as poet-dramatist. Ovid's influence, it has been noted, pervades the works of both Marlowe and Shakespeare.

Despite these literary distractions, Marlowe successfully completed the rigorous studies for his baccalaureate, and in the Easter term of 1584, aged 20, his name was duly entered in the Grace Book of the University as 'Dominus Marlowe'. This was a landmark in his life in more ways than one, for now appear the first extended absences from his college, implying a strong, new, extra-mural interest. These absences can be traced in the Corpus Christi bursar's Audit Accounts Book, which records payments for the weekly shilling stipend *only* when a scholar is in residence. The Audit Accounts can be set against the payments recorded against Marlowe's name at the buttery bar week by week for the purchase of food with his shilling. [16.] So that during William Shakespeare's 'lost years' we can follow Christopher Marlowe's movements from week to week over long periods – a matter that should cause rejoicing to those who have for so long deplored that we know so little about the genius whose dramatic works are revered all over the world in the name of Shakespeare.

Dominus Marlowe now disappears from the university for two-thirds of the next academic year, 1584–85, but by deduction from other documentary sources we know why he was absent and where he went, and almost certainly what he was doing. [17.] His university residence remained erratic from this time forward, although such a protracted period of absence was not repeated.

The important document that sheds a fascinating light on Marlowe's activities during his extended leave from the university is the letter written on 29th June 1587 by the Privy Council to the Cambridge University authorities, in effect commanding them to grant Christopher Marlowe his Master of Arts degree, which was apparently being withheld from him on suspicion that his absences from his college portended that he had turned Catholic. It was rumoured that he had attended Cardinal Allen's Catholic seminary at Rheims during his unauthorized absences from his college studies in 1584–5–6. Rheims was a hotbed of anti-Protestant conspiracies against Queen Elizabeth, which drew young men who had been converted to Catholicism to defect and turn traitor.

The Privy Council's letter, signed by Archbishop Whitgift and Lord Burghley among others of the Privy Council, is too important not to quote in full.

'Whereas it was reported that Christopher Marlowe was determined to have gone beyond the seas to Rheims and there to remain, their Lordships thought it good to certify that he had no such intent, but that in all his actions he had behaved himself orderly and discreetly whereby he had done her Majesty good service, and deserved to be rewarded for his faithful dealing: their Lordships' request was that the rumour thereof should be allayed by all possible means, and that he should be furthered in the degree he was to take this next Commencement: because it was not Her Majesty's pleasure that anyone employed as he had been in matters touching the benefit of his country should be defamed by those that are ignorant in th' affairs he went about.'

(Signed by)   Lord Archbishop (Whitgift)
Lord Chancellor (Sir Christopher Hatton)
Lord Treasurer (Lord Burghley)
Lord Chamberlain (Lord Hunsdon)
Mr Comptroller (Sir James Croft) [18.]

Dated 29th June 1587

In view of the fact that the period of Marlowe's longest absence in 1584–85 co-incided precisely with the germination of the Babington Plot by the Rheims conspirators – John Ballard and John Savage, and the vitally important double agent, Gilbert Gifford, who was actually in holy orders at Rheims at this time – there is every reason to believe that Marlowe's employment 'in matters touching the benefit of his country' had been in connection with gleaning intelligence on the progress of this highly dangerous plot. This had as its main objective the assassination of Queen Elizabeth and the enthronement in her place of Mary, Queen of Scots. The death of Queen Elizabeth was what the entire scheme depended upon, hence there was a vital necessity for espionage surveillance at Rheims where this plot was being hatched, doubtless under the eager encouragement of Cardinal Allen himself.

Gifford had been suborned into the pay of Sir Francis Walsingham, the Queen's Secretary of State responsible for foreign affairs who ran the espionage service, and became Marlowe's employer. As a double agent, Gifford was deeply embroiled in the Catholic conspiracy and totally trusted by the conspirators, while passing their secrets on to Walsingham's special agent, a function which it is likely Marlowe was recruited to perform – acting as a go-between, whose vital task was to shield the double agent from suspicion. In this historical context we may deduce that the brilliant young Marlowe was sent to Rheims, ostensibly to pose as a Catholic convert, in order to liaise with Gifford, and also doubtless to keep a wary eye on this clever, but notoriously devious agent to make sure he did not play false. In a similar role, Sir Francis's young kinsman, Thomas Walsingham, who became Marlowe's great friend and patron, was acting as the liaison between the double agent in London, Robert Poley, and his spy-master, Mr Secretary Walsingham, as Sir Francis was known.

The skilful exposure of this dangerous plot closed the net round all the conspirator. [19] and incriminated Mary, Queen of Scots, which led to her execution at long last in February 1587 – that wished-for conclusion which Lord Burghley and Walsingham had long prayed for and had hardly dared hope would be achieved. Small wonder that the Lord Archbishop of Canterbury and Lord Burghley had hastened to support one whose loyal intelligence service had (we may assume) helped to remove this dire threat to Queen Elizabeth's life! The Queen herself had expressed 'her pleasure' that Christopher Marlowe be held in proper regard in the true light of his patriotic service. No other interpretation of the Privy Council's letter, in the historic circumstances pertaining, is reasonable. It is no routine official stamp of approval. The terms of praise and the Queen's personal endorsement imply a special service rendered.

Lord Burghley, as Chancellor of the University of Cambridge, had access to information on the student body there, and when an intelligent and suitable young man such as Christopher Marlowe had gained his baccalaureate, a confidential approach might be made offering him government service as a secret agent. [20] This is clearly what had happened to Marlowe, and it explains why and how it was that he forsook the path ordained for him to enter the church. Lord Burghley shrewdly used the university as a recruiting ground for this vital government service, and if Marlowe had been hand-picked for this it was obviously because of his intelligence, his integrity, his proven industry in having gained his Bachelor of Arts degree, which was no lightly achieved award, many a student falling by the wayside unable to sustain the rigorous study required; and perhaps also because of his interest in politics. At Cambridge there was avid interest in the works of Machiavelli, who wrote the first treatise attempting to develop a political science, his *Il Principe (The Prince)*, a book that is still read and acknowledged a masterpiece of political thought today. Machiavelli's book had been condemned by the powers-that-be from the Pope downwards, and banned, but it found its way into the universities where it was read avidly. Marlowe was doubtless one who read it secretly.[21] Those who condemned it also read it, and noted its shrewd political advice. We may be sure that Queen Elizabeth and Lord Burghley and Sir Francis Walsingham had read it. They would have appreciated a young man who was so well informed as Marlowe.

And let it be said here, that Christopher Marlowe's employment in the government's secret service was an honourable, a patriotic and a courageous calling, and not, as some critics of Marlowe imply, some kind of lurid descent into working with men of the Elizabethan underworld, shady, devious, and somewhat unsavoury. This biased view ignores all contrary evidence and aims to sensationalize Marlowe's life. There were many sincere and extremely courageous men, some of them the truest patriots and most dedicated Protestants of their day, such as Thomas Cely, [22] and the Flemish merchant Jan Wychegerde,[23] who risked their lives to provide Walsingham with vital information from the trouble spots of Europe where the threats against little Protestant England simmered unremittingly. Of these Marlowe undoubtedly made one, being of Walsingham's confidential inner circle of trusted agents who were maintained out of Mr Secretary's own purse, for the Queen's parsimony allocated limited resources, insufficient in the eyes of this loyal and hardworking minister to ensure the protection of her life. Marlowe's name is not amongst those paid for their intelligence work by the Treasury, which implies that Walsingham maintained him personally. [24] This applies to all those we know to have been employed in uncovering the Babington Plot, which suggests that this had been Marlowe's field of employment also. Coupled with the Privy Council's letter concerning his visit to Rheims at the time of the plotting of this plot, his involvement becomes an irresistible conclusion. [25]

Walsingham employed some whose cleverness at infiltrating the enemy camp made them valuable irrespective of their integrity of character, and on such he set other spies to watch them. He trusted no one except his most confidential agents, and he built up a secret service which was second to none, controlled by his inner core of men of high intelligence and integrity on whom he could rely utterly. Marlowe's intimate connection with the Walsingham family makes it certain that he was of this inner core.

The Marlowe Portrait, now hanging in the dining hall of Corpus Christi College, Cambridge, is an *impresa* portrait in which the sitter's motto and body language are both significant, imparting their cryptic messages to the viewer. Dated 1585 and inscribed 'AETATIS SVAE 21' it precisely fits Marlowe at the time when he would have become a government intelligence agent. As a servant of the Queen he was now entitled to wear the fine clothes in which the sitter is presented, discarding his academic gown as 'Dominus Marley'. This is, I believe, an important statement. The painter, who is of the Spanish School, depicts his young sitter as the Queen's trusted secret agent in this *impresa* portrait celebrating his entry into his new profession. Surely that is the correct interpretation of this fascinating portrait presenting himself as a trusted secret agent of the Queen; his folded arms tell us 'I am one who keeps secrets faithfully' – and a poet; his motto QVOD ME NVTRIT ME DESTRVIT. It celebrates an important advancement for the shoemaker's son. It was indeed a most fortuitous development for his creative work, which was his pre-ordained and true profession.

Having gained his Master of Arts degree, thanks to the timely intervention of the Privy Council, Christopher Marlowe's six and a half years at Corpus Christi as Archbishop Parker's Canterbury scholar ended – but not as his beneficiaries had hoped. He pleaded exemption from proceeding with the commitment to enter the church on the ground of his government service, for which he had already received an unprecedented accolade signed by Archbishop Whitgift, and Lord Burghley, Chancellor of the University, and endorsed by the Queen.

Courtesy of the Master and Fellows of Corpus Christi College, Cambridge

Presumptive Portrait of Christopher Marlowe AETATIS SVAE 21 1585

This genuine Elizabethan portrait was discovered at Marlowe's college in a broken state in 1953. Now restored it is generally accepted as a portrait of Christopher Marlowe aged 21. He had probably been recruited by Lord Burghley's agents to serve in the government's secret service to protect the Queen's life from Catholic plots. This impresa *portrait displays his motto QVOD ME NVTRIT ME DESTRVIT. The sitter's folded arms (a rare posture in portraiture) imparts his message: 'I am one trusted to keep secrets'.*

He could hardly have had more impressive credentials! How could the University refuse to let him go?

It was at this point that Marlowe probably made the decision to present his old Master of Corpus Christi with his portrait as a parting gift. Poor old Dr Norgate must have been greatly disappointed to lose so promising a young churchman, and we can imagine the scene, with Marlowe making an eloquent and sorrowful speech, and offering his portrait to his old Master, whom he would have known well after so many years' residence under the same roof. The gift of his portrait represents the action of a young man who is aware of his destiny as a great poet. Edmund Spenser's portrait also hangs in the University. Old Dr Norgate died only six months later. [26]

The Old Master's Lodge at Corpus Christi formerly housed a little gallery of portraits, and the indication is that this portrait initially hung there in a place of honour. Later when Marlowe was accused of 'Atheism' and the disgrace of his murder became known it would obviously have been removed, and for years remained lost or hidden. It was re-discovered in a badly broken state in 1953 when renovations to the New Master's Lodge were in progress. The portrait's disappearance for untold years and its sudden recovery four centuries later is a fascinating story in itself. [27] This portrait was clearly in the mind of the Poet of the Sonnets when he wrote his *Sonnet 73* in his late years when the thought of approaching death was with him, which he likens to 'black night' symbolized as 'Death's second self'. This important autobiographical sonnet bears oft repetition. Beginning with the memories of his Canterbury choirboy days when he played amid the ruins of the desecrated Abbey near his home, he recalls this portrait celebrating his entry into the Queen's service, and quotes his motto: QVOD ME NVTRIT ME DESTRVIT – 'Consum'd with that which it was nourish'd by'. It is a retrospect on his life.

> That time of year thou mayst in me behold
> When yellow leaves, or none, or few do hang
> Upon those boughs which shake against the cold,
> Bare ruin'd choirs, where late the sweet birds sang.
> In me thou seest the twilight of such day
> As after sunset fadeth in the West,
> Which by and by black night doth take away,
> Death's second self that seals up all in rest.
> In me thou seest the glowing of such fire
> That on the ashes of his youth doth lie,
> As the death-bed, whereon it must expire,
> *Consum'd with that which it was nourish'd by.*
> This thou perceiv'st, which makes thy love more strong
> To love that well, which thou must leave ere long.

Sonnet 73

At the time of our narrative, in 1587, however, Marlowe was on the flood-tide of Fortune. Graced with his M.A. he departed for London and instant fame. The impact made by *Tamburlaine the Great,* first performed that autumn, is impossible to overstate. London's theatre-goers had never heard, seen, experienced anything like it. The plays, (for there are two full-length Parts of this epic work) were quoted, imitated, and parodied for the next seventy years. The references to it in print by his contemporaries would fill a book if all were collected. Perhaps some scholar will undertake it now that we know who wrote *Tamburlaine.* It was certainly a fitting début for England's greatest poet-dramatist!

With Marlowe the young actor Edward Alleyn, who played Tamburlaine, rose also to immediate fame. Following this joint success the new dramatist and his actor formed a theatrical partnership that remained the dominant influence of the Elizabethan theatres for the next six years of Marlowe's brief accredited life. During these years, at a conservative estimate, he wrote not merely the seven plays of his established canon, but at least fourteen plays, many of them published anonymously as was the current practice, besides poetic works. [28]

			First Printed
The True History of George Scanderbeg for the Earl of Oxford's Men		c. 1581/2	printed 1601 (?) [29] lost. Anonymous
Translated: {*The First Book of Lucan* {*Ovid's Elegies*		c. 1582 c. 1582	printed 1600 printed undated
Dido, Queen of Carthage for the Children of the Chapel Royal		c. 1582/3	printed 1594
The First Part of Tamburlaine the Great *The Second Part of Tamburlaine the Great* for the Lord Admiral's Men		c. 1586/7 1587	printed both in one book 1590 Anonymous
Edward the Third (his 'Armada' play) for the Lord Admiral's Men		1588	printed 1596 [30] Anonymous
Arden of Faversham [31] (local history dramatized)		c. 1589	printed 1592 Anon.
The Jew of Malta for the Lord Admiral's Men		c. 1589	printed 1633
Doctor Faustus (Revised 1592?) for the Lord Admiral's Men		c. 1589	printed 1604

The First Part of the Contention betwixt the
Two Famous Houses of York and Lancaster   c. 1590   printed 1594
(Henry VI Part 2)   Anonymous/Pirated
for the Earl of Pembroke's Men

The True Tragedy of Richard Duke of York   c. 1590/1   printed 1595
(Henry VI Part 3)   Anonymous/Pirated
for the Earl of Pembroke's Men

Harey the vj (Henry VI Part l) [32]   early 1592   printed in the Folio
   for the Lord Admiral's Men

Edward the Second   1592   printed 1594
   for the Earl of Pembroke's Men

The Massacre at Paris   1592   printed undated
   for the Lord Admiral's Men   Pirated

Hero and Leander   1593   printed 1598
Unfinished Narrative Poem

This canon of works far more closely accords with what one would expect from the vigorous young Marlowe in the flush of his creativity. The officially accredited canon of his works is based on those plays published under his name, to which is added *Tamburlaine the Great* on internal evidence and contemporary allusions. The same criteria for attributing *Edward the Third* to Marlowe apply. It is among anonymous plays of which the authorship has been widely disputed. I have presented my evidence fully in *Christopher Marlowe and the Armada*. The originals of the *Henry VI* plays have been attributed to Marlowe by F.C. Tucker Brooke, John Bakeless and Allison Gaw in their meticulous analyses of the texts and the historical contexts of their first performances. Their research on these plays has never been equalled. [33]

In addition, Marlowe would certainly have written more poetry than the fragment of *Hero and Leander* and the charming, but slight, *Come Live with Me and be My Love*, which if not published would probably all have perished. Michael Drayton refers to Marlowe as mainly a poet, and so revered among his contemporaries. [34] The present thesis argues that *Venus and Adonis* was his poem, completed before *Hero and Leander*, and already in the hands of the printer when the tragedy struck him down, to which the dedication launching the pseudonym was added just before its publication. This will be pursued in greater depth later. The foregoing establishes sufficiently that here we are dealing with an acknowledged poetic and dramatic genius who had been hailed by his envious fellow playwright Robert Greene as 'Thou famous gracer of Tragedians' in 1592, and by George Peele as 'the Muses darling' in 1593.

Patronage and Friendship

Thomas Walsingham, the young cousin germane of Marlowe's employer, Sir Francis Walsingham, was himself also engaged in the espionage service in a capacity indicative of a close working relationship with Sir Francis. This well-born gentleman became Marlowe's friend and patron. Upon the death of his elder brother, Edmund Walsingham, in 1589, Thomas inherited the extensive family estates in Kent with a beautifully situated moated manor house named Scadbury at Chislehurst.

The Walsinghams were a family with highly cultured tastes in music and literature. Thomas was probably also a poet, and Marlowe soon found himself welcomed into a circle of exceptional courtiers and noblemen whose intellectual interests included not only a love of the arts, but free discussion and questioning of religious tenets and philosophy and embracing all aspects of sixteenth century knowledge, especially scientific subjects such as chemistry, astronomy, mathematics, and navigation and world exploration. Sir Francis Walsingham was greatly interested in world exploration and Richard Hakluyt dedicated his great work, *The Principal Navigations, Voyages, and Discoveries of the English Nation,* to him in 1589. Sir Francis had long been the patron of Thomas Watson, the Latin poet, sonneteer, musician and advanced thinker, who became Marlowe's close friend. Watson's friendship with both Sir Francis and Thomas Walsingham argues intimate social contact between Marlowe and all the Walsingham family, and through them links with Court circles in which the Walsinghams enjoyed a privileged position. Thomas was from his youth a favourite with Queen Elizabeth, and she was very fond of her able Secretary of State, Sir Francis, whom she playfully nicknamed her 'Moor' on account of his dark looks.

Thomas Watson, who had trained in Roman Law, but did not practise, was some seven years Marlowe's senior, a suave and witty man of the world, much travelled in Italy and France, fluent in these languages, and a fine musician. He was a good friend of William Byrd, who set to music the Italian madrigals that Watson collected and translated into English.[35] Doubtless there would sometimes have been singing of these madrigals at the home of the Walsinghams, either at Sir Francis's home at Barnes on the River Thames, or at Scadbury, a delightful setting for such an occasion. Music would naturally have drawn Marlowe and Watson together, and, intellectually, they shared many mutual interests. Watson was evidently also a playwright, though none of his works are known to have survived. In 1589 we find them living near each other in Norton Folgate, which is part of Bishopsgate, with easy access to Finsbury Fields and Holywell, where stood London's first theatres owned by the Burbages, the Theatre and the Curtain.

The Bradley Affray

As so often when evidence survives, it is in the records of the law. In the autumn of 1589, Marlowe and Watson became involved in a fight with Watson's enemy, a thug named William Bradley, who was out for Watson's blood. Watson had gone to the aid of his brother-in-law, Hugh Swift, a lawyer engaged by the innkeeper, John Allen, * (the brother of Edward Alleyn the actor) to recover an outstanding debt of £14 from Bradley. The latter had a record for brawling, and he now called in a pal of his with similar tastes, called George Orrell, a young man of truculent spirit described as one who 'held his neck awry' in that stance that commonly trumpets a challenge to all comers. Orrell visited Hugh Swift and threatened him with a beating up if he dared to take his friend Bradley to court. Swift thereupon lodged an appeal with the Queen's Bench for sureties of the peace against George Orrell 'being in fear of death &c.' [36]

At this stage Tom Watson, it seems, joined forces with Swift and Allen to add the force of numbers in counter-threatening Bradley – who now lodged an appeal for sureties of the peace against Swift, Allen and Watson. Marlowe's name is nowhere mentioned in all this. Whether Watson, who was noted for his witty repartee, had said something that had made Bradley smart with hatred of him, the upshot was that Bradley decided to attack Watson alone, and he was found lurking in Hog Lane, not far from Watson's and Marlowe's lodgings. When Marlowe passed that way in the early afternoon of 18th September, probably on his way to Burbage's Theatre, Bradley either accosted him, or Marlowe, suspicious, may have asked him what he was doing there. Soon swords were drawn and they were locked in a duel. Attracted by the clash of steel a crowd assembled, and Watson himself appeared.

As soon as he saw Watson, Bradley turned to him with the shout: *'Art thou now come, then I will have a bout with thee'*, [37] whereupon he 'did leap upon' Watson, clearly showing with whom his quarrel lay. Marlowe withdrew leaving the two to fight it out.

Watson was evidently an expert swordsman for he slew Bradley piercing him neatly through the heart, though not before he himself had been drawn blood. He knew the law, of course, and they waited by the dead man until the constables arrived to arrest him, when he pleaded homicide in self-defence (he had a wound to show for it) which would gain him the Queen's pardon in due course under Elizabethan law. Both friends were taken to Newgate Gaol there to make their statements and be lodged. [38] Marlowe remained for thirteen days, and then was released on his recognizance of forty pounds, obtained from a lawyer of Clifford's Inn and a horner of East Smithfield known to him.

When the case came up at the next Sessions on 3rd December, Sir Roger Manwood, who was probably Marlowe's boyhood patron for his early educa-

* Foot-note: Although John and Edward Alleyn are brothers each spelt his surname differently as Allen and Alleyn.

tion at the King's School, was one of the judges on the Queen's Bench. Sir Roger must have been gratified to hear that Marlowe's part in this affair had been only peripheral and evidently innocent, for Bradley was obviously spoiling for a fight. He had come to Hog Lane with intent to do Watson an injury, if not to slay him, for he had craftily involved George Orrell, so that his, Bradley's name, was in the clear, and then taken out sureties of the peace against Swift, Allen and Watson in his own name. He was probably aiming to do for Watson exactly what Watson did for him, and then intended to claim immunity by pleading homicide in self-defence. Hoist by his own petard! Marlowe might have remarked, as was *The Jew of Malta* – the play he was probably then writing.

Watson's plea of slaying in self-defence was accepted, and he finally obtained his release from Newgate with the Queen's pardon on 12th February 1589/90 – a weary five months after the duel.

The School of Night

While the Bradley affair was still dragging through the legal procedures, Marlowe's friend and patron, Thomas Walsingham, came into his inheritance on the death of his elder brother in November 1589. It was probably through Watson and Thomas Walsingham that Marlowe became drawn into the circle of intellectuals who were members of Sir Walter Raleigh's 'little academie' or 'School of Night', co-founded by Raleigh and his friend, the young Earl of Northumberland, who was nicknamed the 'Wizard Earl' for his passionate interest in chemistry. He had laboratories installed in his houses at Blackfriars and Syon House, and at his splendid family home, Petworth House, in West Sussex. This studious young nobleman was the same age as Marlowe, and was the friend and patron of the brilliant mathematician and astronomer, Thomas Hariot, who was one of Marlowe's best friends in this group, which argues a close association also, between Marlowe and the Earl, who never stood on rank with men of genius, irrespective of class, and worked, studied and talked with them as equals. When he was eventually imprisoned by King James in the Tower, Hariot and Warner (the latter also Marlowe's friend) and the geographer and explorer Robert Hues, regularly visited him, and became known as the Earl's 'three Magi'.[39] Besides his laboratories which he had equipped with crucibles, furnaces, alembics and 'speculative glasses', the Earl had a magnificent library of books on astronomy, chemistry, mathematics, geometry, navigation, geography, history (including Holinshed's *Chronicles*), archaeology, military and political science, medicine, philosophy, gardening, literature, both classical and modern, and poetry. Here Marlowe could have read all he wanted, and with such a mind he would never have ceased to study. This great library was a store-house of learning rare outside a university and probably wider in its scope.[40]

These were the men whose intellectual pursuits encompassed everything

Henry Percy, 9th Earl of Northumberland
Miniature by Nicholas Hilliard c.1590-93

Born in 1564, he was exactly the same age as Marlowe. He was called 'the Wizard Earl' because of his love of experimenting with chemistry, and dedicated his life to the pursuit of knowledge, especially the study of philosophy and science. These interests are reflected in this impresa *portrait of the young earl in recumbent pose and negligent dress symbolic of the melancholic mood expressed in Chapman's poem, 'The Shadow of Night'. Peele dedicated his poem 'The Honour of the Garter' to him in 1593 in which he named Marlowe 'the Muses darling'. The book lying nearby recalls the earl's great love of reading as manifest in his enormous library.*

their world had to offer. They freely discussed and questioned contemporary thought, eager to expand the limits of sixteenth century knowledge, to follow the enquiring mind whither it might lead them. Theirs was the scientific approach. Such free-thinking was proscribed; inherently it challenged long-held beliefs and ran counter to the church's centuries' long dominance over men's minds. Popularly the free-thinkers were all stigmatized as 'Atheists' by the ignorant, the superstitious and the fearful. During the 1580's they enjoyed relative safety for Raleigh was in high favour with the remarkably broad-minded Queen of England and could do no wrong. His 'School of Night' might be frowned upon by the ultra-conservatives and the ecclesiastical authorities, but no one dared as yet to touch its members.

Thomas Walsingham was, on the available evidence, a cultivated intellectual whose associations suggest that he was a co-member of Raleigh's Academy. Marlowe certainly was, and it speaks volumes for him that he was one of this 'little band of supermen'. Others with him were his friend, the poet and dramatist, George Chapman, who named both Hariot and Hues as among his 'right learned, honest and entirely loved', [41] friends. Chapman was also patronized by Thomas Walsingham. Together with Chapman's special friend Matthew Roydon, also a poet, these formed a circle of true friendship with Marlowe in which intellectual pursuits featured as a strong bond. That Hariot sometimes discussed his mathematical calculations and astronomical researches with his friend Marlowe is evidenced by a note among his voluminous papers on which diagrams, logarithms, mathematical calculations and astronomical projections abound mixed with personal observations. One of these refers to the astronomical work of the Dutch scholar, Gemma Frisius, whose book was among the bequests made by Archbishop Parker to the Library at Corpus Christi College. After quoting Gemma Frisius's work and noting a progression of calculations based on it, Hariot wrote: 'This Morly told me to consider what benefit followeth'. [42] Marlowe's signature spells his name Marley, and he was also known as Morley, Marly, Marlin, Marlyn, Marlo, Marloe and Marlow or Marlowe. Elizabethans varied their spelling even of their names with bewildering inconsistency. Hariot's note seems to reflect a discussion he had with his very good friend Marlowe, in whose company he was often seen.

Marlowe's relationship with the brilliant leader of this group of intellectuals, Sir Walter Raleigh, is not in question. They wrote poems in light-hearted reply on the subject of the shepherd and his nymph. Theirs seems to have been a warm relationship of mutual admiration, and it has been suggested that Marlowe's *Tamburlaine* was in some measure a tribute of admiration for Raleigh. He was a man who epitomized the genius of the English Renaissance perhaps more than any of the brilliant men of his time in his amazing versatility – a man of intellect and action; a poet and a thinker; an enormously courageous and innovative adventurer in all the fields of human endeavour.

100

In 1592, however, Raleigh fell into disgrace with the Queen for having deceived her with his secret marriage to Elizabeth Throckmorton, and was living in seclusion at Sherborne. The free-thinkers were now increasingly under threat, for the forces of reaction were gathering to strike.

Courtesy of the
National Portrait
Gallery

Sir Walter Raleigh, *miniature by Nicholas Hilliard c. 1585,*
when at the height of favour with Queen Elizabeth

Among the habitues of London were Marlowe's fellow writers of the group known as the University Wits, Robert Greene, Thomas Nashe, Thomas Lodge and George Peele, of whom the latter seems to have been his only real friend. Greene was an envious rival who specialized in lampooning Marlowe's dramatic works, joined by Nashe more as a matter of policy for he was ambitious to make a name for himself as a satirist. We owe much of our knowledge of Marlowe's works to the satirical comments these two slipped into their prose writings to amuse their readers.

In 1592 Greene fell mortally sick and as he lay dying he wrote his last work, his moralizing autobiographical tale, *A Groatsworth of Wit*, already discussed, lampooning not only Edward Alleyn, who performed the great roles Marlowe wrote for him in *Tamburlaine, The Jew of Malta, Dr Faustus* and others, but he addressed his fellow dramatists in his bitter, plaintive *Letter.* He paints a pathetic picture of his miserable end brought on by his profligate and godless life, but now exacerbated by the poverty for which he blames the heartless actors who exploited him. To bring the lesson home he exhorts his 'Quondam acquaintance', Marlowe, Peele and Nashe, never again to write for the actors, who will only desert them, he warns, as they have him, leaving him to die penniless.

More important to this relation of Marlowe's life is that Greene, while indulging his dying agonies of conscience and self-recrimination about his own sinful life, had pointed his palsied finger at Marlowe, naming him an 'Atheist' publicly and in print. Crying *'Mia culpa'* in remorse over his past sins, he confesses all! – lechery, drunkenness, blasphemy, dishonesty, mendacity, fraud, and outright Atheism and godlessness – in which last sin he associates Marlowe with himself as one who has said: '(*like the fool in his heart*) There is no God'. But, continues the repentant Greene, '*He has spoken to me with a voice of thunder, and I have felt he is a God that can punish enemies*'. [43] In his terror of Hell-fire, he cries on Marlowe to repent, like himself, before it is too late. He claims Marlowe as a follower of Machiavelli, who was popularly stigmatized as the Arch-Atheist of them all, regarded by the superstitious, ignorant people as the personification of Satan himself! Greene's *Groatsworth of Wit* with its devastating *Letter* was a powerful piece of emotive writing that was widely read, and since in it he addresses Marlowe as 'my friend' his death-bed heart-cry would impress his readers as being the truth about Marlowe – though Nashe later called Greene's book 'a scald, lying pamphlet'. [44] There would be many all too ready to gossip and scandalize about that wicked 'Atheist', Christopher Marlowe, after Greene's popular book appeared in print. It was the first knell of the bell that was ringing his doom.

Meanwhile the campaign against the free-thinkers was mounting. Although Queen Elizabeth let it be known from the time of her accession that she wanted no windows made into men's souls, and she deplored the Spanish Inquisition that burned its heretics in the public orgies of the *auto-da-fé*, it was not so long since her half-sister, 'Bloody' Mary, had lit similar fires in England, and they had never completely been extinguished. The ecclesiastical authorities, now led by the less tolerant Whitgift, had long seen all free-thinking as a potent force that would eventually undermine the *status quo*. Attacks on 'Heresy' and 'Atheism' were powerful weapons in the struggle to retain ecclesiastical power and equilibrium in the volatile state of this period of the Reformation when Puritanism was growing apace and gaining ground. The English Revolution was only half a century hence, and the bishops were feeling increasingly threatened. Their reaction was to take steps to crush whatever seemed to them to be dangerous – and that included the free-thinkers. The climate in England was changing to that of a witch-hunt.

In the early months of 1593 there had been riots in London against the alien communities settling in the City. English xenophobia is easily aroused. Inflammatory verses threatening violence to the foreigners had been pinned on the wall of the Dutch Churchyard, where the immigrants worshipped. At this time a collaboratively written play called *Sir Thomas More* on the subject of riots against aliens was submitted to the Master of the Revels for licensing, but had been rejected unless these riot scenes were rewritten. [45] This brought the playwrights responsible under suspicion of having had a hand in writing the seditious verses threatening the aliens, and a search of all the suspected playwrights' chambers was ordered.

One of these was Thomas Kyd, a friend of Marlowe's, whose play *The Spanish Tragedy* vied with *Tamburlaine* for popularity. When Kyd's room was being searched a manuscript copy of a heretical treatise was found amongst his papers. This had nothing to do with the riots but proved far more incriminating to its owner, for 'heresy' was held to be the greatest evil. Poor Kyd was hauled off to Bridewell there to be stretched on the rack to extract a confession from him concerning his possession of this paper, which was duly labelled, 'Vile heretical Conceits denying the Deity of Jesus Christ our Saviour found amongst the papers of Thos. Kyd prisoner', and underneath was added: 'which he affirmeth that he had from Marlowe'. [46]

Kyd claimed that the paper belonging to Marlowe had become 'shuffled with some of mine (unknown to me) by some occasion of our writing in one chamber two years since'. [47] And now the hunt for the 'Atheist' dramatist Marlowe was really in full cry. A warrant for his arrest was signed on 18th May, but he was apparently not to be found at his lodgings in the plague-ridden city. Two days later he was discovered at Thomas Walsingham's Kentish estate, Scadbury, [48] where on a May morning he was probably writing his unfinished poem *Hero and Leander.*

Marlowe accompanied the messenger bearing the warrant, and as 20th May was a Sunday, when the Star Chamber Court would be closed, he evidently went with him to the Court at Nonsuch and there presented himself before their Lordships of the Privy Council who were always in attendance on the Queen.

In contrast to the dreadful treatment meted out to Kyd, he was not ordered to prison to be put on the rack, but was granted bail and was free to depart with the proviso that he 'give his daily attendance on their Lordships, until he shall be licensed to the contrary'. [49.] This trust in him doubtless reflects his status at Court as an agent.

This freedom continued for nine days, during which time the informer Richard Baines was set on his tracks to assemble as damaging a list of indictments as he could compile on this 'Atheist's' opinions garnered from the sweepings of the gutter, the hearsay and gossip of the ignorant and fearful, anyone who knew, or purported to know, what Marlowe is reputed to have said on the subject of his religious beliefs and other scurrilous subjects, with the aim of defiling his reputation in the eyes of his judges. By the end of May Baines had compiled his dossier on the poet, a document of such virulence that it could not fail to bring this known free-thinker into the clutches of the Star Chamber Court, there to have his confession wrung from him to form the basis of his trial. Heresy in England was still punishable by burning at the stake, and once brought to trial by this dread court few escaped.

Just as Baines had put the finishing touches to his report and delivered it to the Privy Council, whose members, headed by the Lord Chancellor, duplicated their high government office to function as the judicial lords of the Court of Star Chamber, it was learned that their intended victim, the 'Atheist' poet-dramatist Christopher Marlowe, had slipped from their grasp to where no one could touch him. His bail ended suddenly on 30th May – not in his expected re-arrest – but in his murder at Deptford.

❖   ❖   ❖   ❖

This review of the salient features of Marlowe's brief life up to his tragedy in May 1593, when he was just twenty-nine years old, which necessarily omits many interesting details of his well-documented career, demonstrates that his short life-span was intense in its tremendous development, variety and activity.

From his lowly beginnings as the cobbler's son who was selected for a privileged education – which brought him into the company of the élite of his generation, the most gifted youngsters from his own class, rubbing shoulders with the youthful nobility of Elizabethan England – to the teeming years in London, where he obtained the entrée into Court circles through his poetic and intellectual gifts, and, we may confidently assume, by the personal charm that won him staunch friends among the men who were his intellectual peers, that exclusive circle of 'deep brain'd' Elizabethan intelligentsia who clustered around Raleigh, it seemed as though Destiny was drawing together the threads to weave the fabric for the fashioning of an exceptional genius, who would bestride the Renaissance England of his time. What she created was recognized even by his contemporaries as the most gifted of all the gifted poets of his day. To them he was 'the Muse's darling'.

From the home of a humble artisan, to the mansions of the great; from the Canterbury cobbler's shop and his roots in the common people, the bawdy, rumbustious folk of his native city, to the scintillating Court of Queen Elizabeth, whom he served as a trusted secret agent; which gave him opportunities for foreign travel and insight into political intrigue at first hand in some of the courts of Europe. What a background for a dramatist!

When his tragedy struck him down, Marlowe was at the pinnacle of success, without rival, as England's premier poet-dramatist. Yet there was more to come from his pen, for it has been remarked by his orthodox critics that his work reveals that he was on the brink of a new development in his creative writing, wherein

> 'something serene and deeply felt, was gathering into beauty for a second harvest.' [50]

X

THE DEATH OF MARLOWE

my body being dead,
The coward conquest of a wretch's knife,

Sonnet 74

ON 30th MAY, 1593, word would have been hurried to the Privy Council's officers of the law informing them that Christopher Marlowe's life, on the very last day of his bail, had been cut short by a dagger thrust that gave him 'a mortal wound over his right eye of the depth of two inches & of the width of one inch; of which mortal wound' he 'then and there instantly died', to quote the coroner's inquisition.

On that fatal day it seems that the Poet had made an assignation with three men of his acquaintance to meet at a house in Deptford, where they spent all day together. These were, firstly, the experienced espionage agent Robert Poley, who had played the main part in enticing the conspirator Anthony Babington into Sir Francis Walsingham's carefully prepared net to uncover this dangerous plot in 1586, when he worked closely with Thomas Walsingham as his contact man for liaising with Sir Francis.[1] Next was Nicholas Skeres, an agent who was also employed in the Babington disclosure in a minor capacity, and who sometimes undertook work for Thomas Walsingham. The third man was Ingram Frizer, the long-standing family retainer of Thomas Walsingham and his business agent, well known to Nicholas Skeres with whom he engaged in some shady business dealings. We have documentary evidence that both men were clever liars and partners in fraud. [2] It seems an unlikely trio for Marlowe to have chosen to spend the last day of his freedom on bail with, from ten o'clock in the morning until six o'clock in the evening, much of it spent talking together 'in quiet sort'.

Their meeting took place at the house of Dame Elinor Bull, which seems to have been a house catering for private parties wanting a venue to discuss, transact business, or engage in convivial pleasures, where rooms might be hired and meals provided. Their landlady was a respectable dame who had some family connections with the Court.[3] Poley had just arrived in England, probably landing at Deptford direct from the Netherlands for he was currently acting as a government courier carrying Her Majesty's letters in post of 'speciall and secret affayres of great importaunce' between The Hague and the Court, which was at Croydon when he set out on his mission on 8th May. [4]. He returned to the Court at Nonsuch on 8th June bearing his replies, 'being in Her Majesty's service all the aforesaid time' as the note of his payment specifies. [5]. Note this unusual formula which is used *only* for this assignment in the twenty-eight extant records of payment to Poley. This period covers his movements and activities, during which he contrived to put in an appearance at Deptford on 30th May to be in at the kill, and acted as witness at the inquest on 1st June. This was presided over by the Royal Coroner, William Danby, who took precedence over the local coroner because this death occurred 'within the verge', that is, within a circuit of twelve miles from the person of the Queen. [6] The plot thickens from the start.

On 30th May, which was a Wednesday, Poley, Skeres and Frizer spent an eight-hour day with Marlowe at Dame Bull's house, where they had presumably hired a private room, and talked and walked in the garden, and dined and finally they supped. This was Marlowe's last supper for shortly afterwards a quarrel over the bill – cited verbatim as 'le recknynge' in the otherwise Latin inquisition – broke out between Marlowe and Frizer, which ended in an extraordinarily clumsy fracas in which Frizer wounded Marlowe mortally with his dagger above his right eye, disfiguring his face. This would have proved an effective disguise for the corpse.,

'The coward conquest of a wretch's knife' says the sonnet. This is apt, for it was not a valiant fight, nor did it have an admirable purpose; for to squabble violently over the bill when the Poet had a liberal patron and was, moreover, never known to have been short of money as he had secure employment, seems both highly improbable and cast a slur on his end. Thomas Walsingham is described on his tombstone as a man 'famous for his liberal hospitality', [7] so that this fatal dispute between his man servant and his poet over the payment for the day's hospitality due to Dame Bull sounds, frankly, like a put up story concocted by Frizer to explain the murder and exonerate him from blame. His plea was to be slaying Marlowe in self-defence, by which means it was possible to escape the gallows under Elizabethan law.

The inquest on the body took place on Friday 1st June before a jury of sixteen good men and true from the locality; tenement holders in Deptford, Bromley, Greenwich and Limehouse. Two were bakers, one a carpenter, one a grocer, and two were listed as 'gentleman'. Probably none would have known Christopher Marlowe by sight. The witnesses, Ingram Frizer, Nicholas Skeres and Robert Poley, are all described as being of London, 'Gentleman'. Skeres and Poley were both servants of the Queen, as intelligence agents, couriers or court messengers, and Frizer had a wealthy, well-born master, so that the three gentleman witnesses were somewhat superior to the jurymen, which counted for something in this class conscious society. Evidently their story was accepted by these simple men. But the more one ponders the curious tale that is recounted in Coroner Danby's inquisition, the more incredible it seems.

Here is the whole inquisition, as rendered in English by Dr Leslie Hotson, who discovered the document among the unresearched archives of the Public Records Office in 1925 and brought forth this critically important record of Marlowe's murder to the light of day and presented it to our amazed view.

The scabbard

But be contented, when	that fell **arrest**
Without all **bail** shall	carry me away,
My life hath in this	line some interest,
Which for memorial	still with thee shall stay.
When thou reviewest	this, thou dost review
The very part was	consecrate to thee.
The earth can	have but earth, which is his due;
My spirit is	thine, the better part of me.
So then thou	hast but lost the dregs of life,
The prey of	worms, **my body being dead,**
The coward	conquest of a wretch's knife,
Too base	of thee to be remembered.
The	worth of that, is that which it contains,
And	that is this, and this with thee remains.

Sonnet 74

A 16th century Quillon dagger and scabbard mounts (scabbard leather and grip restored) c. 1550, perhaps English, excavated from the River Thames.

Courtesy of the Board of Trustees of The Royal Armouries, H.M. Tower of London

'about the tenth hour before noon (the aforesaid gentlemen) met together in a room in the house of a certain Eleanor Bull, widow; & there passed the time together & dined & after dinner were in quiet sort together & walked in the garden belonging to the said house until the sixth hour after noon of the same day & then returned from the said garden to the room aforesaid & there together and in company supped; & after supper the said Ingram & Christopher Morley were in speech & uttered one to the other divers malicious words for the reason that they could not be at one nor agree about the payment of the sum of pence, that is, *le recknynge,* there; & the said Christopher Morley then lying upon a bed in the room where they supped, & moved with anger against the said Ingram ffrysar upon the words aforesaid spoken between them, and the said Ingram then & there sitting in the room aforesaid with his back towards the bed where the said Christopher Morley was then lying, sitting near the bed, that is, *nere the bed,* & with the front part of his body towards the table & the aforesaid Nicholas Skeres & Robert Poley sitting on either side of the said Ingram in such a manner that the same Ingram ffrysar in no wise could take flight; it so befell that the said Christopher Morley on a sudden & of his malice towards the said Ingram aforethought, then & there maliciously drew the dagger of the said Ingram which was at his back, and with the same dagger the said Christopher Morley then & there maliciously gave the aforesaid Ingram two wounds on his head of the length of two inches & of the depth of a quarter of an inch; whereupon the said Ingram, in fear of being slain, & sitting in the manner aforesaid between the said Nicholas Skeres & Robert Poley so that he could not in any wise get away, in his own defence & for the saving of his life, then & there struggled with the said Christopher Morley to get back from him his dagger aforesaid; in which affray the same Ingram could not get away from the said Christopher Morley; and so it befell in that affray that the said Ingram, in defence of his life, with the dagger aforesaid to the value of *12d,* gave the said Christopher then & there a mortal wound over his right eye of the depth of two inches & of the width of one inch; of which mortal wound the aforesaid Christopher Morley then & there instantly died; And so the Jurors aforesaid say upon their oath that the said Ingram killed & slew Christopher Morley aforesaid on the thirtieth day of May in the thirtyfifth year named above at Detford Strand aforesaid within the verge in the room aforesaid within the verge in the manner and form aforesaid in the defence and saving of his own life, against the peace of our said lady the Queen, her now crown & dignity; And further the said Jurors say upon their oath that the said Ingram after the slaying aforesaid perpetrated & done by him in the manner & form aforesaid neither fled nor withdrew himself; But what goods or chattels, lands or tenements the said Ingram had at the time of the slaying aforesaid, done & perpetrated by him in the manner & form aforesaid, the said Jurors are totally ignorant. In witness of which thing the said Coroner as well as the Jurors aforesaid to this Inquisition have interchangeably set their seals. Given the day & year above named &c.
  'by WILLIAM DANBY Coroner'. [8]

Thus Christopher Marlowe's death was signed and sealed. All that remained was to bury the body in an unmarked grave in Deptford churchyard. Poley and Skeres went their ways, while Marlowe's murderer, Ingram Frizer, returned to prison there to await the Queen's pardon. This arrived with astonishing speed. It was signed by the Queen at Kew on 28th June, so that Frizer would have been a free man in *less than a month*. Compare this with Thomas Watson's imprisonment after slaying William Bradley in self-defence. Watson's case was not heard by the court until 3rd December, forty-six days after Bradley was dead, and he had to wait for a further *sixty-nine days* before receiving his pardon from the Queen. And Watson was himself a lawyer by training, and a fine gentleman, a friend of the Walsinghams whose patron, Sir Francis Walsingham, was then Secretary of State and a man of great influence. Moreover, the man Watson slew was a known brawler and thug, not a famous poet-dramatist whose death would be a national tragedy. This striking contrast has hardly been noted by scholars.

It may be singular that Frizer's plea of homicide in self-defence was heard by the coroner – not by the judges of the Queen's Bench – immediately after the killing and upon view of the body. Whether this is, in itself, unusual I do not know, but this murder cries out for thorough, impartial re-investigation. Frizer's pardon also appears to have been expedited in a manner that suggests it was positively rushed through as fast as decency would allow without arousing suspicious gossip.

Was this unseemly haste to free Marlowe's murderer influenced by the fact that the fraudulent fleecing of a credulous country bumpkin named Drew Woodleff, whom Frizer and Skeres had been successfully duping to extract £200 from the foolish young fellow (who had recently inherited his father's estate) was at this very time going through the courts? The details of this complicated law suit are well described by both Dr Bakeless and Dr Hotson, and need not detain us here, but it is perhaps highly relevant that the date of the bond was 29th June – the very next day after Frizer's release. Was Thomas Walsingham pulling some strings to effect Frizer's speedy release? Bakeless tells us that the bond was 'a statute of CC^{li} vnto a gentleman of worshipp . . the saide Fryser his then Maister.' [9] To wit, Thomas Walsingham!

> 'An allusion to this very paper was discovered by Dr Hotson in a collection of entry books of bonds of recognizance among the Lord Chamberlain's papers at the Public Records Office:
>> June 29, 1593. Drew Woodleff of Peterley, Bucks, gentleman, bound in the sum of two hundred pounds to Thomas Walsingham of Chislehurst, Kent, esquire.
> This was to be paid on July 25, 1593, and when young Woodleff defaulted, the case went to Chancery.' [10]

Bakeless adds the observation that it is not clear whether Frizer's gentleman of worship, Thomas Walsingham, was aware of the fraudulent nature of this transaction, but apparently he stood to benefit from it. 'He bore a high reputation in his own day, but Elizabethan standards of honor were in some respects rather mixed.' [11] It would appear that 'conny catching' was a sport that the Elizabethans in general considered fair game. And, if there is any connection between the advantageous dating of Frizer's rapid release and the legal ratification of this two hundred pounds bond in his master's name on the next day, then it points to one very important aspect of the Deptford affair. Namely, that Thomas Walsingham was capable of exerting extraordinary manipulative power. He appears as a skilful puppet-master pulling all the right strings to effect what he intends to achieve. The very fact that Frizer is busy in his master's affairs *the day after his release from prison for having killed his master's well-loved poet-dramatist* also seems too extraordinary. How is this fact to be explained?

To return to the Deptford murder. Dr Bakeless, Marlowe's greatest biographer, comments drily that 'some scholars have been inclined to question the truthfulness of the coroner's report. There is something queer about the whole episode.' [12] Bakeless himself expresses grave doubts and asks some pertinent questions. He cites the case of the killing of James Feake by the actor Gabriel Spencer who inflicted 'a mortal wound, six inches deep and two inches wide, on the face, that is to say, between the pupil of the right eye, called the ball of the eye, and the eyebrowes, penetrating the brain' on Feake, who nevertheless 'languished & lived in langour, 3 days'. [13] Dr Samuel A. Tannenbaum has produced medical evidence to confirm that such a wound as inflicted on Marlowe would not have killed him 'then & there instantly' as described in the inquisition, but it might have induced a coma. [14] Hence in this medical fact alone, we have evidence that all was not exactly as the three witnesses described it.

From the suggested struggle between Frizer and Marlowe, the latter lying on a bed, therefore at a disadvantage in any fight; the curious passivity of the two men on either side of Frizer who did not intervene; the triviality of the cause of the dispute to arouse such a violent reaction, the more so considering whom we are dealing with – a great poet with many influential friends; the minor cuts on Frizer's scalp which could have been self-inflicted to corroborate his story – these questions are such that only the explanation of a well-planned plot can satisfy.

Add to this the incongruity of these four men spending an entire day in each other's company, who were assuredly not Marlowe's close friends, such as he would choose to spend his last day of freedom on bail with; and it could not have been some important government assignment they were discussing 'in quiet sort' since Frizer was not a secret agent; and bearing in mind that Marlowe was in dire trouble, we begin to smell a device. The absent, shadowy figure to whom all four men stand in differing but significant relationship is, of course, Thomas Walsingham.

Marlowe was innocent of the charge of 'Atheism' levelled against him, which the libellous informer's indictment seeks to fasten on him – which we shall examine in some detail to vindicate him completely – but, although he had powerful and influential friends, these were all liable to be tainted with the same brush, for 'Atheism' was the accusation flung at all the free-thinkers. Raleigh and his circle were suddenly made aware that they also stood in imminent danger, for the informer Baines' report hints at 'great men who in convenient time shall be named.' Here is the last paragraph of Baines' indictment of Marlowe, which even as the four men were deliberating at Deptford was probably already lying on Lord Burghley's desk.

> 'These things, with many other shall by good & honest witness be approved to be his opinions and common speeches and that this Marlowe doth not only hold them himself but almost into every company he cometh he persuades men to Atheism willing them not to be afeard of bugbears and hobgoblins and utterly scorning both God and his ministers as I Richard Baines will justify & approve both by mine oath and the testimony of many honest men, and almost all men with whom he hath conversed any time will testify the same, and as I think all men in Christianity ought to endeavour that the mouth of so dangerous a member may be stopped, he saith likewise that he hath quoted a number of contrarities out of the Scripture which he heath given to some great men who in convenient time shall be named. When these things shall be called in question the witness shall be produced.

RICHARD BAMES' [15] *

If, for a moment, we imagine ourselves as members of Sir Walter Raleigh's secret circle who dared to discuss scientific subjects, and to apply the same speculative inquiring mind to the Scriptures and the mediaeval concept of the world that still enshrined religious tenets, for which the ecclesiastical authorities indicted as heretics those who believed, with Copernicus, that the Earth moved round the Sun and was not the centre of the entire universe, might we not have been aghast at what Baines' Note portended? This informer was gathering ammunition for Archbishop Whitgift's arsenal to wipe out the free-thinkers. And that would mean US. The writing was on the wall, and something had to be done – urgently!

The problem was now, how to extricate Marlowe before he was re-arrested, and with him safeguard the entire 'School of Night' who had long been under attack as 'Atheists'. Lord Henry Howard had disapprovingly named Raleigh, Northumberland and Cobham (who was another nobleman of this group) as 'the infamous Triplicity that denies the Trinity'. [16] All kinds of slanders were current, even such ridiculous allegations as that they taught their members to

---

* Foot-note: Thus Baines signed his name, as Marlowe signed his Christofer Marley.

spell God backwards! Eleanor Grace Clark has eloquently put it: 'ignorance, bigotry, malice and envy all combined to turn the fair fame of these renaissance scientists into the foul legend of criminal atheism.' [17]

There is no space here to do more than touch on the noble work of these brilliant and courageous men, who were laying the foundation of scientific learning. Their magnificent and inspiring story has not received sufficient attention. It is rarely observed that Galileo was the exact contemporary of Marlowe, both born in 1564. At his famous trial he was forced to recant his opinion that the Earth moves round the Sun – and *the date of this trial was 1633.* So long did the forces of repression hold men's minds in thrall. This is the background to the life of the Poet of the *Sonnets* whose personal tragedy, reflected in *Sonnet 74* and confirmed in the huge group of the *Sonnets of Exile,* was the direct result of the repression of free thought. This is the historical context we have to bear in mind in considering the implications of the tale told in the inquisition.

The inquisition poses only three alternatives:

1. That Frizer's story, despite its dubious aspects, is true, and must be swallowed whole, ignoring his known record as a liar and here having a prime motive to lie. He was on trial for his life!

2. That Thomas Walsingham had agreed with certain leading members of the free-thinkers' circle (Raleigh has been named by Dr Tannenbaum as having a demonstrable interest) that Marlowe's mouth must at all costs be stopped before he was delivered to the Star Chamber Court to be tortured for his confession and brought to trial, when not only he, but other witnesses would be called, as Baines had promised. And that this was effected by the plot to assassinate Marlowe, which was organised by Thomas Walsingham, involving his minions, Frizer, Poley and Skeres. Some even see it as a government-inspired assassination.

3. That Thomas Walsingham acted as a true and loyal friend and summoned all his skill, ingenuity, and expertise in espionage to stage a faked murder, using Frizer, Poley and Skeres in a subtle plot; substituting another body whose face was disfigured by the facial wound, to enable Marlowe to escape. Here we come to the Shakespearean authorship theory of the faked murder plot, followed by Marlowe's flight to the Continent, taking ship from Deptford, and his subsequent emergence as the pseudonymous William Shakespeare. .

Option 1 takes some swallowing, firstly, because of the obvious inanities of the account of the actual fight; secondly, because the whole day's business is questionable in our eyes – though not in the jury's who did not know what kind of men they were dealing with. They only saw three proper 'gentlemen' of London who had been enjoying a day's conviviality, mixed perhaps with a little business, which ended unfortunately when one of them became rather drunk and lost his temper. We must remember that Poley was a past master at smooth talking, who had so insinuated himself into the confidence of Anthony Babington that he trusted him implicitly, and even at the end was not sure whether he had betrayed him. The Deptford jurymen would have been putty in his hands – which suggests why he had been urgently called to be there. His skills were needed. Thirdly, to accept Frizer's story we have to find a valid reason for this day-long rendezvous between the intellectual, free-thinking poet Marlowe, who was in grave trouble, and three such very different characters, one of whom had only just landed from a trip to The Hague, to attend some pre-arranged meeting at Deptford. It doesn't add up.

Option 2 seems at first blench to recommend itself for it provides a motive for the murder and seems to answer some of the dubious details of this story. But it has one glaring flaw. Thomas Walsingham was an Elizabethan of good breeding and cultivated tastes, as seen in his liberal patronage of two such poets as Marlowe and Chapman. If he was, by our standards, of questionable honesty in employing a clever rogue like Ingram Frizer, there is no doubt that the latter was devoted to his master. The implication of this option is, indeed, that he was ready to serve him to the death! Loyalty and true friendship were prized in Elizabethan society as the highest virtues. Elizabethan literature testifies abundantly to the sacredness in which friendship was held, and *to betray a friend* was the deepest descent into iniquity conceivable. The fact that George Chapman, who was Marlowe's friend, continued in a warm relationship of friendship under the patronage of Thomas Walsingham after Marlowe's murder does not square with the theory that it was Walsingham, *who was Marlowe's patron and friend,* who plotted his assassination. It would also mean that Walsingham's acceptance of the moving dedication to him of *Hero and Leander* upon its publication by Edward Blount, who was Walsingham's and Marlowe's mutual friend, was an act of sheer hypocrisy. (See this dedication pp. 168-9)

Some scholars favouring this option have suggested that it was a government plot to murder Marlowe because he knew too much. Vague connections with his espionage work are proposed, but no shred of evidence has validated this notion. Eugénie de Kalb, who has done valuable research to reveal Poley's movements at this time, suggests that it was Lady Audrey Walsingham who wanted Marlowe done away with because he knew too much about her intrigues [18] – but Miss de Kalb has got her dates wrong, for in 1593 Thomas Walsingham was still a bachelor, and Audrey Shelton (her maiden name) was not even at the Court. She became Lady Walsingham in 1598, and her political 'intrigues', if they were indeed such, date from the reign of King James. Frizer's later activities in various shady property dealing transactions for Lady Audrey Walsingham are in the tradition of his services as a loyal servant, and extend into the seventeenth century when this lovely lady was one of King

James's favourite court beauties. No one in the corrupt court of King James would have batted an eyelid at such acquisitive dealings. The Walsinghams were all passionately addicted to advantageous intrigues, and when it came to feathering their nest scruples were cast to the wind by many an Elizabethan on the make. Elizabethan social mores were lax on such matters, whereas loyalty to a friend was a paramount virtue. *Friendship was held as sacrosanct.* Hence this option is flawed at its inception, and is unsupported by any evidence.

These suggestions of some kind of plot to murder Marlowe are all a threshing around in the dark with various sinister connotations in vague and formless hypotheses without evidence; but they express the dissatisfaction felt by some orthodox scholars over accepting Frizer's story at face value as the only other alternative open to them, for *Option 3* is for them beyond the pale of contemplation.

Option 3 while seemingly the most fantastic and improbable, on close examination is both the most reasonable and the most probable, indeed, the *only* answer that *fits all the problems raised by the inquisition and precisely reflects the historical context.* It satisfies the obvious motive for a murder plot of *Option 2* – to silence Marlowe and obviate the danger to his friends in the 'School of Night'. And by transforming his death into a faked 'murder', which saved the life of the poet who was also a dear friend, instead of basely destroying him, the noblest and most sacred principle of Elizabethan mores was fulfilled, not desecrated and outraged.

That Thomas Walsingham would have been capable of carrying out such a ruse is not in question. He had years of experience in dealing with espionage affairs and had been privy to his cousin's devious methods of operation, in which he had been trained to think ahead of every situation, to anticipate every exigency in order successfully to outwit and trap dangerous conspirators. Although Sir Francis was now dead, and Sir Thomas Heneage was in charge of the espionage service, and since his inheritance it is probable that Thomas Walsingham himself was no longer active in intelligence work, he would have had a shrewd idea of what the score was regarding Marlowe's predicament. He knew the ropes of old, how to gain access to information, and he knew the qualities of the espionage personnel. Poley was his man for this job, and he knew where to contact him and clearly did so.

Deptford, most conveniently, was a port in those days from which the hoys plied back and forth across the Narrow Seas to the Continent. Forged passports were available for the use of secret agents, who at times needed to travel under assumed identities, pretending to be merchants, or priests and so on. Marlowe himself was still in the secret service, and both he and Walsingham would have possessed expertise regarding the obtaining of false passports, the use of false identities and disguises.

One small but very significant aspect of this affair concerns the delivery of Baines' *Note* containing his detailed indictment of Marlowe. The copy sent to the Queen has the original title scored through and now is headed:

'A Note deliuered on Whitson eve last of the most horrible blas-
phemes vtteryd by Cristofer Marley who within iii days after came
to a soden & fearful end of his life.' [19]

Whitsun eve in 1593 was on 2nd June, so that three days after this *dates his
death on 5th June*. The inference is that this incriminating document had been
either withheld, or removed and then returned later with an erroneous date of
the event given to colour it in such a way as cover this lapse in time. If this is
merely a clerical error – as some scholars argue – it is a strange co-incidence
that this error should have favoured the escape of the hunted man. Every detail
we examine in this curious assassination points us always in the same direction
– that all is not what it seems.

Another fortuitous, and perhaps not so minor, aspect is the presence of
William Danby, the Queen's Coroner, in the case. The Queen was then at her
palace of Nonsuch, near Cheam in Surrey, so that Deptford would have lain just
within the twelve miles radius of the 'verge'. This favourite small palace of
Queen Elizabeth is no longer extant.

Yet another factor in the scenario to give us pause for thought is the choice of
Dame Elinor Bull's house. New light has been shed by the important discovery
by Jane Apple of the draft of Blanche Parry's will, written in Burghley's own
hand for this blind and aged, dearly loved Chief Gentlewoman of Queen
Elizabeth, who had attended the little Princess Elizabeth from her infancy. [20]
Burghley names Blanche Parry 'cousin', so there was some bond of relationship between them. In her will she bequeathes   100 (recoverable as a debt
owing) to her 'cousin' Mistress Bull née Whitney, cited in the prerogative version of the will as 'my cousin Elinor Bull'. [21] This affords the vital clue to
Elinor Bull's identity. Both the Parrys and the Whitneys were armorial Welsh
border families who had long held court offices, and had provided county sher-
iffs and members of Parliament for Herefordshire.

Blanche Parry had died only two years before in 1591, at the grand old age
of 83, when cousin Elinor Bull would doubtless have attended the funeral. She
herself had been widowed the previous year when Richard Bull, a sub-bailiff of
the manor of Sayes Court at Deptford, was laid to rest in Deptford's parish
church of St. Nicholas – the same where the murdered body ostensibly of
Marlowe was buried in the churchyard in an unmarked grave after the inquest [22]

Blanche Parry and Burghley were both people very close to the Queen, privileged members of her royal 'family' – those whom she drew into intimate relationship with herself. Elinor Bull therefore had a very important line of connection with the Court, to its very heart, in fact. Blanche Parry's close connection is seen in that she was godmother to Blanche Whitney, who would have
been the same generation as Elinor, either her first cousin, perhaps even her sister. Blanche Parry was already aged 63 when Elinor Whitney married Richard

Bull in 1571. As Nicholl has percipiently commented concerning Elinor Bull: 'She was someone who could call on court connections if she needed, someone who might serve court connections if they needed.' [23] That is the point. It could not be more aptly put. She is another connection adding her tantalising question mark to this affair: How deeply were those high up in the Court and close to the Queen herself involved? We are getting ever warmer in solving the mystery.

The choice of Deptford was singularly advantageous: it brought Danby in to officiate; it enabled Poley to arrive direct from The Hague by ship; it offered a variety of shipping for a speedy departure for the fugitive poet; and the house of Dame Elinor Bull, with her familial courtly connections, was there offering private rooms for hire which were eminently suitable to their purpose. In short, IF Walsingham were planning such a ruse as is suggested, this was a four star venue for it.

The number of remarkable, fortuitous 'co-incidences' which all helped this clever plot to its successful conclusion are so numerous, and each is so strongly suggestive of a plan which is devised on a *grand scale*, with ramifications apparently right inside the Court (if we judge by the evidence presented) that one begins to wonder – was not only William Danby privy to this intrigue by which the whole legal aspect of the death was expedited in an unprecedented manner, but was Queen Elizabeth herself the Lady of Mercy who extended her white hand to aid the stricken poet?

The immediate reaction will be: This is too far-fetched, too extravagant and fanciful! But is it? Many things, as we follow the course of this strange story to reveal with what consummate skill Marlowe's escape, and his identity behind the name and person of one William Shakespeare were concealed, tend to make one more and more aware that this extraordinarily successful secret must have had the sanction of the Queen from its inception. The fact that such a likelihood lends the whole affair an excitement and romance that lifts it out of the sordid into the realm of almost fairy tale, does not make it less likely. On the contrary, in this baroque period of Gloriana's reign it makes it more likely, more credible.

Queen Elizabeth was a brilliant woman and a wilful one with a mind of her own. She was of the age now when the prospect of love and marriage and children had receded, with which she had toyed for so long, and even her courtly 'lovers' were becoming a fiction. She needed to be kept amused, and she loved the drama. Her lively mind was as dedicated to learning as many a scholar's, and this she appreciated in others. Her attitude towards religion was, above all, one marked with tolerance. She had no sympathy with religious fanatics, and the persecution of the Spanish Inquisition was abhorrent to her. Dr Allen commented that the Queen really had no religion – rather that 'commonsense was the most obvious feature of her religious attitude.' [24] But she believed earnestly in prayer and prayed always regularly and with fervour. She wrote many prayers herself, in Latin, Greek, Italian, French, practising her languages at the same time, 'but the English ones show a poignant and unforced eagerness: 'Thou has set me on high, my flesh is frail and weak. If therefore at any time I forget thee, touch my heart, O Lord, that I may again remember thee'.' [25] She knew the psalms by heart as well probably as ever the choirboy, Christopher Marlowe, did.

This was a very human woman, subject to whims and foibles which, as a Queen, she could indulge, and she had a heart that was easily moved to pity. She had a soft spot for personable young men of talent, and she had always been extremely fond of the young Thomas Walsingham, who had been employed as a court messenger from the age of seventeen, fostered in this by Mister Secretary Walsingham to whom Thomas stood in relationship almost as the son he never had. Thomas evidently rose in the Queen's graces for when he was yet only nineteen she had used him as her special messenger and envoy to bear her love-letter to Alençon (then Duke of Anjou and the heir to the French crown), her 'Frog' with whom a courtship was still in progess, when in July 1582 she wrote him a handsome, denying answer to say (very regretfully) that she could not send him the money that he desired from her to finance his military campaign in the Netherlands, alas! But she says her messenger will proceed afterwards to the French Court to persuade King Henry III that he is in honour bound to finance his brother in this Netherlands venture which would advantage France. In her letter she extols her messenger as a gentleman of good parts, whose service she greatly values, and who is entirely in her confidence; indeed he can answer all Monsieur's questions as though she were speaking herself. [26] His loyalty and his skill in diplomacy she evidently rated highly.

Thomas Walsingham might have risen and gone far, but he seems to have had no political ambitions and preferred to remain in the shadows. It seems to have been his deliberate choice, to live a life of cultured seclusion. When he married he was happy to allow his lovely wife to take the limelight at Court. Thomas Walsingham always kept a remarkably low profile, while remaining constantly high in the Queen's esteem, for she continued to show him many marks of her special favour throughout her life, and at an early age she had given him her intimate confidence and trust. We may reasonably ask: Did this wise young man appeal to the Queen for her help in this hour of need, and was Elizabeth moved to mercy to ensure that her servant, Christopher Marlowe, would be spared a terrible fate? If we judge Elizabeth aright, it would not now have been 'her pleasure' to see this great poet-dramatist cruelly destroyed; he who had performed such signal service to her in the past, when she had defended his good name because he was being 'defamed by those that are ignorant in th' affairs he went about'. [27] Christopher Marlowe had served his Queen loyally ever since, and he had written some superb dramatic works for her entertainment, and promised her many more. That would have been a trump card to win Elizabeth's support! She would certainly have recognized his quality as a poet and dramatist, at that time without rival. We know that she later showed her sincere appreciation of the other half of this famous theatrical team, the great actor Edward Alleyn, the interpreter of Marlowe's admired roles, who retired from the stage at the height of his career in 1597 when he was aged only thirty-one. The Queen is on record as having said how much she missed his performances, which had ever been to her 'great liking and contentment', and she had 'sundry times signified her pleasure that he should revive the same.' It was with her help that he obtained the warrant from the reluctant Justices of the Peace to build his new theatre, the Fortune in Golding Lane, when his theatre, the Rose, was becoming too dilapidated. The Queen peremptorily ordered them 'to permit and suffer the said Edward Alleyn' to build his theatre 'without any your let or interruption toward him or his workmen'. [28] The building went ahead, and in deference to the Queen's expressed wishes Alleyn once more returned to the boards to delight Elizabeth with his performances until the end of her reign.

Since it was the Queen's pleasure to intervene thus decisively on the behalf of Marlowe's actor, Edward Alleyn, (whom Nashe had aptly named the 'Cobbler's Crow'* in his canting allusions to Marlowe and Alleyn) it is reasonable to assume that she would have lent a sympathetic ear to Walsingham's pleas for the saving of her greatest dramatist, whose downfall would have presaged also the dragging down of Raleigh and the brilliant men who studied with him, to the same wretched level of ignomiw and false accusations. That, we may be absolutely sure, would *not* have been Elizabeth's pleasure. And this astute woman would have recognized the danger.

This synopsis precisely fits the picture when we consider what *actually* happened. It is very curious indeed, and no one has ever successfully explained the reason for it, that the Cerne Abbas inquiry into the 'Atheist' opinions of Sir Walter Raleigh and his friends, which was launched following Marlowe's death, was never pursued to its conclusion. The inquiry reached a point in 1594, and then suddenly petered out. Was it Elizabeth's decisive voice that stayed it? She would see no sense in such troublesome investigations of her courtiers and scholars, and this time put a determined brake on the witch-hunting propensities of her Archbishop *before* they went too far – as with Marlowe. Raleigh was still in disgrace for his secret marriage to Elizabeth Throckmorton, but he was eventually forgiven and returned to the Court. And she would not have allowed him to be touched. She wanted *no* windows made into men's souls. It was left to King James to imprison Raleigh and bring him to trial on false charges, in which 'Atheism' was viciously hurled at him, and to impose long imprisonment on Northumberland. During Elizabeth's reign the 'Wizard Earl' had been free as a bird to pursue the delights of the mind, which held no terrors for her. She understood their thirst for knowledge in a way that James, though he prided himself on being a scholar, never could for his mind was still swayed by superstition.

In the light of the foregoing it is more than likely that Walsingham, who had

* Foot-note: 'Crow' is an Elizabethan term for an actor.

a fine perception of Queen Elizabeth's mind and heart, would have opened his own mind and heart to her, pleading on bended knee for her blessing on his project to save his poet Marlowe. In going to the Queen direct he would have shown great wisdom, for Elizabeth loved to be held gracious and she could not abide to be deceived. Her greatest fury was aroused by those who excluded her in this way. The secret marriages with her Maids of Honour contracted by Raleigh and Southampton sent her into paroxysms of rage. They had dared to misunderstand her and to behave in an underhanded way which broke the bonds of mutual trust so dear to her. Walsingham was wiser. He realised that it would, in fact, have been dangerous to attempt to put his plan into action *without* the Queen's confidence and support. She was no fool, and it would not have been easy to deceive her. If Archbishop Whitgift smelt a rat, Elizabeth, if she were in the know, would be able to mollify and draw him off the scent that there had been a plot afoot to extricate the intended victim. He would not dare to impugn the Queen, whereas Thomas Walsingham, who was so obviously associated with all the men at Deptford, was vulnerable. He undoubtedly realised this. Even four hundred years later orthodox scholars have suspected him of some sort of foul play. Walsingham was clearly somehow involved.

So, also, was Frizer vulnerable. He was, in a sense, putting his own life at risk for Marlowe, that is, *unless* he had been assured beyond all possible doubt that he would not be hanged for murder. This brings the strong suggestion that there would have been prior collusion with the Queen's coroner, Danby, to ensure that Frizer's story of the circumstances of the quarrel in which Marlowe was slain by him would be seen by Danby to justify his plea of killing in self-defence, and that it would be such a tale as would impress the jury of his innocence – and, by contrast, of Marlowe's guilt in provoking him.

We can visualize Frizer standing in the courtroom showing his little surface scalp-wounds as evidence of Marlowe's 'malicious ' assault on him – from behind! The expert smooth-talking Poley was there to confirm the story. Nothing must be allowed to go wrong. The jury *had* to be convinced. They were simple men. But Danby, the experienced coroner, was another matter. Would he have been taken in by Frizer's dubious story? He had not risen to be the Queen's coroner through incompetence. I suggest that in order to be *certain* of Frizer's acquittal Danby would have been privily commanded by his royal mistress to give his judicial verdict of slaying in self-defence as agreed. Perhaps with a remuneration from Walsingham, and the acquisition of a suitable body for the purpose. Only then would all the conditions for a totally successful outcome be assured. We now begin to see the ramifications of this extraordinarily subtle plot, devised by the mind of a master-espionage agent who was trained to anticipate every exigency, and to outwit every mischance.

A piece of documentation that curiously underlines the *personal* interest that Queen Elizabeth took in this extraordinary murder case at Deptford is the writ of *certiorari* which Dr Hotson's research discovered in connection with the inquisition.

Elizabeth by the grace of God of England France Ireland Queen Defender of the Faith &c. To our well beloved William Danby, Gentleman, Coroner of our household, greeting. Wishing for certain causes to be certified upon and indictment made in your presence concerning the death of Christopher Morley; upon view of the body of the same Christopher at Detforde Strande in our County of Kent within the verge lying dead and slain, whence a certain Ingram ffrysar, late of London, Gentleman, is indicted (as by the record thence remaining with you it fully appear). And whether the same Ingram slew the aforesaid Christopher in self-defence, & not feloniously or of malice aforethought, so that in no otherwise could he avoid his own death, or not; we command you to send the tenor of the indictment aforesaid with everything touching it and whatsoever names the parties aforesaid in that indictment are known by to us in our Chancery under your seal distinctly & openly without delay, & with this writ. Witness myself at West-minster on the 15 day of June in the year of our reign the thirty-fifth.

POWLE

[Indorsed] The tenor of the record mentioned in this writ appears in a certain inquisition annexed to this writ. [29]

Elizabeth is here requesting, nay, commanding Danby 'to send the tenor of the indictment' together with everything touching it and whatsoever names the parties are known by, to us in our Chancery...without delay'. This implies that the Queen had reason to wish closely to scrutinize Danby's inquisition. Why this *personal* interest on the part of Her Majesty in the sordid details of the murder of a man charged with Atheism by the Star Chamber? It is not an indictment affecting her personal safety such as a Catholic assassination plot, so why is she so interested? No one studying Marlowe's death has ever remarked on this fact. The writ of *certiorari* has been totally overlooked. Yet surely this is a very important document relating to the circumstances of this case. It reveals that the Queen has a *personal* interest in the death of Marlowe which in the context of this hypothesis is very significant. Dr Hotson treats the writ of *certiorari* as merely part of the chronology of the Deptford without making any comment, as though it is normal procedure in connection with the granting of a pardon or slaying in self-defence, but there is reason to think that it was much more than that. He writes:

From these documents the chronology of the case emerges as follows: Ingram Frizer killed Christopher Marlowe on the evening of Wednesday, May 30, 1593. The inquest was held on Friday, June 1; and on the same day they buried Marlowe's body. The writ of *certiorari* was issued out of the Chancery just two weeks later – on

Friday June 15. Thereupon Coroner Danby made his return, and Frizer's pardon was granted at Kew on Thursday, June 28. [30]

He makes no comment on the Queen's express command that the 'tenor' reciting details of the case be sent to her *'without delay'*. Why this haste? When Thomas Watson slew William Bradley in self-defence he waited five months for his pardon! Is not all this full of significance?

I therefore suggest that it is a reasonable hypothesis, that IF such a plot had been devised and carried through, according to Walsingham's plan, to whisk Marlowe away from this position of danger which had reached a point of no return with Baines' *Note*, then Queen Elizabeth would have been privy to it. And having been taken into Walsingham's confidence, this eminently sensible woman would do what was necessary to ensure that his clever scheme was absolutely water-tight. She could rely on his utter discretion. The cat would never be let out of the bag while he was in charge, for she knew well the qualities of this quiet, charming and discreet young courtier, who had had the wisdom to come to her for aid when he needed it.

So it was that Poley was sent for and commanded to play his part as a vital witness at the inquest, – being all this time in Her Majesty's service [31] – this curious rider to his record of payment takes on a new significance; so it was that William Danby was primed to preside officially at the inquest, and Dame Elinor Bull's house was chosen for the venue; and so it was that the Baines' *Note* was discreetly stayed until it could do no harm. That, I suggest, is a logical explanation of this extraordinary event.

This conclusion is consistent with all we know about Elizabeth's character: she was more than usually astute and intelligent, inclined to be merciful even to her enemies, tolerant of religious differences, passionately loving the drama. She would have a manifest interest in saving her favourite dramatist and faithful agent from a horrible and undeserved end. Elizabeth, too, had been called a 'heretic' and an 'atheist' by the Pope and excommunicated, and stigmatized a 'bastard'. She knew what it was to have mud slung at her. She also saw clearly that her erstwhile favourite courtier Raleigh was being aimed at. Marlowe's desperate plight had alerted her to what Whitgift was up to, and she would now, by saving her dramatist, be able to scotch the Cerne Abbas inquiry before it went too far and got out of hand, for she must have known that once begun the persecution would not stop with Marlowe.

These being the desirable ends that all accorded with Queen Elizabeth's personal views, and interests and predilections, can we doubt that it would have been the Queen's 'pleasure' to assist and support Walsingham's plan to save one of the jewels in her crown, 'the Muses darling', her greatest poet-dramatist, Christopher Marlowe? If we admit for a moment, by hypothesis, that we are speaking of Shakespeare, who is thus being saved from a dreadful, premature end, then there can be no doubt in our minds what the Queen's decision would be. Throughout her long reign Elizabeth nurtured what was best in the drama, and this act of mercy was the greatest she ever did for posterity. This is hypothesis, but I ask the reader: Is it not likely to be true?

It is disappointing not to be able to report a final piece of poetic justice to tie up this amazing episode. A Richard Baines who was hanged at Tyburn on 6th December 1594 turns out not to have been our man. [32.] The informer first emerges in the records at Rheims in 1583 where he plotted to poison the entire Seminary by poisoning the well from which their water was drawn! [33]. A ludicrous plan that was discovered in time, which Marlowe lampooned in *The Jew of Malta*. Baines would have relished having his revenge! Fortunately with the Cerne Abbas business firmly quashed, the fanatical witch-hunting receded, defeated. Peace and equilibrium were restored for the duration of Queen Elizabeth's reign.

The foregoing is hypothesis in so far as we cannot expect documentary evidence to come fortuitously to hand, though if we know where to look it may yet emerge. But by cogent reasoning it all hangs together. There are no discrepancies, or incongruities. It all adds up! The characters in this real life drama all behave *in character:* Queen Elizabeth, Thomas Walsingham, Poley, Frizer, and Skeres all fit this scenario, which alone explains the many curious and puzzling factors in an admittedly extraordinary situation, that has remained the most intriguing unsolved murder mystery of the last four hundred years. It is a truism, that life is sometimes stranger than fiction. If to believe this appears difficult, the alternative is to believe Frizer's unlikely tale and to swallow it whole, knowing that it would be 'in character' for him and his confederates to tell a bare-faced lie. We also know, if we listen to what his friends said about Marlowe, and have any appreciation of his marvellous poetic works, that it is incredible that he would have behaved in the manner described by Frizer over the payment of the bill at Dame Bull's house. That alone takes some swallowing, but it is a story that perfectly suits Frizer's necessity to have a plausible excuse for slaying in self-defence.

We must also ask ourselves, if Walsingham, given his influence and relationship of trust with the Queen, his expertise in espionage matters; his knowledge of Poley, Skeres and Frizer as tools for his purpose; his genuine friendship with Marlowe, and his close relationship with the members of the circle of intellectuals endangered by Marlowe's arrest – given all this, if he had *not* lifted a finger to help Marlowe, would it not be even more remarkable? If we compare the dangers of his situation with the not dissimilar experiences of those who were caught up in the toils of the Gestapo in the Second World War, we may well conclude that Walsingham must have done everything in his power to outwit the machinations of Whitgift and his informer. What impresses is the skill with which every detail of this assassination plot slots into place with amazing, perfect timing to achieve the desired result. *And everything that follows in this investigation corroborates it.* Nothing contradicts this premise.

If I have hopefully carried the reader with me thus far, permit me to be so bold as to state it bluntly. *Only a faked death* can answer all the anomalies of the case, which I set down in imitation of the informer Baines' nefarious report on Marlowe, using the 'That' clause, as Paul Kocher calls it:

1. That the trivial cause of his alleged fatal quarrel with Frizer, casting a slur of unprovoked, mean-minded aggression on Marlowe's end, is incredible when we consider who this young man was – a highly praised poet and dramatist; a trusted agent of the government with access to the chief government ministers for whom he worked confidentially; a 'gentleman' in Elizabethan society and a reputable scholar with an M.A. whose friendship was valued by the Elizabethan intelligentsia of courtiers close to the Queen, noblemen, poets, philosophers and scientists.

2. That Frizer's transparent reason for telling this tale to the jury was to get himself off the hook, or he was a dead man.

3. That the close association of Thomas Walsingham with all four men at Deptford cannot be dismissed as irrelevant. Investigation in depth of Thomas Walsingham's connection has been evaded by an apparent academic collusion fearful of what might be discovered.

4. That Marlowe had an urgent reason for disappearing by means of a faked death which would have been the perfect solution to his dilemma.

5. That Thomas Walsingham's qualifications as a past master in espionage, and his access to the inner circle of the Court, would enable him to organize such a ruse.

6. That the necessity to protect Marlowe's free-thinker friends was sufficient motivation for taking urgent action.

7. That all the investigation to date of this murder by scholars in attempts to explain it in terms acceptable to academic orthodoxy – that is, always strenuously avoiding the faked murder hypothesis – has drawn a blank.

8. That the death of Marlowe was immediately followed by the arrival of a new poet named William Shakespeare, whose name was introduced to the public with his *Venus and Adonis* – a poem pre-dating Marlowe's *Hero and Leander,* left unfinished in 1593 and showing marked maturity compared with *Venus and Adonis* which was cleverly presented by the new poet as 'the first heir of my invention.' (This significant publication is treated in some detail in Chapter 22)

9. That Marlowe's dramatic writing, which showed distinct evidence of his growing maturity when tragedy overtook him, carried on without a break *at*

this level with the works of the new poet William Shakespeare, soon blossoming into a greater maturity which reflected undeniable influence of the Italian Renaissance and an intimate knowledge of Italy (see Chapter 23), yet there is no shred of evidence that Shakespeare ever visited Italy.

Can anyone answer these anomalies other than by explaining them by a faked death? I think not.

With this re-assessment of the Deptford murder of Marlowe as neither more nor less than a plot by which to fake his death and enable him to escape into oblivion, we are again firmly on track in this investigation. This historic event is not a wild fancy. It is the essential key to the puzzlingly close relationship between Marlowe and Shakespeare without which we are left uncomprehending and floundering in hypothesis. The faked murder resolves these problems at a stroke, and answers all those unexplained questions that hover around Shakespeare and refuse to lie down. But let us not get carried away because this is an exciting solution. It needs corroboration, and that is what we are seeking here.

The most explicit corroboration of Marlowe's faked death is found in the sonnets which tell the Poet's story of his tragedy and the true friendship that saved him. *Sonnet 74* recounts the facts of this entire episode – the arrest – the bail – the murder by 'a wretch's knife' – and seals it with the moving dedication of his 'spirit', 'the better part of me', to the true friend and patron to whom the sonnet is written as a verse-letter. This all points to Thomas Walsingham alone, who was so undeniably involved with the Deptford incident, which many orthodox scholars suspect was some kind of plot in which he had a hand.

Walsingham is the real Patron of the *Sonnets*, although he is not 'Mr.W.H.', behind whose cryptic identity he is carefully hidden, for the disclosure of his name would have been too dangerous. This is another intriguing aspect of this clever and deliberate mystification, designed originally to mislead his contemporaries, which has for four hundred years also misled posterity. The spirits of Marlowe and Walsingham might well exclaim with Puck –

'Lord, what fools these mortals be!' [34]

ADDENDUM

One aspect of this murder, if it had really been a clever faked murder plot, poses a question to our modern minds. Why was it executed in so complicated a manner with the three men, one of whom then faced trial for murder, only evading hanging by pleading self defence, so that Marlowe had to be shown as the aggressor depicting him as a violent man who attacked Frizer from behind his back? Why this, when he could have been dispatched by an unknown hand in a dark alley?

This is where the subtlety of such a mind as Walsingham's makes itself apparent. A back-alley murder would have pointed the finger at those who would be put into danger by Marlowe's imminent re-arrest and trial, doubtless preceded by torture to obtain his confession and indictment of other freethinkers. Moreover the body of the murdered man would have been examined for identification, and found not to have been Marlowe. This would have been an untidy solution, with the possible consequence of stepping up the witch-hunt. Hence it was decided to stage 'a great reckoning in a little room' with witnesses *to testify that this murdered man was Marlowe,* and an official stamp on the inquisition by no less a person than the Queen's own coroner, followed by a swift burial in an unmarked grave. Thus to write FINIS to the life of this 'Atheist'. A tidy end, no questions asked. It had the stamp of officialdom.

It was an extremely wily plot that took cognizance of all the possible exigencies and hazards, and pulled off a hat trick that has kept us guessing for 400 years. There was, perhaps surprisingly, no aftermath for Thomas Walsingham. So far as we know, not a murmur of suspicion attached to the patron whose servant slew his poet friend and got off scot free after a mere 28 days in jail. The Court, the centre of gossip, one imagines would have buzzed with whispered comments. But so lethal was the taint of 'Atheism' that people were suddenly muffled, shocked into silence, thinking perhaps: There, but for the grace of God, go I. Those who knew Marlowe, knew also that he was innocent of all wrong-doing, and was innocent of 'Atheism' except in the eyes of the ignorant and superstitious bigots. The only effect on Thomas Walsingham seems to have been that he retired himself to Scadbury, to a secluded life away from the limelight of the Court and its intrigues, although perhaps this might have been his personal choice to devote himself to cultural pursuit and study.

One factor alone the Master Plotter had not taken into account. He had not reckoned with the calumny that descended like a black cloud on Marlowe's reputation. Poor Kit. The Sonnets of Vilification speak their testimony, and perhaps most relevant as commentary on this event is *Sonnet 34,* expressing a fierce cry of pain, upbraiding Walsingham for the manner in which the murder plot had been executed, leaving him forever with a besmirched name. He was left to brood helplessly in his exile, unable to refute the story to clear his name, which Walsingham, grieve as he might over what had been done at Deptford, was powerless to amend. This sonnet is discussed more fully later but I include it here as it certainly refers to the murder plot and its consequences for the Poet, and clearly testifies to Walsingham's involvement in the Deptford affair.

> Why didst thou promise such a beauteous day
> And make me travel forth without my cloak,
> To let base clouds o'ertake me in my way,
> Hiding thy brav'ry in their rotten smoke?
> 'Tis not enough that through the cloud thou break
> To dry the rain on my storm-beaten face,
> For no man well of such a salve can speak
> That heals the wound, and cures not the disgrace.
> Nor can thy shame give physic to my grief;
> Though thou repent, yet I have still the loss.
> Th' offender's sorrow lends but weak relief
> To him that bears the strong offence's cross.
>   Ah, but those tears are pearl which thy love sheds,
>   And they are rich, and ransom all ill deeds.

Sonnet 34

This sonnet points to what I had suspected, that Marlowe himself did not know about the details of the plot, and that means that he was not the fourth man at Mistress Bull's house, or, if he were there in the morning, he left early to catch a hoy departing (to 'travel forth without my cloak') from Deptford on a fair wind for the Continent, while Walsingham came to take his place to discuss the final enactment of the plot. Elinor Bull's silence would doubtless have been willingly bought, for as Blanche Parry's 'cousin' she, too, could not have been unknown to Queen Elizabeth and would readily have complied with any command she received. The same would apply to William Danby, the 'well beloved' Coroner of the Royal Household. He would have had the authority to arrange the supply of a body, this being a side-line of sixteenth century coroners. Delivery of a body, recently dead but no longer in *rigor mortis,* and a bag of fresh pig's blood to bedaub the wound as though fresh bleeding would have completed the preparations.

It was not a squeamish age. The substitution of one dead body for another, identified by its clothing, features in *Cymbeline,* – somewhat gruesomely – and notably in *Measure for Measure,* where the Duke (in disguise as a holy friar) actually orders the execution of another condemned prisoner as a substitute to save the life of Claudio, who has been unjustly accused. He even assuages the fears of the Provost of the prison that the substituted decapitated head he is commanded to present to Angelo may be detected, with the reassuring words:

> 'O, death's a great disguiser; and you may add to it.'

This episode in Shakespeare's play is fully discussed in Chapter 21. I see it as a direct reflection of the practical and moral issues involved at Deptford.

Perhaps one of the strangest aspects of the death of Christopher Marlowe, who was unquestionably England's premier poet-dramatist when his life was thus shockingly cut short, is the total silence that descended at the Court, where he must have been known. He was not merely a government agent, like Poley, but also the poet hailed as 'the Muse's darling', with friendships in the circle of the Queen's favourite courtiers. His fete would undoubtedly have been of some interest to many. Yet not a whisper of any opinion expressed at Court has come down from that fertile source of recorded Elizabethan gossip.

Why this unnatural courtly silence?

XI

GORGON, OR THE WONDERFULL YEARE

THE NEWSWORTHY EVENTS of 30th May 1593 were accorded some very curious commentary in the publication, in the autumn of that year, of Gabriel Harvey's extraordinary, cryptic poem *Gorgon, or the wonderfull yeare* – the remarkable year being 1593, in which he proclaims the death of Marlowe as the event that causes him 'wonderment'.

This strange, elegiac extravaganza on Marlowe's death is one of the most incomprehensible literary pieces to come out of the Elizabethan period. It is from the pen of the Cambridge don, Dr Gabriel Harvey, who was a Fellow of Trinity Hall at the time when Marlowe and Nashe and Greene were all at the university contemporaneously for a few years. It was an unhappy period for Harvey when his academic career was injured by the envy of the Fellows, who encouraged the students to make fun of this talented, eccentric and ambitious don, who was sometimes in trouble for his advanced thinking. There were some who wanted him jostled out of his place, and ridicule was the weapon used. Poor Harvey was made the subject of an anonymous student play lampooning him under the title *Pedantius,* which was performed in February 1580/1 just as Marlowe arrived as a freshman. Later in London Greene and Nashe lampooned Harvey mercilessly in their pamphlets and novels. Harvey took his revenge when Greene died in 1592 by publishing the degrading details of his death. Nashe immediately sprang to the defence of Greene's blemished reputation by attacking Harvey in return in his most devastating satirical vein. Thus began a tirade in print of venomous pamphleteering between Nashe and Harvey which was in full cry when Marlowe's death occurred – and Harvey promptly went to investigate.

Harvey apparently discovered some strange 'News' which he elected to publish in the form of a weird poem couched in archaic language which is so obscure that no one can understand it without a gloss, which I have endeavoured to supply, though even so a deal of cloudy darkness remains. It makes no sense at all *unless seen in the light of Marlowe's death as a 'faked murder'* – a compelling reason for extraordinary obscurity!

Harvey obviously greatly admired Marlowe's genius, but disapproved of his 'Babell Pride' (a sin of which Raleigh was also generally accused) and he was, I believe, envious of Marlowe's success and fame, especially of his *entrée* into the esoteric circle of Raleigh's 'little academy' to which Harvey would have loved to belong, but though of outstanding scholarly mind and erudition he had the gift of tactlessness and had signally failed to make a good impression in Court circles. He was also something of a Puritan and censorious of Marlowe's 'Atheism', which Greene's death-bed breast-beating had fastened onto Marlowe, associating him with himself as one who was in dire need of repentance for denying the existence of God – to which Greene confessed abjectly and in print so that all London could read of his conversion. Harvey seems to have believed Greene, so far as his accusations of Marlowe's 'godlessness' went. At the same time, Harvey was shrewdly aware that Whitgift's informers were prowling on the look-out for free-thinkers. After the innocent Kyd was taken and racked, no one felt safe. Fear stalked the streets of London.

This is reflected in the extremely cryptic style of Harvey's poem, in which he cleverly veils his meaning in a jargon of archaic terms of such dense obscurity to safeguard himself, so that he cannot be accused of saying anything. It is indeed a great puzzle. In his *Gorgon*, strangely, Harvey indicates that Marlowe died of the 'Plague'. But it is impossible to credit that he did not know that it was Ingram Frizer who slew him with a dagger, for Gabriel's younger brother Richard Harvey was the rector at Thomas Walsingham's church of St Nicholas in Chislehurst where the family chapel of the Walsinghams lies, and where Walsingham and the members of his household, including Frizer, regularly worshipped on Sundays (attendance was obligatory on pain of swingeing fines for defaulting). Marlowe had probably heard him preach here, which drew the comment that Dick Harvey was 'an asse, good for nothing but to preach of the Iron Age'. [1] Gabriel could have found out all the details from brother Richard, and besides, gossip had long since spread the story, so why did he report Marlowe as killed by the 'Plague'?

My interpretation of this is that Harvey's 'Plague' is his cryptic term for the very real *plague of Fear* that had London in its grip as surely as the deadly plague itself then raging. He uses allegorical terms concocted by himself throughout his poem, and I believe that by the 'Plague' he is signifying the fearful witch-hunt against the free-thinkers, which is what had *really* killed Marlowe.

> 'for faint harts plague themselves.
> *The tyrant Sicknesse of base-minded slaves*
> *O how it dominer's in* Coward Lane?'

(The emphasized passages printed here in Roman type are Harvey's own style of presentation throughout this poem.)

Harvey possessed a remarkably idiosyncratic and intricate mind. No other Elizabethan could have produced this weird poem which is loaded with double meanings and veiled hints about Marlowe's death, with implications that Harvey has received information about goings-on relating to Marlowe which he is longing to impart to the world. It is Strange News indeed which 'some Familiar Spright' had 'buzzed' into his head!

His poem should properly be considered in conjunction with the 26-page epistle he wrote to his friend John Wolfe, *A New Letter of Notable Contents,* to which his sonnet *Gorgon, or the wonderfull yeare* is appended. In sending this curious literary offering to Wolfe he writes by way of explanation:

> 'I terme it a Trifle for the *manner;* though the *matter* be in my conceit, superexcellent; in the opinion of the world, most admirable; for priuate consideration, very notable; for publique vse, passing memorable; for a point, or two, exceeding monstrous. And that is the very disgrace of the *Sonnet,* that the Stile nothing counteruaileth the Subiect, but debaseth a straunge body with vulgar attire, and disguiseth a superlative Text with a positiue Glosse. As it is, it is your owne to dispose or cancell at pleasure.' [2]

Wolfe did publish Harvey's *Gorgon,* taking a calculated risk in doing so, for it speaks to us like the Sphinx, in riddles. Scholars studying it have mostly given up in despair. But now, in the context of this thesis, I believe it is obliquely to be gleaned that Harvey had learnt from brother Richard something about the real facts of Marlowe's 'death', and he is bursting to tell this to the world! But, of course, he dare not do so. So he wraps it up in a cryptic poem so obscure, so deep, that it is submerged and barely discernible even to those who possess the 'key' as to what really happened at Deptford – which until now has been missing.

Harvey's 'News' about Marlowe is in cryptic manner also the gist of his *New Letter* to Wolfe, but this epistle is too long, and too deep a study to be considered here. To date only Virginia F. Stern in her superb monograph *Gabriel Harvey: A Study of His Life, Marginalia and Library* (Oxford, 1989) has managed to dredge up any meaning from its depth, and she has also provided the first meaningful gloss for Harvey's poem *Gorgon* to which I am indebted, only departing from her assessment with regard to his references to the character he names 'Shakerley'.

In two couplets in his poem Harvey cryptically uses the name 'Shakerley'. It so happened that the notorious London braggart Peter Shakerley died and was interred on 18th September 1593. On 16th September Harvey had written his *New Letter* to his friend, but even if Shakerley had died a couple of days before his recorded interment it is doubtful whether the news would have reached Harvey down in Saffron Walden so speedily. Nashe and Harvey had previously used Shakerley as a figure of ridicule in their pamphlet battle, trading insults by comparing each other to this self-important windbag, Nashe firing off first in his *Strange News* with Harvey retorting in his *Pierce's Supererogation.* So there is nothing new in finding Shakerley featured again in Harvey's *New Letter* of 16th September to which the poem *Gorgon* is appended. This time it co-incides closely with the boastful man's death – probably from the plague – lending another layer of cryptic icing to the cake, but I do not think this event had anything to do with Harvey's original inspiration for either the *New Letter* or the poem. However, Shakerley's timely death may have influenced Wolfe to risk publishing Harvey's strange offering, as it presented the perfect red herring that would lend greater safety to the printer and the author. This red herring has successfully led at least one scholar by the nose away from the trail to Marlowe, for Nicholl has fallen right into the trap proposing the untenable theory that the entire poem is merely about Shakerley's recent death and not about Marlowe at all. [3] This facile explanation of *Gorgon* does not stand up to close investigation. Nicholl has not even begun to fathom the depths of this cryptic poem. There is nothing simple about Harvey's intricate and brilliant mind, and he would not have wasted his time in devising a poem of such exraordinary, archaic obscurity about a man like Shakerley, who, for all his *braggadocio* presence in London, was a nonentity. It is of Marlowe and his death that Harvey is writing.

As Bakeless has perceptively suspected, these two, Harvey, the eccentric Cambridge don with advanced ideas that made him the butt of unkind attacks by his Fellows, and the young genius Christopher Marlowe, probably knew each other well at Cambridge. Harvey would, I believe, have been eager to take the brilliant, budding poet-dramatist under his wing, as he had the young Edmund Spenser whom he regarded as his protegé. Spenser's subsequent success was Harvey's pride and joy. A friendship sprang up very likely early in Marlowe's time at Cambridge when he began writing his first play, *Scanderbeg,* at the age of seventeen, about this great Christian warrior-prince of Albania, a strikingly dramatic, heroic subject that would have inspired the young scholar and which Harvey certainly would have approved. Perhaps he even suggested this choice to Marlowe? But the independent-minded, self-motivated Marlowe would not play along in the role of Edmund Spenser and rejected the guiding hand proffered by the opinionated Harvey, who had strong ideas about literary style. This caused disappointment and offence which Harvey seems never to have forgiven. There is a tinge of old bitterness in Harvey's barbed attacks on Marlowe who –

> *'nor feared God, nor dreaded Div'll*
> *Nor ought admired, but his wondrous selfe.'*

At Cambridge we know Marlowe was consciously developing his poetic gift. The dedicated, self-aware, aspiring and perhaps at this time, arrogant, young genius, chose as his literary models Ovid and Lucan, not Gabriel Harvey. Envy of Marlowe's brilliant success is strongly present in this poem's edge of bitterness. He was the fledgling genius who had escaped from Harvey's would-be guiding hand, and followed his own star of destiny unaided. *Scanderbeg* would have been the work which Harvey had ardently discussed with the young dramatist, his first full length play on which he may initially have sought Harvey's opinion, but then rejected him as his mentor. This I see as the reason why we find two references to *Scanderbeg* in Harvey's poem. It had a very special connotation for him personally in relation to Marlowe.

In *Gorgon* Harvey refers to Marlowe as 'Tamburlaine' and as 'Scanderbeg', associating him with his two earliest plays dramatizing the lives of two great warriors who each fought the Turks, which ties in with his *New Letter* where he presents a commentary on the wars against the Turks which were intermittently going on in Eastern Europe, and threatening to spread westwards. He is also deeply concerned about his pamphlet-war with Nashe and seeks Wolfe's advice. There is a temporary lull in which Harvey is licking his wounds, for he had the worst of it. Nashe had taken time off from satirizing Harvey in order to write his religious tract, *Christs Teares over Jerusalem,* to show himself as a good Christian and distance himself from those 'Atheists', his friends Greene (albeit repentant) and Marlowe. He was even holding out the olive-branch to Harvey with offers to patch it all up and let bye-gones be bye-gones, probably aware that such libellous pamphleteering (which of course sold like hot cakes to their gossip-loving readers) was viewed disapprovingly by the authorities, the chief censor of literature being Archbishop Whitgift, who had been Nashe's patron. Sure enough, the Archbishop eventually stepped in to put a stop to it, ordering that 'all Nashes and Doctor Harvyes bookes be taken wheresoever they maye be found and that none of theire bookes bee ever printed hereafter.' [4]

However, Harvey's *Gorgon* escaped censure. Probably even the Archbishop did not understand it! Nashe appropriately called this fantastic poem, Harvey's 'goggle-eyed sonnet'. [5]

What had made Harvey 'goggle-eyed'? I suggest it was when he saw *Venus and Adonis* in the bookshop signed 'William Shakespeare' launching the new pseudonym, which he astutely recognised as such. Having learnt from brother Richard that 'Tamburlaine' had 'vouchsafed to die' - i.e. he had condescended to do so, or agreed, or chosen to die by Frizer's dagger, he introduced the canting character 'Shakerley' into his poem. It has long been accepted by scholars that the 'Shake-scene' of Greene's *Groatsworth of Wit* homophonously represents Shakespeare (a fallacy), but here in Harvey's *Gorgon* I believe we do actually have a homophonous reference to Shakespeare-Shakerley as a cryptic allusion. Scholars recognise that Harvey uses the name cryptically to stand for someone else. Nashe, who was Harvey's sparring partner in their pamphlet battle, has been suggested, but here he hardly fits the bill. In the context of this poem about Marlowe's death, 'Shakerley' is surely intended as an oblique allusion to Marlowe's *second* self – William Shakespeare', the newly-presented author – Harvey's '*Second Shakerley* of Powles', this being St Paul's Churchyard where the bookshops were, and which Kyd tells us was the popular haunt of Marlowe. Harvey emphasizes this also in his apostrophe to Marlowe –

'Weepe Powles, thy Tamberlaine *voutsafes to dye.'*

This is a connotation which this thesis, for the first time, reveals as making sense of this poem. Here, without further ado, is Harvey's 'goggle-eyed sonnet', with a Gloss opposite. All emphasis (in Roman) is Harvey's own.

Sonet

Gorgon, *or the wonderfull yeare*

Gloss:	St Fame *dispos'd to cunnycatch the world,*
l.	*Uprear'd a wonderment of* Eighty Eight:

The Earth *addreading to be overwhurld,*
What now availes, quoth She, my ballance weight?
The Circle smyl'd to see the Center feare:
The wonder was, no wonder fell that yeare.

Wonders enhaunse their powre in numbers odd:
The fatall yeare of yeares is Ninety Three:

2.	Parma *hath kist:* De-Maine *entreates the rodd:*
3.	*Warre wondreth,* Peace in Spaine and Fraunce to see.
4.	*Brave* Eckenberg, *the dowty* Bassa *shames:*

The Christian Neptune, *Turkish* Vulcane *tames.*

5.	Navarre *wooes* Roome: Charlmaine *gives* Guise *the* Phy:
6.	*Weepe* Powles, *thy* Tamberlaine *voutsafes to dye.*

L'envoy

The hugest miracle remaines behinde,

7.	The second Shakerley Rash-Swash to binde.

A Stanza declarative: to the Lovers
of admirable Workes

8.	*Pleased it hath a* Gentlewoman rare,
	With Phenix quill in diamant hand of Art,
9.	*To muzzle the redoubtable Bull-bare,*

And play the galiard Championesses part.
Though miracles surcease, yet Wonder see
The mightiest miracle of Ninety Three

10.	Vis consilii expers, mole ruit sua.

11.	*The Writers Postscript: or a frendly* Caveat
	to the Second Shakerley *of* Powles.

For much of this Gloss I am indebted to Virginia F. Stern's work on Harvey in *Gabriel Harvey: A Study of His Life, Marginalia and Library* (Oxford 1979)

1. A reference to the 15th century scholar Regiomontanus's ominous predictions based on his astronomical and mathematical calculations that the year 1588 would prove fatal to the world. It was the year of the Armada.

2. The Duke of Parma, the Spanish Governor-General of the Netherlands, had recently died. The Duke of Mayenne contested for the vacant governorship, but failed to gain it.

3. Spain and France made peace to everyone's amazement, with the concession of a French port to Spain as part of the deal.

4. Prince Eggenberg (Eckenberg) of Austria defeated the Turks with his united Christian forces against the Infidel, winning victories at sea.

5. Henry of Navarre, now Henry IV of France, formerly the leader of the Protestants against the Catholic party of the Duke of Guise, had embraced Catholicism to bring reconciliation between France's warring factions. Charlemagne falls out with his kinsmen of the House of Guise.

6. Mourn oh ye publishers and booksellers of St Paul's Churchyard, for Marlowe (i.e. Tamburlaine often seen at the bookstalls) 'voutsafes to die'. Harvey chooses the word *vouchsafe* meaning to condescend, to deign to do something. (Middle English: vouchen sauf – to warrant as safe). This event is listed as one of the wonders of 1593!

7. *L'envoy*
Peter Shakerley was a notorious London braggart who died (perhaps from the plague then raging) and was buried on 18th September 1593. Harvey wrote to Wolf two days before Shakerley's demise. Harvey liked to use Shakerley as a type-figure to lampoon Nashe as an empty-headed boaster, but the coincidence of Shakerley's timely death provided topical news as an ideal cover-story enabling Wolfe to bring out his publication of 'Gorgon' in complete safety. It would have been the ideal red herring to lead any clever cryptologist away from the scent of Marlowe's death. Shakerley is used by Harvey as a canting name for another person – *'The second Shakerley'*. We are left to guess who this might be. The clues, of course, are in the poem.

8. Harvey's *'Gentlewoman rare'* has never been identified. It has been doubted whether this allegedly formidable patroness really existed. My guess is, that his reference to her *'Phenix quill'* is significant. Queen Elizabeth was often referred to as the Phoenix. Did Harvey sense her protection of Walsingham in his scheme to engineer Marlowe's escape?

9. Bull-bare – probably this is a pseudo-mythological creature – symbol of threatening power whom the *'Gentlewoman rare'* was able to 'muzzle' and render harmless. Was this Whitgift's power that she curbed? It would have to be something significant to qualify as *'The mightiest miracle of Ninety Three'*.

10. 'Vis consilii expers, mole ruit sua' (Horace: *Odes* Book III, iv)
Force without judgment collapses through its own weight. '

11. A friendly caution to a notable braggart of St Paul's, implying he is a writer, to stay his hand, which may be taken as meaning either Nashe *or* Marlowe. Here we suspect a deliberate mix-up in the poem *Gorgon* with Nashe and Marlowe, as this is what we find in his *New Letter* to which the poem is a postscript. By doing this Harvey is able to drop hints concerning Marlowe, which it would otherwise be too dangerous to do. (In his *New Letter of Notable Contents*, Harvey is at the same time deeply worried about how to proceed in his battle in print against Nashe, and asks Wolfe's advice whether he should accept Nashe's olive-branch. Is he sincere about making peace, or is it just a ploy to make Harvey look foolish?)

Sonet

Slumbring I lay in melancholy bed,
  Before the dawning of the sanguin light:
12.   *When* Echo *shrill, or some* Familiar Spright
Buzzed an Epitaph *into my hed.*

13. Magnifique Mindes, bred of Gargantuas race,
14. In grisly weedes His Obsequies waiment,
    Whose Corps on Powles, whose mind triumph'd on Kent,
15. Scorning to bate Sir Rodomont an ace.

I mus'd awhile: and having mus'd awhile,
Jesu, (quoth I) is that Gargantua *minde*
16. *Conquer'd, and left no* Scanderbeg *behinde?*
17. *Vow'd he not to* Powles *A Second bile?*

18. What bile, or kibe? *(quoth that same early Spright?)*
    Have you forgot the Scanderbegging wight?

Glosse

Is it a Dreame? or is the Highest minde,
19. *That ever haunted* Powles, *or hunted winde,*
    Bereaft of that same sky-surmounting breath,
20. *That breath, that taught the* Timpany *to swell?*

21. *He, and the* Plague *contended for the game:*
    The hawty man extolled his hideous thoughtes,
    And gloriously insultes upon poore soules,
    That plague themselves: for faint harts plague themselves.

The tyrant Sicknesse of base-minded slaves
Oh how it dominer's in Coward Lane?
22. *So Surquidry rang-out his larum bell,*
    When he had girn'd at many a dolefull knell.

23. *The graund Dissease disdain'd his toade Conceit,*
    And smiling at his tamberlaine contempt,
    Sternely struck-home the peremptory stroke.
    He that nor feared God, nor dreaded Div'll,
    Nor ought admired, but his wondrous selfe:
    Like Junos gawdy Bird, that prowdly stares
    On glittring fan of his triumphant taile:
24. *Or like the ugly Bugg, that scorn'd to dy,*
    And mountes of Glory rear'd in towring witt:
    Alas: but Babell Pride must kisse the pitt.

12. Harvey's device of news from the spirit world masks the fact that he has been given confidential information concerning Marlowe's death, which amazes him!

13. *Gargantua* – a giant king of prodigious intellectual powers and physical size.

14. waiment – a Harveyan invention for lament.

15. Sir Rodomant – a flamboyant boaster.

16. *Scanderbeg* – the hero of Marlowe's play, a great Christian leader of his people who freed them from the Turks, a fighter for truth and justice.

17. a Second bile – spleen: black bile engendered melancholy, yellow bile, anger.

18. kibe – an irritant or noxious eruption, especially an ulcerated chilblain on the heel. Is Achilles' heel the connotation intended? He reminds his readers that Marlowe was a Scanderbeg – i.e. a fighter for Christianity, justice and freedom.

19. St Paul's churchyard with its bookshops was Marlowe's favourite haunt.

20. Timpany – drums, or thunder, implying a thundering speech such as a great actor on a stage would give e.g. Alleyn as Tamburlaine.

21. Harvey's *Plague* is analogous of an infectious disease of the mind, not the body – the plague of Fear that enslaves ignorant, superstitious minds.

22. Surquidry – arrogance, haughty pride, presumption. (O.E.D.) Harvey's use of 'girn'd' in this context, probably connotes grinned scornfully.

23. This last verse contains the kernel of Harvey's sonnet entitled *Gorgon* which can only here have the connotation with which Marlowe used it in *Tamburlaine* when Zenocrate's father, the Sultan of Egypt, says he would not fear him 'were that Tamburlaine/As monstrous as Gorgon prince of Hell'. Marlowe had been too proud; he had tempted fate in opposing the power of the arch-prelate Whitgift in his courageous 'Scanderbegging' opposition to bigotted minds, so that eventually he was defeated. The inquisitorial power of the Star Chamber struck him down.

24. the ugly Bugg – This must be another Harveyan invention, for I have not been able to trace it. The creature suggests some sort of metamorphosis like a butterfly, perhaps? There are also connotations of immortality. It scorns to die, or refuses to die. Such an implication is, again, significant in connection with Marlowe.

L'envoy

25.   Powles steeple, *and a* hugyer thing *is downe:*
26.   *Beware the* next Bull-beggar *of the towne.*
27.   —— Fata immatura vagantur.

FINIS

Gloss:

25. St Paul's had one of the tallest steeples ever built, which was struck by lightning in 1562 and destroyed.

26. Bull-beggar – perhaps a Harveyan variant of his 'bull-bare'.
A hobgoblin, or a thing giving a scare associated with witches and spirits

27. 'Fata immatura vagantur'. Premature (untimely) death is all around – or, The Fates are roving prematurely.

It is to be noted that Harvey's 'Glosse' with which he concludes his 'Sonet' is in the third sense of the word as given on the O.E.D., namely: 'A purposely misleading interpretation or explanation' – whereas the gloss I have attempted to provide based on Virginia Stern's pioneer research on Harvey, is in the first sense of the word: 'a brief note or translation of a difficult or technical expression.' [7]

In Harvey's accolade to Marlowe as the 'Highest minde', 'bred of Gargantuas race', we meet the very type of genius who was recognised by Emerson, Carlyle, Goethe and others as the 'greatest intellect', Shakespeare. Choosing his words with utmost care, Harvey cryptically divulges important information. He tells us that Marlowe was not killed by a 'wretch's knife', but by the *'Plague'* that *'dominer's in* Coward Lane', and that he 'voutsafes to dye', implying that this is his self-chosen escape route, perhaps? There is much to ponder here.

The more one mulls over Harvey's weird poem, the more it reveals its hidden meaning now we have the end of the thread in our hands. Was there ever a death, before or since, that merited such a 'Glosse' as this strange 'goggle-eyed sonnet'?

XII

THE PATRON, A TRIPLE PORTRAIT

The identity of the Patron of the *Sonnets* has always been associated with the cryptic dedication to the mysterious 'Mr.W.H.' as the one man to whom the sonnets are addressed, with the exception only of those to the Dark Lady. This has been a basic fallacy blocking advance to the solution of this mystery. I call it a fallacy because the character of the Patron, assuming that this is 'Mr.W.H.', the 'lovely Boy' of the Sonnets, is not credible as a real person. He is full of self-contradictions. On the one hand, he is the Poet's ever-faithful Friend; on the other hand, he is 'lascivious', spoilt, selfish, and a false friend, his character *flawed at base*. The fallacy is, of course, deliberately sown in our minds by the cryptic dedication to one Patron:

TO.THE.ONLIE.BEGETTER.OF.THESE.INSVING
SONNETS.M^r.W.H.ALL.HAPPINESSE.

In pursuit of this 'Onlie Begetter' scholar after scholar has lost his way. Let us look first, then, at what the orthodox academics have made of it.

The two main contenders in orthodox hypothesis, both of them earls, have obvious associations with Shakespeare's works, and while neither is the Patron of the *Sonnets* they each have an important relevance to this study.

WILLIAM HERBERT, 3RD EARL OF PEMBROKE was born in 1580, the son of Henry Herbert, 2nd Earl of Pembroke, who was patron of his company of players, the Earl of Pembroke's Men, for whom Christopher Marlowe wrote three history plays, his *Edward the Second* and two plays on the Wars of the Roses, between 1590 and 1592; these latter two plays, which were published anonymously, are included in the First Folio in revised form as *Henry VI Parts 2 and 3*. Presumably little William Herbert, then a boy of ten or eleven, might have become acquainted with Christopher Marlowe at this time. His mother was Mary Sidney, sister of Sir Philip Sidney, related by marriage to Thomas Walsingham and living with her father-in-law Sir Francis Walsingham, so that family connections with Marlowe's circle are close.

Mary Sidney, who became Countess of Pembroke, was a great patroness of literature. At the death of Thomas Watson, Marlowe dedicated his friend's last work, *Amintae Gaudia,* to Lady Mary with a promise that he would in the future also dedicate his own poetic work to her. Sir Philip Sidney dedicated his *Arcadia,* which he had written while staying at Wilton, the Pembroke's stately mansion, to his sister, the Countess. She is also reputed to have been deeply interested in the study of chemistry or alchemy, and had a laboratory at Wilton for conducting experiments. Lady Mary would have approved her brother's foundation of a literary, free-thinking club named the 'Areopagus'. Sidney was the patron of Giordano Bruno during his sojourn in London during 1583-84.

Sir Philip Sidney's tragic death in the prime of life at the Battle of Zutphen in the autumn of 1586 was mourned as the loss of a great Protestant champion of enlightened mind, who was also one of the foremost literary figures of his brief day – an outstanding scholar-port who was a national hero. Young William Herbert was brought up in this family tradition which was sympathetic to Marlowe's ideas and aspirations.

Some scholars have tried to associate William Herbert with a hypothetical Dark Lady in Mary Fitton, one of the Queen's Maids of Honour, with whom he had a youthful love-affair that ended in mutual disgrace when she bore him an illegitimate child. She was dismissed from Court and William Herbert was cast into the Fleet to cool his ardour. The child died, and they did not subsequently marry. Mary Fitton's two portraits show her to be brown-haired and grey-eyed, so that her eligibility as the raven-eyed beauty of the *Sonnets* is without substance, and this attempt to link the young William Herbert with Shakespeare as his 'Mr.W.H.' falls flat.

He succeeded to his title at the age of twenty-one in 1601. When the First Folio was published in 1623 it was dedicated 'to the most noble and incomparable pair of brethren, William, Earl of Pembroke . . and Philip, Earl of Montgomery', his younger brother. These were also 'brethren' in the sense that they were Brothers in the Freemasons, of whom William Herbert was at that time the Grand Master. (This forms an important link in the chain of evidence finally establishing the First Folio as a Masonic publication). He was, however, not 'Mr.W.H.', although his initials make him eligible for the honour. Those scholars who argue against the theory that William Herbert was the patron of the *Sonnets* – although the dedicatee of the First Folio – point out that an earl would not have been addressed as plain 'Mr'. In real life doubtless this would not be correct, but the dedication of the *Sonnets* is an intentional conundrum, and the creation of doubts, and casting about for eligible 'W.H.'s was probably envisaged as adding to the mystification challenging its solution.

The other main noble contender has the initials backwards – H.W. – and he could equally be said to be ineligible to be addressed as plain 'Mr.', but this has not prevented him from receiving the majority vote as Shakespeare's patron from the orthodox camp.

HENRY WRIOTHESLEY, 3RD EARL OF SOUTHAMPTON was born in 1572 and became an earl as a minor at the age of eight when his father died, and the young Henry was made a Ward of Court and placed in the household of Lord Burghley, who held the lucrative office of Master of Wards. Here he was educated under Burghley's careful supervision until at the age of twelve he was sent to St John's College, Cambridge. There he would have met the budding satirist Thomas Nashe, then a seventeen-year-old 'sizar' at the same college, the lowest class of students who did menial tasks for the wealthy 'fellow-commoners' like young Southampton. Nashe gained notoriety at Cambridge as a young scamp! Southampton later patronized him.

Lord Burghley's responsibilities for his Royal Wards extended to arranging suitable marriages for them, and he used this to advantage the eligible spinsters in his own family by marrying them off to these high-born peers of the realm. With this in mind, Burghley entered a note in his diary on 6th October 1589 observing that Southampton was now sixteen years of age.[1] He already saw the tall stripling as a suitable husband for his grand-daughter, the Lady Elizabeth de Vere, daughter of Burghley's former Ward of Court, the 17th Earl of Oxford, whom he had entrapped into marriage with his own daughter, Anne Cecil in 1571 – a miserable match which proved very unhappy for both of them. Anne was now dead, and Burghley was worried about his grand-daughter who was neglected by the Earl her father. she was already nineteen, three years older than Southampton, but no matter for that; Burghley pushed vigorously ahead with arrangements for the match to the dismay of young Henry Wriothesley who protested that he had no thought of marriage as yet. Pleading his youth, he managed to gain Burghley's reluctant agreement to a year's respite. But, as the end of the year approached, Southampton was still obstinately opposed to the match, and Burghley was desperately casting around for some means by which to incline the young man's mind to the consummation of the proposed nuptials.

Burghley knew well his ward's taste for poetry, and he evidently hit upon the idea of sonneteering the young man into a more malleable mood. The first group of sonnets Nos. 1 – 17, forms a tightly-knit sequence all on the same theme persuading the young man to whom they are addressed of the joys and the advantages of marrying and begetting heirs to his line. Such a young man must have been of noble family to be thus exhorted to perpetuate his name, and Southampton's case precisely fits the logic, which Akrigg,[2] and others support, that these sonnets represent a specially commissioned group; for what poet could have a personal interest in pleading with a young nobleman to take a wife, and go to the lengths on his own initiative of dedicating an entire group of sonnets on the subject to a high-born youth? The idea is implausible.

Nevertheless, Dr Hotson espouses it with enthusiasm, arguing that young William Hatcliffe, playing his part as Prince of Purpoole in the gay tomfoolery of the Inns of Court, required the tongue-in-cheek persuasion of his courtiers through the poetic inspiration of their spokesman, the sonneteer, to plead with him to marry and beget heirs for his 'royal' line.[3]

Since there was no 'princess' around for him to contemplate this seems rather pointless – but then, it was all play-acting. In arguing his thesis, Dr Hotson is, of course, concerned to exorcise all traces of the Earl of Southampton from any connection with the *Sonnets* in order the more firmly to install his candidate, William Hatcliffe, in the seat of honour as Shakespeare's Friend and the 'Onlie Begetter' according to the dedication of the *Sonnets*. He dismisses the Earl of Southampton rather contemptuously as 'that vain, fantastical, amorous and hare-brained sprout of the New Nobility.' [4]

Southampton may have been all of that at the tender age of sixteen when Burghley saw him in his mind's eye as a husband for the Lady Elizabeth de Vere, though if he was precociously amorous it did not incline him to matrimony. Burghley was shrewd enough to realise that Southampton's excuses would be played as a permanent delaying tactic until the young sprout could manage to slip the noose altogether, and he lost no time to assail him with the most appealing and seductive poetry he could commission. The sonneteering vogue was just about to burgeon, and his Lordship did not have to look far for his sonneteer. He was right there, under his nose.

Christopher Marlowe was Burghley's own recruit from Cambridge, who was constantly in and out of the Court on assignments working as agent for either Burghley or Sir Francis Walsingham. Marlowe's quality as a poet and sonneteer as well as a dramatist were well-known to his Lordship's close colleague in government, Sir Francis Walsingham, personally as well as through Thomas Walsingham and his friend Thomas Watson, so that it is inconceivable that Burghley would not have been equally well-informed. Burghley was himself a learned man of cultured taste. The notion that he would cast around for some unknown poet named William Shakespeare in this year 1590 is gratuitous, when he had Christopher Marlowe at his elbow, as must be admitted even by those who believe passionately that Shakespeare wrote these sonnets. Such an assumption for a then unknown actor from Stratford lacks all plausibility. At the date when these sonnets were commissioned addressing the Earl of Southampton – which orthodoxy also favours – Marlowe was very much alive and present at the Court, the most famous poet-dramatist of the day. He cannot be conveniently wished away to give place to Shakespeare.

Everything points to the correctness of this hypothesis. This being so, the date of this group would be 1590, the year in which on 6th October Southampton attained the age of seventeen years, and was already affianced unwillingly to the Lady Elizabeth de Vere, and showing marked, stubborn resistance to the idea of marriage. I suggest that it is no accident or mere chance that the first group of sonnets all exhorting a young man to marry is that numbered 1 to 17 – *exactly seventeen sonnets* – an odd number, however you view it. And its significance is surely this – that this collection of *seventeen sonnets* was Lord Burghley's gift to his Ward of Court on his *seventeenth birthday*.

Henry Wriothesley
3rd Earl of Southampton
AETATIS SVAE 20   1594
*Miniature painted on vellum
stuck onto a playing card with
three hearts on the reverse.
By Nicholas Hilliard*

*Courtesy of the Fitzwilliam
Museum, Cambridge*

Courtesy of the Bodleian Library, Oxford

William Cecil, 1st Baron Burghley, *riding a mule. This* impresa *portrait shows Burghley in his role as Chief Minister of State, holding a sprig of honeysuckle and a pink in his hand, the flowers, the tree and the mule symbolizing loyalty, humility, nobility, fortitude and steadfastness. English school 16th C.*

143

From fairest creatures we desire increase,
That thereby beauty's rose might never die,
But as the riper should by time decease,
His tender heir might bear his memory;
But thou contracted to thine own bright eyes,
Feed'st thy light's flame with self-substantial fuel,
Making a famine where abundance lies,
Thyself thy foe, to thy sweet self too cruel.
Thou that art now the world's fresh ornament,
And only herald to the gaudy spring,
Within thine own bud buriest thy content,
And, tender churl, mak'st waste in niggarding.
    Pity the world, or else this glutton be,
    To eat the world's due, by the grave and thee.

Sonnet 1

Eloquent as these sonnets are, they did not persuade the youth to change his mind. Still obdurate, the following year one of Lord Burghley's secretaries seems to have been similarly commissioned to assail the young nobleman's reluctance towards matrimony by further arguments. An elegant little volume of Latin verse written by John Clapham, entitled *Narcissus,* appeared in 1591 dedicated to Southampton, recounting the Greek legend of the self-loving, beautiful youth who drowned in the pool in which he saw his own reflection and fell in love with it. This 'Short and Moral Description of Youthful Love and Especially Self-Love' was clearly a second attempt to wean the Earl from his avowed preference for bachelorhood to the better state of marriage. To no avail. We note that this was also written by a man in Lord Burghley's employ.

For the unfortunate Southampton the alternative to marriage with Elizabeth de Vere was the payment of a swingeing fine, which Lord Burghley was entitled to exact as compensation for breach of promise. In 1594, when he attained his majority and was still adamantly opposed to this arranged marriage, he was forced to pay £5,000, an excessively punitive sum that placed a crippling burden on his estates. [5] It is to Southampton's eternal credit that he chose to marry for love, not money, when in 1598 he contracted a marriage with Elizabeth Vernon, a cousin of his great friend the Earl of Essex, who had no large dowry to bring him, and incurred the Queen's predictable wrath because he married her in secret when she was already pregnant. They were both cast into the Fleet prison for a spell. The man had honour, loyalty and courage, and there can be little doubt that Marlowe admired him, as the famous dedications of *Venus and Adonis* and *Lucrece* testify.

After these first seventeen sonnets conjuring the noble youth to marry, giving poetic expression to Lord Burghley's arguments, the Earl of Southampton disappears from the *Sonnets.* He does not return in this context, but he makes a reappearance later in this story in another setting of some significance.

144

Who was 'Mr. W.H.'?

We have already posed the question: Are the sonnets presented in their chronological order? This question is particularly bound up with our search for the Patron and the identification of those to whom these poems are addressed. *Sonnets 1 to 17* with which the sequence opens were not the first that were written. They are placed at the beginning because they represent a group distinct and apart, for these are the only commissioned poems. They are not the Poet's personal story, and their position demonstrates this fact and does not indicate that they were written first, although they were relatively early. These first seventeen sonnets have no connection with 'Mr. W.H.' and it is with *Sonnet 18* that the sonnet-story begins, but soon develops into the skilful chronological confusion that obscures the autobiographical story-line and hinders our easy identification of the Patron.

The true Patron of the *Sonnets* is without doubt Thomas Walsingham, Marlowe's known friend and patron who, according to this thesis, saved his life. The sonnet-story that is revealed as we unravel the chronological confusion, as well as every fact and incident in the historical context, bear this out as an inescapable conclusion, that Walsingham, and he alone, is *the Patron* to whom the main body of the poems is addressed, sometimes almost in the form of personal letters, and of him there will be much to tell. But he is not 'Mr. W.H.'

Juxtaposed to him in the *Sonnets* is the portrait of the 'lovely Boy', whose presence is used to obscure the identity of the real Patron by a subtle confusion of the two, which has been achieved by inserting individual sonnets, or a couplet, triplet or quartet of related sonnets from another group into the sonnet-sequence on a different theme, addressed to a different person.

As poems, the sonnets have such power to enter into our imagination, each being such perfection in this idiom, that we are easily beguiled from what had gone before, being now under the spell of the inserted poems which command our whole attention and wean us away from the previous theme. This is often done with such subtlety as to be entirely deceptive of a shift in subject matter, or of the person addressed. Thus we are skilfully misled by the Poet's will-o'-the-wisp.

For instance, *Sonnets 93, 94, 95, 96,* on many re-readings and close scrutiny reveal that they are a quartet of genuinely related sonnets of which *Sonnet 95* is the heart. This group of four sonnets all comment on one theme, which is that the 'lovely Boy' is lascivious and in danger of spoiling the friendship which has existed between himself and the Poet. These four poems are placed directly following the group of the Rival Poet, which *also* speaks of a rift between the Poet and his Patron, but for a *different reason.* Not lasciviousness, but faithlessness in entertaining a rival poet is complained of, which arouses intense, anguished jealousy since this threatens the Poet's secure relationship with his dear Patron. At first sight it seems that the four sonnets are a continuation of this same theme. Not so. They have a different mood, are lighter in emotional tone and bear no relationship to the foregoing highly emotionally-charged poems on the Rival Poet, which are so imbued with hurt and fear of losing the Patron and Friend on whom he is entirely dependent as to rank them amongst the most moving and pathetic of any of the sonnets. The four sonnets *93* to *96* are not only different in mood and subject matter, they are addressed to a *different person,* for here we have not the Patron, but the 'beauteous Youth' whose lascivious and wanton nature finally wrote 'finis' to that relationship of friendship he had enjoyed with the Poet.

The key sonnet in this group of four sufficiently demonstrates this:

> How sweet and lovely dost thou make the shame
> Which, like a canker in the fragrant rose,
> Doth spot the beauty of thy budding name!
> Oh in what sweets dost thou thy sins enclose!
> That tongue that tells the story of thy days,
> Making lascivious comments on thy sport,
> Cannot dispraise, but in a kind of praise;
> Naming thy name blesses an ill report.
> Oh what a mansion have those vices got
> Which for their habitation chose out thee,
> Where beauty's veil doth cover every blot,
> And all things turn to fair that eyes can see!
>   Take heed (dear heart) of this large privilege;
>   The hardest knife ill-us'd doth lose its edge.

Sonnet 95

One of the most fascinating aspects that has emerged during this analysis of the sonnets, in grouping them according to their themes, has been the discovery -which I had in no way anticipated – that Dr Hotson was right. His William Hatcliffe, that beautiful and lascivious gentleman of Gray's Inn, who was elected Prince of Purpoole at Christmas 1587-88, IS HERE! But he is not, as Hotson thought, *the Patron,* who was the Poet's great benefactor, loyal to his Friend in his direst extremity, and deeply and constantly loved by the Poet, to whom the great bulk of the sonnets are addressed, and to whom, in essence, they belong.

The interesting factor that emerges is that it is the poems praising the beauty of the Youth, – then gently chiding him, later admonishing him more sternly for his wantonness, in which he steals the Poet's mistress, but is forgiven – that have been selected to be scattered with a liberal hand throughout the sequence. The poems are, therefore, deceptively dispersed. It is rather as a dramatist might take a sub-plot and interweave this with his main dramatic theme, with the difference that here the purpose is not to tell the story, but to obscure it and prevent easy detection of its import. A clever device, which has deceived us these many long years!

The reason for the amazing success of this deception is easy to see, for the subtle confusion of the themes in Thorpe's published order of the poems gives variety and makes intriguing reading. Therefore we have not felt tempted to tamper with the order, and attempts to re-arrange the sonnets, as by the nineteenth century critic, Charles Knight, have not proved conspicuously successful or improving.

It should be noted also, that when we speak of the order of the sonnets as published by Thorpe, he did not place them in pairs, two sonnets facing each other on the open page as in modern editions. Thorpe's edition was printed in the same way as a prose work, and many of the poems are half on one page and half on the next – sometimes just two lines are continued on the next page. This is because he filled the page up with his type, and whatever did not fit was simply printed on the following page. This casual presentation further obscured the incidence of sonnet pairs, triplets or quartets; but equally the modern editions are misleading in that the two sonnets facing each other sometimes have no real connection, while at other times they are a true pair; or the fact that they are facing each other implies that they ought to be considered as a pair, when perhaps they are not.

Since the sonnet order is intended to obscure the identification of the Patron it has had to be disregarded in order to extract the man we are looking for. The problem has been not only to decide who the Patron can be, but in forming an idea based on the poems of *what kind of person he was,* for the portrait of the man presented as the 'Onlie Begetter' who is named 'Mr.W.H.' is fraught with contradictions that are bewildering and have baffled all students of the sonnets.

Contemplating the almost schizophrenic image that this confused sonnet order presents as Shakespeare's Friend, Stephen Spender has been moved to comment:

> 'The first thing that would strike us is, I think, that he has opposite characteristics. He is divided between his ideal nature, corresponding to his outward beauty, and his actual behaviour, which is shown to be cold, self-seeking, proud and corrupt . . On the one hand the young man is pure essence: on the other hand he is essence tainted at the source.' [6]

These irreconcilable contradictions are only resolved when the realization is borne in on the receptive mind, that this degree of irreconcilability points towards – not a dual personality – but *two different people.* One of these is certainly Thomas Walsingham, and the other is equally certainly Dr Hotson's lovely Youth, the nineteen-year-old William Hatcliffe, the Prince of Purpoole of Gray's Inn, *alias* 'Mr.W.H.' himself.

William Hatcliffe of Hatcliffe in Lincolnshire came of a family with a long history of service to the crown in courtly duties, who had accumulated lands and wealth. He was the son of Thomas Hatcliffe and Judith, daughter of Sir Francis Ayscough (or Askew), one of the wealthiest knights of Lincolnshire. [7] He was christened on 6th September 1568. Of his early education nothing is known, but Hotson surmises that he would, as was the custom for well-born children, have been taken into the household of a nobleman, very probably in William's case into the careful hands of his aunt, Lady Anne Ayscough, the daughter of Edward Fiennes de Clinton, 1st Earl of Lincoln, who was Lord Admiral and Lord Steward of her Majesty's household until his death in 1585. Lady Anne was a favourite at Court, and having no children of her own would have made much of the beautiful boy and nurtured him in those arts and graces that recommended him to the Grayans to elect him as their Prince of Purpoole.

At the age of fourteen years he matriculated at Jesus College, Cambridge, in the Michaelmas term of 1582 in the privileged category of 'fellow-commoner' together with the sons of noblemen who dined at the high table. In the same term the fifteen-year-old Thomas Nashe entered St John's College, while Christopher Marlowe at eighteen was doubtless already writing his first play and making his mark as a poet at Corpus Christi. For the next three to four years they would have been contemporaneous at Cambridge, and it is very likely that Marlowe made the acquaintance of young William Hatcliffe there for he was evidently a young man who was noticed. He was destined to make his mark in London, his beauty immortalized in the *Sonnets*.

Like many young men of good birth Hatcliffe did not take a degree, but proceeded to London in November 1586, aged just eighteen, to enter the 'Third University', as the Inns of Court were known, to study law at Gray's Inn.

The following November 1587, having apparently won the unstinted admiration of his fellow students, the decision was taken to revive the spectacular ceremonies involved in electing a Christmas Prince with his entire Grayan Court. They had found their ideal candidate in the accomplished and exceedingly handsome young William Hatcliffe, whom they duly crowned their Prince of Purpoole. The Inns of Court did not elect a Christmas Prince every year by any means. It was a rare occasion and a costly one. The next extant record we have of such royal pageantry at Gray's Inn is not until 1594, when Henry Helmes became Prince of Purpoole. In 1597 the Middle Temple elected Richard Martin as their Prince d'Amour. Gray's Inn followed with Thomas Perient as Prince of Purpoole in 1614, and Richard Vivien of the Middle Temple became Prince d'Amour in 1635. [8] So that long gaps of many years mark the appearances of these Christmas Princes, and William Hatcliffe's election was a rare honour and an event of considerable magnitude in London.

By December 1587, as Hatcliffe was riding high as Prince of Purpoole, Christopher Marlowe had gained unprecedented acclaim as London's new poet-dramatist, the author of *Tamburlaine the Great* which was on the boards certainly by the late autumn of 1587, and which must have been on everybody's lips as the most thrilling theatrical experience of the time. For Marlowe, with the éclat of the astonishing success of *Tamburlaine* resounding in Londoners' ears, nothing would have been more natural than that he should become the Prince of Purpoole's courtly sonneteer. His friend Thomas Watson had published his collection of one hundred sonnets in 1582 based on French and Italian models as his *Passionate Century of Love,* which may have influenced and inspired Marlowe to develop the English sonnet form which became his own. Marlowe's early sonnets, addressed to the Prince of Purpoole, admirably fit the description of 'sugred Sonnets' mentioned by Francis Meres as passing from hand to hand in manuscript, those hands being the Grayan courtiers' who would have read the poems praising the beauty and virtue of their 'Prince' Will Hatcliffe with great delight, copying and recopying the poems without mentioning their author who was the official 'royal' sonneteer, and would not have signed them.

Dr Hotson points out that 'sugred' meant, not sweet, but eloquent, but he does not remark on the historical aptness, *in this Grayan context,* of Meres' reportage that the sonnets were circulating in manuscript. In his attempt to inject William Shakespeare into this situation as 'Prince' Will's sonneteer at a time when Shakespeare had never been heard of, Hotson has some difficulty and has to call on imagination without any substantiating evidence. At that time William Shakespeare is not known to have been in London, nor is there the slightest need for him when Marlowe was there, just down from the university where he had doubtless already known Hatcliffe, already famous in London and the consummate poet to provide an ideal partnership as sonneteer to the 'Prince' – just as Marlowe was there to be Burghley's sonneteer to importune Southampton. In neither case is there any forcing of the evidence; Marlowe is simply there, physically present, the perfect sonneteer who fits the picture naturally, self-evidently, historically with absolute validity.

The sonnets which address Will Hatcliffe as his exquisite friend, lavishly extolling the beauty and virtues of this very beautiful, young man – those qualities which had earned him the rare honour of being elected as Prince of Purpoole – comprise a very broken and scattered group, which speaks with a distinctive voice. These sonnets are subtly different from those addressed to the Poet's Friend and true Patron, for they have, at first, a certain 'public' character to them. Whilst the beautiful young man is likened to Adonis and extravagantly praised, the plural forms of personal pronouns are used in these poems - 'in every blessed shape *we* know', and 'For *we* which now behold'; with plural nouns, 'dwell in *lovers' eyes',* and *'tongues'* and *'subjects'* - rather as though the sonneteer is speaking for all the 'Prince's Court'. Initially, in placing the sonnets to 'Mr.W.H.' into their separate group, the use of their public voice has been an aid. It is this characteristic, peculiar to these sonnets, that *singles them out* as addressing the Prince of Purpoole, and not just any young man. This particular young man is displayed in the public eye.

The sonnet that begins the sequence chronologically, addressing his first patron 'Mr. W.H.', is also one of the loveliest and most famous.

> Shall I compare thee to a Summer's day
> Thou art more lovely and more temperate;
> Rough winds do shake the darling buds of May,
> And Summer's lease hath all too short a date.
> Sometime too hot the eye of Heaven shines,
> And often is his gold complexion dimm'd;
> And every fair from fair sometime declines,
> By chance, or Nature's changing course untrimm'd.
> But thy eternal Summer shall not fade,
> Nor lose possession of that fair thou ow'st;
> Nor shall Death brag thou wander'st in his shade,
> When in eternal lines to time thou grow'st;
>> So long as men can breathe or eyes can see,
>> So long lives this, and this gives life to thee

Sonnet 18

What could be a more perfect opening accolade to his 'Christmas Prince' than this comparison of his beauty to a summer's day in the depth of winter?

There is also an obvious difference in age, the Poet older, the Youth much younger, which marks these sonnets, which has been of assistance in placing them in their correct theme group. The intense love of beauty is there (as always in Marlowe, almost his signature) and it is this which lends these poems their ardour, but the profound depth of emotion which marks the sonnets to his true Patron and Friend is absent. The word 'love' is used with fashionable extravagance, such expressions of love being especially addressed to patrons and royal personages in sixteenth century society. The young man's beauty is praised with unstinted admiration, and his virtue is declared to match his fair outside. But before long the Poet perceives that this exquisite appearance harbours a spoilt and selfish inner nature, for the 'Prince' plays his friend, the sonneteer, a dirty trick by stealing his mistress, and a second group of chiding sonnets follows in which his disillusionment with his fair friend is expressed. Of these I have already quoted *Sonnet 95*.

Dr Hotson's discovery of 'Mr.W.H.' as William Hatcliffe is another of his extraordinary strokes of genius in historical detection, and my final reason for accepting Hatcliffe as unquestionably the lovely Youth of the Sonnets is the unanswerable evidence of *Sonnet 105*. As Dr Hotson has revealed, this is so utterly and truly Elizabethan that it cannot be gainsaid, for it encapsulates the Hatcliffe coat-of-arms. A Poet of such refinement and sophistication as the

Poet of the Sonnets would not write this witty, emblematic verse playing skilfully on the heraldic device of the Hatcliffes by chance or accident. Every word
was intended and carefully chosen to convey this delightful compliment to the
young 'Prince'. The whole structure of the sonnet is designed around his family coat-of-arms, and we may be sure that this effect – a sophisticated and
admired Elizabethan genre of subtle courtly, complimentary presentation –
would not have been lost on the 'Prince' or on his Grayan courtiers, as it has on
us until Dr Hotson opened our eyes to its significance. Very cleverly Hotson
has hit on a way of mirroring the division of the Hatcliffe coat-of-arms of three
Quatrefoils of Love – that is three *fours* – by an arrangement of the quatrains of
the sonnet into three verses of four lines each, with the couplet as a summation
underneath. These echo and re-echo the words, 'Fair, kind and true', the associated sentiments of the 'True-love grass' or Quatrefoils of his arms.

Dr Hotson has richly demonstrated the significance of emblems and the
symbolic language of the use of emblems to the Elizabethan mind in his books,
Mr. W.H. and his *Shakespeare by Hilliard,* but since his lesson has tended to fall
on deaf ears, I quote from him the following delightful example drawn from
the childhood of Queen Elizabeth – 'the essential Elizabethan', he calls her,
than whom few were more deeply versed in the language of emblems.

'Her devotion to these magical emblems began early. At the
Bodleian Library we see it in 'The Glasse of the Synneful Soule'–
the New Year's gift she created at the age of eleven for her step-
mother Queen Katherine Parr. This she translated from the French,
wrote fair, and bound in a sky-blue cloth, which she embroidered
with flowers, leaves, and figures in gold and silver thread. On both
the covers she enclosed the monogram KP within four-looped true-
love knots; and on the spine presented four true-loves – primroses
of four silver petals, each growing on the same stem with a golden
oak leaf: primroses for True Love, oak for Constancy. These for
Queen Katherine, whose motto is *Amour avec Loyaulte.*
'Thus colour, metal, figure, flower, leaf – literally everything, each
carries its message to Queen Katherine; and to us, but only if we
have learned the language in which that age was eloquent.'[9]

The true-love knot of four decorative loops was greatly valued by Elizabeth
and reappears constantly in the figuration of her jewellery and the ornamenta-
tion of her dress. Hotson remarks: 'What prince of history could match her in
the supreme royal art – the art of winning the love of her subjects?' [10] No
Elizabethan of any education or sensibility was unaware of the messages conveyed by the language of the emblems. Four centuries later we cannot hope
to understand the men and women of this time if ill-equipped to decipher
what is presented to our eyes. Dr Hotson's books are a mine of information
on this complex and entrancing subject, and he provides a wealth of examples
from contemporary sources to bear out his thesis.

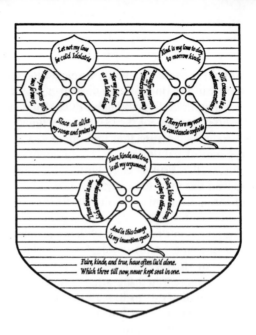

Sonnet 105

1.   *Let not my love be call'd idolatry*
2.   *Nor my beloved as an idol show,*
3.   *Since all alike my songs and praises be*
4.   *To one, of one, still such, and ever so.*

5.   *Kind is my love today, tomorrow kind,*
6.   *Still constant in a wondrous excellence;*
7.   *Therefore my verse, to constancy confin'd,*
8.   *One thing expressing, leaves out difference.*

9.   *'Fair, kind, and true' is all my argument,*
10.   *'Fair, kind, and true', varying to other words;*
11.   *And in this change is my invention spent,*
12.   *Three themes in one, which wondrous scope affords.*

13. *Fair, kind, and true have often liv'd alone,*
14. *Which three till now never kept seat in one.*

Dr Hotson has cleverly emphasised the emblematic format of the Quatrefoils of 'Prince' Will Hatcliffe's coat-of-arms displayed three times, by dividing the sonnet into three verses of four lines each with the final couplet echoing the theme, 'Fair, kind and true.'[11]

Reproduced from Leslie Hotson's MR.W.H. (1964) by kind permission of Mrs Mary Peabody Hotson

This Elizabethan delight in the language of the emblems, which lends itself so sympathetically to artistic and poetic expression, is perfectly exemplified in *Sonnet 105* celebrating Hatcliffe's coat-of-arms of three Quatrefoils 'pierced and slipped argent', i.e. silver, on a ground of azure, the Quatrefoils as the emblems of True-love being emblazoned on a ground the colour of True-love – azure blue. [12]

'Love was the theme of Elizabeth's Court, with every courtier by definition in love high-fantastical with the Queen whose badge was the True-love Knot', declares Hotson. [13] One can see from this how popular the make-believe reign of 'Prince' Will Hatcliffe with his True-love coat-of-arms would have been, and the emphasis on true-love in the sonnets addressing Hatcliffe reflects this. The courts of the Christmas Princes were a faithful imitation of the royal Court of the Queen in fantastic, playful detail, with delightful touches of comic mimicry to enhance the merriment. The ardent love and praise lavished on the 'Prince' who in Hatcliffe personified 'Prince True-Love', as Hotson calls him, is in the exact mood and fashion that fits this concept. The Middle Temple actually named their 'Prince' the Prince d'Amour. The Queen herself attended the 'Court' of the next Prince of Purpoole, Henry Helmes, but only Lord Burghley and five other lords visited 'Prince' Will Hatcliffe's Court of Graya, probably because the Christmas season of 1587-88 was overshadowed by the threat of the Armada. The Middle Temple did not elect a Christmas Prince that year, and probably their reply to the invitation to join the Grayan festivities would have pretended that their 'Emperor' was absent fighting against the Turks, therefore in his place his 'Ambassador' would attend, for this was the 'official' reply sent in 1594 when 'Prince' Henry Helmes invited the Middle Temple to celebrate with them. There was then again no Prince d'Amour to attend in person. We are fortunate to have the detailed records of Henry Helmes' reign extant in Nichols' *Progresses of Queen Elizabeth* of the *Gesta Grayorum* of 1594 describing with delight the fantastic ceremonies of these lavish Christmas Princes, to which we shall have reason to return later. [14]

Sonnet 105 offers just the sort of clever, stimulating exercise in recognition – a challenge to the mind and eye – that the young gentlemen of Gray's Inn would have delighted in. This is surely the clinching argument that 'Prince True-Love' Hatcliffe is indeed the lovely Youth of the Sonnets hymned in this emblematic sonnet by his sonneteer, the spokesman of his loving 'subjects' *(Sonnet 59)*, expressing the adulation of his 'courtiers' in the extravagant praise modelled on the Elizabethan Court. This identification is, to my mind, Dr Hotson at his most perceptive and masterly, and if any critic who thinks he knows his Elizabethans better wishes to query this, he will have to produce a very convincing argument to better this one.

❖ ❖ ❖

Just as we have to understand what the language of the emblems conveyed to the Elizabethans, we have also to appreciate the sense in which terms of endearment were used between Elizabethan men. Over the intervening centuries the terms 'love' and 'lover' have acquired a mainly sexual association. But this was not so in Elizabethan times. Today men do not address other men as 'sweet master', or claim a friend as 'my lover', but this was how Elizabethans spoke without any sexual connotation, just as today a man may call a woman, who is a total stranger, 'love' or 'my love', 'darling' and 'dear', which is accepted as merely a manner of speech, and not as an indication that this strange man is making what is known as 'a pass'. An Elizabethan might understand our modern usage as sexually intended *because* spoken by *a man to a woman,* but in their day when spoken between men such terms indicated friendship, not sexual love. On the surface, this was a chaste and heterosexual society in which extravagant, loving terms denoted courtesy and good manners. The courtly arts and graces were ardently nurtured, and their language reflects this. Even in official letters from the Privy Council to noblemen and government officers serving the kingdom it was usual to sign off 'your loving friends'. [15.] The strict rules of courteous speech and manners were finely developed, percolating down from the Court – a rather necessary aspect of social intercourse when we remember that all 'gentlemen' wore swords, and men not of this class kept a handy dagger in their belts! The Elizabethan Court at the apex of this society had an intimate relationship with the people, and its courtiers indulged in an elaborate cult of love towards the Queen, acting and speaking as though they were in love with her, ardently and passionately. *Love was the language of patronage.*

This convention is reflected in the sonnets to Will Hatcliffe as the Prince of Purpoole. These are flattering, ardent, patently sincere in admiration of his exquisite beauty and his virtues (until the latter are discovered to be false), and they speak not only for the sonneteer, but for the entire 'court', as is evident in the use of the plural personal pronouns, that recur only in these sonnets and in *Sonnet 1* to Southampton: 'From fairest creatures *we* desire increase', where the Poet is speaking also not for himself, but for his patron, Lord Burghley.

In *Sonnet 53* this plural voice is clearly discernible. The term 'shadows' as here used has the Elizabethan connotation of imitation, 'shadowing' the real thing, acting a part.

> What is your substance, whereof are you made,
> That millions of strange shadows on you tend?
> Since every one hath, every one, one shade,
> And you but one, can every shadow lend:
> Describe Adonis and the counterfeit
> Is poorly imitated after you;
> On Helen's cheek all art of beauty set,
> And you in Grecian tires are painted new:

Speak of the spring and foizon of the year,
The one doth shadow of your beauty show,
The other as your bounty doth appear,
And you in every blessed shape *we* know.
  In all external grace you have some part,
  But you like none, none you for constant heart.

Sonnet 53

The 'strange shadows' that tend upon the shadow 'Prince' are his shadow 'courtiers'. A delightful courtly picture is created.

To quote two more from this group to 'Prince' Will Hatcliffe, the martial note struck by *Sonnet 55* aptly reflects the mood of the hour, for at this time, throughout 1587, the Armada threat was steadily mounting, and Marlowe had, I believe, been abroad on missions gathering intelligence on King Philip's preparations and the political situation in France where it was feared aid for the Spanish enterprise might be planned. The flamboyant gaiety of the Grayan's Christmas festivities should be seen against this background of gathering gloom, in which ebullient youth was defiantly having its fling despite all, stating its love of life. The conquest of death in the immortality of verse is the theme this sonnet expresses superbly. Note the use of plurals in both the following sonnets.

Not marble, nor the gilded monuments
Of Princes shall outlive this powerful rhyme,
But you shall shine more bright in these contents
Than unswept stone, besmear'd with sluttish time.
When wasteful war shall statues overturn,
And broils root out the work of masonry,
Nor Mars his sword, nor war's quick fire shall burn
The living record of your memory.
'Gainst death, and all-oblivious enmity
Shall you pace forth, your praise shall still find room,
Even in the eyes of all posterity
That wear this world out to the ending doom.
  So till the judgement that yourself arise,
  You live in this, and dwell in *lovers'* eyes.

Sonnet 55

Time as the devourer of Beauty is a recurring theme in this group.

When in the Chronicle of wasted time
I see description of the fairest wights,
And beauty making beautiful old rhyme,
In praise of ladies dead and lovely knights;

Then in the blazon of sweet beauty's best,
Of hand, of foot, of lip, of eye, of brow,
I see their antique pen would have express'd
Even such beauty as you master now.
So all their praises are but prophecies
Of this our time, all you prefiguring,
And for they look'd but with divining eyes,
They had not skill enough your worth to sing:
  For *we* which now behold these present days,
  Have eyes to wonder, but lack *tongues* to praise.

Sonnet 106

These sonnets have an air of formality. The sonneteer in praising his 'royal' master deliberately uses plurals to suggest that a whole court of 'shadow courtiers' is lost in admiration of this paragon. This mood gives way to an intimate personal note when the 'Prince' and Poet become firm friends, and then rivals for the same mistress. It is very likely that 'Prince' Will was the Poet's first patron as well as his friend, although probably somewhat briefly, for disillusionment soon set in. *

When young Master William Hatcliffe was elected Prince of Purpoole, to be fêted and flaunted around London, Marlowe would have been delighted to act as his official sonneteer, to join in the merriment of the Inns of Court while exercising his poetic talent in praise of this pampered poppinjay, extolling him to the skies. These 'sugred Sonnets' had become justly famous in manuscript for they are little works of perfection written by a consummate poet who had long practised his art, consciously developing his style while at Cambridge. It is very likely that he had read Sir Philip Sidney's sonnet sequence *Astrophel and Stella,* for this would certainly have been known in manuscript in the Walsingham circle to which Marlowe may have been admitted even at this early period, for *Tamburlaine* had already brought him fame. His close association with Will Hatcliffe was probably as ephemeral as the latter's reign as Prince of Purpoole, for disillusionment set in as this 'beauteous and lovely Youth' *(Sonnet 54)* began to reveal his true nature. He was self-indulgent and selfish, beautiful outside but faithless and 'lascivious' within *(Sonnet 40)* and he stole his sonneteer's mistress from him, for which he is chided rather gently at first, his youthful beauty excusing him.

Those pretty wrongs that liberty commits,
When I am sometime absent from thy heart,
Thy beauty and thy years full well befits,
For still temptation follows where thou art.
Gentle thou art, and therefore to be won,

* Foot-note: Evidence that 'Prince' Will became the Poet's patron is seen in *Sonnet 53* where his beauty is associated with his 'bounty' (see page 155).

156

Beauteous thou art, therefore to be assailed;
And when a woman wooes, what woman's son
Will sourly leave her till he have prevailed.
Aye me, but yet thou mightst *my seat forbear,*
And chide thy beauty, and thy straying youth,
Who lead thee in their riot even there
Where thou art forc'd to break a two-fold truth:
  Hers by thy beauty tempting her to thee,
  Thine by thy beauty, being false to me.

Sonnet 41

The italicized words point to the lady in question as having been the Poet's mistress, who, being seduced by the beautiful young 'Prince', had abandoned her lover-Poet. The next sonnet, which clearly is a pair to the above, has an affinity to the Dark Lady group although this seems to be a different mistress.

That thou hast her it is not all my grief,
And yet it may be said I lov'd her dearly:
That she hath thee is of my wailing chief,
A loss in love that touches me more nearly.
Loving offenders, thus I will excuse ye:
Thou dost love her, because thou know'st I love her,
And for my sake even so doth she abuse me,
Suff'ring my friend for my sake to approve her.
If I lose thee, my loss is my love's gain,
And losing her, my friend hath found that loss:
Both find each other, and I lose both twain,
And both for my sake lay on me this cross.
  But here's the joy: my friend and I are one.
  Sweet flattery! Then she loves but me alone.

Sonnet 42

By this intricate and intellectual reasoning, typical of the subtle mind of 'that pure elementall wit. Chr. Marlow', [16] the Poet seeks to subdue his jealous emotions and reconcile himself to the discovery that his mistress is having an affair with this universally admired young man whom he has been so lavishly praising. The loss that touches him 'more nearly', however, is the loss of the 'Prince's' dear friendship, the more so because he was evidently the Poet's patron at this time. The theft of his Poet's mistress is repeated later in the sonnets to the Dark Lady, but then it is far more serious, causing a deep wound that is not easily healed, for the Poet was passionately in love as never before. The mistress of *Sonnets 41* and *42* cannot be the same woman, for although he 'lov'd her dearly' there is not the same emotional intensity as we find in the Dark Lady sonnets, which have an impassioned, and anguished tone of desperation. There is no doubt that Will Hatcliffe is his rival in love also in the Dark Lady sequence, and it would have been entirely in character for him to have deceived his friend, the Poet, a second time with his new mistress, the raven-eyed, seductive siren who has the Poet completely in her thrall. Whereas the mistress of *Sonnets 41* and *42* is more easily given up to his fair friend, for he seems to resign her to him, the loss of the Dark Lady would be unbearable to him; and he pursues her, pleads with her, and evidently does win her back in an on-going and tempestuous love affair in which she is never wholly his, but he is wholly hers.

Significantly, the group of the Dark Lady sonnets, which ends the book of *Shake-speares Sonnets,* is ushered in by *Sonnet 126* which, after a long gap in which Will Hatcliffe does not feature, brings him back again to play his part in the sonnet-story as the Poet's rival lover for the Dark Lady. *Sonnet 126* is the only one which is incomplete, the final couplet is missing. Was this deleted, one wonders, or was it left thus unfinished? This sonnet seems to be the Poet's farewell to his erstwhile friend and first patron, the 'Prince'. His unsatisfactory character has been fully revealed and with this poem the Poet wrote his valediction to Will Hatcliffe.

> O thou my lovely boy, who in thy power
> Dost hold time's fickle glass, his sickle, hour:
> Who hast by waning grown, and therein show'st
> Thy lovers withering, as thy sweet self grow'st.
> If Nature (sovereign mistress over wrack)
> As thou goest onwards still will pluck thee back,
> She keeps thee to this purpose, that her skill
> May Time disgrace, and wretched minutes kill.
> Yet fear her, O thou minion of her pleasure,
> She may detain, but not still keep her treasure!
> Her audit (though delay'd) answer'd must be,
> And her quietus is to render thee.
> (   )
> (   )

Sonnet 126

The brackets appear in Thorpe's original. The term 'Boy' is applicable to a grown man, as it is today, but in *Sonnet 62* and *63* in this group to Hatcliffe, the Poet deliberately exaggerates his own age in the typical sonneteering convention that was widely used, and when he speaks of himself as 'Beated and chapp'd with tann'd antiquity' this is an instance of poetic licence, for these sonnets only make complete sense when seen in the context of 1587-88. This dating, which is Dr Hotson's, is wholly consistent with the identification of Marlowe as the Poet of the Sonnets, for he would have been in the vanguard of the development of the English sonnet, as he was in the vanguard of the development of English blank verse, and of English dramatic poetry which we know as Shakespearean. The quality that is universally recognised as the hallmark of Marlowe is his creativity as an originator and innovator of new forms in our literature and drama. Even if he had really died in 1593 it would be very strange if he had contributed nothing to the great sonneteering vogue that took off in 1591 when he was still very much alive.

The group that now asks our attention is that of the Dark Lady, for Will Hatcliffe is undoubtedly present in them although they are not addressed to him. *Sonnet 144* is one of the most famous of this group which was printed by W. Jaggard in his piratical collection of miscellaneous poems, *The Passionate Pilgrim* in 1599.

> Two loves I have of comfort and despair,
> Which like two spirits do suggest me still:
> The better angel is a man right fair,
> The worser spirit a woman colour'd ill.
> To win me soon to hell my female evil
> Tempteth my better angel from my side,
> And would corrupt my saint to be a devil,
> Wooing his purity with her foul pride:
> And whether that my angel be turn'd fiend,
> Suspect I may, yet not directly tell;
> But being both from me, both to each friend,
> I guess one angel in another's hell.
>   Yet this shall I ne'er know, but live in doubt,
>   Till my bad angel fire my good one out.

Sonnet 144

The close affinity with *Sonnet 42* is obvious; it is a reworking of the same theme in a similar but different context. The friend who is 'a man right fair' is named in two sonnets in this group which play on the word 'will' connoting sexual desire as an Elizabethan term for this, and the name of the Poet's rival, *Will*. This is unmistakably the lascivious and lovely Youth, Will Hatcliffe, who has seduced or been seduced by the Dark Lady, who is the Poet's passionately adored mistress, as is clearly indicated in this witty word-play. This interpretation fits the picture perfectly without any straining of the facts in this historical context.

> Whoever hath her wish, thou hast thy *Will*,
> And *Will* to boot, and *Will* in over-plus,
> More than enough am I that vex thee still,
> To thy sweet will making addition thus.
> Wilt thou, whose will is large and spacious,
> Not once vouchsafe to hide my will in thine?

Shall will in others seem right gracious,
And in my will no fair acceptance shine?
The sea, all water, yet receives rain still,
And in abundance addeth to his store,
So thou being rich in *Will,* add to thy *Will*
One will of mine to make thy large *Will* more.
　Let no unkind, no fair beseechers kill;
　Think all but one, and me in that one *Will.*

Sonnet 135

The italicizing of the name *Will* follows Thorpe's edition so this is clearly the intention of the author. This is how Elizabethan printers presented all proper nouns, and it underlines the felicitous identification by Hotson of Will Hatcliffe as the somewhat disturbing presence that has puzzled us for so long, for the shadow 'Prince', having cast his long shadow over the true Patron obscuring him from recognition, has also penetrated the Dark Lady!

Will Hatcliffe's exquisite looks and charming person are testified by his election as the Prince of Purpoole, making him peculiarly eligible to fit the portrait of the 'lovely Boy', and such a stunning young man would obviously stand to make an easy conquest of the lady he was intent on seducing, especially when robed in the added glamour of the princely role he was playing. His is a pervasive presence in the sonnets, although, as I suspect, of limited duration, even as his elevation to the throne of Graya was but temporary. Something of the ephemeral nature of his princely glory, as of his youthful beauty, is caught in these sonnets that return insistently to the theme of 'devouring Time' as the enemy most to be feared, which is strongly present in this group.

However, there is more required if we are to accept Will Hatcliffe with complete confidence as the 'lovely Boy' of the Sonnets. Arguing back from the poems to match the identification with the long-sought quarry requires to be supported by some documentary evidence confirming his dubious character. We need to know whether it is indeed true that the lovely Youth's character is not so noble as his beautiful face and figure suggest. It is nothing less than a perfect fit for the portrait of the 'lovely Boy' that we are seeking. Was Will Hatcliffe, the Prince of Purpoole, really an exceedingly beautiful young man possessing a flawed character?

Meticulously researching the history of Hatcliffe's life, our expert Elizabethan sleuth, Dr Hotson, has come up with the corroborating evidence. [17.] The record testifies that this favoured gentleman was indeed weak and feckless by nature, a self-indulgent and spoilt man who lacked true nobility of character.

Early in 1596 when he was aged twenty-seven William Hatcliffe married Dorothy Kay, a girl of eighteen, daughter of the late John Kay, Esquire, of Hackney, who had held office as one of the Clerks of the Green Cloth at Court. At her coming of age Dorothy would receive certain lands and messuages and £100 – a modest substance. Probably it was a love-match, but even had she

160

been wealthy it might not have saved Hatcliffe from final ruin. He was evidently given to lavish spending and neglect of his estates. Hotson concludes: 'It is clear from the start that young Hatcliffe proved incapable of husbanding his estate and keeping out of debt.' [18] His self-indulgent nature and love of luxurious living and ostentation – possibly also gambling, though this is unproven – led to the steady dissipation of his inheritance. He had been brought up as pampered and to expect everything to drop into his lap. Perhaps his brief glory as Prince of Purpoole and the munificent praise of his sonneteer had turned his head. As a member of the country gentry he was elected to the House of Commons and sat for Grimsby in the Parliament of October 1597 to February 1598, but without making his mark there in any way. By the time he died in 1631 there was virtually nothing left of the Hatcliffe estate. It had all been sold over the years to clear his accumulating debts. His brief will shows no forethought for the two unmarried daughters and the son he left behind. Noting his will, Hotson comments:

'The one particular in his mind is "all my fine linen" (which the inventory lists as his most valuable asset next to the corn and hay in his barn). If Will Hatcliffe fleeted his time carelessly like a prince "clothed in purple and fine linen", the disappearance of his heritage is no mystery.' [19]

The portrait fits, does it not? His sonneteer and large-hearted Friend had perceptively assessed the self-centred soul that inhabited this beauteous mansion, and history reveals Will Hatcliffe predictably following the path of his personal destiny from a glorious beginning to a rather degraded end. It is the kind of confirmation gratifying to the historian, but there is sadness in this tale of human frailty.

> They that have power to hurt, and will do none,
> That do not do the thing they most do show,
> Who moving others, are themselves as stone,
> Unmoved, cold, and to temptation slow:
> They rightly do inherit heaven's graces,
> And husband nature's riches from expense;
> They are the lords and owners of their faces,
> Others but stewards of their excellence.
> The summer's flower is to the summer sweet,
> Though to itself it only live and die,
> But if that flower with base infection meet,
> The basest weed outbraves his dignity;
>   For sweetest things turn sour by their deeds:
>   Lilies that fester, smell far worse than weeds.

Sonnet 94

This sonnet praises chastity which, though cold 'as stone', was a highly rated virtue, and condemns lasciviousness, the theme of this quartet of sonnets in the Hatcliffe group. All the sonnets to Will Hatcliffe are presented together under *The Themes of the Sonnets Analysed,* where they are extracted from the sequence; the identification is emphasised when they are seen separated from the rest of the sonnets as in Groups A & B in 'The Book of the Sonnets' that concludes this book.

Having separated the 'lovely Boy' from the Patron, we now turn to discover what we can about Thomas Walsingham, to test whether he does indeed fit the portrait of the Poet's true Friend and Patron, the man whom he addresses as both his 'Lord' and 'dear friend', who was ever faithful to him in his hour of need.

❖   ❖   ❖   ❖

THE PATRON

THOMAS WALSINGHAM was evidently born in 1563, the third son of Sir Thomas Walsingham III, of a distinguished family coming originally from Walsingham in Norfolk, who settled in Kent during the fourteenth century and acquired large landed estates around Chislehurst, where they built a fine moated manor house, Scadbury. Thomas's grandfather, Sir Edmund Walsingham, was Lieutenant of the Tower and was granted monastic lands by Henry VIII.

Sir Francis Walsingham, cousin germane of Thomas, was one of the most important and powerful statesmen of Queen Elizabeth's government, sharing with Lord Burghley the main responsibilities of day-to-day government, sharing with Lord Burghley the main responsibilities of day-to-day government of the realm. Thomas's two elder brothers, Guildeford (who predeceased his father) and Edmund both worked for the government in some capacity as intelligence agents for Sir Francis Walsingham, who built up a remarkable intelligence organisation with agents as far-flung as Turkey in order to feed him with information on which to base English foreign policy, for which he had responsibility as Secretary of State. For this he employed members of his family. Loyalty to the crown, utmost discretion and skill in intelligence work seem to have been Walsingham family attributes. [20]

162

Thomas also entered the intelligence service and from the age of seventeen he was already acting as a government courier to the French court bearing her Majesty's letters relating to those 'special and secret affairs of great importance' which were entrusted to the agents in Walsingham's secret service. By the time he was twenty he had been back and forth to the French court half a dozen times. Doubtless he was fluent in French, for these missions often entailed a lengthy sojourn at the French court. [21]

As has been previously mentioned, when he was nineteen the Queen chose Thomas Walsingham for her messenger and envoy on a very special mission to Bruges, in July 1582, to attend the Duke of Anjou (Alençon), her 'Frog' as she called her suitor, to bear her love-letter to him. [22] This called for some diplomacy. The main object of Elizabeth's letter to her beloved 'Monsieur' (written in French of course) was to inform him how deeply she regretted (with many crocodile tears – that splashed onto the paper as she wrote) that she could not send him the large sums of money he was requesting from her to finance his military campaign in the Netherlands. However, she had thought of a plan to help him in this matter, and was sending her trusted and charming messenger, who knew her mind in all things and could answer any questions he might wish to put as though she were there to speak herself, whom she had enjoined to proceed afterwards to the French court to persuade Monsieur's brother, King Henri III, to supply the moneys he so desperately needed. It is his brother Henri, Elizabeth suggests, who is the right and proper person to aid Monsieur by financing this military expedition, for it is France who would stand to benefit most from his warlike exploits which will ensure peace for their country and Monsieur is rendering a great service to his brother, the King.

Queen Elizabeth's eulogy of her messenger, to whom she had entrusted a diplomatic mission of considerable importance despite his youth, sheds a valuable light on this somewhat enigmatic gentleman. Her confidence in him, and the special favours that she bestowed on him throughout his life, indicate that Thomas Walsingham was a young man blessed with charm and good looks, and he seems to have possessed in good measure the Walsingham quality of rare discretion. Elizabeth loved young men who were charming and handsome, and if they were endowed with precocious wisdom she knew how to use them to advantage. Sir Philip Sidney, Sir Francis Walsingham's son-in-law, had also been entrusted with a most important diplomatic mission to all the courts of Europe as the Queen's envoy when he was aged only twenty-three. [23] His youth and exceptional grace made such a favourable impression that unprecedented success was achieved. This was the inception of the Protestant League, conceived to counterbalance the Holy Roman Catholic League. Queen Elizabeth had an appraising eye for a proper man to embellish her court and to represent her kingdom and do it honour.

Thomas Walsingham's mission for the Queen to Alençon is given emphasis here because of its importance in establishing the rather special relationship of personal trust that seems to have existed between this discreet young courtier and his royal mistress. He seems to have remained constantly in Elizabeth's love and grace throughout her reign. Yet, surprisingly, after such an advantageous early beginning from which he might have risen high, he remained obscure. This charming gentleman never features in the political intrigues of the Court, but preferred to withdraw himself to live a private life from the time he came into his inheritance of the Walsingham estates; from which he emerged but once in a role of public responsibility to take command of the defence of Kent in the second Armada threat of 1596. The impression given is of a studious, artistic temperament.

In November 1589 his elder brother Edmund died without issue after only five years as the lord of Scadbury, and Thomas succeeded as the last surviving son, being 'aged 26 years and more' as the inquisition post mortem states. [24.] His christening record is missing, and my research on the contradictory statements on his age show these to be in error, but the post mortem can be taken as conclusive evidence. He was therefore born in 1563, and would have been a few months to a year older than Marlowe. [25.] It is likely that Marlowe and Thomas Walsingham first became acquainted through their work in the secret service, but we do not know when their close friendship matured. Armada year, 1588, a crucial time when dangers were faced and Sir Francis's intelligence service was stretched to its limits, is a time when mutual friendship may have drawn closer, and when Thomas inherited his estate is a probable time for him to have become the acknowledged patron of his poet-friend.

While Sir Francis Walsingham was alive Thomas worked closely with him in the capacity of his trusted right hand in the secret service, so far as we may judge, for he contributed, probably significantly, to the successful scheme for the uncovering of the most dangerous of the conspiracies against the Queen's life, the infamous Babington Plot, to which, I have suggested, Christopher Marlowe also contributed at Rheims. [26.] The whole intelligence operation was conducted with such skill that all the conspirators were deftly netted, including the Queen of Scots. It was the coup of the century, and ensured that England was thenceforth free from serious Catholic conspiratorial attempts on the Queen's life. It cleared the way for the Armada confrontation, which was the greatest turning point bringing security to England and peace for the rest of Elizabeth's reign.

The part played by the Walsinghams in safeguarding her life, both Sir Francis and his young cousin Thomas, must have been appreciated by the Queen, even though it presented her with the dilemma she had always hoped to evade – the problem of the execution of Mary. She handled this with consummate play-acting to fool the European heads of government who expressed horror at the act. Elizabeth knew how to get away with doing what she wanted, or found it necessary to do, no matter what others said, or thought.

Sir Francis was extremely fond of his young cousin Thomas, and from the time of the elder Sir Thomas's death in April 1584 he seems to have looked upon him with a father's eye.

Sir Francis Walsingham, Secretary of State
After J. de Critz the Elder (?)

At the funeral of Sir Francis Walsingham in 1590 Thomas is named as the chief mourner, and the eclogue written by Thomas Watson to honour his death is dedicated to Thomas Walsingham. Some lines in this Latin poem, *Meliboeus,* imply that Thomas Walsingham was also an accomplished poet, although no verses by him are known, and they would have been left, as was the custom, in manuscript. [27.] In having such friends as Watson and Marlowe, and belonging to the family circle of Sir Francis, whose son-in-law Sir Philip Sidney was one of the foremost poets and writers of the time and an early patron of Edmund Spenser, there can be no doubt that Thomas Walsingham was a young man of exceptionally cultured tastes in literature, poetry, music and art, as the extant inventory of Scadbury Manor endorses. This, dated 1727, upon the demolition of Scadbury Manor, lists a large collection of paintings and several maps, suggesting an interest in exploration. Included are '17 large Indian pictures' which formerly hung on what was called the 'White Staircase'. Virginia Stern's research links the 'White Staircase' with the wonderful water-colour paintings (exactly 17 in number) by John White, who accompanied the colonising expedition to Virginia organised by Sir Walter Raleigh. [28.] If this evidence is accepted it provides an additional link between Thomas Walsingham and Raleigh's close associates. If Thomas Walsingham was Shakespeare's Patron, all these pieces of evidence and information assume considerable importance.

Scadbury was a fine example of a Tudor moated manor, similar in style to the present Ightham Mote, near Sevenoaks in Kent, and it lay in extensive and beautiful grounds which are now a protected nature reserve. [29.] In 1597 Queen Elizabeth visited Scadbury on what seems to have been a private visit, for it was not part of her royal progress; and as a mark of her continued grace and favour she knighted her host, Sir Thomas Walsingham, and planted trees in the avenue in commemoration of her stay. Rooms in Scadbury Manor were thereafter known as 'the Queen Elizabeth Room' and 'the Maids of Honour Chamber'. This portended, I believe, the Queen's gracious consent to Sir Thomas's proposed marriage to one of Her Majesty's Maids of Honour, the Lady Audrey Shelton, of an old Norfolk family with large estates also in Suffolk. Audrey's grandfather, Sir John Shelton, had married an aunt of Anne Boleyn, also named Anne Boleyn, and they had sheltered Elizabeth during the time of her persecution by her half-sister Mary, so that there was a close family bond. Thomas Walsingham could hardly have chosen a more acceptable bride. Can we have any doubt that Queen Elizabeth's visit was in connection with these proposed nuptials to which she was asked to give her blessing?

I have not been able to trace a record of their marriage to date, but it probably was celebrated in the spring of 1598 when the poem *Hero and Leander* was published in dedication to Sir Thomas Walsingham and his Lady as an epithalamium, and the birth of their son Thomas in 1600 also supports this date. He was their only child. Audrey was already aged thirty when they married, but she evidently remained very beautiful well into her advanced years, for she emerges as one of the noted beauties of King James's court, where she features in the masques written by Ben Jonson to give opportunities for the ladies of the court, including the Queen, to disport themselves in play-acting. King James chose her for his 'Valentine' in 1616 when she was aged forty-eight, which suggests such a woman of whom it might be said, 'age doth not wither her'. [30]

Lady Walsingham Junior is first recorded in the records of Queen Elizabeth's court in 1599, when she accompanied the Queen on her summer progress, and their stay at the Countess of Derby's country mansion, Harefield, found them housebound by the English weather – it poured! An impromptu entertainment was thereupon devised in which Audrey Walsingham played the part of 'a guileless lady' who presented the Queen with a 'robe of rainbows', accompanying her presentation with the speaking of suitably guileless verses – which may have been composed by Audrey herself. [31] This is the charming creature Sir Thomas Walsingham took to wife.

The Rival Poet

The year 1598 saw the publication of Marlowe's exquisite poem Hero and Leander, based on Musaeus' tale of these ill-starred legendary lovers, which contains the most beautiful poetic description of the consummation of the love act by two virgin lovers that has ever been written. This unfinished poem, which he must have been writing at Scadbury at the time of his arrest in 1593, was published in two separate editions in 1598; firstly, Marlowe's lovely unfinished fragment of two sestiads only, dedicated to Sir Thomas Walsingham posthumously on Marlowe's behalf by the publisher Edward Blount, a cultured gentleman publisher who was the friend of both Marlowe and Walsingham; immediately followed by a newly-completed edition of the poem with four additional sestiads by George Chapman, dedicated to Lady Audrey Walsingham.

These two publications, I have previously suggested, [32] were intended as the epithalamium to the wedding that year, 1598, of Sir Thomas Walsingham and Lady Audrey Shelton, by the Patron's two poets, Christopher Marlowe and George Chapman.

The dedication to Thomas Walsingham by Edward Blount is a moving remembrance of Marlowe which testifies to the dear friendship that existed between Patron and Poet.

To the Right Worshipful SIR THOMAS WALSINGHAM, KNIGHT

Sir, we think not ourselves discharged of the duty we owe to our friend when we have brought the breathless body to the earth; for, albeit the eye there taketh his ever-farewell of that beloved object, yet the impression of the man that hath been dear unto us, living an after-life in our memory, there putteth us in mind of farther obsequies due unto the deceased; and namely the performance of what-

167

soever we may judge shall make to his living credit and to the
effecting of his determinations prevented by the stroke of death.
By these meditations (as by an intellectual will) I suppose myself
executor to the unhappily deceased author of this poem; upon
whom knowing that in his lifetime you bestowed many kind
favours, entertaining the parts of reckoning and worth which you
found in him with good countenance and liberal affection, I cannot
but see so far into the will of him dead, that whatsoever issue of his
brain should chance to come abroad, that the first breath it should
take might be the gentle air of your liking; for, since his self had
been accustomed thereunto, it would prove more agreeable and
thriving to his right children than any other foster countenance
whatsoever. At this time seeing that this unfinished tragedy hap-
pens under my hands to be imprinted, of a double duty, the one to
yourself, the other to the deceased, offering my utmost self now and
ever to be ready at your worship's disposing.

EDWARD BLOUNT

'At this time' sounds like a reference to Walsingham's projected or recent marriage. Thus five years after Marlowe's 'death' his *Hero and Leander* was delivered to the world, a lovely uncompleted fragment, in the beautifully printed edition of Blount in association with the printer Adam Islip, now in the Folger Shakespeare Library. It is in the expanded edition with the completion by George Chapmen, however, that we strike gold, for here is that very situation of a patron with his two poets which Shakespearean scholars have scoured literary history for in vain to explain the jealousy expressed in the Sonnets of the Rival Poet. They have independently identified Shakespeare's rival as George Chapman, that metaphysical poet who most aptly fits the description of the poet portrayed in *Sonnets 80* and *86.* [33]

Chapman's Dedication to Lady Walsingham of his completion of Marlowe's poem is worthy of our close study. Typical of his didactic style he digresses to give a pedantic appraisal of the Lady's commendable reputation at Court – a kind of welcoming of her as his Patron's bride, perhaps? This is the venerable and learned George Chapman speaking, a man full of high principles, good intentions and honest endeavours, but, (as he himself recognises) somewhat lacking in courtly graces, having a 'silly' (simple, unworldly) disposition.

To My Best Esteemed and Worthily Honoured Lady, the LADY WALSINGHAM
One of the Ladies of her Majesty's Bed-Chamber

I present your Ladyship with the last affections of the first two
Lovers that ever Muse shrined in the Temple of Memory; being
drawn by strange instigation to employ some of my serious time in
so trifling a subject, which yet made the first Author, divine Musaeus,

168

eternal. And were it not that we must subject our accounts of these common received conceits to servile custom, it goes much against my hand to sign that for a trifling subject, on which more worthiness of soul hath been showed, and weight of divine wit, than can vouchsafe residence in the leaden gravity of any money-monger; in whose profession all serious subjects are concluded. But he that shuns trifles must shun the world; out of whose reverend heaps of substance and austerity, I can, and will, ere long, single, or tumble out as brainless and passionate fooleries as ever panted in the bosom of the most ridiculous Lover.

[Here Chapman is referring to his comedy All Fools *which he was probably already writing, and which he dedicated to Sir Thomas Walsingham.]*

Accept it therefore (good Madam) though as a trifle, yet as a serious argument of my affection: for to be thought thankful for all free and honourable favours, is a great sum of that riches my whole thrift intendeth.

Such uncourtly and silly dispositions as mine, whose contentment hath other objects than profit or glory, are as glad, simply for the naked merit of virtue, to honour such as advance her, as others that are hired to commend with deepliest politic bounty.

It hath therefore adjoined much contentment to my desire of your true honour to hear men of desert in Court, add to mine own knowledge of your noble disposition, how gladly you do your best to prefer their desires; and have as absolute respect to their mere good parts, as if they came perfumed and charmed with golden incitements. And this most sweet inclination, that flows from the truth and eternity of Nobles, assure your Ladyship doth more suit your other ornaments, and makes more to the advancement of your name and happiness of your proceedings, than if (like others) you displayed ensigns of state and sourness in your forehead, made smooth with nothing but sensuality and presents.

This poor Dedication (in figure of the other Unity betwixt Sir Thomas *and yourself) hath rejoined you with him, my honoured best friend, whose continuance of ancient kindness to my still-obscured estate, though it cannot increase my love to him, which hath ever been entirely circular, yet shall it encourage my deserts to their utmost requital, and make my hearty gratitude speak; to which the unhappiness of my life hath hitherto been uncomfortable and painful dumbness.*

By your Ladyships vowed in most wished service

GEORGE CHAPMAN

It is typical of Chapman's dedicatory style to speak of his 'still-obscured estate' and the 'unhappiness' of his life and his 'uncomfortable and painful dumbness' which he harps on in his other dedications in this self-deprecating manner. [34] Success in a worldly sense constantly eluded him, and he was most unlucky in his other patrons, for the Earl of Essex was executed and Prince Henry died young. It also seems as though Marlowe's pleas (in the sonnets) resulted in Chapman having been asked by Walsingham to refrain from dedicating further works to him for a time, as appears from his dedication of a play in 1608 to be considered later. However, he clearly remained a life-long friend of the Walsingham family.

Both the above dedications contain hints that the marriage was a fairly recent event. Blount compares the creation of works of literature to the birth of children, and Chapman makes an allusion to his patroness' union with his 'honoured best friend' when he speaks of 'the other Unity betwixt *Sir Thomas* and yourself'. Both dedications contain hints at the wishes of the 'dead' author of *Hero and Leander* as though Marlowe had communicated his desire to have this poem presented as an epithalamium to his Patron. Blount states that he was moved to undertake this 'by an intellectual will', and Chapman claims he was 'drawn by strange instigation' to spend his 'serious time in so trifling a subject' – the term 'trifles' denoting poetic works of an entertaining and romantic nature.

The implications are that Chapman and Blount, both of whom were close to Walsingham, and both associated with the esoteric club of the free-thinkers, knew that Marlowe was not really dead. In Chapman's continuation of *Hero and Leander,* the Third Sestiad has an extraordinary passage which critics have found puzzling, for it seems to inform us that Marlowe had asked him to complete the work.

> Then, ho, most strangely-intellectual fire,
> That, proper to my soul, hast power t' inspire
> Her burning faculties, and with the wings
> Of thy unsphered flame visit'st the springs
> Of spirits immortal! Now (as swift as Time
> Doth follow Motion) find th' eternal clime
> Of his free soul, whose living subject stood
> Up to the chin in the Pierian flood,
> And drunk me half this Musaean story,
> Inscribing it to deathless memory:
> Confer with it, and make my pledge as deep,
> That neither's draught be consecrate to sleep;
> Tell it how much his late desires I tender
> (If yet it know not), and to light surrender
> My soul's dark offspring, willing it should die
> To loves, to passions, and society. [35]

This characteristically cloudy passage is slipped into the story, having no relevance whatsoever to what went before or what comes after, but it is obviously something Chapman felt impelled to express. It has defied sensible explanation since his reference to the author of 'half this Musaean story' can only mean Marlowe who had written the first part of *Hero and Leander*, and if Marlowe had really asked Chapman to complete his unfinished poem then 'his late desires' must have been imparted in 1593 – five years ago! In that case, how did he have foreknowledge of his murder so that he could ask this of his friend George? In the context of Marlowe's actual death in 1593 the passage can only make sense if some supernatural message had been received from the dead Poet's spirit. However, this divining of the wishes of dead poets by supernatural telepathy is just what Chapman specialized in – as is implied in *Sonnet 86*.

When Chapman began the greatest work of his life, his translation of Homer's *Iliad* and *Odyssey*, he tells us that the inspiration to undertake the tremendous labour for this masterpiece came to him in a vision in which the spirit of Homer appeared to him, with his bosom full of fire. In contemplation of the high ambition he had conceived of englishing the Homeric tales, he had taken a night walk on a hill near his home at Hitchin, when this vision came to him,

'suddenly, a comfortable light
Brake through the shade; and, after it, the sight
Of a most grave and goodly person shined,
With eyes turn'd upwards, and was outward blind;
But inward, past and future things he saw;

His sacred bosom was so full of fire,
That 'twas transparent; and made him expire
His breath in flames, that did instruct (me thought)
And (as my soul were then at full) they wrought.' [36]

It was Chapman's thoughts of Homer, as he deliberated in the solitude of the night concerning the great project before him, that had called the Elysian spirit to visit him 'in a sweet gale' to communicate inspiration and encouragement. Chapman was 'a convinced believer in the Platonic doctrine that poetry is divinely inspired'. [37]

It is in this light that the invocation to Marlowe's spirit may be interpreted as having inspired him to complete the unfinished fragment; at the same time Chapman employs this cryptic method to tell Marlowe that a terrestrial message had been received by his friend George, who saw himself as the poet 'chosen' by Kit to finish his poem (which was, I believe, a grievous misunderstanding!) rendering a pledge in return to his 'dead' friend that their joint work would achieve immortality.

Marlowe's *Hero and Leander*, although incomplete, is nevertheless aesthetically a beautiful fragment that can stand alone, for the story is brought to a conclusion with the consummation of their love by the two virgin lovers, which is, in a sense, their wedding night, making it a perfect offering as an epithalamium. This fragment had originally been entered on 28th September 1593 in the Stationers' Register to John Wolfe, the good friend of Gabriel Harvey and, like Blount, an erudite man, a cut above most publishers. Wolfe probably intended publishing it in its unfinished state. However, for some reason he withheld it, perhaps because of the odium into which Marlowe's name fell after the murder story became common knowledge, and at some unknown date he passed his copyright to Edward Blount, who published it early in 1598 with his dedication to Sir Thomas Walsingham.

Blount's edition had evidently preceded that containing Chapman's continuation, for the Stationers' Register entry for this on 2nd March 1598 to the publisher Paul Linley states that the copyright had been 'Assigned over unto him from Edward Blount', who must have already brought out his own edition of the incomplete poem.

George Chapman, it seems, honestly believed that Marlowe had expressed 'his late desires' to the effect that he should now undertake to complete the poem for their joint Patron's impending marriage – but, unfortunately, this was a mistaken assumption. What had really happened, I suggest, is that it was not Marlowe, but Walsingham who had requested Chapman to finish the poem, in order therewith to give pleasure to his bride and flatter her by bringing her into the patronage of his two poets. This alone can explain the storm of jealousy that broke forth in the Sonnets of the Rival Poet. In these the Patron is bitterly accused of having turned towards another poet in preference to himself. It was one of those misunderstandings of the motive behind an action that can sometimes lead us to unbearable grief, especially when deep emotions of mutual love and loyalty are stirred. This *exactly* mirrors the mood and the words of these anguished sonnets.

From Marlowe's point of view there would have been no need to complete his poem by another's hand. It was, in fact, tantamount to gilding the lily, for this exquisite, little masterpiece is a sufficient offering to his Patron without any addition, a thing of such rare perfection that even Chapman's poetic gifts – which have here risen to the challenge of Marlowe's inspiration with more felicitous passages than usual in Chapman's knotted and intricate versification – cannot match it. Furthermore, Marlowe's fragment had already been separately published in a very fine edition. So why should he have sent a message to George asking him to finish it? This could add no lustre to Marlowe's name *per se,* but it certainly enhanced Chapman's reputation for his critics have unanimously acclaimed that his four sestiads of *Hero and Leander* are among the finest verse he ever wrote. Inspired by the sheer beauty of Marlowe's verse, he excelled himself, for his completion is singularly free of Chapman's grosser faults. Nevertheless, when the poem is read right through there is a marked difference in style in the two parts. As the editor of Chapman's *Poems,* Phyllis Brooke Bartlett, has commented: 'Readers of the completed *Hero and Leander* (1598) have always received a severe jolt when moving on to the third sestiad, where Chapman's contribution begins.' [38]

Chapman would, I believe, genuinely have thought that Marlowe wished him to finish this 'trifle', for honest George would have been incapable of appropriating his friend's work (dead or alive) dishonestly out of self-interest. With all his failings and foibles, Chapman, as his biographer Millar Maclure remarks, 'was a good man'. [39] There is complete openness in his invocation to Marlowe's spirit, and his pledge 'that neither's draught be consecrate to sleep' was liberally honoured, for *Hero and Leander* in its completed form went into nine editions: 1598, 1600, 1608, 1613, 1616, 1617, 1622, 1629, 1637. It was on everybody's lips. John Taylor, the 'Water Poet', tells us that he recited passages from *Hero and Leander,* as he plied his oars, to the delectation of his customers.

This enormous success was not anticipated, and it is evident that Marlowe heard of the completion of his poem with utter dismay, fearing that the mighty Chapman's contribution would eclipse his own. Arthur Acheson, who identified Chapman as the Rival Poet, wrote: 'All students of the Sonnets will agree with me when I say that Shakespeare's personality as we find it there revealed, is of much too magnanimous and gentle a spirit to gratuitously assail a fellow poet with such bitterness as we find in many passages indicating Chapman'. [40] *A sufficient cause must have existed.* And this we have in the Marlowe-Chapman rivalry regarding *Hero and Leander.*

In completing the poem, Chapman had also divided Marlowe's original continuous verse into two sestiads, adding four more of his own and giving each sestiad an introductory 'Argument' in verse. This is how the completed version was printed in the spring of 1598 in Paul Linley's edition. There can have been no more delightful epithalamium offered to any patron and his lady than this presentation edition in an elegantly printed little vellum-covered book, neatly tied with a pair of knotted thong-like ribbands that keep the book closed when not being read, as in the rare 1598 copy in the British Museum – one of only two extant. Blount's Dedication to Sir Thomas Walsingham begins the book, preceding Marlowe's two sestiads, followed by Chapman's Dedication to Lady Walsingham introducing his continuation of the love-story; and this joint format, elegantly bound together, and the date of the transfer of the copyright on 2nd March 1598 to Linley, combine to suggest that it was *this* edition that was presented as the epithalamium by his two poets on their Patron's wedding.

These facts fully qualify as cause for the passionate emotional reaction provoked, which finds its outpouring in the fourteen Sonnets of the Rival Poet. George Chapman's characteristics are easily recognised in the allusions to his style: 'the proud full sail of his great verse' is a perfect description of the splendid passages launching his first *Seven Books of the Iliad,* which also appeared in 1598 dedicated to the Earl of Essex, as the first instalment of his life's work.

Courtesy of The British Library

Title page of Chapman's *Homer,* 1596

'Chapman's *Homer* is one of the great achievements of the Elizabethan age, a monument of skill and devotion . . through the whole work there breathes a spirit of sleepless energy that amply atones for all crudities and conceits', [41] is the verdict of posterity, and this deathless work was equally greeted with admiration and acclaim by his contemporaries, so that, to Marlowe, Chapman must have appeared a formidable rival.

> O how I faint when I of you do write,
> Knowing a better spirit doth use your name,
> And in the praise thereof spends all his might,
> To make me tongue-tied speaking of your fame.
> But since your worth, wide as the ocean is,
> The humble as the proudest sail doth bear,
> My saucy bark (inferior far to his)
> On your broad main doth wilfully appear.
> Your shallowest help will hold me up afloat,
> Whilst he upon your soundless deep doth ride;
> Or, being wreck'd, I am a worthless boat,
> He of tall building and of goodly pride.
>   Then if he thrive, and I be cast away,
>   The worst was this: my love was my decay.

Sonnet 80

The sea imagery used in the Sonnets of the Rival Poet is particularly apt when applied to Chapman, as this criticism of his dramatic works by William Lyon Phelps shows: 'When the mighty spirit of Chapman – for he had a mighty spirit – does get the better of its environment, and finds its true voice, we are swept along resistless on the rushing torrent. At its worst, Chapman's thorny style leads us into a great wood; at its best, it has a deep-sea quality, now a succession of rolling swells, and now infinitely calm "too full for sound and foam". It is at such times that we fully understand Webster's acknowledgement of how much he had learned from "that full and heightened style of Master Chapman".' [42]

> Was it the proud full sail of his great verse,
> Bound for the prize of all-too-precious you,
> That did my ripe thoughts in my brain inhearse,
> Making their tomb the womb wherein they grew?
> Was it his spirit, by spirits taught to write
> Above a mortal pitch, that struck me dead?
> No, neither he, nor his compeers by night
> Giving him aid, my verse astonished.
> He, nor that affable familiar ghost
> Which nightly gulls him with intelligence,

As victors of my silence cannot boast;
I was not sick of any fear from thence.
But when your countenance fill'd up his line,
Then lack'd I matter that enfeebled mine.

Sonnet 86

J.M. Robertson writes: 'Chapman alone meets the claim that he was 'by spirits taught to write/ Above a mortal pitch', the 'affable familiar ghost' and 'compeers by night''; these being his friends in the 'School of Night', such as Matthew Roydon and Thomas Hariot, to whom Chapman dedicated works in friendship, not patronage, whose appreciation of his work aided him. These clues, Robertson maintains, were clearly intended by Shakespeare to point to Chapman. [43.] With Marlowe in mind the words 'that struck me dead' gain a new significance as we read this sonnet.

More recently, Millar Maclure, commenting on the hypothetical identification of Chapman as the subject of these poems, writes: 'If we cast him as the "rival poet" of Shakespeare's *Sonnets* . . "that affable familiar ghost/ Which nightly gulls him with intelligence" of No. 86 does sound a little like Chapman's "heavenly familiar", and if we give any countenance at all to the "School of Night" we must perforce be struck by the reference to that curious advisory committee of "compeers by night" who aid the rival to shake out "the proud full sail of his great verse". But to what person who might conceivably be "Mr.W.H." did Chapman, at any time before 1609, address such verses or "fill up his line" with that beloved countenance? In the present state of our knowledge we are forced back upon hypothetical lost manuscripts, accepted at an unknown date by an unknown person, and that will not do.' [44.]

With Marlowe in the picture there is no difficulty in cracking this dilemma, for it does not exist. That Chapman remained on intimate terms of friendship with Thomas Walsingham is testified by the dedication to Sir Thomas of his comedy *All Fools,* generally acclaimed as his best, which was acted at Blackfriars Theatre in 1599, and was undoubtedly that piece that he had promised to Lady Walsingham he would 'tumble out' for her of 'brainless and passionate fooleries as ever panted in the bosom of the most ridiculous Lover'. Plays were never published until their stage life was well spent, and *All Fools,* published in 1605, had probably been dedicated in manuscript in 1599 as it was later printed: 'To My Long Loved and Honourable Friend, Sir Thomas Walsingham, Knight'.

In 1608, when their little son Thomas was aged eight years, Chapman published his tragedy *The Conspiracy of Charles, Duke of Byron,* and included the young heir in his dedication to Sir Thomas.

To My Honourable and Constant Friend SIR THOMAS WALSINGHAM, KNIGHT, and to My Much-loved from his Birth, the Right Toward and Worthy Gentleman his Son, THOMAS WALSINGHAM, ESQUIRE.

176

Sir, – Though I know you ever stood little affected to these unprofitable rites of Dedication (which disposition in you hath made me hitherto dispense with your right in my other impressions), yet, lest the world may repute it a neglect in me of so ancient and worthy a friend, having heard your approbation of these in their presentment, I could not but prescribe them with your name; and that my affection may extend to your posterity, I have entitled to it, herein, your hope and comfort in your generous son, whom I doubt not that most reverenced mother of manly sciences, to whose instruction your virtuous care commits him, will so profitably initiate in her learned labours, that they will make him flourish in his riper life, over the idle lives of our ignorant gentlemen, and enable him to supply the honourable places of your name; extending your years and his right noble mother's, in the true comforts of his virtues, to the sight of much and most happy progeny; which most affectionately wishing, and dividing these poor dismembered poems betwixt you, I desire to live still in your graceful loves, and ever,

The most assured at your commandments,
GEORGE CHAPMAN

Had Sir Thomas tactfully intimated to George Chapman that he did not desire to receive 'unprofitable rites of Dedication' from him, having been moved by the anguish expressed in the Sonnets of the Rival Poet? Marlowe was, of course, unable to dedicate any works publicly to his Patron, for to associate Shakespeare's works with Walsingham would have attracted unwelcome attention that was far too dangerous. He could only pour out his heart in his sonnets. After *Hero and Leander* there is a marked gap of seven years duration in which Chapman did not dedicate any works to Sir Thomas, whilst remaining in a relationship of warm friendship with the family.

The two *Byron* plays are considered to be Chapman's masterpieces in tragedy, and it is a testimonial to Walsingham's cultivated tastes that of all his dramatic works – seven comedies and seven tragedies, which are fair mixture of dross and gold, – Chapman chose to dedicate his best comedy and his best tragedies to Walsingham, who, we are told, had been heard to express his admiration of the tragedies by *Byron* in their 'presentment', i.e. when he saw them in performance.

The long-standing friendship between Thomas Walsingham and George Chapman tells us something about the Patron, for Chapman has been described as a man 'of most reverend aspect, religious and temperate', [45] renowned for his great learning, one to whom 'the deep search for knowledge' afforded 'a rapture of delight'. [46] Their mutual attraction also tells us something about Marlowe. Chapman had an obvious kinship with intellectual men, as with the learned Ben Jonson, with whom he developed a close friendship and working

177

relationship, even sharing a spell in prison with him in 1605 when their collaborative play *Eastward Hoe* drew the ire of King James for their overt criticism of his Scottish courtiers.

The complex psychological problems that surround the Sonnets of the Rival Poet are, I suggest, clearly perceived for the first time in the triangular relationship high-lighted by the completion of *Hero and Leander.* Walsingham, it must be remembered, was in a peculiarly vulnerable position through his obvious connections with the three men who were present at the Deptford murder only five years earlier. There may have been an element of self-protection in his desire to have *Hero and Leander,* the first dedication of a work by Marlowe to him since the scandal of 1593, now completed by another hand and published as an offering to his bride. Walsingham would have viewed this as a double compliment; to Lady Audrey, and to Marlowe as a mark of admiration for his unfinished poem, which was completed by one who was considered among the greatest poets of his day, and a good friend of Marlowe. This must have appeared to Walsingham as both eminently suitable in the circumstances, and as acceptable to the 'dead' Poet. That, I suggest, is how Walsingham and Chapman viewed the matter.

The Sonnets of the Rival Poet put a different complexion on it.

That both the Patron and the Poet were deeply wounded by the misunderstanding of the motives involved is seen in the Sonnets of Reconciliation – numbers *117, 118, 119* and *120* – that provide the corollary to the fourteen Sonnets of the Rival Poet in which Marlowe finds release for the searing experience of jealousy, anxiety and hurt that this (to him unwarranted) imposition of another's hand on his poetic work wrought in him. He expresses his contrition, after the situation had been explained, most eloquently and movingly.

> What potions have I drunk of siren tears
> Distilled from limbecks foul as hell within,
> Applying fears to hopes, and hopes to fears,
> Still losing when I saw myself to win!
> What wretched errors hath my heart committed
> Whilst it hath thought itself so blessed never!
> How have mine eyes out of their spheres been fitted
> In the distraction of this madding fever!
> O benefit of ill! Now I find true
> That better is by evil still made better,
> That ruin'd love when it is built anew
> Grows fairer than at first, more strong, far greater.
>   So I return rebuk'd to my content,
>   And gain by ills thrice more than I have spent.
>
>   *Sonnet 119*

This sonnet is followed by a very lovely conclusion to this quartet of remorseful and revealing poems.

That you were once unkind befriends me now,
And for that sorrow which I then did feel
Needs must I under my transgression bow,
Unless my nerves were brass or hammered steel.
For if you were by my unkindness shaken
As I by yours, you've pass'd a hell of time,
And I, a tyrant, have no leisure taken
To weigh how once I suffered in your crime.
O that our night of woe might have remembered
My deepest sense, how hard true sorrow hits,
And soon to you, as you to me then tendered
The humble salve which wounded bosoms fits!
But that your trespass now becomes a fee,
Mine ransom yours, and yours must ransom me.

Sonnet 120

The word 'crime' is here referring to a trespass, not something actually criminal; it has been used to fit the rhyme. In the reference to 'as you to me then tendered' is revealed the great generosity with which Walsingham always responded to his Poet's grief, ever giving him swift, warm-hearted consolation. This beautiful sonnet contains a great deal for us to ponder. It gives a marvellous insight into the relationship between the Patron and his Poet. Are there recollections of the tragedy of 1593 in his moving reference to 'our night of woe'? This poem is redolent with the memories of a great deal of sorrow that these two friends have shared.

It is with the completion of Marlowe's *Hero and Leander* by George Chapman for the Patron's wedding that certainty is reached, for here is the very man in the precise context that Shakespearean scholars have been seeking to explain the Sonnets of the Rival Poet. *Sonnet 83* declares the triangular relationship that has taxed scholars in their vain search for just such a situation among Elizabethan poets and patrons in relation to William Shakespeare.

I never saw that you did painting need,
And therefore to your fair no painting set,
I found (or thought I found) you did exceed
The barren tender of a Poet's debt:
And therefore have I slept in your report,
That you yourself, being extant, well might show
How far a modern quill doth come too short,
Speaking of worth, what worth in you doth grow.

179

This silence for my sin you did impute,
Which shall be most my glory, being dumb,
For I impair not beauty, being mute,
When others would give life, and bring a tomb.
　　Therelives more life in one of your fair eyes,
　　Than *both your Poets* can in praise devise.

[My emphasis]　　　　　　　　　　　　Sonnet 83

With the identification of the metaphysical poet, George Chapman, as the Rival Poet who alone perfectly fits this scenario, another ghost long troubling Shakespearean scholars has finally been laid. The triangular relationship between Thomas Walsingham and his two poets, which is so forcibly and poignantly exposed in these sonnets, is the ultimate and, surely, irrefutable confirmation that Thomas Walsingham is the Patron of the *Sonnets*.

The three patrons here identified are each supported by firm evidence. The identification of Thomas Walsingham is confirmed on three counts which fit all the attributes required by the true Patron as depicted in the *Sonnets* once his person has been separated from both the 'lovely Boy', and the young Earl of Southampton whose seventeen sonnets are the formal opening theme of the book.

1.　Walsingham was a gentleman of the requisite social standing and he is known to have regarded his Poet as also a dear friend.

2　.He alone of possible candidates was the known patron of two leading rival poets, Christopher Marlowe and George Chapman, whose joint composition of *Hero and Leander* provides a sufficiently poignant cause for the jealousy expressed in the Sonnets of the Rival Poet.

3.　Walsingham alone of possible candidates can be deemed to have been intimately involved in that 'disgrace' with which the Poet of the Sonnets was tragically afflicted.

These credentials are impeccable.

HERO AND LEANDER
(The End of Marlowe's Part)

By this, Leander, being near the land,
Cast down his weary feet, and felt the sand.
Breathless albeit he were, he rested not
Till to the solitary tower he got;
And knock'd, and call'd: at which celestial noise
The longing heart of Hero much more joys
Than nymphs and shepherds when the timbrel rings,
Or crooked dolphin when the sailor sings.
She stay'd not for her robes, but straight arose,
And, drunk with gladness, to the door she goes;
Where, seeing a naked man, she screech'd for fear,
(Such sights as this to tender maids are rare,)
And ran into the dark herself to hide,
(Rich jewels in the dark are soonest spied).
Unto her was he led, or rather drawn
By those white limbs which sparkled through
                        the lawn.
The nearer that he came, the more she fled,
And, seeking refuge, slipt into her bed;
Whereon Leander sitting, thus began,
Through numbing cold all feeble, faint and wan.
'If not for love, yet, love, for pity-sake,
Me in thy bed and maiden bosom take;
At least vouchsafe these arms some little room,
Who, hoping to embrace thee, cheerly swum:
This head was beat with many a churlish billow,
And therefore let it rest upon thy pillow.'
Herewith affrighted, Hero shrunk away,
And in her lukewarm place Leander lay;
Whose lively heat, like fire from heaven fet,
Would animate gross clay, and higher set
The drooping thoughts of base-declining souls,
Than dreary-Mars-carousing nectar bowls.
His hands he cast upon her like a snare:
She, overcome with shame and sallow fear,
Like chaste Diana when Actaeon spied her,
Being suddenly betray'd, div'd down to hide her;
And, as her silver body downward went,
With both her hands she made the bed a tent,
And in her own mind thought herself secure,
O'er cast with dim and darksome coverture.

And now she lets him whisper in her ear,
Flatter, entreat, promise, protest, and swear:
Yet ever, as he greedily assay'd
To touch those dainties, she the harpy play'd,
And every limb did, as a soldier stout,
Defend the fort, and keep the foeman out;
For though the rising ivory mount he scal'd,
Which is with azure circling lines empal'd,
Much like a globe (a globe may I term this,
By which Love sails to regions full of bliss,)
Yet there with Sisyphus he toil'd in vain,
Till gentle parley did the truce obtain.
Wherein Leander on her quivering breast,
Breathless spoke something, and sigh'd out the rest;
Which so prevail'd, as he with small ado
Enclos'd her in his arms and kissed her too.
And every kiss to her was as a charm,
And to Leander as a fresh alarm,
So that the truce was broke, and she alas,
(Poor silly maiden) at his mercy was.
Love is not full of pity (as men say)
But deaf and cruel, where he means to prey.
Even as a bird, which in our hands we wring,
Forth plungeth, and oft flutters with her wing,
She trembling strove, this strife of hers (like that
Which made the world) another world begat
Of unknown joy. Treason was in her thought.
And cunningly to yield herself she sought.
Seeming not won, yet won she was at length;
In such wars women use but half their strength.
Leander now like Theban Hercules,
Enter'd the orchard of Th'Hesperides,
Whose fruit none rightly can describe but he
That pulls or shakes it from the golden tree.
And now she wish'd this night were never done,
And sigh'd to think upon th' approaching sun;
For much it griev'd her that the bright day-light
Should know the pleasure of this blessed night,
And them, like Mars and Erycine, display
Both in each other's arms chain'd as they lay.
Again, she knew not how to frame her look,
Or speak to him, who in a moment took
That which so long, so charily she kept;
And fain by stealth away she would have crept,

And to some corner secretly have gone,
Leaving Leander in the bed alone.
But as her naked feet were whipping out,
He on the sudden cling'd her so about,
That, mermaid-like, unto the floor she slid;
One half appear'd, the other half was hid.
Thus near the bed she blushing stood upright,
And from her countenance behold ye might
A kind of twilight break, which through the hair,
As from an orient cloud, glimps'd here and there;
And round about the chamber this false morn
Brought forth the day before the day was born.
So Hero's ruddy cheek Hero betray'd,
And her all naked to his sight display'd:
Whence his admiring eyes more pleasure took
Than Dis, on heaps of gold fixing his look.
By this, Apollo's golden harp began
To sound forth music to the ocean;
Which watchful Hesperus no sooner heard,
But he the bright Day-bearing car prepar'd,
And ran before, as harbinger of light,
And with his flaring beams mock'd ugly Night,
Till she, o'ercome with anguish, shame, and rage,
Dang'd down to hell her loathsome carriage. [1]

Here Marlowe's *Hero and Leander* ends. We may assume that it was his arrest at Scadbury on Sunday 20th May 1593 that also arrested his composition and ushered in his tragedy.

This poem, therefore, would have held a special place in his affections as the last work written under his own name Christopher Marlowe.

XIII

THE SONNETS OF EXILE

When in disgrace with Fortune and men's eyes,
I all alone beweep my outcast state,
And trouble deaf heaven with my bootless cries,
And look upon myself and curse my fate,

Sonnet 29

IN THE LIGHT of what the sonnets tell us we can assume that Marlowe took ship from Deptford on 30th May for the Continent on what was clearly to be a long journey, making his way overland, probably through France to Italy, for there is distinct evidence of an Italian influence in the plays from this time onwards. Dr Hotson's invaluable researches, again, have pointed to a likely connection with the court of Duke Orsino, the subject of a later chapter.

The Sonnets of Exile cannot be interpreted in any other way than to accept that this tragic journey was what can only be described as banishment from his home, his country, his friends, and from his beloved Patron to whom he owed his escape, and his very life. These poems form a huge group when extracted from the body of the collection, numbering thirty-six sonnets to which, if we add the four that also speak of his anonymity, we have by far the largest group – forty sonnets which tell their undeniable message of enforced absence from his Patron, to whom these are addressed, who seems at first to be his sole point of contact with his former life, his friends and wonted haunts which he recollects in grief with an evident sense of homesickness. As he journeys the sense of his disgrace and anonymity weighs heavily on him and finds expression in these sonnets.

This group begins with *Sonnet 26,* which declares the Poet's inexpressibly deep gratitude to his Patron, and, as so many of these, takes the form of a verse-letter.

> Lord of my love, to whom in vassalage
> Thy merit hath my duty strongly knit,
> To thee I send this written ambassage
> To witness duty, not to show my wit;
> Duty so great, which wit so poor as mine
> May make seem bare in wanting words to show it,
> But that I hope some good conceit of thine
> In thy soul's thought (all naked) will bestow it;
> Till whatsoever star that guides my moving
> Points on me graciously with fair aspect,

And puts apparel on my tatter'd loving,
To show me worthy of thy sweet respect,
   Then may I dare to boast how I do love thee;
   Till then, not show my head where thou mayst prove me.

Sonnet 26

In the context of this thesis it is not too fanciful to imagine this sonnet as being written on board the ship that was bearing the Poet away on his flight into exile. This is followed by a group of sonnets that describe what is clearly a long journey overland.

Weary with toil, I haste me to my bed,
The dear repose for limbs with travel tired;
But then begins a journey in my head
To work my mind, when body's work expired;
For then my thoughts (from far where I abide)
Intend a zealous pilgrimage to thee,
And keep my drooping eyelids open wide,
Looking on darkness which the blind do see:
Save that my soul's imaginary sight
Presents thy shadow to my sightless view,
Which like a jewel (hung in ghastly night)
Makes black night beauteous, and her old face new.
   Lo thus by day my limbs, by night my mind,
   For thee, and for myself, no quiet find.

Sonnet 27

How heavy do I journey on the way,
When what I seek (my weary travel's end)
Doth teach that ease and that repose to say:
Thus far the miles are measur'd from thy friend.
The beast that bears me, tired with my woe,
Plods dully on, to bear that weight in me,
As if by some instinct the wretch did know
His rider lov'd not speed, being made from thee.
The bloody spur cannot provoke him on,
That sometimes anger thrusts into his hide,
Which heavily he answers with a groan
More sharp to me than spurring to his side;
   For that same groan doth put this in my mind,
   My grief lies onward and my joy behind.

Sonnet 50

When in disgrace with Fortune and men's eyes,
I all alone beweep my outcast state,
And trouble deaf Heaven with my bootless cries,
And look upon myself and curse my fate,
Wishing me like to one more rich in hope,
Featur'd like him, like him with friends possess'd,
Desiring this man's art, and that man's scope,
With what I most enjoy contented least:
Yet in these thoughts myself almost despising,
Haply I think on thee, and then my state,
Like to the lark at break of day arising
From sullen earth, sings hymns at Heaven's gate,
    For thy sweet love remember'd such wealth brings,
    That then I scorn to change my state with kings.

Sonnet 29

When we consider that this is the great Shakespeare envying 'this man's art, and that man's scope', we have to admit the existence of circumstances in his life that engendered this deeply despondent mood. The creative artist, never satisfied with his work and always seeking perfection, speaks in the line: 'With what I most enjoy contented least' – an indication that he was continuing to write plays in exile for London's theatres. If so, there must have been someone who was looking after his works and bringing them to the boards. The Italianate influence in the mature plays that now flowed from his pen is strikingly apparent and has been noted by all critics of the Shakespeare canon of the period from 1594 to the early 1600's.

Evidence of communication through messengers that kept him in touch with his Patron is seen in *Sonnet 44* and *Sonnet 45*, which are a true pair.

If the dull substance of my flesh were thought,
Injurious distance should not stop my way,
For then, despite of space, I would be brought
From limits far remote where thou dost stay.
No matter then although my foot did stand
Upon the farthest earth remov'd from thee,
For nimble thought can jump both sea and land
As soon as think the place where he would be.
But ah, thought kills me that I am not thought,
To leap large lengths of miles when thou art gone,
But that so much of earth and water wrought,
I must attend time's leisure with my moan,
    Receiving nought by elements so slow,
    But heavy tears, badges of either's woe.

Sonnet 44

There is a witty playing on the four elements of earth, water, fire and air, in true Renaissance style, but there can be no doubt that real messengers are also being referred to, probably the agents of Walsingham.

> The other two, slight air, and purging fire,
> Are both with thee wherever I abide,
> The first my thought, the other my desire,
> These present absent with swift motion slide;
> For when these quicker elements are gone
> In tender embassy of love to thee,
> My life, being made of four, with two alone
> Sinks down to death, oppress'd with melancholy,
> Until life's composition be recured,
> By those swift messengers return'd from thee,
> Who even but now come back assured
> Of thy fair health, recounting it to me.
>   This told, I joy; but then no longer glad,
>   I send them back again and straight grow sad.

Sonnet 45

The next sonnet-pair show how sadly he misses his friends, and express a touching sense of homesickness. The words 'love' and 'lovers' and the emotive expression of 'desire' in these poems spoken as between men are the Renaissance concept of Platonic relationships of dearest friendship. This aspect of the Renaissance is discussed in some detail in Chapter 14

His reference to 'precious friends hid in death's dateless night' cannot be read literally. It is not his friends who have died; it is the Poet himself who is 'dead' to the world he had known, where he can no longer reveal himself.

> When to the sessions of sweet silent thought,
> I summon up remembrance of things past
> I sigh the lack of many a thing I sought,
> And with old woes new wail my dear times' waste:
> Then can I drown an eye (unus'd to flow)
> For precious friends hid in death's dateless night,
> And weep afresh love's long-since cancell'd woe,
> And moan th' expense of many a vanish'd sight.
> Then can I grieve at grievances foregone,
> And heavily from woe to woe tell o'er
> The sad account of fore-bemoaned moan,
> Which I new pay as if not paid before.
>   But if the while I think on thee (dear friend)
>   All losses are restor'd, and sorrows end.

Sonnet 30

Thy bosom is endeared with all hearts,
Which I by lacking have supposed dead,
And there reigns Love and all Love's loving parts,
And all those friends which I thought buried.
How many a holy and obsequious tear
Hath dear religious love stol'n from mine eye,
As interest of the dead, which now appear
But things remov'd that hidden in thee lie.
Thou art the grave where buried love doth live,
Hung with the trophies of my lovers gone,
Who all their parts of me to thee did give:
That due of many, now is thine alone.
  Their images I lov'd, I view in thee,
  And thou (all they) hast all the all of me.

Sonnet 31

The implications are that when this poem was written the fugitive Marlowe was in contact solely with Walsingham, through whom he heard news of his friends. This suggests that it was during an early period of strictly observed concealment when the anguish of this was still fresh with him.

In *Sonnet 33* the Poet tells us that he had once enjoyed considerable fame – 'triumphant splendour' had graced his brow with the plaudits of his contemporaries, but this is now lost, obscured by some dark cloud of fate that has blotted out his brief sun of glory. This man, therefore, is no nonentity. The imagery of mountains and 'pale streams' in this lovely sonnet suggest that he may have written it when travelling through the Alps on his way to Italy, which is the itinerary his exile suggests.

Full many a glorious morning have I seen,
Flatter the mountain-tops with sovereign eye,
Kissing with golden face the meadows green,
Gilding pale streams with heavenly alchemy;
Anon permit the basest clouds to ride
With ugly rack on his celestial face,
And from the forlorn world his visage hide,
Stealing unseen to west with this disgrace.
Even so my sun one early morn did shine
With all triumphant splendour on my brow;
But out alack, he was but one hour mine,
The region cloud hath mask'd him from me now.
  Yet him for this, my love no whit disdaineth:
  Suns of the world may stain, when heaven's sun staineth.

Sonnet 33

Sonnet 36 speaks of enforced separation and disgrace – 'those blots' on his reputation which he must bear. There is also a hint that the Patron is in some way implicated, and it would be dangerous for the Poet to acknowledge him publicly for this would besmirch his good name also.

Let me confess that we two must be twain,
Although our undivided loves are one,
So shall those blots that do with me remain,
Without thy help, by me be borne alone.
In our two loves there is but one respect,
Though in our lives a separable spite,
Which though it alter not love's sole effect,
Yet doth it steal sweet hours from love's delight.
I may not ever more acknowledge thee,
Lest my bewailed guilt should do thee shame,
Nor thou with public kindness honour me,
Unless thou take that honour from thy name.
    But do not so: I love thee in such sort,
    As thou being mine, mine is thy good report.

Sonnet 36

Sonnet 71 is from the small group about the Poet's self-inflicted anonymity, which obviously relates also to his life in exile.

No longer mourn for me when I am dead,
Than you shall hear the surly sullen bell
Give warning to the world that I am fled
From this vile world with vilest worms to dwell;
Nay, if you read this line, remember not
The hand that writ it, for I love you so,
That I in your sweet thoughts would be forgot,
If thinking on me then should make you woe.
O if (I say) you look upon this verse,
When I (perhaps) compounded am with clay,
Do not so much as my poor name rehearse,
But let your love even with my life decay,
    Lest the wise world should look into your moan,
    And mock you with me after I am gone.

Sonnet 71

If these sonnets are indeed the autobiographical poems of the Poet who wrote them, poems which have been pronounced 'astonishing' because of the 'impression they make of naked autobiographical confession'; which 'Shakespeare wrote out of his own life, in his own person'; and which 'can be read biographically despite all the difficulties and confusions inherent in such an approach': then it is remarkable that they compellingly underline the validity of the hypothesis that Shakespeare is none other than the pseudonymous poet-dramatist, Christopher Marlowe, whose tragic story they tell. The handful of eleven Sonnets of Exile presented already corroborates this most movingly.

It is a historical fact that Marlowe was struck down by cruel Fate when in the glory of his fame, was indicted of 'Atheism' and disgraced, was arrested and granted bail, and was apparently murdered in a highly suspect incident with distinct implications that his patron, Thomas Walsingham, was somehow involved, and the weapon used was 'a wretch's knife' *(Sonnet 74)*. The hypothesis then follows that his death was faked, and that he fled into exile and anonymity, in which his true Friend and Patron succoured him, to whom he is bound in deepest gratitude. All this is testified in the Sonnets of Exile, not vaguely, but quite precisely.

No such tragic circumstances of exile and disgrace ever afflicted William Shakespeare, yet Dr Hotson, not having the right Poet and Patron in his sights, has nevertheless made another remarkable discovery that relates to this period of grief. Following his Sherlock Holmesian instinct he has once again uncovered gold. He audaciously proposes that the most famous miniature that Nicholas Hilliard ever painted, of the unnamed *Young Man among Roses,* is a portrait of Shakespeare's patron, whom he identifies as 'Mr.W.H.' *alias* Will Hatcliffe.[1] His reasoning in support of the identification of the subject of the Hilliard portrait is drawn from his expert reading of the symbolic language of this exquisite *impresa* portrait, which he has interpreted in marvellous detail to show that the figure, the pose, the dress, the setting are no mere ornament or artistic design, but that every detail depicted is giving us the one message, repeated over and over again, that the *Young Man among Roses* represents the embodiment of *True Friendship* affirming that *he will never desert his friend in his adversity.*

Dr Hotson has amassed contemporary evidence to demonstrate that the Young Man in the portrait is not a lover sighing for his lady, as might be imagined from his languishing, romantic pose in pensive mood, for if that were the case he would be presented in déshabille, whereas this young man is impeccably dressed, denoting that he is a Friend, and above all a *True and Constant Friend.*

Believing that 'Mr.W.H.' was the one and only patron addressed in the *Sonnets,* whose schizophrenic personality Hotson perforce accepts – as have all critics of the *Sonnets* hitherto – he nevertheless recognizes that the recurring theme of the poems is the affirmation of *Truest Friendship* between Poet and Patron, and that some nameless troubles beset Shakespeare at some time in which his True Friend (Mr.W.H.' *alias* Will Hatcliffe) remained faithful to his sonneteer. For Dr Hotson the emblematic theme of *Sonnet 105* ('Fair, kind and true is all my argument') is seen as confirmation that the portrait of a *Young Man among Roses* depicts William Hatcliffe as the True Friend, who was once praised by his sonneteer as 'Fair, kind and true'. But this, as has been revealed, was *not* the real character of the spoilt young Prince of Purpoole, who was the Poet's first patron, 'Mr.W.H.' – the beautiful mirage used to conceal the identity of the true Patron, Thomas Walsingham.

Once we have disentangled the strands and have in our view the three separate men addressed in these poems, a different picture emerges. Will Hatcliffe's dubious character makes him no longer eligible for the portrait of the True Friend, nor does the weight of grief expressed in the Sonnets of Exile conceivably reflect the relationship of Hatcliffe and his sonneteer. Hilliard's exquisite portrait miniature is, however, strangely evocative of the *real* sonnet-story here told, and no picture could more perfectly reflect the relationship of the afflicted Poet and his true Patron than Hilliard's little masterpiece does. When its pictorial symbolism is deciphered to disclose its full meaning, this beautiful portrait captures the very essence of the sonnets themselves.

We will accordingly follow our trusty guide Dr Hotson, once more as he unravels the mysteries of the symbolic language of the *impresa* for us as understood in the Renaissance. Quoting from William Camden, the antiquary and teacher of Ben Jonson at Westminster School, an expert on this subject:

'An Impress (as the Italians call it) is a device in picture with his motto, or word, borne by noble and learned personages, to notify some particular conceit of their own. There is required in an Impress (that we may reduce them to a few heads) a correspondency of the picture, which is as the body, and the motto, which as the soul giveth it life. That is, the body must be of fair representation, and the word in some different language, witty [i.e. full of meaning] short, and answerable thereunto; neither too obscure, not too plain, and most commended when it is an hemistich, or parcel of a verse.' [2]

All these conditions Hilliard's miniature fulfills to perfection (See Frontis). In every *impresa* we are challenged 'to find correspondency of the picture with the motto, which gives it life and notifies some particular conceit of the sitter who chose it, and is also likely to have chosen the costume and its colours, the essential pose, and the accessories too – although the limner may certainly have contributed suggestions', Dr Hotson informs us. [3]

Studying the body language of the *Young Man among Roses* there is a great deal that is significant, which would immediately be recognized as revealing him to be 'The Picture of True-loving Friendship'. Firstly, he is shown with his hand on his heart, as understood in classical, Renaissance allegory;

'The Romaines . . Shadowed [Friendship] in the shape of a young man whose head was bared . . putting his finger to his harte.' [4]

Many examples are presented by Hotson to confirm this. Hence bare-headed with hand on heart conveys the message that the young man is a True Friend. This is further emphasised by the colours chosen for his costume: White for his ruff, his cuffs, his stockings, and his pumps, and his doublet is white satin with black hatching; Black for his short cloak, nonchalantly slung over his left shoulder.

'On the picture of sincere white Friendship in the symbols-book are painted the words MORS ET VITA, Death and Life: meaning that "a perfect friend . . is for ever inseparable: for however great the change of fortune, whether for better or for worse, he is glad to live and die for the sake of a true love".' [5]

'White, as everyone knows', writes Hotson, 'is the colour of Truth or Faith; and Black is Constancy, for black will take no other hue: "Galen . . attributeth . . to the blacke constancie."' [6]

White and Black were the personal colours of Queen Elizabeth. They signify 'True Friendship Eternal'. Lyly in his *Endymion* writes: 'the love of men to women is a thing common and of course: the friendship of man to man infinite immortal.' [7]. He is referring to the Renaissance ideal of Platonic friendship which imbues the *Sonnets* with their ardour for it was extolled as the highest and deepest relationship to which man could aspire, as in the beautiful *Sonnet 116* describing this state as 'the marriage of true minds'. This Renaissance concept is superbly portrayed in Hilliard's miniature.

The tree on which the Young Man leans is not merely 'a tree', it also conveys its message symbolising Constancy, Steadfastness, being rooted and immovable. From Bodenham's *Politeuphuia* (1587) Hotson quotes:

'The greatest treasure in adversitie, is the truth of a friend immoveable.' [8]

And adversity is signified by the rose-briers in which the Young Man is standing, which are blooming with *white roses*. These are not just a lovely decoration to enhance the picture's beauty, they convey a very important message, declaring that 'he is not one "at need that leaves a man sticking in the briers", or that "hath left his friend in the briers".' [9] Also 'the White Rose was the type of Love and Faith' in heraldry. [10]

To return to the figure of the Young Man standing with *his legs crossed.* Even this pose has significance. This, after much searching, Dr Hotson discovered as depicting the god Apollo, who is, significantly, the god of True Friendship, and in this pose he is presented in his identity as *Apollo Loxias,* the 'wry-legged god' of the Delphic oracles: 'in images of Delphic Apollo Orthos, the *crossing of his leg* was a recognised symbol of his oblique or "riddling" oracles.' [11]

The symbolism of Apollo has further meaning, revealed by Littleton: 'Apollo was called *Loxias;* who in his replies was loxos, that is *oblique,* and speaking ambiguously, so that he may be taken divers ways.' [12]. In other words, we have here the connotation of things hidden, and not obviously told – 'of the truth which "Apollo hath clouded in hid sense" or "wrapp'd up in cross doubtful terms".' [13]

This is precisely what we see presented in *Sonnet 31* written by the Poet to his Patron with this concept of him as *Apollo Loxias* in mind, the god of True Friendship, who also keeps things 'clouded in hid sense'.

> As interest of the dead, which now appear
> But things remov'd *that hidden in thee lie.*

Searching yet deeper, the indefatigable Dr Hotson found what he was seeking as absolute corroboration in Principio Fabricii's six books of allusion, devices and emblems on the life, works and actions of the late Pope Gregory XIII – he who reformed our calendar, which was in use on the Continent but left England behind ten days adrift for another century. At last, with a thrill of discovery, Hotson's search was rewarded, and he writes: 'on its page 112 I found Bonifazio's engraving of Apollo's temple: suppliants kneeling before the god's oracular cortina, while in the background on a pedestal is great Apollo radiant in glory, standing *with his legs crossed.*' [14.]

Greek coins also show Apollo in this stance. Hence the association with Apollo is strong. The Young Man's circular great ruff, like a white wheel, further accentuates the identification with the Sun-god, for 'the white of his ruff, of his long stockings, and his pumps – on his right, the East – is set against the black of his short cloak – on his left, the West – similarly to denote Phoebus: his white figure emerging from the black like the God of Day from Night.' [15]

These are the colours of Apollo, the white Swan and the black Raven (or Crow) both being sacred to Phoebus-Apollo:

> The snow-white Swan betokens lightsome Day,
> The coal-black Crow, of darky Night is sign.
> R. Tofte: *Laura* (1597) [16]

Yet one further emblematic identification with the god Apollo, who was also the *god of the Dance,* is the depiction of the Young Man in the costume worn for dancing, the short doublet, long silk stockings and light pumps, and a short cloak. The Elizabethans not infrequently affected to have themselves painted as the personification of a Greek god, redolent with all the symbolism of the deity they had chosen. Every detail and nuance in this miniature *impresa* portrait is declaring that he is presented as the *god of Friendship,* Apollo, for the cumulative evidence from Renaissance literary sources assembled by Hotson makes the identification of the sitter as a personification of Apollo irresistible, Hotson draws attention to the intentional elongation of the sitter's legs (misinterpreted by some critics as Hilliard's artistic device to fill the enlarged oval of his frame) quoting from Algarotti:

'The legs and thighs of the Apollo Belvedere, somewhat longer than just proportion would allow, contribute not a little to give him that light grace *(sveltezza)* and agility which suit so well with the comely motion *(movenza)* of that God.' [17.]

To my mind this clinches the identification.

Finally, we come to the most significant message, the soul of the *impresa* as Camden expressed it, which is the motto. Here it is appropriately in a different language, Latin:

'Dat poenas laudata fides' [18]

This is a hemistich or half-line of verse from a famous speech in Lucan's *De Bello Civili VIII*, of which Marlowe had translated the First Book whilst still at Cambridge, so this epic work was very familiar to him.

Dr Hotson explains the significance of this:

'It recalls a classical and most extreme test of True Friendship. Put directly, it is this: When your father's great benefactor and faithful friend comes to you in defeat, *hunted with overwhelming power by his deadly enemy,* what do you do? Loyally to succour and support him will certainly get you the revenge of his conqueror. The fidelity which one of your advisers recommends is all very fine, but as a coward and a traitor you prefer to follow the worldly-wise counsel of the other. He tells you not to put your neck in the noose for friendship, but to join cruel Fortune in crushing your friend: turn on him, murder him, and claim the reward. The grim story is the Fall of great Pompey.' [19.]

(The italics are mine, not Dr Hotson's).

The speech from which the hemistich is taken is that spoken by the eunuch, Pothinus, who

'with base breath
Durst thus presume to counsel Pompey's death' [20]

'Dat poenas laudata fides, dum sustinet' inquit
'Quos fortuna premit?' [21]

which Dr Hotson renders:

'He said, "*We all praise fidelity; but the true friend pays the penalty* when he supports those whom Fortune crushes".' [22]

In other words, the *Young Man among Roses* identifies himself by his motto as one who has *chosen to pay the penalty for aiding his friend,* who is 'hunted with overwhelming power by his enemy', rather than to follow the worldly-wise advice of such men as Pothinus, who 'with base breath' had counselled King Ptolemy to *murder his friend.* Is the implication that there had been some who *did* counsel Walsingham to murder Marlowe to get rid of him before the Star Chamber could get him into its power irrevocably? The choice of this hemistich from Lucan as his motto for this *impresa* portrait may now be seen as extraordinarily significant, for the circumstances that Lucan describes are remarkably similar to the tragedy of Marlowe and the dilemma that Walsingham was faced with. His motto declares that he *chose to aid his friend, and to bear the risks involved.* He also bore the censure that would have been whispered by those who suspected that he *had* murdered his friend, using as his ready instruments the three men involved, his own servant Frizer, and his secret agents Poley and Skeres. There are some scholars today who still believe that Walsingham was responsible for organising Marlowe's murder, while for Dr Tannenbaum it was Raleigh who was under suspicion, although Walsingham's involvement is also assumed. [23]

The sonnets tell us over and over again that Walsingham was no King Ptolemy who took Pothinus' advice and murdered his friend, great Pompey. He was a True Friend in adversity, and every detail in this *impresa* portrait declares the *same message* that we read in the sonnets, that his Patron was the personification of True Friendship, Fidelity, Constancy. They speak of his God-like Love and his steadfastness in succouring his Friend in his adversity, and as *Apollo Loxias* he contains the hidden truth, which only the initiated understand.

Is there any other Elizabethan man known to us who fits this *impresa* portrait with such absolute perfection, to whom this motto would equally apply? It must be admitted that all this fits Thomas Walsingham as Marlowe's Patron in a manner that is almost uncanny in its beautiful precision. Uncanny, that is, until we remember that this is Renaissance England, and the Elizabethans lived dangerously, and made an art of doing so.

It is now necessary to reinterpret Hotson's allusion to Lucan's *De Bello Civili VIII* to show how it precisely fits the identification of both Walsingham and Marlowe.

The story of Pompey is inapplicable to the man in the portrait representing the Faithful Friend, personified as the god Apollo, for it is Pompey who is the fugitive, who was *betrayed* by Ptolemy.

> 'Who will think himself beholden to one that is distressed? and when doth not fortune chaunge friendship? Ptoleme, unthankful Ptolome . . how false was this world to Pompey, who had not now earth enough for his sepulture, to whom before the earth was too little for his conquests: but rare is the bird whose feathers do not moult, and happie is that man whose glorie doth not eclipse.'
> William Fulbecke: *Historicall Collections of the continuall factions, tumultes and massacres of the Romans and Italians.*

This applies precisely to the fate of Marlowe, but in no way does it apply either to William Shakespeare of Stratford-upon-Avon, or to Master William Hatcliffe. Dr Hotson tries to make it applicable to Hatcliffe because his armorial crest was a Lion holding Pompey's Sword, thus associating Hatcliffe with the fugitive Pompey, who cannot at the same time be identified with the god Apollo. This is to stand his argument on its head, and it is not surprising that scholars have not accepted this tenuous hypothesis but have rejected it as one of Hotson's whims. The remarkable thing is that the portrait fits the Walsingham-Marlowe situation perfectly in every detail!

This interpretation of the famous Hilliard miniature of the unnamed *Young Man among Roses* as a portrait of the Patron of the *Sonnets* will, I believe, find eventual wide acceptance. Confirming this identification, I have built on what Dr Hotson has researched and proposed; but narrowly missed his mark by arguing that Hatcliffe is the subject of this *impresa* portrait because his armorial crest is Pompey's Lion – a well known heraldic symbol. But the *sitter* in the portrait does *not represent* Pompey, who is *identifiable in this context as the fugitive*, Marlowe. The sitter personifying Apollo is the Patron, who saved Pompey (Marlowe) and bore the burden, as the hemistich from Lucan declares: *Dat poenas laudata fides* (We all praise fidelity but the true friend pays the penalty). The hemistich precisely clinches it for Walsingham as the true Friend.

In taking Hotson's brilliant premise, and adjusting the sights, the true picture is revealed. No portrait of Thomas Walsingham is known, but if one were to be discovered I would take a bet on it that he would resemble the *Young Man among Roses* to a hair, that rich brown, curling hair, like 'buds of marjoram' *(Sonnet 99)*, for this *impresa* portrait represents the very essence of such a man as is portrayed in the sonnets, – not the 'lovely Boy', but the Patron who was faithful to his friend, the fugitive Poet (Pompey) for whom this delightful portrait was painted bearing its heart-warming message of solace and support. The dating given tentatively by Roy Strong to this portrait is *circa* 1587 to 1588, but such precise pinpointing of the years must be hypothetical at best. [24] If this is Thomas Walsingham – and who else could he conceivably be without destroying its entire *impresa* structure in which each detail was carefully devised by the unnamed sitter and exquisitely limned by Hilliard for his client? – then the painting could not date earlier than 1593.

With what joy this delightful portrait was received by the exiled Poet when it was sent to him as the token of his Patron's faithfulness, we read in the two sonnets which follow the sonnet-pair already presented above, *Sonnet 44* and *Sonnet 45*, that tell of 'swift messengers' bringing news of his Patron's health to the exiled Poet. This placement suggests that one of these messengers also brought him the portrait that is the subject of the next two sonnets.

> Mine eye and heart are at a mortal war
> How to divide the conquest of thy sight;
> Mine eye, my heart thy picture's sight would bar,

My heart, mine eye the freedom of that right;
My heart doth plead that thou in him dost lie,
(A closet never pierc'd with crystal eyes),
But the defendant doth that plea deny,
And says in him thy fair appearance lies.
To 'cide this title is empannelled
A quest of thoughts, all tenants to the heart,
And by their verdict is determined
The clear eye's moiety, and the dear heart's part,
   As thus: mine eye's due is thine outward part,
   And my heart's right, thine inward love of heart.

Sonnet 46

Betwixt mine eye and heart a league is took,
And each doth good turns now unto the other;
When that mine eye is famish'd for a look,
Or heart in love with sighs himself doth smother,
With my love's picture then my eye doth feast,
And to the painted banquet bids my heart.
Another time mine eye is my heart's guest,
And in his thoughts of love doth share a part.
So either by thy picture or my love,
Thyself away, art present still with me,
For thou no farther than my thoughts canst move,
And I am still with them, and they with thee;
   Or if they sleep, thy picture in my sight
   Awakes my heart to heart's and eye's delight.

Sonnet 47

This charming tribute to his Patron matches in subtle legal word-play the intricacy of the allusive pictorial language of the *impresa,* which his eye and heart must have dwelt on long in deciphering, assimilating and appreciating every emblematic nuance to his great joy and contentment, taking infinite comfort from this beautiful pictorial presentation and its heart-warming message. The fact that his gratitude for this wonderful message is couched in legal language is not to be construed as evidence that the Patron was the Grayan law student Will Hatcliffe, for all well-educated gentlemen had a good grasp of the law and its legal terminology. Thomas Walsingham was a member of the Middle Temple, and Marlowe's father, who loved to dabble in legal affairs, would have understood the terms used in these sonnets although he was only a shoemaker – but a literate one, whose interest seems to have been more in legal affairs than in his cobbler's shop!

Hilliard's miniature is justly famous for its beauty, but we can now see how much we have been missing in not being able to read its intricate emblematic messages. Significantly, Dr Hotson comments, 'since this is a "heroical device", the motto must "notify some particular conceit" (of the sitter) beyond the general instruction of "True-loving Friendship" as an emblem. This "conceit" should be a personal allusion "to be understood by some but not by all": a kind of signature.' [25]

All this the portrait and its motto fulfil to perfection when applied to Thomas Walsingham as the Patron of the *Sonnets* in the context of this thesis – for the *un*written part of the hemistich – the *hidden message* – declares its secret consolation that *'he supports those whom Fortune crushes'* which precisely fits the circumstances appertaining to Marlowe and Walsingham.

Out of the searing experience of his tragic downfall Marlowe wrote to his Patron in words that sum it all up in his *Sonnet 110* – and we should not be misled by his use of theatrical imagery, which was widely used by people in all walks of life. And Marlowe was a dramatist and his Patron was a lover of the drama.

> Alas, 'tis true, I have gone here and there,
> And made myself a motley to the view,
> Gor'd mine own thoughts, sold cheap what is most dear,
> Made old offences of affections new.
> Most true it is, that I have look'd on truth
> Askance and strangely: but by all above,
> These blenches gave my heart another youth,
> And worse essays prov'd thee my best of love.
> Now all is done, have what shall have no end;
> Mine appetite I never more will grind
> On newer proof to try an older friend,
> *A God in love,* to whom I am confin'd.
> > Then give me welcome, next my heaven the best,
> > Even to thy pure and most, most loving breast.

[My emphasis]   *Sonnet 110*

If ever woeful circumstances of human error – enmeshed in the evil forces of bigotry and repressive authoritarian power as the setting of this tragedy – and the minds and temperaments of a great poet and his cultured patron accorded to fit the painter's hand to inspire an emblematic portrait of singular beauty, this is it. The *Young Man among Roses* perfectly epitomizes the true Friend and noble Patron, Thomas Walsingham, who did not leave his hunted and persecuted friend, the Poet, 'sticking in the briers', but remained faithful, to shine upon him in his adversity like the Sun-god Apollo, the god of True Friendship – 'A God in love', indeed. In Walsingham, Marlowe found his ideal friend and soulmate, and the *Sonnets* truly are his monument.

198

XIV

POET, 'PRINCE' AND PATRON

THE RELATIONSHIP between the Poet of the Sonnets and his Patron has been bedevilled from the first by the mistaken identification of 'Mr.W.H.' as the sole patron – 'the onlie begetter' – who was both 'lascivious Youth' and noble Friend rolled into one. It is essential to reassess these important relationships for an understanding of the Poet, particularly in so far as the question of his sexuality is concerned, which is here subjected to scrutiny.

Despite the fact that this sonnet-sequence is dedicated to a 'Mr.W.H.', and both his 'Prince' and his Patron are male recipients of the greater part of these sonnets, the one form of love they do *not* celebrate is homosexual love. This will surprise some, but it is demonstrable. The sexual love of the *Sonnets* is heterosexual throughout. Any other reading derives from the reader, not from the Poet, *who must be judged essentially as an Elizabethan.*

The circle to which Marlowe belonged was steeped in the Platonic concept which Renaissance culture espoused with enthusiasm – that the highest form of human love is between men in a Platonic relationship. Chastity is extolled as the most admired virtue in all the plays and poems of Marlowe and Shakespeare, and this is what is strongly reflected in these autobiographical sonnets, which were written in an age which was not besotted with sex as is our modern age, in which sexual incontinence is divested of any moral implications.

A modern man addressed in the terms used to the 'Prince' or the Patron would feel decidedly embarrassed, and immediately assume that he was being solicited. But the Elizabethan man viewed this without inhibition, and accepted it as a first rate compliment. He felt secure in his manhood and his male sexuality, though he wore a lace ruff, a richly embroidered doublet, and his legs were elegantly encased in long stockings, with a ring in his ear, gold chains and ostentatious jewellery – but, a cod-piece and a sword at his belt! He studied to move gracefully and to excel in dancing, doing balletic leaps in the galliard when the men often performed solos, and displaying both his masculine strength and his courtly grace and courtesy when he lifted his lady high in La Volta.

To-day, boys who would secretly love to learn ballet dancing shrug their shoulders and deny themselves fulfilment in this virile art, afraid to be called 'effeminate' and become the object of jeers and teasing by their peers. In many ways the Elizabethan age was less inhibited, more natural and robust in its attitude. Homosexuality was a capital offence under the Tudors. Though seldom prosecuted, it would certainly have to be practised in secrecy. Marlowe demonstrably did not commend it, as quotations from his works clearly show. Chastity was a virtue he ardently extolled, as did Shakespeare. His sincerity is not in doubt, for he hated hypocrisy.

Henry VIII, in a fit of reformatory zeal, had unwisely legislated to abrogate the long established, officially licensed brothels, which were previously under the protection of the law and had regularly been inspected in the interest of hygiene and the prevention of the spread of venereal diseases. The district in which these licensed brothels were formerly located was the Liberty of Southwark. Here the theatres and Paris Garden, the home of bear-baiting, were situated, for the liberties were outside the jurisdiction of the strongly Puritan City Fathers. Southwark lay in the See of the Bishop of Winchester, and his association with the brothels had long been delightedly seized upon as a popular subject for lampoon, the prostitutes being dubbed 'Winchester geese'. Elizabethan bawdry was the rumbustious expression of the vitality of that age. We know that Marlowe came from a home in which bawdy tales were relished – his father was a great purveyor of such – and the inns and taverns of Canterbury, as of London, were the haunts of Doll Tearsheet and her sisterhood. The very language of the Elizabethans is uninhibited in its extraordinarily, rich vocabulary of oaths and swear words, used with ribald enjoyment from Queen Elizabeth down, but this was all heterosexual jesting.

The Elizabethan love of ribaldry was in diametrical contrast to the strict etiquette of decorum, the conventional rules of manners that governed all polite society. Ribaldry and decorum exemplify the rich diversity of this period. The prevailing tension of opposites created the fertile soil from which sprang the Elizabethan drama in all its vitality and sparkling wit, that we find most highly developed in the mature Shakespearean plays, for the man who conceived them bestrode this Elizabethan world, from the simple cobbler's home, in which we know ribaldry thrived, to the Court where decorum was *de riguer,* at least on the surface. All well brought up children had the code known as decorum implanted by exhortation and repetition *ad nauseum* to mould them in the image of cultured society so that they would grow up to succeed at Court and amongst the upper classes on whom so many depended for patronage. I suspect that part of Marlowe's charm that endeared him to the aristocracy who welcomed him into their circle lay in the naturalness with which he broke decorum with his wit and ribald humour, as well as for the intellectual quality of his 'aspiring mind'. Did not Michael Drayton call him 'neat Marlowe', meaning one who is close to nature, natural, possessing unaffected charm.

A particular difficulty for the modern mind is our ignorance about the role that patronage played in Elizabethan society. Patronage was the mainstay of the Elizabethan poet, writer and artist, and those who did not find permanent patronage fared badly, living from hand to mouth, or tied to financial dependence on a theatrical company who exploited the dramatist – a situation that Greene so bitterly railed against. In the case of Marlowe, his expressions of gratitude and praise for his Patron are coloured with an intensity and depth of feeling far beyond the general, which springs from the well of his tremendous debt of love and gratitude owed to Walsingham, and his consequent dependence on him at an unusual level. The circumstances were unique, and there is nothing with which we can compare the *Sonnets* in the whole of Elizabethan literature for this very reason.

These poems are imbued through and through with what we recognise as Marlowe's love of beauty, and that characteristic, passionate sensibility which is present in all his plays and poetry, as has been noted by one of his most percipient critics, A.W. Ward:

> 'The element in which as a poet he lived was passion: and it was he who first inspired with true poetic passion the form of literature to which his chief efforts were consecrated. For with few and faint exceptions this element had hitherto been strange to English tragedy . . . After Marlowe had written, the days of cold horrors and soulless declarations had alike been left behind; the stage was peopled with living men and women, full of hatred and love, desire and remorse, of aspiration and despair, whose language was the confession of their souls.' [1]

Thus from his early writings Marlowe emerges as a man of a passionately responsive nature capable of deep feelings – or else how could he so eloquently have expressed them? – and we begin to discern the Poet of the *Sonnets* in this young man of genius who created English tragedy in its truest sense. C.L. Barber's apt portrait of the Poet drawn from his superb *Essay on the Sonnets* reveals a man in whom Christopher Marlowe's features are readily recognizable: his is a 'complex, resonant personality which, for most purposes in life, is over-responsive, over-eager'.

> 'His fluidity, his almost unbearable openness to desire and to life, are described in *109* in the course of a moving plea:
>
> > Never believe, though in my nature reign'd
> > All frailties that besiege all kinds of blood,
> > That it could so preposterously be stain'd
> > To leave for nothing all thy sum of good.
>
> The sort of knowledge of the heart and its turnings which finds expression in the plays appears in these sonnets with a special if limited intensity – the intensity involved in seeing, in one's single life, the broken lines made by Eros.' [2]

In considering the complex personality of the Poet of the Sonnets, one aspect of his nature emerges clearly – Love and Beauty are of vital importance to him. One might say that he was in love with Beauty. Nothing moved him more deeply and passionately than beauty perceived in people, in nature, in things living or inanimate, in jewellery, in colours and perfumes, in flowers, in music – eagerly communicated to his senses in sight, sound, smell, touch and taste. Beauty was the 'Mother of the Muses' to Marlowe from his beginnings, the very source of his poetic inspiration.

Love, no less than Beauty, was the shrine at which he worshipped. The *Sonnets* are essentially a celebration of Love in its various forms united with Beauty. This is symbolized in their arrangement and form of presentation, culminating in his passionate love for the Dark Lady and the final comment of two sonnets presenting the little Love-God discovered innocently asleep, who, once awakened, can cause havoc in human lives. In essence, the *Sonnets* have one great dual themes, Love and Beauty, Beauty and Love. In this union his poetry is conceived in Beauty, brought to birth in Beauty: it is the Platonic concept expounded by Socrates in the famous Dialogue of the *Symposium*.

The *Sonnets* present the Poet's experiences of Love: faithless love that is not true love, but wounds the heart; physical, sexual love, in which his dark mistress is the incarnation of his passionate desire for a consummation and union with Beauty, which he can never find with her for she is sinful and impure, and his sexual desire for her torments him because it is at war with his yearning for perfection; and, at the other end of the see-saw, is the ideal of pure love between true friends whose hearts and souls are one, the Renaissance ideal of Platonic Love extolled by Plato as the highest form of human love – that 'marriage of true minds' symbolized in his relationship with the Patron, the faithful friend who did not leave him 'sticking in the briers' but succoured him in his hour of direst need.

The beautiful and faithless 'Prince' Will, whose disturbing presence weaves in and out of the Poet's love-life, is a symbol of lascivious, selfish love, a kind of Narcissist image, incapable of giving the *true love* of friendship. His glamorous person proved utterly beguiling to the Poet's mistress, and this rivalry in his love-affair caused him much anguish. Yet he forgives his friend's trespass with a touching magnanimity because his beauty and youth move the Poet, and he cannot bear to castigate him too severely. His large capacity for human understanding and his own humility are aspects of his nature that infuse the *Sonnets* with their rare quality.

As C.L. Barber has noted, despite the Poet's deep sense of heartfelt loss, (in addressing Will Hatcliffe's betrayal) he does not 'turn injury into anger. Shakespeare turns injury into poetry'. [3] This is wonderfully expressed in *Sonnet 40*:

> Take all my loves, my love, yea take them all:

In this witty rationalization of his injury he finds solace, bringing a salve to his wounds through his art. His sensitivity and acute perception of the heart enables him to comprehend human frailty with a generosity that few of us have the objectivity to do when hurt; qualities that made him such a marvellous dramatist. Finally disappointed in his 'Prince', who showed himself unworthy and incapable of that 'true love' that marks genuine friendship, the Poet turned to find another patron under whose *aegis* – the essential patronage which was the Elizabethan poet's life-line – he could bring to birth his poetic and dramatic works. He found him in Thomas Walsingham who fulfilled the role of the Renaissance patron to perfection – a man of exceptional cultural refinement and taste, whose magnanimous nature matched Marlowe's own.

In the sixteenth century, chivalry, which was the cultural inspiration of the mediaeval writers and poets, was still greatly admired and had not relinquished its influence on the educated classes, when, at the same time, the Renaissance patron emerged, bathed in the glow cast by the rediscovery of the classical culture of ancient Greece and Rome. It was in this intermingling of two cultural influences that the rich literature of Renaissance England found its inspiration. The 'new' classical culture had a totally uninhibited view of physical beauty, delighting in the beauty of the naked human form, both male and female, and presenting the hedonistically sensual gods in their catholic tastes, some, such as Jove and Neptune, bestowing their lustful attentions on beautiful boys and lovely maidens indiscriminately; and allusions to this were fashionably reflected in Elizabethan literature aimed to please the classically educated tastes of the Renaissance patron, who was yet clad in his chivalric armour. The impact of the new classical influence on the chivalric ideals of purity and chastity that enshrined sexual continence as the highest virtue, resulted in a heightened literary and poetic indulgence in the sensual description of human beauty as a kind of sublimation of hedonism, tasted and enjoyed as an art form. The *Sonnets* are suffused with this Renaissance spirit in full measure.

It is characteristic of Elizabethan literature that it fashionably extolls beauty, both female and male, in terms of poetic hyperbole. When an Elizabethan writer describes a young man with effeminate adjectives, lavishly praising his exquisite looks, the modern reader naturally senses sexual innuendo, concluding this to be evidence of a covert homosexuality when it is merely evidence of the height of fashion in elegant writing. That ever fashion-conscious writer and obsessive womanizer, Robert Greene, conformed as readily as any. His biographer, J.C. Jordan, cites Greene's description of a man in a song sung by the courtezan Infida in his *Never Too Late* (1590):

'Here we have a poem, written as a description of a man, which, except that it is sung by a courtezan to entice her lover, and that it contains what might easily be said to be adaptations to the sex of the singer, cannot in any way be distinguished from the conventional descriptions of women. There are the same cherry cheeks, vermilion lips, silver-white neck, and flaming eyes which fill the fond one's thoughts with 'sweet desires'; there is the same appeal for mercy that may be found in any other Elizabethan song of the kind sung by a man. Indeed, we wonder whether there was any clear-cut difference as to how the descriptions should read, and whether all such descriptive poems were not made purely in accordance with a convention which would fit either men or women.' [4]

The conventional feminine ideal was blonde beauty. Women were almost invariably golden-haired and blue-eyed – Sidney's Stella and the Dark Lady of the *Sonnets* being notable exceptions – while men were conventionally amber-haired. It is these standard conventions that are satirized in *Sonnet 130* in wickedly Marlovian vein:

> My Mistress' eyes are nothing like the Sun,
> Coral is far more red than her lips' red.
> If snow be white, why then her breasts are dun;
> If hairs be wired, black wires grow on her head.
> I have seen roses damask'd, red and white,
> But no such roses see I in her cheeks;
> And in some perfumes is there more delight
> Than in the breath that from my Mistress reeks.
> I love to hear her speak, yet well I know
> That music hath a far more pleasing sound.
> I grant I never saw a goddess go:
> My Mistress when she walks treads on the ground.
>> And yet, by heaven, I think my love as rare
>> As any she belied with false compare.

This sonnet was certainly written tongue-in-cheek in mocking take-off of the ridiculous lengths in hyperbole to which some of the sonneteers went in eulogizing their fair lady. When done with artistry, however, hyperbole was much admired. That excellent poet, Sir Walter Raleigh, was especially praised for his courtly poems to Queen Elizabeth which abound in hyperbole, his amorous odes being esteemed 'most lofty, insolent and passionate'. [5] Reading them gives the impression (as intended) that he is desperately in love with her. In his long poem addressed to the 'dear Empress of my Heart' he descants on his secret and ardent desire for the 'Conquest of your Beauty'. [6]

Queen Elizabeth was Sir Walter Raleigh's patroness, and it is in this sense that his poems to her are to be understood. His passionate poetry was doubtless one of the enchantments by which he rose so high in the Queen's favour after arriving at the Court 'a bare gentleman', [7] and was soon to be reckoned among the most influential men in the entire country. But one is not to assume from his ardent wooing in his love poetry to her that he gained the Virgin Queen's bed. But certainly her ear, her admiration, affection and generous patronage; and he earned, at least partly thereby, great wealth and power, as well as the envy and enmity that his enormous success engendered.

This was the Elizabethan art of playing the courtier, which was not seen as demeaning or false flattery. It was an admired convention of life, and bearing this in mind we now turn to the famous sonnet addressed to the 'Master-Mistress of my passion' – here the word 'passion' being used in its Elizabethan sense meaning a poem. The friend addressed is undoubtedly 'Prince' Will, whose exquisite beauty was displayed to the public gaze, as hinted in the poem, to whom such a tribute to his 'royal' personage would have been most suitable. The witty sexual innuendo in the *double entendre* of the couplet would have delighted the Grayan 'courtiers'!

> A woman's face, with Nature's own hand painted,
> Hast thou, the Master-Mistress of my passion;
> A woman's gentle heart, but not acquainted
> With shifting change, as is false woman's fashion;
> An eye more bright than theirs, less false in rolling,
> Gilding the object whereupon it gazeth;
> A man in hue, all hues in his controlling,
> Which steals men's eyes and women's souls amazeth.
> And for a woman wert thou first created,
> Till Nature as she wrought thee fell a-doting,
> And by addition me of thee defeated,
> By adding one thing to my purpose nothing.
> > But since she prick'd thee out for women's pleasure,
> > Mine be thy love, and thy love's use their treasure.

Sonnet 20

With this sonnet I place its opposite number in the Dark Lady group.

> Love is too young to know what conscience is,
> Yet who knows not conscience is born of love?
> Then, gentle cheater, urge not my amiss,
> Lest guilty of my faults thy sweet self prove.
> For, thou betraying me, I do betray
> My nobler part to my gross body's treason:
> My soul doth tell my body that he may
> Triumph in love; flesh stays no farther reason,
> But rising at thy name doth point out thee
> As his triumphant prize. Proud of this pride,
> He is contented thy poor drudge to be,
> To stand in thy affairs, fall by thy side.
> > No want of conscience hold it that I call
> > Her 'love', for whose dear love I rise and fall.

Sonnet 151

These poems are nothing if not explicit. One cannot really misunderstand them. They give the lie to the supposition that the Poet of the *Sonnets* was a homosexual. His relationship with the 'Prince' who was 'the Master-Mistress' of this sonnet is plain. Comparing his beauty to a woman's was clearly accepted as a compliment. This was the fashion of the time. He was also evidently parading his vaunted beauty publicly as the glorious Prince of Purpoole, who 'steals men's eyes and women's souls amazeth'. At the same time, his masculinity is wittily referred to, and this gorgeous, much fêted young gentleman is the rival who steals the Poet's mistress! Nothing effeminate about him there. This sonnet epitomizes the Elizabethan attitude towards the sexes.

Evidence of Marlowe's Heterosexuality

Marlowe has frequently been called a homosexual. Before such an emotive allegation is made we must be very sure of our facts. The evidence when examined (and it has never before been fully researched) does not uphold this. If he were inclined to homosexuality one would expect to find indications of this in his adolescent writings when his sexual attitudes were being established. We are fortunate in being able to study his youthful poetic works, written at Cambridge, and we can also draw conclusions from what was undoubtedly an early, full scale dramatic work, probably his very first written when he was seventeen or eighteen. The play is now lost, but its source can be consulted, for this was, again, a dramatization of history. These early works all show only heterosexual attitudes, without any doubt and, indeed, most emphatically.

At Cambridge the youthful Marlowe began consciously to develop his poetic style by translating from the Latin authors, Lucan and Ovid. These were tasks he set himself for his own edification and interest; they were indulgences worked at surreptitiously, for the university would not have approved these activities, especially if they had known what he chose for the subject of his translations! He could have selected from a wide range of classical literature, including works having a homosexual element, but he deliberately chose Ovid's *Amores,* which are as heterosexual a collection of poems as one could imagine. Anyone reading these forty-eight love-poems, which are of varying length, some as much as three pages, representing a choice celebration of *erotica* mainly devoted to the poetic description of Ovid's love-affair with his mistress, Corinna, will not gain the impression that their self-employed translator was a young man interested in homosexuality!

Many of the Amores are explicitly erotic poems. Marlowe named his translation *Ovid's Elegies,* perhaps to mask their erotic nature. They were eventually published in an undated, surreptitious and unauthorized edition bearing the imprint 'At Middlebourgh' in the Netherlands, where much illicit literature was printed and smuggled abroad. The book was condemned by Archbishop Whitgift and the Bishop of London and copies consigned to the flames, but several have survived. [*]. It was evidently a popular book.

206

Young Marlowe was learning his sex education from the heterosexual Ovid, of that there can be no question at all. These poems are totally uninhibited and quite explicit. A selection of two are given below to provide a sampling of this luscious literature in which the young poet was employing his leisure hours.

Elegy V. Book I

In summer's heat and mid-time of the day
To rest my limbs upon a bed I lay;
One window shut, the other open stood,
Which gave such light as twinkles in a wood,
Like twilight glimpse at setting of the sun,
Or night being past, and yet not day begun.
Such light to shamefast maidens must be shown,
Where they may sport, and seem to be unknown.
Then came *Corinna* in a long loose gown,
Her white neck hid with tresses hanging down,
Resembling fair *Semiramis* going to bed,
Or *Laïs* of a thousand wooers sped.
I snatch'd her gown; being thin, the harm was small,
Yet striv'd she to be cover'd therewithal.
And striving thus as one that would be cast
Betray'd herself, and yielded at the last.
Stark naked as she stood before mine eye,
Not one wen on her body could I spy.
What arms and shoulders did I touch and see,
How apt her breasts were to be press'd by me!
How smooth a belly under her waist saw I!
How large a leg, and what a lusty thigh!
To leave the rest, all lik'd me passing well,
I cling'd her naked body, down she fell;
Judge you the rest; being tir'd she bade me kiss;
Jove send me more such afternoons as this.

Ovid also tells of unsuccessful sexual liaisons.

Elegy VI. Book III

. . .
She on my neck her Ivory arms did throw
Her arms far whiter than the Scythian snow.
And eagerly she kiss'd me with her tongue,
And under mine her wanton thigh she flung.
Yea, and she soothed me up, and call'd me sire,
And us'd all speech that might provoke, and stir.

Yet like as if cold Hemlock I had drunk,
It mock'd me, hung down the head, and sunk.
. . .
Why mock'st thou me? she cried, or being ill
Who bade thee lie down here against thy will?
Either th' art witch'd with blood of frogs new dead,
Or jaded cam'st thou from some other bed.
With that her loose gown on, from me she cast her,
In skipping out her naked feet much graced her.
And lest her maid should know of this disgrace,
To cover it, spilt water on the place.

The young Marlowe was clearly getting his sexual education from Ovid!
Marlowe's *Hero and Leander* is redolent with recollections of his translation
of the *Amores* but they are here transmuted by his innate delicacy, and the
passionate intensity of first love is exquisitely depicted, touched with an
integrity of feeling which lifts this erotic poem into a sphere far above Ovid's
sensuous eroticism. There is a streak of genuine purity and idealism in
Marlowe's make-up, which, warring with his passionate nature, creates turbu-
lence in him.

Marlowe's first play, or so I judge it, now lost, was sold to the Earl of
Oxford's men. *The True History of George Scanderbeg,* tells of a Christian
Prince of Albania who saved his country from the Turks. [9] The source he used
was evidently the account by John Shute in his *Two Very Notable
Commentaries* (1562). The British Library's copy of this rare book has mar-
ginal annotations in an Elizabethan hand that may well be Marlowe's. In it we
find this description of Scanderbeg :

> 'Scanderbeg was of a goodly stature, and fayre, wel sewtrid of al
> his membres and of an excellent complexion, wel able to endure
> hete, cold, and al kinde of trauaile, as touching ye vertues of his
> minde, he was wise, circumspect, and magnanime, ful of liberalitie,
> and cortesie, and juste both in dede and worde, as moughte be pos-
> syble, valiante & merciful, apte to forgeue wronges if it were
> required of him, he was an enemie of al vice, and especially of that
> of the Citie of *Gomorra,* he wolde neuer suffer his souldiours to
> slay women nor children of his enemies, nor that anye woman
> shoulde be enforced, in prosperitie he was neuer proude, nor in
> aduersitie neuer discoraged . . ' [10]

This history relates the extraordinary life of this noble Albanian prince who
was taken hostage as a child to the court of the Turkish emperor, who brought
him up and trained him in arms to become a marvellous warrior, treating him
with great favour, giving him charge of his armies. Being secretly converted
to Christianity, he escaped to join his own people and led them to victory

against the Turks. It is an inspiring and dramatic story. Scanderbeg was a man of pristine valour and chivalry, a brilliant military tactician, heroic and intelligent. He taught his soldiers his values, and was especially noted for his hatred of the sin of sodomy. One has the sense that Scanderbeg was a hero-figure for the youthful Marlowe. I have already mentioned this play in relation to Gabriel Harvey, who knew the young Marlowe at Cambridge, perhaps more intimately than we realized, and associated him with this character, naming him 'Scanderbeg' and 'the Scanderbegging wight' in his *Gorgon*. Certainly no young homosexual would have chosen to dramatize the life of George Scanderbeg!

Since Marlowe's earliest known play dramatized the life of the virtuous Christian Prince Scanderbeg, who hated the sin of sodomy, and who loved his wife dearly, and in *Tamburlaine* (who likewise mightily fought the Turks) Marlowe introduces out of his *own* invention the love-story of the great Scythian warrior and Zenocrate, it cannot then be argued that he was a homo-sexual *because* he chose to dramatize the tragic life of a homosexual English king in his *Edward the Second*. Yet that is what some of his critics have claimed, despite the evidence in this play of scornful comments from the rebel noblemen utterly despising Edward for his abject attachment to Piers Gaveston, who is shown in anything but a favourable light. He is a corrupter of the 'pliant king', and a base-born fellow with base principles, while Edward cuts a weak, pathetic figure, an unfit king, who is taunted and spurned by his noblemen.

Young Mortimer.	The idle triumphs, masks, lascivious shows,
	And prodigal gifts bestow'd on Gaveston,
	Have drawn thy treasury dry, and made thee weak;
	The murmuring commons, overstretched, break.
Lancaster.	Look for rebellion, look to be depos'd:
	Thy garrisons are beaten out of France,
	And, lame and poor, lie groaning at the gates;
	The wild Oneil, with swarms of Irish kerns,
	Lives uncontroll'd within the English pale;
	. . .
Y. Mort.	Who loves thee, but a sort of flatterers?
Lancaster.	Thy gentle queen, sole sister of Valois,
	Complains that thou has left her all forlorn.
Y. Mort.	Thy court is naked, being bereft of those
	That make a king seem glorious to the world,
	I mean the peers, whom thou shouldst dearly love;
	Libels are cast against thee in the street;
	Ballads and rhymes made of thy overthrow.

King Edward the Second 11.960-981

The horrendous murder of the pitiful king devised by Lightborne – surely one of the most coldly cruel and fiendishly evil characters ever created – by driving a red hot iron rod up his anus, is sufficient evidence that this is not the dramatist's self-identification with the practice of homosexuality. The scene arouses the most powerful emotions of pity and horror in the audience of any scene ever written. I do not believe that anyone who was himself a homosexual could have written this play. How can any sentient person argue this?

The touching love and loyalty of the youthful King Edward III for his deposed and murdered father, despite his depraved and condemned life, ends this play on a note of deep compassion which does not excuse or exonerate the king's faults, but sees them as expiated in his tragic death, and brings just retribution to his murderers. This play is the strongest dramatic condemnation of homosexuality that has ever been written; although Marlowe himself remains the dramatist standing in the wings, presenting these historical characters with compassionate humanity, weaving his theatrical magic with tolerance and understanding for human frailty.

His treatment of the French King Henry III in *The Massacre at Paris* similarly depicts the utter scorn which other characters in the play show towards him for his indulgence of his homosexual courtiers, while his portrait of the king is nevertheless sympathetic.

> *Guise.* I love your minions! dote on them yourself,
> I know none else but holds them in disgrace.
> 11. 779-780

The sole origin of the identification of Marlowe as a homosexual is the informer Baines' infamous dossier on him in which he reports that the Poet had been known to express the opinion 'That all they that loue not *Tobacco* & *Boies* were fooles.' (This is fully discussed in Chapter 16 'The Poet Vilified and Vindicated'). Those who have credited Baines' 'Note' have attempted to deduce homosexuality from Marlowe's works, citing the little scene that opens *Dido Queen of Carthage*, showing Jove dallying with Ganymede as 'evidence'. They seem not to have realised that this scene fulfils the essential dramatic purpose of presenting the reason for Juno's jealousy which underlies the tragedy of this play; it is not gratuitously introduced. In the context of this Greek legendary tale it shows Jove in his traditional, hedonistic character, in a little scene so delicately handled it could not give offence to a Victorian prude. Artistic licence would baulk at altering the nature of Jove! Is every writer on classical mythology supposedly a homosexual? The argument is fatuous. Similarly, these hunters for 'evidence' of Marlowe's alleged homosexuality point to the episode in *Hero and Leander* in which the god Neptune tries to seduce Leander as he swims the Hellespont. Leander repudiates his advances in alarm: 'You are deceiv'd; I am no woman, I', which angers the god. Once again, this episode has a dramatic purpose in the story, for had

Marlowe completed the poem he would, I believe, have harked back to Neptune's rejection to present Leander's watery death as the god's jealous revenge for spurning his amorous advances. The poem has another such digression, which has nothing to do with homosexuality. This relates the courtship of a beautiful country maid by the god Mercury, which equally has a dramatic purpose. The moral of this episode is to show *why true lovers are star-crossed.* These two commentaries drawn from the classics establish the style in which the poem is conceived by the author. They are an essential part of the artistic intent.

One might ask, what are we to make of the heterosexual evidence in *Edward the Third?* This apocryphal play – long believed to be at least partly by Shakespeare – has now been attributed unassailably to Marlowe, as his first English history play written in 1588 in celebration of the great victory over the Spanish Armada, in which he himself fought with the English navy. [11] In this play, King Edward III, who was a notorious womanizer, relieves the castle of the Countess of Salisbury which was held by the Scots, who at once flee upon the arrival of Edward with his army, whom the Countess then entertains, her husband being absent fighting in France. Edward is immediately smitten by the Countess' beauty and sets about determinedly to seduce her, ordering his courtier, Lodowick, to compose a love poem to her declaring his illicit love. It was Marlowe's first essay in romantic comedy, foreshadowing the great romantic comedies he was to write later. It is the only play of this early period that is not a tragedy, which was still his main inspiration.

In King Edward's speeches there are strong echoes of the Scythian conqueror Tamburlaine's famous invocation to Beauty as he contemplates the power that Zenocrate's beauty has over him, which is given opposite in full for comparison. Tamburlaine's soliloquy is one of the best loved of all the great speeches in the play and would have evoked immediate recognition in his Elizabethan audiences.

TAMBURLAINE'S SOLILOQUY

Ah, fair Zenocrate! – divine Zenocrate!
Fair is too foul an epithet for thee,
That in thy passion for thy country's love,
And fear to see thy kingly father's harm,
With hair dishevell'd wip'st thy watery cheeks;
And, like to Flora in her morning's pride,
Shaking her silver tresses in the air,
Rain'st on the earth resolved pearl in showers,
And sprinklest sapphires on thy shining face,
Where Beauty, mother to the Muses, sits,
And comments volumes with her ivory pen,

Taking instructions from thy flowing eyes;
Eyes, when that Ebena steps to heaven,
In silence of thy solemn evening's walk,
Making the mantle of the richest night,
The moon, the planets, and the meteors, light;
There angels in their crystal armours fight
A doubtful battle with my tempted thoughts
For Egypt's freedom and the Soldan's life,
His life that so consumes Zenocrate,
Whose sorrows lay more siege unto my soul
Than all my army to Damascus' walls;
And neither Persia's sovereign nor the Turk
Troubled my senses with conceit of foil
So much by much as doth Zenocrate.
What is beauty, saith my sufferings, then?
If all the pens that ever poets held
Had fed the feeling of their masters' thoughts,
And every sweetness that inspir'd their hearts,
Their minds, and muses on admired themes;
If all the heavenly quitessence they still
From their immortal flowers of poesy,
Wherein, as in a mirror, we perceive
The highest reaches of a human wit;
If these had made one poem's period,
And all combin'd in beauty's worthiness,
Yet should there hover in their restless heads
One thought, one grace, one wonder, at the least,
Which into words no virtue can digest.

The First Part of Tamburlaine the Great Act V, scene 1, 11. 135-173

Edward the Third is probably the next play he wrote after *Tamburlaine* for in the hectic activity of Armada year he would hardly have had much time to devote to dramatic composition. The speech below is one of the many stylistic identifications of authorship that mark *Edward the Third* so clearly as Marlowe's work containing many echoes of Tamberlaine's soliloquy.

King Edward.   Now, Lodowick, invocate some golden Muse,
To bring thee hither an enchanted pen,
That may for sighs set down true sighs indeed,
Talking of grief, to make thee ready groan;
And when thou writest of tears, encouch the word
Before and after with such sweet laments
That it may raise drops in a Tartar's eye,
And make a flintheart Scythian pitiful;

> For so much moving hath a poet's pen:
> Then, if thou be a poet, move thou so,
> And be enriched by thy sovereign's love.
> For, if the touch of sweet concordant strings
> Could enforce attendance in the ears of hell,
> How much more shall the strains of poets' wit
> Beguile and ravish soft and human minds?
>
> *Lodowick.* To whom, my Lord, shall I direct my style?
> *King Edward.* To one that shames the fair and sots the wise;
> Whose body is an abstract or a brief,
> Contains such general virtue in the world.
> Better than beautiful, thou must begin;
> Devise for fair a fairer word than fair,
> And every ornament that thou wouldst praise,
> Fly it a pitch above the soar of praise.
> For flattery fear thou not to be convicted;
> For, were thy admiration ten times more,
> Ten times ten thousand more the worth exceeds
> Of that thou art to praise, thy praises worth.
> Begin; I will to contemplate the while:
> Forget not to set down, how passionate,
> How heart-sick, and how full of languishment,
> Her beauty makes me.
>
> *Lodowick.*   Write I to a woman?
> *King.* What beauty else could triumph over me,
> Or who but women do our love lays greet?
> What, thinkest thou I did bid thee praise a horse?
>
> *King Edward the Third* Act 2 scene 2 11.65-98

With this parting shot of ironic wit the King leaves Lodowick to his composition, while he himself muses on his passionate love and the art of composing a love poem. The gallant and beautiful Countess, who foreshadows Lucrece in her chastity, skilfully outwits the lecherous King Edward and shames him out of his infatuation by her dramatic offer to kill herself rather than to submit to his illicit desires. This episode reveals Marlowe's undoubted gift for romantic tragi-comedy, and it may with far more validity be cited as evidence of his heterosexuality, together with the cumulative evidence of his other early works, than the examples cited as alleged evidence of his homosexuality.

Such arguments as applied to detection of Marlowe's sexuality may now be seen as the fallacious opinings of critics who have a distorted image of Marlowe in their sights. We are dealing with a dramatist of protean mind, which reflects, as light through a prism, all the many-coloured and multi-faceted aspects of human nature, and whose restless and supremely innovative genius from its first emergence is characterized by the continual search for new material for his pupil pen, preferably in contrast to what he had done before. It is a trait remarked on by Dr Bakeless. This was, I suggest, the attraction that drew him to follow his dramatization of *Scanderbeg* with that of *Tamburlaine*, both tremendously successful fighters against the Turks but of totally opposing characters, the one a virtuous Christian Prince who was canonized as a saint by his people after his death, the other a cruel and tyrannical, but brave, pagan. Similarly, his dramatization of the decidedly heterosexual King Edward III, whose womanizing exploits brought some scandal on the crown, and the only play from his pen prior to 1593 that is not a tragedy, he followed up with his dramatization of the tragic history of Edward II. This he would first have noted during his research in Holinshed, where the two reigns overlap, for Edward III became king in his minority upon his unhappy father's deposition. It is the compassion with which Marlowe deals with Edward II's sexual crime, that his modern critics have misinterpreted as the dramatist's self-identification with the pitiful, homosexual king. In this gross misunderstanding of the dramatist's art and soul, they have condemned Marlowe for this 'Shakespearean' quality of blessed broad-mindedness and humanity. Such misconceptions are rooted in historical prejudice.

The two sharply contrasted English history plays, *Edward the Third* and *Edward the Second*, the one an extravagantly heterosexual, successful and popular monarch, the other his tragic, homosexual father – fascinating material for a student of humanity such as our poet-dramatist – provide effectively the missing link in the chain of Marlowe's development as a dramatist from early Marlowe to mature Shakespeare.

In assessing what kind of man this genius was on such an emotive subject as his sexuality, it is the historical period in which he lived that provides the landscape in which we try to comprehend the mind and nature of this essentially Elizabethan, late English Renaissance poet whose sonnet-sequence reveals his life and character. The language in which he expresses himself is Elizabethan English, and just as we need some guidance in the language of the emblems, so we have to appreciate what the word 'lover' meant as used between Elizabethan men. In *Julius Caesar*, Brutus addresses the assembled crowd as 'Romans, countrymen and lovers!', and he names Caesar his 'best lover'. [12] In *Coriolanus*, Menenius speaks of his good friend Coriolanus as his 'lover'. Never has there been an age when friendship was more highly valued, this ethic receiving its inspiration from Renaissance Neoplatonism. It is in this sense that the term is constantly used in the *Sonnets* also; and only in this sense as spoken between men, plain, frank, in the language of love addressing a patron.

> *Menenius.* I tell thee, fellow,
> Thy general is my lover. I have been
> The book of his good acts, whence men have read

His fame unparallel'd haply amplified;
For I have ever verified my friends –
Of whom he's chief – with all the size that verity
Would without lapsing suffer.

Coriolanus Act 5 scene 2 11.14-19

Those who see a sexual connotation in the sincere expression of ardent adoration of the Patron in the *Sonnets,* denying that such emotional attachment can be innocent, are really denying that a deeply-grounded love can ever exist between two people without also developing into a sexual relationship. Such an assertion is the most ignorant nonsense, for love is by definition a transcendent power. Parental love, brotherly and sisterly love, the love between true friends – which is perhaps the rarest of all – are as real and true and deep, often far *more* so, than that which is sexually evoked, of which the flame burns fiercely and is often as quickly spent. Whilst sex is an undeniably potent force in human relationships, it is the emotional need for love, appreciation and sympathy that is of prime importance, particularly in highly-developed beings whose yearning for a true love is paramount. Love and sexual attraction are not necessarily the same. Yet this is the fallacious assumption behind the misinterpretation of the language of love used in the *Sonnets* as *evidence* of homosexuality. Many people go through life without ever finding a true soul-mate, though most will find a sexual partner who may be more or less satisfactory. Equally is it rare for marriage to be a true union at a spiritual level. Disillusionment boosts the divorce rate.

To find a true-loving relationship with a true and faithful friend is an unaccountable blessing. In Marlowe's case, who was so blessed, there must have been those intrinsic qualities in his own nature which called forth the loving friendship that was offered so whole-heartedly, and the relationship he had with Thomas Walsingham gained in depth and poignancy through the danger from which his Patron saved him – virtually he owed him his life, so that the ties that bound him were immeasurably strong and bespeak a friendship of complete trust and harmony.

The Renaissance Platonic Ideal

The Renaissance brought with it, alongside the rediscovery of the rich heritage of the Greek legends with their pantheon of pagan gods displaying uninhibited hedonism and plural sexuality, the knowledge of Plato and the Greek philosophers whose teaching the poets, writers and intellectuals of Elizabethan England took to their hearts. The Platonic ideal was a powerful inspirational influence on the mores of the time, elevating friendship to the most sacred of human relationships. Shakespeare's plays are full of examples, and we see it also among women in the delightful portraits of Rosalind and Celia in *As You Like It.*

Whilst Plato extolled beauty of heart and spirit as the ultimate, far beyond mere physical beauty, and, as though to emphasize this, presents his ideas through the mouth of Socrates, a physically very ugly man, he also taught that the path to the elevated, ideal state of Platonic Love was through the contemplation of beauty in all its manifold forms in the physical world as well as the spiritual. In his adoration of beauty, the Poet of the Sonnets reveals himself as one who is aspiring to attain the ideal state of Platonic Love. Many of these sonnets are his outpourings in eulogistic language celebrating the beauty that his soul loved and which his eye saw in the 'lovely Boy', as well as in Walsingham, who must also have been an exceedingly handsome man as is evident in *Sonnets 98* and *99*, which praise his beauty and are certainly addressed to Walsingham, not Hatcliffe. But it was Walsingham's spiritual qualities that the Poet loved above all, and his enduring soul-love for his magnanimous Patron is wonderfully expressed in one of the most justly famous of all the sonnets.

> Let me not to the marriage of true minds
> Admit impediments. Love is not love
> Which alters when it alteration finds,
> Or bends with the remover to remove.
> O no, it is an ever fixed mark
> That looks on tempests and is never shaken;
> It is the star to every wand'ring barque,
> Whose worth's unknown although his height be taken.
> Love's not Time's fool, though rosy lips and cheeks
> Within his bending sickle's compass come;
> Love alters not with his brief hours and weeks,
> But bears it out even to the edge of doom.
>   If this be error and upon me proved,
>   I never writ, nor no man ever loved.
>
> *Sonnet 116*

This beautiful sonnet takes on an even deeper meaning in the context of the tragedy that was the Poet's life-experience, when he speaks of love that 'alters not . . But bears it out even to the edge of doom'. In Marlowe and Walsingham we have that rare example of two friends who are in the perfect relationship of Platonic Love, as commended by Plato and Ficino and Pico della Mirandola as the highest condition to which man can aspire. The sonnets eulogizing physical beauty always associate this with virtue in his patrons in celebration of 'soul love' between faithful friends – that 'dear religious love' referred to in *Sonnet 31*. This is the Platonic concept: it is in his adoring contemplation of beauty and virtue that the artist gives birth to his inspired poetic works. A patron was seen to be the more greatly honoured, the more brilliant the poetic works that were produced by those he patronized, giving status and merit to the patron. In this one can see a strong incentive for Walsingham's protection of his Poet, though in his case unselfishly for he was also obscured by the same anonymity as his Poet. This man of fine discrimination and artistic judgment may have sensed the importance of saving Marlowe for posterity.

'The Vision of Eros' is how W.H. Auden describes this perfect spiritualized love, which Wordsworth had glimpsed in his *Ode to Immortality,* where it is, however, an entirely depersonalized vision as a love of Nature and the beauty of the natural world that brings a glory into the child's life. 'It would seem that, in our culture, this vision is not uncommon in childhood', he writes, and we cannot doubt that the transcendent power of beauty was felt by the child, Christopher Marlowe, as much as by the young Wordsworth, and it remained the inspiration of his life. Auden continues:

> 'The vision of Eros, on the other hand, is concerned with a single person, who is revealed to the subject as being of infinite sacred importance. The classic descriptions of it are found in Plato's *Symposium,* Dante's *La Vita Nuova,* and some of these sonnets of Shakespeare. . .
>
> 'The Vision of Eros is probably a much rarer experience than most people in our culture suppose, but, when it is genuine, I do not think it makes any sense to apply to it terms like heterosexual or homosexual. Such terms can only be legitimately applied to the profane, erotic experiences with which we are all familiar, to lust, for example, an interest in another solely as a sexual object, and that combination of sexual desire and *philia,* affection based upon mutual interests, values, and shared experiences which is the securest basis for a happy marriage.
>
> 'That, in the Vision of Eros, the erotic is the medium, not the cause, is proved, I think, by the fact, on which all who have written about it with authority agree, that it cannot long survive an actual sexual relationship.' [13]

Dante took his Vision of a chaste, higher love conceived for his ideal woman, Beatrice, to extremes, elevating her to an angelic spirit, until finally, as Leslie Fielder tells us, 'Beatrice represents, in some sense, Christ! At this point the Inquisition moved in to expurgate his little book.' [14]

Our Poet of the Sonnets is not inclined to such aesthetic, visionary extremism; he is more intensely beauty-loving, making a religion of worshipping beauty of face and form as well as beauty of mind and soul, and to him Beauty itself is, in a sense, sacred. Because his 'Prince' was flawed, having beauty only in his physical appearance and not in his inner nature, the Poet finally rejected his patronage and friendship. He could no longer give him the love owed to a true friend, but he mourns this as a sad loss, for it represents a betrayal of the sacred image.

217

The works we know as Marlowe's and Shakespeare's demonstrate an attitude towards sex of uncompromising integrity. *Lucrece, Cymbeline, Tamburlaine, Edward the Third* present us with heroines who will choose death rather than sexual defilement, and, in contrast, we have the horrible lasciviousness of Goneril. These creations of the dramatist's art demonstrate an intensely felt approach that is typically Elizabethan, but in the *Sonnets* is expressed personally. Although no Puritan, his strong hatred of lust and lasciviousness is a notable characteristic. It is an undeniable fact that our Poet has a self-tormenting, ambivalent attitude towards the sex act, a love-hate, guilt-ridden longing, yet aversion to its consummation. This, in itself, would preclude a sexual aspect intruding into his perfect relationship with his beloved Patron.

> Th' expense of Spirit in a waste of shame
> Is lust in action, and till action lust
> Is perjur'd, murd'rous, bloody, full of blame,
> Savage, extreme, rude, cruel, not to trust,
> Enjoy'd no sooner but despised straight,
> Past reason hunted, and no sooner had,
> Past reason hated as a swallowed bait
> On purpose laid to make the taker mad:
> Mad in pursuit, and in possession so,
> Had, having, and in quest to have, extreme,
> A bliss in proof and proud and very woe;
> Before, a joy propos'd, behind, a dream.
>   All this the world well knows, yet none knows well
>   To shun the heaven that leads men to this hell.

Sonnet 129

This sonnet is about lust, the dark side of sexual love, in which the Poet sees sex, when aroused, as cruel, a predatory monster. It is part of the sequence to the Dark Lady, and these strong feelings of self-revulsion are an expression of his guilt-feelings about his association with a harlot – for so she is – who is an 'unclean' woman. There is, nevertheless, something very beautiful in his relationship with her; in his poems there is implicit his descent from his longing for a union with true beauty to the passionate love he conceives for this fallen woman, in which he becomes her helpless devotee, enslaved by a beauty that is 'black' – not in actuality but because this is an Elizabethan term describing a harlot, as the term 'proud' used in this context means sexual lust. In this case, his Dark Lady does also possess beautiful black eyes which captivated him. Yet he perforce admits the power of sexual lust that drives him to seek her, and he passionately hates the thought of her unfaithfulness to him with her other lovers. That is his torment. The feelings of self-disgust that overwhelm him are reflected in his castigation of himself for having descended to the level of his 'gross body's treason'.

Contrasting his turbulent love affair with his dark-eyed mistress, in which the faithless 'Prince' Will is also involved, the celebration in the sonnets of his great love for his Patron is the more touching. Here we have a love which is true, which shines through the convention of lavish praise owed to a patron, expressing a devotional love between male friends whose chaste relationships is no more in question than is their constancy, tested in dangerous circumstances, and who have attained a relationship which is surely as perfect as any that frail creature man can aspire to. His tribute to their enduring, deep, mutual affection is echoed in many of the sonnets to Walsingham with a sincerity and depth of feeling never found in the sonnets to 'Mr.W.H.', beautiful though he is.

> What's in the brain that ink may character,
> Which hath not figur'd to thee my true spirit?
> What's new to speak, what now to register,
> That may express my love, or thy dear merit?
> Nothing, sweet boy, but yet, like prayers divine,
> I must each day say o'er the very same,
> Counting no old thing old, thou mine, I thine,
> Even as when first I hallowed thy fair name.
> So that eternal love in love's fresh case
> Weighs not the dust and injury of age,
> Nor gives to necessary wrinkles place,
> But makes antiquity for aye his page,
>   Finding the first conceit of love there bred
>   Where time and outward form would show it dead.

Sonnet 108

There remains the question of identity of the tantalizing raven-eyed siren who occupies all but exclusively the last twenty-five sonnets in the sequence; and she has probably been the subject of more fantastical conjecture than any woman in history. The story of the Dark Lady with whom Marlowe fell hopelessly and tormentedly in love will now be considered in the light of what these sonnets – and Dr Hotson – reveal to our gaze. It is an entrancing portrait that emerges.

219

XV

BEAUTY HERSELF IS BLACK

THE DARK LADY'S group of twenty-five consecutive sonnets addressed to her, with the exception of the introvert *Sonnet 146,* 'Poor soul, the centre of my sinful earth', is placed at the end of the sequence for aesthetic, not for chronological reasons, for many of these were amongst the earliest ever written. She is closely associated with Marlowe's first patron, 'Mr.W.H.', in his role as the Prince of Purpoole, for 'Prince' Will is the 'Will' who features as the Poet's rival for her love and favour in *Sonnets 133* to *136* (a quartet of sonnets on one theme, which is how he often seems to have composed them) and *Sonnet 143,* written when the 'Prince' appears to have abandoned her. This triangular relationship of the beautiful black-eyed siren with her 'Prince' Will and her Poet is marvellously borne out by historical evidence here to be reviewed, in which we find the Dark Lady and the Prince of Purpoole brought face to face in a context appropriately spiced with sexual innuendo.

The commencement of the Dark Lady sonnets therefore also dates from a youthful episode during the Prince of Purpoole's brief reign of splendour in the Christmas season of 1587-8. This was evidently a period of prolific sonnet-writing for him, underlining Hotson's view that Shakespeare would have been in the van of the sonneteering vogue. This fits, for Marlowe was the greatest literary trend-setter of his age, and, moreover, his friend Tom Watson had introduced the art of sonneteering from the Italian and French models in his *Passionate Centurie of Love,* published in 1582, which were 18-line poems, which Marlowe adapted to the 14-line sonnet. With Sidney he may claim to be the creator of the English sonnet, another 'Shakespearean' achievement, dating from the year when he was twenty-three, and in love, and had just launched 'Shakespearean' drama with his *Tamburlaine the Great.*

As previously suggested, the mistress who is the subject of three sonnets featuring Will Hatcliffe also as rival lover, which are separated from the Dark Lady group, cannot refer to the same woman, for there is no mention of her black eyes, which are such a striking feature of the Dark Lady's beauty, nor is the Poet so hopelessly enthralled by this fair mistress. Although he 'lov'd her dearly', the intensity of emotion and of jealousy that has him in its grip over the Dark Lady affair is absent. These are: *Sonnet 40:* 'Take all my loves, my love, yea take them all'; *Sonnet 41* 'Those pretty wrongs that liberty commits'; and *Sonnet 42* 'That thou hast her it is not all my grief'. We may conclude that the placing of these three sonnets separately from the Dark Lady group indicates that this is another sweetheart he had. Presumably the affair ended when Will

Hatcliffe stole her from him, and the Dark Lady affair followed almost immediately.

For the 23-year-old Marlowe falling in love with this dark-eyed siren was an experience that virtually 'bowled him over'. This is evident from the two sonnets describing this experience, *Sonnet 23* and *Sonnet 24*. These are placed immediately following the start of his sonneteering to his new patron, 'Prince' Will, with five sonnets in which he explores the sonneteering convention, *(Sonnets 18, 19, 20, 21* and *22)* this placement associating the Dark Lady with the Grayan 'Court'. I believe this is a deliberate placement giving us a clue to her identity, which is substantiated in the analysis of the sonnets' themes under the heading 'First Love' using Hotson's unique, tried and tested method of identification, which immediately throws a new light establishing that the object of his love is none other than the Dark Lady to whom he became enslaved. (See pages 451 - 455)

Again, we have to remain aware in our search of the historical context of the poems. Four hundred years ago the word 'black' had no racist connotation, and it is not used in its ethnic sense in the sonnets, but always figuratively. The Elizabethans associated colours with the popularly accepted Renaissance cultural kaleidoscope that allocated certain images, qualities, attributes, humours, characters and concepts to different colours – as already seen in the *impresa* portrait by Hilliard – conveying distinct messages visually in art, or to the reader or listener. There is absolutely nothing remotely racist to be read into the sonnets that harp so constantly on the word 'black'. The Dark Lady we are seeking to identify was, in fact, *not* black, and anyone seeking her in this ethnic sense is doomed to fail. She was apparently Welsh, although she had beautiful black eyes and black hair to match, no doubt, although her hair is not important to the Poet because it has no reference to her *name,* as we shall see.

Who the Dark Lady was has, I submit, been finally and conclusively solved by our remarkable Elizabethan Sherlock Holmes, Dr Hotson, who has once again come up with the only feasible solution to this long-standing teaser. Following the trail of his established line of research, elucidating the Elizabethan word-connotations which the Poet associates repeatedly with his black-eyed mistress we are shown how to 'read' these. Hotson leads us to the revelation that the word 'bright' which the Poet applies paradoxically to his *dark* mistress is traditionally associated with the names Lucy, Luce or Lucia, which mean 'brightness'. [1]. The name Lucy (and its variants) also represents 'eyes', and Hotson produces a mass of evidence testifying to the association of 'eyes' with the name Lucy. The ode written in Italian to Lucy, Countess of Bedford, in translation is simply entitled 'The Eyes' [2]. Hence, he concludes, 'eyes' and 'bright' point to her name – Lucy, or Luce or Lucia.

Hotson has taken his cue from the sonnets to the Dark Lady which are laden with references to *eyes, sight, looks, blindness* and *brightness* – all of which connote the name Lucy. The word 'eyes' or 'eye' occurs twenty-four times in these twenty-five sonnets, sometimes supported by 'looks, 'sight', 'blindness' or 'brightness' in some form or other, forming a *repeated theme* – which we had hitherto been too blind to notice! So let us see these sonnets afresh with Hotson.

> Therefore my Mistress' *eyes* are raven black,
> Her *eyes* so suited, and they mourners seem   *Sonnet 127*

> My Mistress' *eyes* are nothing like the Sun   *Sonnet 130*

> Thine *eyes* I love, and they as pitying me,
> Knowing thy heart, torment me with disdain,
> Have put on black, and loving mourners be,
> . . .
> Nor that full Star that ushers in the Even
> Doth half that glory to the sober West
> As those two mourning *eyes* become thy face: *Sonnet 132*

> Me from myself thy cruel *eye* hath taken   *Sonnet 133*

> Thou *blind* fool Love, what dost thou to mine *eyes*
> That they behold, and see not what they see?
> . . .
> If *eyes*, corrupt by over-partial *looks*,
> Be anchor'd in the bay where all men ride,
> Why of *eyes'* falsehood hast thou forged hooks?
> . . .
> Or mine *eyes* seeing this . .
> . . .
> In things right true my heart and *eyes* have erred, *Sonnet 137*

> Wound me not with thine *eye* but with thy tongue
> . . .
> Tell me thou lov'st elsewhere, but in my *sight*,
> Dear heart, forbear to glance thine *eye* aside,
> . . .
> Her *looks* have been mine enemies,
> . . .
> Kill me outright with *looks*, and rid my pain.   *Sonnet 139*

> Be it lawful I love thee as thou lov'st those
> Whom thine *eyes* woo as mine importune thee,   *Sonnet 142*

> O me! what *eyes* hath love put in my head,
> Which have no correspondence with true *sight*,
> . . .

If that be fair whereon my false *eyes* dote,
What means the world to say it is not so?
. . .
Love's *eye* is not so true as all men's: no,
How can it? O how can love's *eye* be true,
That is so vex'd with watching and with tears?

. . .
O cunning love, with tears thou keep'st me *blind,*
Lest *eyes* well seeing thy foul faults should find. *Sonnet 148*

Bear thine *eyes* straight, though thy proud heart go wide.
                                                        Sonnet 140

Commanded by the motion of thine *eyes.*   *Sonnet 149*

Swear to thy *blind* soul that I was thy *Will*   *Sonnet 136*

For I have sworn thee fair, and thought thee *bright,*
Who art as *black* as hell, as dark as night.   *Sonnet 150*

O from what power hast thou this powerful might,
With insufficiency my heart to sway,
To make me give the lie to my true *sight,*
And swear that *brightness* doth not grace the day:
                                                        Sonnet 152

And to enlighten thee gave *eyes to blindness*   *Sonnet 152*

But at my mistress' *eye* Love's brand new-fired,
Where Cupid got new fire; my mistress' *eyes*   *Sonnet 153*

Elucidating the reason for this constant, recurring emphasis in these sonnets on 'eyes', and on 'sight' and blindness', with 'brightness' added, which distinguish the sonnets in this group, (although posing no obvious clue, for eyes do traditionally speak of love and Cupid is blind) undeterred, Hotson, the born investigator, pursues his search and tracks down the story of St Lucy, a noble virgin of Syracuse in A.D.300, which yields significant information to fill out the picture making it a perfect photofit for a lady called Lucy, or Luce or Lucia.

> 'Lucia, St Lucy . . she plucked out her eyes when they threatened
> to become a snare to her lover . . they were afterwards restored to
> her more beautiful than before. She is regarded as the special
> patroness of those who suffer from diseases of the eyes.

St Lucy (December 13) . . is invoked by persons afflicted with diseases of the eyes, because, rather than accept the hand in marriage of a lover who desired her for the sake of her beautiful eyes, she plucked them out and sent them to him . . Nevertheless her sight was restored to her the next day . . In Christian art she is generally represented as bearing a dish or platter with two eyes on it.

St Lucy. Many paintings represent her bearing her eyes in her hand or on a salver. Some artists have even represented her blind.' [3]

Hotson next goes on to investigate the significance of blackness and brightness. Not merely *eyes,* but especially *black eyes, black beauty,* are the Poet's theme. Intrigued by this unusual juxtaposition of 'brightness' with darkness and a beauty that is 'black', Dr Hotson pursues his unremitting quest to discover the traditional qualities associated with this recurring imagery concerning the Dark Lady.

Hotson postulates: ' "Bright" and "brightness" certainly carried *Lucy* to the Elizabethan reader.' [4]. Ben Jonson's refrain in Epigram XCIII, 'To Lucy, Countess of Bedford' confirms this:

> LUCY, you brightnesse of our spheare, who are
> Life of the *Muses* day, as their morning-starre!
>
> . . . .
> LUCY, you brightnesse of our spheare, who are
> The *Muses* evening, as their evening-starre!

Dr Hotson's copious cullings from Elizabethan literature support this. From these I give a small representative selection to demonstrate that *Lucy* clearly connoted 'brightness' to the Elizabethans.

> 'That same other Damzell, *Lucy* bright'
> 'For *Lucy's* sake, that lady bright . . as ever man beheld with eye'
> 'To Sir *Thomas Lucy,* Bright spark of wit and courage'
> 'LUCY, the bright' (To Lucy, Countess of Bedford) [5]

But even this affirmation of the soundness of his line of research is not enough for Dr Hotson. He notes that 'Shakespeare adds the apparent paradox: this "bright" woman is in fact as *dark as night'* [6]. And consulting the Calendar, Old Style, he makes this discovery:

> 'We find Lucy *on the darkest night of the whole year:* December 13, the winter solstice – "Lucy bright, the shortest day and the longest night". ' [7]

Pursuing 'black' he finds that traditionally 'black' people, namely those having black hair, dark eyes and swarthy complexion were held to be lustful. Hotson offers:

'At a Pale man draw thy knife; from a Blacke man keepe thy wife .
. . the pale peevish, the blacke lusty.' [8]

'A mayden blacke is alwayes proud.' [9]

'Pride' in a woman is also associated with sexual promiscuity, and with harlotry. Her 'black' colour repeatedly referred to, together with reference to her 'foul pride' all reveal the Dark Lady as a courtezan. Hotson's research has highlighted the wealth of symbolism that is present in the sonnets which, even whilst expressing the Poet's turbulent emotions, are poems imbued with his wit and his wide awareness of folklore and traditional wisdom. He makes fullest use of this rich source for his poetic inspiration, combining Christian tradition, English folklore and Renaissance myth. Our appreciation of these poems and of the Poet who wrote them is thereby enhanced. We can now understand all that the Poet intended to convey in the lines in *Sonnet 147*:

> For I have sworn thee fair, and thought thee *bright*,
> Who art as *black* as hell, *as dark as night.*

It is the winter solstice he is evoking together with her name and her profession, which is a source of anguish to him, for she whom he loves is impure. In *Sonnet 144* he describes her as wooing his friend's 'purity with her foul pride', yet he loves her.

> Thou art as tyrranous, so as thou art,
> As those whose beauties *proudly* make them cruel,
> For well thou know'st to my dear doting heart
> Thou art the fairest and most precious jewel.
> Yet, in good faith, some say that thee behold,
> Thy face hath not the power to make love groan;
> To say they err, I dare not be so bold,
> Although I swear it to myself alone.
> And to be sure that is not false I swear,
> A thousand groans but thinking on thy face,
> One on another's neck do witness bear
> Thy *black* is fairest in my judgment's place.
> > In nothing art thou *black* save in thy deeds,
> > And thence this slander, as I think, proceeds.
>
> *Sonnet 131*

Hence we learn that it is her deeds that are 'black', and this figurative use of the word is played on in his descriptions of her 'raven black' eyes, which have enthralled him, for our Poet was infatuated from the first encounter:

> In the old age *black* was not counted fair,
> Or if it were it bore not Beauty's name:
> But now is *black* Beauty's successive heir,
> And Beauty slander'd with a bastard shame;
> For since each hand hath put on Nature's power,
> Fairing the foul with Art's false borrow'd face,
> Sweet Beauty hath no name, no holy bower,
> But is profan'd, if not lives in disgrace.
> Therefore my Mistress' *eyes* are *raven black,*
> Her *eyes* so suited, and they mourners seem
> At such who, not born fair, no beauty lack,
> Sland'ring Creation with a false esteem.
>   Yet so they mourn becoming of their woe,
>   That every tongue says Beauty should look so.

Sonnet 127

Thus primed with his clues, Hotson pursues his inspired search for a black-eyed 'fallen woman' named Lucy or Luce, and through unremitting and intelligent research he traces a gentlewoman of the Court named *Luce Morgan,* who afterwards became a courtezan! This Luce Morgan was in high favour with the Queen at the time of her courtship with Alençon, her name first appearing in the Accounts of the Great Wardrobe in 1579. In this first bequest she received 'Eleven yards of silk grosgrain given by our Commandment to Luce Morgan to make her a Gown of our great wardrobe.' [10] Further similar bequests to her are found until New Year's Day of 1581/2. After this she disappears, apparently, from the Court. She would probably have been aged about nineteen when first attending the Queen at Court, thus she was some four years older than Marlowe, which again fits precisely, for the Poet refers to himself as 'some untutor'd youth' in his Dark Lady's estimation.

As Hotson himself suggests, Luce Morgan's skill on the virginals would have endeared her to her royal mistress, who had a constant need of music. Queen Elizabeth was herself a fine player and brought a connoisseur's appreciation to the musicianship of others. Her musician Ferdinando Heyborne *alias* Richardson was in daily demand, [11] but at such times when she was attended only by her Ladies, to have a skilled player of the virginals present would have been much to her liking, and doubtless Luce Morgan filled that niche ably. The presents to her of dress materials, silk grosgrain, velvet and russet satin with black velvet in each of the three years when she was one of the Queen's intimate attendants testify to the favour in which she was held. [12] Her music was no less appreciated by her doting Poet-lover, who lovingly describes her playing in *Sonnet 128,* the second in the series, in which he calls her his 'Music'.

> How oft, when thou, my Music, music play'st
> Upon that blessed wood whose motion sounds
> With thy sweet fingers when thou gently sway'st
> The wiry concord that mine ear confounds,
> Do I envy those jacks that nimble leap
> To kiss the tender inward of thy hand,
> Whilst my poor lips, which should that harvest reap,
> At the wood's boldness by thee blushing stand.
> To be so tickled they would change their state
> And situation with those dancing chips
> O'er whom thy fingers walk with gentle gait,
> Making dead wood more bless'd than living lips.
>> Since saucy jacks so happy are in this,
>> Give them thy fingers, me thy lips to kiss.

By 1587 when Marlowe first arrived in London in the late summer of that year, Luce Morgan was no longer a Court favourite, having likely succumbed to the advances of a courtier seducer. Sir William Knollys refers to the on-going danger from the predatory debauchers of the Court beauties, who preyed with 'wolfish cruelty and fox-like subtlety on the tame beasts' [13] to encompass these young ladies' downfall. Her dismissal would soon have followed, but she managed to find a husband, a man named Parker, whose name she did not use, preferring to be known as Luce Morgan. She bore a Welsh name, and such black-eyed beauties are to be found among the Welsh, a musical nation. With such attributes of enchantment she set up in the profession as a courtezan in a house in Clerkenwell, where we can see her as one of those 'Who chaine blind youths in trammels of their haire' and sing their 'Calipsoes charmes'. [14] At the time when Marlowe and 'Prince' Will were her clients she was probably a rather high class courtezan. She must have been of good family to have qualified for the Court.

The sonnets making play with the term 'will', meaning sexual desire, and the 'Prince's' name Will, make it clear that he had followed his Sonneteer to this mistress' love-nest, and with his vaunted fair beauty became her fast favourite. The vulnerable and passionate Poet was no match for the flamboyant and wealthy 'Prince' Will. Moreover, one has the impression that the young Marlowe was a somewhat shy lover, overpowered by his emotional subjection to her charms. In *Sonnet 128* the lines referring to his 'poor lips which . . by thee blushing stand' have a hint of *double entendre*. This courtezan with the 'raven black' eyes was no conventional beauty, but she exercised a powerful enchantment over Marlowe. There is a deal of anguish in these sonnets expressing his crying need to be loved in return.

Lo, as a careful housewife runs to catch
One of her feathered creatures broke away,
Sets down her babe and makes all swift despatch
In pursuit of the thing she would have stay,
Whilst her neglected child holds her in chase,
Cries to catch her whose busy care is bent
To follow that which flies before her face,
Not prizing her poor infant's discontent;
So runn'st thou after that which flies from thee,
Whilst I, thy babe, chase thee afar behind.
But if thou catch thy hope, turn back to me
And play the mother's part: kiss me, be kind.
    So will I pray that thou may'st have thy *Will*,
    If thou turn back and my loud crying still.

Sonnet 143

    The fickle 'Prince' Will, it seems, abandoned her finally, who had at first ousted his friend the Sonneteer, and the Dark Lady sulked, wanting her glamorous lover back, and was cruel to her doting Poet-lover, perhaps blaming him for 'Prince' Will's departure. But evidently at first 'Prince' Will was really smitten by her dark beauty, for preceding the sonnets playing on *'Will"* – 'Whoever hath her wish, thou hast thy *Will*' (Sonnet 135) and 'If thy soul check thee that I come so near, Swear to thy blind soul that I was thy *Will*' (Sonnet 136) – are two sonnets couched appropriately in legal terms, for Will Hatcliffe was a Grayan, which speak of them as *both* enslaved to this black-eyed tormentress.

Beshrew that heart that makes my heart to groan
For that deep wound it gives my friend and me;
Is't not enough to torture me alone,
But slave to slavery my sweet'st friend must be?
Me from myself thy cruel eye hath taken,
And my next self thou harder hast engrossed;
Of him, myself, and thee I am forsaken,
A torment thrice three-fold thus to be crossed.
Prison my heart in thy steel bosom's ward,
But then my friend's heart let my poor heart bail;
Who e'er keeps me, let my heart be his guard;
Thou canst not then use rigour in my jail.
    And yet thou wilt, for I being pent in thee,
    Perforce am thine, and all that is in me.

Sonnet 133

So now I have confess'd that he is thine,
And I myself am mortgag'd to thy will;
Myself I'll forfeit, so that other mine
Thou wilt restore to be my comfort still.
But thou wilt not, nor he will not be free,
For thou art covetous, and he is kind;
He learn'd but surety-like to write for me,
Under that bond that him as fast doth bind.
The statute of thy beauty thou wilt take,
Thou usurer that putt'st forth all to use,
And sue a friend came debtor for my sake,
So him I lose through my unkind abuse.
    Him have I lost, thou hast both him and me:
    He pays the whole, and yet am I not free.

Sonnet 134

At this stage in Luce Morgan's game she was still evidently a very desirable courtezan who had her special clients, and these sonnets were written early in the Poet's relationship with 'Prince' Will before his disillusionment with this young man's character had set in. The precise situation is intriguing, but it would seem that the Dark Lady had cast her charms to hook the young Prince of Purpoole into her net and preferred this wealthy young man to her poor Poet.

GESTA GRAYORUM

Corroboration that this really is the Prince of Purpoole, 'Prince' Will Hatcliffe in 1587-8, and Luce Morgan, who became notorious as 'Black Luce' of Clerkenwell – *alias* Hotson's fair 'Mr. W.H.' and Hotson's Dark Lady – is strikingly provided in the extant records of the reign of the next Prince of Purpoole, Henry Helmes, who was not elected until 1594. His Court of Graya was honoured with a visit from Queen Elizabeth, who that year was persuaded to play up to this mock Prince of Purpoole and his 'Court'. John Nichol's *Progresses of Queen Elizabeth* has preserved a full and fascinating account of the 'royal' proceedings at Gray's Inn that year under the title *Gesta Grayorum.* [15]. In the inaugural ceremonies for 'Prince' Henry Helmes we find listed all those 'homagers and vassals' of the Prince of Purpoole, who were called to his Court of Graya to do him homage and pay their tribute. There is one lady included – she is named *'Lucy Negro,* abbess of Clerkenwell'. The term 'Negro' from the Italian for *black* does not, however, tell us she is a negress; of such there were probably none known in sixteenth century London, whereas Italian words had entered the common language, so that no such confusion would have occurred. She was, of course, Luce Morgan!

The entire ceremony is a delight. It is all done in mock seriousness according to a well established Grayan tradition: the 'Solicitor, having certain great old books lying before him' from which he reads to the newly-elected Prince of Purpoole of the extent of his 'provinces and territories . . the particulars whereof do here appear in your Excellency's records in the book of Dooms- day remaining in your Exchequer, in the 50th and 500th chest thereof.' He then reads out the list of 'homagers and vassals' by name with the details of their 'Tenures and Services belonging to the same', who are then called (probably by trumpets) in turn to the 'Prince's' footstool to kiss his hand and do 'homage to his Highness in solemn manner, kneeling according to their order'. In fact, the 'solemn manner' of the proceedings must have been broken by chuckles and uproarious gusts of laughter!

> *'Mariotto Marquarillo de Holborn* holdeth the manors of High and Nether *Holborn* by cornage in *capite*, of the Prince of *Purpoole*, and rendering on the day of his Honour's coronation, for every of the Prince's pensioners, one milk-white doe, to be bestowed on them by the Prince, for a favour, or New-Year's-night-gift; and ren- dering yearly two hundred millions sterling.'

(Note the ridiculously large sum of money!)

And next follows, accompanied no doubt by a murmur of excitement:

> *'Lucy Negro*, abbess de *Clerkenwell*, holdeth the nunnery of *Clerkenwell*, with the lands and privileges thereunto belonging, of the Prince of *Purpoole* by night-service in *Cauda*, and to find a choir of nuns, with burning lamps, to chant *Placebo* to the gentle- men of the Prince's privy-chamber, on the day of his Excellency's coronation.' [16]

How this would have delighted the listening 'courtiers'! And their 'Prince'! Luce Morgan, doubtless still beautiful in 1594 when she would have been about thirty-four years of age, clad in her nun's garb in her role as Abbess de Clerkenwell, her raven-black eyes shining and flashing their coquetry at the gentlemen of the 'court' as she passed to kneel at the Prince of Purpoole's foot- stool and kiss his hand, doubtless caused quite a sensation.

And so the merriment continues. The long list of 'signiories' concludes with more delightful tomfoolery, including sexual innuendo that would have caused ripples of laughter through the assembled 'court'.

> *'Amarillo de Paddington* holdeth an hundred ox-gangs of land in *Paddington*, of the Prince of *Purpoole*, by petty-serjeantry, that when the Prince maketh a voyage royal against the *Amazons*, to subdue and bring them under, he do find, at his own charge, a thou- sand men well furnished with long and strong morris-pikes, black bills, or halberds, with morions on their heads; and rendering year- ly four hundred millions sterling.'

'*Baldwine de Islington* holdeth the town of *Islington,* of the Prince of *Purpoole,* by grand-serjeantry; and rendering, at the coronation of his Honour, for every maid in *Islington,* continuing a virgin after the age of fourteen years, one hundred thousand million sterling.' [17]

Since Luce Morgan was at the Court of Graya in 1594 it is to be expected that she would have been there six years earlier, when she was younger and even more beautiful, to pay her homage to will Hatcliffe as Prince of Purpoole, with his poet-friend Christopher Marlowe present, who was head-over-heels in-love with the dark-eyed courtezan there intent on seducing the beautiful young 'Prince' Will. We can imagine the emotion that was stirring in the Poet's breast, which he poured into his sonnets to the Dark Lady. That the *Gesta Grayorum* records a repeat performance (by popular request?) of Luce Morgan as 'Abbess de Clerkenwell' in 1587-8 cannot really be doubted.

So here we have the Dark Lady and the 'Lovely Boy' almost thrown together! Scholars wishing to reject this evidence must then produce equally viable evidence for an alternative 'Mr.W.H.' and another Dark Lady – or retreat into total disbelief in the *Sonnets* seeing these poems as mere figments of Shakespeare's imagination without foundation, or historical, or personal significance.

But Luce Morgan, 'Black Luce' who was at the Court of Graya in 1594, cannot be wished away. These high-class courtezans were often young women of good family who became seduced, and once 'fallen women' took up trading on men's lust – perhaps in revenge for their stolen chastity. Chastity was much prized in Elizabethan times – something that may be difficult to appreciate in this permissive age when it has become the least valued, the most scorned possession of the liberated young women, and men, of to-day. But the Elizabethan man, even whilst he was an avid hunter whose game was the breaking of maidenheads, deeply respected chastity where it was successfully preserved against his predatory assault. Chastity was the battle-ground of the sexes, as honour was the battle-ground of real war amongst men, each in their way cruel and merciless. That is how Marlowe saw this field of human 'warfare'. The delectable and courageous Countess of Salisbury in *Edward the Third,* and the poetic narrative depicting the chaste *Lucrece* are not his only celebrations of chastity as a virtue for which death itself was not too high a price to pay. The entire Marlowe-Shakespearean canon reflects the Elizabethan mores governing sex.

Several portraits of courtezans scattered amongst the multifarious characters of the plays testify that he knew and had shrewdly observed the ladies of this most ancient profession: beginning with the enchanting Bellamira in *The Jew of Malta* with her ponce Pilia-Borzia; the nameless Courtezan in *The Comedy of Errors;* to his most rounded portrait, Doll Tearsheet in *Henry IV Part 2* – who, I suspect, is in part based on his youngest sister Doll or Dorothy Marlowe, a proper little tear-away who married Thomas Graddell, the inn-keeper of 'The George' in Canterbury. The bawd or brothel-keeper Mistress Overdone makes a brief appearance in *Measure for Measure,* and the Bawd in *Pericles* is a sharply observed portrayal of such a type.

John Lyly, Marlowe's predecessor from the King's School, Canterbury, made his name with his courtly novel *Euphues* about a lady of the Court, Lucilla, who turned courtezan, which became a best-seller and set the fashion in novel writing. The gossip-collector John Aubrey relates the history of just such a famous real-life courtezan, the well-born Elizabeth Broughton, of a respectable Herefordshire family, who 'was a most exquisite beautie, as finely shaped as nature could frame; and had a delicate wit'. She became the kept woman of Richard, Earl of Dorset, but 'at last she grew common and infamous, and gott the pox, of which she died.' [18]

Inevitably, this was the slippery path down which Luce Morgan descended, and Hotson traces her sad decline. By 1595 Thomas Lodge in *A Figge for Momus* has a character relate of another, 'For I knew him well, he had the pox by Luce', [19] although this may be mere poetic licence for she survived at least another thirteen years. Thomas Heywood in about 1599 in his *Edward IV, Part I* puts a speech into the mouth of a character called Spicing who is about to pay Nature's debt on the gallows, and aiming 'to die like a man' recalls the whores of his day:

> 'Commend me to blacke *Luce,* bouncing *Besse,* & lusty *Kate,* and the other pretty morsels of man's flesh'. [20]

Kate Arden was a well known prostitute of the time, and 'bouncing Besse' was either Bess Lister, or Luce Morgan's rival, Elizabeth Holland, a notorious courtezan of Islington. Mistress Holland was charged in 1595 with keeping 'a common house of bawdrye' [21] but pleaded not guilty before the Queen's Bench, although eventually the law caught up with her, and at her trial at the Middlesex sessions of February 1596/7 she was sentenced to be 'carted' to Newgate. During her carting she would be pelted with stinking fish and such missiles as came to hand, and for good measure her punishment was a whipping with a cruel knotted four-lashed whip. [22]

Luce Morgan seems to have evaded justice until the end of the century, and Dr Hotson suggests she may have enjoyed some degree of protection through Court influence, but on 15th January 1599/1600 she was eventually arrested and her sentence, appreciably more lenient than that meted out to Elizabeth Holland, ordained :

> 'Item yt is ordered that Luce Morgan *alias* Parker for that she is a notorious and lewde woman of her bodye and otherwise of evill conversacion shalbe presentlie committed to Brydewell there to be sett to worke till she shall become bounde with good & sufficient sureties for her good behaviour during her naturall lief.' [23]

232

The Elizabethan gentleman Philip Gawdy, whose extant letters home to his father in Norfolk are an invaluable source of information on London gossip, reported in December 1600 on some of the ladies of these illicit brothels :

'There is heavy news out of Bridewell, for Mall Newberry and Mall Digby have been carted three days together, when one of them had like to have been killed with a blow of a stone upon her forehead . . Luce Morgan lives in reasonable discredit still, but yet she keeps herself from coaching or carting.' [24]

It is not known how long she remained in Bridewell but it seems she regained her freedom and continued her trade unmolested thereafter. She died before 8th October 1610, according to John Davies of Hereford. [25] The *Sonnets* appeared in print by the summer of 1609, but there is no evidence to tell us whether Luce Morgan ever saw herself immortalized as the Dark Lady before her life ebbed away, a rather superior courtezan who was Marlowe's mistress during his hey-day in London before his own tragedy overtook him.

Taking note of her surname, Morgan, Dr Hotson has produced yet further evidence to seal the identification of the Dark Lady. The sea imagery that is used in the sonnets to her makes clear that the lady in question is a harlot, and also reflects the connotations of her surname, Morgan, which derives from the Welsh word for the sea – *mor.* Hence the Welsh name *Morgan* means Sea-man[26] In the sea imagery of *Sonnet 135* the Poet adds a touch of the word 'more' (mor), and we recall that in Canterbury there were Welsh-speaking families, and with the vicinity of the sea this was one of the Welsh words he is most likely to have known. (The italics follow Thorpe's edition)

> The sea, all water, yet receives rain still,
> And in abundance addeth to his store;
> So thou being rich in *Will* add to thy *Will*
> One will of mine to make thy large *Will* more.

Under 'The Themes of the Sonnets Analysed' 'more' connoting Morgan is further explored. In *Sonnet 137* we read of *'eyes* corrupt by over-partial looks' which are –

'anchored in the bay where all men ride'.

Having an association with a harlot, even of superior class, inevitably had its penalties for the Poet, which he reaped in due course in a gonorrhoeal infection, the less virulent form of venereal disease, for which the prescribed cure was the taking of medicinal baths. His sickness is frankly declared in three of the sonnets. In the first of these, *Sonnet 147,* there can be no doubt that our poet is speaking from anguished personal experience of the pangs of love, and the wretchedness of his physical condition that has fastened on him as a result of his love-affair with a harlot.

> My love is as a fever, longing still
> For that which longer nurseth the disease,
> Feeding on that which doth preserve the ill,
> Th' uncertain sickly appetite to please.
> My reason, the physician to my love,
> Angry that his prescriptions are not kept,
> Hath left me, and I desperate now approve.
> Desire is death, which physic did except.
> Past cure I am, now reason is past care,
> And frantic mad with ever more unrest,
> My thoughts and my discourse as mad men's are,
> At random from the truth vainly express'd.
> > For I have sworn the fair, and thought thee bright,
> > Who art as black as hell, as dark as night.

The sonnet-pair which concludes the entire sequence bewails his sickness, depicting Cupid's 'love-kindling fire' being quenched with medicinal water that –

> . . grew a seething bath, which yet men prove
> Against strange maladies a sovereign cure.
> But at my mistress' eye Love's brand new-fired,
> The boy for trial needs would touch my breast.
> I sick withal the help of bath desired,
> And hither hied, a sad distemper'd guest.
> > But found no cure; the bath for my help lies
> > Where Cupid got new fire; my mistress' eyes.

Sonnet 153

So the sonnet-sequence winds to its end with a frank and unabashed confession that the Poet is paying the price of his love for the 'black' beauty who has him in her toils, and whom he cannot help loving despite all. His enslavement to her becomes increasingly desperate, her 'foul pride' being an expression of his revulsion against her professional use of her sex, which has brought its Nemesis in infecting him with this disease.

> Oh from what power hast thou this powerful might,
> With insufficiency my heart to sway,
> To make me give the lie to my true sight,
> And swear that brightness doth not grace the day?
> Whence hast thou this becoming of things ill,

That in the very refuse of thy deeds
There is such strength and warrantise of skill,
That in my mind thy worst all the best exceeds?
Who taught thee how to make me love thee more,
The more I hear and see just cause of hate?
Oh, though I love what others do abhor
With others thou shouldst not abhor my state.
    If thy unworthiness rais'd love in me,
    More worthy I to be belov'd of thee.

Sonnet 150

This genius of many contradictory facets who possesses an inherent strain of purity in his nature is, nevertheless, absolutely head over heels in love with this enchanting courtezan, whose 'sinful loving' he embraces with adoration. But then, he is not only the Poet of Beauty, but also of Passion – a truly 'kaleidescopic personality', as C.L. Barber has called him.

When we read the *Sonnets* in the illumination of their own rational, this is a passionate hetrosexual, personal testament, howsoever complex, in which the Poet indulges his love of beauty and movingly expresses his sinful love for his black-eyed Mistress, to whom he is tied as strongly by his sexuality as he is bound in his 'dear religious love' to his Patron, the faithful Friend and soul-mate who shared his tragic eclipse.

If he had a sexual problem, it was not a homosexual aberration, but the vene-real disease he contracted through his passionate love for a beautiful harlot.

And surely it is not for us to judge him. Let him or her cast the first stone who is only utterly pure in heart and life before presuming to castigate the Poet who wrote such a treasury of love for our contemplation, our delight, and our edification.

Babington with his Complices in S. Giles field

Babington and his Companions. *This band of dedicated conspirators had the Pope's blessing and he named them his 'White Sons'. The whole object of the conspiracy was to assassinate Queen Elizabeth and place Mary Queen of Scots on the throne – a prospect over which Mendoza, the Spanish ambassador in Paris, gloated.*

In translation the Latin words issuing from Babington's mouth are :
'These are my companions whom danger itself led'.

Above the scaffold: One is punished in that in which one sins.

> To this I witness call the fools of time,
> Which die for goodness, who have liv'd for crime.

Sonnet 124

XVI

THREE SONNETS BY THE QUEEN'S SECRET AGENT

ONCE AGAIN we are indebted to the incisive research of Dr Hotson, this time turning to his *Shakespeare's Sonnets Dated* (1949), to elucidate the meaning of three sonnets that had proved intractable. He alone has revealed their precise historical context – which, again, fits Marlowe with amazing precision!

In the placement of *Sonnet 107,* the first of these 'difficult' sonnets, numbered deliberately as the one hundred and seventh in the sequence, he has given us proof positive that this is the Poet's own personal and very carefully chosen order of presentation. If we want to understand the mind of this greatest poet-dramatist this question is not incidental, but of prime importance, for not only does he reveal himself as essentially an Elizabethan in this, his sonnet-presentation to his contemporary readers, but there are fascinating autobiographical implications to be gleaned from the subtlety of his sequential device. As Hotson has noted: 'the poet's arrangement of the sequence is a matter just as essential to his art as his ordering of the thought within each poem.' [1]

Hotson has shown that *Sonnet 107* is so placed in mental association with *Psalm 107,* that beautiful psalm which paints with vivid imagery the sufferings of mankind and offers praise to God for deliverance from dangers and tribulations, especially from *dangers at sea. Psalm 107* was one of the most popular in the Psalter. [2]

To the Elizabethans, from Queen Elizabeth downwards, the *Book of Psalms,* the Psalter, was familiarly known and constantly resorted to as comfort in times of trouble, and many psalms were known by heart. The Earl of Essex recited two verses of *Psalm 51,* one of the seven 'Penitential Psalms', at his execution, and Lady Jane Grey at hers managed the entire nineteen verses by heart, beginning:

'Have mercy upon me, O God, according to thy lovingkindness: according unto the multitude of thy tender mercies blot out my transgression.
Wash me throughly from mine iniquity, and cleanse me from my sin.'

This was known as the 'neck verse' which, in Latin, accurately and fluently read, might save a felon from the noose – a feat easily achieved by Ben Jonson when he slew his fellow actor, Gabriel Spencer.

The Elizabethans had Henry VIII's Reformation to thank for their knowledge of the Psalms. Hotson tells us: 'The Book of Common Prayer, for the use of every parish in the land, begins: 'The Psalter shall be read through once every Month, as it is appointed, both for Morning and Evening Prayer' .. in the beautiful version of Myles Coverdale, who introduced into English the phrases *lovingkindness* and *tender mercy.* The Psalter's one hundred and fifty psalms were thus appointed to be distinctly and audibly read twelve times every year – an annual one thousand eight hundred psalms, or five psalms each day, in every church.' [3]. Christopher Marlowe, the Cathedral choirboy, would undoubtedly have had them by heart, and growing up in Canterbury with its sizeable Huguenot community, he would be aware that it was a point of their religion to know all the Psalms by heart. He would have learnt them as easily as breathing while singing them daily. Richard Noble in his fascinating study, *Shakespeare's Biblical Knowledge* (1935) has culled one hundred and fifty references to the Psalms from the plays that would have sounded an echo in the psalm-singing Elizabethans.

Queen Elizabeth was a devotee of the Psalter and knew many of the Psalms by heart. She also sometimes composed her own psalms and sacred songs, and in 1588 when the mighty Armada was defeated she contributed a psalm of her own composition to be sung as part of the thanksgiving service for their deliverance from the Spanish threat, held in St Paul's Cathedral on 24th November 1588. Dr Hotson quotes from this and explains the special significance of her choice of word and phrase:

> 'Look and bow down thine ear, O Lord,
> From thy bright sphere behold and see
> Thy handmaid and thy handiwork
> Among thy priests off'ring to thee.

'Few souls in that vast and exalted throng could fail to recognize that in these words she drew on the 86th Psalm – which begins *Bow down thine ear, O Lord,* and later prays *help the son of thine handmaid* – or fail to see that she chose it *because the 86th is the first psalm* appointed in the Prayer Book *for Day 17:* the Queen's Accession Day, the 17th November, "the day of the gladness of her heart", the day thirty years ago last Sunday when Mary's death both ended for us the burning of Christians for heresy and rid us of Spanish Philip; the day "wherein our Nation received a new light after a fearful and bloody eclipse". To the sound of *Bow down thine ear, O Lord* every bell in England this month rings out joy unceasing for Day 17, "wherein God gave a rare Phoenix to rule this land". In the royal choice of "her own" psalm to render thanks for this second Great Deliverance, what felicity, what richness of evocation for her loving people!' [4]

This is the background we must be aware of in order to appreciate the significance of the precise placement of *Sonnet 107* (which is certainly not chronological in the sonnet-sequence), which, for the Elizabethan reader, would immediately have associated it with the great psalm of thanksgiving for deliverance from present dangers that had been sung, chanted and spoken throughout the country in churches and homes as news of the defeat of the dreaded Spanish Armada rang through the land.

Armada Year: A Psalm, a Sonnet, and a Play

Psalm 107 is one of the longest in the Psalter, its theme being praise of God for his manifold mercies in succouring suffering mankind in all kinds of dangers, but its chief glory lies in the famous passage describing perils at sea. Marlowe's Bible would have been the Bishops' or the Genevan Bible. I have quoted from the latter as the text of *Psalm 107* is nearer to that of the Authorised Version of 1611.

PSALM 107

verse

23	They that go downe to the sea in shippes, and occupie by the great waters,
24	They se the workes of the Lord, and his wonders in the depe.
25	For he commandeth and raiseth the stormie winde, & it lifteth vp the waues thereof.
26	They mounte vp to the heauen, & descend to the depe, so that their soule melteth for trouble.
27	They are tossed to and fro, and stagger like a drunken man, and all their cunning is gone.
28	Then they crye vnto the Lord in their trouble, and he bringeth them out of their distress.
29	He turneth the storme to calme, so that the waues thereof are stil.
30	When they are quieted, they are glad, & he bringeth them vnto the hauen where they wold be.
31	Let them (therefore) confesse before the Lord his louing kindenes, and his wonderful workes before the sonnes of men. ⁵

For a man who has recently travailed in storms at sea (and during the Armada campaign they endured some mighty storms!) his sense of vivid recall would wring a heartfelt response. It has been revealed by my researches, to be published in *Christopher Marlowe & the Armada,* that he took part in the great naval campaign, so that this psalm would have a special personal significance for him, and it evidently influenced his numbering of *Sonnet 107* with this association in mind. Dr Hotson's identification of *Sonnet 107* as the Poet's 'Armada Sonnet' once again emphasises the autobiographical content of these poems for it related to a most momentous experience in his young life. [6]

The Armada campaign was the greatest naval confrontation that history had ever seen to date. Naval warfare was still in its infancy, and no one knew what the outcome of these great sea-battles might be, or what was the best way of fighting a naval battle. This was to prove a testing ground for more than mere strength, but of tactics which were to influence the future of navies. The two forces confronting each other were very different. The English navy consisted of faster, more manoeuvrable fighting ships built to Hawkins' new design, and having guns of lighter, but more rapid fire-power with longer range. The Spanish navy was composed of the high-built galleons of traditional design, armoured with iron cannon throwing huge cannon balls of shorter range, and somewhat less accuracy, though devastating when landing; and their aim was to grapple the enemy and finish the fight with hand-to-hand combat on the decks. The English sought to avoid this, concentrating their fire-power to force the break-up of the Spanish defensive formation and eventually to pound their ships sufficiently to sink them. Theirs was basically a ship-sinking tactic of naval warfare.

The most striking feature of the formidable Spanish Armada with its towering black-painted ships was their unique defensive battle formation, which took roughly the shape of a crescent moon. It was a defensive manoeuvre of great strength in which the 'horns' of the crescent faced the enemy with their strongest ships in these exposed positions, while the body of the fleet was protected. If an enemy ship entered the bay of the crescent moon, Spanish ships would immediately surround and grapple it. The English wisely never permitted this, although much of the cannonade was at very close quarters in order to maximize fire-power and there were some extremely hot fights, in which the Spanish engaged in defiance of strict instructions from King Philip to keep the Armada intact to provide naval cover for Parma's expected invasion of England.

The Spanish Armada's crescent-moon battle formation was the novel feature of this great naval confrontation that seized the imagination of those reporting news of the battles, which was blazoned throughout Europe – not always accurately! The mighty Armada was seen as the 'Spanish Bull' presenting its horns to the English 'matadors' harrying it with their mobile navy which Howard formed into four squadrons under himself as Admiral, Drake as Vice-admiral, and Hawkins and Frobisher. The Protestant zealot 'J.L.' (probably James Lea) in his book *The Birth, Purpose and mortall Wound of the Romish holie League* in 1589 made great play with the description of the Armada 'Moon' as he fulminated against the Holy Roman League led by the Pope with the King of Spain, the Duke of Guise, and the Duke of Parma, who were poised to join forces in anticipation of the great Spanish victory. To 'J.L.' it was a battle between David and Goliath, Christ and Anti-Christ.

'Now to make this League an able Bodie, to beare downe the

aduersaries of Antichrist both by land and sea, her head was beautified with a horned Moone of huge and mightie shippes, readie to
ioyne with the bloody Guise, and also to vnite them to the Prince of
Parma, that in a moment they might swallow vp little England . . '

And referring to the sacred banners of Catholic saints borne by each ship, and
after which the vessel was named:

'. . whose Mooned Cronet was deckt with sundrie pendants of painted Saints . . But all in vaine: for the breath of the Lords mouth hath
dimmed the brightnesse of her Moone, and scattered those proud
shippes, whose masts seemed like Cedars to dare the Sunne.' [7]

Throughout Europe news of the 'invincible' Spanish Armada's moon-
shaped battle formation, and eventually of its hopeless defeat, spread and
aroused amazement combined with dismay or elation according to which side
the hearer supported. The great confrontation had been watched with keenest
interest to see what the outcome of this vital Protestant-Catholic battle would
be, not least because of the prophetic crash of great empires and kingdoms that
was forecast to take place in the fatal year 1588, for which fearful predictions
had been prophesied for over a hundred years. Catastrophic events were
expected to happen, the world order would be turned topsy-turvy and calamities
of every kind would follow thick and fast! All Europe knew of the doomful
prophecies pronounced a century ago and confirmed by the great mathematician known as Regiomontanus, *alias* Johan Müller of Königsberg, who had
worked them out with Biblical testimony to culminate in this fatal year, 1588.
These mathematical calculations were supported by the ominous portents
discerned by the astrologers, who calculated that an eclipse of the sun would
take place on 16th February 1588, followed by a total eclipse of the moon when
it was at full, on 2nd March, and a second eclipse of the moon on 26th August
– three eclipses in one year! And all this to the accompaniment of the baleful
conjunction of Saturn, Jupiter and Mars in the moon's house. [8]
By the time the Armada, Philip of Spain's instrument designed to hale that
great Jezebel, Elizabeth, from her throne, was ready to set sail against England,
all Europe was in the grip of apprehension as to the dreadful disasters that
would befall, for *this* was that very fateful year, 1588. (This is what Gabriel
Harvey referred to in his *Gorgon, or the wonderfull yeare,* which is not 1588,
but 1593, the year of the death of Marlowe that he sees as the most amazing
event!).
King Philip was not ruled by superstition, however. He heard only the voice
of God commanding him to proceed against the Protestant Queen who defied
the Pope. Many in Europe saw this battle of the Armada, indeed, as a sort of
Armageddon. In England the effect of these predictions engendered such
despondency and apprehension that the government ordered the astrologer and

physician, John Harvey, brother of Gabriel Harvey, to write a treatise denying these dreadful auguries, which was published in 1588 to pour cold water on the mounting alarm with counter-arguments cleverly advanced 'especially in abatement of the terrible threatenings and menaces, peremptorily denounced against the kingdoms and states of the world.' [9]

Against this background of the Armada's moon battle-formation, and the fearful portents widely believed of infinite disaster to befall in 1588, we have to consider the Poet's 'Armada' sonnet.

Sonnet 107

Not mine own fears, nor the prophetic soul
Of the wide world, dreaming on things to come,
Can yet the lease of my true love control,
Suppos'd as forfeit to a confin'd doom.
The mortal Moon hath her eclipse endur'd,
And the sad augers mock their own presage;
Incertainties now crown themselves assur'd,
And peace proclaims olives of endless age.
Now with the drops of this most balmy time
My love looks fresh, and Death to me subscribes,
Since spite of him I'll live in this poor rhymen,
While he insults o'er dull and speechless tribes.
   And thou in this shalt find thy monument,
   When tyrants' crests and tombs of brass are spent.

The first two lines clearly refer to the world-wide prophecies believed for the year 1588 – in dreams the future was said to be revealed – and these 'sad augers mock their own presage' for they were not fulfilled. 'Incertainties' about the future were turned to 'endless peace' for the 'mortal Moon ' – the Armada (not the planet, which also had its eclipses in 1588) had suffered its eclipse. There is an accolade to Queen Elizabeth in 'olives of endless age' (capitalized in Thorpe's edition) as one of her popular synonyms was Olivia, deriving from the acclaim of her people when they cried: 'O live! Long live our Queen!' [10]

The word 'mortal' in Elizabethan English had the connotation fatal, deadly – as in 'J.L.'s' *'mortall Wound of the Romish holie League'*. The 'mortal moon' of the Armada was a death-dealing moon, hence it was 'mortal', fatal, deadly. In contrast the Poet speaks of 'this most balmy time', balm being the healing herb with which wounds are salved – and the Elizabethans knew their herbs. His reference to 'tyrants' crests' is also apt, for the members of the Holy Roman League were all tyrants. [11] Everything in the highly-charged language of this sonnet fits Dr Hotson's identification of it as the Poet's personal celebration of the victory over the Spanish Armada perfectly.

242

There is another school of thought, however, that favours the interpretation as the celebration of the release of the Earl of Southampton, seen as Shakespeare's sole patron, from the Tower on the accession of King James in 1603. The line 'Suppos'd as forfeit to a confin'd doom' has been the stumbling block to acceptance of Hotson's interpretation. However, we have only to compare Shakespeare's use of this very word in *Sonnet 110* to see that it does not mean 'imprisoned' as we today understand it:

> Mine appetite I never more will grind
> On newer proof to try an older friend,
> A God in love, to whom I am confin'd.

Here the sense is 'limited, circumscribed'. In *Sonnet 107* 'a confin'd doom' also means a *limited* life, one doomed to an end. For many who engaged in the mortal fight against the Armada their doom was 'confin'd' in this very sense, for their lives were sealed by death. This literally expresses the Poet's view of the fate awaiting him and his friend if the battle turned against them, and Englishmen and women generally, in the event of a successful Spanish invasion when they would have met a 'confin'd doom'. [12]

Critics arguing that Southampton is identified claim that Queen Elizabeth's death in March 1603 is referred to in the line: 'The mortal Moon hath her eclipse endur'd', because 'Moon' is referred to as female, and Thorpe capitalizes this word – but so he does 'Olives', in which case the Queen would be both dead and alive! and he also capitalizes 'Augurs'. Dr Hotson has sufficiently demonstrated from Elizabethan literature that it would be unthinkable to describe Elizabeth as 'The mortal Moon' (however feminine, and the moon is traditionally also a female orb) for 'mortal' connoted 'deadly' or 'fatal', and moreover it was not mannerly to refer to a monarch's mortality, nor would a poet refer to the reign of so popular a queen as Elizabeth as suffering 'eclipse' [13] Elizabeth I's long and scintillating reign was widely recognised as a blessed era in English history by all her contemporaries of Protestant persuasion. In no sense was she a tyrant, so that reference to 'tyrants' crests' is meaningless in 1603. When Southampton was convicted of high treason the Queen showed him mercy in revoking his execution on grounds of his youth and political naiveté in following the leadership of that hot-headed lordling Essex, out of loyalty to him rather than conviction. So that although 1603 brought his release and the restoration of his rights, there could hardly have been grounds for grievance against the Queen (as implied in such an interpretation of this sonnet) and his imprisonment was mercifully brief. One might say he owed his life to the Queen's mercy, for Essex's foolish behaviour could have led him nowhere but to the block, and Southampton must have expected it. Since his death sentence had already been commuted to imprisonment, the line 'and Death to me subscribes' is not applicable.

In the context of 1603, 'the prophetic soul/Of the wide world dreaming on things to come' has no application comparable to the dire auguries of 1588, nor do 'the sad augurs mock their own presage', for the accession of James I was popularly acclaimed. Londoners put on a fantastic show to welcome him in their 'Magnificent Entertainment' and any apprehension was soon allayed. England was already at peace, so that the line 'And peace proclaims olives of endless age' has no significance. The case for this interpretation as a reference to Southampton in 1603 falls down at every point.

On the other hand, Dr Hotson's identification of the theme of *Sonnet 107* associated with *Psalm 107* as the celebration of the defeat of the Armada, based on his meticulous research, is confirmed doubly and trebly by recent evidence concerning Marlowe's involvement with the Armada campaign.

THE 'ARMADA' PORTRAIT
AETATIS SVAE 24   1588
Shown on opposite page: Presumptive Portrait of Christopher Marlowe

This is the Grafton 'Shakespeare' Portrait, so-called because the unknown sitter is the exact contemporary of Shakespeare – and of Marlowe – dated 1588, Armada year. It has now been suggested that it is, in fact, a second portrait of Christopher Marlowe, painted in celebration of the victory over the Spanish Armada in which he took part. It is probably by a Flemish immigrant artist in Canterbury painted while Marlowe was recuperating from the strenuous naval campaign. This would account for the wan appearance of the young man who had survived the privations endured when their food ran out and the beer turned sour, and the dreaded ships' fever (a kind of gastric enteritis) ravaged the crews after the fighting was over and claimed more dead men than during the entire naval campaign.

This young man looks like a slimmer version of the twenty-one year-old sitter in the Corpus Christi Portrait of Marlowe. All the facial features are similar: the wide brow and identical hairline; the size and shape of the nose, nostrils, and mouth with a small moustache; the chin with its faint, narrow line of beard shadowing it; the shape of eyes and eyebrows – the left eyebrow being partly erased from the scrubbing with soda water administered by the lady who once owned the portrait in her attempt to clean it. This has removed some of the surface pigment. The portrait is an entirely unrestored genuine Elizabethan portrait, whreas the Corpus Christi portrait has been completely restored and overpainted. The Grafton Portrait is of the Flemish or English school, whilst the Corpus Christi Portrait is of the Spanish School favouring heavy contrast of light and shade, known as *chiaroscuro*, as opposed to the 'dry manner' eschewing dramatic light for a 'natural' looking portrait of the English and Flemish school.

For a comparison of the two portraits of 1585 and 1588 showing the strong likeness of the sitters, see *In Search of Christopher Marlowe* (1965 and 1993) by A.D. Wraight and Virginia F. Stern.

The 'Grafton Shakespeare Portrait'

There is no known connection with Shakespeare except the age of the sitter.
It has been claimed as a portrait of Shakespeare because the young man
'looks like a poet'. Discovered at Grafton Regis and has a curious history.
See Wraight and Stern: In Search of Christopher Marlowe, pp. 214-22

CHRISTOPHER MARLOWE AND THE ARMADA

Whatever William Shakespeare was up to in 1588 we do not know, except that he was evidently at Stratford-upon-Avon for the legal case *Shakespeare v. Lambert,* but of Christopher Marlowe's involvement there is recently discovered documentary evidence. In *Sonnet 107* the emphasis on the personal pronouns tells us of the Poet's personal participation in this great naval conflict:

> Not *mine own* fears . .
> . . . . and Death *to me* subscribes,
> Since spite of him *I'll live* . .

These lines impart a sense of the exultation of a young man who had taken part in these great battles against the 'mortal Moon', and had felt death brush past him — and had survived! This whole poem is an exultation over death, and the threat of the Spanish Armada which had mercifully been defeated.

Such was the impact of the stirring events of 1588 on the young poet-dramatist that he also wrote a play in celebration of the great English victory. This is the apocryphal play *The Raigne of King Edward the third* published in 1596 by Cuthbert Burby with several succeeding editions. It was clearly a popular play with contemporary readers, hence seen as fitting subject for satirical allusions couched in their canting language invented for the express purpose of lampooning Marlowe and his great actor, Edward Alleyn, by Robert Greene and his pal Thomas Nashe. These two identified *Tamburlaine the Great* as Marlowe's play – which was also published anonymously, and they have similarly identified *Edward the Third* as his popular play, in which the youthful Edward Alleyn – two years younger than Marlowe – played the Black Prince, who shares the honours of the leading heroic role jointly with his gallant father, Edward III; an unusual arrangement of a play with two heroes – which is perhaps why critics have not recognized that this was written by Marlowe.

The play is unequivocally identified as Marlowe's first English history play on three counts. Firstly, by the canting contemporary allusions made by Greene and Nashe which appeared from 1590 onwards. Secondly, by the strong stylistic affinity with Marlowe's known works, in particular *Tamburlaine the Great* which he had but recently completed; there are numerous tricks of dramatic technique and versification which identify the play as unmistakably from his hand. (The play has had only superficial examination from earlier critics, none of whom has noticed its Armada association.) Thirdly, by its remarkable Armada reflections that link it with the Armada Report written by Marlowe for Lord Admiral Howard, which is the subject of my *Christopher Marlowe & Armada.* [14.] It is very likely that he drew initial inspiration for his choice of this reign from contemplation of the magnificent Tomb of the Black Prince in Canterbury Cathedral.

Courtesy of The Dean and Chapter of Canterbury
Photograph by Tony Whitcomb

The Tomb of the Black Prince. *This magnificent tomb must often have drawn the boy Christopher Marlowe to contemplate the effigy of the Prince, named 'the Soul of Chivalry', who probably inspired his first English history play,* Edward III, *dramatizing the brilliant military exploits of the Black Prince and his father King Edward, who was given the title 'Sovereign of the Seas' by Parliament for his defeat in 1340 of the French navy at the Battle of Sluys – a great historic sea-battle which Marlowe transformed into his dramatic celebration of the English victory over the Spanish Armada in 1588. This popular play launched the fashion for English history plays between 1588 and 1606, comprising more than one fifth of all contemporary plays.*

247

That Marlowe wrote *Edward the Third* to celebrate the victory over the Spanish Armada, against which he had himself fought, is revealed by the text. He chose the reign of Edward III because this king was reputed to have founded our navy. Parliament had awarded him the title 'King of the Sea' for his total defeat of the French navy at the battle of Sluys in 1340, thereby gaining the supremacy of the seas for England. The most remarkable aspect of this play – establishing the dramatist's intent to use this historic reign as his vehicle for the joyful celebration of the great victory over the Armada – is his deliberate depiction of the naval victory of Sluys, fought with bows and arrows, *in terms of a sixteenth century naval battle fought entirely with cannon and gunfire.* Since he was using Holinshed's Chronicles as his source, he could not have been ignorant of the historic facts, but he ignores Holinshed's extremely detailed account of the naval battle and, instead, he writes a dramatic, paraphrased account of the Armada campaign, *which can be compared naval 'accident' by naval 'accident' with his own first-hand account of the Armada battles,* which he wrote for Lord Admiral Howard specifically for presentation to Sir Francis Walsingham. This manuscript report, representing the only first-hand contemporary account in English of the whole naval campaign, has been compared calligraphically with the 'leaf' from Marlowe's play, *The Massacre at Paris,* now in the Folger Library, believed to be his autograph, and both are compared with Marlowe's signature of 1585. The resemblance is undeniably impressive. And the fact that the report is dramatized in his play further supports this. It is further supported by the fact that this unique Armada report was written at the behest of the Lord Admiral for Marlowe's boss in the intelligence service, Sir Francis Walsingham (as Lord Howard's letters to Sir Francis testify), for whom Marlowe had undoubtedly written many reports. There is a treasure trove of research awaiting those who will devote themselves to investigating Marlowe's intelligence activities fully. His Armada report reveals him as a highly trusted government agent. If he is our great dramatist Shakespeare is this not exactly what one would expect to find? His 'Armada' description of the battle of Sluys is put into the mouth of the French Mariner, who also recounts his first sighting of King Edward's invasion fleet as it approaches the French coast. His speech to the French King John is couched in words that would at once have alerted his Elizabethan audiences to what was in store for them:

> *Mariner:* Near to the coast I have descried, my Lord
>
> . . .
>
> The proud Armado of King Edward's ships:
>
> . . .
>
> Majestical the order of their course,
> Figuring the hornèd circle of the moon:
>
> Act 3, scene 1. 11. 62-72

This is a mere foretaste. The long speech that follows, wherein the Mariner describes the defeat of the French navy, couched in 'Armada' terms, leaves no possibility for doubt that this is Marlowe's 'Armada' play, written in conscious celebration of the great English victory in which he had himself played a part.

This topical play would undoubtedly have been chosen for performance at Court that Christmas when on 29th December 1588 the Lord Admiral's Men, with Edward Alleyn playing the Black Prince, presented it before the Queen and her Lord Admiral who was patron of this company. Lord Howard would have been delighted by the French Mariner's 'Armada' speeches, doubtless identifying for the Queen the dramatic account of the 'accidents' at sea depicted in it, which recall their experiences during the campaign most movingly in evocative poetic language – and accurately, for all the evidence combines to support the dramatist's personal involvement in the naval battle.

In two fascinating studies, *Shakespeare at Sea* (1964) augmented by *A Glossary of Shakespeare's Sea and Naval Terms including Gunnery* (1965), Professor A.F. Falconer has unwittingly provided further evidence of Marlowe's Armada involvement. By his assemblage of an amazing wealth of quotations taken from Shakespeare's works, he reveals the dramatist's knowledge of the navy of his time, of storms at sea, of shipwrecks, of winds and tides and many other aspects of life at sea, which is so familiar and accurate as to imply that he must have had first-hand experience on which he could draw freely when composing his dramatic works. The Armada campaign was not long, but it was concentrated; this naval experience clearly made a deep impression on the sensitive and responsive young Marlowe. That William Shakespeare ever had such experience is totally unknown. There is no evidence that he ever went to sea, hence this is once more a matter of arguing back from the plays to invest him with the qualities and knowledge that fit him to be their author.

In Marlowe's case, we have documentary evidence of a singularly exciting and fascinating kind to substantiate it. This, once again, brings the figure of Christopher Marlowe into clear focus as the dramatist responsible for the plays attributed to his pseudonym, William Shakespeare. With every new piece of research, the twin stars of Marlowe and Shakespeare are drawn ever closer to form one brilliant conjunction.

Sonnets 123 and *124* provide an impressive demonstration of the effectiveness of the Hotson approach. No one had been able to fathom the meaning of these sonnets, but our intrepid researcher has brought them clearly into focus, setting them firmly in their historical context. This sonnet-pair has as its theme political events abroad, and they reveal a high degree of political awareness, such as one would expect to find in a government agent whose profession would take him fairly frequently abroad. Having correctly identified the precise circumstances in the contemporary political scene that are alluded to in the poems, Dr Hotson perforce assumes that William Shakespeare would have been thus astutely informed. That is as may be, but there is no need to hypothesize about Marlowe. These two sonnets are the only ones which were written directly out of his personal experience as an intelligence agent. The first of this sonnet-pair was inspired by an assignment in Italy that evidently took him to Rome – as is argued here by hypothesis.

Sonnet 123 illustrates Dr Hotson's method clearly, interpreting the topical context of this poem, and taking the Poet's word *literally,* not figuratively as one is tempted to do when not understanding what is referred to. In this sonnet the Poet speaks of 'pyramids', and not having an Elizabethan understanding of this term the critics have missed the historical significance, which Hotson has supplied. [15]

The Poet's 'pyramids' refer to one of the latest wonders of his sixteenth century world. In Elizabethan English the word 'pyramid' meant an obelisk, such as Cleopatra's Needle, not a pyramid like that of Gizeh. And in the years from 1586 to 1589 such obelisks or 'pyramids' were much in the news in Western Europe as the subject of fashionable gossip. They were 'news' for conversation and table talk at Court and up and down the country.

The 'pyramids' referred to in this sonnet are certainly those gigantic obelisks of great antiquity in Rome, originally brought from Egypt by Caligula, one of Rome's most flamboyant and tyrannical emperors. Pope Sixtus V decided to restore tham from their long fallen, broken state, and had them re-erected by his brilliant engineer, Dominico Fontana. The tremendous feat of construction and erection, which had been declared impossible by both Michelangelo and Antonio da Sangallo, and extolled in poetry by Torquato Tasso, brought to rebirth one huge obelisk in each of the years 1586, 1587, 1588 and 1589, to be gaped at and talked about as the great, new wonders of the world! They drew crowds of eager sightseers to view them.

Pope Sixtus was so pleased with them, he had his portrait painted showing the famous 'pyramids' in the view through the window behind him, just as Queen Elizabeth had herself painted in her 'Armada' portrait showing the naval battle in progress in the seascape seen through the window behind her.

Courtesy of The Vatican Museum

Pope Sixtus V, *Scuola Romano 16th century. Felice Peretti was of humble birth but rose to become Cardinal of Montalto and then succeeded Pope Gregory XIII. He was a crafty politician and became enormously wealthy. His policy was the aggressive extension of Catholic power over Protestant states, but his notable eccentricity found satisfaction in expressing his personal admiration for Queen Elizabeth to the bafflement and dismay of staunch Catholics. He was inordinately proud of the erection of the 'pyramids' brought to Rome by the Emperor Caligula as seen through the window.*

The 'Armada' portrait of Queen Elizabeth, *English School* c. 1588.
This portrait, attributed to George Gower, depicts the Queen as 'Empress of the World' following the defeat of the Spanish Armada, seen in the seascape through the window on the horizon in its crescent formation with English ships in the foreground.

> This royal throne of kings, this sceptred isle,
> This earth of majesty, this seat of Mars,
> This other Eden, demi-paradise,
> This fortress built by Nature for herself
> Against infection and the hand of war,
> This happy breed of men, this little world,
> This precious stone set in the silver sea,
> Which serves it in the office of a wall,
> Or as a moat defensive to a house,
> Against the envy of less happier lands;
> This blessed plot, this earth, this realm, this England.
>
> *Richard II Act 2 Sc. 1*   *ll.40-50*

Since the reference in *Sonnet 123* is to 'pyramids' in the plural, Dr Hotson dates this sonnet to 1589 when all four would have been erected, and their description as 'novel' suggests that they were still a 'new' interest. [16] News of these engineering feats as each huge obelisk rose in its place was carried to the European courts, and became current gossip. To the Catholics they were a feather in the cap of the Pope. Eager travellers hied to Rome to see for themselves these wondrous 'pyramids' and, if lucky, hoped to witness their erection. That Marlowe was interested in them we know from *Dr Faustus* in which reference is made to them when Mephistophiles promises to transport Faustus to Rome to see its wonders, a city which, we must remember, it was dangerous for Protestants to visit. Here he is describing to Faustus the castle on the Ponte Angelo,

> Within whose walls such store of ordnance are,
> And double cannons fram'd of carved brass,
> As match the days within one complete year;
> Besides the gates, and high pyramides,
> Which Julius Caesar brought from Africa.
>
> Doctor Faustus 11. 853-7

Julius Caesar replaces Caligula in Marlowe's play probably because he would be the only Roman ruler known to the Elizabethan playgoers. Bakeless dates this play also to 1589, the year that *Sonnet 123* was written as Hotson suggests, the year following the defeat of the Armada. [17] Both *Dr Faustus,* in the comic scene satirizing the Pope, and this sonnet express popular anti-Catholic views which must be seen in the light of their historical context when the Catholic threat had been newly repulsed, in which Marlowe was actively involved.

From the mid-1500's, as the conflict between Protestant Reformists and the Roman Catholic Church sharpened, English Protestants found themselves unwelcome when they visited Rome. The scholarly Thomas Wilson was arrested as a heretic when he was there in 1555, and when Thomas Sackville visited Rome in 1564 he was thrown into prison. Secret agents, however, travelled under the protection of assumed names and guises, as merchants, scholars or priests with the right colour of religion when their assignments took them into such enemy territory, hence Marlowe could have enjoyed a rare advantage in personally viewing Pope Sixtus's wonderful 'pyramids' – a rather special privilege for a Protestant Englishman not long after the defeat of the Spanish Armada. The inspiration of this sonnet implies a personal viewing to prompt this contemplative poem.

Sonnet 123

> No! Time, thou shalt not boast that I do change.
> Thy pryamids built up with newer might
> To me are nothing novel, nothing strange,
> They are but dressings of a former sight:

251

Our dates are brief, and therefore we admire
What thou dost foist upon us that is old,
And rather make them born to our desire,
Than think that we before have heard them told.
Thy registers and thee I both defy,
Not wond'ring at the present, nor the past;
For thy records, and what we see doth lie,
Made more or less by thy continual haste.
   This I do vow and this shall ever be,
   I will be true despite thy scythe and thee.

In taking the Poet's word literally and teaching us to see with the eyes of the time, Hotson has revealed a fascinating picture of our Poet, the Queen's agent, as he might well have stood surveying Time's pyramids and composing a sonnet woven from his thoughts – for surely this sonnet was not written from hearsay in far away London? The sense of the Poet actually viewing these admired 'pyramids' is far too strongly present. The scene as I have suggested it, is conjectural, but it has the smack of authenticity which says, not only is this possible, it is probable, given the time, the background, and the Poet himself correctly identified.

Sonnet 124, the pair to the sonnet above, is even more undeniably associated with Marlowe by Dr Hotson's findings, for the subject which inspired this intensely political poem is taken direct from his experience as a government intelligence agent familiar with the political intrigues and events that rocked France, whither I believe his last assignment, in the period just prior to the outbreak of the naval war with Spain with the arrival in English waters of the Armada, must have taken him. His task then was probably the important one of assessing the degree of instability in France, for Walsingham feared that the French Catholic Holy Leaguers might join forces with Spain to attack England, unless their own preoccupation with the civil wars that intermittently raged in France ensured that they had their hands too full to lend support to King Philip's invasion plans. And so it turned out, for the French Huguenots and the Catholic factions were thoroughly embroiled in conflict, plot and counter-plot. Later Marlowe was to dramatize the complex French political scene in *The Massacre at Paris*.

Without a knowledge of the contemporary political background, with which Marlowe was so familiar, this sonnet remains obscure; but Dr Hotson's explanation, which follows, will throw light on this obscurity. [19]. In *Sonnet 124* the Poet draws comparisons between his own constancy and faithfulness (his 'faithful dealing' for which the Queen and Privy Council had praised him), which the final couplet of *Sonnet 123* avows as 'true' despite Time's scythe and the uncertainties and disasters born of deceit and ruthlessness that marked the contemporary political scene.

If my dear love were but the child of state,
It might for Fortune's bastard be unfathered,
As subject to Time's love, or to Time's hate,
Weeds among weeds, or flowers with flowers gather'd.
No, it was builded far from accident;
It suffers not in smiling pomp, nor falls
Under the blow of thralled discontent,
Whereto th' inviting time our fashion calls.
It fears not policy, that heretic,
Which works on leases of short-number'd hours,
But all alone stands hugely politic,
That it nor grows with heat, nor drowns with showers.
    To this I witness call the fools of Time,
    Which die for goodness, who have liv'd for crime.

We need to analyse this poem line by line, so much is packed into the metaphors alluding to events and personalities of the time. Dr Hotson's research has clarified its meaning, comparing and matching recent political events in France, which establish its date of composition in conjunction with *Sonnet 123* to which it is an undoubted pair, and comparing this historical background with the precise words of the sonnet: an astute exercise in observation and historical knowledge. He began by asking: Who was 'Fortune's bastard' whose fate it was to suffer 'in smiling pomp' and who fell 'Under the blow of thralled discontent, Whereto th' inviting time our fashion calls'? The fashion of the time was indeed then, as again in our century, political murder.

> 'Very little familiarity with the momentous events of Shakespeare's times is required to recognize the ruler he is thinking of. A prince who, suffering shameful deprivation of his royal power, had with smiles dissembled his fierce resentment. A prince who, after waiting his time, deftly murdering his two capital enemies and reporting his deliverance to his politic Queen Mother, himself fell under the blow of the assassin who thought him a tyrant. This 'fortune's bastard', this victim of 'time's hate', is Henry of Valois, King Henry III of France, favourite child of Catherine de Medici, and sometime suitor for Elizabeth's hand.' [19]

This was not her 'Frog' but his elder brother, who sued for Elizabeth's hand while he was yet Duke of Anjou, but it came to nothing and he subsequently became Henry III upon the death (possibly by poison?) of his brother Charles IX, only to be murdered in turn by the poisoned dagger of a Jacobin friar.

This is the dramatic scene that ends Marlowe's French political play *The Massacre at Paris* and testifies to his intimate knowledge of the troubles of this volatile period in French contemporary history, which is also the subject of this sonnet. Hotson writes informatively on the events of Henry III's reign:

> 'The first great "accident" or misfortune that befell him was Paris' famous Day of the Barricades, May 12, 1588, which the Venetian ambassador in Madrid called "l'accidente di Francia contra quel povero Re" – the accident of France against that poor King. On that day the people of Paris rose against their King in support of his enemies, the Duke of Guise and the Holy Leaguers, who already had strong foreign backing in Pope Sixtus and Philip of Spain. Escaping immediate deposition by a hair's breadth, Henry managed to get away. He was obliged, however, to convoke the hostile States General, which sat throughout the autumn scorning him as a do-nothing king, and preparing to make their "Caesar", the Duke of Guise, master of the throne.' [20]

This is the period of contemporary French history that Marlowe chose to dramatize, selecting and including the bloody massacre of the Huguenots that took place on St. Bartholomew's Eve in 1572, and evoked horror in the hearts of all Protestant Europe. This ghastly event was engineered by the Guise and Catherine de' Medici, the Queen Mother, while her eldest son, Charles IX, was on the throne as her puppet, to be succeeded in like capacity of impotence by her second son, Henry III. Marlowe's portrait of this ambitious woman is coloured with Huguenot sympathy, which he had strongly imbibed from his Canterbury boyhood whither so many of the persecuted Huguenots fled. He shows her as an evil woman plotting with the Cardinal of Lorraine, brother of the powerful Duke of Guise who aspired to the throne, whilst the newly-crowned Henry is dallying with his court favourites, his 'minions', of whom the Guise scornfully declares: 'I know none else but holds them in disgrace'. It is a similar situation to that in *Edward the Second* and, in slightly variant form, in Richard II, in which a weak and self-indulgent king loses the respect of his noblemen as a prelude to disaster.

> *Catherine.* How likes your grace my son's pleasantness?
> His mind, you see, runs on his minions,
> And all his heaven is to delight himself;
> And whilst he sleeps securely thus in ease,
> Thy brother Guise and we may now provide
> To plant ourselves with such authority
> As not a man may live without our leaves.
> Then shall the Catholic faith of Rome
> Flourish in France, and none deny the same.

> Cardinal. Madam, as in secrecy I was told,
>   My brother Guise hath gathered a power of men,
>   Which are, he saith, to kill the Puritans;
>   But 'tis the house of Bourbon that he means,
>   Now, madam, must you insinuate with the King,
>   And tell him that 'tis for his country's good,
>   And common profit of religion. [21]

Of course Marlowe's dramatization presents a grossly over-simplified scenario of the complex political machinations, the devious waverings, the about-turns of policy which preceded and eventually led to the terrible massacre, and his portrait of the scheming Queen Mother is painted in lurid colours; nevertheless his grasp of the main stream of the political currents is masterly. This play, and the sonnet that reflects these same events, reveal unmistakably the sophisticated mind of the intelligence agent who was a student of politics, and had undoubtedly read Machiavelli at Cambridge. Machiavellian characters also abound in the early Shakespeare plays.

After a scene in which Henry showers royal favours and position on the Duke Joyeux, when the Guise openly taunts the King for his love of his 'minions', anger blazes between them, and the Guise determines that he will have Henry murdered, exclaiming: 'Par le mort Dieu, il mourra!' But Henry anticipates him, fearing his treachery, and urged by his friends he discloses his intent:

> Henry. . . . though I seem mild and calm,
>   Think not but I am tragical within.
>   I'll secretly convey me unto Blois;
>   For, now that Paris takes the Guise's part,
>   Here is no staying for the King of France,
>   Unless he mean to be betray'd and die:
>   But, as I live, so sure the Guise shall die. [22]

Henry has made up his mind to become king at last in more than name, and he strikes first. The Guise is murdered – and Henry declares over his dead body: 'I ne'er was King of France until this hour.' [23] But it was a short-lived victory. Henry III was himself murdered in August 1589. This gives us a bottom-line dating for the sonnet.

We perceive the thread of his thought that this sonnet, drawing on his study of foreign politics as Walsingham's agent, ties together in the final couplet:

> To this I witness call the fools of Time,
> Which die for goodness, who have liv'd for crime.

Having glanced at the murder of Henry III, who fell 'Under the blow of thralled discontent', he finally recalls such poor dupes of the Catholic plotters as young Anthony Babington, whose name was given to the plot that aimed to assassinate Queen Elizabeth, to the uncovery of which I believe Marlowe's intelligence work at Rheims had contributed during 1585-6. Babington and his band of conspirators, ardent Catholics who were designated 'the Pope's white sons', paid the terrible price of a traitor's death, dying 'for goodness' (their religious faith) though they had 'Liv'd for crime', intending to assassinate the Queen of England.

This political sonnet, with its pair *Sonnet 123*, are thus seen to have direct relevance to Marlowe's work as a government agent, travelling abroad on assignments to gather intelligence for Mr Secretary Walsingham's foreign policy, acutely observing the political developments on the Continent. Their dating by Hotson to the year 1589 provides the historical background that confirms these as Marlowe's sonnets, written probably as he returned from an assignment towards the end of that year, when he was aged twenty-five and was already an experienced and active secret agent.

Sonnet 124 and *Psalm 124* are linked in the same way as are *Sonnet 107* and *Psalm 107*. Both psalms were used throughout England in thanksgiving to God for survival and safe delivery from death or danger of individuals or of the nation. *Psalm 124* would probably have been specifically used in thanksgiving services at the time of the Babington Plot in thanks for the preservation of the Queen's life, as well as at the services for the nation's delivery from the Spanish Armada, for it also refers to enemies that would have 'swallowed vs vp quicke' if the Lord had not defended them: 'Then the waters had drowned vs.' But they were saved, and the psalmist cries:

> Praised be the Lord, which hath not giuen vs as a praye
>   vnto their teeth.
> Our soule is escaped, euen as a birde out of the snare of
> the foulers: the snare is broken and we are deliuered. [24]

Queen Elizabeth had escaped the snare laid for her. Can it be doubted that these would have been in Marlowe's mind, familiar as he was from his boyhood with the psalms and their specific uses?

Although the events reflected upon in *Sonnet 124* are not directly connected with the Armada, they certainly impinged on it, if we accept the implication of the evidence of Marlowe's involvement with the Armada and the lead-up to it; that his task had been to report on the situation in France, whether danger might be expected from that quarter with the Holy Leaguers joining forces with Philip and Parma to invade England. That that unfortunate country lay in the grip of 'thralled discontent', finally leading to the murder of Henry III, is the gist of *Sonnet 124*. All this ties in with his recollection of 'the fools of Time' whose Catholic plots had not succeeded, but brought Mary Queen of Scots to the block as the tragic prelude to the Armada, all events associated with Marlowe's professional involvement in these stirring times. Its association with *Psalm 124* is clearly appropriate and supports the view that his work at Rheims was indeed connected with the protection of Queen Elizabeth's life from this assassination plot.

Marlowe's patriotism and pride in his profession is demonstrated also in his introduction of an English agent in the last scene of his French political play *The Massacre at Paris.* It is not too fanciful to see in this character the person-ification of the dramatist himself. He is given no lines to speak – his is simply a physical presence, and we visualize him kneeling to the dying King Henry III as he addresses him:

Enter the English Agent

King Henry. Agent for England, send thy mistress word
　　　　　　　What this detested Jacobin hath done.
　　　　　　　Tell her, for all this, that I hope to live;
　　　　　　　Which if I do, the papal monarch goes
　　　　　　　To wrack, and th' antichristian kingdom falls:
　　　　　　　These bloody hands shall tear his triplecrown,
　　　　　　　And fire accursed Rome about his ears;
　　　　　　　I'll fire his crazed buildings, and enforce
　　　　　　　The papal towers to kiss the lowly earth.
　　　　　　　Navarre, give me thy hand: I here do swear
　　　　　　　To ruinate that wicked Church of Rome,
　　　　　　　That hatcheth up such bloody practices,
　　　　　　　And here protest eternal love to thee,
　　　　　　　And to the Queen of England specially,
　　　　　　　Whom God hath bless'd for hating papistry.

This play and the three sonnets here considered are assertions of Marlowe's deeply-felt patriotism and devotion to the great Protestant Queen he served. The numbering of *Sonnets 124* and *107* in association with those Psalms used nationally at time of danger highlights the Poet's intention in their placement. There is nothing haphazard in this beautiful arrangement, which spoke its message to the Elizabethan reader familiar with the Psalter, proclaiming that these sonnets tell of deadly dangers that threaten the Protestant world – the Armada, and dire plots against the lives of a friendly French monarch, and their own Queen Elizabeth.

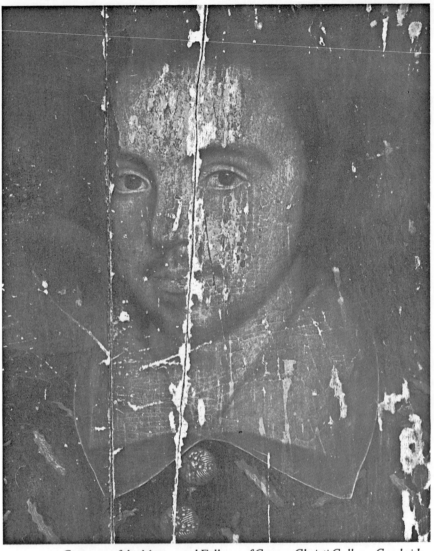

The 'Broken' Portrait of Christopher Marlowe, *discovered in 1953 during renovations to the Master's Lodge.*

In a pile of builders' rubble, a passing undergraduate noticed two pieces of wood washed clean in a downpour of rain to disclose the painted surface. On examination it turned out to be a genuine Elizabethan panel portrait, but how it got into the rubble remains a mystery. The Old Master's Lodge housed a small gallery of portraits, and this portrait may have been set into the panelling of the room. Its obscure fate reflects Marlowe's fall into disgrace in 1593 when the panel might have been turned with its face to the wall. Such an explanation would confirm that it is a genuine portrait of Christopher Marlowe, which he had donated to his old Master on leaving Corpus Christi in 1587, graced with his MA, as a gesture of gratitude and regret that he was not proceeding to holy orders as his scholarship required, but was entering the secret service of the Queen's government. The portrait, now restored, hangs in the dining hall of the College.

THE VINDICATION

XVII

THE POET VILIFIED AND VINDICATED

'Tis better to be vile than vile esteemed,
When not to be, receives reproach of being.

Sonnet 121

MARLOWE'S REPUTATION has been vilified on three counts: that he was a blaspheming Atheist, a man given to violence, and a homosexual. These accusations all stem from the Star Chamber witch-hunt of 1593. They have been sheepishly followed by latter-day credulous critics. I shall present evidence here that the premise of every one of these base intimations is flawed by error at its inception. Not one of these accusations stands up under close investigation. Marlowe has been condemned by bigotry, ignorance, superstition and envy in his own day, and by prejudice in modern times when the words of his enemies have been credited to an unwarranted degree. His friends thought otherwise – yet their testimony has gone unheeded, and evidence from his remarkably well documented life has been misinterpreted.

Following the news of his death in the Deptford incident came virulent censure by the Puritan revilers of the theatres, which were seen as cess-pits of iniquity (under Cromwell they were all closed down), who seized gloatingly upon Marlowe's murder as welcome news to hold up his violent end as the fearful example of God's visitation on a man who was both an Atheist and a writer of plays – a conjunction that was grist to their mill! As Bakeless points out: 'A charge of atheism and heresy was almost a necessity for them.' [1]

Robert Greene in his *Groatsworth of Wit Letter* had sounded the first blast, naming Marlowe as a disciple of Machiavelli and a believer in 'Diabolicall Atheisme', and by 1597 the Puritan campaign had joined to complete the destruction of his fair fame, opening with vitriolic, thunderous noise in Thomas Beard's *Theatre of God's Judgement*. (He refers to Marlowe as Marlin, by which he was also known.)

> 'Not inferior to any of the former in Atheism & impiety, and equal to all in manner of punishment was one of our own nation of fresh and late memory, called *Marlin,* by profession a scholar, brought up from his youth in the University of *Cambridge,* but by practice a playmaker, and a Poet of scurrility, who by giving too large a swinge to his own wit, and suffering his lust to have the full reins, fell (not without just desert) to that outrage and extremity, that he denied God and his son Christ, and not only in word blasphemed the Trinity, but also (as it is credibly reported) wrote books against

it, affirming our Saviour to be but a deceiver, and *Moses* to be but a conjurer and seducer of the people, and the holy Bible but vain and idle stories, and all religion but a device of policy. But see what a hook the Lord put in the nostrils of this barking dog: It so fell out, that in London streets as he purposed to stab one whom he ought a grudge unto with his dagger, the other party perceiving so avoided the stroke, that withall catching hold of his wrist, he stabbed his own dagger into his own head, in such sort, that notwithstanding all the means of surgery that could be wrought, he shortly after died thereof. The manner of his death being so terrible (for he even cursed and blasphemed to his last gasp, and together with his breath an oath flew out of his mouth) that it was not only a manifest sign of God's judgement, but also an horrible and fearful terror to all that beheld him. But herein did the justice of God most notably appear, in that he compelled his own hand which had written those blasphemies to be the instrument to punish him, and that in his brain, which had devised the same.'[2]

There followed a spate of Puritan writers whose versions of his death became increasingly fanciful and inaccurate in their gloating over the fatal dagger thrust that pierced the brain of this vile Atheist-playmaker. Charles Norman in his biography *The Muse's Darling* (1947) describes the tide of calumny that engulfed Marlowe's memory:

'The outburst of Puritan wrath against Marlowe is without parallel in literature. No vile epithet was too vile for his detractors to use, yet most of them wrote only from hearsay, or merely embroidered one another's accounts, hardly one able to contain his gloating . . In the tragic end of the poet who blazed the trail that Shakespeare followed they saw only the terrible justice of heaven appropriately meted out, and added fuel to the fiery legend which has persisted to this day of Marlowe as the very archetype of an Elizabethan roaring boy – hot-blooded, bellicose, wearing pride like a feather in his hat, and iniquitous before God and man. In truth, he sat for this portrait, distorted though it is; but there was something else, as we have seen.'[3]

The 'something else' Charles Norman refers to is the evidence contained in his poetry and plays, of a man of fine sensibilities, a nature that is in love with beauty, informed by high intelligence, and capable of a depth of human feeling that bespeaks a noble being – the antithesis of an Elizabethan roaring boy, which is how he is seen by those who credit the Deptford tale of his violent death without having considered this suspect evidence thoroughly, ignoring the evidence of his many friends, preferring to accept the words of the base informer Richard Baines, the envious and vengeful Thomas Kyd, and the dubious trio at Deptford as the truth.

An entire thesis could be written on Marlowe's alleged brush with Atheism, which, like the term 'heresy', was used to connote any questioning of orthodox religious tenets. The Socinian treatise discovered among Kyd's papers was an account of a theological debate conducted half a century earlier, based on the beliefs of a Unitarian heretic (tentatively identified as John Assheton) who was asked to write down his views when arrested under Archbishop Cranmer, and did so using the name Arrian. John Proctour replied to Arrian refuting this heresy from the standpoint of the orthodox Trinitarian. [4]

Presumably Marlowe would have used the treatise as a basis for serious discussion, point by point, with the members of Raleigh's circle. We learn from the informer's indictment of another contemporary named Richard Cholmeley, who was unfortunate enough to have attracted the attention of the heresyhunters and was also apprehended about this time, 'that Marloe tolde him that hee hath read the Atheist lecture to Sr Walter Raliegh & others'. [5] We have a record of a discussion on the nature of the soul which was reported to the Cerne Abbas inquiry into the atheistic opinions of Raleigh and his friends in 1594, which reflects the interest of these intellectuals in such speculative debates. From this Raleigh emerges as a philosophical investigator into spiritual matters whose interest was to discover what the essence of the spirit is and how it can be understood by man. Bakeless tells us that, 'In June 1594 Raleigh spent a whole night discussing religion with the Jesuit, John Cornelius . . then under arrest at Wolverton.' [6] This was a courageous act. Raleigh, Hariot, and his close friend Marlowe, were all men whose minds were 'stirred by the Renaissance speculative impulse . . to prove all things [and] to test by stringent dialectic the most sacred conceptions. The 'Atheist lecture' read by Marlowe to Raleigh was thus probably a closely reasoned discussion in scholastic form of first principles', declares Dr Boas. [7]

These are the considered opinions of Marlowe's greatest biographers. Such a serious interest in debating theological concepts does not square with the obscene rubbish claimed to represent Marlowe's 'Atheist opinions' contained in the infamous *Note* compiled by the informer Richard Baines, which is mainly a scurrilous libel. On the other hand, that Marlowe was a proselytizer of his ideas on religious tolerance and against religious bigotry and superstition, willing men 'not to be afeared of bugbears and hobgoblins', [8] we can well believe of him. That he ardently hated hypocrisy in a religious guise and sought to expose the cynical political manipulation of the devoutly religious populace by power-seeking, ambitious men to gain popular support for their factions, is reflected in his works. Raleigh observed this at first hand when fighting in the religious civil wars in France. Doubtless Marlowe noted it whilst working as an agent on the Continent where religious wars continually erupted. His perceptive eye for the motives underlying the actions and attitudes of men, seeing beneath the surface of outward appearances, is what made him such a brilliant dramatist. There can have been little that escaped him.

Marlowe's friend, the mathematician Hariot, is said to have calculated that there is error inherent in the Biblical time-scale concerning Adam. This idea is stated in Richard Baines' *Note* enumerating Marlowe's 'Damnable judgement of Religion and scorn of God's word', which begins with the statement of his opinion: 'That the Indians and many authors of antiquity have assuredly written above 16 thousand years whereas Adam is proved to have lived within 6 thousand years'.[9] A natural observation for a man of an advanced scientific turn of mind, and in a totally different key from the blasphemous scurrilities which Baines otherwise lists as examples of Marlowe's alleged opinions. Baines' profession was that of informer, whose task was to produce a list of statements purporting to be his victim's heretical opinions that would bring him into the power of the Star Chamber Court. These consist of such lewd blasphemies and preposterous obscenities that it is only remarkable that the so-called *Baines Libel* has been taken seriously by any modern scholar.

It has, however, been taken totally seriously – crediting *every* statement made by Baines as emanating from Marlowe and actually representing his serious thoughts on religion, by Paul Kocher in his *Christopher Marlowe: A Study of his Thought, Learning and Character* (1962). Kocher claims that when Baines was compiling his Note he was, in fact, 'transcribing Marlowe with minutest accuracy'.[10] If the word 'transcribing' means anything then Kocher is alleging that Baines prepared his *Note* by copying from a paper or treatise written by Marlowe – though Kocher does not divulge how Baines got hold of this hypothetical document. If he had had such a document, then he would not have needed to write his *Note* for Marlowe's manuscript *would have provided all the damning evidence he could have wished for.* This does not seem to have occurred to Kocher, who returns insistently to the existence of this hypothetical manuscript. This is based solely on contemporary rumour that arose, I suggest, from the hearsay that 'a paper' belonging to Marlowe had been discovered in Kyd's room which turned out to be heretical, and since Marlowe was a writer and a scholar it was assumed that he had written it. Gossip eventually exaggerated it into a 'book'.

Pursuing the existence of this hypothetical manuscript, however, and as his 'evidence' that Baines is actually reporting Marlowe's opinions with 'minutest accuracy' – obscenities and all – Kocher produces a mass of quotations from contemporary and ancient writers, both historians and ecclesiastical authors, who express very similar ideas to those that Baines quotes in his *Note* as Marlowe's opinions. Kocher thereby demonstrates that these ideas were certainly not original to Marlowe, but he takes this as 'proof' that Marlowe had read widely in the anti-Christian literature available, which was quoted by these ecclesiastical and historical writers, and these works had 'all left their mark on him.'[11]

For instance, Kocher quotes from the 'respectable divine', the Reverend

Henry Smith, who wrote a defamation of the Prophet Mohammed revealing a mind producing parallel statements of an obscene nature applied to Christ in the Baines *Note*.

> 'Mahomet himselfe was such a fleshly fellow, as though modest eares are loth to heare, yet because the filthinesse of this Prophet may not be concealed, I must utter it: He committed buggerie with an Asse, Bonfinius writeth it. Againe, he committed adulterie with another mans wife . . As Mahomets religion is defended by force of sword and fraude . . so likewise did it begin . . and was established through wiles, deceit, subtiltie, and lies. For first hee hauing the falling sicknes, perswaded his wife and others, that it was the power of God, and the presence of the Angel Gabriel that caused him to fall downe. Sergius the hereticall Monk was at hand, and bare false witnesse to the same (saith Zonaras) . . He had three companions all of a confederacie to deuise and face out his lies with him. When hee perceiued that men gaue eare to him, hee fained that the Angell Gabriel had carried him to Jerusalem, and thence to haue lifted him up to heauen, and there to haue learned his law . . ' [12]

Thus, quoting chapter and verse from such ecclesiastical historians as Bonfinius and Zonaras, the Reverend Henry Smith makes his points. One begins to see why Marlowe turned his back on joining the fraternity of reverend churchmen! These are such people as he would have called 'religious caterpillars'. [13] But this is not how Mr Kocher sees it. He argues that it was this kind of 'edifying' literature that influenced Marlowe: *'Into these ideas he breathed the living reality of his convictions, and dared to utter them abroad at the risk of his career and his life that other men might share the truth.'* [14] (My italics).

Here are items from Baines' *Note*, transcribed with 'minutest accuracy' from Marlowe's hypothetical treatise – according to Kocher – declaring the 'truth' for which he claims Marlowe was prepared to risk his life!

- That Christ was a bastard and his mother dishonest.
- That the woman of Samaria & her sister were whores & that Christ knew them dishonestly.
- That St John the Euangelist was bedfellow to C[hrist] and leaned alwaies in his bosome, that he vsed him as the sinners of *Sodoma*.
- That the Angel Gabriell was baud to the holy ghost, because he brought the salutation to *Mary*.
- That he was the sonne of a Carpenter, and that if the Jewes among whome he was borne did crucify him theie best knew him and whence he came.
- That Christ deserued better to dy then Barrabas and that the Jewes

made a good choise, though Barrabas were both a thief and murtherer.[15]

Kocher makes much of the evidence of a good working knowledge of the different editions of the Bible revealed in the last two items, the Geneva Bible, the Bishops' Bible and the Vulgate, and he generously concedes: 'Marlowe seems entitled to whatever credit for originality there may be in the elaboration of these particular points and the use of these particular texts, but *the volume of similar abuse of Jesus* among the pagan classics and the Jews *is immense*. It is so much like what was suffered by Moses and Mohammed that only a few representative examples need be offered. Celsus, for one, said that Christ lived *'a most infamous life'* and *'was punished by the Jews for his crimes'*. [16] (My italics). Compare this with Baines' *Note*.

Kocher proves by numerous quotations from contemporary sources that the abuse of Jesus available in print was 'immense'. But the conclusion he draws from this fact is not only fallacious, it is ridiculous, and contradicts all we know about Marlowe, who was never an imitator but essentially a highly original thinker. Bakeless, Marlowe's definitive biographer, sees originality as Marlowe's hallmark. He was the innovator of new forms in our literature, a man who set fashion, not a follower of other men's fashions. Kocher's claim to have made a study of Marlowe's *'Thought, Learning and Character'* is thrown into doubt.

I suggest that it was not Marlowe, *pace* Mr Kocher, but Baines who had been reading this libellous clerical literature to extract anything suitably obscene and morally shocking with which to lard his indictment of Marlowe, and it is these items that he is intent on fastening onto the free-thinking poet-dramatist whom he sees as a vile 'Atheist'. Baines' *Note* is not some rarity, as Kocher implies. He calls it 'unique'! It is a *typical* informer's indictment. Libellous accusation has been the favoured method used down the ages to blacken the reputations of those whom the authorities saw as a threat to their own security and power, and to aid their dominance of the minds of the people in matters religious and philosophical. We have only to look back at Socrates to see it at work. Kocher himself cites evidence of the practice of character assassination from ancient times, but he fails to draw the logical conclusion.

'How badly fared the reputations of heresiarchs and apostates in the first centuries of the Christian era can be read in the pages of Eusebius' *Ecclesiastical History,* Irenaeus' *Against Heresies,* or Hippolytus' *Philosophumena*. . . Coming down to more recent times, everyone remembers what the Catholics thought of Luther, what stories the Protestants circulated about the witchcraft and abominations of the popes, and what filth a bishop like John Bale could write about the Catholic saints. Later on, the leaders of the more bizarre Puritan sects became victims of the same tradition.'[17]

RICHARD BAINES' NOTE (B.L. Harleian MS. 6848 ff. 185/186)

A note Containing the opinion of on[e] Christopher Marly Concerning his Damnable Judgment of Religion, and scorn of gods word.

That the Jndians and many Authors of antiquity haue assuredly writen aboue 16 *thousand yeares agone wher as Adam is proued to haue lived w*^t*hin* 6 *thowsand yeares.*

He affirmeth that Moyses was but a Jugler, & that one Heriots being Sir W Raleighs man can do more then he.

That Moyses made the Jewes to travell xl yeares in the wildernes, (w^{ch} *Jorney might haue bin Done in lesse then one yeare) ere they Came to the promised land to thinent that those who were privy to most of his subtilties might perish and so an everlasting superstition Remain in the hartes of the people.*

That the first beginning of Religioun was only to keep men in awe.

That it was an easy matter for Moyses being brought vp in all the artes of the Egiptians to abuse the Jewes being a rude & grosse people.

That Christ was a bastard and his mother dishonest.

That he was the sonne of a Carpenter, and that if the Jewes among whome he was borne did Crucify him theie best knew him and whence he Came.

That Christ deserved better to Dy then Barrabas and that the Jewes made a good Choise, though Barrabas were both a thief and murtherer.

*That if there be any god or any good Religion, then it is in the papistes because the service of god is performed w*th *more Cerimonies, as Elevation of the mass, organs, singing men, Shaven Crownes & cta. that all protestantes are Hypocriticall asses.*

That if he were put to write a new Religion, he would vndertake both a more Exellent and Admirable methode and that all the new testament is filthily written.

That the woman of Samaria & her sister were whores & that Christ knew them dishonestly.

That St John the Evangelist was bedfellow ı C[hrist] and leaned alwaies in his bosome, that he vse him as the sinners of Sodoma.

That all they that loue not Tobacco *& Boies wer fooles.*

That all the apostles were fishermen and bas fellowes neyther of wit nor worth, that Paull only ha wit but he was a timerous fellow in bidding men to t subiect to magistrats against his Conscience.

*That he had as good Right to Coine as the Queene England, and that he was acquainted w*th *one poo a prisoner in newgate who hath great Skill in mixtur of mettals and hauing learned some thinges of him ı ment through help of a Cunninge stamp maker to Coi ffrench Crownes pistolets and English shillinges.*

*That if Christ would haue instituted the sacramer w*th *more Ceremoniall Reverence it would haue b had in more admiration, that it would haue bin muc better being administred in a* Tobacco *pipe.*

That the Angell Gabriell was Baud to the holy ghos because he brought the salutation to Mary.

That on[e] Ric Cholmley hath Confessed that he wa perswaded by Marloe's Reasons to become an Atheis

*These thinges, w*th *many other shall by good ε honest witnes be aproved to be his opinions and Comc Speeches, and that this Marlow doth not only houl them himself, but almost into every Company h Cometh he perswades men to Atheism willing them nc to be afeard of bugbeares and hobgoblins, and vtteri scorning both god and his ministers as J Richari Baines will Justify & approue both by mine oth an the testimony of many honest men, and almost al me with whome he hath Conversed any time will testify tl same, and as J think all men in Cristianity ought h indevor that the mouth of so dangerous a member ma be stopped, he saith likewise that he hath quoted number of Contrarieties oute of the Scripture w*^{ch} *ı hath giuen to some great men who in Convenient tin shalbe named. When these thinges shalbe Called ı question the witnes shalbe produced.*

RICHARD BAMES [Baine

266

The destruction of reputation by false report is still used in totalitarian states to convict those whom the authorities wish to silence. The Nazis used libel to defame courageous, liberal-minded people, especially if they were Jews when these would be specifically obscene. Under Stalin the KGB labelled their victims in the self-same tradition. The more 'shocking' the libel that could be concocted and made to stick, the more 'efficient' the prosecutor appeared in the eyes of the state he served.

Baines was obviously out to prove himself an efficient prosecutor in Marlowe's case whom he recognised as a quarry of some importance. He had himself also been a student of Divinity in the Seminary at Rheims (a fact that Kocher totally ignores) hence the 'fidelity with which the Baines note preserves the Biblical language' which Kocher finds so 'striking' is equally traceable to Baines' hand, as to Marlowe's. But to Kocher, 'The inference is unmistakable that Baines is really transmitting the words of Marlowe, if not with absolute accuracy, then at least with substantial accuracy.' [18] Kocher does not believe that Baines, or some other 'fabricator', would have been 'clever enough to piece together the . . texts into a damaging Scriptural argument and then diabolical enough to father it on Marlowe.' [19]

O, sweet innocence! Presumably Mr Kocher has been living in an ivory tower and does not recognise the face of oppression, but even the most meagre acquaintance with the outside world testifies that vicious persecution of the innocent accompanied by torture and unbelievable cruelty is still flourishing. Amnesty International affords the horrifying evidence from many quarters of the world of politically motivated police brutality. Many of these innocent people have survived to tell the tale of preposterous libels and obscenities that have been invented by the secret police of corrupt modern states (not sixteenth century, but twentieth century members of Baines' tribe) who have been 'diabolical enough to father' vile accusations onto their hapless victims. The Elizabethan informers cannot be credited with such scruples as Kocher asserts they possessed, with Baines seen as a decent chap who is reporting Marlowe's opinions honestly. Nor is it necessary to credit Baines with any extraordinary degree of cleverness (and we may take it he was cunning, as evidenced by the plot he devised at Rheims to kill off the entire community of the Catholic Seminary by poisoning the well where they drew their water) since the texts that Kocher has researched detailing Biblical and anti-religious blasphemies were equally available to Baines as they would have been to Marlowe, had he been interested to read them – which is doubtful, for to him they would have been beneath contempt. But they would have proved most interesting and satisfying reading to Baines, providing him with just the very thing he needed for his nefarious profession.

The unwitting contribution to the rehabilitation of Marlowe's reputation that Charles Nicholl's book, *The Reckoning: The Murder of Christopher Marlowe* (1992) has made is to a reassessment of the significance of Baines' *Note* by the evidence he has assembled revealing 'a glimpse into the mind of Richard

Baines.' This cites Baines' confession made when he was a prisoner of Cardinal Allen at Rheims Seminary in 1583, where he had been apprehended the previous year after his poison plot had been discovered. In his confession Baines describes the methods he used to suborne young Catholics (very similar to those cited concerning Marlowe and Cholmeley below) and his own descent into apostasy when he found his studies of divinity and 'holy writers . . . began daily to wax more and more tedious and loathsome'. [20] He confessed:

> 'I most delighted in profane writers, and the worst sort of them, such as either wrote against the truth, or had least taste of religion . . . I had a delight rather to fill my mouth and the auditors' ears with dainty, delicate, nice and ridiculous terms and phrases, than with wholesome, sound and sacred doctrine.' [21]

He indulged in 'jesting and contempt, against the seminary and against the Catholic faith', and spoke 'wicked words', scoffing at divine service, and 'began to mock at the lesser points of religion'. Progressing from there to 'utter divers horrible blasphemies in plain terms against the principle points of religion' he reached outright 'atheism and no belief at all', declaring this to be 'the highway to heresy, infidelity & atheism, as to my great danger I have experienced in mine own case.' [22]

Compare this with Baines' *Note* on Marlowe. Is there any need to comment further? Clearly this man had personal experience to draw on for his damning *Note*. He seems miraculously to have escaped from Rheims having (as I suspect) made a deal with Cardinal Allen to pursue the downfall of Walsingham's best secret agents by giving false evidence against them to the Privy Council to incriminate any who became vulnerable. This is, of course, precisely what he achieved in the case of Marlowe. I cannot prove it. No one can. But, given all we know about Marlowe and the circumstances of his tragedy, together with what we know about Baines, the inference is soundly based. This, I suggest, is the true explanation of the Baines *Note* that has brought such odium on the name of Marlowe to this day.

What Kocher's research has proved, which is of considerable value, is that *not one* of the obscene opinions accredited to Marlowe in Baines' *Note* is original to Marlowe. *Every single one of these specifically scurrilous anti-Christian statements has been lifted from some clerical authority.* And not only were they available in print, but several of them were widely known and are even quoted in Elizabethan secular literature – always adding the appropriate expression of horror in quoting them so as to dissociate the writer from the blasphemous statement, e.g. 'my heart trembleth to thinke them.' [23]

What is much to the point is that several of the self-same 'opinions' crop up with only minor variations in the indictment against Richard Cholmeley prepared by an anonymous informer, who was presumably from the same stable as Baines, who tacks these accusations onto the end of his report, almost as an after-thought, or as if he had been told to do this – perhaps by Baines who was his superior? Identically Cholmeley is accused of making –

'a Jeste of the Scripture with these fearfull horrible & damnable speeches, that Jhesus Christe was a bastarde, St Mary a whore & the Anngell Gabriell a Bawde to the holy ghoste & that Christe was justly persecuted by the Jewes for his owne foolishnes that Moyses was a Jugler & Aaron a Cosoner the one for his miracles to Pharao to prove there was a god, & the other for takinge the Earerings of the children of Israell to make a golden calfe with many other blasphemous speeches of the deuine essence of god which I feare to rehearse.' [24]

In the above we have evidence of the professional informer's stock-in-trade abuses based on the texts so readily available, as Kocher has clearly demonstrated. Such standard indictments can be found in use by all repressive agencies, varied according to whether it is a Marxist or an extreme right-wing dictatorship that is using these instruments of state suppression. That Baines, whose profession was to trap heretics and so-called 'Atheists' and freethinkers, and who had had a theological training, would relish poring over this clerical literature to research the juiciest obscenities with which to incriminate his victims is not to be doubted. His previous activities at Rheims testify to his sly and ruthless nature, and on the evidence of his *Note* he was a religious bigot. The Elizabethan informer's mentality is typified in the labelling of the scholarly Arrian treatise found amongst Kyd's papers as 'vile hereticall Conceiptes'. [25]

It is likely that Baines had been present at Kyd's torture as the interrogator in charge, and when Marlowe's name was disclosed he would immediately have recognised him as of far more importance as a potential victim than the miserable Kyd, who was soon released. His aim was undoubtedly to make an efficient job of nailing his indictment on this important free-thinker and gratifying his master, the Archbishop, and he would have no incentive to harbour any scruples as to how he achieved this.

Commenting on the clerical texts he has researched, Kocher points out: 'One must emphasise again that the men who wrote such abuse were reputable, excellent authors, most of them churchmen', and he seeks to equate Marlowe with these religious bigots. He adds: 'It seems a little hard on Marlowe to require him to have more charity in his soul than did the ministers of God in his own century.' [26]

A perverted kind of generosity to Marlowe, for it is the imputation to him of the scurrilous opinions in the informer's dossier based on the commentaries of these 'reputable' churchmen that is 'a little hard'. What Kocher has conveniently forgotten is that Marlowe was not a churchman, but had turned away from a profession tainted with religious fanaticism, pedantry and hypocrisy, and, one might add, with lewdness. Nor was Marlowe a mere 'reputable, excellent author'. He was a genius! His aspiring mind soared as far above the minds of these men with their obscene religious clap-trap as the mind of Socrates, or Giordano Bruno, or Dante Alighieri – or Sir Walter Raleigh and Northumberland and their brave fellow free-thinkers.

Kocher follows the fashion among scholars to pretend that the circle of free-thinkers led by Raleigh was just a figment of gossip. It is perfectly in order to credit any unsubstantiated gossipy recorded note on Marlowe's 'Atheism' – as in Henry Oxinden's commonplace book that he 'was an atheist & had writ a booke against Scripture', [27] (which becomes Kocher's hypothetical manuscript on which Baines allegedly based his *Note*) but those same scholars who credit this recorded gossip, dismiss with scepticism the recorded gossip concerning Raleigh's 'little academie' as a dubious myth. There is an astonishing reluctance to believe that it existed at all. Yet the organisation of the free-thinkers was necessarily esoteric and secret, which it would have been highly unsafe to advertise, and more than reported rumour can hardly be expected. But that does not cast doubts on the reality of the circle. It rather testifies to the fact that such a club of intellectuals had to be secret, not open, and this accurately reflects the climate of the times. The late sixteenth century was marked by terrible exhibitions of religious intolerance with the active suppression of free thought and scientific questioning.

We are told that Raleigh and Northumberland held their meetings behind closed doors. Inevitably curious servants noted it, and pricked up their ears, and prying, ignorant, fearful minds commented. Something leaked out, and was exaggerated, distorted. Rumour spread that they met secretly for evil practices, such as raising the devil learning to spell GOD backwards! In conditions of secrecy superstition ran riot.

These same conditions vulgarized and distorted the truth about Marlowe's opinions, which the informer Baines took full advantage of in collecting his damning indictment against the poet-dramatist. Raleigh and his circle of 'heroicall spirits' were a rare breed of courageous free-thinkers who represented the essence and core of the late English Renaissance. They were generally accused by their contemporaries of the sin of 'pride' – for daring to think freely – and stigmatized as 'Atheists', which was particularly flung at Raleigh, Northumberland, Hariot and Marlowe. This implies that Marlowe was a leading light in the circle. The particular form of their heretical thinking was allegedly the denial of the Holy Trinity. Speculative debate on this taboo subject was probably the theme of the 'Atheist lecture' that Marlowe is reputed to have read to Sir Walter Raleigh's circle.

Kocher's firm belief that Marlowe had written a serious polemic based on the ubiquitous obscenities against Christianity in the Baines *Note,* and had then read this nonsense to the noble-minded Northumberland and Raleigh and his 'deepe-brain'd' friends is an incredible concoction. He even conjures up a picture of the attentive Baines listening to Marlowe's lecture and taking down his notes *verbatim,* [28] – though where this lecture is supposed to have taken place we are not told by Kocher, nor yet how the informer could have managed to insinuate himself into the secret meeting of the 'School of Night'. Or was he listening at the key-hole? But then, Kocher does not seem to believe that this free-thinkers' club actually existed although the references to it are as well documented as those to Marlowe's alleged Atheist book, which Kocher finds no difficulty in accepting as gospel.

As evidence of the existence of this 'book' he cites what he calls 'the "That" clause' in Baines' *Note*:

> 'On minute examination it appears that the statements attributed to Marlowe, even as they stand, reveal a progress and transition of ideas which strongly suggest that they form parts of an organized dissertation against Christianity. . . Particularly interesting is the "that" clause into which each statement is cast, (e.g. "That the first beginning Religioun was only to keep men in awe") resembling the typical section or chapter heading of the Renaissance treatise on theology. Thus the list as a whole has all the air of a series of formal propositions, each capable of support by a section of detailed argument, and all articulated into a single overarching design.'[29]

How, then, does Kocher account for the fact that the informer's note indicting Richard Cholmeley of Atheism is couched in *exactly the same format*? Each statement in this informer's document also begins with a 'That' clause!

> 'That hee saieth hee doeth entirely hate the Lord Chamberleyn & hath good cause to so doe.
>
> 'That he saieth & verely beleveth that one Marlowe is able to showe more sounde reasons for Atheisme then any devine in Englande is able to geve to prove devinitie & that Marloe tolde him that hee hath read the Atheist lecture to S^r walter Raliegh & others.
>
> 'That he saieth that hee hath certen men corrupted by his p[er]suasions who wilbee ready at all tymes & for all causes to sweare whatsoever seemeth good to him, Amonge whom is one Henry younge & Iasp[er] Borage& others.
>
> 'That hee so highly esteemeth his owne witt & Iudgment that hee saieth that noman are sooner devyned and abused then the Councell themselves.
>
> 'That hee can goe beyonde & Cosen them as hee liste . . . '

There are twelve 'That' clauses in this informer's report called: *Remembraunces of wordes & matters against Ric. Cholmeley.* (B.L. *Harl. MS.* 6848 F. 190 recto and verso)

Kocher is obviously ignorant of this document, although it belons to the same Harleian manuscript collection as the Baines *Note*. His thesis is exposed as based on limited, narrow research directed by his prejudiced approach. He has jumped to false conclusions based on gossip and bigotry in Marlowe's day. These are the very things that almost destroyed this greatest genius of our dramatic literature.

Renaissance Influences

One of the greatest free-thinkers of the age was Giordano Bruno, whose influence on Marlowe was profound. This one time Dominican friar eluded the grasp of the Holy Roman Inquisition by travelling and lecturing in the countries where a more tolerant attitude prevailed under Protestant influence, but returning to Italy in 1592 he was arrested, imprisoned for eight years and finally burnt at the stake in 1600. At his trial before the Inquisition the witnesses called were his fellow prisoners, poor devils who testified that he had uttered scurrilous speeches concerning Jesus Christ, which are on a par with the blasphemies attributed to Marlowe in Baines' *Note*. This 'evidence' sealed Bruno's fate as one for burning.

The inquisitorial denigration of this martyr to scientific thinking has been compounded by John Bossy in his book *Giordano Bruno and the Embassy Affair* (1991). Taking his cue from the testimonies of Bruno's traducers in the modern trend to credit the evidence of the enemies of the free-thinkers, Bossy has presented this great, original thinker as a renegade priest who was besotted with an implacable hatred of Jesus Christ, much as Kocher presents Marlowe. This false premise is contradicted by the genuine religious opinions of Bruno reported by the Venetian nobleman, Giovanni Mocenigo, who knew Bruno.

> 'The world, Mocenigo recorded him as saying, was in a terrible state;
> Catholicism, though better than any other version of Christianity,
> needed a complete shake-up; if it was to survive it would have to
> renounce force and return to preaching the gospel.'[30]

This is hardly an anti-Christian declaration, and it is the real Bruno speaking his mind to a friend. He is severely critical of the corruption of the Christian ecclesiastical authorities. Like most free-thinkers he was almost ecumenical in his views on religion, hating narrow, fanatical sectarianism, but certainly neither hating Christ nor Christianity. The obvious question that Bossy does not ask is: Why should an astute and brilliant philosopher like Bruno have been such a fool as to regale his fellow prisoners with opinions guaranteed to bring him to the stake? He omits to compare the testimonies of the pathetic prisoners, who doubtless had no choice in the matter, with Mocenigo's statement, and the only writings of Bruno's prolific output to which he pays attention is his *Cena de le ceneri*. In this Bossy interprets the wine-bibbing scene at the dinner party as a satirical commentary on the Eucharist, claiming that

272

the unflattering picture of the assembled Oxford doctors dribbling into the wine-cup is intended as an anti-Christian lampoon. For this extraordinary assumption there is no evidence at all. Indeed the wine-bibbing scene is all of a piece with Bruno's typical fastidiousness and misanthropic impatience with such specimens of humanity as he is depicting here. His writings expand on his idiosyncratic, unorthodox views on religion which are passionately and deeply felt; in his *Cena* these are laced with his fierce intellectual scorn for the bigoted know-alls with whom he came to dispute. It is not surprising that he was advised to expunge the scene from his publication, for it would have made him a host of enemies! But this had nothing to do with an attack on the celebration of the Eucharist with which Bossy imbues the scene in order to inject the fashionable 'shocking' element into his book. Whatever else he was, Bruno was a genius, and this does not come across in Bossy's book which utterly misrepresents both his vision and his heroism.

As a renowned mystical philosopher and adept Renaissance magus, Bruno was warmly welcomed by the English intellectuals. He was invited to lecture and discuss his ideas with them at gatherings including Sir Philip Sidney, Sir Walter Raleigh, and Thomas Watson and his patron Sir Francis Walsingham, with many other distinguished Englishmen. Marlowe was then a nineteen-year-old student at Cambridge, but he doubtless read Bruno's works written during his year in England and dedicated to Sir Philip Sidney, which would have been in Walsingham's library, if not also among Watson's books and in the great library of the 'Wizard Earl'. [31]

Bruno made a deep impression on the circle in London led by Sir Philip Sidney, until his untimely death three years later when Raleigh succeeded him as the head of an esoteric academy. Bruno was a dedicated religious magician, who practised 'good' magic as taught by Hermes Trismegistus, the Thrice-great Messenger of the Gods of Egyptian origin, a personification of Thoth, who among his many facets was also the god of science, hence a cult grew up around this deity in the Renaissance. Bruno sought his aid in the discovery of divine and scientific truth. This eccentric ex-Dominican monk astounded his listeners when he gave his inspired exposition of the innumerable worlds of the infinite universe, a concept which he had by sheer force of his intuitive imagination attained and grasped (although even four hundred years ago this idea was already ancient.) For Bruno this was a religious truth. His vision of a God who was the creator of an infinite universe, whose ineffable purity, omnipotence and omniscience forbade the notion that his Almightiness could be contained in the body of an earthly man, would have dazzled Marlowe. The concept of God as pure Divinity is central to Bruno's theology which also embraced the heady Hermetic principle of Man as potentially divine through the power of his intellect.

Bruno's teaching envisaged a universal religious and moral reform, which his ardent spirit longed for. He detested the religious intolerance of the Protestant and Puritan zealots, as much as of the Catholics, and claimed they had destroyed the moral teaching of the ancient philosophers and especially of the old Egyptian religion which gave men moral laws by which to order their lives. He believed that the marvellous magical religion of the Egyptians would one day return, reforming the warring Christian sects, who were creating havoc and dissention in his world. This would eventually be controlled by the restitution of good moral law.

The Nolan, as Bruno liked to call himself, was far from being an Atheist, but rather a deeply and passionately religious crusader whose religion was imbued with occultism. 'The infinite universe and the innumerable worlds', writes Frances Yates in *Giordano Bruno and the Hermetic Tradition,* 'are for him new revelations, intense accentuations of his overpowering sense of the divine. Or they are ways of figuring the unfigurable, of grasping and holding within, the infinite divine reality. For Bruno uses thought in a Hermetic way, a semi-magical way, as a mode of reaching intuitive knowledge of the divine.' [32]

All this is a million miles away from the obscene anti-Christian blasphemies cited by Kocher as being Marlowe's opinions, of which we find no trace in any of Marlowe's works. But there are surely echoes of Bruno's voice heard in Faustus' passionate cry -

'Tis magic, magic, that hath ravish'd me. (1. 136)

Faustus, too, longs to possess all knowledge by means of magic, but his desire is sinful for he aims to obtain power for himself thereby. Faustus is partly based on a historical personage around whom legends had accrued, but some acquaintance with Bruno's ideas probably fired Marlowe's imagination to realize this masterpiece of his dramatic conception. In Prospero there is an even closer link with Bruno, for 'this irritable magician', as Frances Yates calls him, 'regarded himself as a missionary of reconciliation', [33] and what is the theme of *The Tempest* but reconciliation? And what is Prospero but a kind of Renaissance magus?

Bruno spent one of the happiest years of his troubled life in London where he found the intellectual climate remarkably congenial under the benign rule of Elizabeth. In the early 1580's the free-thinkers were fairly unmolested in their intellectual pursuits, and he found himself 'understood in the innermost recesses of the Queen cult', and became an ardent admirer of the great Elizabeth. [34] He recorded his London experience in *The Ash-Wednesday Supper* which he partially fictionalizes, setting it in the house of Sir Philip Sidney's great friend Fulke Greville (although it actually seems to have taken place at the house of the French Ambassador, de Mauvissière), recounting in his inimitable mixture of humour, satire and didactic exposition his philosophical encounter with the 'Aristotelian pedants', the doctors who came there to dispute with him and heartily disapproved of the Nolan's unorthodox ideas, which he expounded with great liveliness and originality, employing the imagery of mythological beasts and emblems to illuminate and impart his ideas.

Met with a blank wall of rejection, Bruno asks: How can such intolerant minds be brought to reason? 'By weakening with arguments their conviction that they know, and in a subtly persuasive manner drawing them away as much as possible from their bigotry'. [35] Doubtless the learned pedants found him to be a 'rather threateningly tolerant writer', [36] or speaker, as Yates calls him, for Bruno jarred with their assiduously cultivated intolerance to which they clung as to a protective cloak whose thick folds were gathered fearfully around themselves. They were non-plussed by this extraordinary man who grasped knowledge through mystic experience, which fuelled his astonishing, vivid imagination to burst into inspiration.

Had Marlowe ever heard him lecture he would have been transported by the Nolan's inspirational poetic leap into infinity, in which he becomes a traveller in the infinite reaches of the universe. Something of this is found in Marlowe's early works, which had doubtless brushed off from his reading of Bruno. 'His concept of God as 'a sphere of which the centre is everywhere and the circumference nowhere' is basic for Bruno, for whom the innumerable worlds are all divine centres of the unbounded universe.' [37] Compare this with Marlowe's pulsating vision of a God who 'never sleeps, Nor in one place is circumscriptible' in the *Second Part of Tamburlaine.*

This concept, drawing its inspiration from Renaissance Hermetic philosophy in its Christianized form, is here associated with Christ as Godhead in a rich amalgam of religious sources. The Mohammedan King Orcanes rails fiercely against the perfidious Christian King Sigismund for breaking his sacred oath made in Christ's name by attacking his depleted defences whilst his main army is away fighting the enemy, the Scythian upstart, Tamburlaine. This episode is based on contemporary histories of Timurlane, or Tamburlaine, and is not Marlowe's invention, but he uses it to expose the hypocritical abuse of religion which he detested. This passage is of great value in shedding light on Marlowe's thinking.

> *Orcanes.* Can there be such deceit in Christians,
> Or treason in the fleshly heart of man,
> Whose shape is figure of the highest God?
> Then, if there be a Christ, as Christians say,
> But in their deeds deny him for their Christ,
> If he be son to everlasting Jove,
> And hath the power of his outstretched arm,
> If he be jealous of his name and honour
> As is our holy prophet Mahomet,
> Take here these papers as our sacrifice
> And witness of thy servant's perjury!
>   *(He tears to pieces the articles of peace)*
> Open, thou shining veil of Cynthia,
> And make a passage from th' empyreal heaven
> That he that sits on high and never sleeps,

Nor in one place is circumscriptible,
But everywhere fills every continent
With strange infusion of his sacred vigour,
May in his endless power and purity,
Behold and venge this traitor's perjury!
Thou, Christ, that art esteem'd omnipotent,
If thou wilt prove thyself a perfect God,
Worthy the worship of all faithful hearts,
Be now reveng'd upon this traitor's soul,
And make the power I have left behind
(Too little to defend our guiltless lives)
Sufficient to discomfit and confound
The trustless force of those false Christians!
To arms, my lords! on Christ still let us cry:
If there be Christ, we shall have victory.

Tamburlaine the Great, Part Two   Act 2 scene 2 11.36-64

Orcanes' small force is victorious against the perfidious Sigismund, so Christ is vindicated by the Mohammedan prince! Marlowe's presentation of men of other races and other religions who were reviled by the 'reputable' churchmen of Kocher's thesis is imbued with the broad tolerance of his mind which is in striking contrast to the intolerance of the general Elizabethan attitude. This places Marlowe in direct opposition to such writers as the clerical author Du Plessis Mornay, whom Kocher commends as 'surely one of the most temperate of men'. [38.] Here this 'most temperate of men' gives his opinion of Mohammed, the prophet of Allah, which we may compare with Marlowe's above. In this one example Kocher's false premise is revealed for the nonsense it is.

> 'Whether he were a good man or no, let the people of Mecha (who woorshippe him at this day) judge, which condemned him to death for his Robberies and murthers. And he himself confesseth himself to bee a sinner, an Idolator, an adulterer, giuen to Lecherie, and subject to women.' [39]

Du Plessis reflects the popular view of Mohammed, so that Marlowe, had he been of this mind, would have pandered to popular opinion in flinging mud at the Mohammedans, but never does he indulge in anything of the kind in any of his dramatic works. Quite the contrary, he is concerned to teach his audiences a broader, more tolerant view, and he does this *consistently.* It is therefore inconceivable that he would have indulged in the kind of blasphemous scurrilities against Christ that are presented by Baines as Marlowe's 'opinions'. Marlowe's credo, like Bruno's, like Raleigh's, like Northumberland's, was religious tolerance and freedom of thought – to question, to examine philosophical and religious concepts, to discover new scientific knowledge by inquiry and experiment. Marlowe spoke for himself and his compeers in his circle of English Renaissance intelligentsia when he wrote this splendid passage:

> Nature, that fram'd us of four elements
> Warring within our breasts for regiment,
> Doth teach us all to have aspiring minds:
> Our souls, whose faculties can comprehend
> The wondrous architecture of the world,
> And measure every wandering planet's course,
> Still climbing after knowledge infinite,
> And always moving as the restless spheres,
> Will us to wear ourselves, and never rest,
> Until we reach the ripest fruit of all,
> That perfect bliss and sole felicity,
> The sweet fruition of an earthly crown.

> *Tamburlaine the Great, Part One*   Act 2 scene 7   11.18-29

Only the last line brings it back to Tamburlaine's earthly ambition, the rest is pure intellectual aspiration expressing the essence of Renaissance man's impulse to *know* and shake off the trammels of mediaeval strictures on his advance into the realm of science. Compare this with the Baines *Note!*

What had been the real influences on the advanced-thinking Marlowe? This is the crucial question we are addressing, a question which is of even more importance in the light of this thesis which presents him as the pseudonymous Shakespeare.

Giordano Bruno was undoubtedly an important influence on this youthful genius. We also have to consider Marsilio Ficino, the great fifteenth century Florentine scholar, philosopher and theologian, whose writings carried the influence of Italian Renaissance Neoplatonism through Western Europe, and contributed vitally to the development of the literature and philosophical-religious thought in Renaissance England, and who had been a tremendous influence on Bruno. Both these men are totally ignored by Kocher.

Ficino's most famous and influential book, *Theologia Platonia de Immortalitae Animae,* published in 1482, in which he expounded his synthesis of Platonism and Christianity, would certainly have been avidly read by Marlowe at Cambridge. This book has been described as 'one of the greatest events in European literary history', [40] which had a tremendous impact on all educated Europe. Ficino's philosophy was the true 'fountain-head of Renaissance Neoplatonism' [41], and his influence was largely instrumental in effecting the gradual change from Aristotle to Plato. The debate was not yet concluded and in Marlowe's day was still being hotly contended at Cambridge, where Gabrial Harvey became a protagonist in academic battles over Aristotelian principles for which he was accused of nonconformity. I believe that Bakeless is right in suspecting that the relationship between Dr Harvey, then a controversial figure among the Cambridge dons, and the youthful Marlowe were closer than we have as yet been able to discover. If so they would doubtless have discussed Ficino's ideas together.

Ficino's most important contribution to the theological-philosophical development of the Renaissance was the reconciliation he established of two distinct concepts, deriving from Thomas Aquinas and Dante, in which he substitutes the Christian God for the Platonic Idea of the Good and Beautiful – 'the Neoplatonic mystical abstraction of the All as the god of the ladder of love'. [42] This is also present in Bruno's complex philosophy. Ficino managed skilfully to evade accusations of heresy by always clothing his arguments in Biblical language, but when he finally published his essays, *Liber de Vita,* in 1489, in which he discussed his belief in astrology and necromancy (compare Bruno again) he was sailing dangerously near the wind! The stern displeasure of Rome was aroused, and Ficino only escaped its disastrous consequences by writing his *Apologia,* but this was not quite enough to mollify the papal ire. His fate might eventually have been that of Bruno but for the staunch loyalty of his powerful patron Lorenzo de' Medici, whose admiration for his old tutor Ficino was unbounded. He wrote a little volume of eloquent testimonials defending him, and the papal rumblings finally subsided.

Ficino was fortunate from the first in having the munificent patronage of Cosimo de' Medici, who obtained for him the texts of the Hermetic books for him to translate, all the *Dialogues* of Plato, and the *Enneads* of Plotinus. He also gave him a small estate at Careggio, and there Ficino gathered around him an esoteric circle of intellectuals who called themselves 'The Careggian Academy'. On 7th November 1474 they held a symposium on the lines of Plato's, which Ficino described in his second *Commentary on the Symposium,* an event which became famous and spread Ficino's name far and wide as the *alter Plato.* Ficino did indeed model his entire life on Plato, even burning his early works as had Plato.

In Ficino's Neoplatonic philosophy, aesthetics form an essential part, hence the influence his ideas exerted on Renaissance literature. So admired was Ficino by the Elizabethan poets that Edmund Spenser always kept his *Commentary* by him as his handbook, and its influence pervades the *Faerie Queene.* George Chapman's 'Hymnes' in his poem *The Shadow of Night* are full of Ficinian influence. His writings brought the knowledge of Dionysius the Areopagite into the philosophical-literary culture of Elizabethan England, and Sir Philip Sidney's ardent response is seen in the name he gave to his esoteric club 'The Areopagus' in the 1580's, which was antecedent to Raleigh's 'School of Night'. These 'little academies' all probably took their inspiration from Ficino's 'Careggian Academy'. The tradition for such esoteric clubs had great appeal for Renaissance intellectuals and is delightfully parodied in *Love's Labour's Lost,* in which the 'School of Night' pokes fun at itself. It is impossible that this play could have been written by a rank outsider such as the common actor William Shakespeare, who could not have gained access to their closed circle to write this witty parody.

Ficino's second patron, Lorenzo de' Medici, established him as master of The Platonic Academy of Florence, where a flame was kept perpetually alight before the bust of Plato. Ficino was not only a great classical scholar but also a physician and priest, and his influence extended to the theologians of Elizabethan England as well as to poets, writers and the intellectual laymen. His brilliant, handsome and high-born pupil, Count Pico della Mirandola, became his disciple and carried on Ficino's work after his death exerting also a notable influence. If we compare the writings of these men with Baines' *Note* the contrast is so vast that the proverbial coach and horses could be driven through! It is not possible that the same mind could think in such blatant contradiction, let alone 'risk his life' to spread the blasphemous 'truth' contained in the Baines *Note*.

For anyone who knows Marlowe's works, there can be no doubt as to which of these sources provided him with his inspiration. Not Baines' obscenities based on the clerical authors, but Ficino, Bruno, Castiglioni, Petrarch, Ovid, Virgil were among the inspirational influences informing his genius. In fact, Kocher himself, when he turns to analysing the religious ideas expressed in Marlowe's plays, *Tamburlaine, Dr Faustus* and *The Jew of Malta,* finds not an iota of evidence supporting Baines' accusations. All he can cite is what he calls the 'if' clause in *Tamburlaine:* 'if there be a Christ, as Christians say' (quoted above) and 'The God that sits in heaven, if any god, For he is God alone, and none but he', *(Tamburlaine Part Two,* Act 5 scene 1, 1.1200). Kocher finds that the plays, in fact, present orthodox Christianity. We know from Bakeless' definitive research on the sources used for *Tamburlaine* that Marlowe based the conflicts between Christian and Mohammedan forces in detail on his historical sources; as also his depiction of Tamburlaine's cruelty and monstrous treatment of his vanquished foe, the Turkish emperor Bajazeth.

Marlowe's chief inspiration for his dramatic works was history, which he adhered to faithfully, unless for valid artistic reasons, to recreate historical characters and their lives for his audiences. The historical Tamburlaine, or Timurlane, had assumed the role and title of 'The Scourge of God', giving himself the divine authority to conquer and ruthlessly punish his enemies. This is history which Marlowe dramatized. Tamburlaine was, in any case, not a Christian, and the 'if' clauses imply the pagan scepticism of pagan characters in the plays. Kocher himself admits: 'the philosophy is eminently suitable to the Scythian conqueror and may therefore be a dramatic convention.' [43]

Once Kocher turns his attention to the plays he shows a sensitive responsiveness to the wonderful poetry and dramatic art of Marlowe, and rises to the inspiration of his subject. In fairness to Kocher I give this final quotation from his thesis in which he is really contradicting his own premise regarding the Baines *Note* as an accurate rendition of Marlowe's religious opinions. Here he is commenting on *Tamburlaine:*

'What is most surprising, in view of the Baines note and other testimonies, is that Marlowe in writing like a Christian theologian
should write so magnificently. There is no question but that it is
magnificent. And so we arrive at the realization that however bitterly Marlowe may have hated Christian dogma there were some
elements in it, notably its teaching about God, which could enlist
the highest fervor of his imagination. This truth should warn us
not to over simplify the problem of Marlowe's attitude toward religion.' [44]

It is a great pity that Kocher did not temper his judgement by making a study
of Ficino's and Bruno's ideas and their influence on Marlowe. This lack of
breadth has given his thesis a totally false bias, whilst his whitewashing of
Baines as a decent man whose word is to be believed leads him to make some
preposterous conclusions. Seeing Marlowe's mind in the baleful and distorting
light cast by Baines, Kocher misrepresents him as 'the prophet of the new irreligion'. [45] His myopic obsession with Baines' *Note* has misled him to miscon-
strue with a lamentable lack of historical perspective what *free thought* represented in Elizabethan times. He actually equates 'free thought' with the licence
to slander Christ and debase Christian beliefs, regarding such an expression of
'free thought' as (strangely) admirable and courageous, if foolhardy, on the part
of Marlowe. By imputing the opinions of the Baines *Note* to Marlowe he perceives him as some kind of early Marxist-Leninist revolutionary bent on
destroying religion as the 'opium of the people' which keeps them doped and
incapable of revolutionary ardour. This is sadly to compound his error.

Although the free-thinkers were passionately interested in scientific discovery and freedom to pursue the search for knowledge, these men were profoundly conservative in their political allegiance to the Queen. There was no
latent revolutionary impulse to rock the boat, or to weaken the organs of state.
Not one of them was an extreme Puritan or had political ambitions to change
the *status quo*. They shared only an ardent desire for religious tolerance.
Northumberland was a most courageous campaigner for religious toleration,
and at his trial in 1606 one of the charges against him was his persistent cham-
pionship of the Catholics as a persecuted minority, braving the terrible religious
intolerance of the time.

Kocher's unhistorical view of Marlowe as preaching propaganda for some
kind of early Marxist-leftist revolutionary 'irreligion' is summed up as follows:

'For free thought was stirring in England in a vague, unorganized
way during the last fifty years of the century. Underneath the into-
nations of the orthodox writers, one can hear it rising, this mutter
of revolutionary dissidence. For the most part it was scattered and
anonymous. But in Marlowe we can see the quintessence of it

drawn together and revealed. This is the unique historical importance of the Baines Note, to which we have never sufficiently awakened. Of whom among the Elizabethans have we such another record? Not Raleigh, not the scientists, nor any of Marlowe's fellow dramatists, nor any other literary Englishman whose work we know. For revolutionary impact and scope it stands alone, an extraordinary document in the history of English free thought.' [46]

This 'extraordinary document . . of English free thought' is – the Baines *Note!*

Kocher's excited panegyric of meaningless rhetoric in praise of the Baines *Note* – an informer's libel that is a mere re-hash of ideas raked up from the 'immense volume' of similar obscenities current among 'reputable, excellent' ecclesiastical writers as examples of anti-Christian criticism – can be dismissed as glorified dross. There is nothing extraordinary or 'unique' about Baines' *Note,* for we find the same stock-in-trade indictments added almost as an addendum to the note on Richard Cholmeley (prepared by a rather less skilful anonymous informer who was probably Baines' underling carrying out his boss's instruction on how to nail an indictment) showing that responsibility for these scurrilities can be fairly and squarely laid at the door of the informer. They are not mutual confirmation that Marlowe said these things (as Kocher contends) but mutual confirmation of the informer's obscene touch, which we can find repeated in the tactics of agents of repression even today. Indeed, their methods have hardly changed over the centuries.

Only compare Baines' *Note* with the Nolan's vision of a reformed religion, purified of intolerance and hypocrisy, bringing with it a more blessed state based on moral law in which peaceful and useful activities would thrive and all warring between religious sects be banished, and the conclusion is clear. Religious tolerance and hatred of hypocrisy are reflected in Marlowe's plays, and religious conflicts are exposed as the political tool of powerful factions. This same political acuity allied to this same ethic runs right through the Shakespearean canon.

XVIII

A MURDERED REPUTATION

'Mad slanderers by mad ears believed be', wrote the Poet in *Sonnet 140.* The *Sonnets* once again corroborate that they are the confessional and autobiographical poems of Christopher Marlowe as the hidden pseudonymous author, for they assert most passionately and unequivocally that some terrible scandal afflicted the Poet's name, which (being officially 'dead') he was powerless to refute. Nor could his Patron speak against these slanders, for he also had to lie low for his own safety. The scandal, of course, was Atheism, rated a fatal heresy.

> Your love and pity doth th' impression fill
> Which vulgar scandal stamp'd upon my brow,
> For what care I who calls me well or ill
> So you o'er-green my bad, my good allow?
> You are my All the world, and I must strive
> To know my shames and praises from your tongue;
> None else to me, nor I to none alive,
> That my steel'd sense or changes right or wrong.
> In so profound abysm I throw all care
> Of others' voices, that my adder's sense
> To critic and to flatterer stopped are.
> Mark how with my neglect I do dispense:
>   You are so strongly in my purpose bred,
>   That all the world besides me thinks y'are dead.

Sonnet 112

The last line follows Thorpe's edition, which is somewhat obscure, and I suggest it may have been purposely altered for this 1609 publication to leave a hint, but not declare definitely that the Poet is thought to be dead by the world. The line has been too freely altered from Thorpe's version by some modern editors to make it really nonsensical as in 'That all the world besides, methinks, they're dead' (?)

That the Poet feels that he has been horribly maligned and misjudged is clear from *Sonnet 121,* one of the bitterest outpourings in this entire sequence.

> 'Tis better to be vile than vile esteemed,
> When not to be, receives reproach of being,
> And the just pleasure lost, which is so deemed,
> Not by our feeling, but by others' seeing.
> For why should others' false adulterate eyes

Give salutation to my sportive blood?
Or on my frailties why are frailer spies,
Which in their wills count bad what I think good?
No, I am that I am, and they that level
At my abuses, reckon up their own.
I may be straight though they themselves be bevel;
By their rank thoughts my deeds must not be shown.
    Unless this general evil they maintain,
    All men are bad and in their badness reign.

Sonnet 121

Had Marlowe perhaps inherited something of that 'sportive blood' from the gregarious, lively busy-body shoemaker of Canterbury, who was his father? That he may sometimes have indulged in witticisms and what religious zealots might take for irreverend jesting would be in character, though it had a serious purpose behind it. Marlowe's proselytizing, like Bruno's, was directed towards broadening men's minds and preaching religious tolerance by his oblique methods. In saying provocative things in defence of the arch-enemy Roman Catholicism, he was showing that every religion has its commendable aspects – the Catholics in their more splendid ritual, 'as Elevation of the mass, organs, singing men, Shaven Crownes & cta. That all protestants are Hypocriticall asses.'[1] Similarly, his jest that the prodigal son 'held his purse so neere the bottom in all pictures' that it could only have contained four nobles, which was 'either a jest or els fowr nobles then was thought a great patrimony'.[2] (This last is reported by Kyd in his second letter to be typical of Marlowe's table talk.)

This reportage, together with the citation of error in the chronology of Adam in the Bible, which being written by men was not an infallible book, are examples that are doubtless genuine, and their object can be seen to sow the seeds of healthy scepticism which militates against the over-zealous self-righteousness and bigotry that feed the intolerance underlying all inter-religious conflicts. But not one of these is either blasphemous against Christ or God, nor obscene or scurrilous. They criticise men, not the deity, and they smack of Marlowe's noted wit. That he was possibly a bit of a show-off in company, and that he had talked at times too rashly to people outside their esoteric circle about his unorthodox views is confirmed in his confessional sonnets.

O for my sake do you with Fortune chide,
The guilty goddess of my harmful deeds,
That did not better for my life provide
Than public means, which public manners breeds.
Thence comes it that my name receives a brand,
And almost thence my nature is subdued
To what it works in, like the dyer's hand.
Pity me then, and wish I were renew'd,

Whilst like a willing patient I will drink
Potions of eysell 'gainst my strong infection;
No bitterness that I will bitter think,
Nor double penance to correct correction.
  Pity me then, dear friend, and I assure ye,
  Even that your pity is enough to cure me.

Sonnet 111

Thus even here, in the troubled question of his unorthodox religious beliefs, we receive confirmation that this *is* Marlowe, for the cap fits. Seemingly he had turned for a time, at any rate, from the orthodox dogma of the church under whose *aegis* he had grown up and received his education, to espouse, or to lean towards the Arrian Heresy, of which Raleigh was also suspected, and which Bruno held for much of his life.

He has confessed it frankly –

Most true it is, that I have look'd on truth
Askance and strangely:

Sonnet 110

This is his recollection in exile of his conversion to a form of Unitarianism under the enchantment of the teachings of Giordano Bruno and the Renaissance scientific questioning that underlies the humanist philosophy. Bruno was at heart a monotheist or Unitarian as opposed to a Trinitarian. The Modern Unitarian church is a Christian denomination that rejects the doctrine of the Trinity and emphasises freedom and tolerance in religious belief. Bruno held somewhat similar views.

The Informer's Libel

Baines' Note has a curious history that has never yet been investigated thoroughly. A second copy was made by a scribe's hand from Baines' autograph *Note,* and this fair copy was destined to be presented to the Queen as indicated by the inscription on the back: 'Copye of Marloes blasphemyes As sent to her H.' This is the copy that had the original heading deleted, which read simply,

'A note contayninge the opinion of one Christopher Marlye concernynge his damnable opinion and Iudgment of Religioun and scorne of Gods worde'. ³

This has been scored through and replaced with the puzzling misdating of the death at Deptford already referred to in Chapter 10. Scholars have passed this off as a scribe's error, but it is not the *only* deletion. This copy of the *Note* has been substantially altered with several important deletions, which would certainly not have been done by a scribe. These are as follows.

Firstly, Baines' allegation of homosexuality, which is the thirteenth item or 'That' clause in the list, is firmly scored through. Secondly, the fifteenth item, which refers to Marlowe's alleged claim to the right to coin money is scored through; and finally the entire last paragraph in which Baines recommends that 'the mouth of so dangerous a member be stopped' with the promise that 'great men' will 'in convenient time' be named, is deleted. No one has ever queried these deletions to wonder, Who might have made them? And why? In the light of this thesis they take on a special significance.

Clearly these deletions were made by an authoritative hand, for only someone in high office would have tampered with the copy of the *Note* to be delivered to the Queen. I believe that authoritative hand was Lord Burghley's. This official fair copy would have been made for him to deliver to the Queen. To begin with the last item, Burghley would have known that it would certainly not have been Her Majesty's pleasure to have the 'great men' of her court arraigned and investigated. The threat points to Raleigh and Northumberland and Lord Strange and possibly others whom Marlowe's 'confessions' might expose were he to be tortured and brought to trial. Elizabeth would not have countenanced it, so out went Baines' summary (of which he was doubtless very proud!) with firm scratches of the quill.

Burghley, who certainly knew all about Baines and the nature of the man, would have recognised the informer's slur in the charge of homosexuality, and felt that he was overstepping his brief again which was typical of Baines' whole career in espionage and government secret police work. He seems to have been employed in the latter after his disastrous espionage activities at Rheims in 1583, when he concocted the ludicrous plot to kill off the entire inhabitants of the Catholic seminary by poisoning the well, for which he was apprehended and imprisoned, first in the town gaol and then held privately in the Seminary, when he wrote his self-revealing confession. There is no evidence to indicate how the matter ended, or how he regained his freedom. [4] It is remarkable that Baines escaped worse punishment than imprisonment, and why he is found back in England, apparently employed once again in government service on policing duties for the Court of the Star Chamber, remains a mystery. Had he craftily sold his promise to Cardinal Allen at Rheims that, if released, he would act in some useful capacity to bring such skilful, trusted espionage agents as Marlowe to their downfall? Acting as a double agent deviously undermining the smooth working of the English espionage network? This seems the only logical explanation for his remarkable escape from Rheims, which left Dr Boas puzzled when he researched this extraordinary Rheims incident. Such a crafty ploy precisely fits Baines' devious mind. It represents a cunning variant of the role of double agent, betraying his victims not to the Catholics but to their own side, with lies and insinuations to tar them with suspicion and distrust. For this is exactly what we find Baines doing in his malicious pursuit of Marlowe, the first evidence of which is in connection with illicit coining.

In January 1592 Marlowe and Baines were in Flushing together and actually sharing a room in a lodging-house. It was doubtless a case of necessity makes strange bed-fellows! What Baines was doing there is not clear, but it seems that Marlowe was on an assignment for Lord Burghley to discover the source(s) of illicit coining from which the renegade English Catholic armed force at Nijmegen under the command of the traitor, Sir William Stanley, were getting their supplies of illicit money. [5] At Flushing Marlowe made contact with an expert goldsmith, who demonstrated to him how coins could be cast, using for his sample the base metal pewter, so that the resulting Dutch shilling was of no value. Baines, as his room-mate, got wind of this – perhaps he dogged Marlowe, spying on him – and he forthwith reported Marlowe's dealings with the goldsmith, one Gifford Gilbert (a strange inversion of the name of the double agent at Rheims, but apparently there is no connection) to the governor of Flushing, Sir Robert Sidney. Sidney had the two arrested and they were sent, together with Baines, under escort back to England to be delivered to Lord Burghley. On his arrest Marlowe and Baines made mutual counter accusations about coining and defecting to the Catholic enemy, and it is clear that no love was lost between them. In this mood they arrived on Burghley's mat to answer for their conduct.

Burghley sorted out the matter of the charge of coining and other accusations, though we can only guess how, for no records survive. It was probably too secret. Illicit coining was a serious crime punishable by death – by boiling in oil! But all we know is that no punitive consequences transpired from this affair. This points to the conclusion that Burghley knew all about Marlowe's alleged coining escapade at Flushing. As Lord Treasurer he was closely concerned in matters of illegal coining and had sent his agent to investigate what appeared to be a serious coining operation in the Netherlands, fuelling a Catholic military threat. That interfering busy-body Baines thought he had caught Marlowe red-handed, but he had only succeeded in putting his foot in it, upsetting Burghley's well laid plans and doubtless upsetting his temper too. However, it would not have been prudent to disclose to such a man as Baines what Marlowe's connection with himself in the matter was. The wily elder statesman knew how to play his cards close to his chest, and Baines was left to continue in his official capacity probably none the wiser. It was, after all, only a pewter Dutch shilling. That is how I see the logic of this episode.

Baines ought to have drawn some conclusions from this affair, but here he was once more determined to fasten a coining charge on Marlowe. The item in the *Note* reads:

> 'That he had as good Right to Coine as the Queen of England, and that he was acquainted wth one Poole a prisoner in newgate who hath great Skill in mixture of mettals and hauing learned some thinges of him he ment through help of a Cunninge stamp maker to Coin ffrench Crownes pistolets and English shillinges.' [6]

This sounds like a rendition of what Baines was accusing Marlowe of in Flushing, which he is determined to revive now to his advantage. One detects the annoyance with which the corrector scratched out the offending words. Marlowe's encounter with 'one Poole', identified by Eccles as John Poole, was put to good use during his brief sojourn in Newgate at the time of the Watson-Bradley duel. [7] John Poole, besides having skill in metals and coining was acquainted with a Catholic priest from Rheims, so Marlowe would have a professional interest in cultivating his acquaintance. This he would also doubtless have reported to Lord Burghley at the time, so Baines' *Note* would have imparted no news but would have ruffled the old man's temper.

The case for identifying the correcting hand in the *Note* with Lord Burghley is a strong one on several counts. Although Marlowe worked in espionage directly under Sir Francis Walsingham during his lifetime, he was also Burghley's man. Elizabeth's two chief ministers worked in harness, but not always in harmony, as is evidenced by a rift over the Armada tactics. It seems Marlowe was sent to monitor the phoney peace negotiations that Burghley and the Queen supported in the face of ardent opposition by the 'war party', headed by Lord Admiral Howard and Drake and Sir Francis Walsingham as well. Their argument was all for pre-empting the Spanish threat by attacking Spain first in her own waters – a full-scale follow-up of Drake's singeing of the King of Spain's beard at Cadiz. But the cautious Burghley and the Queen were playing for time, and, dismissing strong and popular criticism, pressed ahead with sending a top-ranking peace commission headed by the old Earl of Derby to negotiate 'peace' terms with the Duke of Parma at Bruges, proposed of course by Spain where King Philip was arming his Armada furiously. Queen Elizabeth was not so blind that she did not realise what was going on, but this was a game she thoroughly understood and she played the prelude to the Armada her way, with her elder statesman's full support. Tucker Brooke first suggested that Marlowe had been sent by Burghley with the peace commission to report back to him. That this is what actually happened is evident in the Armada report he wrote for Lord Admiral Howard to be presented to Sir Francis Walsingham, in which he devotes the first two pages to a lengthy account *justifying* Queen Elizabeth's conduct of the peace negotiations despite King Philip's obvious double-faced policy in proposing them. This would *not* have been according to Lord Howard's instruction to his report writer. He would probably have fumed upon first reading it! But Marlowe would have known how to pacify him with cogent arguments to persuade him how graciously the Queen would view this report, and had they not won the war after all? It gives us invaluable insight into the trust and the political clout that such a high-placed intelligence agent as Marlowe wielded. And is this not what we would expect if he were Shakespeare? [8]

That Lord Burghley valued Marlowe's services highly cannot be doubted. We have also to put into the picture the commission of the *Sonnets* for the young Earl of Southampton three years earlier. This, again, indicates that

Marlowe and Burghley enjoyed a rather close relationship. I have no doubt that it was Burghley who was mainly responsible for granting Marlowe bail upon his arrest under the warrant of the Star Chamber, when he was by good luck brought to the court at Nonsuch because it happened to be a Sunday. Burghley would, I believe, have been very worried at this turn of events threatening Marlowe. Sir Francis Walsingham had held certain advanced opinions, in particular reflected in his keen interest in world exploration. One would not label this extremely busy man a free-thinker, but his family were certainly touched with free thought, both in his son-in-law Sir Philip Sidney and in Thomas Walsingham. Significantly, Burghley was the lifelong friend of Sir Nicholas Bacon, who died in 1579, the father of Francis and Anthony Bacon, and Lord Keeper of the Great Seal. As the sequel to this book reveals, he was the founder of Freemasonry. It was the Freemasons who sheltered Marlowe and provided the total protection that enabled him eventually to return from his exile. Sir Nicholas Bacon, a great free-thinker, was also Burghley's brother-in-law. Their closeness suggests Burghley would have had sympathy for Marlowe in his dire trouble.

Thomas Walsingham had been almost a son to Sir Francis, and would have been intimately known to Lord Burghley. Burghley had a good acquaintance of Dame Elinor Bull, to whom he was probably related, for both named Blanche Parry 'cousin'. [9.] Burghley's affectionate, life-long relationship with Queen Elizabeth is not in doubt. These two enjoyed mutual trust. William Danby, Coroner of the Queen's Household, is named 'well beloved' by her. We can discern a chain of association deep inside the Court of people who could have combined to form a protective circle to save the brilliant, young poet-dramatist who had so loyally served the Queen and Lord Burghley. This close-knit human chain linked Thomas Walsingham – the Queen – William Danby – Lord Burghley – Dame Elinor Bull. This is conjecture, but, given the circumstances, the people and the place and time, it is both logical and possible.

There were of course many in high positions at Court who viewed the free-thinkers with the utmost suspicion. Burghley, if he were a party to Marlowe's escape, would have played a lone hand. It was a matter of the utmost secrecy. Baines' *Note* would have impressed his masters – powerful, reactionary, bigoted men who had instigated this persecution. For them he penned his item attributing the remark to Marlowe –

'That all they that love not *Tobacco* & Boies were fooles.'

This was calculated to make their lordships sit up with a jolt. What have we here? Not only an Atheist, but one who commends sodomy! Which is exactly what Baines intended. The only real 'fool' in the case, if he had ever commended such a thing, would be Marlowe himself, for sodomy was punishable by death under Tudor law enacted in Henry VIII's reign.

Immediately preceding this item Baines has placed the alleged remark attributed to Marlowe –

'That St John the Euangelist was bedfellow to C[hrist] and leaned alwaies in his bosome, that he vsed him as the sinners of *Sodoma.*'

The charge made here is of scandalous criticism of Christ in the context of a series of shockingly obscene and blasphemous statements defaming him, concluding with this – all of which are specifically and maliciously *anti*-Christian. The alleged *commendation* of a homosexual relationship with boys, however, is a sudden *volte-face,* allying himself with Christ upon whom he had heaped odium; a contradiction in attitude. This had escaped the notice of this cunning informer! I suggest that Baines was determined to slip in the accusation of sodomy, the most damning charge he could bring, and he cleverly tacked it onto the remark about tobacco, which was fashionably used by Raleigh and Hariot, who was addicted to his pipe; thus lending it a spurious authenticity, which has misled the modern scholars to credit this item.

Marlowe's earlier biographers and critics, J.H. Ingram, C.F. Tucker Brooke, and John Bakeless did not allow themselves to be convinced by Baines' accusation. It is his later critics who have turned so incredibly credulous, spuriously arguing his homosexuality from *Edward the Second* as supposedly supportive evidence for the thirteenth item in Baines' *Note.* The question of Marlowe's sexuality needs no further comment. The evidence of his writings reviewed reveals what his attitude to sodomy really was. It contrasts starkly with Baines' accusation.

So far as Baines was concerned, his brief was to nail this important 'Atheist', against whom he appears to have also had a personal vendetta, and there was no surer way of doing this than to charge Marlowe with sodomy. It was the favourite weapon of the informer reserved for the most desired victim. Sexual depravity of every sort, from adultery, incest, fornication with devils, to sodomy and even buggery with animals, were the charges used with venomous success against important religious figures seen as dangerous rivals by the prosecuting churchmen. Such indictments of sexual depravity are among the oldest and most powerful weapons in the informer's arsenal.

The 1590's were very different from the 1580's when England basked in a liberal period of Elizabeth's benign reign, with the free-thinking Philip Sidney and Raleigh riding high in favour with the Queen. Suddenly the climate changed as a fierce *fin de siècle* gathering of the forces of reaction swept through Western Christendom eventually to spend itself in the fury of the Thirty Years War. With this the scientific age was born.

To enable us to arrive at a realistic assessment of what the Baines *Note* portends regarding the significance of the obscene allegations it offers, it is essential to be fully aware of this historical context in which the tragedy of Marlowe was played out. It has been given too scant consideration by his critics and biographers, especially in its wider implications, but it is central to our understanding of what happened. Throughout Europe reaction against the free-thinkers was on the move in the last decade of the sixteenth century and even in Elizabeth's England the clouds were gathering ominously.

To fill out this picture a digression concerning the power and function of the Court of Star Chamber, the English equivalent of the Inquisition, is in order.

THE COURT OF STAR CHAMBER was created by the Tudors by an Act of 1487, 3 Henry VII, to provide a strong arm of the law deriving its power and authority directly from the king and the Privy Council. It operated independently of the English common law courts to which it stood in the relation of a higher judiciary, despite the fact that it did not impose the death sentence. Nevertheless its judgments were regarded to be of 'greater terror and amazement to offenders', [10] for they included brutal and inhuman punishments from whipping and branding, cutting off of ears, amputation of hands when the stumps were cauterized by plunging into hot pitch, to severe and often exorbitant fines. Nor did those charged by the Star Chamber necessarily escape the death penalty eventually, as in the case of the Earl of Essex who received 'the overture of his ruin' [11] from the Court of Star Chamber, and was finally, executed. This court alone was empowered to use torture.

This powerful higher court was, in fact, the judicial arm of the Privy Council, who served as its members, and it was from its inception presided over by the Lord Chancellor and the Archbishop or his bishop, aided by the Lord Treasurer, the Keeper of the Privy Seal, temporal lords and chief justices, who finally numbered about thirty judges during the reign of Queen Elizabeth. The Court of Star Chamber was greatly augmented under Cardinal Wolsey, Archbishop of York, when he was also Lord Chancellor heading this court, who elevated it to its position as the supreme court of the land with powers as wide as its constitution was vague. [12] Although particularly concerned with jurisdiction in cases of riot and unlawful assembly, libel and slander, forgery, perjury, fraud, duelling, and disputes between English and foreign merchants, and testamentary cases, in practice its jurisdiction was unlimited. All offences, including treason, murder, and heresy, could be examined and punished at the discretion of the sovereign and the Privy Council under the Star Chamber Court.

Its most important difference was that the procedure of the Star Chamber was not according to the common law of England, and therein lay the terror in which its name was held. It operated without any jury, being its own prosecutor and judge, and the accused were allowed no benefit of legal counsel; it could proceed on rumour alone without prior evidence; it was empowered to apply torture, and confessions so extracted were regarded legal; it proceeded from the assumption that any person arrested, for whatever reason, might be examined for other alleged misdemeanours by a method called 'scraping the conscience'. Witnesses were heard in secret, and if any evidence was given by a witness who later recanted, the evidence given (probably under duress) nevertheless carried the full weight irrespective of any subsequent retraction.

290

No wonder that this 'great and high Court of Star Chamber' was seen as 'but an usurpation of monarchy upon the common law of England, and in the prejudice of the liberties granted to the subject by the Great Charter'.[13] It was one of the more despotic legacies bequeathed to the nation by the vigorous Tudor dynasty of Henry VII and his son Henry VIII.

In the 1590's Elizabeth's then Archbishop of Canterbury, John Whitgift, a man of very different calibre from the benign, tolerant Matthew Parker, was intent on using the power of the Star Chamber to stifle the beginnings of English scientific and metaphysical inquiry, which he saw as dangerous to the stability of state and church, the breeding ground of heresies which must be stamped out ruthlessly. Doubtless he recalled how

> 'the grave archbishops and bishops, finding the heresy of the *Erastites* to creep into this kingdom held it the surest way for suppression to bring it to this bar; [i.e. the Star Chamber] where the bishop of Winchester's confutation, London's sharpest reprehension, the archbishop's wholesome discipline, together with the grave judicial medicines, stopped the current of those flowing streams which would have been like to have brought an inundation upon Christ's church and people.'[14]

Perhaps he even quoted this precedent at the meeting of the Privy Council when the warrant for Marlowe's arrest was despatched, proposing it was high time that their lordships took the matter seriously and decided to apply such 'grave judicial medicines' to these free-thinkers that were spreading their ideas in the realm.

In the heightened atmosphere of the witch-hunt of this period a particularly unpleasant individual came into his own province of power as the cruel persecutor of the Roman Catholics, the notorious Richard Topcliffe, whose name appears in the special commission against the Jesuits issued by the Privy Council on 26th March 1593. We note this date. Because the frequent use of the rack in the Tower was noticed and aroused indignant comment, being held odious by the population, Topcliffe was granted authority to torture priests in his own house. He boasted that he had a rack made to his own design 'compared with which the common racks in use were child's play'.[15] His diabolical treatment of the saintly Jesuit priest, Robert Southwell, would be incredible if it were not confirmed in Topcliffe's own handwriting. Southwell was arrested in 1592 and eventually executed in 1595. His writings in poetry and prose on sacred themes were illicitly published and widely read. Gabriel Harvey praised them as 'elegant and pathetical', and Ben Jonson was among his most ardent admirers.

This was the atmosphere of the 1590's in which Marlowe was hunted. Topcliffe has been described as 'a monster of iniquity'.[16] Baines was in the same profession, and both men obtained confessions under torture to gain the 'evidence' they needed. Such men are not disposed to be nice about whether it represented the truth or not, and Kocher's view, that Baines was far too decent a chap to have insinuated matter into Marlowe's indictment unless he really had said these things, is naive.

In the Star Chamber Archbishop Whitgift would have precedence over Lord Burghley. It is difficult, if not impossible, to draw a clear distinction between the overlapping duties of the Privy Council and the Star Chamber Court. The Privy Councillors wearing their Star Chamber 'hats' did not all sit at the same session, but probably took turns in these duties. The Star Chamber Court was located in the outer quadrangle of the Palace of Westminster, and was doubtless so-named because 'all the roof thereof was decked with images and starres gilded'. [17.] Its sessions were from nine o'clock until eleven every morning during the law terms on Wednesdays and Fridays; and the officers permanently in charge there were the clerk, three attorneys and an examiner. It employed its own pursuivants or messengers, who were sergeants-at-arms, to deliver warrants and apprehend malefactors.

Henry Maunder, who was sent to arrest Marlowe, is designated 'one of the messengers of her Majesty's Chamber' on the warrant dated 18th May, which was a Friday during the law term when the Star Chamber would have been in session, so that he would be one of their sergeants-at-arms. As Marlowe did not answer the summons until 20th May, which was a Sunday, he probably rode the fifteen miles from Chislehurst to the Queen's Court, then at Nonsuch, where the Privy Council would also be present to attend on the Queen's person. The record of Marlowe's appearance before their lordships is accordingly found in the Acts of the Privy Council:

> 'This day Christofer Marley of London gentleman, being sent for by warrant from their Lordships, hath entered his appearance accordinglie for his Indemnity therein, and is commaunded to give his daily attendaunce on their Lordships until he shalbe lycensed to the contrary.' [18]

The absence of any threat in the wording of this entry does not indicate, as Bakeless assumed, that there was no intention to proceed against him. It rather indicates that Marlowe was well known to their lordships, who allowed him his freedom while investigating the charge against him. Those who saw him when he was delivered under arrest are not likely to have been the full Privy Council, for it was a Sunday. It may have been only Lord Burghley himself with one or two others present at Court. The Privy Council record does not name the member or members who presided.

Thomas Walsingham and Marlowe were familiar with the methods employed and they could have been under no illusion that his bail meant that he was safe. There would have been days of fearful apprehensive waiting during which their desperate plans were laid. When Baines' *Note* was finally completed its delivery was somehow delayed or intercepted, as is evident from the curious alteration of the dates on the official copy, which were almost certainly not made by the same hand that made the deletions of the items already discussed, for the purpose behind the deletions in the text and the alteration of the dates is quite different. This interceptor, as I shall call him, was most probably Thomas Walsingham or someone who was acting for him. He would have noted the virulence of the contents so that whatever escape plans had been formulated had to be urgently expedited, for there would have been only one outcome from such an indictment.

Baines had done his devilish work well.

God's Holy Fool

Marlowe was peculiarly vulnerable through his characteristic independence of mind; his brilliance, which evoked envy and spiked Greene's attack on him in print, and exposed him in the distorted and lurid light that superstition finds most congenial; his privileged association with the Court circle that held its meetings in secret behind closed doors, which engendered suspicions; and his rash proselytizing, by which he foolhardily spoke his mind to some who were not ready to receive his message of religious tolerance.

Through the characters in his plays he had the temerity to express controversial ideas that nevertheless passed the censor because they are spoken 'in character' by the personages in his plays, and not as emanating from the dramatist. Thus, speaking in the character of Machiavel in his prologue to *The Jew of Malta* he declared for all the world to note in an admixture part Marlowe, part Machiavel:

> I count religion but a childish toy,
> And hold there is no sin but ignorance.

This bold statement was certainly intended to make his audiences take note and think. Marlowe is expressing criticism of the contemporary malpractice of religion at its most hypocritical in this tragedy masquerading as 'black comedy', a witty, diverting, sharply satirical commentary on sectarian and racist intolerance and religious hypocrisy cleverly presented in a fast-moving dramatic entertainment which finally draws the moral that dishonesty does not pay.

Marlowe was not, I believe, attacking the worship of God as divine creator of the universe, for this was not compatible with his philosophy or his nature. He was a profoundly moral human being whose sparkling wit complemented a deeply serious and searching attitude of mind and soul questing for moral justification. His early plays before 1593, though immensely popular, are not superficial entertainment but speak to their audiences at many levels. All address problems reflecting human behaviour with an underlying theme of moral integrity. This is the characteristic of the entire Shakespearean canon, which has established these plays as the greatest ever written and gives them their universal and eternal appeal. They will never be outdated. Marlowe's message that bigotry and sectarian hatred are rooted in ignorance is as relevant today as it was in his own day.

Throughout history there have been those who have felt the heavy obligation to speak out and tell the truth as they perceived it – and take the consequences. Such people have been called 'God's holy fools'. The prophets told the unpalatable truth about injustices and moral wrongs they saw around them, and were prepared to suffer for it. The disciples of Jesus were all cast in this mould and suffered as witnesses to his divine truth, and after them comes an endless procession of saints and martyrs, many of them obscure and unsung, who dared to speak out and were silenced. The supreme example is Jesus himself, who spoke the message he was born to deliver knowing he would have to pay the ultimate price.

This immensely brave, foolhardy and scary profession is of an ancient human tradition. Giordano Bruno followed it in his own fashion and paid the price, which Marlowe escaped. We should not lightly forget that his genius was nurtured in the Anglican church to which his education had initially dedicated him, and if he did not preach from a pulpit it was nevertheless a kind of preaching in which he indulged. He turned reproving eyes on the established church to make courageous criticism exposing contemporary religious malpractice.

Harry Levin has summed up this remarkable poet-dramatist's special contribution as a reforming influence in his time with true insight:

> 'The doubts and aspirations that Marlowe voiced, the aesthetic impulses and scientific curiosities, may be less typical of their time and place than has commonly been supposed; but to that extent he is the more original, and plays an even more strategic role than had been previously recognized. His combination of sensuous perception and speculative intelligence is not to be valued less because it is rare. Civilization is shaped and changed by genius and not by mediocrity.' [19]

Marlowe was not only a dramatic-poet of genius, he was one of those deeply thoughtful people who, seeing the world to be a badly managed place, have felt impelled to declare that there must be a better way of running the human show. Such people are pioneers who either become successful leaders, or are crushed. They inevitably make enemies. In this, too, Marlowe was treading his path of destiny.

We have not yet finished with Marlowe's enemies, for Kyd's evidence must now also be examined in order to answer the charges brought and to test their

294

truth; for Kyd's two extant letters have been credited word for word by Marlowe's modern critics, with few exceptions, as presenting a true picture of him by his erstwhile 'friend', Thomas Kyd, although it is clear he had no love for Marlowe and had an obvious reason for maligning him.

Poison Letters

Thomas Kyd, the dramatist who wrote *The Spanish Tragedy,* a revenge play in blank verse that rivalled *Tamburlaine the Great* in popularity for many years, was by profession a noverint, or copier of manuscripts, for which a stylish Italic hand was used. Dr Tucker Brooke has compared the Italic hand in which the copy of the Arrian heresy found among Kyd's papers is written, with the Italic hand Kyd uses for the Latin quotations with which he embellished his first Letter to Sir John Puckering, and he claims that these could be an identical autograph. [20]

This is a feasible hypothesis. Marlowe, being perhaps very busy, and having doubtless ready cash from his government work was possibly doing his less affluent friend, the noverint, a small favour by employing him to copy this paper for him, having maybe borrowed it from Northumberland's library where a copy existed, and intending to use the treatise as the reference for his lecture to the members of Raleigh's coterie on the dogma of the Trinity, which we know interested them. This would explain why this paper allegedly belonging to Marlowe was lying among Kyd's own, for its presence seems otherwise hard to explain, though human carelessness is always a factor, and this Kyd used as his explanation to his interrogators.

Kyd's two Letters to Sir John Puckering were written after his release from prison when, doubtless still bearing the injuries of his racking, the pathetic man sought to return to the service of his lord (the reactionary Earl of Sussex, not Lord Strange as some believe)[21] and found the door shut because the taint of 'Atheism' still clung to him. It was to 'shake the viper off my hand into the fire' that Kyd wrote to Puckering, pleading for a good word to be put in for him with his lord to exonerate him from the fatal charge and clear his name.

Upon his release from prison Kyd's burning interest must have been to find out what had happened to Marlowe, on whose behalf he had suffered so unjustly. One can imagine his chagrin on learning that Marlowe, unlike himself, had been neither imprisoned nor racked, but was allowed his freedom on his recognizance. Such favoured treatment for the man who was guilty and for whom Kyd had borne the ordeal of torture! Naturally, he would have made every effort to discover the details of Marlowe's death. He would learn that Marlowe had a quarrel with Ingram Frizer, had lost his temper and attacked him from behind (oh, reprehensible!) and Frizer had then in his own defence stabbed him, for which the jury had acquitted him of murder.

These facts, of which Lord Puckering would have been aware, Kyd makes full use of in his first Letter, presenting Marlowe as 'intemperate & of a cruel heart', aiming to gain sympathy for himself as the innocent victim of so 'malicious' an Atheist. He writes, interspersing his Letter with Latin tags (here translated into English in the Italicized passages) which are chosen to emphasize his case :

> 'That I should love or be familiar friend with one so irreligious, were very rare, when Tully saith, *Those are worthy of friendship in whom there resides a cause why they should be esteemed*, which neither was in him, for person, qualities, or honesty, besides he was intemperate & of a cruel heart, the very contraries to which my greatest enemies will say of me.' [22]

He adds piously,

> 'It is not to be numbered amongst the best conditions of men, to tax or to upbraid the dead *Because the dead do not bite*, But thus much have I (with your Lordship's favour) dared in the greatest cause, which is to clear myself of being thought an Atheist, which some will swear he was.' [23]

Kyd names Hariot, the mathematical genius, and his friend Warner as those with whom Marlowe was most frequently seen in company (they at least thought his friendship well worth cultivating) and he hints that they may be of Marlowe's heretical opinion – he himself will neither accuse nor excuse them – but if Lord Puckering should wish to interrogate them he would learn that he, Kyd, is *not* 'of that vile opinion'.

At the end of his wordy Letter he complains that some had suspected him of being the cause of 'the former shipwreck' – meaning that he was believed to have implicated Marlowe by his confessions on the rack. He also offers to turn informer.

> 'I shall beseech in all humility & in the fear of God that it will please your Lordship but to censure me as I shall prove myself, and to repute them as they are indeed *Since of all injustice none is more pernicious than that of those who, when they most deeply deceive, do it in such manner that they shall seem good men.* For doubtless even then your Lordship shall be sure to break open their lewd designs and see into the truth, when but their lives that herein have accused me shall be examined & ripped up effectually, so may I chance with Paul to live & shake the viper off my hand into the fire for which the ignorant suspect me guilty of the former shipwreck. And thus (for now I fear me I grow tedious) assuring your good Lordship that if I knew any whom I could justly accuse of that damnable offence to

the awful Majesty of God or of that mutinous sedition toward the state I would as willingly reveal them as I would request your Lordship better thoughts of me that never have offended you.'[24]

Kyd's heart is chock full of bitterness, this much is clear, and he sees Marlowe and his friends as his enemies whom he is ready to inform against. The whole tenor and purpose of his first Letter is to distance himself in every way possible from friendship with the 'Atheist' Marlowe, and to ingratiate himself with Lord Puckering as one who hates all Atheists and will willingly assist in bringing them to justice. The 'mutinous sedition' he refers to is the verse inciting the Londoners to riot against foreigners, which had brought the officers of the law to search his room – whereupon Kyd was areested and racked.

Now that Marlowe's star is fallen, Kyd feels he can malign him with impunity, being an Atheist and a dead one, and he set about doing so with cunning. The man he depicts in his Letters is not recognisable as the man befriended by Walsingham, Blount, Watson, Hariot, Warner, Chapman, Roydon, Raleigh, Northumberland, Lord Strange, with whom his acquaintance ranged from sincere amity to the deepest bonds of friendship. The stigma of Atheism has remained with Kyd and he is prepared to go to any length in order to recover his lost reputation, 'the greatest cause' as he calls it. That is a potent motive, and one may forgive the poor, injured man for bartering Marlowe's reputation dead, and already sullied by circumstance and rumour, for his own reputation living. Kyd is astute enough to forestall what Lord Puckering may think on reading his Letter *(the dead do not bite)*. Kyd is no fool, and he is also one of the most successful dramatists of his time, and here he is out to impress and win Lord Puckering's sympathy for his own innocence; so by blackening Marlowe he seeks by contrast to whiten himself. If such was his intention, however, Kyd's Letters do not cast a favourable light on his own character, let alone Marlowe's.

When Lord Puckering took him up on his offer to disclose all he knew about Marlowe's Atheistic beliefs and remarks, Kyd wrote a second Letter, in which he reports his recollections of Marlowe's table talk: 'to jest at the divine scriptures, gibe at prayers, & strive in argument to frustrate & confute what hath been spoke or writ by prophets & such holy men.' [25] This sounds as though it may have been in part serious conversation, in part jesting table talk. We know that the young lads at Cambridge used to make a practice of turning the wrong way at the Creed when in chapel out of sheer devilment! If when the wine flowed Marlowe's noted wit indulged in a bit of irreverent fun recollected perhaps from his student days, who are we to deny Shakespeare his cakes and ale? But this is not to assume that his jesting was obscene and blasphemous.

Such human behaviour is in a different category from the scurrilities of Baines' *Note*. Kyd's notes of Marlowe's table talk are all in this jesting vein free from obscenity, with one exception. This is the repetition of an item in Baines' *Note* that is one of the informer's stock-in-trade obscenities designed to bring in implications of sodomy as blasphemy – here claiming 'St John to be our Saviour Christ's Alexis, I cover it with reverence and trembling that is that Christ did love him with an extraordinary love.' We should remember that Kyd had been interrogated on the rack, probably by Baines. Homosexuality is not presented in this instance by either Kyd or Baines as something that Marlowe *approved* – in both instances the statement is intended to present Marlowe as an obscenely blasphemous critic of Jesus.

The fact that Kyd offered Lord Puckering his willingness to inform on Marlowe and his friends suggests that Baines would have found him a co-operative respondent during his interrogation – aided by the persuasive turn of the screw – and this item was very likely implanted in Kyd's mind by Baines. If Marlowe's mind had really been of this calibre of crudeness, which is in such stark contrast to the refinement of his poetic works, he would never have found honourable welcome in the inner circle of the Elizabethan intelligentsia.

The chronology of events is all-important in considering Kyd's Letters. Both are undated but were written after Marlowe's death. Gossip about the sordid events at Deptford would soon have spread through the tavern talk of the sixteen jurymen relating how Marlowe had attacked his friend 'maliciously'. Kyd, still smarting painfully in body and mind from his unjust racking and the taint of Atheism, and now desperate to regain his lord's patronage, would have been predisposed to believe every word he was told about Marlowe's death. He seizes upon these 'facts' to colour his Letters with emphasis (twice repeated – once in each Letter) on the allegedly reprehensible character traits of the dead Marlowe, depicting him as just such a nasty individual as Frizer's story implies, assuring Puckering that this 'Atheist' was a man of 'intemperate' nature and 'of a cruel heart', contrasting his own gentle disposition. In his second Letter he returns gratuitously to this theme harping on an alleged mean streak in Marlowe's character in a context in which it is quite irrelevant:

'That things esteemed to be done by divine power might have as well been done by observation of men, all which he would so suddenly take slight occasion to slip out as I & many others, in regard to his other rashness in attempting sudden privy injuries to men, did overslip though often reprehend him for it & for which God is my witness, aswell by my lord's commandment, as in hatred of his life & thoughts I left & did refrain his company.' [26]

Here he mixes in a reference to 'sudden privy injuries' with a report on opinions of scepticism of a scientific nature. The very phrase he uses suggests the unprovoked attack on Frizer as being in Kyd's mind. Marlowe's manner of death in the sordid Deptford quarrel was obviously a source of gratification to Kyd.

If Kyd's portrait of the dead poet as a nasty, rather vicious person were really true then it would be a matter of amazement that Marlowe had so many friends

298

who loved him and cherished his memory. Blount refers to him tenderly as 'the man that hath been dear unto us, living an after-life in our memory'. Of no other contemporary poet do we have such clear documentary evidence that he was cherished as a man held in the warmest esteem by his patron as his friend, not just for his poetry, and admitted to the society of the noblemen whose inner circle was penetrated by a select few. Blount's moving dedication to Thomas Walsingham of *Hero and Leander* has no parallel in Elizabethan literature as a testimony of genuine friendship between patron and poet here expressed from the patron's side, not from the poet's, of which latter there are numerous examples in the dedications of literary works by poets suing for noble patronage. Blount's dedication is in a different category. It is unique.

That the exiled Poet of the *Sonnets* loved his friends in return and missed them sorely is most touchingly testified in *Sonnets 30* and *31*. These included the learned and venerable George Chapman, who was a devout Christian to whom such obscene blasphemies as are imputed to Marlowe would certainly have been offensive. This argues that he never made such remarks at all, and that Kyd and Baines are lying.

The aspersions Kyd casts on Marlowe's character and unworthiness of friendship are in complete contradiction of this evidence. We know from his own admission that Kyd intensely disliked Marlowe, and whatever friendship had existed – and it was probably always tinged with envy – was turned to hatred by the injustice of his injurious treatment, which is reflected in the palpable bias and malice expressed in his Letters, which derive an obvious, strong motivation for untruthfulness from his turbulent feelings. If Kyd is lying on one count, there is every reason to conclude that he is lying on other counts, and his Letters are consequently worthless as evidence on which we can base a reliable assessment of Marlowe's true character.

Scholars have been swayed to accord more weight to the maliciously motivated reports written by Kyd to Lord Puckering because it represents handwritten documentary evidence. If it is in writing it must be true, is a common assumption. It is also argued that Kyd knew Marlowe personally. Yes, he knew him, and he knew that he was lying and went out of the way to excuse himself – but it was in 'the greatest cause'.

> Reputation, reputation, reputation! O, I have lost my reputation!
> I have lost the immortal part of myself, and what remains is
> bestial.
> *Othello* Act 2 scene 3 11.254-55

So cried Cassio. The man who put those words into his mouth had also wrung them from the bitter experience of his own heart.

XIX

THE DISTORTED IMAGE

THE ASSESSMENT of Marlowe's character by modern scholars has been detrimentally affected in a slowly mounting crescendo by Baines' and Kyd's testimonies, for they are seen to be corroborated by the story told in the inquisition of his alleged violent quarrel with his murderer Ingram Frizer. Marlowe is today increasingly presented as a man given to violence and 'sudden rages', his reputation engulfed by the libels of the informer and the perfidious, pathetic Kyd, together with the tale of the loyal servant of his patron who was facing the gallows for slaying a great poet in reprisal for a couple of minor scalp wounds. The questions tentatively raised by Bakeless, and the medical evidence presented by Tannenbaum, have been superseded by blind acceptance of the dubious documentary evidence with no questions asked. The distorted image prevails.

Charles Norman on reading Marlowe's works sensed that in the maturing of his genius 'something serene and deeply felt in him was gathering into beauty for a second harvest', but he also wrote:

> 'We know from his work that his spirit was kin to exultation; but we learn from the records of his life that he was quick to grasp sword, voice turning ugly and provocative, fist clenched for threat or striking; that he was a scorner of the unlearned, a scholar and a blasphemer.' [1]

His biographers have not really known what to make of him. The fear of questioning and objectively investigating his death to the fullest limits, in case it turns out that he really did not die, and therefore the inevitable corollary presents itself that he was the pseudonymous author Shakespeare, has apparently paralyzed further research into the circumstances. Bakeless has commented: 'As witnesses, both Baines and Kyd command very little confidence.' [2] But it has been left at that. After tossing the arguments surrounding his death to and fro, all have opted for a safe harbour. Let sleeping dogs lie, is good counsel. Marlowe safely dead and libelled is preferable to having all those books on Shakespeare outdated. Whether consciously perceived or not, the motive is there.

So it is that the Bradley affray, an innocent affair so far as Marlowe is concerned, is misrepresented as an example of his violent nature; whereas he became involved in a quarrel that was *not* his own, from which he withdrew when the real protagonist appeared on the scene to confront the notorious brawler Bradley (as the legal records testify) who was harbouring malicious intent against Marlowe's friend, Tom Watson. Today this is coloured by comments which aim to link this incident with the quarrel at Deptford when he met his death as 'the coward conquest of a wretch's knife.' The Bradley affray is commonly cited as supportive 'evidence' to uphold the distorted image of Marlowe as a man of violence, in this case ignoring the legal records that establish his innocence.

By contrast, we know that the self-confessedly hot-tempered Ben Jonson actually killed a fellow actor, Gabriel Spencer, and only escaped hanging for his crime by reading his 'neck verse', proving that he was an educated man – the loophole provided under Elizabethan law. [3] Yet nowhere do we find such a passage stating that Jonson 'was quick to grasp sword, voice turning ugly and provocative, fist clenched for threat or striking', although Ben himself says that he once beat John Marston over the head with a pistol. [4] Ben was inclined to be physical, but this is never held against him as a reprehensible trait. It was an age where resort to the sword might be a matter of life or death. Duelling, though forbidden, nevertheless frequently took place surreptitiously. The Earl of Southampton fought an extremely bitter duel with Lord Grey at a secret rendezvous abroad, but he is never accused of having a violent nature. [5] By comparison, Marlowe's brief duel with Bradley was *on the evidence* in self defence, and more than this cannot be argued without bias.

When Marlowe was returning home one evening in May 1592 he bandied words with two constables of Shoreditch, who subsequently lodged a plea for sureties of the peace against the dramatist, who, they said, had threatened them with opprobrious words. [6] This is again seen by some of his biographers as 'evidence' of a man habitually given to unruly behaviour. Yet William Shakespeare's indictment in November 1600 by one William Wayte, who claimed sureties of the peace against him, and a writ of attachment ordering his arrest was issued by the Sheriff of Surrey, is never held to show him in the light of an unruly and violent character. Wayte's petition names him first: 'William Shakspere, Francis Langley' (and two aggressive ladies) 'Dorothy Soer and Anne Lee', who had apparently threatened him with violence. [7]

Such incidents were common enough, but why elevate Marlowe's altercation with the constables of Shoreditch (doubtless marked with his noted wit!) as an example of his allegedly violent nature? Perhaps the day will yet come when this incident is seen in the light of *Much Ado About Nothing,* presenting the originals of Dogberry and his fellows who tried to 'comprehend' Marlowe – perhaps a bit drunk? – as he was wending his way homeward from the alehouse; not as an instance of his nasty and violent nature (which is a myth of Kyd's pathetic Letters) but as the inspiration for delightful comic invention. This, as is demonstrated in Chapter 21, 'Canterbury Tales', is how Marlowe often drew from life to create his own divine comedy.

We must now consider the case of *Corkyn v. Marlowe,* which is the most important documentary evidence on Marlowe to have been discovered in recent years. It finally scotches all the spurious tales of his alleged violent nature in an unquestionably valid, impartial, legal record of the man as he really was, testifying to the way he actually behaved in his life. It is a revelation!

The Rose of Reconciliation

On what was probably his last visit home to Canterbury in September 1592, the City's legal archives, researched by Dr William Urry, have disclosed Marlowe's involvement in an incident which throws a unique and fascinating light on his temperament, wherein we recognise 'that pure elementall wit, Chr. Marlow', as Thorpe called him, who was also the Poet of the Sonnets – a delightful young man with a wonderfully forgiving nature.

The documents relate an interesting civil case of a breach of the peace in the City's Westgate Ward involving Christopher Marlowe and the tailor, William Corkyn, who was also a chorister of the Cathedral. We do not learn what their quarrel was about, but it is testified that on 10th September Corkyn had assaulted Marlowe and 'did there and then beat, wound and maltreat, and other atrocities *(enormia)* did then and there inflict upon the said Christopher Marlowe'; [8] which injuries the said Christopher Marlowe revenged on 15th September, inflicting 'loss', but (be it noted) he did *not wound* Corkyn in return. Corkyn thereupon promptly filed a suit against Marlowe for 'damages to the extent of £5'. [9] What these 'damages' were we are not told, but at a guess it was to Corkyn's clothing. Marlowe thereupon turned the tables by filing his counter-suit for Corkyn's previous assault on him.

Dr Urry, who discovered these documents (they are presented in his posthumously published *Christopher Marlowe and Canterbury,* 1988) has argued that both suits filed by the protagonists, *Corkyn v. Marlowe,* and *Marlowe v. Corkyn,* refer to the same incident, although the legal records clearly state two different dates – that Corkyn beat up Marlowe on *'decimo die Septembris',* and that Marlowe returned the compliment on *'quinto decimo die Septembris'.* [10] Dr Urry should be the last to suggest that they are incorrect, for he subscribes emphatically to the view that a legal document constitutes 'unassailable' evidence, and *if* this all occurred on one date how is it that Marlowe, armed with 'staff and dagger' was the wounded party? And what would he be doing going around armed in this manner anyway? Whereas on the later date it had a purpose – he was out to pay Corkyn back, but as it turns out, in a surprising way!

From the legal depositions it is possible to reconstruct a pretty clear picture of what had happened on 10th and 15th September. It was, I suggest, the following: On 10th September the two men, Marlowe the poet and Corkyn the musical tailor, who were old friends and had probably been choirboys together, were walking near the West-gate when what was obviously a heated argument broke out, and Corkyn, perhaps getting the worst of the argument in words resorted to physically belabouring Marlowe, as the deposition informs us.

City of   The Grand Jury present for Our Lady the Queen that
Canterbury William Corkyn of the City of Canterbury 'taylor', on the
              tenth day of September in the thirty-fourth year of Our
              Lady Elizabeth by the Grace of God, of England, France,
              and Ireland, Defender of the Faith, here in the City of
              Canterbury aforesaid, in the parish of St Andrew and in the
              Ward of Westgate in the aforesaid city, did make an assault
              upon a certain Christopher Marlowe, gentleman, and the
              same Christopher Marlowe did there and then beat, wound
              and maltreat, and other atrocities [*enormia*] did there and
              then inflict upon the said Christopher Marlowe, to the
              grave damage of the aforesaid Christopher and against the
              Peace of Our present Lady the Queen, etc.[11]

The wounded and maltreated Marlowe presumably went limping home to
nurse his injuries, but he did not lodge a complaint for assault then. Instead he
decided to teach his bellicose friend a lesson (perhaps Corkyn had always been
a bully?) to show him he was no longer willing to put up with his bullying
attacks and atrocities (verbal ones?) So five days later on 15th September he
met Corkyn at the same spot, but this time armed with 'staff and dagger'.
However, it is clear that he appeared thus with intent to give Corkyn a fright,
for *he did not injure him physically in any way,* as Corkyn had done to him, as
is unquestionably established by Corkyn's suit which *makes no mention of
physical hurt.*

City of   William Corkyn sues Christopher Marlowe, gentleman, on
Canterbury plea of transgression. And pledges to prosecute *viz.* John
              Doo and Richard Roo. And the plaintiff by Giles Winston
              his attorney makes plaint that the said defendant on the fif-
              teenth day of September, in the thirty-fourth year of the
              reign of Our Lady Elizabeth by the Grace of God, of
              England, France and Ireland, Queen, Defender of the Faith
              here in the City of Canterbury aforesaid, in the Parish of St
              Andrew, and in the Ward of Westgate of the aforesaid city,
              did by force of arms [*vi et armis*], *viz.,* with staff and dag-
              ger, make an assault upon the aforesaid plaintiff, and
              against the Peace of the said Lady the Queen. Wherefore
              the said plaintiff says he has suffered loss, and has incurred
              damages to the extent of £5, and hence produces his suit.[12]

If there had been physical injury sustained this would have been mentioned
without question. The claim of £5 is damage to property, and in this instance
presumably refers to clothing. Did Marlowe use his dagger to cut off
Corkyn's buttons? (As does the Cutpurse in *The Massacre at Paris* who cuts

off the buttons from Mugeroun's cloak). [13.] A suitable punishment for a tailor! Just such reflections of real life in Canterbury woven into his plays have been discovered by Urry. There appears to have been some element of Marlowe's typical humorous wit in this tit-for-tat, as is implied by the surprising outcome of this case.

Damage to property tends to rate above mere physical injury in the law, and Marlowe's hurts were doubtless mended by the time the case came to court on 25th and 26th September, when the tailor's suit for damages was preferred, and Marlowe's counter-suit for injuries was thrown out. But happily, when the civil case *Corkine v. Marlowe* came up for its final hearing on 9th October, the two protagonists had already mended their quarrel and had once more become good friends. By mutual agreement, then and there, the case was dropped, and the two men, reconciled in friendship, left the court. Probably it had all been schoolboy stuff really! But there is a delightful corollary.

Dr William Urry, when first discovering these legal documents in the Canterbury archives, recounts:

> 'Town Serjeant Nower started a new plea book on 28 September, still entering matter concerned with last year's cases. Shortly after Marlowe quitted the court, close to entries for cases heard on 12 October, a rosebud was dropped into the new plea book where it was recently found, its shape pressed into the pages. This bud, a strange irrelevance among all this legalism, was about to blossom into a late rose of the summer of 1592.' [14]

How did it get there? Was it placed there by the Poet as a symbol of his reconciliation with his friend, the musical tailor? Or had it just dropped accidentally from the buttonhole of the clerk writing the document? It was customary for clerks of the court to wear a rose in their lapels. Or is this where Marlowe had 'plucked' it to lay between those very pages of the plea book as a symbol of their happily renewed friendship? It would be typical of him, would it not? The gesture of a great poet. This Tudor rosebud, long since withered, is solicitously kept in a case in the Cathedral Library, an inestimable historic treasure.

William Corkyn's son, also named William, was a lutenist and composer of songs. He set Marlowe's 'Come Live with Me and be my Love' to music, and this delightful air was published in 1612. A common interest in music united the Corkyns and Marlowe, and if they did once get into an argument that led to a court case, it was soon mended.

Ironically and sadly, for I knew him as one who loved Marlowe, it is William Urry – whose searches in the Canterbury archives discovered the rosebud in the plea book, relating the Poet's reconciliation with his friend, William Corkyn, the singing tailor – who has misinterpreted this fascinating find and deeply misunderstood its implications. Under the weight of academic pressures the distorted image of Marlowe as a man of violence has bedevilled his brilliant research, and Urry's biographical work presents the most fierce distortion to date of Canterbury's greatest son as a man of violent temperament.

Urry's book is in the fashionable tradition of sensationalizing Marlowe's life. He presents his association with the secret agent Robert Poley as though this man were of prime importance in the Poet's life. Poley, in Urry's view, hovers around Marlowe 'like an evil spirit. He forges letters, dabbles in ciphers, intercepts correspondence, snaps up fees and bribes. He was the very genius of the Elizabethan underworld.' [15]

There is no hint here that the aforesaid forged letters were written by Poley on the express instructions of Sir Francis Walsingham and Lord Burghley to obtain from Mary Queen of Scots her acquiescence to the plot to murder Queen Elizabeth, and thus to incriminate her. Anthony Babington was the ringleader of this most dangerous conspiracy which had regicide as its *main objective,* with the assassination of Elizabeth to be followed by the enthronement of Mary as Catholic Queen of England. Poley was entrusted with the vitally important task of insinuating himself into the confidence of Babington in order to discover their intentions and bring the conspirators to justice. But to Urry the extremely skilful agent Robert Poley is only seen as bringing with him 'an evil odour of fraud, crime and double dealing' wherever he goes. 'Utterly deceiving Anthony Babington, he was principal agent in sending that youth to the scaffold.' [16]

Well, poor misguided youth though he was, it was either Babington's life, or Queen Elizabeth's, so with whom are we being invited to take sides? By the same judgment, one can denigrate those brave soldiers, policemen and CID agents who protect us today against terrorism. Poley's profession involved living dangerously, but it was not 'of the Elizabethan underworld'. He was a government agent – as were Marlowe, and Thomas Walsingham, and the immensely brave Thomas Cely, who suffered in the Spanish galleys for his services to his country. If Poley's private life was somewhat questionable in his illicit love-affairs, his morals were no better and no worse than those of some prominent men in our society today; and in his professional capacity he was a trusted servant of his government and served posterity extraordinarily well in what he achieved. He was instrumental in saving not only the life of Queen Elizabeth, but, I contend, also the life of Shakespeare by the part he played at Deptford.

Marlowe himself is also seen by Dr Urry only in the sensational and baleful light cast by Baines' *Note* and Kyd's Letters; above all, he credits the legal document of the Deptford inquisition, accepting these as evidence because they represent historic documents, never for one moment allowing that written records can also tell lies – and all of these have a questionable context. He concludes his book:

'there is no need to invent a plot to put Marlowe out of the way. He was the victim of his own temperament. Four times at least he was involved in violent struggles with men: at Hog Lane in September 1589 when William Bradley was slain: in May 1592 when he scuffled with the constable and sub-constable of Shoreditch; at Canterbury in September 1592 when he fought with William Corkyn; and now at Deptford. For every case which came to the notice of the courts there may have been many times when Marlowe was involved in other incidents – 'sudden privy injuries to men'.

'Quod me nutrit me destruit'. The portrait at Cambridge may or may not be a likeness of Marlowe, but the motto inscribed there is a likeness of his fate. That brilliant mind, tensed like a coiled spring, ready to soar into flights of genius, was equally ready to erupt in a fire of uncontrollable temper. Now, at the last, goaded by worry and the prospect of disaster, he attacked a man who turned and killed him in self-defence. The surges of excitement generating his mighty verse were very close to the sudden rages which convulsed him. The same passion which sustained him as a poet destroyed him as a human being.' [17]

Here we have the distorted image of Marlowe writ large and boldly to which the last five decades have been moving, steadily grinding his face into the dust. It is hardly necessary to point out that it is coloured with bias. Marlowe's duel at Hog Lane was not his quarrel – it was Watson's and he slew Bradley, who was a thug. There is no justification for describing Marlowe's altercation with the Shoreditch constables as a 'scuffle'; it was verbal threats that Marlowe made, probably in jesting high spirits! Corkyn assaulted Marlowe first (when he was unarmed) and wounded him, which Marlowe revenged inflicting 'loss' to the value of £5, but *no* physical injuries *although* he was then armed with both staff and dagger (the former, I imagine, to trip Corkyn up, and the latter to threaten him with and then slash the tailor's garments?) And it all ended in a charming reconciliation. This is the legal record which has no taint of suspicion. Whereas what Baines and Kyd state was obviously prejudiced; and what Coroner Danby recorded stands in an especially questionable context. But this is not how Dr Urry views it. He writes:

> 'There survives . . an official and quite unassailable document to depend upon for a record of Marlowe's last day – the famous record of the coroner's inquest.' [18]

I beg to differ. Danby's inquisition is not an 'unassailable document' on which we can depend for the historical truth. Bless Dr Urry, but he has got it wrong. Danby's Inquisition, Baines' *Note* and Kyd's Letters have here been subjected to some sharp scrutiny which has established that they cannot possibly be blandly accepted as giving a true picture of the Poet, who was hailed by his contemporaries and friends as 'the Muses darling', [19] that 'pure elementall wit,

Chr. Marlow',[20] and 'kynde Kit Marloe' [21.] His fellow poet Michael Drayton called him 'neat Marlowe,' [22] the word 'neat' meaning unsophisticated, natural, a man without pretensions. Edward Blount described him as 'the man that hath been dear unto us'; the brilliant Hariot and the noble Chapman cherished him as a dear friend; Raleigh and Northumberland welcomed him into their circle; he was a beloved friend to his patron, and was warmly received into the cultured family of the Walsinghams who were close to the Queen who had commended him for his 'faithful dealing'; he was the valued friend of Thomas Watson whose Latin poetry had won him the patronage of Sir Francis Walsingham. Those by whom Marlowe was admired and loved as a friend included the cream of Elizabethan society. Their verdict on him had no axes to grind. When we consider Marlowe's writings, it is clear that his friends judged him aright for in them we read his heart, his mind and his spirit, which speak to us of nobility, not baseness.

Whereas with Shakespeare scholarly opinion accepts his great works as representative of the man himself, and the mundane facts of his life are disregarded as having any relevance to his character, with Marlowe it is the opposite. His works are dismissed as representing the man. It was not always so with Marlowe. His earliest biographers J.H. Ingram and C.F. Tucker Brooke have passed judgements of breadth and understanding. Tucker Brooke wrote as late as 1930:

> 'Hero and Leander in particular has biographical significance. It forbids us to believe that Marlowe was fundamentally or finally intemperate, as Kyd called him, or of a cruel heart. Nor can we easily suppose that its placid beauty was achieved while the author was employing his less poetical hours as a libertine, a secret agent, or a revolutionist.' [23]

Ingram declined to be impressed by Marlowe's detractors: 'the only basis for imputing 'hellish sins' to him is puritanical malice, – supported by libel and forgery.' He points out that Marlowe was 'the companion, the compeer, and the admired of all that was best of his time.' [24]

The gradual descent into the latter-day fashionable detrimental view of Marlowe's character was given impetus by Dr Boas' publication of Kyd's Letters. Boas, being also Kyd's biographer, naturally tended to see them as valid testimony to be accepted as irrefutable documentary evidence. He set the pattern that others have followed.

> 'Kyd, in the letter first printed by me in 1899, told Puckering that Marlowe's associates were "Harriot, Warner, Roydon, and some stationers in Paules churchyard". Harriot is the well-known mathematician who had long been in Sir Walter Raleigh's service, and Warner was probably Walter Warner, a mathematical friend of Harriot. Nash has Harriot in mind when he declares in Pierce

Pennilesse, "I heare say there be Mathematicians abroad, that will proue men before Adam". It is to Harriot also that the Jesuit pamphleteer, Robert Parsons, referred in his *Responsio ad Elizabethae edictum* (1592), as "Astronomo quondam necromantico" the preceptor of the "schola frequens de Atheismo" which Walter Raleigh notoriously held in his house. In the English summary of the *Responsio* the words used are:

"Of Sir Walter Rawley's schoole of Atheism by the waye, & of the Coniurer that is M[aster] thereof, and of the diligence vsed to get yong gentlmen of this schoole, where in both Moyses, & our Sauior, the olde and the new Testamente are iested at, the schollers taughte amonge other thinges, to spell God backwarde."

'It is worth noting that when on Whitsun eve, 2 June 1593, the informer Richard Baines brought charges of blasphemy against "Christopher Marly" (Harl. MSS.6868 ff.185-6), he too brings Moses, Harriot, and conjuring into close relation.' [25]

Dr Boas then proceeds to quote the relevant items from Baines' *Note,* and he finds 'a remarkable family likeness' in the words used by Baines and Kyd. He concludes:

'Can it be doubted that out of the statements of Baines and Kyd taken together, and supplemented by the less specific allegations of Nash, Parsons, and others, a fairly consistent picture can be framed?' [26]

Dr Boas, a great scholar, is impressed, but he had forgotten one important factor. All these sources represent Marlowe's enemies. None of them is a reliable witness. To Baines and Kyd he adds a Jesuit pamphleteer, while Nashe was sweating in fear to dissociate himself from the fatal taint of 'Atheism' that clung to Marlowe and all the free-thinkers whom Nashe, with an eye to his own safety, satirizes for daring to pursue speculative scientific questioning. Everyone of Dr Boas's witnesses were men who had an axe to grind; all were enemies of free thought. Dr Boas is entitled to his point of view, but, if we step back for a moment, let us consider what he is inviting us to accept as valid evidence of his 'consistent picture'.

Are we to believe the Jesuit pamphleteer, Parsons? the informer Baines? the broken, pathetic Kyd in his remarks about his dead (and hated) former friend, Marlowe? And the subtle Poley, who once confessed, 'I will sweare and forsweare my selfe rather then I will accuse my selffe to doe me any harme'? [27] the cunning Skeres, who was involved in a well-documented case of chicanery together with his friend Frizer? And Frizer, whose urgent problem was to extricate himself from a charge of murder?

The whole matter hangs on the credibility and honesty of these witnesses. Frizer's acquittal on his plea of slaying in self-defence required that Marlowe be presented as his base-minded, unprovoked attacker. He was clearly taking no chances to escape the gallows. The story he told, with the smooth-talking Poley and Skeres as his witnesses, had to stick – and stick it did for four hundred years.

The final word may be allowed to Marlowe's greatest biographer, Dr John Bakeless, whose deep study of the Poet's life and works entitles him to an authoritative opinion on whether the inquisition is an 'unassailable document to depend on'. The 'discovery of the document relating to Marlowe's death raises as many questions as it answers', [28] comments Bakeless. *It is by no means an open and shut case.* And Dr Samuel Tannenbaum quotes the opinions of several eminent physicians to support his view of the obvious untruthfulness of the coroner's report:

> 'The Coroner's inquest was a perfunctory matter . . his story cannot be accepted as a faithful account of what actually transpired . . One who knows the anatomy and pathology of the human brain knows that it is almost impossible for death to follow immediately upon the infliction of such a wound . . The Coroner's "grim tale" of Marlowe's violent and untimely end, therefore, is not a true account of what happened.' [29]

If anyone still contends that the coroner's inquisition records the true facts, then one salient question requires an answer. Why were Poley, Skeres, Frizer closeted with the intellectual Poet for eight hours on that fatal day? They were not his close friends. If it is argued that this was in connection with some government plot, then what was Frizer doing there? He was not a secret agent. A satisfactory explanation for this day-long conference has never been given. It is merely claimed that the inquisition is infallible because it is 'official'. Officialdom, apparently, cannot err, and, above all, it must not be questioned!

Finally, we have the testimony of the sonnets in which the tragedy of Christopher Marlowe is shadowed forth unmistakably. In *Sonnet 74* he tells us that he viewed as utterly base the sordid affair at Deptford, whereby the story was put about that he had died 'the coward conquest of a wretch's knife'. If this was *not* true, then the whole edifice maligning Marlowe collapses like a house of cards.

To admit that one has been mistaken is never easy, but it is honourable. There will assuredly be those with the necessary stature who will accede this, and will be ready to consider the evidence presented, and to judge it on its merits with fairness and without prejudice. More than this one cannot ask. Even if Marlowe were not Shakespeare, he is one of our very greatest poet-dramatists and thinkers, who has been monstrously maligned and misrepresented. This reassessment aims to adjust the focus, so that we can at last see him as he really was, when –

> reckoning Time, whose million'd accidents
> Creep in 'twixt vows, and change decrees of Kings, [30]

will bring redress, and restore his vilified image. The cumulative evidence here presented reveals what logic has long indicated, but no academic scholar has dared to think – that the maligned poetic genius, 'Marley the Muses darling' was none other than our 'gentle Shakespeare'.

Courtesy of the Cathedral Library, the Dean and Chapter of Canterbury
Photograph by Tony Whitcomb

'The Rose of Reconciliation'
Discovered by Dr. William Urry when Archivist
to the City of Canterbury
The Elizabethan rosebud of 1592 preserved and pressed in the Plea Book.
A perfect specimen, only the colour has changed to black

THE CONFIRMATION

XX

FINGERPRINTING THE AUTHOR

THE QUESTION of how to establish with certainty the authorship of anonymous literary works is one for which a solution is wanting. At present the only accepted yardstick in authorial disputes is the parallelism, which is not free from some degree of subjective influence, for it depends on the critical judgment of the investigator, and what one critic sees as a parallel thought or expression, another may reject. It lacks true scientific basis, but it is the best we have to date and is widely used. The development of a perfected scientific method in this age of the computer cannot be far away, however, for in 1887 the American physicist, Dr T.C. Mendenhall, had come very near to it.

Interest in Mendenhall's method, which is based on the frequency distribution in the text of words according to length, was recently revived by the studies of Dr C.B. Williams, who published two papers on an allied method: *'A note on the statistical analyses of sentence lengths as a criterion of literary style'* in *Biometrika, 31,* pp.356-61 (1940); and *'Statistics as an aid to literary studies'* in *Penguin Science News, no.24,* pp.99-106 (1952). Dr Williams later heard of the somewhat similar work that Dr Mendenhall had done more than half a century earlier, and he has kindly given permission to reprint his paper describing Mendenhall's technique published in 1970 in *Studies in the History of Statistics and Probability,* pp.241-249, entitled *'A note on an early statistical study of Literary Style'*.

Dr Mendenhall's research was first published in 1887, and then reissued in *The Popular Science Monthly,* December 1901 under the title *'A Mechanical Solution to a Literary Problem'* for a wider readership. In this he described the application of his method to the works of Shakespeare and the writings of his contemporaries, including Bacon, which he undertook on behalf of a gentleman from Boston, Augustus Heminway, who expected thereby to prove that Francis Bacon was the real author of the Shakespearean canon. To everyone's amazement it was not Bacon, but Marlowe who emerged as Shakespeare's identical twin – a totally unforeseen result!

It is this work that C.B. Williams has critically reassessed in his most recent paper in 1970, given below in its entirety with its graphs, and including his introductory references to the work of G. Udny Yule in this field, for the interest of those who may wish to experiment in developing a computerized technique for this aspect of literary study.

A scientific solution to this important problem would have far-reaching consequences for literary studies – not least for Shakespeare. An experiment based on Mendenhall's simple system on computers has evidently never been tried. One wonders why not?

A NOTE ON AN EARLY STATISTICAL STUDY OF LITERARY STYLE

By C. B. WILLIAMS

In *Biometrika* for January 1939, G. Udny Yule discussed the frequency distribution of sentence length in samples of the writings of different authors. After showing that each author had a fairly characteristic distribution, he turned to the value of the method in cases of uncertain or disputed authorship. Thus, in the case of *De Imitationi Christi*, he showed that the frequency distribution of sentences with different numbers of words more closely resembled that of works by Thomas à Kempis than that of works by de Gerson.

In *Biometrika* for March 1940 I showed that the skew distribution found by Yule could be brought almost to a symmetrical form by using a geometric or logarithmic scale for the number of words per sentence, thereby simplifying the mathematical comparisons. In this note I mentioned that some years previously (about 1935) I had made a number of frequency distributions from different authors using the number of letters per word as the variable, but that I had not found any striking differences. I considered Yule's use of the number of words per sentence as a better technique, giving a greater range of possible variation and comparison.

In a letter written to me in June 1939 Yule said: 'I booked up some ten years ago a number of distributions of word-length by the number of syllables only. Monosyllables are always considerably in the majority (if I remember rightly I omitted "a" and "the"), and different authors diverged a good deal, but, so far as I can recall, the range from Bunyan to a *Times* Leader was not so very striking.'

Neither Yule nor myself was aware that quite extensive investigations in this line had been made and published in summary more than fifty years previously, giving frequency distributions of word lengths (by the number of letters per word) for several authors, and suggesting that similar distributions of the numbers of syllables per word, or the number of words per sentence, might well help to throw light on cases of doubtful or disputed authorship.

Through the kindness of Mr Rushworth Fogg of Glasgow I was put on the track of a paper published in 1901 by Thomas Corwin Mendenhall,* in which he gives a reference to a still earlier paper published in 1887, both of which I have been able to examine.

Mendenhall states in his first paper (1887) that five or six years previously he had seen a suggestion in a book by Augustus de Morgan, possibly his *Budget of Paradoxes*, that it might be possible to identify the author of a book, a poem or a play by the average length of the words used in the construction. Mendenhall, however, considered that the method which he had adopted in this publication, of using the frequency distribution of words of different lengths, was better, as while the average number of letters per word is easily obtainable from his data, the shape of the distribution provides considerably increased possibilities of comparison.

Augustus de Morgan was Professor of Mathematics at University College, London. His *Budget of Paradoxes* was first printed as weekly notes in the *Athenaeum* and republished in book form in 1872, after the author's death. I have examined the second edition (1915), but, although it contains a few references to cases of disputed authorship, I cannot find any suggestion about the use of the average number of letters per word. It may be in one of his earlier works, or perhaps in one of his *Athenaeum* notes that was not reprinted in book form.*

It is interesting to note than Mendenhall, who was primarily a physicist was attracted to the frequency distribution technique by its resemblance to spectroscopic analysis, which in 1887 was much to the fore in scientific circles. He writes: 'It is proposed to analyse a composition by forming what may be called a "word spectrum" or "characteristic curve" which shall be a graphic representation of the arrangement of words according to their length and the relative frequency of their occurrence.' The mathematics of the comparison of frequency distributions was very little understood at the time when he was writing.

Mendenhall first discusses samples taken from different books by the same author to see if they resemble each other sufficiently closely to make comparisons between one author and another likely to be profitable. Most of the evidence is given in the form of thirteen diagrams and, unfortunately, in only very few cases are actual numbers presented.

Mendenhall's first seven graphs deal with various combinations of ten samples, each of one thousand words, from Dickens's *Oliver Twist* and Thackeray's *Vanity Fair*. In his second figure the distribution of five separate samples of 1000 words from *Oliver Twist* are shown superimposed, and there is no doubt as to their general resemblance. In another (Fig. 1 in this paper) he shows one graph for the whole 10,000 words from *Oliver Twist* and another for *Vanity Fair*. There is very little difference in the average length of the words (Dickens, 4·324; Thackeray, 4·481), but *Vanity Fair* has rather more words of 3 and of 7–10 letters, while *Oliver Twist* has more of 1, 2 and 4–6 letters. Mendenhall was somewhat disappointed by the lack of difference and commented 'it is certainly suprising that...so close an agreement should be found. This is particularly striking in the words of 11, 12 and 13 letters, the numerical composition of which is as follows:

Number of letters	11	12	13
Dickens	85	57	29
Thackeray	85	58	29'

Undaunted by this small difference he next tried two groups of words from John Stuart Mill's *Political Economy* and his *Essay on Liberty*, in which he 'expected to find more longer words than in the novelists'. 'But I confess to considerable surprise in finding from the very beginning that, although on the whole the anticipation was realized, the word which occurred most frequently was not the three-letter word, as with both Dickens and Thackeray, but the word of two letters.' The explanation he says 'is to be found in the liberal use of prepositions in sentence-building'. The results, given in two separate diagrams, are here combined into one (Fig. 2).

Mendenhall next studied two addresses given by a Mr Edward Atkinson on 'Labour Questions' to two different audiences, one consisting of working men and the other students of a Theological College. There was 'a marked difference in style', but the word-length distributions (from two samples of 5000 words) were very similar. He comments that 'Mr Atkinson's composition was remarkable in the shortness of the words used'. The average length was 4·298 letters; which is, however, only 0·044 shorter than the samples from Dickens.

For comparison with all the above studies of works in the English language, Mendenhall gave a distribution of the first 5500 words in Caesar's *Commentaries*, in Latin. He finds a mean word length of 6·065 letters and an entirely different form of curve with peaks at 2, 5 and 7 letters (see Fig. 3). This is of course connected with the Latin construction of adding to the main root for inflexions instead of using additional small words.

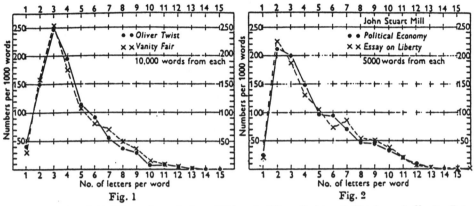

Fig. 1. Samples of 10,000 words each from Dickens's *Oliver Twist* and Thackeray's *Vanity Fair*. Redrawn from Mendenhall (1887, fig. 7).

Fig. 2. Samples of 5000 words each from two works of John Stuart Mill. Redrawn from Mendenhall (1887, figs. 8, 9).

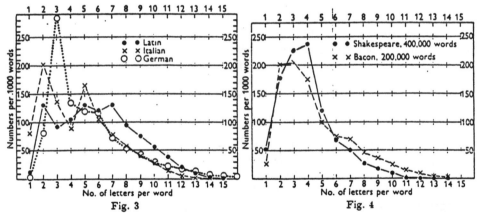

Fig. 3. Examples of distribution of word length in languages other than English. (1) Latin, (2) Italian, (3) German. Redrawn from Mendenhall (1887, fig. 13 and 1901, fig. 2).

Fig. 4. Comparison of frequency distribution of word length in two very large samples from the plays of Shakespeare and works of Bacon. Redrawn from Mendenhall (1901, fig. 7).

He considers that, for a really reliable estimate of the characteristic curve for an author, a sample curve of 100,000 words might be necessary, and concludes his first paper as follows: 'Many interesting applications of the process will suggest themselves to almost every reader; the most notable, of course, being the attempt to solve questions of disputed authorship, such as exist in reference to the letters of Junius, the plays of Shakespeare, and other less widely known examples. It might also be used in comparative language studies,

315

in tracing the growth of a language, and in studying the growth of the vocabulary from childhood to manhood.'

'If striking differences are found between the curve of known and suspected compositions of any writer, the evidence against identity of authorship would be quite conclusive. If the two compositions should produce curves which are practically identical, the proof of a common origin would be less convincing for it is possible though not probable, that two writers might show identical curves.'

It was not until 14 years later than Mendenhall returned to the problem in a paper in *Popular Science Monthly*, published in December 1901. In this he repeats some of the discussion and diagrams from his earlier paper dealing with Dickens, Thackeray, John Stuart Mill and Mr Atkinson; but in addition to his earlier diagrams showing analysis of a Latin work he gives examples of single authors in Italian, Spanish, French and German (see Fig. 3). The French and Spanish curves, possibly by the idiosyncrasies of the authors chosen, have their peaks in the 2-letter words; the Italian has two peaks at 2 and 5 letters; while the German has a peak at 3 letters, but with more longer words, reaching one word of 27 letters.

After this introduction, he settles down to a discussion of the value of his technique in the study of the authorship of the plays of Shakespeare. For this the length of nearly two million words were counted from the works of Shakespeare and of some of his contemporaries. Most unfortunately the data are all condensed into half a dozen small diagrams, and not one table of the actual numbers is given. Does his evidence still exist, hidden away somewhere?

Mendenhall says: 'The result from the start, with the first group of 1000 words, was a decided surprise. Two things appeared from the beginning: Shakespeare's vocabulary consisted of words whose average length was a trifle below four letters, less than any writer of English previously studied; and his word of greatest frequency was the four-letter word, a thing never before met with' (Fig. 4).

A comparison of the diagrams with those of Thackeray and Dickens shows that Shakespeare had a higher proportion of words with 1, 2, 4 and 5 letters, and a lower proportion of words with 3 letters and of 6 letters upwards; which accounts for the fact that while his peak is higher, his average number of letters per word is lower. In modern terminology, he would have a smaller standard deviation.

Altogether about 400,000 words were counted including 'in whole or in part, nearly all his most famous plays', and it was found that this characteristic curve is most persistent— that based on first 50,000 words differing very little from the whole count. In a diagram giving two examples of 200,000 words each, it is practically impossible to separate the two lines, in spite of the fact that Mendenhall says the differences have been of necessity slightly exaggerated in order to make them show at all!

A comparison was next made of Shakespeare's prose and his poetry as exemplified by *The Rape of Lucrece* and *Venus and Adonis*. The prose gave more shorter words, particularly of 2 letters, and fewer words of 5, 6 and 7 letters; but both gave the characteristic peak at the 4-letter word. Mendenhall writes: 'At first this was thought to be a general characteristic of his time, but this was found not to be so.'

A study was then made of a number of works by Francis Bacon, including his *Henry VII* and his *Advancement of Learning*, with a total of nearly 200,000 words. The frequency distribution was quite different from that of Shakespeare (see Fig. 4) with the peak at the 3-letter word, with more 2-letter words, fewer with 4, 5 and 6 letters, and more longer words with 7–13 letters. Mendenhall here comments that 'the reader is at liberty to draw any conclusion he pleases from this diagram. Should he conclude that, in view of the extra-ordinary difference in these lines, it is clear that Bacon could not have written the things ordinarily attributed to Shakespeare...the question still remains, who did?'

An examination of the works of Ben Johnson, in two groups of 75,000 words, showed once more a peak at the 3-letter word; but an extensive study of the plays of Beaumont and Fletcher showed that on the final average the number of 4-letter words was slightly greater than those of 3 letters, although the excess was by no means persistent in smaller samples. The final curve was not unlike that of Shakespeare, and Mendenhall suggested that the 'lack of persistency of form among small groups' might be due to the dual authorship.

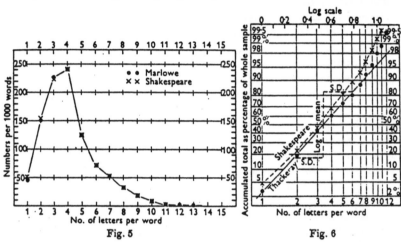

Fig. 5. Comparison of frequency distribution of word length in two large samples from the plays of Shakespeare and of Christopher Marlowe. Redrawn from Mendenhall (1901, fig. 9).

Fig. 6. The number of letters per word, on a logarithmic scale, from works of Thackeray and Shakespeare (as shown by Mendenhall) plotted against the accumulated total as a percentage of the whole sample on a probability scale. It indicates some resemblance to a log-normal distribution for words up to about 8 letters, but differing above this level.

When, however, he turned his attention to the plays of Christopher Marlowe 'something akin to a sensation was produced among those engaged in the work'. 'In the characteristic curve of his plays Marlowe agrees with Shakespeare about as well as Shakespeare agrees with himself' (Fig. 5).

Finally, Mendenhall pointed out that a dramatic composition *Armada Days* written by Prof. Shaler of Harvard, in which the author endeavoured to compose in the spirit and the style of the 'Elizabethan days', gave a curve (from only about 20,000 words) with 'excess of the 4-letter word and in other respects decidedly Shakespearian'. Mendenhall does not give this curve or any figures.

DISCUSSION

We are not concerned here so much with the results that Mendenhall obtained, or with their repercussions, but rather with the general value of the technique. There appears to be little doubt that he was the first to act on the suggestion of de Morgan, and that his own method of using the frequency distribution, instead of merely the average length of word, was a distinct improvement, although the average length would not normally be given

317

to-day without the standard deviation. The skew form of the curve makes this latter measure less reliable than it might otherwise be.

Mendenhall's sampling method was to take blocks of 1000 words each 'at the beginning of the volume and, after a few thousand words had been counted, the book was opened near the middle and the count continued'. This method is not above reproach, but, in view of the large number of samples and the general close resemblances, it is unlikely that a more randomized method would produce any measurably different result. In the case of the plays of Shakespeare the sampling was large enough to justify the statement that it included nearly all the most famous plays 'in whole or in part'.

That Mendenhall appreciated the difference between the statistical method and evidence based on selected phraseology believed to be characteristic is clear from the following quotations: 'The chief merit of the method consisted in the fact that its application required no exercise of judgement' and that 'characteristics might be revealed which the author could make no attempt to conceal, being himself unaware of their existence'; and again, 'the conclusions reached through its use would be independent of personal bias, the work of one person in the study of an author being at once comparable with the work of any other'.

That Mendenhall saw the wide range of possibilities is clear from his statement: 'it is hardly necessary to say that the method is not necessarily confined to the analysis of a composition by means of word-length: it may equally be applied to the study of syllables, of words in sentences, and in various ways.' And I have already quoted his suggestion as to its value in comparative studies.

Two additional comments may be of interest. The curve of the frequency distribution of words of different lengths is in every case skew, with the peak usually at 3 or 4 letters per word, and the tail running off generally to 15 or 16, but sometimes to higher than this. In my contribution to the study already mentioned, I showed that by the use of a logarithmic scale the skew distributions of sentence length became approximately symmetrical, and so the distribution resembled a log-normal. It is of interest to see if Mendenhall's figures for word length show a similar relation. We can, however, note beforehand that the length of a sentence is under the conscious control of a writer, who may stop when he pleases. The lengths of words are not so controlled and selection of words for reason of their length alone is not likely to occur.

Most unfortunately only three sets of numbers are given by Mendenhall, all in his first 1887 paper. They are for 1000 words in *Oliver Twist* and two sets of the same size for *Vanity Fair*. Taking the latter we find that the accumulated totals up to each successive number of letters per word, expressed as percentages of the whole, are as shown in Table 1.

When these results are plotted on to log-probability paper the result is as shown in Fig. 6. There is an approximately straight-line relation up to about 8 letters per word, but above that there is a definite departure. The straight-line portion suggests a log-normal distribution with a mean log at 0·53 and a standard deviation of approximately 0·26. On an arithmetic scale this is equivalent to a geometric mean of about 3·4 and a standard deviation of × or ÷ 1·8.* The arithmetic mean is 4·5 letters per word.

* When a frequency distribution is skew on an arithmetic grouping of the data but approximately symmetrical when a geometric scale is used, the standard deviation cannot be expressed on an arithmetic scale as ' + or − '. The use of the expression '3·4, × or ÷ by 1·8' implies that approximately 33% of the observations will be between 3·4 and 3·4 × 1·8; 33% will be between 3·4 and 3·4 ÷ 1·8; and approximately 17% will be above, and below, these limits.

In his second paper Mendenhall gives five graphs showing Shakespeare's frequency distribution per 1000 words in comparison with other authors. With a lens and a fine scale it is possible to read the numbers to about three units, but unfortunately the results so obtained from the five diagrams do not agree. This is possibly because (as he admits in one case) Mendenhall exaggerated the differences in the diagrams in order to separate the two lines. I have made an estimate from each of the five diagrams, and the average values are given in Table 2.

Table 1

No. of letters per word	No. of words out of 2000	Accumulated no. of words total	Accumulated total % of 2000
1	58	58	2·9
2	315	373	18·7
3	480	853	42·7
4	351	1204	60·2
5	244	1448	72·4
6	154	1602	80·1
7	152	1754	87·7
8	100	1854	92·7
9	63	1911	98·9
10	43	1960	98·0
11	16	1976	98·8
12	15	1991	99·6
13	4	1995	99·8
14	5	2000	100·0

Table 2

Letters	Words	Letters	Words	Letters	Words
1	47·6	6	71·2	11	3·4
2	175·8	7	52·6	12	2·0
3	225·0	8	31·6	13	1·0
4	237·6	9	18·4	14	0·4
5	124·4	10	9·0	—	—

When the accumulated totals are plotted on log-probability paper as in the previous case, the result (Fig. 6) indicates a fairly regular departure from the straight line, although once again the break is more distinct above 7 letters per word.

I have also attempted to get, from Mendenhall's diagram of five samples of 1000 words each from *Oliver Twist*, some measure of the error of his results.

The frequency distribution of words of certain lengths in the five samples is approximately as given in Table 3.

If the size of the sample were increased sixteen times—to 80,000 words—without altering the pattern of the material sampled, the S.E. of the mean would be reduced to a quarter of the above—or approximately 2·1, 1·1, 2·1, 1·5 and 0·8 for words of 3–6 letters respectively. The error is smaller in the less frequent words, but greater in proportion to the mean.

319

Thus for the comparison of two samples of this size—assuming the same order of variation in each—the s.e. of the difference would be approximately 1·4 times the above or 2·9, 1·7, 2·1 and 1·1. Thus differences in number of words per 1000 would have to be of the order of 5·7, 3·3, 4·1 and 2·1 to be significant at the 1 in 20 level, and 7·5, 4·4, 5·4 and 2·8 to be significant at the 1 in 100 level. The five samples on which the above rough estimate is made were, however, consecutive samples of 1000 words from one work; when different works, written at different periods by the same author, are combined the error of the mean would almost certainly be greater.

A careful examination of Mendenhall's diagram giving the comparison of the distributions of Shakespeare and Marlowe suggests measurable differences only in words up to 5 letters, Marlowe differing from Shakespeare approximately as follows: 1 letter, 5 less; 2 letters, 3 less; 3 letters, 3 more; 4 letters, no difference; and 5 letters, 5 more. All the other

Table 3

No. of letters	Five samples	Mean	s.e. of mean for 5000 words
3	221, 232, 236, 254, 268	242·2	8·36
4	170, 175, 183, 186, 198	182·4	4·82
5	95, 102, 120, 122, 123	112·4	5·80
6	83, 92, 94, 97, 103	93·8	3·28

word lengths are indistinguishable in the diagram. These differences may have been exaggerated in the diagram. The numbers are in words per 1000 in large samples—in the case of Shakespeare over 200,000 words, but in the case of Marlowe the size of samples is not given. On the other hand, the comparison of Bacon with Shakespeare (see Fig. 5) shows a difference of nearly 60 words per thousand with 4-letter words.

It would seem likely that real differences between authors would show themselves as sequences of departures in the same direction for several consecutive word lengths. One can imagine one author differing from another in an unconscious preference for longer words or for shorter words, but it is unlikely that one author would prefer words of, say, 11 letters in preference to 12, while another author would prefer the 12 to the 11. Thus, rapid changes of departure directions in sequence would be less convincing than blocks of departures of similar sign as evidence of real differences, and would be more likely to be due to error.

Mendenhall, in his 1887 paper, calls attention to the fact that in an analysis of Dickens's *Christmas Carol*, words of 7 letters appeared to be unduly numerous, due to the fact that the character 'Scrooge', frequently referred to, is a word of this length. It would be desirable to leave names of persons and places out of any tabulation.

REFERENCES

MENDENHALL, T. C. (1887). The characteristic curves of composition. *Science*, 9 (214, supplement), 237–49.
MENDENHALL, T. C. (1901). A mechanical solution of a literary problem. *Pop. Sci. Mon.* 9, 97–105.
DE MORGAN, A. (1872). *A Budget of Paradoxes.* London (2nd edition 1915).
WILLIAMS, C. B. (1940). A note on the statistical analyses of sentence length as a criterion of literary style. *Biometrika*, 31, 356–61.
WILLIAMS, C. B. (1952). Statistics as an aid to literary studies. *Penguin Science News*, no. 24, pp. 99–106.

XXI

CANTERBURY TALES

CHRISTOPHER MARLOWE is in some ways an intensely autobiographical writer, and the evidence of the *Sonnets* is strikingly confirmed by the plays. Only recently has it been realised to what extent his dramatic works reflect his Canterbury background. Dr William Urry, himself born and bred in Marlowe's native city, noticed the Canterbury associations that had lain undetected in such an unlikely play as *The Jew of Malta* which, despite its exotic subject, is actually set within the walls of his own familiar city for many of its scenes.

> 'Without the exercise of very great ingenuity a description of much
> of Elizabethan Canterbury can be extracted from this play.' [1]

Dr Urry substantiates this by quoting Marlowe's references to the Dark Entry that leads from the Cathedral Cloisters to the King's School, and the Abbey of St Augustine standing just without the gates of the city, where Barabas entertains the Turks. Once we are alerted to the hand of the author, there are surprising instances in the Shakespearean canon reflecting the life and background of the Kentish dramatist, Christopher Marlowe, beside which the efforts to discover Warwickshire reflections pale into insignificance.

The use of incidents from his local background and personal experience, particularly when there is an element of comedy to be extracted from the situation, is a typical trait. Dr F.S. Boas has researched the incident of the nefarious plot of the spy, Richard Baines, to kill off the entire Catholic Seminary at Rheims by poisoning the well from which they drew their water, which misfired and landed Baines in prison. [2] It was this, Boas suggests, that was lampooned in *The Jew of Malta* where Barabas poisons wells, and then the entire nunnery to which his renegade daughter Abigail has fled, turning Christian, by leaving a pot of poisoned pottage as a charity gift at the 'dark entry'. Marlowe adapts this incident to create an episode of black comedy. We detect the same eye for adapting humorous incidents from real life as material for his immortal pen in the 'Canterbury Tales' gleaned from the archives by Dr Urry during his time as Archivist to the City of Canterbury, which reappear woven into the comic invention of two of Shakespeare's greatest comedies.

A Canterbury Pyramus and Thisbe

From the Canterbury archives Dr Urry produces the story of a real life 'Pyramus and Thisbe' affair concerning a young wench named Dorothy

321

Hocking, who led a miserable life as the drudge of her step-parents, who kept her closely confined at home. To escape this slavery she made a contract of marriage through a hole in the wall dividing the back-yard of her step-parents' house from that next door, with a young man called Richard Edmundes who had become enamoured of her. The next-door neighbour and his wife, being sympathetic to Dorothy's plight, assisted by bringing Richard Edmundes to the yard and witnessing the hole-in-the-wall betrothal of the young couple. Having thus obtained a 'husband' young Dorothy gained her independence from her tyrannical parents, but once free she had no more use for Edmundes and refused to consummate the marriage, denying she had ever plighted troth to him, so the case was brought to court under breach of promise. [3]

We may be grateful for the litigious nature of Canterbury citizens, who invoked the law at the drop of a hat – going to court was almost an Elizabethan hobby! – so that these, sometimes hilarious, stories have found their way into the legal records. The details unearthed by Dr Urry are gems of human comedy bringing Elizabethan Canterbury vividly to life. He recounts this story with delight, which is found in Andrew Butcher's informative and valuable Introduction to Urry's posthumously edited book *Christopher Marlowe and Canterbury*. Dorothy's next-door neighbours were Robert Holmes and his wife, who became the midwife in this affair. It seems that it was Mistress Holmes who took the initiative:

'she drew Dorothy from "her mothers busynes in his mothers backsyde" to speak with her secretly at the hole in the wall. Soon they agreed to send for Richard Edmundes and Robert Holmes found him, playing bowls, in "the backsyde of goodman podiches house", and took him at once to talk with Dorothy. Holmes' wife took Dorothy's hand through the wall and made Richard take it by the finger, asking "knowe youe who this is that hath youe by the finger", and Dorothy answered "no not yet". Robert Holmes said "it is Richard Edmundes" and Dorothy asked "what . . he wold have with her". Richard first asked whether her father and mother were in the house and, learning that they were not, he said "well my wench I beare youe good will and if thow canst find in thie harte to love me and wilbe ruled by me I will delyver thee out of thye miserie. And she answered she could find in her hart to love him above all men. Then Edmundes axed her howe ould she was, saieing, I thinck you bee neere hand 16 or 17 yeares of age, and she said yea that I am, for I am neerer 20 yrs ould but my age is kept from me. Then Edmundes said unto Dorothee have youe made any contract before this tyme to anye others so that we can laufully go together, and she answered no. Then said Edmundes, can you finde in your harte to forsake father and mother and all men lyving for my sake and she answered yea." ' [4]

Robert Holmes then called his journeyman, Harry Jenkinson, from the house to act as witness to the betrothal, which was made with mutual plighting of troth then and there, with holding of hands through the hole in the wall, and in proper manner, 'viz. "I Dorothee take youe Richard to my husband forsaking all other for your sake and thereuppon I give you my faith and trouthe." ' Richard returned the same plight, and 'he "called for drinck and dronck to Dorothie" and gave her "an ould angell" in token of their betrothal which Dorothy received thankfully but, for fear of her parents discovering it, asked Robert Holmes to keep for her and after a few words concerning the speedy dispatch of their marriage, they departed.' [5]

This wall with a hole in it, through which the lovers speak, which was 'probably one of those walls made up of stones and earth, bonded with hair and coated outside with lime and roughcast, while a capping of thatch kept out the wet', as Dr Urry, has suggested, [6] features prominently in the mini-play of 'Pyramus and Thisbe' played at the court of Duke Theseus as an entertainment for the three newly-married couples in *A Midsummer Night's Dream,* a play which has several Kentish associations beside its famous Pyramus and Thisbe story. There is even an ancient tradition that a man with an ass's head was born in Kent. [7] These Kentish reflections are all found in the play's comic and fairy aspects.

Wall.	In this same interlude it doth befall
	That I, one Snout by name, present a wall;
	And such a wall as I would have you think
	That had in it a crannied hole or chink,
	Through which the lovers, Pyramus and Thisby,
	Did whisper often very secretly.
	This loam, this roughcast, and this stone, doth show
	That I am that same wall; the truth is so;
	And this the cranny is, right and sinister,
	Through which the fearful lovers are to whisper.
Theseus.	Would you desire lime and hair to speak better?
Demetrius.	It is the wittiest partition that ever I heard discourse, my lord.
	. . . *Enter Pyramus*
Pyramus.	O grim-look'd night! O night with hue so black!
	O night, which ever art when day is not!
	O night, O night, alack, alack, alack,
	I fear my Thisby's promise is forgot!
	And thou, O wall, O sweet, O lovely wall,
	That stand'st between her father's ground and mine;
	Thou wall, O wall, O sweet and lovely wall,
	Show me thy chink, to blink through with mine eyne.
	. . .

Enter Thisby

Thisby.	O wall, full often hast thou heard my moans,
	For parting my fair Pyramus and me!
	My cherry lips have often kiss'd thy stones,
	Thy stones with lime and hair knit up in thee.
Pyramus.	I see a voice; now will I to the chink,
	To spy an I can hear my Thisby's face.
	Thisby!
Thisby.	My love! thou art my love, I think.
Pyramus.	Think what thou wilt, I am thy lover's grace;
	And like Limander am I trusty still.
Thisby.	And I like Helen, till the Fates me kill.
Pyramus.	Not Shafalus to Procrus was so true.
Thisby.	As Shafalus to Procrus, I to you.
Pyramus.	O, kiss me through the hole of this vile wall.
Thisby.	I kiss the wall's hole, not your lips at all.

Act 5, scene 1. 11.153-200

And so the fun continues. Limander is an obvious malapropism for Leander, in which Marlowe is poking sly fun at himself which would have delighted Sir Thomas Walsingham and Lady Audrey for whom *Hero and Leander* was an epithalamium for their wedding, and this comic rustic play is given at Theseus's wedding. *A Midsummer Night's Dream* was first printed in 1600. One wonders whether it had, in fact, been written as his wedding offering to Sir Thomas and Lady Audrey in 1598 to match (and to rival) George Chapman's offering of *All Fools* (promised to Lady Audrey in his dedicatory letter to her). Both plays might have been given at private performances at Scadbury, and it is just what one would have expected Marlowe to have produced in the circumstances. The Kentish references are in that case especially appropriate as Walsingham was a Kentish gentleman with a delightful Kentish seat.

The tale of Dorothy Hocking and her eager swain, Richard Edmundes, even as recorded in the legal document is anything but 'dry'. It actually reads like a comedy. The ingredients are all there, and were recognised by 'that pure elementall wit' Kit Marlowe, who probably heard it more than once from his father, who spent much of his time in and out of the law courts involved in minor legal duties. The case dates from 1564 when Christopher was born, but such a rare piece of local gossip would, one may be sure, have lingered on among the tavern tales and local tittle-tattle tinged with scandal beloved of the Canterbury raconteurs. All we know of his life suggests that John Marlowe was one of this lively, extrovert, tale-telling crew, loving nothing better than an appreciative audience.

John Bakeless recounts a marvellously funny story – a piece of real bawdry – involving John Marlowe's friend Lawrence Applegate, which came into the law courts in the following year, 1565. John Marlowe was called upon to depose in a case alleging slander by Applegate against two irate ladies who were anxious to silence the gossip impugning the chastity of the daughter – Marlowe's neighbour in the case – which was becoming the talk of the neighbourhood. John Marlowe, a young married man at the time with a one-year-old son, Christopher, had received the confidences of his friend, the tailor, Lawrence Applegate, who boasted to him that he had many times enjoyed the favours of Goodwife Chapman's daughter, Godliffe, in sundry places. Applegate had on one occasion loaned the sum of two shillings to her mother, Goodwife Chapman, who now refused to repay the debt, whereupon he had his revenge on her, as he told John Marlowe in the presence also of his wife Catherine, 'for that I occupyed godliff hir Daughter fower times wch was for everie tyme vjd.' (The old shilling was 12d so that 2 shillings equalled four sixpences). One can imagine the guffaws of bawdy laughter that greeted this! Applegate was so delighted with this story that he repeated it to John Marlowe's two apprentices, to their delectation! It soon came to the scandalized ears of Goodwife Chapman, whose daughter Godliffe, now being married, was the more anxious to deny such naughty goings-on, and promptly took Applegate to court. [8]

Through John Marlowe's life-long association with the law courts as a sideline to his shoe-making, and the fact that the tailor, Applegate, was his friend and confidant, it is highly probable that such stories of local scandal would have been the cause of merriment in the Marlowe household over the years. If Lawrence Applegate enjoyed repeating his waggish tale, we may be sure that John Marlowe would have been quite as ready with a store of anecdotes for willing ears to hear. Christopher, from an early age, was absorbing what he heard, later to be transmuted as material for his dramatic works. The Applegate affair, being too bawdy, did not provide such material, but it gives us, not a fanciful, but a real insight into this lively community and the family atmosphere in which Marlowe grew up. They were not a straight-laced lot!

It is inconceivable that a dramatist coming out of Canterbury, and from such a background, could have been lacking in a sense of humour. Yet that is what Marlowe's critics have constantly averred, because they judge him on his tragedies alone, [9] although even in these we can detect the latent vein of rich comedy and wit that is waiting in the wings. His responsiveness to his Canterbury environment and the extent to which this is directly reflected in the plays is shown here to be a well-established trait.

The Merry Wives of Canterbury

The second comic incident from the Canterbury archives which Dr Urry's researches have unearthed concerns the malodorous reputation of Canon William Darrell, a former vice-dean of the Cathedral, who was eventually suspended from his canonry for various 'unrecorded misdemeanours'. Gossip among the goodwives of Canterbury features in this tale about a notorious Canterbury harlot named Clemence Ward, and her scandalous relations with Canon Darrell, which reappears translated in *The Merry Wives of Windsor* as one of its most famous comic incidents.

> 'At about harvest time in 1575, one Goodwife Thomasina Newen went round to the Northgate ward of Canterbury to the house of Goodwife Pratt, and sat working with her at her door. Near by a new-made widow, Goodwife Culverhouse, gave milk to her child. They gossiped of Clemence Ward, saying "Yt is a pity she is not carted out of the town." One story which they told about her was repeated a few months later with slight variations in the kitchen of the house of Goodwife Joan Moyse, a widow and "impotent woman" aged fifty, when Clemence Ward's landlord, John Foster, kindly went to see if Goodwife Moyse lacked for anything. As Goodwife Moyse rambled on, retelling a story told previously by a Mrs Hunt, as she recalled, she conjured up a scene of two people staggering through Christchurch Gate into the cathedral precincts on the way to Canon Darrell's house at the far east end, by the city wall, carrying between them a laundry basket over which a coverlet was spread. They went along the great length of the "Centuary" or cemetery of Canterbury Cathedral, through the Norman gateway to the inner cemetery until they came to the Oaks in front of Canon Darrell's house. There they set the basket down, in among the oak trees. The laundry basket was going, said Goodwife Lea, "to Mr Darrell's chamber". Before long either Mr Whyting or perhaps Mr Wade, one of the cathedral lay clerks, approached with some foreknowledge of what was in the basket. He drew out his dagger and plunged it into the basket and, with a wound in her arm from the dagger, out leapt Clemence Ward.' [10]

This choice piece of gossip dates from the year when Archbishop Parker died, when Christopher Marlowe was aged eleven and undoubtedly already a Cathedral chorister and a fee-paying commoner at the King's School waiting hopefully for a scholarship. The story would certainly have reached the ears of the Marlowes, whose personal connections with the Cathedral through their son would have made this scandal doubly interesting. Perhaps it was the first revelation to young Christopher of the hypocrisy and sinfulness that hid beneath a clerical coat, which is reflected repeatedly in his plays, as when Gloucester calls the Bishop of Winchester 'wolf in sheep's array' and a 'scarlet hypocrite!' in *1 Henry VI* (Act 1, scene 3, l. 56).

This clerical scandal being so gleefully gossiped around Canterbury in the mid 1570's and probably long after, is likely to have been our dramatist's inspiration for Falstaff's glorious laundry-basket drubbing in *The Merry Wives of*

Windsor, a play which prominently features gossiping and plotting wives – the Goodwives of Canterbury, perhaps, up-graded to middle-class status? The parallel is particularly felicitous. This play, although carefully set geographically in Windsor and its environs, also contains the marvellously funny and sharply observed characters of Sir Hugh Evans, the Welsh parson, and Dr Caius, the French physician, a deft portrait from life of a fellow of French-speaking Huguenot origin, both of them drawn from Canterbury's immigrant community, whose manner of speech and accents are so faithfully presented in this delightful play.

If we add to these two Canterbury incidents reflected in *The Merry Wives of Windsor* and *A Midsummer Night's Dream,* the graphic description of the 'Shakespeare Cliffs' at Dover in *King Lear,* the evidence of an otherwise inexplicable association with Canterbury and Dover, Marlowe's own stamping ground, cannot be lightly dismissed.

The Shakespeare Cliffs of Dover

As a boy Christopher Marlowe must often have gone to Dover to visit his maternal grandparents, the Arthurs, and there can be no doubt that he wrote the detailed description of the White Cliffs of Dover out of his own vivid recollection. Edgar leads the blinded Earl of Gloucester, who longs to end his misery by throwing himself over the edge of the cliff, to what he pretends is the very edge of this dizzyingly high precipice. It is a marvellous piece of evocative writing.

> *Edgar*   Come on, sir; here's the place. Stand still. How fearful
> And dizzy 'tis to cast one's eyes so low!
> The crows and choughs that wing the mid-way air
> Show scarce so gross as beetles. Half-way down
> Hangs one that gathers samphire – dreadful trade!
> Methinks he seems no bigger than his head.
> The fishermen that walk upon the beach
> Appear like mice; and yond tall anchoring bark
> Diminish'd to her cock; her cock, a buoy
> Almost too small for sight. The murmuring surge
> That on th' unnumb'red idle pebble chafes
> Cannot be heard so high. I'll look no more;
> Lest my brain turn, and the deficient sight
> Topple down headlong.
>
> *King Lear* Act 4, scene 6. 11. 11-24

Photograph by Virginia F. Stern

The Shakespeare Cliffs. *Marlowe's maternal grandparents, the Arthurs, lived at Dover, and as a boy he must often have visited this important seaport, the Gateway to the Continent and the world beyond. His boyhood memories are reflected in his plays. The ship the 'Flying Dragon' rode in Dover Harbour during these years, and he later sailed her into his play* The Jew of Malta, *just as in* Edward III *he introduced the 'Nonpareille', the ship on which he fought in the Armada campaign. The vivid description in* King Lear *recollects what he would have seen and absorbed when lying perhaps in the grass on top of the sheer cliffs gazing down, or scanning the horizon for approaching ships.*

Kentish recollections abound in Part 2 of the trilogy, which several scholars attribute to Marlowe's hand in origin, this being one of the Pembroke plays written about 1590-91. Admittedly, the Kentish Rebellion of 1450 led by Jack Cade in protest against the swingeing taxation imposed by King Henry VI sets the scene, geographically, mainly in Kent, but the intimate knowledge of the county betrays the dramatist's personal connection with this, his home county. Act 4, scene 1, is set on 'The Coast of Kent', and in the opening speech the Lieutenant refers to their recent fight at sea in which they took sundry prisoners who are brought on stage:

> . . . whilst our pinnace anchors in the Downs,
> Here shall they make their ransom on the shore.
>
> ll. 9-10

The Downs is the name given to the stretch of sea along the Kent coast bordering the Downlands which top the cliffs above Sandwich, one of the Cinque Ports, and stretch for miles along this coastal region and inland into Kent. The Small Downs is the sheltered stretch of sea north-east of the Straits of Dover, roughly between Deal and Ramsgate. One can walk across the springy downland grass from Canterbury to the coast at the nearest point between Deal and Sandwich in a bare ninety minutes, a pleasant exercise that the boy Christopher Marlowe must often have taken.

In Act 4, scene 2, the rebels are gathering their force on Blackheath, mostly stout-hearted Men of Kent, and as they arrive John Holland cries out:

> I see them! I see them! There's
> Best's son, the tanner of Wingham
>
> ll. 20-21

Wingham lies only five or six miles directly east of Canterbury. Best, the tanner of Wingham, may have been known to the Marlowes for the tanners were an allied trade to shoemakers and belonged to the same guild. Bringing in an actual tanner's son known to him in the guise of his antecedent in the famous Cade Rebellion of 1450 would have been the kind of personal touch that delighted Marlowe. At present this is hypothetical for I have not researched to discover any tanners of Wingham named Best in the Canterbury archives, but future search may yet reveal treasure. Later in the same scene, the illiterate rebels take their envious revenge on the harmless clerk of Chartam (so spelt in the First Folio, which is modern Chartham a mile due West of Canterbury, mistakenly rendered as Chatham by modern editors) [11] for being literate.

> Cade. . . How now! Who's there?
> Smith. The clerk of Chartam. He can write
> and read and cast accompt.

Cade.	O monstrous!
Smith.	We took him setting of boys' copies.
Cade.	Here's a villain!
Smith.	Has a book in his pocket with red letters in't.
Cade.	Nay, then he is a conjurer.
Dick.	Nay, he can make obligations and write court-hand.
Cade.	I am sorry for't; the man is a proper man, of mine honour; unless I find him guilty, he shall not die.
	Come hither, sirrah, I must examine thee. What is thy name?
Clerk.	Emmanuel.
Dick.	They use to write it on the top of letters; 'twill go hard with you.
Cade.	Let me alone. Dost thou use to write thy name, or hast thou a mark to thyself, like a honest plain-dealing man?
Clerk.	Sir, I thank God, I have been so well brought up that I can write my name.
All.	He hath confess'd. Away with him! He's a villain and a traitor.
Cade.	Away with him, I say! Hang him with his pen and inkhorn about his neck.

Act 4, scene 2. 11.80-105

The highly-educated Marlowe had probably suffered jeering from less favoured boys who ganged up against him for his privileged education at the King's School. And again, when the rebels capture Lord Say, Jack Cade arraigns him on a similar charge of malpractices in a Marlovian vein of tragi-comedy.

Cade	Thou has most traitorously corrupted the youth of the realm in erecting a grammar school; and whereas, before, our forefathers had no books but the score and the tally, thou hast caused printing to be us'd, and, contrary to the King, his crown, and dignity, thou hast built a paper-mill. It will be proved to thy face that thou hast men about thee that usually talk of a noun and a verb, and such abominable words as no Christian ear can endure to hear. Thou hast appointed justices of the peace, to call poor men before them about matters they were not able to answer. Moreover, thou hast put them in prison, and because they could not read, thou hast hang'd them, when, indeed, only for that cause they have been most worthy to live.

Act 4, scene 7. 11. 30-39

Cade is referring to the loop-hole provided for educated men, who, under Tudor law, could escape hanging for a felony by reading their Latin 'neck verse'. Lord Say's speech replying to Cade's accusations contains a patriotic eulogy of Kent which is not likely to have come from the pen of the Warwickshire-born William Shakespeare.

> *Say.* Hear me but speak, and bear me where you will.
> Kent, in the Commentaries Caesar writ,
> Is term'd the civil'st place of all this isle.
> Sweet is the country, because full of riches;
> The people liberal, valiant, active, wealthy;
> Which makes me hope you are not void of pity.
>
> 11. 55-60

Henry IV Part 1

No such equivocation as for the *Henry VI* trilogy concerning its attribution to Marlowe exists for the two-part history of *Henry IV.* Therefore the introduction in *Part One* of a scent set in Kent, which has no historical basis, is entirely the dramatist's choice of geographical venue and represents his own invention. This is the scene in Act 1 when Ned Poins persuades Prince Hal to join with him in playing a trick on Falstaff to expose this outsize buffoon's cowardice and talent for lying, by pretending to support a scheme to rob some travellers of their money; but then withdrawing secretly, leaving Falstaff to gain the loot from the unwary travellers, they immediately return disguised and set upon him to rob him in turn. This would provoke Falstaff to an exaggerated tale of how he was robbed by a huge number of fearful villains with whom, of course, he fought most valiantly until the insuperable odds overpowered him and they got away with the loot, – when in reality he had taken to his heels, like the arrant coward he conceals under his swagger, as soon as the attackers (the disguised Poins and Prince Hal) appeared.
Poins sets the plot a-foot:

> *Poins.* But my lads, my lads, to-morrow morning, by four o'clock
> early, at Gadshill! There are pilgrims going to Canterbury
> with rich offerings, and traders riding to London with fat
> purses. I have vizards for you all; you have horses for
> yourselves. Gadshill lies to-night at Rochester; I have
> bespoke supper to-morrow night at Eastcheap.
>
> 11. 120-125

Act 2, scene 1 is set in an inn yard at Rochester, where Gadshill is pumping the dishonest chamberlain of the inn for information about travellers who have passed that way:

Chamberlain. Good morrow, Master Gadshill. It holds current that I told you yesternight: there's a franklin in the Weald of Kent hath brought three hundred marks with him in gold; I heard him tell it to one of his company last night at supper, a kind of auditor; one that hath abundance of charge too – God knows what. They are up already and call for eggs and butter; they will away presently.

11. 50-58

Probably Marlowe knew of just such an inn in Rochester.

Some of these Kentish references are more significant than others, but it is the cumulative instances of Kentish reflections that make this evidence weighty. Scholars have combed the Shakespeare plays for Warwickshire references, but ignore the Kentish ones – although the 'Shakespeare Cliffs' are somewhat difficult to ignore. We now ask the question, Where did Shakespeare learn the French which is used so liberally in several of the plays?

Courtesy of the Dean and Chapter of Canterbury
Photograph by Tony Whitcomb

The Tomb of King Henry IV in Canterbury Cathedral

Henry V

Marlowe heard French spoken in his native Canterbury from his infancy, and some of the Huguenot immigrants gave lessons in French to Canterbury's English children for a modest fee. The shoemaker, John Marlowe, ambitious for his bright little son's advancement may have sent him to attend such French classes. Language skills were highly prized in Elizabethan times. Later Marlowe would have used his knowledge of French and had opportunities to perfect it on his assignments abroad for the government. The courtship scene in *Henry V* reveals a good knowledge of French in the conversation here between King Henry, Princess Katherine and her lady-in-waiting, Alice.

King.	Do you like me Kate?
Katherine.	Pardonnez-moi, I cannot tell vat is like me.
King.	An angel is like you, Kate, and you are like an angel.
Kath.	Que dit-il? que je suis semblable à les anges?
Alice.	Oui, vraiment, sauf votre grace, ainsi dit-il.
King.	I said so, dear Katherine, and I must not blush to affirm it.
Kath.	O bon Dieu! les langues des hommes sont pleines de tromperies.
King.	What says she, fair one? that the tongues of men are full of deceits?
Alice.	Oui, dat de tongues of de mans is be full of deceits – dat is de Princess.

. . . .

King.	Come, thy answer is broken music – for thy voice is music and thy English broken; therefore Queen of all, Katherine, break thy mind to me in broken English. Wilt thou have me?
Kath.	Dat is as it shall please le roi mon père.
King.	Nay, it will please him well, Kate – it shall please him, Kate.
Kath.	Den it sall also content me.
King.	Upon that I kiss your hand, and I call you my queen.
Kath.	Laissez, mon seigneur, laissez, laissez! Ma foi, je ne veux point que vous abaissiez votre grandeur en baisant la main d'une, notre seigneur, indigne serviteur; excusez-moi, je vous supplie, mon trés puissant seigneur.
King.	Then I will kiss your lips, Kate.
Kath.	Les dames et demoiselles pour être baisées devant leur noces, il n'est pas la coutume de France.

Henry V Act 5, scene 2, ll. 107 &c.

There is a fair sprinkling of French in *Henry V* and one all French scene between the Princess and Alice. And in Marlowe's *The Massacre at Paris* King Henry III cries: Par le mort Dieu, il mourra! and the Guise leads the massacre with: Tuez, tuez, tuez! but this is a truncated text. Besides French-speaking Huguenots there was also in Canterbury 'a strong Welsh contingent, represented by families of Davys, Joneses, Vaughans, Williamses and Evanses, some of whom still spoke their native language among themselves.' [12]

In *Henry V* we meet the redoubtable Welsh captain, Fluellen; a faithfully observed portrait which Garrett Mattingly thinks may have been based on a real life character, Sir Roger Williams (did he hail from Canterbury?) who was commanding the English battalion defending Sluys against the Duke of Parma in 1587, where the beleaguered garrison were having a hard time of it waiting for the relief that never came. Mattingly writes of Williams in his moving chapter on the bitter loss of Sluys in *The Defeat of the Spanish Armada* (1959):

> 'Williams was a professional soldier who had spent most of the past fifteen years campaigning in the Netherlands. He was a Welshman, a bantam gamecock of a man who wore on his morion the longest plume in either army "so that his friends and his foes might know where he was", a man so like Captain Fluellen in his level head and blazing temper, forthright tongue and indomitable heart, even in the quirks of military pedantry that adorned his speech, that one must believe that William Shakespeare either knew him personally or drew heavily on the reminiscences of someone who did.' [13]

There is no evidence that William Shakespeare had served in the Netherlands or had ever left England; whereas Marlowe was a valued and trusted espionage agent in the summer of 1587, Sluys fell at the beginning of August. From the time he left Cambridge graced with his Master of Arts, he would have been actively employed gathering intelligence for Walsingham and Burghley in the run-up to the Armada, which kept the intelligence service fully occupied; probably he was working on the Continent for much of that summer and up till the outbreak of hostilities in the following July 1588 he may well have been back and forth many times. [14]

There were Welsh Williamses and Welsh-speaking Evanses resident in Canterbury, and there Marlowe would readily have picked up the Welsh lilt with his quick ear and the accent and the tricks of speech so faithfully reproduced in the words spoken by Fluellen and by Sir Hugh Evans, the Welsh parson in *The Merry Wives of Windsor.* Evans talks of 'pribbles and prabbles' and pronounces 'b' as 'p', look you, as does the valiant Fluellen, of whose delectable speech a few samplings must suffice.

Enter Fluellen and Gower

Gower   . . . but why wear you your leek today? Saint Davy's day is past.

> *Fluellen.* There is occasions and causes why and wherefore in all
> things. I will tell you, ass my friend, Captain Gower:
> the rascally, scald, beggarly, lousy, pragging knave,
> Pistol – which you and yourself and all the world know
> to be no petter than a fellow, look you now, of no merits
> – he is come to me, and prings me pread and salt yester-
> day, look you, and bid me eat my leek; it was in a place
> where I could not breed no contention with him; but I
> will be so bold as to wear it in my cap till I see him once
> again, and then I will tell him a little piece of my desires.'
>
> Act 5, scene 1. 11.1-13

Fluellen also talks of 'pibble-pabble' here expounding his philosophy of war:

> *Fluellen.* It is the greatest admiration in the universal world, when
> the true and aunchient prerogatifes and laws of the wars
> is not kept; if you would take the pains but to examine
> the wars of Pompey the Great, you shall find, I warrant
> you, that there is no tiddle-taddle nor pibble-pabble in
> Pompey's camp; I warrant you, you shall find the cere-
> monies of the wars, and the cares of it, and the forms of
> it, and the sobriety of it, and the modesty of it, to be oth-
> erwise.
>
> Act 4, scene 1. 11.64-74

Mattingly is right! Such a man was known to the dramatist, else how could
he have drawn him so to the life? Canterbury was often filled with soldiers
returning from the wars, or going thither, so that the boy Marlowe would have
had a long experience of observing these types who are so marvellously portrayed in *Henry V,* essentially a soldier's play, peopled with heroes, villains,
cowards, cunning rascals, all immortalized. And where and how did William
Shakespeare pick up his excellent French in Stratford-upon-Avon? Take this
passage in which a French prisoner bargains with Pistol for his life with the
Boy translating:

> *Boy.* He prays you to save his life; he is a gentleman of a good
> house, and for his ransom he will give you two hundred
> crowns.
> *Pistol.* Tell him my fury shall abate, and I the crowns will take.
> *French Soldier.* Petit monsieur, que dit-il?
> *Boy.* Encore qu'il est contre son jurement de pardonner aucun
> prisonnier, néanmoins, pour les écus que vous l'avez
> promis, il est content à vous donner la liberté, le fran-
> chisement.
> *Fr. Sold.* Sur mes genoux je vous donne mille remercimens; et je

m'estime heureux que je suis tombé entre les mains d'un chevalier, je pense, le plus brave, vaillant, et trés distingué seigneur d'Angleterre.

Pistol. Expound unto me, boy.

Boy. He gives you, upon his knees, a thousand thanks; and he esteems himself happy that he hath fall'n into the hands of one – as he thinks – the most brave, valorous, and thrice-worthy signeur of England.

Pistol. As I suck blood, I will some mercy show. Follow me.

Act 4 scene 4. 11.43-63

Ancient Pistol was probably also a Canterbury type.

The Merry Wives of Windsor

The life-like portraits of immigrants draw us back to this marvellous comedy again. Here, in the delightfully comic scene in which Parson Evans is waiting apprehensively for Dr Caius, with whom he has an assignment to fight a duel but is heartily wishing he hadn't got himself into this miserable situation, the Welshman tries to cheer his spirits by singing to himself.

Evans. Pless my soul, how full of chollers I am, and trempling of mind! I shall be glad if he have deceived me. How melancholies I am! I will knog his urinals about his knave's costard when I have goot opportunities for the 'ork. Pless my soul!

He sings.

> To shallow rivers, to whose falls
> Melodious birds sing madrigals;
> There will we make our peds of roses,
> And a thousand fragrant posies.
> To shallow-

Mercy on me! I have a great dispositions to cry.

Sings.

> Melodious birds sing madrigals -
> Whenas I sat in Papylon -
> And a thousand vagram posies.
> To shallow......etc.

Act 3 scene 1. 11.9-24

Marlowe is parodying his own 'Come live with me and be my Love' in comic vein! This delightful lyric and its tune would have been well known in Canterbury for it was set to music by William Corkine, a chorister of the Cathedral and son of the tailor with whom Marlowe had a quarrel that landed them in court and ended in a charming reconciliation. [15]

The Gallic temperament of the hot-tempered Dr Caius, who fancies himself as a suitor for the lovely Anne Page, makes a marvellous foil for the Welsh parson, and one cannot doubt that somewhere among the Canterbury Huguenot immigrants his real-life prototype was strutting the cobbled streets in high dudgeon over some imagined insult to his dapper person.

> *Cauis.* You jack'nape; give-a this letter to Sir Hugh; by gar, it is
> a shallenge; I will cut his troat in de park; and I will
> teach a scurvy jack-a-nape priest to meddle or make.
> You may be gone; it is no good you tarry here. By gar, I
> will cut all his two stones; by gar, he shall not have a
> stone to throw at his dog.

Caius also speaks his native French, and rules his servants with peppery impatience. He objects to Mistress Quickly singing.

> Caius. Vat is you sing? I do not like des toys. Pray you, go and
> vetch me in my closet un boitier vert – a box, a green-a
> box. Do intend vat I speak? A green-a box.
> *Quickly.* Ay, forsooth, I'll fetch it you.
> Caius. Fe, fe, fe, fe! ma foi, il fait fort chaud. Je m'en vais ... la
> cour – la grande affaire.
> Quick. Is it this sir?
> Caius. Oui; mette-le au mon pocket; depêche, quickly. Vere is
> dat knave, Rugby?
> Quick. What John Rugby! John!
> *Rugby.* Here, sir.
> Cauis. You are John Rugby, and you are Jack Rugby. Come,
> take-a your rapier, and come after my heel to the court.
>
> Act 1 scene 4.11.39-46

Is this not Canterbury? It certainly is not Stratford-upon-Avon.

Measure for Measure

In *Measure for Measure* there is a remarkable direct recollection of the events at Deptford in the scene in which the Duke intervenes to save Claudio from execution on the orders of Angelo, 'the righteous man', to whom the Duke has abrogated the government of his dukedom while he departs on a faked journey, intending to return in disguise. Presently, he returns as a holy friar to observe how Angelo is making out. Claudio, who is guiltless of any crime other than to have begotten a child on the lady to whom he is betrothed, but has, for reasons connected with her dowry, been unable to marry, is condemned to death by the puritanical Angelo for this unpardonable licentiousness. The death sentence on Claudio is held by the Duke to be tyrranical. His purpose is to expose Angelo as the very opposite of a man of vaunted high morals for he conceals under his puritanical cloak a nature far more lascivious than Claudio's.

But the saving of Claudio's life is a race against time, for, in proof of his execution, Angelo has invoked the grisly mediaeval custom of having the executed man's head sent to him.

The Duke, in his disguise as a holy man, enlists the help of the sympathetic provost of the prison in a plot to save the life of the unjustly condemned Claudio. In the following scene he persuades the Provost to switch his execution with that of a death-deserving criminal who is to die a few days later than Claudio, and to send the head of this criminal, Barnardine, to Angelo instead of Claudio's, thus gaining time for his return as the Duke, when he will pardon Claudio and expose Angelo's hypocisy.

> *Duke.* I crave but four days' respite; for the which you are to do me both a present and a dangerous courtesy.
> *Provost.* Pray, sir, in what?
> *Duke.* In the delaying death.
> *Provost.* Alack! How may I do it, having the hour limited, and an express command, under penalty, to deliver his head in the view of Angelo? I may make my case as Claudio's, to cross this in the smallest.
> *Duke.* By the vow of mine order, I warrant you, if my instructions may be your guide. Let this Barnardine be this morning executed, and his head borne to Angelo.
> *Provost.* Angelo hath seen them both, and will discover the favour.
> *Duke.* *O, death's a great disguiser; and you may add to it.* Shave his head and tie the beard; and say it was the desire of the penitent to be so bar'd before his death. You know the course is common.

[My italics]   Act 4 scene 2. 11.152-169

Frizer improved the effect of the 'great disguiser' Death, adding to it at Deptford by the wound on the face. The Provost is, however, yet fearful and remonstrates saying: 'Pardon me, good father; it is against my oath.' The Duke then goes further than he had intended, all but revealing his identity by showing the Provost a letter bearing the Duke's seal and signet, stating that he will return within four days, when the Provost's action in saving Claudio's life will be applauded, not censured.
He adds:

> *Duke.* Put not yourself into amazement how these things should
> be: all difficulties are but easy when they are known.
> Call your executioner, and off with Barnardine's head. I
> will give him a present shrift, and advise him for a better
> place. Yet you are amaz'd, but this shall absolutely
> resolve you. Come away; it is almost clear dawn.

Act 4 scene 2 11.190-196

We may also be amazed, but by and by it will be clear dawn with us and much new light will be shed, not only on the sonnets but also on the plays of this superb dramatist. In *Measure for Measure* the character of Abhorson, the executioner, and many things spoken by others, take on a new meaning. However, there is no need to execute Barnardine before his time, for the fortuitous death of another prisoner provides the body.

> *Provost.* Now sir, how do you find the prisoner?
> *Duke.* A creature unprepar'd, unmeet for death;
> And to transport him in the mind he is
> Were damnable.
> *Provost.* Here in the prison, father,
> One Ragozine, a most notorious pirate,
> A man of Claudio's years, his beard and head
> Just of his colour.

At which the Duke exclaims:

> O, 'tis an accident that heaven provides!
> Dispatch it presently.

Act 4 scene 3 11.62-73

Thus Angelo is foiled on his intended victim. Do we perhaps have an indication here that the body at the Deptford inquest could have been provided by the agency of Danby, and is he shadowed in the character of the Provost? Elizabethan coroners were known sometimes to sell bodies illicitly when no relatives or aquaintances of the deceased were to be found. The interesting character of Angelo may, perhaps, have been modelled to some extent on

Whitgift, who began his brilliant ecclesiastical career by drawing attention to himself as a fire-eating preacher of great power with puritanical leanings, which Puritanism the genius of his aspiring ambition counselled him to tone down and lay aside, for he could see that under such a sovereign Queen Elizabeth only the middle road would lead him to the goal on which he had fixed his covetous eye – the Archbishop's throne. Once he was firmly established in his seat of power, riding on a rising wave of reaction against the free-thinkers, he began to show his true puritanical nature in the witch-hunting he attempted to launch in the 1590's. It is a strange anomaly of this progressive movement, that Puritanism emerged as analogous with intolerance, bigotry and superstition. Under the Puritan Protectorate of Cromwell more 'witches' and 'wizards' were burnt than at any time in our history.

Measure for Measure is an exposure of the injustice and inhumanity of such a puritanical authority when given a free hand. In this context we may see the Duke as embodying the liberal and humane philosophy of Elizabeth, who moved to save the 'most gentle Claudio' from a hypocritical and puritanical authority – and who was prepared to use the subterfuge of another man's dead body to effect his act of mercy. The close parallel is there for us to pick up if we know that happened at Deptford. There is much in this play, in the presentation of its characters and plot, and in the thoughts expressed by the Duke and others, which reveals new depths in the drama when seen as the work of the dramatist who had suffered 'The slings and arrows of outrageous fortune' in his own life.

Did Marlowe ever succumb to the temptation to reveal himself overtly as the author of the dramatic works given to the world as by *William Shakespeare?* In one play there is evidence of this, which, though cryptic, is absolutely specific.

As You Like It

In this play the character of the clown, Touchstone, has a special significance. His name is deliberately chosen, designating the stone which alchemists used to reveal the true value of metals in their search for gold, by touching or stroking with the stone. Preceding his revealing altercation with the country bumpkin, William (of whom protagonists of the numerous Shakespearean authorship theories have long held that he represents William Shakespeare) Touchstone makes the point of *'touching'* William, indicating that a revelation of truth is about to be made.

Touchstone	[*to William*] Give me your hand, Art thou learned?
Will.	No, sir.
Touch.	Then learn this of me: to have is to have; for it is a figure of rhetoric that drink, being pour'd out of a cup into a glass, by filling the one doth empty the other; for all

your writers do consent that *ipse* is he; now, you are not *ipse*, for I am he.

> *Will.* Which he, sir?
>
> *Touch.* He, sir, that must marry this woman. Therefore, you clown, abandon . .

Act 5, scene 1. 11.35-43

Touchstone having revealed that he is *ipse*, the man himself, which follows a reference to *writers*, is then telling William to cease courting his intended bride, Audrey, that is, *to lay claim to her as his own.* In a previous scene Touchstone had indicated that Audrey represents the audiences who clapper-claw his plays without really understanding them, or by whom they are written.

> *Touchstone.* Come apace, good Audrey, I will fetch up your goats, Audrey. And How, Audrey, am I the man yet? Doth my simple features content you?
>
> *Audrey.* Your features! Lord warrant us! What features?
>
> *Touch.* I am here with thee and thy goats, as the most capricious poet, honest Ovid was among the Goths.
>
> *Jaques.* (*Aside*) O knowledge ill-inhabited, worse than Jove in a thatch'd house!
>
> *Touch.* When a man's verses cannot be understood, nor a man's good wit seconded with the forward child understanding, it strikes a man more dead than a great reckoning in a little room. Truly, I would the gods had made thee poetical.
>
> *Audrey.* I do not know what 'poetical' is. Is it honest in deed and word? Is it a true thing?

Act 3, scene 3. 11.1-13

In this pregnant passage we are handed multiple clues if we are alert to receive them. The lack of understanding of his verses that 'strikes a man more dead than a great reckoning in a little room' could hardly be plainer, for 'le recknynge' (a precise English word used in the Latin inquisition on Marlowe's death) was evidently repeatedly used during the proceedings at Deptford when the body lay there in the view of the jury, since it is used in the record. The gossip about this event was spread, we assume, by the members of the jury who were there present. It was 'le recknynge' that was the cause of the quarrel that ended in his 'murder'. Touchstone, we are to understand, represents the author himself, and here he is, like Marlowe, in exile, to which he draws attention by likening himself to Ovid amongst the Goths, who also spent a period in exile. Audrey, his intended bride, is ignorant and not 'poetical', hence she does not understand him, as his audiences equally fail to understand him.

341

We now meet the character Sir Oliver Mar-text (whose name is thus written and hyphenated in the First Folio!), the vicar of the next village whom Touchstone has engaged to come to the greenwood to marry him to Audrey; but when he arrives, the wedding is abruptly called off by Touchstone, and he dismisses poor Mar-text unceremoniously. Significantly, (Marlowe's Text?) has scarcely a line to speak beyond his defiant cry, after Touchstone cancels the wedding and departs with Audrey leaving Mar-text alone on the stage, when he declares stoutly: 'Tis no matter; ne'er a fantastical knave of them all shall flout me out of my calling.' And he stumps off in high dudgeon.

What is the meaning of all this horse-play? Why is the marriage called off? If Touchstone *(alias* the real author) were to be married by Mar-text (Marlowe's Text) to Audrey (the Elizabethan audiences) it would be far too risky. The cat would be out of the bag.

In addition to all this there is a direct quotation from Marlowe's *Hero and Leander* of a famous line spoken by the love-sick Phoebe in the very next scene:

> Dead shepherd, now I find thy saw of might,
> Who ever lov'd that lov'd not at first sight?

Act 5, scene 1 11.80-81

A poet was commonly termed a shepherd by the Elizabethan writers. Hence this is a direct invocation of the 'dead shepherd', Christopher Marlowe, whose *Hero and Leander* was a well-loved and popular poem in its day, one of the most widely read. It is hardly to be wondered why the play *As You Like It* was refused a licence for publication when it was entered in the Stationers' register on 4th August 1600. A note beside the entry reads: 'to be staied'.[16] It was the only play out of four that were entered in the Register on that day which remained permanently under this caveat. It was never published, and perhaps never performed, until it appeared in the First Folio. Had someone recognised that if these cryptic fooleries were seen in print someone unfriendly to the author could too easily pick up the scent, and realise who Shake-speare really was? Even if he then escaped a second time, there were those who had assisted his escape by 'murder' who were far too vulnerable for the risk to be lightly taken.

However, the 'dead shepherd' is stirring in the plays, as may be judged by the remarkably high proportion of plots he chose which mirror his own fate, revolving round the theme of exile, including characters who are the victims of slander, and apparently die, and are believed dead, but return to life to find reconciliation and happiness, which we encounter in play after play. The plots of the Shakespeare plays are almost all second-hand, largely or in part derived from the stories of the Italian writers, Boccaccio, Bandello, Cinthio and Ariosto and from the novels of his contemporaries, Lodge and Greene. This was the fashion that other dramatists also followed, using as sources contemporary and ancient literature, and reworking in dramatic form existing stories, in which banishment was a popular theme; even re-emergence to life after supposed death is not the sole preserve of Shakespeare's works. It is not suggested that the incidence of these themes in the plays represents 'proof' of their authorship by the exiled and supposedly 'dead shepherd', Christopher Marlowe. What I draw attention to here is merely the frequency of these themes in the plays of one great dramatist – William Shakespeare.

The choice of story to dramatize is that of the dramatist, who, in the case of the dramatist Shakespeare, seems peculiarly drawn to any subject embracing these particular themes, either singly or all of them in one play. The moving scenes of reconciliation of long-lost brothers and sisters, mothers, fathers and dear friends are a memorable feature of his plays, capable of drawing tears from the audience. It is only by its emergence in time, and by its preponderance, that this theme may be judged to have some significance – perhaps as another auto-biographical touch?

Dramatizations of history are in a separate category, and are excluded from my list of plays, namely, the great English history cycle, which numbers ten in all, and also the four plays based on Roman and Greek history or legend, *Julius Caesar, Anthony and Cleopatra, Coriolanus,* and *Troilus and Cressida,* although banishment and slander feature. Omitting these fourteen plays the rest of the Shakespearean canon is presented below, listing the incidence of the themes of banishment, slander, and supposed death that occurs in these remaining twenty-three plays.

Conjectural dates of composition of the plays listed follow orthodox hypothesis, unless stated otherwise, showing incidence of themes of exile, slander, supposed death.

Approximate Date written	Themes of Exile, Slander, Supposed Death	First Printed
Before 1594 (?)		
Love's Labour's Lost	None. Revised for publication in 1598. (First written, I believe, before 1593)	1598
Titus Andronicus	Quintus and Martius slandered and murdered; Lucius banished.	1594
The Two Gentlemen of Verona	Julia supposed dead; Valentine banished.	Folio
The Comedy of Errors	Emilia, and the Twins supposed dead.	Folio
The Taming of the Shrew	None.[17]	Folio
1594-1597 (?)		
Romeo and Juliet	Romeo banished; Juliet supposed dead.	1597 (pirated) 1599

343

A Midsummer Night's Dream	Thisbe supposed dead.	1600
The Merchant of Venice	None.	1600

1597-1600 (?)

Much Ado About Nothing	Hero slandered, supposed dead.	1600
The Merry Wives of Windsor	None.	1602(pirated) Folio
As You Like It	Duke exiled; Rosalind banished; Touchstone, Celia, Orlando flee into voluntary exile.	Folio

1601-1608 (?)

Hamlet	Hamlet supposed dead.	1603 (pirated) 1604
Twelfth Night	Sebastian and Viola supposed dead.	Folio
Measure for Measure	Claudio supposed dead.	Folio
All's Well that Ends Well	Helena supposed dead.	Folio
Othello	Desdemona and Cassio slandered, both murdered.	1622
King Lear	Kent banished; Edgar slandered, hunted.	1608
Macbeth	Malcolm, Donalbain, Fleance, MacDuff flee into exile.	Folio
Timon of Athens	Alcibiades slandered, banished (This is a historical personage)	Folio
Pericles	Pericles, Thaisa, Marina all supposed dead.	1609

After 1608(?)

Cymbeline	Posthumus banished, slandered, supposed dead; Imogen slandered, supposed dead; Belarius exiled, slandered; Guiderius and Arviragus supposed dead.	Folio
The Winter's Tale	Hermione slandered, supposed dead; Perdita supposed dead.	Folio
The Tempest	Prospero exiled, slandered, supposed dead; Miranda exiled with her father, supposed dead; Ferdinand supposed dead; Alonso supposed dead.	

We began this chapter with Dr Urry's reference to *The Jew of Malta* as Marlowe's autobiographical recollection of Canterbury, for he chose to set his drama in his native city. So we end with this intriguing, youthful work, which is in a unique genre compounded of satire, romance and romantic tragedy, outrageous comedy, bitter tragedy, and even partakes of the Elizabethan morality play. It was not published, so far as we know, until 1633, long after the death of Edward Alleyn, who seems to have held the copyright as his own property and who alone in his lifetime acted the Jew Barabas. When Marlowe added the Prologue that appears in Thomas Heywood's edition of 1633 is not known, but I surmise it was probably written for a private performance of the play at Thomas Walsingham's home, perhaps to mark an anniversary, such as that of the 'death' at Deptford on 30th May? The tongue-in-cheek satire of this intriguing Prologue suggests as much.

Enter Machiavel

Machiavel: Albeit the world think Machiavel is dead,
             Yet was his soul but flown beyond the Alps;
             And, now the Guise is dead, is come from France,
             To view this land, and frolic with his friends.
             To some perhaps my name is odious;
             But such as love me, guard me from their tongues,
             And let them know that I am Machiavel,
             And weigh not men, and therefore not men's words.
             Admir'd I am of those that hate me most;
             Though some speak openly against my books,
             Yet will they read me, and thereby attain
             To Peter's chair; and when they cast me off,
             Are poison'd by my climbing followers.
             I count religion but a childish toy,
             And hold there is no sin but ignorance.
             Birds of the air will tell of murders past;
             I am asham'd to hear such fooleries.
             Many will talk of title to a crown:
             What right had Caesar to the empire?
             Might first made kings, and laws were then most sure
             When, like the Draco's, they were writ in blood.
             Hence comes it that a strong-built citadel
             Commands much more than letters can import:
             Which maxim had Phalaris observ'd,
             H'ad never bellow'd in a brazen bull
             Of great ones' envy: o' th' poor petty wights
             Let me be envied and not pitied.
             But whither am I bound? I come not, I,
             To read a lecture here in Britain,

But to present the tragedy of a Jew,
Who smiles to see how full his bags are cramm'd;
Which money was not got without my means.
I crave but this, – grace him as he deserves,
And let him not be entertain'd the worse
Because he favours me.

There is much to ponder in this clever speech. Line 14 confounds this Machiavellian statement with Marlowe's credo, craftily linked here with the notorious and equally much maligned Machiavelli, who was always represented to the ignorant hoi polloi as the Arch-Atheist. Marlowe was presented as one who studied Machiavelli's banned book, the famous political treatise *The Prince*. It is still read by politicians today, but when it was published in the fifteenth century it contained too many home truths for the Pope to stomach. Students at Cambridge were surreptitiously reading it when Marlowe was there, and Greene's *Groatsworth of Wit* associates Marlowe with such forbidden studies when he sets out deliberately to stigmatize him as an Atheist: 'Is it pestilent Machiuilian pollicy that thou hast studied?'

The reference to 'Peter's chair' denotes the Archbishop's throne in Canterbury Cathedral, bringing this play back again to Marlowe's native city. If the death of the 'Guise' is a cryptic reference to its late occupant, Archbishop Whitgift, who died in 1604, this would suggest a celebration after Marlowe's safe return from exile when he came to Britain to 'frolic with his friends'. His initial return visit from exile is documented cryptically by Thorpe in summer 1600, which may have been temporary until it could become permanent with Whitgift's death, which would indeed call for a celebration.

There are multiple, unmistakable autobiographical hints in this witty prologue, and it is not surprising that it was not published until 1633. If we take on board the cryptic messages contained in this pregnant passage, it points Marlowe's flight into exile towards Italy, and in particular to Florence and Northern Italy which had been the home of Machiavelli. Thither we shall follow him, eventually to the Florentine Court of the Grand Duke of Tuscany, uncle and foster father to the orphaned prince, Virginio Orsino, Duke of Bracchiano, for whom Marlowe wrote *Twelfth Night* in celebration of Orsino's visit to Queen Elizabeth in the Christmas of 1600-1.

PART TWO

THE AFTERMATH

THE AFTERMATH

INTRODUCTION

WE NOW ENTER an area in which hypothesis must be relied on to guide us. This is not without precedent. The orthodox case for William Shakespeare of Stratford-upon-Avon relies heavily on hypothesis.

It begins with the hypothesis that he was educated at Stratford-upon-Avon's Free Grammar School, for which no evidence exists other than the traditional tales, that start some seventy years after William Shakespeare's death, with Betterton's information gleaned in his home town confirming that his education was sadly limited. The hypothesis is then necessarily developed that he was largely self-educated. Books, however, were neither cheap nor widely available in such a backwater as little Stratford, and no evidence exists to show that he moved elsewhere before 1593. On the other hand, evidence shows that his father was in straitened circumstances and probably could not afford to have his son educated, nor to lose his support at home. In 1585, when he was aged twenty-one, he became the father of twins, and in 1588 he is named in a lawsuit together with his parents and is still domiciled at Stratford-upon-Avon. Of personal data there is then a blank until March 1595, when he is listed as one receiving payment for the Lord Chamberlain's Men for their performances in the Christmas season of 1594-5 – a prominent position placing him with the leading actor-shareholders of the company, Kempe and Burbage. Despite this prominence, he is not known to have been a member of that company in their records of 1592, 1593 or earlier in 1594, nor has he been traced in any other acting company of the period. This is suggestive of a sudden entry into the players' company at an unusually high level for a man without any previous acting experience.

The sudden emergence of William Shakespeare as an actor is as inexplicable as his sudden emergence as a poet-dramatist of genius. The inter-relationship of these two facts will be put under scrutiny in the following chapter. All the evidence regarding William Shakespeare's known circumstances is taken into careful consideration in developing the ensuing hypothesis concerning his relationship with Christopher Marlowe as his playbroker and 'front man' – a scenario that fits the man from Stratford to a tee!

The common basis of all the multifarious, rival Shakespearean authorship theories is that the identity of the Divine Author, Shakespeare, – a 'concealed poet' deemed to be Bacon, or the Earl of Oxford, or Derby, or Rutland &c., – had been grafted onto the person of the mundane man from Stratford, who cannot sustain this image. For all these hypothetical 'Shakespeares' a pseudonym would have sufficed adequately to enable them to remain unidentified with their poetic and dramatic works – as it did for Voltaire. Only in the case of Christopher Marlowe was there an urgent reason for such an elaborate measure as the adoption of a 'front man' of the same name in order to provide a protective cloak of permanent anonymity for the persecuted Poet.

How did it come about? No one knows. But within the context of this thesis in which all the foregoing evidence indicates that we are on the *right* track at last, since the facts agree with all that the sonnets tell us, corroborated strongly by Dr Hotson's research as well as all that is known about Marlowe's life, we may conjecture with some confidence to present a logical, convincing hypothesis of the manner, firstly, of how William Shakespeare's entry into this history was effected; and, secondly, of where our true author, Christopher Marlowe, went on his journey into exile, and what his activities were during the period of his obscurity.

Orthodox opinion does not for one moment consider the possibility that the name *William Shakespeare* was a pseudonym. This is the very basis of the present thesis, arguing that this is the only reasonable explanation of the conflicting evidence, or lack of it, and it *alone* fits the story that the sonnets tell; that it was a vitally necessary pseudonym for a genius who was in great trouble – the poet-dramatist who was Shakespeare's universally acknowledged forerunner, the 'Morning Star' of the great Elizabethan dramatic era, and hailed as the darling of the Muses.

In the ensuing investigation, it will be self-evident that when Shakespeare is referred to as the *author of the works* known to the world in that name, it is never the Stratford actor who is intended, but our pseudonymous Poet, Christopher Marlowe. As has been remarked, a pseudonym takes on a strong identity of its own, and the name *Shakespeare* is henceforth, for all time, the Author, who is the concealed Poet of the Sonnets, Christopher Marlowe. There are two men encompassed by that name, but only one great poet-dramatist.

In developing this thesis beyond the 'death' of Christopher Marlowe, it is, in the present state of research, necessary to resort to hypothesis, but never is such hypothesis permitted without valid and persuasive evidence to support it. In submitting this thesis, clues are constantly put forward indicating areas of research which offer the prospect to the objective researcher of yet further corroborative evidence in support of the hypothesis. The prospect for future Shakespearean scholars is exciting and most, most worthwhile, for here we are on the track *at last* of the historical truth that has eluded us for so long concerning our greatest poet-dramatist, whose life has been deliberately shrouded in an enigma for reasons of protection, that no longer apply. It is time to rescue him from oblivion and set him free.

XXII

ENTER WILLIAM SHAKESPEARE

IN THE LITTLE TOWN of Stratford-upon-Avon everyone within his class of traders and craftsmen would have known each other, and this would certainly have been true of the tanner, Henry Field, in the allied trade of tanning leather, and the glover working in leather, John Shakespeare, father of William. Henry Field's son Richard had gone to London as a lad to be apprenticed for the space of seven years to the Huguenot printer, Thomas Vautrollier, of excellent repute, who had settled in London on being admitted to the Company of Stationers in 1564. By 1570 he was established with a famous Black Letter press in Blackfriars, where he published books of notable quality such as would have excited the interest of the London intelligentsia and free-thinkers. During his career Vautrollier was sometimes in trouble with the Star Chamber – for publishing Giordano Bruno's *Last Tromp* dedicated to Sir Philip Sidney, and he was twice fined 10s for publishing Luther's *Sermons* without a licence. An erudite man, he also translated books himself. His fame as a printer of fine books spread, and on the recommendation of the General Assembly of the Church of Scotland he was invited by King James to print under his royal grant of 'a licence and privilege', if he would come to Scotland. [1]

In about 1580 Vautrollier took up King James's invitation and journeyed to Edinburgh taking a large number of books with him, and leaving his printing press in the capable hands of his wife, and Richard Field who apparently married Vautrollier's daughter Jakin in 1588. When Vautrollier died in 1587 Field succeeded him as master-printer at the house in Blackfriars, using the same device as his trade mark – an anchor with the motto *Anchora Spei* (Anchors of Hope). It seems that he soon became a widower for in the records of the Stationers' Company of 1590 Field is listed as married to Vautrollier's widow. He carried on the Vautrollier tradition, specializing in the publication of French and Spanish books. The first entry to him in the Stationers' Register on 24th December 1588 is for 'a booke in *French*, intitled: "Le politique reformé".' [2] This might well have been of interest to Marlowe in his contacts with the French court as an agent for Walsingham at this time. He would probably have been interested in other books Field brought out, such as North's *Plutarch*, Puttenham's *Arte of English Poesie*, a handsome edition in Italic print of Ovid's *Metamorphoses*, and Harrington's translation of *Orlando Furioso*.

Immigrant communities tend to keep close contact, and it is likely that Thomas Vautrollier and his family knew Huguenots living in Canterbury, which city was the gateway and hostelry for the stream of travellers passing through it on their way in and out of the kingdom to and from the Continent. Vautrollier was undoubtedly a man of progressive ideas, as evidenced in his publications. Frances Yates has shown in her fascinating book *The Rosicrucian Enlightenment* (1972) that progressive printers on the Continent were members of secret societies, such as the Family of Love, which gave protection to those holding progressive views, for the printers who published advanced works were in the firing line of repressive authorities. Their presses were at the risk of being closed down or destroyed, and the printers faced persecution. Yates' evidence is relevant.

'We know that the Family of Love was a secret society, which undoubtedly had a real existence and organization arising out of the situation in the Netherlands in the late sixteenth century. We know that many well-known people were secretly members of this sect or society, which allowed its members to belong ostensibly to any religious denomination while secretly maintaining their affiliation with the Family. These attitudes of the Family of Love have something in common with those of Freemasonry. We know that secret membership of the Family was widespread among printers, that, for example, the great Antwerp printer, Plantin, was a member of this sect and keen on propagating it through publishing works of those in sympathy with it. . . the De Bry family of printers, who had connections with the Plantin firm, might have been Familists.' ³

Many of the advanced works of Francis Bacon were first published on the Continent by progressive Continental printers. It was De Bry who in 1590 printed Thomas Hariot's report on *The New Found Land of Virginia,* which he dedicated to Raleigh, and for which De Bry executed the beautiful engravings of John White's watercolour paintings of Indian life and flora. The originals of these exquisite paintings had probably once adorned the so-named 'White Staircase' in Thomas Walsingham's manor house, Scadbury, as has been suggested by Virginia Stern. ⁴ These progressive intellectuals shared interests and maintained communications with each other in a world of close circles wherein free thought was stimulated and protected, and this embraced the Continent. There was contact across Europe by correspondence among the *illuminati* or *cognoscenti,* as the free-thinkers were known. This is the historical background we have to bear in mind.

Clearly Richard Field had inherited both his philosophy and ideals, as well as his business and his wife from the progressive printer, Thomas Vautrollier. Mutual ideological sympathy as well as the excellence of his press would have attracted Marlowe to bring his *Venus and Adonis* to Richard Field, who registered the poem anonymously, as was common practice, on 18th April 1593, one month before Marlowe's arrest. This poem became the vehicle for the launching of his protective pseudonym, 'William Shakespeare', the signature added to the dedication, but not on the title-page. The poem may already have been set in print so that only the page of dedication to Southampton needed to be added, for it was published very shortly after the Deptford 'murder' – perhaps only a week or ten days later. There can be little doubt that Richard Field lent his co-operation to the launching of the pseudonym. This collusion in secrecy was entirely in the tradition of progressive printers.

Precedents for the adoption of pseudonyms by those who were fleeing from religious persecution are found in the lives of several notable free-thinkers of the period who had their writings published by progressive printers on the Continent. Research on the heretics who adopted pseudonyms is presented in George Huntston Williams' book, *The Radical Reformation* (1962). These included, Casper Schwenkenfeld *alias* Eliander; Paulo Ricci *alias* Camillus Renatus; Bernardino Ochino *alias* Antonius Corvinus; Sebastian Costello *alias* Martin Bellius; Michael Servitus *alias* Michel de Villeneuve, whose heretical book *The Restoration of Christianity* brought him to the stake when the author's identity was discovered. Hunted by the Inquisition he fled to Geneva and threw himself onto the mercy of Calvin, who responded by doing the work of the Inquisition for them and burning him. Giordano Bruno had enjoyed a long run of freedom to express his unorthodox religious ideas without the pro-tective cloak of a pseudonym, welcomed and fêted in London and Paris (whence he eventually had to flee), in Poland and Germany; but by 1592 he was languishing in a prison in Rome, and died at the stake in 1600. Marlowe must have been well aware of the dangers he faced.

Field ran no risk so long as the pseudonymous identity of William Shakespeare remained a close secret, for his poem was not a heretical writing. Hovering near the stricken Poet, and perhaps instrumental in successfully launching the pseudonym so that there was no breath of suspicious gossip as to who this new poet, William Shakespeare, might be, was also Francis Bacon. Marlowe was an important member of Bacon's secret society, the Freemasons, alongside his membership of Raleigh's parallel circle, The School of Night; the former an ethical, ecumenical, highly secret organisation with strict rules to ensure the protection of its members; the latter a free-thinkers' debating acad-emy devoted to the pursuit of the study of advanced learning. Freemasonry is the subject of the sequel to this book, in which irrefutable evidence is presented revealing that the First folio, dedicated to the then Grand Master of the Freemasons, the Earl of Pembroke, was a Masonic publication, and its defer-ment until seven years after the death of William Shakespeare of Stratford-upon-Avon was a deliberate precaution. But this is to anticipate.

In 1592 Francis Bacon and his brother Anthony, recently returned from the Continent, had begun working for the Earl of Essex as his political advisers, Anthony continuing to provide intelligence for the Earl as he had done for Lord Burghley and Sir Francis Walsingham during his long residence abroad, mainly in France. It was probably Anthony Bacon who had first got to know Marlowe through their intelligence work, and introduced him to Francis, whereupon these three like-minded men collaborated in the development of Freemasonry. We have no evidence that the Earl of Essex was among those of the nobility who became Freemasons, but his personal association with both the Bacon brothers who headed this society and were deeply concerned about Marlowe's plight, and the fact that Essex's bosom friend was the young Earl of Southampton with whom he had been brought up by Lord Burghley as a Ward of Court, suggests that the latter's co-operation in accepting the dedication of the new, pseudonymous poet would readily have been obtained.

Essex was by now married to Frances, daughter of Sir Francis Walsingham and widow of Sir Philip Sidney, a notable free-thinker in his day. She was Sir Francis's only child, and her cousin Thomas Walsingham stood in this relationship as a son from the time of his own father's death in 1584. At Sir Francis Walsingham's funeral in 1590 Thomas was chief mourner; indeed Watson's funeral ode to his patron, Sir Francis, is dedicated in the Latin original to Thomas Walsingham, and in the English translation to Lady Frances, as though to a son and a daughter of the deceased. We have here an undeniably close family circle including Thomas Walsingham, into which Essex had married.

It is sometimes argued by scholars that Shakespeare's allegiance, if he had any, was to the Essex faction. At this time there may have been a shift in his allegiance from Raleigh to Essex if the latter aided him in the important matter of effecting the secure establishment of the pseudonymous dedication to Southampton. We have no definite evidence to go on, but there is a hint that Raleigh was critical of Marlowe over his too outspoken comments about scientific matters (condemned as heresy) obliquely expressed in a satirical poem called *The Lie*, which is attributed to Raleigh. This exceedingly bitter poem of thirteen verses ends obscurely on an apparently personal note.

> So when thou hast, as I
> Commanded thee, done blabbing–
> Although to give the lie
> Deserves no less than stabbing –
> Stab at thee he that will,
> No stab the soul can kill.

It has been conjecturally dated to 1596, two years after the Cerne Abbas inquiry. I am not proposing to discuss this further, but there is an invitation to research here.

The Earl of Southampton is known to have actively assisted the escape from justice of the Danvers brothers, Sir Henry and Sir Charles Danvers, for their murder of Henry Long in a violent quarrel in October 1594, when they sought refuge from the hue and cry by fleeing to Southampton's country house, Titchfield. The Earl hid them, and then managed to see them shipped safely to France, where they lived in exile until their eventual pardon. Southampton had to face the judicial investigation concerning their escape, but fortunately, his step-father, Sir Thomas Heneage (who was in charge of the espionage service after the death of Sir Francis Walsingham in 1590) had great influence with the Queen and Privy Council, and was thus able to persuade them to exonerate Southampton. [5] This incident shows that he was a young man willing to take risks *to help friends in need, to escape the clutches of the law.*

How close Southampton's friendship with Marlowe was we do not know, though he must obviously have had some relationship with the 'famous gracer of Tragedians' whose plays the theatre-loving young Earl would certainly have seen and admired, and who had written him seventeen sonnets in which some degree of intimacy is reflected. *Venus and Adonis* shows signs of being an early poem, written probably in 1590 at the time of the sonnets to Southampton, but was left in manuscript until brought to Field. The speed with which the publication of this poem followed the Deptford 'death' of Marlowe would have helped the subterfuge; and the smoothness with which all this was orchestrated reflects the willingness of several influential hands to help the persecuted poet-dramatist. Concern about Marlowe's danger would undoubtedly have percolated through the Court from the moment the news of his arrest was known.

Although he was immediately granted bail, Marlowe could not have entertained any doubt that he was in grave danger and that this period of respite was but the skilful playing of the fish on the hook in order to entrap yet bigger fish in the circle of free-thinkers. Marlowe and Walsingham would therefore have lost no time in laying their plans, and for Marlowe this included the adoption of a pseudonym to ensure the continued performance of his plays, giving them life, 'Where breath most breathes, even in the mouths of men.' His main thought next to his own safety would have been for his works.

There is a recollection of this in *Sonnet 48:* 'How careful was I when I took my way./ Each trifle under truest bars to thrust', one of these 'trifles' being his *Venus and Adonis.* Someone, perhaps even Marlowe himself, had evidently visited Field to obtain his co-operation and his silence in the matter of publishing the poem under the chosen pseudonym. It is conceivable that it may have been agreed in discussion there and then that one William Shakespeare of Stratford-upon-Avon, a man well-known to Field, would be enlisted to act as broker for the plays under his name. The hand of Fate, so evident in Marlowe's life, may perhaps have brought William Shakespeare to London at this very time under the small cloud of trouble that the traditional tales tell us beset him and made him leave his home town for a spell to seek his fortune in the great city of London.

This very year, 1593, was a peak period of economic depression in Stratford that had the little town in its grip for the whole decade of the 1590's. In 1593 John Shakespeare was still burdened with debts from which he seems to have been unable to struggle free, and by the time of his death in 1601 almost half of the population of Stratford were impoverished. This background lends credence to the traditional story of William Shakespeare's poaching incident and the evasion of troubles in Stratford that impelled his flight to London. In such circumstances, a man with a family to support would have leapt at an offer of a secure position with an acting company as their broker for playscripts of assured quality to be brought to him from a regular source, and, moreover, money to invest as a shareholder – for that is how we find William Shakespeare placed from the very first when he joined the Lord Chamberlain's company with no evidence of any prior experience as an actor.

One of the few people who would have been known to him, arriving as a stranger in the metropolis, would have been his fellow townsman, Richard Field. Orthodox scholars have also assumed that William Shakespeare came from Stratford-upon-Avon to his old acquaintance Richard Field to offer him his poem, composed as 'the first heir of my invention', asking Field to print it with a dedication to the Earl of Southampton. In that case, one might well imagine that Field would have raised a surprised eyebrow. Could such talent have been hidden in little Stratford all this time?

Scholars have combed the records for evidence of William Shakespeare grooming himself for the authorship of the works, beginning with his astonishing emergence as the writer of *Venus and Adonis*. But there is none. All is pure hypothesis. In such a case the scales are weighted against him. On the other hand, absolutely everything we know about William Shakespeare as a man, from documentary evidence, testifies that this man from Stratford was ideally suited to the role of front man for the pseudonymous, persecuted author. He was discreet and trustworthy, for the Burbages commended him as a 'deserving' fellow as housekeeper of their theatrical business; he was not a Londoner, hence not known in the city or in theatrical circles, and Stratford-upon-Avon was far enough away to shield him in some obscurity; he was shrewd and would safeguard his own interests, and he must have possessed integrity as well as native wit. Moreover, it was a rare piece of luck that he possessed such an appropriate name, easily adapted to the implication of the spear-shaker who shakes his spear at ignorance. Ben Jonson's reference in his dedicatory encomium in the First Folio expresses it when he describes Shakespeare as seeming 'to shake a Lance,/ As brandish't at the eyes of ignorance', and Marlowe declared this same Renaissance concept, so characteristic of the freethinkers, in his Prologue to *The Jew of Malta*, 'I hold there is no sin but ignorance'. The hyphenating of the name Shake-speare also connotes this. Finding his ideal man in William Shakespeare of Stratford-upon-Avon may have been the silver lining to Marlowe's dark cloud in those troubled days.

The choice of pseudonym is very important to a writer, as was the choice of the patron for this first work launching the pseudonym. The seventeen sonnets to the young Earl of Southampton in 1590 reveal a degree of intimacy between the Poet and Henry Wriothesley somewhat reminiscent of the admonishing tone used towards young 'Prince' Will Hatcliffe.

Music to hear, why hear'st thou music sadly?

Sonnet 8

Make thee another self for love of me,

Sonnet 10

O that you were yourself, but love you are
No longer yours, than you yourself here live,

. . .

O none but unthrifts, dear my love you know,
You had a Father, let your Son say so.

Sonnet 13

This is surely not the unknown man from Stratford speaking to the scion of a noble house, but the cajoling voice of the famous poet-dramatist, Master of Arts of Cambridge University, who numbered Raleigh and the Earl of Northumberland among his friends, and who knew Lord Burghley's mind in matters of State, as also in this personal affair; a man familiar with the Court and a trusted servant of the Queen's government. Such a man could adopt a tone of authority with the young Earl with ease and grace. Such a man could write the dedicatory epistle for his *Venus and Adonis* to the Earl of Southampton with complete naturalness. Its object was twofold: to launch his pseudonym, and to draw suspicion away from his patron, Thomas Walsingham, who stood exposed by his close connection with the Deptford 'murder'.

TO THE
RIGHT HONORABLE HENRIE WRIOTHESLEY,
EARLE OF SOUTHAMPTON, AND BARON OF TITCHFIELD

RIGHT HONOURABLE,
I KNOW not how I shall offend in dedicating my unpolisht lines to your Lordship, nor how the worlde will censure mee for choosing so strong a proppe to support so weake a burthen, onelye if your Honour seeme but pleased, I account my selfe highly praised, and vowe to take advantage of all idle houres, till I have honoured you with some graver labour. But if the first heire of my invention prove deformed, I shall be sorie it had so noble a god-father: and never after eare so barren a land, for feare it yeeld me still so bad a harvest, I leave it to your Honourable survey, and your Honor to your hearts content which I wish may alwaies answere your owne wish, and the worlds hopefull expectation.

Your Honors in all dutie,

WILLIAM SHAKESPEARE.

356

The introduction of the name is carefully presented as though this is a real person, and appears only as a signature to the dedication. On the title-page is printed VENUS AND ADONIS and underneath it his chosen motto:

Vilia miretur vulgus: mihi flavus Apollo
Pocula Castalia plena ministret aqua

Which in Marlowe's translation from Ovid's *Amores* reads:

Let base conceited wits admire vile things,
Fair Phoebus lead me to the Muses' springs.
About my head be quivering myrtle wound,
And in sad lovers' heads let me be found.
The living, not the dead, can envy bite,
For after death all men receive their right.
Then though death rakes my bones in funeral fire,
I'll live, and as he pulls me down mount higher.

These words speak a passionate challenge to Death. It is surely remarkable that the passage has an almost prophetic ring when applied to Marlowe's tragedy. The motto was a cryptic choice, for only those knowing the whole poem and his own tragic circumstances could appreciate the significance of culling the first two lines from this passage as his motto for the publication launching his pseudonym upon the world. Marlowe's *Elegies* were banned in England, considered too erotic, but the amorous poem *Venus and Adonis* went into sixteen editions between 1593 and 1640, spreading the fame of the new poet, William Shakespeare, far and wide.

William Shakespeare Emerges as an Actor

The summer of 1593 saw the escalation of the plague, which had been simmering in sporadic outbursts since 1592, into the full-blown epidemic of the long plague that lasted until the summer of 1594. The unprecedented upheaval caused to the actors' companies, who were forced to go on tour when all the London theatres were closed by government order, created the ideal conditions for William Shakespeare's unobtrusive entry into the Lord Chamberlain's company with whom Edward Alleyn, Marlowe's close associate in the theatrical world and the greatest and most influential actor of his day, had been working all through the plague year.

Alleyn's own company, the Lord Admiral's Men, had mostly gone abroad on a Continental tour, but Alleyn had opted to remain behind having recently married Philip Henslowe's step-daughter, Joan Woodward, having also gained what I believe was a half share or moiety in the ownership of the Rose theatre of Bankside thereby. He had begun his management of this company when it

357

was still Lord Strange's Men, which in quick succession became the Earl of Derby's Men when Lord Strange succeeded to his title until, at his tragic death in 1594, they passed to the patronage of the Lord Chamberlain. This is when Shakespeare joined them.

Some idea of the enormous disorganisation resulting from the plague, which affected all the actors' companies based in London, is obtained from Philip Henslowe's letters to his 'sonne', as he affectionately called his son-in-law Edward Alleyn, who was on a protracted tour of the country at the head of Lord Strange's Men. Henslowe, and Alleyn's young wife, remained in London, his Rose theatre shut down, gradually becoming poorer, as he sadly complains, for even his tenants could no longer pay their rents. He writes to Alleyn that the Earl of Pembroke's Men, who had not gone on tour, were so impoverished that they were reduced to selling off their stock of theatrical properties and apparel; [6] and their valuable playscripts were sold to the publishers, including Marlowe's *Edward the Second,* and the two plays on the Wars of the Roses which later became *Henry VI, Parts 2 and 3* in the First Folio.

In the period of flux and reorganisation as the plague receded during 1594 the entry of William Shakespeare would have been easily effected, and anyone offering money for a share in an acting company, with perhaps the added bonus of a good playscript, would have been eagerly welcomed. The testimony of Betterton concerning William Shakespeare's prowess as an actor was that 'the top of his performance was the Ghost in his own *Hamlet',* [7] as gleaned on his fact-gathering visit to Stratford-upon-Avon *circa* 1690, which suggests strongly that his acceptance into such a top-rating company as the Lord Chamberlain's Men was not on the basis of his ability (or his experience, of which there is no evidence) as an actor. He was seemingly able to buy himself in as a share-holder from the outset, for his name immediately appears as one of the payees for the company listed in the Chamber Accounts together with the seasoned actors, Kempe and Burbage, who now headed the reformed Lord Chamberlain's Men. This first mention of his name shows him in the light of a company shareholder receiving payment for performances given at Court on 26th and 27th December 1594, for which they did not receive remuneration until 15th March 1594/5. It is the only time Shakespeare is ever mentioned in this capacity as a company payee, but here he is, though apparently still fairly new to the company:

'To Willm Kempe Willm Shakespeare & Richard Burbage
seruantes to the Lord Chambleyne . . .' [8]

Commenting on this, 'the first official notice of Shakespeare as a player', F.E. Halliday writes: 'If he were with Strange's before this, as he may have been, it is odd that he should not have been mentioned in the cast of *The Deadly Sins,* in the Licence of 1593, or by Alleyn in his correspondence, for after all Strange's had acted one of his plays, and perhaps more, while Greene's oblique attack and Chettle's apology of 1592 testify to his importance.' [9]

This is a lucid comment from a great orthodox Shakespearean scholar, but it reflects the *in circulo* thinking that bedevils the orthodox concept of Shakespeare of Stratford-upon-Avon as both the actor and the author. The play that Strange's Men had acted to which Halliday refers is that named by Henslowe in his *Diary* as *harey the vj* performed as a new play at the Rose on 3rd March 1591/2, which Dr Allison Gaw has identified as Marlowe's play, later combined into the *Henry VI* trilogy as *Part 1;* and Greene's 'oblique attack' has been irrefutably proved to be an attack, not on William Shakespeare as 'Shake-scene', but on his hated 'king of the stage', Edward Alleyn, while Chettle's apology (for having printed Greene's libellous tirade) is equally concerned with Alleyn, not Shakespeare.* In 1592, when Greene's vitriolic attack in print became a major London scandal, Shakespeare had not yet made his appearance, as Halliday's evidence demonstrates.

All the evidence we have suggests that William Shakespeare was not an experienced or talented actor, but that he was accepted into the Lord Chamberlain's company by negotiation and on the basis of some perquisite, such as down-payment of a sum of money for a share in the company, and probably including the offer of the playscript of *Titus Andronicus* and a promise of further plays of this quality for which he would be broker.

The inference of the interesting theatrical history of *Titus Andronicus* suggests that it was with this 'Shakespeare' play that William Shakespeare came to buy himself into the players' company he joined, and which became his permanent home. The title-page of John Danter's 1594 quarto edition of *Titus Andronicus* states: 'As it was Plaide by the Right Honourable the Earle of Darbie, Earle of Pembrooke, and Earle of Sussex their Seruants', testifying that *it changed hands three times,* though not in that order, for it was the Sussex's Men who played it first as a new play. We are able to trace this play's early theatrical history precisely in Henslowe's *Diary,* beginning with the Christmas season of 1593-4 when the official restriction of playing during the long plague was lifted as colder weather reduced the incidence of infection and people longed for some festive entertainment.

At this Christmas there is no sign of the Earl of Derby's Men (as Lord Strange's had become on the 15th September) for they had probably gone to play at one of the Earl's stately homes in Lancashire for Christmas as was their wont, and Edward Alleyn returned to London alone awaiting the home-coming of his own company from abroad.

Meanwhile he was acting with the resident company at the Rose, who were the Earl of Sussex's Men, and this company first presented *Titus Andronicus* as

---

* Footnote: Greene's reference to one 'Shake-scene' has now been definitively identified as Edward Alleyn, not Shakespeare. See pp. 32 – 36, citing my research in *Christopher Marlowe and Edward Alleyn* (1993) where the evidence is set forth in detail in Chapters V, VI, VII, and further confirmed in Chapters VII and IX. The case is irrefutable.

a new play, giving three performances in January 1593/4, as recorded by Henslowe:

> In the name of god Amen begninge th 27 of ....[sic]
> desemb[er]1593 the earle of susex his men

———▶ *ne*   Rd at titus & ondronicus the 23 of Jenewary ....iij^{li} viijs

              Rd at buckengam the 27 of Jenewar ....xviijs

———▶   Rd at titus & ondronicus the 28 of Jenewar............xxxx s

              Rd at abrame & lotte the 31 of Jeneway 1593........xijs

              Rd at the Jewe of malta the 4 of febery 1593 ....ls

———▶   Rd at titus & ondronicus the 6 of febery 1593........xxxx^S [10]

We have to remember that Henslowe's 1593 is really 1594, for the Elizabethan New Year did not begin until Lady Day, 25th March. Henslowe is very inconsistent in his dating of the New Year, but in this instance he is observing the Elizabethan Calendar. The performance of *The Jew of Malta* is a sure indication that Alleyn was acting with the company temporarily, for this was his own playscript and no one else ever played the part of the Jew, Barabas, while Alleyn was alive. His personal standing as an actor meant that he was always in demand, and at such times of flux owing to the plague disruption he was able to move freely from one company to another, whilst always retaining his allegiance to his patron, the Lord Admiral.

Titus Andronicus was, I believe, that work on which Marlowe had collaborated with Kyd when 'wrytinge in one chamber twoe years synce', as Kyd had told Lord Puckering in his first Letter, in which he was probably exaggerating the distance of time in order to distance himself the more from his former association with his 'Atheist' friend Marlowe. The 'Lord' for whom Kyd worked in the last years of his life was undoubtedly the Earl of Sussex, who perfectly fits his description of this nobleman's horrified reaction to Marlowe's 'Atheism' when news of this became current early in 1593. Kyd dedicated his last work *Cornélie* to the Countess of Sussex, probably in the pathetic hope that his Lady would intervene on his behalf with her Lord to reinstate Kyd in his patronage after the disgrace of his involvement with Marlowe's Atheism had led to his dismissal.* *Titus Andronicus* is in the same genre of revenge tragedy as Kyd's highly successful *The Spanish Tragedy.* The play was, I suggest, still

* Foot-note: In my biography *In Search of Christopher Marlowe* (1965) I had followed the suggestion of other scholars who claim that Lord Strange was Kyd's 'Lord'. I there cited Kyd's part-authorship of the play Sir Thomas More as evidence to clinch this identification. However, since there were altogether six playwrights involved in writing this collaborative play, and they were certainly not all in Lord Strange's patronage, for whose company it was being written, this could not be said to apply to Kyd either. Lord Strange would not have cast Kyd off simply because of his association with Marlowe, the 'Atheist'. This behaviour consorts with the views of Sussex, a thoroughly orthodox and reactionary nobleman.

in process of writing and Marlowe had taken the script with him to finish it but, as was a common custom, the unfinished play may have been promised as a new play to the Sussex's Men, so that the completed script was owed to them. This could have been given to William Shakespeare to deal with the company, since Kyd, if not yet dead, was dying, and Marlowe was dead to the world. Shakespeare very likely retained ownership of the playscript when presenting it to Sussex's Men, who lost no time in performing it as soon as the restrictions on the theatres were lifted.

However, it was not Sussex's Men, an inferior company, with whom ideally William Shakespeare was to remain as the pseudonymous author's broker, but with Derby's Men, who were in the patronage of the young Earl who had been a member of Raleigh's 'School of Night' and who had known Marlowe. This company was to remain through all its vicissitudes under the successive patronage of noblemen sympathetic to the free-thinkers. When Derby died soon after attaining his earldom, they passed briefly to the old Lord Hunsdon, Henry Carey, then Lord Chamberlain, a good friend of the Derbys, and on his death in July 1596 to his son, Sir George Carey, who was a member of Raleigh's circle, who did not immediately gain the vacant office of Lord Chamberlain, which was given to the old Lord Cobham, so that the players were for a while Lord Hunsdon's Men. Danter's quarto of *Romeo and Juliet* of 1597 names Shakespeare's company as 'the L. of Hunsdon his Seruants'. On the death of Cobham, the coveted office of Lord Chamberlain passed to their patron, Lord Hunsdon, and they became once again the Lord Chamberlain's Men.

What is important, I suggest, in all this change of patronage is that it was always in the service of noblemen associated with the free-thinkers of the Raleigh-Northumberland-Hariot-Marlowe circle that this company of players remained until the accession of King James, when they were elevated to the King's Men – and King James became, probably by Bacon's persuasion, a Freemason 'by royal prerogative'. And it was *this* company with which Shakespeare worked all his professional life.

How did he transfer from the Earl of Sussex's Men to the Lord Chamberlain's? Perhaps by means of his interest in *Titus Andronicus* is a suggestion that the theatrical history of this play offers as a feasible scenario in a reconstruction that is necessarily largely hypothetical, though based on the recorded evidence available. Henslowe's *Diary* provides us with the evidence again of the next stage in the theatrical history of this play which records the change-over of ownership of the playscript from Sussex's Men to the Lord Chamberlain's. In these transactions the play probably remained with William Shakespeare as broker. The implication is that the deal made was for Sussex's Men to release the play, they having had the benefit of the highest box office receipts for its performance as a *new* play, which always boosted the takings (and as will be seen it now had a much lower box office rating) while the broker William Shakespeare retained an interest in it for himself, by allowing the Sussex's Men to perform it, but not to own it. This time it is being performed not at the Rose, but at the theatre at Newington Butts.

> In the name of god Amen begininge at newing
> ton my Lord Admeralle men & my Lorde chamberlen
> men As ffolowethe 1594

3 of June 1594	Rd at heaster & asheweros	viijs
4 of June 1594	Rd at the Jewe of malta	xs
5 of June 1594	Rd at andronicous	xijs
6 of June 1594	Rd at cvtlacke	xjs
8 of June 1594 ne-	Rd at bellendon	xvijs
9 of June 1594	Rd at hamlet	viijs
10 of June 1594	Rd at heaster	vs
11 of June 1594	Rd at the tamynge of A shrowe	ixs
12 of June 1594	Rd at andronicous	vijs
13 of June 1594	Rd at the Jewe	iiijs [11]

Thereupon follow two days' break from playing, and when Henslowe resumes his records on 15th June the poor box office receipts experienced at Newington Butts, where even a new play only took 17s, are dramatically upgraded, so that one may assume they are back at the Rose. The reason for their ten days' playing at the outlying Newington Butts theatre is obscure. The Lord Admiral's Men being now returned, we may also assume that it is this, Alleyn's own company, which is now resident at the Rose, for the repertoire they play consists only of Lord Admiral's plays. [12] Gone are *Titus Andronicus* and *Hamlet* (this is Kyd's old play which Nashe identifies satirically as Kyd's work in his Preface to *Menaphon*). Gone also *The Taming of a Shrew* (as distinct from *The Shrew*) an old play which plagiarizes Marlowe's works wholesale stealing entire passages from his plays, and gone is what Henslowe calls *'heaster & asheweros'*, but *The Jew of Malta* remains as always with Alleyn. What is interesting is that all these old plays which later re-emerge rewritten by Shakespeare were in the possession of the Lord Chamberlain's Men, so that William Shakespeare had access to these scripts and could send/lend them to his concealed master dramatist who returned them new-minted for the benefit of the Lord Chamberlain's to perform.

What is also interesting is that Edward Alleyn is the one constant figure in the association with *Titus Andronicus,* first with Sussex's Men, with whom he was playing *The Jew of Malta,* and then with the Lord Chamberlain's together with his own company. Did he perhaps lend a helping hand in these transactions? It may well be that Alleyn acted as midwife to the establishment of William Shakespeare as an actor, for Alleyn had known Marlowe intimately, as my research presented elsewhere has established. [13] It would have been too dangerous for the new poet-dramatist Shakespeare to have become associated with Alleyn's company, which was famous for its performance of Marlowe's plays, *Tamburlaine, Dr Faustus, The Jew of Malta, The Massacre at Paris,* all written with Edward Alleyn's particular histrionic gifts in mind, of some of which he himself owned the playscripts. We know that Alleyn purchased a copy of the *Sonnets* when they were hot off the press in 1609. Did he know something?

This reconstruction of how William Shakespeare came to be ensconced securely in the Lord Chamberlain's company is hypothetical, but it rests on the evidence of theatrical history, and is supported by the entire foregoing thesis of the autobiographical story of the *Sonnets,* making one logical and credible whole. I may be wrong about the part *Titus Andronicus* played in this scenario, but it is both plausible and self-evident that this could have happened. This play is in the same category as Kyd's popular gory drama *The Spanish Tragedy.* Scholarly arguments attributing *Titus Andronicus* to William Shakespeare in collaboration with Kyd have been advanced, even though no shred of evidence for William Shakespeare's acquaintance with Thomas Kyd exists. In Marlowe's case such evidence does exist. In the context of the present thesis it is yet another piece of evidence supporting his authorship of the whole Shakespearean canon, beginning with this revenge tragedy *Titus Andronicus* in 1594, the most Marlovian of all the Shakespeare plays, and more frequently accredited to his hand than any other by disputing scholars. *Titus Andronicus* is a play of some significance in this thesis and is further discussed in the sequel to this book in the light of Dame Frances Yates' remarkable research in her *ASTRAEA: The Imperial Theme of the Sixteenth Century* (1975).

The long plague would have played its part in this story by providing advantageous conditions that facilitated the unobtrusive establishment of the pseudonymous Poet's effective front man. William Shakespeare now being installed with the Lord Chamberlain's company, with whom he remained until his retirement at the age of about forty-eight, we will, for the moment, leave him there, and follow our Poet as he journeys into his exile, to see if we can detect where he is going, and what he may be doing.

363

XXIII

THE ITALIAN YEARS

WE NOW EMBARK on a period of obscurity when we have to rely on what the *Sonnets of Exile* convey to us, supported by the internal evidence of the Italian-inspired plays of the mature Shakespearean canon. Significantly, this evidence clarifies and explains textual problems, and it underlines unequivocally that the thesis presented is 'on course', for orthodox scholars have themselves presented evidence of an unmistakable Italian influence in the plays of the very period we are now investigating. Once again, our redoubtable guide, Dr Hotson, is at the helm, this time steering us on a voyage to Italy.

Having settled his affairs with Richard Field, and leaving his fate (rather unwisely) in the hands of the three men who were Walsingham's agents, we may assume that Marlowe left the shores of England from Deptford at some time during that fatal day, and it was probably on board ship that he wrote his first verse-letter to his Patron to acknowledge the enormous debt of gratitude he owed him, addressing his dear friend and benefactor with a full heart:

> Lord of my love, to whom in vassalage
> Thy merit hath my duty strongly knit,
> To thee I send this written ambassage
> To witness duty, not to show my wit;
> Duty so great, which wit so poor as mine
> May make seem bare in wanting words to show it,
> But that I hope some good conceit of thine
> In thy soul's thought (all naked) will bestow it;
> Till whatsoever star that guides my moving
> Points on me graciously with fair aspect,
> And puts apparel on my tatter'd loving,
> To show me worthy of thy sweet respect.
> > Then may I dare to boast how I do love thee,
> > Till then, not show my head where thou mayst prove me.

Sonnet 26

A long journey lay ahead of him, one that he had taken some four years before with eager interest to view Rome's antique 'pyramids', but this time with a burden of insupportable grief, for he knew it was destined to divide him for an indeterminately long period by 'large lengths of miles' of 'both sea and land' from his Patron, his homeland and all whom he knew and loved there. Much of it he travelled on horseback, the bitter taste of banishment making the prospect ahead bleak and daunting.

The evidence adduced from the Italian reflections in several of the plays attributed to the next few years, suggests that it must have been to Italy that he travelled, in particular, to Northern Italy, his first place of residence probably the ancient city of Verona. The first fruit of the Italian experience was almost certainly *The Two Gentlemen of Verona,* which was not printed before the First Folio, but was an early play in the 'Shakespearean' canon and is deemed by orthodox scholars as 'historically significant' in the development of Shakespeare's art.

> 'It was a beginning; it was an experiment which led to much, it was
> a repertory of dramatic ideas; it brought Italy and romance into
> Shakespeare's comedies.'[1]

So wrote Edward Dowden. It is also the first play for which a plot was chosen in which we encounter the theme of banishment and, added to it, supposed death, though here handled with a light touch.

The dating of Shakespeare's plays is arbitrary, even those appearing in quarto editions providing but an upper limit of composition before the date of publication. Often plays underwent revision, thus obscuring their origin as earlier works. The 1598 quarto of *Love's Labour's Lost* declares it to be 'newly corrected and augmented'. This delightfully witty comedy was, I believe, written before 1593, distilled from Marlowe's experience of the court of the French King Henry of Navarre,[2] which he has idealized, changing the name of this Protestant hero to Ferdinand, to replicate just such an esoteric academy of noblemen as the English 'School of Night'. He satirizes this with tongue-in-cheek comic invention, including a take-off of the tremendous sonneteering vogue sweeping London from 1591. It was obviously written for private performance to delight his free-thinking friends, perhaps to be played before his patron, Walsingham, at Scadbury for the Christmas festivities of 1592-3. By contrast, *The Massacre at Paris* is a bitter tragedy dramatizing the political intrigues of the factions at the court of France jostling for power under the cloak of religion. It was the last play he sold to Edward Alleyn and given its first performance at the Rose on 30th January 1593, which Marlowe would probably have attended.

If we had the original forms of both these contrasted plays we would be able to note his dramatic development, in particular the emergence of that witty lighter vein that marked the burgeoning maturity of his genius at the time when his personal tragedy overwhelmed him. Clear evidence of this leap in his achievement is seen in the two sestiads of *Hero and Leander,* which far outdoes his achievement in *Venus and Adonis,* which was probably written in 1590/91. Not to disparage the latter, of the two poems *Hero and Leander* is the incomparable masterpiece. Dr Boas has been moved to comment in assessing Marlowe's superb achievement in *Hero and Leander:*

'If we are to speculate about what might have been, we may perhaps regret that Marlowe did not make a play out of the tragic story, and provide what might have been a companion piece to Romeo and Juliet, as Edward II is to Richard II.'[3]

In a different genre, I believe *Hero and Leander* is the pair to *Romeo and Juliet*. Having his unfinished romantic poem in mind, it would have been the natural evolutionary next step for him to take from the romantic comedy of *The Two Gentlemen* to a romantic tragedy about two star-crossed lovers, also set in Verona. His love of reworking a theme, providing either a like companion piece, or the same in contrasted mode, is a typical trait that emerges strongly when we see the complete cycle of the works from early Marlowe to late Shakespeare.

The Italian influence in the plays is doubly important; it points us in the right direction for his years of exile; and in this fortuitous exposure to the great centre and birthplace of the Renaissance his dramatic art was enormously enriched. Marlowe was the brilliant child of the English Renaissance that flowered late; but to come to Italy itself where it had all begun and become immersed in the Italian atmosphere was a bonus that was reaped in the golden comedies and romantic tragedies of this middle period, which he based on the novels of Boccaccio and Fiorento, both Florentines, Bandello, a Lombard, and Giraldo Cinthio, from Ferrara. These Northern Italian writers were responsible for the development of 'a very distinctive species of literature which is peculiarly characteristic of Renaissance Italy.'[4] To this Marlowe responded with all the sensitivity of his poetic nature, and it added a new dimension to his genius which we recognise in the heightened quality of his dramatic writing from this period onwards. The collection of tales by Ser Giovanni Fiorento entitled *Il Pecorone* gave him the whole plot of *The Merchant of Venice;* and Cinthio's *Hecatomiti* gave him the tragedy of *Othello,* neither source translated into English in Shakespeare's day so he must have read them in Italian. Cinthio also provided the story of Isabella's troubles for *Measure for Measure; The Two Gentlemen of Verona* is mainly based on the Spanish novel *Diana* by the Portuguese writer Jorge de Montemayor; *Romeo and Juliet, All's Well That Ends Well, Twelfth Night, Much Ado About Nothing* derive substantially from Italian sources; and *The Taming of the Shrew* and *Cymbeline* draw in part from Italian writers. These were so popular that they were translated into French, German, Spanish and English, but it is the Italian influence in the stories and their settings that is striking. The legend of *Romeo and Juliet* was Englished as a narrative poem by Arthur Brooke, *The Tragical History of Romeus and Juliet* in 1562, described as a 'tedious work', which Marlowe had obviously read, but his main source remains the Italian original of Bandello. Sir Sidney Lee gives a perceptive appreciation of the essentially Italian inspiration of this enchanting play.

'At times Shakespeare's choice of Italian plots sets his work in the full tide of the Italian literary stream. The story of Romeo and Juliet, which Bandello first told to Europe . . has a right to be reckoned a national legend of Italy. . . [It] was the theme of Shakespeare's earliest venture in tragedy of the great romantic kind. In his dramatic treatment of it, he gave indubitable promise of his glorious fertility and power. Manifold are the original touches of poetry, insight and humour in Shakespeare's version of the Italian novel. Yet who can deny the Italian glow which lives in Shakespeare's radiant picture of youthful love?' [5]

Professor Ernesto Grillo is the Italian authority who has contributed most significantly to the identification of the intimate, first hand knowledge exhibited in the Shakespeare plays. Apart from those plays based directly on the works of Italian writers, altogether thirteen of the plays are set partly or wholly in Italy. From these Professor Grillo has shown that the dramatist had an amazing familiarity with the customs, history and topography of Northern Italy. Modern scholars have accused Shakespeare of ignorance when he refers to travel by boat for *inland* cities. In fact, he knew better than they! Verona lies on the River Adige, which in the sixteenth century was navigable and had communications with many of the cities of northern Italy, including Milan. Communication by water was extensively used in preference to roads. 'Milan itself was situated on several canals, by means of which it was possible to travel from city to city.' [6] Knowledge is shown of the ancient waterways of Verona, Milan and Padua in *The Two Gentlemen of Verona,* in *The Tempest* and *The Taming of the Shrew.* The latter has a reference to a sailmaker of the inland town of Bergamo. Grillo informs us that 'the city of Bergamo has been famous for that industry until recent times'. [7] Shakespeare's alleged ignorance about communications by water between these inland cities turns out to be remarkably accurate knowledge. Professor Grillo suggests that the picture described to Sly *(Shrew, Induction, ll.* 53-5) resembles Correggio's famous *Giove ed Io,* which was exhibited from 1585 to 1600 'to the public in the palace of the sculptor, Leoni, in Milan, where it was admired by numerous travellers.' [8] Shakespeare knew that 'Padua possessed a great University [and] was under the protection of Venice, while Mantua was not'; that Pisa was wealthy and noted for its 'grave citizens'; that the Florentines were known as merchants who used letters of credit in their commercial dealings and that their currency was in 'ducats', and that they were expert mathematicians. He also knew of the envious friction that existed between the Florentines and Siennese, and he uses a phrase 'which is pure Italian' referring to Florentines and Siennese as having each other 'by the ear *(si pigliano per gli orecchi)*'. [9] Grillo detected that the plays abound in proverbs of Italian origin, such as the saying 'sound as a fish' in *The Two Gentlemen of Verona* – a straight translation of the Italian *'sano come un pesce'.* [10] Shakespeare refers to Milan's

367

'royal court' and speaks of the city correctly in contemporary parlance as 'the fair'. Grillo finds that the dramatist evokes the spirit of each city in which his play is set with uncanny accuracy. In Venice he conjures a picture of: 'The darkness of morning, the narrow and mysterious 'calli', Brabantio's house with its heavy iron-barred doors, the Sagittary, the official residence of the commanders of the galleys, the hired gondolier witness of gallant intrigues, the gondola where the lovers had been seen, the galleys sent on a multitude of errands, the armaments, the attendants with torches, the special night guards, the council chamber, the senators' [11.] He knew that the Venetians called the doge their beloved 'Signor Magnifico'. All these convince Professor Grillo that Shakespeare must have actually been to Northern Italy at some time.

In *The Taming of the Shrew* the Italian form of marriage is celebrated between Petruchio and Kate. The sumptuous description of the furnishing in Gremio's house is based on a sixteenth century villa, not an English home which by comparison was primitive, and 'not even Elizabethan courtiers could boast of possessing such refinements', declares Professor Grillo: 'These magnificent 'objets d'art' were only to be found in Italy, in the palaces of the aristocracy of Milan, Genoa, Turin'. [12.] The English engaged Italian craftsmen to come to England to beautify their homes. It would be very typical of Marlowe to revel in the description of these beautiful artefacts:

> My hangings all of Tyrian tapestry;
> In ivory coffers I have stuffed my crowns;
> In cypress chests my arras, counterpoints,
> Costly apparel, tents, and canopies,
> Fine linen, Turkey cushions boss'd with pearl,
> Valance of Venice gold in needlework,
> Pewter and brass, and all things that belongs
> To house and housekeeping.

Act 2, sc.1. 11.341-8

In *The Merchant of Venice* 'the topography is so precise and accurate that it must convince even the most superficial reader that the poet visited the country, acutely observant of all its characteristics', writes Grillo. [13.] Portia tells Nerissa that their journey to Belmont (Monte Bello) is twenty miles, which is accurate when measured in the 'Lombardy mile' which was in use in that region and is longer than our English mile in which this distance would measure some thirty miles. Grillo points out that the name Gobbo is that of the kneeling hunchback at the base of the pillar in Venice on which the decrees issued by the Republic of Venice were displayed – another purely Venetian touch using a Venetian name. He was clearly especially familiar with Verona for in that city the law courts were located in the Villafranca, which Shakespeare translates literally as Freetown in *Romeo and Juliet* when the

Prince orders the brawling factions of the Capulets and Montagues to present themselves before the law officers. Grillo asserts moreover that this degree of familiarity in Shakespeare's play is confined specifically to Italy.

In view of the inescapable evidence of the dramatist's knowledge of things Italian, other orthodox scholars have also come to the conclusion this argues first-hand experience although evidence for Shakespeare is totally lacking. Regarding his sources, Professor Grillo, who is of course an orthodox Shakespearean scholar, writes: 'It seems as if Shakespeare must somehow or other have learned enough Italian to read and understand our writers ... It has been argued that in Elizabethan England translations of Italian books abounded, but certainly Shakespeare's knowledge of life and customs in Italy was not entirely derived from them'. [14.] Professor Grillo has convincingly argued the presence of our exiled Poet in Italy with overwhelming internal evidence from the plays.

Even when his sources are not the stories of the Italian writers, the scenes of many of the comedies and tragedies hardly leave Italy: Padua, Verona, Venice, Mantua, Milan, Florence, Pisa and, in historical drama, Rome – all feature. The names of his characters are often altered from those of his source, and are rechristened with Italian names. In the pastoral comedy, *As You Like It*, the Forest of Arden is of indeterminate geographical location, the tale being taken from Thomas Lodge's *Rosalynde* (1590), but Marlowe changes the hero's name, Rosander, to the Italian Orlando, linking this play in which banishment is the dominant theme with his sojourn in Italy. Touchstone (the author as previously demonstrated in deciphering the cryptic horse-play of the comic characters) likens himself to Ovid who was banished among the Goths.

In *The Winter's Tale* the statue of Hermione is ascribed to the hand of the Italian artist, Julio Romano, one of the gifted pupils of Raphael, who is known to us today only as an artist. But the sixteenth century biographer of the Italian artists, Vasari, described him as highly commended for his sculpture. In the play, Hermione's real-life 'statue' is extolled as 'a piece many years in doing and now newly perform'd by that rare Italian master, Julio Romano, who, had he himself eternity and could put breath into his work, would beguile Nature of her custom, so perfectly he is her ape; he so near to Hermione, hath done Hermione, that they say one would speak to her, and stand in hope of answer.' [15]

But it is that most delightful of all his comedies, *Twelfth Night,* based on a tale told by Bandello, which also appeared in many versions by various other Italian writers, that most concerns us. This play is 'a fantasy of which all the elements are dyed in Italian colours', [16.] though it was written for a memorable and most important English première, as our marvellously informative guide, Dr Hotson, will presently reveal. So, following him, we will not linger any longer amongst the Italian inspired comedies and tragedies, but hie us to the court of Duke Orsino, or, to give him his full title, Don Virginio Orsino, Duke of Bracciano, at his castle in the mountainous region north of Rome surrounding Lake di Bracciano.

Dr Hotson gives us a glimpse of this ancient fortress, the 'mighty ancestral castle' of Bracciano from a description of the journey made thither by Pope Clement in 1597:

> 'Passing by way of La Tolfa, riding by rocky declivities, and crossing the Mignone which threads these mountains with its waters clear and most cold, we entered the fair and delectable country of Monte Verano, famed for the best vineyards, green with thick and very rich grain.

> 'Proceeding a little farther, we met some seventy well-mounted musketeers of the Duke of Bracciano, and afterwards another cavalcade escorting the ambassador of Tuscany, who was come to Bracciano to receive the Pope, since at that very time Don Virginio, the duke of that place, was gone pilgrimaging on foot with but two or three, in fulfilment of a vow, to Madonna Santissima di Loreto.

> 'At sight of Bracciano, which was by night, the castle with a handsome *gazzarra* of guns great and small saluted the Prince; while the soldiers, beating drums in the outskirts of the town, bowed to the Pope and the cardinals as they passed, and then with a fine volley made all the neighbouring vales resound. Meantime the highest points showed blazing with fires and beacons, which made of dark night well-nigh the brightest daylight.

> 'Our Master was lodged in that very ancient stronghold, where one sees the effigies of the greatest heroes known to fame of the most noble family of the Orsini. The accommodation, besides the largeness of the rooms and the noble hangings, was marvellous for the apartments and good attendance – many Roman gentlemen being there – for the quantity and choiceness of the viands, and for the quiet.' [17]

'And for the quiet' – what a wonderful place to come to for composing his plays, if indeed this is where the exiled Poet found a haven. Doubtless the Duke would possess a fine library of Italian, French, Spanish and Latin books, for he spoke no English. He was absent on a pilgrimage to the shrine of San Loreto when Pope Clement arrived on this visit – probably a shrewd politically motivated absence, for his relations with Pope Clement tended to be rather strained, but he diplomatically saw to it that his Holiness was received with all honour. Don Virginio was, in fact, often absent for he spent much of his time at the Pitti Palace in Florence assisting his uncle, the Grand Duke, who had brought him up and to whom he was as a son.

Pope Clement was the successor to Pope Sixtus V, he who had erected the 'pyramids' in Rome and had entertained a sneaking admiration for Queen Elizabeth – letting fall such remarks as: if only she had been a Catholic, there was no Prince in all Europe he would rather serve! But as she was a Protestant he was, of course, her implacable enemy. It was to Pope Sixtus that Virginio Orsino became affiliated in marriage when in April 1589 at the age of sixteen he was wedded to Sixtus's grand-niece, Flavia Peretti. The magnificent marriage ceremony in Rome for this youthful pair was hymned with five sonnets as an epithalamium from the pen of Italy's most celebrated poet, Torquato Tasso. [18]

The marriage had been arranged by Virginio's uncle, Ferdinand, the Grand Duke of Tuscany, who became a father figure to the young Prince after the tragic events of his parents' tempestuous marital affairs, which were later dramatized by John Webster in his famous revenge tragedy, *The White Devil.* When he was about seven years old, Virginio's father, Paolo Giordano Orsino, Duke of Bracciano, had murdered the boy's mother in a fit of jealousy, and it is this murder, and, more particularly, Orsino's infatuation with the beautiful Vittoria Accorambona, that provide the main plot of Webster's play. In order that he can marry the object of his passion, the beautiful Vittoria (named the White Devil), Orsino had her husband also murdered; but eventually both the Duke and Vittoria were murdered in revenge by the Orsini kinsmen, mainly in zealous protection of the young Virginio Orsino's inheritance. Surviving these tragic events, the boy was carefully nurtured by his uncle, the Grand Duke, together with his orphaned cousin, Maria de' Medici, who was later to become Queen of France.

The Grand Duke Ferdinand arranged these advantageous political marriages for his young protegés, allying the house of Orsini to that of the powerful Pope Sixtus V, who was low-born but had risen in despite of this to the papal throne and possessed enormous wealth. Flavia Peretti brought her young husband a dowry of a hundred thousand crowns, a veritable fortune, and as a happy bonus it turned out to be a real love-match, the first fruit of which was the birth of twins, a boy and a girl, like to 'An apple cleft in two', as Shake-speare wrote in *Twelfth Night.* In the second year of their marriage Don Virginio Orsino commissioned a poem from the pen of Torquato Tasso to honour his beloved duchess, and he remained the patron of the admired Italian poet all his life.

It was to this cultured and virtuous Italian nobleman that, on the evidence to be presented, we may assume Marlowe came, probably to serve him in some capacity in intelligence work. The arena of Marlowe's hypothetical activities on the Continent demands the research of expert investigation by dedicated scholars determined to follow all clues that have become apparent. The task is challenging, but now that we know where to look it is possible to hope that some new evidence may be brought to light. There are over 100,000 letters in the Orsini archives awaiting careful research, many of them in cipher – an unexplored treasure trove, which, so far as I know, only Dr Hotson has mined with the able assistance of both Dr G. Degli Azzi, and Prince Lelio Orsino himself who tracked down the vitally important letters in the Orsini archives, then in the Archivio Storico Capitolino in Rome, relating to Don Virginio's visit to Queen Elizabeth in 1600/1 when *Twelfth Night* was performed. [19]

However, Marlowe did not, I believe, proceed to Orsino's castle in the mountain fastnesses of Bracciano immediately on reaching Italy. Having traversed the Alps from France, if we are to take the description of *Sonnet 33* as his response to an Alpine scene when he observed the sun shining with 'sovereign eye' on 'mountain tops' and 'gilding pale streams with heavenly alchemy', he would then have descended to the plain of Northern Italy to reach Verona. This ancient city nestles at the foothills of the Alps, and there, it seems, he lingered for some time writing the Veronese plays, *The Two Gentlemen of Verona* and *Romeo and Juliet*.

Settling here and having an address at which post could reach him, he probably learnt for the first time of the scandalous reports blemishing his character and reputation which followed from the Deptford affair. His deep distress at this situation, and the bitter realization that this was the price he would have to pay for escaping with his life – namely, a 'murdered' reputation – is expressed in *Sonnet 34*. Since this is placed directly following his Alpine journey in *Sonnet 33*, we may assume that he heard this news soon after his arrival at Verona. The *Sonnets of Exile* seem to be presented, on the whole, in their chronological order although frequently interrupted by small groups of sonnets from a totally different chronological sequence, especially from the early period when 'Mr.W.H.' was his patron, as will be made clear in the analysis of the Sonnet Themes in the final pages of this book.

It seems evident from *Sonnet 34* that Marlowe had not known the details of the plot that Frizer and the witnesses, Poley and Skeres, were to present at the inquest as the facts of how he came to be 'murdered'. Frizer's prime interest was to escape the gallows by convincing the coroner and jury that he had been the victim of a malicious attack by Marlowe, the unprovoked aggressor – a tale totally contrary to the true character of the Poet. It was a nasty scenario. Walsingham doubtless was horrified and blamed himself for not having foreseen the outcome, but was powerless to refute the story that was spreading on the wings of malicious gossip. He received a verse-letter from his Poet expressing his bitter grief and anguished reproach.

> Why didst thou promise such a beauteous day
> And make me travel forth without my cloak,
> To let base clouds o'ertake me in my way,
> Hiding thy brav'ry in their rotten smoke?
> 'Tis not enough that through the cloud thou break
> To dry the rain on my storm-beaten face,
> For no man well of such a salve can speak
> That heals the wound, and cures not the disgrace.
> Nor can thy shame give physic to my grief;

Map of Northern Italy

Sonnet 33

Full many a glorious morning have I seen,
Flatter the mountain-tops with sovereign eye,
Kissing with golden face the meadows green,
Gilding pale streams with heavenly alchemy;
Anon permit the basest clouds to ride
With ugly rack on his celestial face,
And from the forlorn world his visage hide,
Stealing unseen to west with this disgrace,
Even so my sun one early morn did shine
With all triumphant splendour on my brow;
But out alack, he was but one hour mine,
The region cloud hath mask'd him from me now.
*   Yet him for this, my love no whit disdaineth:*
*   Suns of the world may stain, when heaven's sun*
*   staineth.*

Though thou repent, yet I have still the loss.
Th' offender's sorrow lends but weak relief
To him that bears the strong offence's cross.
    Ah, but those tears are pearl which thy love sheds,
    And they are rich, and ransom all ill deeds.

Sonnet'34

This moving sonnet is an outpouring of emotions and recriminations that precisely fit these circumstances, and *it only makes complete sense when seen in this context*. It is a revealing autobiographical testimony that gives us insight into the turmoil that was in the Poet's heart following the Deptford deception with its woeful consequences. His consolation may be seen in the marvellous release of creative energy that found expression in the great dramatic works that now flowed from his pen.

He probably visited the famous cities of North Italy at this time – Padua and Venice, both lying east of Verona within easy reach, and, further south along the eastern side of the Appenines, Bologna, and near the Adriatic coast, Ravenna. He would doubtless have wanted to go to Florence where the Grand Duke of Tuscany ruled, hoping to gain employment at the Pitti Palace. What sort of employment would have kept him during his years of exile? Obviously his skill in intelligence would have been his mainstay, as it had been all his working life, and he would have had contacts abroad from his previous assignments, some of whom he might have been able to trust and use now. In this respect, Anthony Bacon, the elder brother of Francis Bacon, would undoubtedly have assisted him, as would Thomas Walsingham who would equally have known some reliable contacts on the Continent among men who were also free-thinkers.

Anthony Bacon had lived abroad, mainly in France, for nearly twelve years, working in intelligence for Sir Francis Walsingham and Lord Burghley, Marlowe's employers. There can be no doubt that Marlowe knew him well and, as we shall see later, they collaborated closely in the development of Freemasonry. Anthony Bacon returned to England in 1592, and had then entered the service of the Earl of Essex, who was ambitious to establish himself as a political force in the Queen's Privy Council on which he had gained a place. Anthony acted as his secretary and supplied Essex with foreign intelligence in advance of that which Lord Burghley received for the government. In this situation, being now permanently based in England, Anthony Bacon needed sources abroad to furnish him with intelligence, and one of these is likely to have been Marlowe, who was a Brother in Freemasonry with him. Protection from unjust persecution and aid for their members in times of trouble are basic principles of Freemasonry even today.

During his last year in France, Anthony Bacon had been able to procure the release from prison of an English Catholic, Anthony Standen, who was one of

Walsingham's spies, who had been imprisoned in Bordeaux on suspicion of having treasonable correspondence with Spain. Later he introduced Standen to Essex as an intelligence agent he could highly recommend, whereupon Essex engaged Standen's services for many years. [20] An amusing story relating to Standen sheds light on the activities of such espionage agents and their special skills in disguise and the necessary mastery of foreign languages by the men in this demanding profession. When working in France, Standen assumed the name of 'La Faye', and in one of his letters to Anthony Bacon he recounts with glee how he had fooled some Englishmen into believing that he was a real Frenchman who understood no English, so that he was able to listen to their English conversations as an uncomprehending innocent to pick up useful hints. Intelligence agents regularly worked under assumed identities and false names, and clearly Marlowe would have had very special reasons for adopting these precautions and maintaining them with assiduous skill and care to prevent the detection of his true identity.

With this in mind, it is of intriguing interest to consider another intelligence agent whom Anthony Bacon introduced to the Earl of Essex in 1595. This man purported to be a Frenchman named Monsieur Le Doux, who was highly recommended by both Anthony and Francis Bacon as a skilful intelligencer who had some experience of Italy. It was to Italy that Essex was wanting to send an agent on an extensive fact-finding assignment. The account below is taken from Thomas Birch's *Memoirs of the Reign of Queen Elizabeth,* for which his research was largely based on the voluminous letters of Anthony Bacon now in the archives of Lambeth Palace Library. I quote this at length because I strongly suspect that this agent, described as 'a French gentleman', was none other than Christopher Marlowe. If Standen could pass himself off as a Frenchman, we may be sure that Marlowe would have been equally capable of it!

By 1595 Marlowe had, on the evidence of the Italian influence in his plays, spent some time in Italy, and doubtless his French was sufficiently fluent for him to pass as the French gentleman, Monsieur Le Doux – which sounds like a *nom-de-guerre.* Did Essex know the secret of Marlowe's escape? It is possibly on the cards that he would have known if Southampton knew of it. In any case, if Monsieur Le Doux had been presented in person to the Earl, his experience and skill at disguise and impersonation would have prevented detection. Evidently he was accepted into the Earl's service for this most interesting mission on which further research is in progress following up the clues of this intriguing 'hunch', which is the most hopeful that we have to date.

The following extract from Birch's *Memoirs* gives us a picture of just the kind of activity in which Marlowe might have been engaged at this very period, using his expertise in intelligence for Essex in association with the Bacons.

'The earl of *Essex* having engag'd *Monsieur Le Doux,* a French gentleman, who had come to England to serve him as an intelligencer abroad, gave him a passport, dated at London February 10th 1595, [21.] which he renew'd at Richmond on the 10th March, [22.] giving him instructions in French for his conduct, directing him to send accounts of important occurrences, and upon his arrival at the place where he design'd to reside, as at the emperor's court or elsewhere, to advertise not only the state of it, but whatever he could learn concerning the affairs of *Italy* and *Turky*. The most remarkable points, which he should inform himself of, were . . '

Here I have paraphrased the lengthy, detailed instructions drawn up for Monsieur Le Doux, either by Anthony, or possibly in this instance by Francis Bacon, who was apparently also involved in devising this assignment. Francis had become the impetuous Earl's political and diplomatic mentor, hoping to groom him for a position of enhanced influence in the Queen's government, to seek the realization of his ambitions in high office in the arena of government rather than in military glory. Francis Bacon was a great maker of lists, and his pedagogic tone is detectable in the directives set forth in this document. Monsieur Le Doux was to supply the Earl with information covering:

'Deaths of princes and great personages
Friendships &/or enmities between states
Of wars – how conducted, what land &/or sea forces
Of peace treaties – conditions &c
Of alliances and confederacies
Of embassies sent from one prince to another
Of troubles and seditions
Of alliances between princes of Germany and Italy
Of favourites and chief counsellors used by princes
Of sums of money raised by princes in the bank
&c.

'And in case *Monsieur Le Doux* should find a proper opportunity of going into *Italy,* and particularly to that source of all news, *Rome,* to make some stay there, he should there be especially upon the watch to discover the most secret motions, that could in any measure affect England and Scotland, and the two princes of those two kingdoms. And since the earl's misfortune had been, that God had never permitted him to see *Italy,* the garden of Christendom, he particularly recommended to *Monsieur Le Doux,* that for his lordship's satisfaction he would take a little pains to draw up a particular description of every principality in *Italy,* specifying in each of them the following points: The grandeur and the extent of them: The revenues, and when they arise: The strong places, with their garrisons: What number of soldiers are maintain'd by each state:

The sea ports: The great rivers and famous cities in each principality: The commodities produc'd by each country, and whither they
are exported: What merchandises they import from abroad, and
from whence: What laws or customs each state is governed by: and
what counsellors and officers the prince most employs.'[23]

It is quite a list. Was it perhaps as a direct result of this assignment that
Marlowe travelled further south in Italy towards Rome, and thus came to the
court of the Duke of Bracciano? Orsino's principality lies just north of Rome,
a long way from Florence, and there must have been some special reason that
took Marlowe to this region which, as subsequent evidence suggests, later
brought him into the service of the Duke.

Orsino was an anglophile, who liked to employ Englishmen as mercenaries
in his army. Knowing this, it is a logical probability that Marlowe would have
shed whatever foreign identity he might have assumed, such as Monsieur Le
Doux, for instance, and presented himself as an English agent to the Duke,
probably with some letter of introduction that had been arranged to effect his
acceptance under his chosen guise. This contact would have been of vital
importance to Marlowe in his assignment. The Tuscan court of Orsino's uncle,
The Grand Duke, at Florence, where Orsino was often present to assist him,
was the political centre of Italian affairs of state, which Marlowe would have
aimed to penetrate. If he was indeed the mysterious Monsieur Le Doux, the
recipient of this important assignment, it is inconceivable that he would have
failed to gain his entrée into the court of the Duke of Bracciano and, through
him, the Tuscan court at Florence.

At the present stage of research the foregoing is a hypothesis based on reasonable deductions. Hopefully the decipherment of some of Anthony Bacon's
letters, many of which are written in a numerical cipher, will yet reveal what
everyone who has followed this story with bated breath must be expectantly
awaiting – conclusive evidence of Marlowe's presence and activities in the
years following 1593. For the present we remain wondering, was he Monsieur
Le Doux?

The key figure in this part of the story is Don Virginio Orsino, who, I
believe, employed Christopher Marlowe. Tantalizingly, the Orsini archives,
consisting of a vast reserve of letters, many of them in cipher, may well harbour
the vital information linking the Poet in his exile with the Italian Duke. What a
find that would be! The hunt is now up in both these great archives with scrupulous impartiality. Historical documentary evidence alone will serve. We are not
trying to substitute a myth about Marlowe to replace the myth about
Shakespeare of Stratford. The truth and nothing less is being aimed at.

XXIV

THORPE WRITES A LETTER

WHETHER MARLOWE returned to England for visits in the interim before his eventual return from exile is conjectural in the present state of research, but in 1600 we have definite evidence of his presence in London.

Dr Hotson's research has established that it was during the Christmas season of 1600-1 that the play *Twelfth Night* received its first performance at the Court on 6th January to honour the presence of Don Virginio Orsino, Duke of Bracciano, as the noble guest of Queen Elizabeth. [1.] It is in connection with the impending visit of this cultured Italian Prince, who is so delightfully and faithfully personated in the play in the character of Duke Orsino, that Marlowe had evidently come to London to make the necessary preparations. Two pieces of documentation point to his presence in London in the autumn of 1600 – the first, a cryptic letter written by Thomas Thorpe; the second, the entry of a play in the Stationers' Register.

The first to consider is the letter, a puzzle by Thorpe, the deviser of the cryptic dedication of the *Sonnets*. In 1600 he published Marlowe's translation of the *First Book of Lucan* and wrote a cryptic dedication of this book to Edward Blount, the publisher of Marlowe's *Hero and Leander* in 1598. Blount is cited by Eleanor Grace Clark as a member of Raleigh's 'School of Night' [2.] and as such would have known of Marlowe's escape from the coils of the Star Chamber Court. Thorpe had evidently got wind of the true situation, for his dedication takes the form of a very curious letter to Blount in which he informs him that he has seen Marlowe alive and in person, and has received a manuscript or 'booke' that he is going to bring to Blount. Since Thorpe's strange letter is a *published* dedication to Blount, this imposes the necessity to veil his information, using his considerable ingenuity in cryptic language that can be read two ways. It is the kind of thing Thorpe hugely enjoyed, especially as here he is flaunting a piece of one-up-manship to the world. He seems to have been the sort of chap who delighted in handling any publication that gave him an opportunity for cryptic teasing.

> *To his Kind, and True Friend:*
> Edward Blunt.

> Blount: *I purpose to be blunt with you, and out of my dullnesse to encounter you with a* Dedication *in the memory of that pure Elementall wit,* Chr. Marlow; *whose ghoast or* Genius *is to be seene walke the* Churchyard *in (at the least) three or foure sheets.*

378

Me thinks you should presently looke wilde now, and grow
humourously frantique upon the tast of it. Well, least you should,
let mee tell you.

This spirit was sometime a familiar of your own, Lucans first
booke translated; *which (in regard of your old right in it) I have*
rais'd in the circle of your Patronage. But stay now, Edward *(if I*
mistake not) you are to accommodate your selfe with some fewe
instructions, touching the property of a Patron, that you are not yet
possest of; and to study them for your better grace as our Gallants
do fashions. First, you must be proud and thinke you have merit
inough in you, though you are ne're so emptie; then when I bring
you the booke take physicke, and keepe state, assigne me a time by
your man to come againe, and afore the day, be sure to have
chang'd your lodging; in the meane time sleepe little, and sweat
with the invention of some pittiful dry jest or two which you may
happen to utter, with some litle (or not at al) marking of your
friends when you have found a place for them to come in at; or if
by chance something has dropt from you worth the taking up weary
all that come to you with the often repetition of it; Censure scorne-
fully inough, and somewhat like a travailer; commend nothing
least you discredit your (that which you would seeme to have)
judgement. These things if you can mould your self to them Ned *I*
make no question but they will not become you. One speciall
vertue in our Patrons of these daies I have promist my selfe you
shall fit excellently, which is to give nothing; Yet, thy love I will
challenge as my peculiar Object both in this, and (I hope) manie
more succeeding offices: Farewell, I affect not the world should
measure my thoughts to thee by a scale of this Nature: Leave to
thinke good of me when I fall from thee.

Thine in all rites of perfect friendship,

THOM. THORPE

The Churchyard he mentions is, of course, St Paul's where the booksellers
had their stalls, the favourite haunt of Marlowe. Thorpe's pregnant piece has
heretofore been interpreted as a light-hearted quip as between one publisher
and another, just teasing Ned Blount with the news that his rival, Thorpe, has
managed to acquire the manuscript of Marlowe's *Lucan* (formerly in Blount's
copyright it seems) which he has now brought out and sent abroad on the
bookstalls, the 'three or foure sheets' being the pages of the book. Such an
innocent reading evades scrutiny of what the artful Thorpe is really saying. If
that were all that Thorpe intended to convey, it hardly warrants the heavy
cryptic implications – which will cause Blount to 'looke wilde' and 'grow
humourously frantique', with the suggestive hints at secrecy, advising him to

change his lodgings and find 'a place for them [his friends] to come in at'. This is certainly more than the publication of *Lucan*, even if it were filched from Blount (whose 'old right' in it could not have been of great moment since he had allowed it to lapse without publication) would warrant.

When we now see this in the light cast by the *Sonnets* it becomes abundantly clear what Thorpe is *really* telling Blount. The BIG NEWS with which he is bursting is that he had indeed seen Marlowe's 'ghoast or *Genius* . . walke the Churchyard in (at the least) three or foure sheets'. Is this, perhaps, intended cryptically as referring to his garments? Was Marlowe, perhaps disguised as a Moor in loose flowing robe, swathed in 'sheets'? One would not put it beyond him! He was probably a very good actor, and if this were a long-expected visit to London in which he wanted to be able to move around freely, he may well have been careful to adopt a disguise that would completely conceal him. But the crafty Thorpe had seen through it, putting two and two together, having probably always wondered how such a man as that 'pure elementall wit, *Chr. Marlow*' could have become involved in a mean, paltry quarrel to be fatally stabbed for his pains by Sir Thomas Walsingham's servant. The implication of Thorpe's letter is that he had a manuscript or 'booke' to bring to Blount which Thorpe had received from Marlowe, whose exotic disguise (if such it was) had not fooled the astute Thorpe. He had obviously known Marlowe personally in days of yore, and he had called his bluff; or else Marlowe, wanting Thorpe's help, had disclosed himself and commissioned him, so to speak, for the publication of this 'booke'.

Thorpe seems to have been a man sympathetic to the publication of cryptic works. He later published the *Sonnets* with their cryptic dedication, which even orthodox scholars have suggested were possibly withdrawn or suppressed, although they do not connect this with the fear of revelation of their authorship which would have been the real reason for their suppression. As with the *Sonnets*, I see the attempted publication in 1600 of *As You Like It* as a case of that 'suborn'd informer' of *Sonnet 125* whispering in the Poet's ear, urging him to drop hints that he is alive in the pseudonymous Shake-speare.* We know that his play was unaccountably withheld from publication with the caveat 'to be staied'. Significantly, this date co-incides with Thorpe's cryptic letter to Blount. This co-incidence suggests that the 'booke' to which he is cryptically referring is probably none other than the playscript or book of *As You Like It*, which fits the bill perfectly. It cannot be Thorpe's publication of the *First Book of Lucan* for this *contains the letter from Thorpe* that refers to the 'booke' he is promising to bring to Blount – which cannot mean *itself*.

Thorpe had already acquired Marlowe's *First Book of Lucan* which provided him with a vehicle for writing his cryptic letter to Blount, giving his quirky spirit the satisfaction of indulging in the kind of publicly displayed cryptic

---

* Foot-note: The 'suborn'd informer' of Sonnet 125 is more fully discussed on pages 487-490

game he enjoyed. Apparently he obtained the copyright of *Lucan* when Paul Linley, who printed *Hero and Leander* for Blount in 1598, died sometime in the earlier months of 1600. [3.] The entry in the Stationers' Register of 26th June 1600 gives a long list of books belonging to Linley that were transferred to J. Flasket, the printer who succeeded Linley and took over his copyrights and his house at the Black Bear in St Paul's Churchyard. Among these are listed 'HERO and LEANDER and the j booke of LUCAN by MARLOWE', [4.] the latter being subsequently sold to Thorpe, who must have published it immediately after he had seen Marlowe's 'ghoast', for his letter to Blount is written to impart his BIG NEWS.

In his letter Thorpe advised Blount: 'You are to accommodate your self with some fewe instructions, touching the property of a Patron, that you are not yet possest of'. What this property is he makes clear in his statement: 'when I bring you the booke'. Evidently Thorpe has been entrusted with a manuscript which he is to give to Blount for the purpose, I suggest, of obtaining his advice, or blessing, on its publication, which Thorpe would then undertake. That the playscript, commonly called a 'book', of *As You Like It* did, just at this time, get as far as application for its licence by the Stationers' Register is a fact – but there it was stayed.

Let us look at the facts more closely. Under the date 4th August 1600 in the Stationers' Register is listed *'As you like yt'*, followed by three more plays: *Henry the Fifth, Every Man in His Humour* and *Much Ado About Nothing,* all of which are bracketed together with the injunction 'to be staied' written against them. [5.] All the last three were shortly licensed for publication, however. On 14th August Thomas Pavier was granted a licence for *Henry the Fifth,* and Ben Jonson's play was licensed to Burby and Burre, while *Much Ado* was licensed on 23rd August to Wyse and Aspley. [6.]

No name for the presenter of the manuscript of *As You Like It* is given, so we do not know who had an interest in it. Above the entry of this play are two plays under the heading: 'my lord chamberlens menns plaies Entred *viz*': then follow, *A moral of 'clothe breches and velvet hose'* and *Allarum to London.* A note by Edward Arber who did the enormous work of transcribing the Stationers' Registers states: 'The next entry ('As you like yt/ a booke') has nothing to do with the preceding. The ink of it is now of a different colour'. [7.] He therefore dissociates this play from the Lord Chamberlain's Men's entry. The other plays mentioned were all published with the usual advertisement for the company, 'As it hath been sundrie times publikely acted by the right honorable the Lord Chamberlaine his servants', [8.] or some such variant, showing that these had all had their season on the boards and were not new plays. But *As You Like It* was a new play. It had never been presented by the Lord Chamberlain's Men at the time of its entry in the Stationers' Register, and it is doubtful whether it was ever performed publicly before its appearance in the First Folio. There are no contemporary references to it. It alone remained 'staied' in 1600. Why was this? I suggest the following.

Evidently, Marlowe, conscious of the cryptic allusions to his authorship with which the play abounds, thought it best not to give it to the Lord Chamberlain's Men through his broker William Shakespeare, but gave the play instead to Thorpe with, it is to be inferred, some instruction that he should discuss its possible publication with Blount first. The inference is that Blount, who knew the dangers and was fully aware of Marlowe's circumstances and Walsingham's involvement, and who was probably himself a member of the 'School of Night', would have made an informed judgment on the play's cryptic messages and would advise Thorpe, as to whether he would *sanction its appearance in print as safe.* The publication of the First Folio was a joint venture with which Blount would later be closely involved as a prime mover, ensuring the cryptic concealment of its author; and so carefully presented have the cryptic references in the First Folio been that they have obscured its author to this day! A unilateral publication of such a potentially revealing play-book was another matter. It is highly likely that he would have strongly advised against printing it in 1600 when Archbishop Whitgift was still alive. However, if Thorpe did go to see him as promised, it seems that, whatever Blount may have advised, Thorpe did not take notice of. He was a law unto himself, a very independent gentleman in whom eccentricity was a trait of his character.

Dr Hotson's research on Thomas Thorpe has revealed that he was regarded as something of an oddity in the publishing fraternity. In fact, his friends had given him the 'by-name' of Odd! [9.] This may be taken as meaning either an odd fellow, a bit eccentric, highly individual, one who does not go with the crowd; or it may connote 'high esteem, meaning (like rare) "singular or distinguished".' [10.] In support of this Hotson quotes a contemporary verse ending with the line, 'For still odd fellows are the wisest men.' [11]. Thorpe may also 'have earned the by-name *Odd* through his recent piratical publication, as *The Odcombian Banquet,* of the many amusing verses contributed by the wits to the *Crudities* of "odd Tom" Coryate of Odcombe.' [12]

This Odd fellow would, one feels, have appealed to Marlowe, and in him he found a ready ally for the publication of the *Sonnets* in 1609. This being an undeniable fact, we may reasonably infer that it was to Thorpe that he took his manuscript in 1600, which was none other than the 'book' of the play *As You Like It,* also a risky publication for Thorpe to handle, asking him to show it to Blount before committing it to the press. That Blount had felt unable to give it his blessing is a foregone conclusion, so that, in the event, it was probably the eccentric and independent-minded Thorpe who, despite his friend Ned's advice, decided to go ahead and obtain a licence for it. He very likely indicated his intentions to do so, whereupon Blount, acting in his free-thinking friends' best interests exerted his influence, and saw to it that the Stationers' licence was withheld – and the play was stayed for twenty-three years.

This interpretation of Thorpe's letter, linking it with *As You Like It,* fits the circumstances precisely in the light of the sonnet-story. The implication is that Marlowe knew the 'Odd' fellow Thorpe's peculiar penchant for cryptic publications, and this is why he took the *Sonnets* to him, and found him a willing accomplice in devising the cryptic dedication. Thorpe would have delighted in that challenge, just as in reading his dedicatory letter to Ned Blount we detect his glee!

It is a hypothetical question whether Blount was, as suggested, the censor-figure for the free-thinkers, but he might well have been concerned lest the true story of the events at Deptford were now to be leaked. If Thorpe had put two and two together so might others. The facts cited tell their own story for us to interpret. Someone took *As You Like It* to the Stationers' Company to register it for publication, and someone saw to it that it was stayed. I suggest that these persons were Thorpe – and Blount. When we consider Thorpe's letter, the mention of the 'booke' he will bring to Blount cannot be the *First Book of Lucan* which contains the letter referring to the said 'booke', and the reference must be something that warrants the portentous and crafty secrecy in which Thorpe wraps the event – and the link with the staying of *As You Like* It fits the time and the circumstance. All conditions are met.

Orthodox Shakespeareans dismiss the significance of the cryptic allusions in the play, doggedly insisting that Touchstone's comments, and the horse-play with William, Audrey, and Mar-Text are just part of the comedy with no cryptic messages intended. This insistence on a naive appreciation of what is obvious, and not subtle, is the only way to deny that double meanings are used by Shakespeare. But we are not all so naive, nor am I clever enough to have invented this subtle interpretation if it were not actually there in the text. Touchstone himself cries out in exasperation:

> 'When a man's verses cannot be understood, nor a man's good wit seconded with the forward child understanding, it strikes a man more dead than a great reckoning in a little room.' [13]

It is the only play in the entire canon that makes a *direct* reference to Marlowe's death, and names him the 'dead shepherd', at the same time quoting from his *Hero and Leander*. Let us credit the Elizabethans with being more astute and quick to see allusions than we are, hence the danger, *especially if the play were seen in print*. Today a great deal of Shakespeare's wit passes us by, and to much of it we are kept blind by the conventional teaching of orthodox thinking about Shakespeare as the man from Stratford.

Since, in the event, there were no untoward consequences from the publication of Thorpe's cryptic letter in *Lucan*, this may have encouraged him and Marlowe in the publication of the *Sonnets* nine years later, by which time Whitgift had died, and they evidently felt justified in thinking that some people were being over-cautious about allowing his works to appear under the now well-established name, Shake-speare, even if they did contain cryptic hints concerning the real author.

Again in 1609 there were no unpleasant repercussions, though the edition seems to have been either limited or soon suppressed, for these beautiful poems appeared only in this single edition for a period of thirty years whereas today they are still best sellers.

The next question is, What was it that brought Marlowe to London in 1600? This is the story now to be unfolded.

Courtesy of Don Filippo Orsini
From the family portraits of the Orsini

Don Virginio Orsino, Duca di Bracciano

XXV

A GRAND FLORENTINE WEDDING

THE YEAR 1600 was an eventful one for Don Virginio Orsino, for his well-loved cousin and childhood playmate, Maria de' Medici, was to be married to King Henry IV of France, the erstwhile Protestant hero who, as the King of Navarre, had fought so valiantly against the Guise's Catholic faction, which had been supported by the powerful Queen Mother of France, another Maria de' Medici, whose sons had been her pawns when they successively and briefly in turn occupied the French throne before being picked off by assassins. Two of them had been suitors for Queen Elizabeth's hand despite the fact that she was a Protestant, for where political power vied with religion the former took precedence. So it had been with Henry of Navarre; when he finally gained the throne of France he easily renounced his Protestantism in order to win the vital allegiance of the Parisians by embracing Catholicism. 'Paris is worth a mass', he had declared, and the Pope duly annulled his marriage to Marguerite de Valois for having failed to bear him any children. To fulfil that function the Grand Duke Ferdinand saw his opportunity for a most important political alliance by offering him his niece Maria de' Medici to present him with heirs, and besides, a handsome dowry that cancelled all Henry's debts and set him up both solvent and enriched with essential cash to spend. Naturally the offer was accepted.

The wedding was to take place in Florence by proxy in the autumn of 1600, and though Henry himself would not be present, (he did not even turn up to meet his bride on her arrival in France) the affair was celebrated with unprecedented magnificence marking the importance of this alliance. Of course Queen Elizabeth was immediately informed to her great pleasure, for it provided a balance of power in Europe. Tuscany was not to be reckoned in the pocket of either Philip of Spain, or the present Pope Clement, a politically ambitious Aldobrandino, to whom the Tuscan alliance made with his predecessor Sixtus V was a thorn in his side.

One aspect of the Tuscan alliance with Pope Sixtus resulting from the marriage between Don Virginio Orsino and Sixtus's grand-niece Flavia Peretti had been a Papal decree granting Orsino precedence over all the Italian nobility of his rank, and at the same time making peace between the rival Orsini and Colonna families by ordaining that the elder of the chiefs of these families had precedence of the other. [1] Such matters still rankled in sixteenth century Italy, whose fierce tribal rivalries are reflected in the tragedy of *Romeo and Juliet*.

When Ippolito Aldobrandino was elected Pope in 1592 to become Clement VIII, he lost no time in rescinding what Sixtus had ordained by passing his own

Papal decree of precedence, which degraded Don Virginio Orsino from his position of primacy to a place with the rest of the Roman barons. This was to have repercussions at the grand wedding of Maria de' Medici, magnificently described by Doctor Hotson in *The First Night of Twelfth Night* (1954) shedding radiance on Orsino and this play.

To mark the occasion the facade of the great Cathedral of Florence was covered with huge murals gorgeously painted on wood presenting the history of the Medici rulers of Florence and the three Medici Popes, surmounted by the heraldic arms of the Pope, the Holy Roman Emperor, the King of Spain, the King and Queen of France whose wedding it was, the Grand Duke of Tuscany, and the Papal Legate who would perform the ceremony. There were days of splendid feasting, of tournaments and hunting, of grand balls, with masques and plays and a unique performance of a specially composed *dramma per musica* by Italy's Jacopo Peri, presenting in music and song the story of *Euridice*, the libretto by the poet Ottavio Rinuccini. [2] It was the birth of opera.

One wonders whether our exiled Poet saw and heard this first public performance of an opera? Certainly he must have seen the gorgeous galley which the Grand Duke Ferdinand (probably the richest man in Europe, whom the English had given the appropriate cipher-name *Riches)* [3] had especially ordered, at no charge spared, for the journey by sea to her new homeland that the new Queen of France would make after the wedding. This was a ship of 'extraordinary length, with twenty-seven sweeps a side manned by slaves all in crimson velvet, the ship completely covered to the water-line with beaten gold. The cabins in the poop curtained and hung with gold silk-brocade and gold tissue. Opposite her throne stood jewelled scutcheons of arms, the fleurs-de-lys of diamonds. It was the marvel of Europe.' [4]

Dr Hotson quotes from *Antony and Cleopatra* as evidence that the fame of this magnificent gilded vessel had reached William Shakespeare in London, yet how much more likely and plausible that our Poet had actually seen this wonderful galley, which is so closely mirrored in his description of Cleopatra's fabulous barge:

> The barge she sat in, like a burnish'd throne
> Burn'd on the water. The poop was beaten gold;
> Purple the sails, and so perfumed that
> The winds were love-sick with them; the oars were silver,
> Which to the tune of flutes kept stroke, and made
> The water which they beat to follow faster,
> As amorous of their strokes. For her own person,
> It beggar'd all description. She did lie
> In her pavilion, cloth-of-gold, of tissue,
> O'er picturing that Venus where we see
> The fancy out-work nature.

Act 2, scene 2. 11.195-205

The new Queen of France was no Cleopatra, however. Certainly Henry IV would have received a detailed description of his bride in advance, an unsophisticated girl who affected few jewels despite her great wealth, and lacked 'grace' or 'princelike majesty', being somewhat 'full-faced, of a reasonable personage', and to sum up, was 'as the Italians say, *bona roba:* a good bedfellow, for one that is not over curious. She is for the most part merry, and liketh well of the French fashion of courting'. [5] With all the lavish show of magnificence to launch this unexceptional, somewhat buxom Italian girl on her destiny as Queen of France, there was also a touch of high drama in the occasion which is the point of our story.

Don Virginio Orsino knew full well that Pope Clement's Legate, Cardinal Aldobrandino, would endeavour to enforce the new Papal decree of precedence in the procession to the Cathedral, whereby Orsino was degraded from his place of honour before the cross. But this young nobleman had secretly determined not to yield this place at any cost, – no, not here in his own city of Florence at the grand wedding of his cousin! Choosing his moment, and ably seconded by two Medici princes in his plan, he boldly placed his mount directly in front of the cross, forcing Marzio Colonna, to whom the position as Champion or *Antesignano* now belonged, to give way to him and move forward in the procession. [6] Don Virginio is thus installed in the position of honour at the head of the Orsini, and there he is determined to stay. Here let Hotson take up the story for he does it superbly.

Profound sensation. The Legate, outraged, sends his Grand Master of Ceremonies, Paolo Alaleone, to remind the Orsino of the new Papal decree: That his place is forward. Don Virginio replies that any such decree does not apply to him. Checked here, the Legate appeals to the Grand Duke, who manifests surprise, and ignorance of any difficulty. Under the Aldobrandino's angry insistence, however, he can do no less for appearances' sake than to send a message by his noble cupbearer, recommending obedience to the Pope's mandate. But he might know that Don Virginio will not obey. And if the Legate imagines that he will, he is deceived. Don Virginio budges not an inch. More than that, reports Bentivoglio, 'in resolute terms he sent to tell the Cardinal that 'He [Orsino] was at Florence, and not at Rome. And that even in Rome he would never have submitted himself to this decree.'

Language of this unbending sort angers the Legate still more, and forces his hand; he must play his trump. He calls for his coach. He will return to Rome, and not perform the marriage!

Deadlock; and the situation is deteriorating rapidly. But that able statesman Ferdinand has a formula, even for a case like this. He gives Don Virginio a message for the Princess Maria, publicly desiring that it be conveyed at once to her at the palace. Excellent.

The Duke of Bracciano bows to his uncle's wish – 'I shall in all my best obey *you'* – and three princely Medici backs are turned on the red-robed Aldobrandino and all his pomp as they ride off. [7]

The Grand Duke's face-saving device saves the day, and later Don Virginio still has the honour of bearing the 'Golden Rose' at his cousin's wedding ceremony. Thereafter, the whirl of entertainments, feasts, dancing, tilting and theatricals, until it is time to accompany the new Queen in her golden galley from Leghorn to Marseilles to deliver her to her husband, providing Orsino with a useful respite. But of course the matter is not forgotten. The Pope will be told of it, and soon Orsino's defiance of the Papal decree becomes the talk of Italy.

It was in this situation that Orsino, anxious to evade doing penance to the Pope, had conceived the plan of fulfilling an ambition – to go to England to see the fabulous Protestant Queen whom Sixtus had been bold to admire, and whom Pope Clement held in implacable hatred, even cherishing hopes of a revival of Spain's 'Great Enterprise' against England that had been dashed in 1588. Having hurled defiance at this Pope, Don Virginio was minded to go further and, weighing the consequences of his recent action, felt that he might reap some advantage by showing Clement that he had powerful friends in the very camp of his greatest enemy. Such a move would be a coup indeed! On arriving in France he discreetly made contact with Queen Elizabeth's agent at the French court, Sir Ralph Winwood, informing him of his desired intention to visit the English court, which Winwood promptly passed on to the Queen's government in a letter that gives notice of Orsino's intention; but no date for the visit is vouchsafed. [8]

We know of no written reply, but this would be just the kind of political game that was dear to Elizabeth's heart – to sow seeds of uncertainty in the minds of her enemies that would keep them guessing about her strengths. The tetchy young Philip III of Spain, successor to the dedicated, monkish Philip II who had sent the Armada to hale her off her throne, and Pope Clement must be kept on tenterhooks by suspicions and doubts. Driving a wedge between them by nurturing alliances, and especially to be on good terms with the independent and enormously wealthy Grand Duke of Tuscany, was entirely to her advantage. Naturally, his princely nephew, the valiant Don Virginio Orsino, Duke of Bracciano, whose rare qualities were extolled by all who knew him, would be most warmly welcomed. His brave show of spirit at Florence would have been reported to Elizabeth and would greatly enhance him in her eyes. And his visit would, moreover, provide an excellent opportunity to show the world that all this gossip claiming that she was sick, decrepit or dying was nonsense! She had her sixty-seventh birthday on 7th September 1600, but what of that? She would show them that she could still enchant a young nobleman of twenty-eight – and she did.

Queen Elizabeth's entertainment of Orsino proved to be one of the most brilliant of her long reign, especially notable to us for the first performance of *Twelfth Night* on Twelfth Night, 6th January 1600/1, in the presence of Duke Orsino and written undoubtedly to honour him as Elizabeth's special guest on the occasion of this unique visit of a Catholic prince to the Court of the great Protestant Queen. It was Hotson's discovery of the error in the Historical Manuscripts Commission in the papers of the Duke of Northumberland, mis-dating by one year the report on –

'A full narrative or description of the reception and entertainment of the Muscovite ambassador and of an Italian nobleman, the Duke of Bracciano, who were received at the Court of Queen Elizabeth ... upon Twelfth-day, January 6, 1601-2', [9]

that triggered his connection of this event with the royal wedding in Florence in October 1600, and the Duke's consequent visit to the Court of Gloriana. With the correction of the date to January 6, 1600-1 everything fell into place to reveal the brilliant first night of *Twelfth Night* in honour of Orsino, con-firming every detail of time and place. We share fully in Hotson's thrill of discovery as he exclaims: 'What a find!'

Orsino's curiosity to see the English Queen may have been whetted when an important visitor from England arrived at the Pitti Palace in Florence in the early spring of 1600. This was Mr William Cecil, the son and heir of Thomas Cecil, Lord Burghley, and nephew of Sir Robert Cecil, the younger son who had succeeded their father, the great Lord Burghley, as Elizabeth's chief minis-ter of state. [10] When don Virginio reached London the following winter he was given reciprocal hospitality at the home of the Cecils, [11] so perhaps the invita-tion to visit England might have been extended in Florence sowing the seed of his later decision.

When Orsino took the momentous decision to extend his fortuitous trip to France by visiting the Queen of England he wrote to his Contessa, who was confined at home, [12] soon to present him with his sixth son. He also wrote to his uncle, the Grand Duke, whom he had not previously consulted, hoping that he would give him his consent and blessing to this rather risky enterprise. [13] The Grand Duke, however, remained prudently detached from his nephew's escapade, but it nevertheless proved a most lucky throw of the dice, which later brought Orsino advantages and prestige beyond anything he could have fore-seen.

For the present, this intrepid young politician was playing a lone hand, and he travelled almost alone having 'made show to depart with the galleys, but afterwards came disguised to Avignon; he hath a purpose to pass through France, and, as I understand, into England, and the Low Countries, in which places he doth desire to pass his time during the time of this Pope.' [14] So wrote Ralph Winwood reporting to Cecil in a letter that reached London about 10th December 1600. After bidding his cousin Maria farewell at Lyons, Orsino had apparently pretended he was returning to Italy with the galleys. Instead he proceeded towards England by a leisurely route. As Dr Hotson tells us: 'He travelled modestly, *incognito* – a company of five souls. Two gentlemen: the Grand Duke's *maestro di stalla* (Master of the Horse, or Stables), Signore Giulo Riario, and a Spanish youth, Don Grazia de Montalvo; his secretary, Emilio Fei; and a servant.' [15] He sent word to his uncle Ferdinand's London agent, the wealthy Florentine merchant, Filippo Corsini, who prepared his house in Gracechurch Street to receive the travellers.

By 1st January 1600/1 he was ready to embark for England, arriving on Saturday, 3rd January 'after dinner . . in the London house of Signore Corsini, whom presently I sent to her Majesty to let her know of my arrival, and to beg her to be pleased that I might privately kiss her hands. Signore Corsini spoke with Secretary Cecil [*Secil*], who is the one who governs this kingdom, and with the Lord Chamberlain, who replied – after conferring with the Queen – that her Majesty welcomed my coming hither more than that of any gentleman who has ever arrived in her realm; and that for Tuesday (the 16th in our style, in theirs the 6th, Twelfth Day) she would appoint me audience, albeit not so private as I had desired.' [16] Orsino was writing home to his Duchess, whom he addresses lovingly as 'Signora Consorte amatissima'. He continues: 'Her Majesty has twice a day sent only principal gentlemen to visit me, causing them ever to tell me that I should consider myself not merely at Florence in the house of the Grand Duke, but at Bracciano in my own.' [17]

Later Orsino was to write again at length to recount his flattering reception at the Court, which was at Whitehall Palace that Christmas, where the Queen danced with him, and a comedy was performed which, he tantalizingly writes, he will describe to her by word of mouth when he sees her again. That this comedy was none other than the delectable *Twelfth Night,* featuring the noble Duke Orsino himself, acknowledged one of the most valiant princes of Europe, (who is presented in the play as in love with Olivia, *alias* Queen Elizabeth, in the tradition of gallantry of Gloriana's Court where all her courtiers were by definition in love with the Virgin Queen) is established by Dr Hotson's reassessment of the play, placing it in the context of the Elizabethan Court at this Christmas Saturnalia of 1600/1.

This authentic glimpse of a historical world premiere with the commentaries from people who were present at these Christmas festivities, highlighted for us by Dr Hotson's enthralling research, is included here at some length because it strongly supports the present thesis. The richness of our Poet's drama reflects his experience of the Renaissance courts of Orsino and Elizabeth, and one felicitous flowering of that influence is to be seen in the comedy he wrote to honour both his Italian lord and his royal English mistress. *Twelfth Night* was conceived, I suggest, as a New Year's gift to them both when he was evidently also celebrating his return home from his long exile.

XXVI

'THE FIRST NIGHT OF TWELFTH NIGHT' BY LESLIE HOTSON

WHEN SHALL WE ever again have an opportunity to observe, as favoured visitors transported across the time span of four centuries, the scene of Elizabeth's brilliant Court in the enjoyment of the first performance of a play by Shakespeare? This is what Dr Hotson has recreated for us in such delightful detail, supported by historical data, that we cannot doubt its authenticity. It is perhaps the most exciting of all his many remarkable Elizabethan discoveries. *Twelfth Night* was undoubtedly written especially for performance on Twelfth Night, 6th January 1600/1 to honour the visit of Duke Orsino to the Court of Queen Elizabeth. Yet he had arrived in London only three days before – secretively, *incognito,* unheralded by public acclaim, though evidently by prior confidential arrangement with Queen Elizabeth herself. This argues that the play could certainly not have been written by the London actor, William Shakespeare. On the other hand, every aspect surrounding *Twelfth Night* lends credence to its composition by Marlowe. The glittering occasion of its première was of unique importance, which we shall retrace here to reveal its authentic significance for the return of our Poet from his exile.

That *Twelfth Night* was especially written to be played on this Saturnalian night is testified by the wealth of comic mimicry of characters prominent at the Elizabethan Court that Christmas, and the compliments to the noble Italian guest present. Besides Don Virginio Orsino, there was another important foreign visitor, the Ambassador from Boris Godunov, the Tsar of all Russia, whose visit was specifically to negotiate a treaty of friendship with England. The day appointed for the confirmation of 'The league between the Muscovites and the English (by eating bread and salt with the Queen)' [1] was 6th January, Twelfth Day or Epiphany, concluding with the Saturnalia of Twelfth Night. This was the day Queen Elizabeth had also promised Orsino that he would be royally received (although not so privately as he had wished) and entertained by her at the Court. The exotic presence of the Russian Ambassador on the same day proved to be an added entertainment for Orsino, who found this extraordinary visitor wondrously amusing, as we can glean from his letters.

Grigori Mikulin, Boris Godunov's envoy, was a huge mountain of a man who, despite his exalted position, was really no more than the Tsar's *kholóp,* or serf, bound to obey his royal master in every point of protocol according to the lengthy and precise instructions he had been given, which even set down 'a catalogue of detailed replies to be made to every conceivable question he might be asked.'[2] These he had to memorize, and the 60-page report he wrote 'To the Lord Tsar and Great Prince of All Russia, Boris Fedorovich' gives a blow by blow account of all his doings in England. Fascinating! Mikulin, for all his great size, obviously lived in fear of putting a foot wrong, and showed himself susceptible to the least gesture that might be construed as a slight or dishonour to his person as the representative of his great Lord, the Tsar.[3] It was rumoured that if he did not carry out his duties exactly as he was commanded, he would be beheaded upon his return to Russia.[4] His striking manner (literally) of salutation to the Queen, and to those noblemen who attended him on her behalf, was to kneel down on both knees and, bending forward, he knocked his forehead on the ground.[5] One can imagine the sensation this created at Court every time the huge man abased himself in this way. They must have had strict instructions not to laugh!

According to his brief, Mikulin had to be the sole important guest of the Queen at the feast when she entertained him (or the Tsar would feel insulted), although he was not allowed to sit at the same table with her royal Highness, being himself but his master's bond slave, but had to have his board and chair placed at her side.[6] This put his hostess to some inconvenience, but she managed it all superbly, arranging the banqueting of Mikulin and Orsino in separate but adjacent rooms. She sat alone with Mikulin, attended by her most high-born lords who had been especially commanded to be at Court to wait on her at table to impress her Russian guest, where he was offered the ritual bread and salt with a great flourish, and the Children of the Chapel sang to them during dinner – which doubtless helped to compensate for any lack of conversation between hostess and guest. When the meal was served the Queen washed her hands with great ceremony and, as Mikulin himself reports to his Lord, the Tsar: 'having washed, she ordered the silver ewer with water to be taken to Grigori; and to her Majesty's favour Grigori prostrated himself, but did not wash his hands, and said, "Our great Lord the Tsar calls Elizabeth the Queen his beloved sister; and it doth not befit me, his bond-slave, to wash my hands in her presence". Thereupon the Queen waxed merry, and commended Grigori in that he honoured her so highly as not to wash his hands before her.'[7]

Evidently the Queen was secretly enjoying herself no end, whilst keeping a suitably straight face. This little ceremony Orsino was able to observe from the open door, where he awaited those noblemen who were serving the Queen's table, including the Lord Admiral, and apparently it amused him highly for he promises in his letter to his Contessa to relate in detail 'of her hand-washing, for this description alone would fill four sheets.'[8] The bread and salt being eaten, the peace treaty concluded, it had been pre-ordained that Mikulin would be dismissed and would not be invited to stay for the evening's entertainment, which would end with the performance of the play. This was an honour clearly designed especially for the Queen's Italian guest who was placed at the Queen's side for the dramatic entertainment. So Mikulin was sent home, well fed and his master's business despatched, leaving the dramatist a free hand to delight his audience as his Saturnalian inspiration might take him. These orders of the day must have been known to him, for our Poet was able to take advantage of the huge Muscovite who cut a figure of ridicule at the Court, and he brings him into his play archly, but subtly, so as not to cause offence in case it were reported back to him.

A contemporary description of Mikulin tells us that he was 'of tall Stature very fatte with a great face and a blacke bearde cutt round: of a swarfye Colour of his face, and his gate maiesticall.' [9] His towering height was further increased since 'his buskins were of Redd leather with highe heeles', and his figure was enveloped in a gorgeous gown or kaftan of cloth of gold, which was 'laced' with pearls, and reached his ankles. On his head this Russian bear wore 'a great furre Capp' and underneath this he wore a second cap (presumably for use indoors) 'imbroidered very richly with greate pearles'. [10] What a gift to a dramatist! But the satire would have to be skilful, for no wind of *byezchéstiye* or 'scorn' must reach the apprehensive Mikulin. [11] His touchiness on matters of protocol had been experienced.

Hotson has detected the hilarious (and subtle) take-off of Ambassador Mikulin in the arrival of Cesario (Viola in her masculine disguise) who, as Duke Orsino's personal ambassador to the Lady Olivia, arrives at her gate demanding entry so that he can convey Orsino's embassy of love to her. Olivia, having forsworn the company of men while she is in mourning for her father and brother, at first commands Malvolio to refuse Cesario entry. He presently reports back to her Ladyship that the young gentleman answers 'very shrewishly' and will not be denied, for he –

> 'would seem to have "some hideous matter to deliver, the courtesy of it is so fearful", but – just like the very great fat Muscovite – holds the olive-branch in his hand, brings no overture of war, no taxation of homage. Admitted at length in audience, and primed to the teeth with his memorized speech as full of peace as matter, he is instantly miffed at not being told at once which is "the honourable Lady of the house"; whereupon, after a step or two with "gait majestical", and a hand spread below the chin for the "round black beard", comes the loaded line, in a russified and ominous voice – *"Let me sustain no scorn; I am very comptible * even to the least sinister usage."* And the next speech hits off Mikulin's by-rote answers, dictated by his puppet-master the Tsar: *"I can say little more than I have studied, and that question's out of my part".* ' [12]

Hotson comments: 'What a delicious drollery we have been missing – the little boy-actress aping that Russian colossus.' [13]

* Foot-note: 'accountable', in the sense taking account of, susceptible.

The play was given as the last entertainment of the evening in the specially prepared Great Hall or Noon-hall of Whitehall Palace, where the carpenters had been busy erecting the seating for a performance *in the round*. Dr Hotson has resuscitated this historic first night to show us exactly how the play was presented before that elegant assembly in the candle-lit Noon-hall, the court seated on wooden tiers or 'degrees' constructed to varying heights against all four walls, the rows below the tall arras-hung windows, which were thus 'curtained' against the night sky and the winter cold, reaching under these windows to only three tiers in height, whilst against the walls they were as high as ten tiers – up 'in the gods' – to accommodate all the spectators. The play was performed on the floor space in the centre of the hall, where it had been preceded by a splendid ball. Dancing was the Elizabethans' favourite pastime.

Don Virginio found this dramatic presentation 'in the round' sufficiently novel to comment on in his letter to his Duchess where he describes how the 'degrees with ladies – *gradi con dame* – stood *atorno atorno*': that is, all round and round about the chamber. [14.] There would be no scenic changes once the portable, light-framed 'mansions' representing Olivia's house and Orsino's house had been placed, with a stage-property box hedge for the concealment of the comic trio who secretly observe Malvolio in the letter-scene. The Elizabethan theatrical 'mansions' were beautifully painted, having wide windows with curtains which could be drawn or opened to hide or show the persons within.

Queen Elizabeth's dais under its canopy was placed somewhat forward of the surrounding courtiers ranked against the walls. Here she sat for the performance with her honoured guest, Duke Orsino, beside her, to whom she would have translated as required in her fluent Italian, for he spoke no English. [15] He would quickly have picked up the plot for it was taken from a well known Siennese comedy, *Gl' Ingannati* (The Deceived) which was popular in the Duke's own Tuscany. [16] The play soon offers a pointed compliment to the Duke when Viola, upon landing in Illyria, questions the Captain who has saved her from drowning after her shipwreck.

> *Viola.* Who governs here?
> *Captain.* A noble duke, in nature as in name.
> *Viola.* What is his name?
> *Captain.* Orsino.
> *Viola.* Orsino! I have heard my father name him.

And his relationship of hopeless love for Olivia-*alias*-Elizabeth immediately establishes the courtly tradition of ardent love for the Virgin Queen.

> *Captain.* .... but a month ago I went from hence,
> And then 'twas fresh in murmur – as, you know,
> What great ones do the less will prattle of –
> That he did seek the love of fair Olivia. [17]

But this fair, virtuous lady has taken a vow to renounce the company of men as she is in deep mourning for her dead brother: 'she will admit no kind of suit – No, not the Duke's' [18] It is a compliment to the Queen who had been wooed by kings and princes to no avail. Throughout the play deft touches in the portrait of Olivia reveal how well the Poet knew Elizabeth's tastes and idiosyncracies. Olivia, as Hotson points out, is a representation of the Queen in her youth, as the mirror of her days held up to compliment her. No less is Orsino complimented and drawn to the life. The Duke's first-born children were twins, a boy and a girl, who are mirrored in the twins, Viola and Sebastian:

> An apple cleft in two is not more twin
> Than these two creatures. [19]

The plot of *Gl' Ingannati* was ideally chosen for it revolves around the comedy of these twins and the resultant mix-up. Orsino's valiant exploits in battle against the Turks are also remembered in a glancing reference. He gained fame at the siege of Giavarino in 1585 for his valour, and in 1589 he led a Florentine naval expedition for the Grand Duke with the aim of capturing Chios from the Turks, and though this sea-battle went against him, Orsino distinguished himself by his cool-headed courage in successfully extricating his ships in the retreat. He received a bullet-wound as memento, gaining personal honour and glory even in defeat. [20] Orsino's love of music is also strikingly featured. The Duke would easily have recognized himself.

In Illyria

Twelfth Night is one of the most romantic comedies in the canon. It opens on the theme of fervent love, and its main characters are all in love – with a liberal seasoning of confusion of identity and sex to spice it. Despite Dr Hotson's in depth research which has put the record straight, the play's setting in Illyria is still seen by Shakespearean directors as just a make-believe land. Beguiled by the romantic sound of this name, Illyria is imagined to be some kind of Arcadia, and misconstruing the title of the play, *Twelfth Night or What You Will*, some critics suppose that this choice of title indicates that only a superficial connection is intended with the festival of Twelfth Night. Hotson has utterly routed this fallacious interpretation by showing that its very setting, Illyria, is chosen *because* this part of the Dalmation-Croatian coast was noted for its riotous, wine-bibbing inhabitants – the ideal country for Twelfth Night's wassailing and carousing. The dramatist purposely set his comedy in this land of hard drinkers and riotous livers, and to his educated Elizabethan audience Illyria would immediately have conjured up the land in which the mad licence permitted during the Saturnalia would traditionally flourish; [21] while *What You Will* obviously carries a sexual connotation. Illyria was also notorious for its pirates. [22] Antonio is accused of piracy, though he refutes the charge.

The underlying moral theme of the whole comedy of *Twelfth Night* is that of man's enslavement to drink, which provides much hearty laughter but is also warned against as the path to ultimate degradation. Sir Toby Belch is a typical Illyrian in his devout drinking of healths to the Lady Olivia, his fair niece.

> 'I'll drink to her as long as there's a passage in my throat and drink in Illyria. He's a coward and a coystrill that will not drink to my niece till his brains turn o' th' toe like a parish top.' [23]

But Olivia scolds him out for a 'rudesby'. The two carousing, toping knights, Sir Toby Belch and his boozing companion Sir Andrew Aguecheeke are true denizens of Illyria. Both men are well-named, but Aguecheeke has been completely misunderstood, and is always represented as a sickly, pale, thin, drip of a man with his lank, finely spun blonde hair hanging 'like flax on a distaff'. This image is not at all as our Poet conceived him. Hotson has established that this 'foolish knight' is, in fact, of Spanish blood and, far from being a pale, sickly sort of fellow – which his name Aguecheeke is misconstrued to mean – he is 'as tall a man as any's in Illyria', [24] a hard-drinking, beef-eating dolt, fit companion for the bibulous Sir Toby Belch; hefty rather than skinny, and proud of his bulging calves for he fancies himself as a nimble dancer. His lank, sparse hair, straight but doubtless black, is referred to sarcastically (not literally) as flax on a spindle, signifying his slender wit for people with thin hair were reputedly bird-brained. Sir Toby values him mainly for his wealth, of which he is intent on fleecing him, for he has an income of three thousand ducats a year, and – as Hotson points out – these are 'Spanish ducats, legitimate booty for an Englishman like himself.' [25] (Sir Toby is, in fact, an Illyrian but he bears a good English name that depicts him to the life.)

Sir Toby's answer to Maria's scolding for his association with this doltish knight, in whom she can see no virtue, is significant:

> *Toby.* What, wench, *castigliano vulgo!* [26]

In other words, *vulgo:* to spread about: spread the castilians, *viz.* spend them lavishly. [27] This is his sole, mercenary interest in cultivating Sir Andrew's company and feeding his ridiculous love-suit to Olivia, leading him by the nose to imagine he stands to gain her hand if he only hangs around long enough, while the two of them spend their time and his money drinking at the charge of his Spanish ducats, or castilians.

Hotson concludes: 'Since Aguecheeke's income is in castilians, the simpleton must be supposed a Spaniard: and if so, we have hitherto failed to catch his descriptive Spanish name under its anglicized spelling.' [28] This is brilliant deduction! Hotson alone has spotted the Spanish origin of his name concealed by the typical Elizabethan spelling according to the sound of the Spanish *'Aguchica*, Little-wit, shortened from *agucia chica* or *agudeza chica',* [29] which is far removed from the English 'Aguecheeke' with its apparent connotation of agues and sickliness, being merely the Elizabethan spelling of *agu-chica*. It will be objected that Sir Toby also calls him 'Agueface', to which Hotson replies that this connotes *Agua-fáce*, which is Spanish for 'Makes water'. Most appropriate for a hard drinker! Sir Toby is referring to Aguecheeks' large capacity for drinking. Sir Andrew's two great accomplishments are his drinking and his dancing, which are deliciously sparked off by Sir Toby:

> Why dost thou not go to church in a galliard and come home in a coranto? My very walk should be a jig; I would not so much as make water but in a sink-a-pace. What dost thou mean? Is it a world to hide virtues in? I did think, by the excellent constitution of thy leg, it was form'd under the star of a galliard. [30]

Note the reference to 'make water', and the spelling of 'sink-a-pace', which is the French *Cinque-a-pace*, or five steps, also thoroughly anglicized. Aguecheeke is not only noted for being a great drinker, but a great quarreller. Moreover, he combines this with being a notorious coward when it comes to a proper fight. Toby declares that 'if he were open'd and you find so much blood in his liver as will clog the foot of a flea, I'll eat the rest of th' anatomy.' [31]

It would have highly delighted an Elizabethan audience to be presented with a Spaniard as the butt of the comedy, held up to ridicule as an arrant coward, as a dim-witted ass, and artfully fleeced of his castilians by the bluff, hard-drinking Sir Toby. Aguecheeke is himself aware of his poor mental equipment and is well described by Hotson as an 'artless zany "always enjoying a joke, never understanding it".' [32] Maria's witty banter easily puts him down and, crestfallen, he decides he will go back home, at which Sir Toby asks in consternation: 'Pourquoi, my dear knight?' This is beyond Sir Andrew: 'What is "pourquoi" – do, or not do?' He confesses ruefully: 'I am a great eater of beef, and I believe that does harm to my wit.' [33]

One can imagine the Queen's Yeomen of the Guard, the tall, red-coated Beefeaters, wincing at that one! For the Queen's stalwart Yeomen were stationed at all the entrances to the Noon-hall at the first performance of *Twelfth Night* (as our Poet would have well known they would be). We can now see that the beef-eating Aguecheeke, a tall man but slow-witted, served as a take-off of both Spaniards and English Beefeaters. [34] Feste, the clown, refers to them also as the 'myrmidons' who, being red-coated, might be mistaken by a drunkard for the red-latticed ale-house in his hitherto obscure quip: 'and the Myrmidons are not bottle-ale houses'. Hotson interprets this: 'Lurch absently into one of them for another drink, and you'll wish you hadn't.' [35] He cites Marston's: 'as well known by my wit as an alehouse by a red lattice', from his *Antonio and Mellida*. [36] Every contemporary allusion that he identifies, Hotson copiously corroborates with evidence from literary sources to support it.

The entire play abounds in topical, witty jests and apt allusions and quips that accurately reflect the time, the people and the place, the Saturnalia of Misrule at the Court on Twelfth Night, when those in authority were fair game as the butt of the fun, and it was permissible to indulge in endless jokes at the expense of others' foibles and idiosyncracies, misdeeds or failings, even ridiculing them without mercy. The chief butt chosen to provide the comedy for this particular Saturnalia is unmistakably and wickedly portrayed in Malvolio – an identification which clinches the play as the Whitehall performance of *Twelfth Night or What You Will* on 6th January 1600/1, the *double entendre* of the word 'will' having a special application to the character of Malvolio and the original he is lampooning. Dr Hotson has identified for us who this highly-placed personage at the Court was.

Who Was Malvolio?

In the Steward of the Lady Olivia's household is depicted the elderly Comptroller of her Majesty's Household, Sir William Knollys (later to become Earl of Banbury) [37] who was observed to have grown lecherous in his dotage, for he was making overtures of love to one of Queen Elizabeth's favourite Maids of Honour, Mary Fitton, offering to make her Lady Knollys as soon as his present aged and ailing wife had vacated her elevated position, who, however, though apparently sick unto death was inconsiderately refusing to give up the ghost. Knollys love-letters to Mary Fitton are extant. [38] That young lady, aged twenty-two to Knolly's fifty-three, was playing fast and loose with her own good name carrying on a hot love-affair under Knollys' nose with the young Lord William Herbert, soon to become Earl of Pembroke. Toby's arch comment that 'Mistress Mall's picture' is 'like to take dust' voices the rumour that Mistress Fitton was with child by her young aristocratic lover, which presently became a major Court scandal. The name Malvolio can readily be seen to fit Knollys to perfection, Mall being a common Elizabethan nickname for Mary, and *volio* or *voglio* connoting 'I want', hence *Malvolio* may be read as 'I want Mall'. [39]

Knollys, known about the Court as 'Mr Controller', had responsibility for the expenses of the Queen's household for all the meals served, and for the routine domestic management of the palace in a supervisory capacity, overseeing the hundreds of servants, most of whom were men in Elizabethan times. As his symbol of office Mr Controller carried a long, white staff. He was a member of the Privy Council, hence an important man to target as this Twelfth Night's fool. I believe that the Walsinghams gave Marlowe the inspiration for this, having regaled him with Court gossip which he would avidly have sought in order to embellish his play with authentic touches for the night's revelry.

The similarities between Malvolio and Knollys are skilfully etched into the portrait and are unmistakable. Knollys was known for his Puritan opinions, and his estates in Oxfordshire included the town of Banbury, famed for its association with psalm-singing weavers, fanatical in their Puritan zeal, and its

398

excellent cakes and ale. Sir Toby is given a bull's eye hit-line in his retort to Malvolio when he appears in nightcap and gown to order them to cease their midnight carousing:

> 'Art any more than a steward? Dost thou think, because thou art virtuous, there shall be no more cakes and ale?' [40]

There is a tale told in a jest-book of 1650 that Lord Knollys' lodging in the palace was adjacent to that of the Ladies and Maids of Honour who 'us'd to friske and hey about in the next roome, to his extreame disquiete a nights, though he had often warned them of it; at last he getts one to bolt their owne backe doore, when they were all in one night of their revells, stripps off his shirt, and so with a payre of spectacles on his nose, and *Aretine* in his hand, comes marching in at a posterne doore of his owne chamber, reading very gravely, full upon the faces of them.' To force them to be quiet he is said to have 'often traverst the roome in this posture above an houre.' [41] The story is unconfirmed, but it sounds as if it might well be the origin of that fantastical scene in which Malvolio descends upon the Illyrian revellers in his nightgown, his Puritan decorum scandalized by such licence, to scold them roundly: 'Have you no wit, manners, nor honesty, but to gabble like tinkers at this time of night?' [42] It is a glorious scene of Misrule in which the high-spirited Sir Toby is irrepressible and only plays up the more, telling Malvolio to go 'rub your chain with crumbs'. [43] The sweet revenge Maria exacts is the famous gulling letter wherein Malvolio is hooked, thinking he reads a confession of the Lady Olivia's love for him.

> 'M.O.A.I. doth sway my life'. Nay, but first let me see, let me see, let me see. [44]

Malvolio, of course, is intent from the first moment on making the clue yield his name. 'If I could make that resemble something in me! Softly! M.O.A.I. . . M – Malvolio. M. why that begins my name! A should follow, but O does.' He never solves the riddle but comes to his conclusion regardless that it *must* apply to him: 'to crush this a little, it would bow to me, for every one of these letters is in my name.' [45] All eagerness to believe that he is the man on whom fortune has (deservedly!) smiled, our gull is soon hooked.

Dr Hotson, never to be outclassed by any Elizabethan conundrum he sets his mind to solve, has deciphered Maria's clever clue for us. 'M.O.A.I. doth sway my life' is a perfectly true statement. He points out that the key word 'element' recurs more frequently in *Twelfth Night* than in any other of Shakespeare's plays, [46] the dramatist having scattered the clue to his fustian riddle right through his text for the alertest minds in his audience to pick up, and as a reward for these brightest wits the fun of Malvolio's gulling must instantly have trebled their delight.

Here then, for the modern ignoramus (I confess to having been one myself) is the solution of the riddle: 'Maria has cleverly chosen those 'fustian' designations of the (four) elements whose initials appear in his name: *Mare* – Sea, *Orbis* – Earth, *Aer* – Air, and *Ignis* – Fire. M.O.A.I.' [47] Hotson expounds the intricacy of the riddle's precise construction in depth:

'Fire hot and dry, air moist and hot we call;
Seas cold and moist, earth dry and cold withal.

'Her 'dish o' poison' dupes the self-loved *MALVOLIO* into imagining himself Controller of Lady Olivia, although every fool knows that she is swayed only by *Mare, Orbis, Aer*, and *Ignis*. And the order of Maria's arrangement of the elemental four is thoroughly appropriate. According to accepted theory, Woman is cold and moist, Man, hot and dry; in the elements swaying Olivia, therefore, *Mare* must take first place. Also she commands Malvolio ('*I may command where I adore*'): consequently *Mare* leads and *Ignis* comes last. Moreover, in mourning her brother, Olivia's controlling emotion is grief: and 'Grief like water cold and moist' is again *Mare*.' [48]

The little conundrum is a brilliant piece of wit. The word 'adore' is also pointed. As Hotson explains:

'This riddle is an essential part of the practical joke on Malvolio. Elaborate plots to make somebody look a fool constituted a principal Court pastime in the holidays. The current courtier's slang for the jest was to *dor* someone – "that villain dors me" – or to give someone the *dor* . . the term is obviously borrowed from the Dutch: *een door*, a fool. . . Shakespeare . . brings in the *dor*-ing, but so lightly and deftly that we have failed to notice it – in the foolish Sir Andrew's innocent echo of Sir Toby's boast of Maria's love for him: "She's a beagle true bred, and one that adores me: what o' that?"
    Sir Andrew: "I was a-*dor*'d once too". ' [49]

Self-love was a sin much deprecated by the Elizabethans, and it is Malvolio's self-love that makes him such an easy prey to fall into Maria's skilfully baited trap. 'In their mad "allowed foolling" ' the quarry Malvolio (Mr Controller Knollys) is mercilessly 'slaughtered in gross and in detail' [50] as revealed by Hotson as he uncovers the relentless pin-pricks and stabs of pointed identification with which the character is larded thick and richly. 'Sir Toby prepares the unmistakable victim both with "*Mal-voglio*'s a Peg a Ramsey", and by singing *There dwelt a man in Babylon* – the ballad of the Elders' lust for fair young Susanna'. [51]

Is not this a deliciously wicked comment on –

'the fifty-three-year-old Mr Controller, who, though troubled with a wife, fancied himself a fit husband for the belle of the young Maids of Honour, and longed for Mall while she made an ass of him with a handsome rival less than half his age? If she brought scandal on the Queen's Court, he had brought something worse – ridicule. The favourite refrain to the tune of Peg a Ramsey fitted him almost beyond belief:

When I was a bachelor I led a merry life;
But now I am a married man, and troubled with a wife
. . .
Give me my yellow hose again, give me my yellow hose!
For now my wife she watcheth me: see yonder where she goes!

Yellow hose, or long stockings, are infallibly indicated for this "Peg a Ramsey" Mr Controller, the married man who would a-wooing go . .' [52]

Following the instructions in the gulling Letter Malvolio presents himself before the Lady Olivia continually smiling (leering) dressed in yellow stockings, – 'a colour she abhors' exults Maria, [53] and it was also the colour Queen Elizabeth detested. Her personal colours were black and white, but yellow was the colour of the flag of Spain, her old enemy, and it was the colour of that traitor, the Duke of Norfolk, who was executed in 1572. 'Yellow was also the proper wear of jealous-foolish husbands, the English by-word for "jealousy" was "to wear yellow stockings and cross-garters". ' [54]. Both long stockings and cross-gartering were out-of-date by 1600, the latter style favoured only by 'old men, Puritans, pedants, footmen, and rustic bridegrooms' – all very apt for Mr Controller.

Malvolio, by his ridiculous behaviour in Olivia's presence is believed to be mad, which brings us back to the mad, riotous kingdom of Illyria in which the comedy of this appropriately named *Twelfth Night* is set. Dr Hotson comments:

'Wise men hold that there is a no great wit without a mixture of madness. Further, that "there is a pleasure sure in being mad which none but madmen know". "Wild, madding, jocund, and irregular", the world of *Twelfth Night* is a very mad world, exceeding mad. Small wonder that the epithet mad appears here more often than in any other play of Shakespeare's. Sir Toby in drink speaks nothing but madman; witty Maria is a finder of madmen; self-loving Malvolio, both sad-mad and madly-used; Lady Olivia in love, merry-mad; the startled Sebastian not only asks, "Are all the people mad?" but is forced to the conclusion, "I am mad or else the lady's mad." And Feste, mad by vocation, seconds the notion by calling her *Mad-donna*. The piece is shot through with the mad mood of hilarity – only heightened by a humourless Malvolio, who holds with the Preacher: "I said of laughter, it is mad; and of mirth, what doeth it?" ' [55]

Toby's Illyrian friend Fabian joins them in 'the mad jest on Malvolio'. Even his name is significant, deriving from the Elizabethan term, 'a flaunting fabian', one who is 'a riotous, lavish roister'. [56]

All the names in *Twelfth Night* have significance. Sir Toby Belch is well-named in both his surname and in his Christian name: 'the prime aura of suggestion to Sir Toby's name and nature is the Biblical one, from the Apocrypha: in itself an affront to Puritan-sympathizers such as '*Mal'-voglio* and Mr Controller Knollys. For the Puritans vehemently rejected the Apocryphal books. . . Aside from the Angel, and the Devil – who killed his bride's seven previous grooms – the salient points in Toby's story were two: (a) his fish, and (b) his postponed wedding night.' [57] To drink like a fish is a common saying even today, but it is less well known that the Church in A.D. 398 prescribed that the first night of marriage be held in abstinence. George Chapman wrote: 'it is the use/That the first night of marriage the bridegroom spares the bride', [58] and this custom was familiarly referred to as the 'Toby'night', during which the bridegroom took his consolation in a heavy drinking bout. Sir Toby is given to celebrating every night as a 'Toby-night', and Feste remarks to Maria: 'If Sir Toby would leave drinking, thou wert as witty a piece of Eve's flesh as any in Illyria.' [59] In other words, he might *then* be actually brought to the marriage bed.

One aspect of the cross-wooing around which the plot of *Twelfth Night* revolves, which Hotson's dating of the play to 1600/1 has revealed, is that 6th January 1600/1 fell in Leap Year, for by the Old Style calendar it was still 1600 until Lady Day, 25th March, when the Elizabethan New Year began. Hence the ladies have all the success in wooing. Olivia woos Cesario, thinking he is a man, and gains her husband in Sebastian. She is also represented in the gulling Letter as wooing Malvolio. Maria wins her Toby as the reward for her clever trickery of Malvolio, which so delights him that he marries her. Viola in the guise of a boy is able to confess her love for Orsino, and wins him. [60]

The Noon-hall of Whitehall Palace

The magnificent setting for this important première was the great candle-lit Noon-hall in the palace which was built for his own use by Cardinal Wolsey. Alas, this was destroyed by fire in 1698. Its name derives from its exact South-North orientation, with a great clerestory window at either end and tall bay windows along the entire length of the side. For the performance of the play the Queen's daïs was positioned at the South end. The text of the play

402

reflects the orientation of the Great Hall, the South position of the Queen's throne, the windows of the Hall that were hung with arras against the cold January night, the location of the adjacent Chapel – all are unmistakeably referred to in the play, so that Dr Hotson has been able to reconstruct precisely how the comedy was staged.

The stage properties, consisting of two beautifully painted, delicately constructed little 'mansions', were placed thus: Olivia's house (East) and Orsino's house (West), each 'mansion' having two entrances and/or exits, with all the surrounding floor space providing the playing area. [61] This staging is confirmed by the text, as, for instance, when Olivia dismisses Cesario from her house, she directs him back to his master Orsino's home with a scornful gesture: 'There lies your way, *due West'*.[62] When Fabian admonishes Sir Andrew for his lack of valour, by which he has put himself at the farthest point from his lady's favour, he tells him: 'You are now sailed into the North of my lady's opinion', [63] and we detect a meaningful glance at the Queen (whom Olivia identifies) seated on her throne at the South of the Great Hall.

We are given a precise picture of the great Noon-hall in Feste's remarks, when he impersonates the cleric Sir Topas who comes to torment Malvolio as he is imprisoned for his alleged madness in Olivia's house (which is curtained to conceal him).

Malvolio.	(*within*) Who calls there?
Clown.	Sir Topas the curate, who comes to visit Malvolio the lunatic.
Malvolio.	Sir Topas, Sir Topas, good Sir Topas, go to my lady.
Clown.	Out, hyperbolical friend! How vexest thou this man! Talkest thou nothing but of ladies!
	. . .
Malvolio.	Sir Topas, never was man thus wronged. Good Sir Topas, do not think I am mad; they have laid me here in hideous darkness.
Clown.	Fie, thou dishonest Satan! . . Say'st thou that house is dark?
Malvolio.	As hell, Sir Topas.
Clown	(*looking about him, round the brilliantly-lighted Noon-hall with its bay windows and clerestories blocked with hangings*) [This is Hotson's inserted direction] Why, it hath bay windows transparent as barricadoes, and the clerestories toward the south north are as lustrous as ebony; and yet complainest thou of obstruction?*

*Foot-note: Malvolio had previously complained that his cross-gartering created some obstruction in his legs.

Malvolio.	I am not mad, Sir Topas. I say to you this house is dark.
Clown.	Madman, thou errest. I say there is no darkness but ignorance. [64]

We hardly need reminding that this play is from the pen of 'that pure elemen-tall wit, *Chr. Marlow*', but here he announces again his credo: 'I hold there is no sin but ignorance', and it is from the mouth of his clown, Feste, just as he used the clown Touchstone in *As You Like It* to express himself and give clues. As a free-thinker Marlowe interpreted this literally in its Rennaissance scientific application to the pursuit of knowledge, but as a Divinity student he would have been well aware of its religious significance for the Festival of Light which had been celebrated in the service in the Chapel earlier that day, 6th January, named Epiphany in the Christian calendar.

The Feast of the Epiphany celebrates the divine nature of Christ in the ado-ration of the Three Kings who acknowledged the infant Jesus as their divinely-born King, the Messiah or Saviour of the world; hence the ritual of the Epiphany ceremony represents man's liberation from darkness and sin by the illumination of the light of divine knowledge symbolically *expelling blind ignorance by God's light.*[65] This idea is brilliantly woven into the fooling that Feste plays out with Malvolio in his cell of darkness, but it contains the *double entente* of Marlowe's favourite credo – and he often speaks through his Fool. Shakespeare's Fools require a study to themselves in the light of this thesis.

The Epiphany service was the beginning of that day of splendour at the court. That morning in the Queen's Chapel at Whitehall the Epiphany service had been conducted with the entire Court dressed in sparkling white going in ordered procession to the Chapel, where the Archbishop of Canterbury, Marlowe's old enemy Whitgift, assisted by the Bishop of London, in their white and gold copes, led the service to the singing of the Children of the Chapel with Dr John Bull playing the organ. [66] The Queen went down to kneel at the communion table to present the traditional gifts of gold, frankincense and myrrh. Don Virginio Orsino, in flagrant disobedience of the Papal authority, watched the ceremony from the upper closet overlooking the Chapel on the Queen's side, while Mikulin was placed to watch from the window overlooking the Chapel on the opposite side. [67]

It seems the Archbishop Whitgift and his Prelate were to be present at the performance of the play that night. Whitgift was a keen lover of the drama – and he also kept a fool – often having plays and entertainments performed pri-vately at his palaces of Lambeth and Croydon. In this sense he was not a Puritan! Hotson accepts that the dramatist would have known about these arrangements, and he suggests: 'With so handsome a body of Clergy present, Shakespeare must give them something more'[68] over and above the comic antics when Feste impersonates Sir Topas, the curate. The Biblical and religious allusions in *Twelfth Night* are numerous, beginning with the first scene between

Olivia and Cesario, when the lady, intrigued, relaxes her adamant rejection of Orsino's suit, curious to hear this persistent and attractive young messenger of love.

> | | |
> |---|---|
> | *Olivia.* | What are you? What would you? |
> | *Viola.* | . . What I am and what I would are as secret as maiden head – to your ears divinity; to any other's profanation. |
> | *Olivia.* | Give us the place alone; we will hear this divinity. Now, sir, what is your text? |
> | *Viola.* | Most sweet lady – |
> | *Olivia.* | A comfortable doctrine, and much may be said of it. Where lies your text? |
> | *Viola.* | In Orsino's bosom. |
> | *Olivia.* | In his bosom? In what chapter of his bosom? |
> | *Viola.* | To answer by the method: in the first of his heart. |
> | *Olivia.* | O, I have read it; it is heresy. [69] |

When we recall that this was played in the presence of Whitgift, the author of his tragedy, its irony strikes one as neat. The play is a rich tapestry of wit incorporating a wealth of seasonal, Biblical and traditional allusions, topicality of persons, place, events and time with which it is packed. These include echoes of Rabelais, and references to the ancient Twelfth Night sport of Hunt the Fox, and the holiday pastimes of gambling with dice in trey-trip, spinning the tee-totum, or four-sided top, and every witty detail declares the inspiration of its name, *Twelfth Night.*

To conclude, we cannot pass over the fact that *Twelfth Night* is the most musical of all Shakespeare's plays. This is in perfect accord with the Queen's expressed wishes when she was making her preparations for the Twelfth Night entertainment of her important visitor. When she was briefing her Lord Chamberlain, Lord Hunsdon, her 'good George', he took copious notes concerning the Queen's requirements. These included the memorandum:

> To confer with my Lord Admiral and the Master of the Revells for taking order generally with the players to make choyse of [?the] play that shalbe best furnished with rich apparell, have greate variety and change of Musicke and daunces, and of a Subiect that may be most pleasing to her Ma*je*stie.' [70]

Elizabeth would have wanted especially to impress her noble Italian visitor of whose love of music she would probably been advised. A most cultured gentleman this, a Florentine from the sophisticated nobility of the Medicis, noted patrons of art and music and literature, in whose capital city of Florence the first opera had just been performed in honour of his cousin's splendid wedding, of which she would have been given detailed information. This she had to match! Much thought and planning preceded Orsino's visit. This is reflected in

405

Olivia's lines: 'he says he'll come. How shall I feast him? What bestow of him?' [71] spoken in anticipation of Cesare/Viola's visit.

In *Twelfth Night* the Queen was given all that she asked for, from its first moment, opening with Orsino's languishment in love for his Olivia to the accompaniment of delicious music. This equally reflects the love of music of the real Orsino, of which there is ample evidence. The whole comedy is richly interspersed with music and song; no less than nine songs and two musical interludes. One song was especially reserved for the Queen's own singer, Robert Hales, the 'Orpheus of the Court', for whom she had requested ' to have one place expresly to shewe his owne voyce' [72] and a very lovely song it is, that was reserved for him. Here is the musical catalogue of *Twelfth Night:*

Opening music to Orsino's speech: *'If music be the food of love'*

Songs:	*O mistress mine* – sung by Feste	
	Hold thy peace – catch sung by Toby, Andrew and Feste	
	Three merry men be we }	
	There dwelt a man in Babylon }	sung by Sir Toby
	O' the Twelfth day of December }	
	Farewell dear heart, since I must needs be gone	sung by Toby and Feste in alternate lines answering each other (cf. an opera!)

Musical interlude while the singer Robert Hales is fetched.

Song: *Come away, Come away, Death*   – sung by Robert Hales

Music on the pipe and tabor to Feste's dance.

Song: *I am gone, sir, and anon, sir*   – sung by Feste

When that I was a little, tiny boy   – sung by Feste

The play begins and ends with music, and is filled with music, which we may be sure was all 'most pleasing to her Majestie' as also to Duke Orsino. The queen would no doubt have appreciated the bawdiness in Feste's famous and haunting final song, for Elizabeth was a true woman of her time. The Elizabethans responded with gusto to ribaldry, and it may not be generally realised that Feste's delightful song, hey-hoing about the wind and the rain, is really a very bawdy song about sex and drunkenness, which incapacitates a man, robbing him of his virility. This musical gem is actually a piece of Elizabethan ribaldry all about sex as Hotson so delightfully explains. [73]

To the 'little tiny boy' his 'bauble' or member is but a 'foolish toy'; then as he grows to manhood he can use it to cuckold another man, and when he misbehaves men will 'shut their gate' against him, and he is left out in 'the wind and the rain'; when he 'came, alas! to wive', his wife drove him to drink, 'for

406

the rain it raineth every day'. And finally he is incapable, having come 'unto my beds' with 'drunken toss-pots'. And so the story of mankind goes on for 'A great while ago the world begun, With hey, ho, the wind and the rain'. The haunting, plaintive song tells a tale with a moral about the evils of drunkenness to end the night in the well-loved minor key.

Bawdry tickled the Elizabethan sense of humour and *Twelfth Night* has its full quota of sexual innuendo in the utterances of Feste. 'Historically the Fool and the indecency cannot be parted'. Hotson reminds us. [74] Nature, it was believed, had blessed fools with extra virility to compensate for their little wits. Hence ribaldry is the province of the Court Fool who makes play with his bauble to point his jokes. He is, of course, no fool but an exceedingly witty man. The sweet-voiced singing fool of the Lord Chamberlain's men was Robin Armin, who played not only Feste but Lear's Fool as well. 'Knavish, licentious speech is common to both roles; and Armin's rendering of Feste's song proved so popular that an additional Stanza was sung in *Lear – He that has and a little tiny wit.*' [75]

If one were looking for a contrasted companion piece in the works for the *Twelfth Night,* then I suggest *King Lear* is that: the one, a riotous comedy about a mad, mad world set in Illyria; the other, a deep and heart-rending tragedy about madness in this real world of mad-cruel men and women who destroy each other in the madness of their wickedness. And in each play the Fool plays a significant part.

In his book *The First Night of Twelfth Night* Leslie Hotson has uncovered layer upon layer of allusive textual delights to heighten our appreciation of this gloriously witty comedy. It is a scintillating historic occasion that Dr Hotson's research has captured, and it is tantalizing to allow the imagination to picture Sir Thomas Walsingham, with his Lady who had recently given birth to their son, little Thomas, in 1600, watching this latest theatrical offering of his Poet. It is conceivable that Marlowe would have insinuated himself into the audience, suitably disguised, to see the first performance of his play. He had woven into his comedy the 'shadow' representations of two royal personages whom he had served, and who were both present watching his Saturnalian comedy. How could he have stayed away? When we recall that it was (by hypothesis) this cultivated Italian prince, whom he had served abroad, and this remarkable Queen of England whose confidential agent he had for many years been, it is obvious that for him the vital interest of this unique occasion cannot be overestimated.

Twelfth Night is one of Shakespeare's all-time favourites, for its infectious comedy and romance come across the intervening centuries with a perennial freshness, even when we do not understand every witty nuance. Now, given its Elizabethan perspective, the fun and enchantment of this superb comedy can be more fully appreciated by modern audiences. The foregoing has merely dipped selectively into Leslie Hotson's *The First Night of Twelfth Night* – a book that should never be allowed to go out of print. Students of Shakespeare will find it an invaluable repository of information and delights which illuminate the text of *Twelfth Night* and reveal its historical setting in a way no other research has ever done.

The only documented evidence to a performance of *Twelfth Night or What You Will*, identifying the play by name, is in the diary of John Manningham, a law student of the Middle Temple, where the play was performed the following year at Candlemas, 2nd February 1601/2. There is nothing to suggest that this was its *first* performance, however, although this is how some orthodox scholars choose to interpret it. They cite two references to 'the Sophy', the popular name for the fabulously rich Shah of Persia, as important evidence for dating it. These may possibly reflect a recent play about the Shah. But it is Orsino who is a central character, not the Shah, nor Sir Robert Shirley who returned in 1599 from a visit to the Persian court in a ship aptly named 'The Sophy'. This kind of titivation of old plays is typical of the way in which the actors constantly revised their stock by adding 'topical tips'. (See Henslowe's *Diary* for payments for alterations and additions to old plays). These two minor references could be slipped in by the actors themselves without any reference to the original author, and they are not gems of blank verse, but mere bits of textual commentary, as evidenced in Fabian's –

'I will not give my part of this sport for a pension of thousands
from the Sophy,'   (2. 5. 1.174)

and Sir Toby's comment boosting Sir Andrew Aguecheek's bogus prowess in fencing in order to frighten Viola the more: 'They say he has been a fencer to the Sophy.'(3. 4. 1.271).

These are just examples of topical references used to spice a play's fashionable appeal for the audience. But *two* such references *cannot negate the mountain of evidence* produced by Hotson's research linking this play with Orsino and an especially brilliant Twelfth Night celebration in the Duke's honour on 6th January 1600/1.

XXVII

The Elizabethan Enchantment

IT IS A PROFOUND disappointment that Don Virginio did not describe or name the play he saw in the great Noon-hall that night when writing to his Duchess, but, promising her that he will tell her about it, he refers to it as *'una commedia mescolata, con musiche e balli'* [1] – a mixed comedy with music and dances. This is, at least, an appropriate brief description of *Twelfth Night*. Probably there were additional interludes of music and dancing introduced by way of relaxation for the audience corresponding to our intervals, when they could break their silence and talk, and the Queen would impart to Don Virginio any part of the story he might not have fully understood, especially the finer points of the wit.

Don Virginio makes abundantly clear in his letters to her that his visit to the English Court was an altogether enchanting experience. His enthusiasm for the elegancies of the Queen's reception and prestigious treatment of him personally is infectiously communicated, and his admiration for the scale and splendour of the courtly ceremonial suggest that Elizabeth had made special preparations to present her royal household to him at its most magnificent. Orsino's description of his meeting with her on the morning of Twelfth Day before the Epiphany service in the Chapel at Whitehall leaves no doubt about the charming impression the Queen made on him:

> 'The Queen came to the door, and I presently approached in all humility to do her reverence; and she drew near me with the most gracious cheer, speaking Italian so well, uttering withal such fine conceits, that I can maintain that I might have been taking lessons from Boccaccio or the [Tuscan] Academy. Her Majesty was dressed all in white, with so many pearls, broideries, and diamonds, that I am amazed how she could carry them. . . then all the Court set forward in order toward the chapel. The order is such that I am having the whole noted in writing; nor do I believe I shall ever see a court which, for order, surpasses this one.
>
> 'I attended her Majesty to a room next the chapel, where I stayed in company with many gentlemen; and as we stood in excellent conversation, we heard a wondrous music.' [2]

When Orsino wrote to his Duchess about his splendid entertainment by the Queen on this day of Epiphany he was careful to omit mention that he had observed the service (but it nevertheless eventually leaked out and came to the ears of the Pope), but he related to her of the banquet after the service, of how the Queen dined separately with the Muscovite Ambassador, 'of whose ridiculous manners I shall give an account', he promises – but, again, by word of mouth when he sees her. [3] After the banquet Don Virginio was conducted back to his lodgings to rest until the evening, when Lord Worcester, the Queen's Master of the Horse, and the Earl of Cumberland came to sup with him. Of the latter he wrote: 'with him I had some speech which will be to the taste of his Highness [the Grand Duke, his Uncle Ferdinand] since that man is the greatest corsair in the world.' [4] Drake had died in 1596, and the Earl of Cumberland was his natural successor in privateering achievements – against the Spaniards, of course, so that here Don Virginio was enjoying himself hob-nobbing with the Protestant enemy! But there was little love lost between Tuscany and Spain.

Supper concluded, he was escorted back to the Palace where he was met by the Queen's Secretary of State and chief minister, Lord Burghley's hunch-backed son, Sir Robert Cecil, who invited him to 'salute all the ladies of title after the French fashion *(first, kiss the fingers, next, kiss the lips, then embrace the waist).*' [5] Soon the Queen arrived, and he was invited to accompany her, she discoursing in excellent Italian all the while as they proceeded to the place for the evening's grand entertainment. 'Her Majesty mounted the stairs, amid such sounding of trumpets that methought I was on a field of war, and entered a public hall [the Noon-hall] where all round were rising steps with ladies, and diverse consorts of music.' [6]

The Queen had previously given order 'To send for the Musitions of the Citty to be reddy to attend' [7] at the Court on Twelfth Day and Night, being the finest consort of musicians of the day. For such V.I.P. receptions the Elizabethans used what was known as 'the broken consort', consisting of treble and bass viols, lute, cittern, flute, pandora and hautboys. Don Virginio remarked in his letter to the Duchess that there were two instruments being played that were unknown to him. [8] It was the time of the peerless William Byrd, of Orlando Gibbons, Morley, Dowland, Weelkes, among those immortal composers of Elizabethan England, and this country was then famous both for music and dancing. Dancing was the national pastime, and at the Court no entertainment was complete without the inclusion of dancing, as also in the country at large. Before the play at Whitehall there was a 'Grand Ball', and after the dancing, the floor being cleared, the players' company of the Lord Chamberlain – namely the company of Shakespeare and Burbage – presented themselves to the Queen and Court, advancing with formal obeisances before taking up their positions in the 'mansions' and making their entrances for the beginning of the play to the strains of music to accompany Orsino's famous opening lines:

> 'If music be the food of love, play on,
> Give me excess of it, . . ' [9]

Sheer enchantment!

410

During the play the Queen sat on her throne forward on the daïs with Don Virginio beside her as her guest of honour. She had ordered a stool to be placed for him, which he declined and remained standing beside the daïs, but, at her request as a mark of honour, he wore his hat in her presence in which she graced him as her peer in rank. Elizabethan dramatic performances were often enlivened with interludes of acrobatics, juggling and tumbling, known as 'activities', but in the case of *Twelfth Night* appropriately it was music and dances that featured, for only these are mentioned by Don Virginio in his letter.

After the play, which was the last entertainment of the evening, the Duke was invited to join the Queen and her ladies in partaking of a light and delicious collation 'all of confections', [10] a very courteous gesture. By the time he went to his lodgings it was 'two hours after midnight'. [11] He had been assured that he was to see the Queen again, in private this time, and he hoped from what she had said that she would give him the favoured opportunity to hear her play and sing. Clearly Don Virginio's love of music was as great as the Queen's, and in this respect *Twelfth Night* was a play that had catered equally to their tastes.

Meanwhile various visits had been arranged for him. He was banqueted at his home by Lord Cecil; he went to Hampton Court escorted by Sir Walter Raleigh and Lord Cobham; and he joined an excellent hunting party arranged by William Howard, Lord Effingham, the son of the Lord Admiral. Finally he spent a day viewing the Tower of London with its great Arsenal and Wardrobe. Grays Inn were planning to entertain the popular and much admired Italian prince, but he now felt he dared not remain much longer in England for political reasons, and began to prepare for his departure, when he received word from the Queen that he was invited to come again to the Palace.

The Queen sent her coaches and three gentleman to escort him. Upon his arrival, as he wrote to his Duchess, 'her Majesty received me with so gracious a countenance that I could not ask for more, and led me into a chamber with all the ladies and gentlemen, where a most beautiful ball took place.' [12] That night the Queen danced with the Duke more than she had been known to dance for the past fifteen years. She kept him continually entertained with her conversation, drawing his critical attention to those of her Court whose dancing particularly excelled. She insisted that he be *seated* by her side, bidding him to be covered as a mark of her great respect for him. Every kind of compliment was extended him. Obviously this cultured Florentine prince had made a great hit with her, and she was bent on charming him as completely as she could. That she succeeded in this is clearly established by his final comment on his experiences of the English court and its remarkable Queen during this unique visit:

'The morning after [Monday, the 12th], it was signified to me that her Majesty wished to enjoy me in private, to use her own word; and after dinner she dispatched two of her most confidential gentlemen to fetch me and convey me in a close carriage; and by way of a back garden gate they brought me in to her Majesty. What the Queen did I am saving for you at my return; but I shall only say that it seemed to me I had become one of the paladins who used to enter those enchanted palaces.' [13]

What a charming accolade to this unsurpassed queen – 'enchanted palaces'! Hotson comments: 'These are not expressions of an English courtier or poet, intended to please the Queen's ear, but a cultivated foreign nobleman's confidences to his wife. Their sincerity is unmistakable.' [14]

Don Virginio departed the next day having, for his part, gained a great reputation at the English Court. The general admiration of all is summed up in the comment: 'a very courtlike and compleat gentleman'. [15]

It had indeed been a fabulous visit. In the first-hand descriptions that Hotson has garnered from the letters of this Italian nobleman to his 'Signora consorte amatissima', which he has printed in the original Italian in an Appendix in his book, and the records of history of the time, we are given an intimate picture of the Elizabethan Court as it really was at its most festive and glorious. Don Virginio remarks that he knows of no court in Europe that can match it for the meticulous keeping of 'order' in its ceremony. It is a great tradition that has been handed down to us, in which England still excels, for the ceremonial occasions surrounding the British royalty are unsurpassed for their marvellously maintained 'order' to this day.

Elizabeth, too, achieved a resounding personal victory, having excelled herself in graciousness towards the Duke. On his return home by way of the courts of Europe he divulged news of the English Queen in Paris and Brussels, praising the glories of her Court, her admirable personal qualities, her wisdom, her learning, her command of languages, her musicianship, her grace in dancing – all sweet music to Elizabeth's ears when she heard it. It was a brief happy hour which she shared with Don Virginio in full, generous measure. And for him it was more than a passing pleasure for it eventually brought unexpected blessings.

At first, however, the Duke had to face the wrath of Pope Clement. He was given 'a public penance to perform in the Duomo at Florence', [16] and had to humble himself and repent his sins – but it proved worth it. Dr Hotson states: 'the general voice whispered that Don Virginio had been entrusted by his uncle or by Henri of France with a secret diplomatic mission to Elizabeth . . the Spaniards tormented Ferdinand about it – gave him "many blows" while he swore that his nephew's visit had borne no official character, and had actually displeased him.' [17] Nevertheless, these persistent rumours combined to shed a glow of admiration on the young Orsino for his daring, and he soon found that the prestige that the Queen of England's white hand conferred brought him enhanced respect from everyone – including his enemies. Philip III, after first threatening to cut off his stipend, ended by increasing it handsomely by another three thousand escudos and awarding him the Order of the Golden Fleece. [18] A man who had the friendship of the Queen of England deserved such respect!

For Elizabeth, alas, tragedy followed hard upon the heels of the enchantment she had woven for Orsino. Hardly had he sailed away than the simmering discontent of the Earl of Essex, debarred the Court in disgrace, although a free man, boiled over in the Essex rebellion. On Sunday 8th February the Earl took to the streets with his band of followers calling on the City of London to rise up in arms in his support, shouting false slogans: 'For the Queen! For the Queen! A plot is laid for my life!' [19] Cecil put a stop to this nonsense by despatching a messenger to denounce the Earl as a traitor, and not a man in the City stirred to follow him. They only smiled upon him in pity.

His treachery was the unbearable grief that broke Elizabeth's heart. Essex was executed on 25th February 1600/1, just fifty days after the celebration of Twelfth Night with all its brilliance and mirth. His cruel remark, spoken as he fulminated in impotent rage because he could not get his own way with the Queen, 'that her conditions were as crooked as her carcass', had been reported back to her. [20] Those wounding words, it was said, put the seal on Essex's fate if he had hoped to cajole the Queen to extend him mercy and forgiveness; and they diminish him.

On the other hand, Elizabeth's calmness and fortitude in her handling of the wayward and unregenerate Essex stamp her with the greatness which this crisis highlights. Hotson adds information on Grigori Mikulin's reaction to the Essex rebellion that sheds a gentle light on this massive Russian bear who at once came forward offering to fight for the Queen against her enemies. He made no mention of this in his reports to the Tsar, worried perhaps, as Hotson suggests, that he had 'no instructions to cover a contingency so unforeseen. . . We learn of it only through Elizabeth's own letter to Boris Godunov. She remembered, both to be grateful and to do the loyal Grigori all the good in her power with his master.' [21] Mikulin, for his part, spoke in ardent praise of the Queen and of his entertainment in England, 'which doth very much increase the reputation of our country among the Russes', wrote the English agent, Robert Barne, from Archangel. [22]

Elizabeth was a woman who was sustained by the love of her people and her Court, and the glow of the aftermath left by the visit of Don Virginio Orsino, and the touching loyalty of Grigori Mikulin must have helped her to surmount in some measure the awful unfaithfulness of Essex, whom she had dearly loved above all others; but it was an injury she could not long survive. After putting a brave face on it for a while, her spirits deserted her, and she went into a rapid decline. She died only two years later, on 24th March 1602/3, the last day of the Elizabethan Old Year.

XXVIII

RETURN FROM EXILE

THE COMPOSITION of *Twelfth Night* for the visit of Don Virginio Orsino to London was the catalyst of the return. How did the play come to be written? And when?

Dr Hotson necessarily resorts to hypothesis here. He assumes that the actor, William Shakespeare, was summoned by the Lord Chamberlain, and was commissioned, so to speak, to write a play having 'greate variety and change of musicke and daunces, and of a Subiect that may be most pleasing to her Ma*j*estie.' [1] These were his guide lines for the choice of play to be presented on Twelfth Night.

The Lord Chamberlain's 'particular matters' noted in his memoranda for the elaborate preparations for the Twelfth Day celebrations are very revealing for our purpose. They included the 'order' for furnishing the chambers for the banqueting of Mikulin and Don Virginio Orsino. He notes such details as:

'To give order that the Cowncell chamber boord be furnished with playted napkins, after the French fashion' [2]

This was where Don Virginio was to dine. And for the separate chamber where the Queen would dine with Mikulin he made note:

'To proportion the heigth of the Chaire of Estate to be [of a] heigth fitt for her Ma*j*estie to sitt at dinner and to appoint fowre knightes to remove the Table' [3]

He makes a note 'To warne all the gentlemen ordinary and Ext*raordinary* to attend [her] Ma*j*estie in their best and richest apparell.' [4] Great preparations are in hand! Sir Edward Stafford's French cook (he had been ambassador in France and had brought back a French chef) was to be called in 'to dresse the dinner and supper that is to be made for the *Duke of Brachiana.*' He was 'To speake to Mr Comptrouller [Sir William Knollys] that the Bankett [of confections at the Queen's lodging after the play] be made of better stuffe fitt for men to eate and not of paper shewes as it is wont to be.' [5] The lords are named and their duties apportioned for waiting at table, and for bringing to Court the Muscovite Ambassador and the Duke of Bracciano. Among those to fetch the latter was William Cecil who had been to Florence early in 1600, and timing for arrival at Court is stipulated as 'after 11 of the Clock.' [6]

The detailed instructions given to 'good George', Lord Hunsdon, are very lengthy, precisely orchestrating the events planned for the grand day, including the music, and reveal how that splendid 'order' of Queen Elizabeth's Court was achieved by meticulous planning, which so impressed Orsino. It is a long and fascinating document providing insight into the running of the Court, including intimate details that show the Queen's sharp eyes missed little that went on in her royal household, even to her command 'makeing cleane the glas windowes to give good light.' [7]

The Lord Chamberlain's memoranda are, unfortunately, not dated, but it is clear that when they were written the arrival of the Duke of Bracciano *was expected in time for his attendance at Court on 6th January.* Yet the only documentary evidence of his intended visit to England are Winwood's two letters from Lyons to Sir Henry Neville, the first of which reached London on 10th December, [8] and the second on 24th December, neither of which gives any indication when the Duke might be expected to arrive. Here is the information given in his second letter:

'I have been entreated by a gentleman who doth accompany Don Virginio into England (whereof in my letter of 20th November I advertised) to address them by some letter to someone who would vouchsafe to make them have the sight of the Court and access to her Majesty. I have given them a letter to your Lordship.' [9]

This is sufficiently vague – 'some letter to someone'. No hint of any date of arrival. It leaves open the vital question of just how welcome the Duke might be, how to be received, how entertained? It is a mere formal letter of introduction which is not even at the highest level in the English government. Such an approach surely would not have satisfied the Duke who was putting his reputation at risk in this venture. Yet by the time the Lord Chamberlain was making his long and detailed memoranda for the 'order' on Twelfth Day, the Queen *knew* that her Italian visitor would be there for she was making precise arrangements for his entertainment. She even names the noblemen – those who were to fetch the Duke and bring him to Court (Lord Darcy, William Cecil, George Buc, Edward Gorge); those who were to meet him 'at the gate' [10] (the Earl of Rutland, with his two brothers, and two more). This entire party were to accompany him at Court and bring him home again at night. Upon arrival the Duke was to walk beside the Queen to her Closet at the Chapel, and (if he so wished) to remain there to observe the Epiphany service through its window, then to walk back beside her to the Great Chamber where she would dine alone with Mikulin, waited on by her most high-born noblemen, who would afterwards dine with the Duke in the adjacent Council Chamber, where the sumptuously laid table with the 'playted napkins after the French fashion' stood ready. The Queen meanwhile would doubtless retire after her dinner leaving the Duke to banquet with the gentlemen.

The Duke's every move was carefully plotted, his treatment was to be princely and prestigious. These meticulous arrangements appear to be the final ratification of an expected visit that had been decided some time before.

Mikulin, we know, did not receive his invitation (or command) to attend on her Majesty at Court until 4th January, only *two days* before Twelfth Day, as though this, the appointed day for the ratification of the treaty with Russia, had been kept hanging fire until the Duke of Bracciano *had arrived.* Even the notice of his arrival just three days before Twelfth Day, when he at once sent word to the Queen, sounds like confirmation of a pre-arranged date, declaring: I'm here, I've come as arranged.

But there had been *no* such arrangement according to the records. It was all left vague and unconfirmed with 'some letter to someone'. How did the Queen know that the Duke would be making every effort to arrive in time for Twelfth Day and Twelfth Night for which she had evidently been making such especial preparation?

The Elizabethan nobility traditionally returned home to their country mansions for Christmas, so all these would have to have been called to attend at Court to take up their several ordained duties on that grand day. They would have been warned in advance of the three days' notice that Orsino's arrival gave (one presumes) or else there would have been frenzied posting up and down the country to bring them to the Court in time. It must be said that the young Lord William Herbert did not respond to the Queen's summons, but sent reply that he only received word on Monday, (a fortuitous delay?) and travelling from Wilton House in Wiltshire he could not reach the Court in time for Tuesday morning. [11] But he had good reason for seeking an excuse since Mistress Mall Fitton was with child by him. Best to keep away.

It is in the Lord Chamberlain's memoranda that the Queen's requirement for a play especially embellished with music and dances is noted, and if this were written down *only three days before the play's performance,* this is indeed short notice; too short for such a sophisticated piece reflecting the wealth of topical allusion that this play embraces. In order to accommodate this problem Dr Hotson hypothesizes, basing his dating for the writing of *Twelfth Night* by William Shakespeare of the Lord Chamberlain's Men on the receipt of Winwood's second letter (quoted above) on Christmas Day, a letter which gives no indication of any date of arrival. He suggests that the Lord Chamberlain granted Shakespeare an interview on 26th December, when the company were also playing at Court, and informed Shakespeare then of the expected visit of a certain Italian prince whom the Queen wished to entertain lavishly. [12] On this hint he surmises that Shakespeare at once began with all speed to research concerning the Italian duke (who was to arrive *incognito,* mark you); found a suitable Italian play, *Gl' Ingannati,* originating from the duke's own Tuscany, which fortuitously featured twins to compliment him; wrote it all; had the play censored by the Master of the Revels (we may assume the Lord Chamberlain would approve it, having in a manner commissioned it, as Hotson suggests); memorized and rehearsed it, and so it was ready for performance on Twelfth Night. In support of this speedy achievement Hotson cites other examples of plays – including the original *Gl' Ingannati* itself, written in only three days –

as evidence that the thing could be done. [13] He concludes that ten days' time would be ample, basing this on the assumption that the Lord Chamberlain was, indeed, expecting Orsino to arrive in time for Twelfth Night, when Winwood's letter mentions no such date.

It is not for me to dispute whether such a feat is possible. Burning the midnight oil or candle much can be achieved, even by those of us who are no genius. But in this case, all we have are Winwood's vague letters. How did Queen Elizabeth *know* that the Duke would be there by 6th January, and how did the author of *Twelfth Night* get to know this so that he wove the enchantment of his play so precisely around the person of the Duke Orsino, *and* chose the setting as Illyrian Twelfth Night revelry? Let us look at the facts again.

Don Virginio, we know, was travelling to England *incognito* and secretly with his small party of four from France, two Italians of his household, a Spanish youth, and his servant. We even know the names of all of them, except for his servant. They did not arrive in London until after dinner on Saturday, 3rd January – barely three days before *Twelfth Night* was performed. It was neat timing, allowing him a brief period in which to rest from his travels, if indeed, as I strongly suspect, he had somehow made a pre-arrangement to arrive in London for Twelfth Day celebrations as desired by the Queen. He attended mass on the Sunday at the French Ambassador's house and received visits from English noblemen at the house in Gracechurch Street, whilst the Queen set all in motion for his splendid entertainment at Court on Tuesday, commanding Grigori Mikulin to present himself on the same day.

Even given ten days, and not three from Orsino's arrival in London, no dramatist not already acquainted with this Italian nobleman's life and habits and tastes could have so aptly incorporated them into his play. The character of Orsino is integral to the play's conception, not something added as a finishing touch. His speech opens the play presenting him at once as the exemplar of a cultured Renaissance prince shown in the throes of romantic love in the fashionable manner of the day. The words spoken by Olivia-*alias*-Elizabeth are a charming accolade to him:

> . . I suppose him virtuous, know him noble,
> Of great estate, of fresh and stainless youth;
> In voices well divulg'd, free, learn'd, and valiant,
> And in dimension and the shape of nature
> A gracious person. [14]

The play was surely written as a personal tribute, a New Year's gift from the Poet to his Italian prince and his Queen. Hotson has shown that when Orsino, seeing Olivia, rhapsodizes: 'Now heaven walks on earth', it is intended for the ears of Elizabeth to whom such eulogies were part of the conventions of the Court. [15] If Marlowe, as Orsino's envoy, had seen the Queen, he may have promised a special play for the occasion. Did her command to her Lord

417

Chamberlain perhaps reflect this foreknowledge?

We have to remember, too, that the Christmas season was the peak of the year for the theatres, with the additional responsibility for the leading companies of fitting in performances at Court. A Court performance had to be especially polished, it might not be a rushed last-minute affair. Allowing for the Master of the Revels' censorship, the Lord Chamberlain's approbation of it (which Hotson, with justification, takes for granted) as against the other plays submitted by rival companies, it could not have been a race against time that brought *Twelfth Night* in all its brilliant perfection to Court. The play must, I suggest, have been written, rehearsed and ready well in advance *knowing* that Twelfth Night was the pre-arranged date.

The implication of Thorpe's letter to Blount gives an approximate date for Marlowe's presence in London, and what had brought him to London was, I suggest, the diplomatic task of ascertaining what kind of welcome Don Virginio Orsino would receive at the hands of Queen Elizabeth in the event of his arrival at the Court. In a word, he was Orsino's envoy, sent to negotiate a favourable reception for his noble master, and to discuss acceptable dates for such a visit.

Lucan was published *after 26th June,* the earliest date when Thorpe could have obtained the copyright from Flasket, and *before 4th August,* when *As You Like* It was entered in the Stationers' Register – assuming that this was the 'booke' that Thorpe brought to Blount. From these dates the months of July and August are those most clearly indicated as the likely period when Marlowe may have been in London, before returning to Florence to report his news to Orsino. Don Virginio knew very well that the question of the order of precedence would arise at Florence, and he had predetermined to lay his fortune at risk in claiming his place of honour in defiance of Pope Clement. He would wisely plan with forethought, weighing the consequences, while determined to answer the urging of his valiant spirit. Would this intelligent Duke not have taken the precaution to send his envoy to London in advance to ascertain *at first hand* what his reception at Gloriana's Court might be? He was, after all, a Catholic prince and would need to *know* her reaction for certain. In his own land such religious tolerance was hardly to be thought of, though the court of Tuscany was more liberal than most. Only personal contact could ensure what degree of warmth his arrival would be granted. Writing letters in such a case would not be suitable. It stands to reason that the Duke would not have taken the considerable political risk in coming to the English Queen's Court, in which he greatly displeased his uncle, the Grand Duke, *unless* he had been assured unequivocally of an especially gracious welcome, the more so since he would be in bad odour with the Pope even before going.

Assuming that our exiled Poet had spent some time at the Duke's court at Bracciano, we may be sure that Orsino would have been curious to learn from this Englishman as much as possible about the English Queen. Some of Pope Sixtus's sneaking admiration for the fabulous Protestant Queen who snapped her fingers at Philip II's Armada had clearly rubbed off on his young grand-nephew-in-law. It is evident that Don Virginio had nurtured a desire to visit England long before the events at Maria de' Medici's wedding precipitated the realisation of his ambition. One can readily see how such a plan as was finally undertaken began to formulate in the Duke's mind.

An eminently sensible precaution would have been to send his personal envoy secretly ahead to Elizabeth to negotiate his reception well in advance, and if Marlowe were at Bracciano he may have suggested it himself, had the Duke ever confided in him a desire to see the English Queen. From my researches on the part he played in the Armada it is clear that Marlowe was an astute politician who was capable of exerting influence, and was accustomed to give advice, for the government intelligence agents were no mere dumb pawns in the intricate political games in which they were involved. Marlowe would have been able to give the Queen a first-hand account of the noble Duke, his person, his valour, his tastes, his love of music; she would have been shown one whom she would recognise as a prince after her own heart, one who would go back to Italy *via* Europe to report of the splendour of Elizabeth's Court, and the glorious reality of Elizabeth herself, not an aged, decrepit woman, as was widely reported in Catholic countries, but a great Queen in full possession of herself at sixty-seven. It would prove a mutually beneficial visit. [16]

The Queen would have been greatly interested to learn at first hand of the incredibly lavish plans for the celebration of Maria de' Medici's wedding in Florence in October. Dr Hotson has suggested that these were seen to constitute a challenge to her to outdo in splendour what the young French Queen had enjoyed to launch her. She, Queen Elizabeth, would show Europe what she could present in courtly magnificence, and (above all) in personal charm, which the Italian girl seems conspicuously to have lacked. It is clear from what *actually* happened that this is how the Queen saw the Duke's visit – as a golden opportunity which she hugged to her heart.

And who better to present this to her than the experienced intelligencer, her former devoted agent, Christopher Marlowe? If he had been present at Bracciano, as there is good reason to suspect, his services to the Duke would have been especially valuable in such an enterprise as he was contemplating. If he had been there in his service, Orsino would have found in him his ideal agent for assessing the situation at Elizabeth's Court, and her personal reaction to a proposed visit from this Catholic prince. Arriving before 4th August it would have been a propitious time to make such overtures, allowing Orsino ample time to plan ahead. How does this fit in with the other events of this historical time span?

The Muscovite Ambassador Grigori Mikulin does not feature prominently in *Twelfth Night* and could not be allowed to do so in case of *byezchéstiye* being perceived, so the touch here is light, and it took a Hotson to detect it! But etched in with our dramatist's notable wit he is surely there, though it is doubtful that Marlowe would still have been in London when he arrived with his retinue of a dozen large Russian retainers and his secretary, Ivan Zinoviev, on 18th September. [17] Mikulin came on an extended visit being 'dyetted for eight moneths space, at the sole charges of the company of the Muscovie Merchants' [18] for trade was much to the fore in these negotiations. Mikulin visited Queen Elizabeth first at Richmond where her Court then was. But he did not receive his invitation to the state dinner at Whitehall, where the final ratification of the treaty of friendship with Russia was to be made on 6th January, until 4th January, *two days' notice*, as he wrote to his Lord, the Czar. [19] This treaty would benefit mutual trade and tilt the balance of power with Denmark to England's advantage, but its ratification *appears* to have awaited the safe arrival of Queen Elizabeth's most highly favoured guest, the Florentine prince, the Duke of Bracciano, as though it was for *him* that Elizabeth was planning to present all this magnificence for her Twelfth Day and Night celebration.

The details about Mikulin, his *'costumi ridicolosi'* or ridiculous manners, of which the Duke promises to recount to his Duchess when he sees her, [20] would provide an added source of amusement to the Italian prince, whose sense of humour is manifested in his delightful letters. His royal hostess purposely entertained them together, which seems to indicate that she knew very well what sort of gentleman this prince was, how he would relish this experience of witnessing the huge Russian envoy at her Court.

The gossip at Court concerning Sir William Knollys' farcical courtship of young Mary Fitton, and her scandalous affair with Lord William Herbert, were all on-going in July/August – ripe for dramatic treatment in a play written to celebrate the reign of the Lord of Misrule on Twelfth Night. Mistress Fitton was already six months pregnant by Christmas. The scenario fits.

Having laid the foundation for the Duke of Bracciano's highly favoured reception by the Queen, Marlowe would have speeded back to Florence with his good news to reach Don Virginio before the wedding – an event not to be missed in any case. It took place on 14th October (New Style) or 4th October (Old Style) so that he would have made his departure from London at least three weeks before, not staying long enough to witness the arrival of the mountainous Muscovite with his delegation – but this little take-off could have been slipped into the play at a later stage. Most likely Marlowe would want to return in advance of Orsino's arrival. There would be no reason for him to dawdle back with the Duke's party, whose leisurely progress gives every indication of a carefully timed arrival in London in mind.

Confirmation by his envoy would have put the seal on Orsino's resolution boldly to defy Pope Clement's decree, and to follow this up with his visit to the great Protestant Queen – a brave throw of the dice! It would be a unilateral decision, made without involving the Grand Duke in any way. He wrote to his uncle only after having taken the step, informing him of his intention to visit the English Court, and asking for his blessing – but he did not get it.

At Lyons he had very properly approached Queen Elizabeth's agent Winwood, informing him of his intention to visit the Queen of England, hoping

420

to have audience with her. But this was a formality. The real approach had, I suggest, already been made and agreed by personal contact through his envoy. The very vagueness of Winwood's information supports this premise – that Orsino's approach to him was for form's sake, diplomatically masking the fact that contact had been privately made and the date already agreed.

The inspiration for the uproarious comedy of *Twelfth Night* reflects renewed contact with Queen Elizabeth's Court, although it may be argued that he could have obtained all his information and Court gossip from Sir Thomas Walsingham, and Lady Audrey. She had given birth to their son that summer, probably in July 1600, for in that month she was presented with a purse of gold by the Queen, which suggests a gift for the baby's christening. [21] Both Sir Thomas and Lady Audrey feature at Court in the New Year's gifts lists of 1599/1600, when they gave the Queen a gift of fine garments and received gilt plate in return, and at New Year 1600/1 when Lady Audrey received another purse from the Queen valued at £20. 12s. 8d. [22]

If we may pursue the hypothesis further, it is very likely that the play may have been part-written at Scadbury, with the delighted approval of Walsingham if his Poet had showed him the playscript, which would then be delivered to Master William Shakespeare for rehearsal for the Christmas season. But when? Here we must indulge in hypothesizing as Shakespearean scholars are so fond of doing. Assuming that Marlowe arrived on his mission in London during July – a happily timed co-incidence when Thomas Walsingham's little son would have been born – doubtless he would have composed a poem for his Patron's heir, but if left in manuscript it has not survived. It would have been an emotionally rich experience for the exile to make renewed contact with his homeland and his friends. Important decisions were forged at this time

First he must see his mission completed, preferably in an interview with the Queen herself, when he would most likely have been accompanied by Thomas Walsingham. It would have been arranged through Walsingham, who was in high favour with the Queen as evidenced in the gifts of New Year presents exchanged, and her special present to Lady Audrey that July. Walsingham could have negotiated the entire business on behalf of his Poet, but a private, secret meeting with Orsino's envoy would have been most desirable to Queen Elizabeth, and there is no reason to doubt that she was aware who William Shakespeare really was. In that case a disguise would be a formality.

His mission accomplished, and the 'booke' of *As You Like It* left with Thorpe, he would have sped back to Florence – as I reckon it, a journey of about three weeks, leaving at the end of August.* He must reach Don Virginio, at all events, in good time before the date of the wedding, when Orsino planned to deliver his challenge to the Pope in the satisfaction of the knowledge that Queen Elizabeth was awaiting him with the promise of an especially warm welcome, inviting him to attend her in the forthcoming Christmas season to be pre-

* Footnote: Allowing for the ten days' discrepancy of the Gregorian calendar.

sent *before* 6th January, Twelfth Day, when she planned to receive him royally. How royally, however, he had not imagined for his request upon his arrival had evidently been for a private meeting. He was to be pleasantly surprised by the lavish public reception honouring him that was planned, including a play written especially for his visit showing him in the accepted courtly relationship with the Queen of England – Duke Orsino suing for the hand of the Lady Olivia, with many personal compliments woven into the delightful entertainment.

Once the grand wedding celebrations in Florence were over, and the new Queen of France delivered in her golden galley, the Poet need not have lingered a moment longer, but hied him back to England, the playscript of *Twelfth Night* probably already part-written, to put the finishing touches to it in London, incorporating all the latest Court gossip, before delivery for rehearsal by the Lord Chamberlain's Men at some time in November, well before the Christmas season was underway.

This hypothetical reconstruction is based firmly on all that *Twelfth Night* and the historical context tell us. It is an entirely credible scenario. The marvellous historical background is filled in, and the play's delightful exploitation of the Court gossip is given in intriguing and impressive detail in Dr Hotson's fascinating book to seal the irrefutable evidence of its composition to honour Duke Orsino's visit on 6th January 1600/1. His revelation of this Twelfth Day and the first performance of *Twelfth Night* in its authentic historical context has once more confirmed that the story the *Sonnets* tell of the Poet's exile and adoption of a pseudonym to veil his anonymous existence must be true, for it is based on internal evidence and a wide consensus on the influence of Italy detected in the plays of this period, and here specifically highlighting a personal association with Duke Orsino that is undeniably embedded in the text of *Twelfth Night.* How else to explain it?

Thus far there are no flaws in the hypothesis, every new piece of evidence confirming what went before to present a credible, coherent and convincing whole, embracing also Italy as the land of his exile, an environment in which his maturity blossomed.

In conclusion, it would be impossible to over-emphasize the richness of the feast that Leslie Hotson has presented for our delectation and information in *The First Night of Twelfth Night,* from which I have here only been able to cull the most significant evidence, briefly presented. There is much more in this research detailing a historical and literary case of undeniable validity and importance for our appreciation of Shakespeare's witty comedy and its Elizabethan context. His book should be essential reading for all who direct this play for stage performance. This has never yet happened, although it has been in print since 1954, for, inexcusably, his illuminating research has been treated dismissively by scholars writing on, or preparing editions of *Twelfth Night,* who prefer the well-worn rut of established academic teaching about the play to this exciting fresh evidence revealing the connection with Orsino and dating it *precisely* to Twelfth Night, 1600/1.

Hotson's genius has recreated *Twelfth Night* in all its glorious comic invention as no one has ever done before. His work is truly a tribute to Shakespeare's genius. He has brought to life the scintillating occasion at the Court of Queen Elizabeth when she received a visit extraordinary from the Italian Catholic prince, Don Virginio Orsino, that concludes this part of the investigation in glowing colours.

With Malvolio – though without the need 'to crush this a little' – we can declare,

'Daylight and champain discovers not more. This is open.' [23]

Twelfth Night brought the Poet home again, establishing renewed contact with the Court and his friends, who protected him. But this is not the end of the story, which is to be continued in the sequel to this book, where the approach is made not through the *Sonnets* as here, but by a totally different route leading us to the selfsame conclusion, that William Shakespeare was the pseudonym used to conceal the persecuted poet-dramatist Christopher Marlowe. It proves – and I do not use that word lightly – that this concealment was absolutely deliberate and strictly maintained, which is why it has taken us 400 years to uncover it; and that the First Folio was a Masonic publication.

We must now put the entire sonnet-sequence to the test, analysing each sonnet to ascertain that it fits the story of Marlowe's life naturally, without forcing a single word or nuance, which is pursued in 'The Book of the Sonnets' that ends the first leg of this journey.

PART THREE

THE BOOK OF THE SONNETS

THE SONNETS LISTED IN THEIR
THEME-GROUPS

THE THEMES OF THE SONNETS ANALYSED

IT WAS THE ANALYSIS of the sonnet-sequence by dividing these poems into their themes that first alerted me to the story they conceal. We are now submitting the entire 154 poems to the supreme test to see whether each sonnet readily applies to the life of Christopher Marlowe. Does the whole book of the *Sonnets* fit him as the glove fits the hand for which it is made? That is the question to be answered.

Thorpe's edition of the *Sonnets* is the authority to which all modern editors must bow. I have followed this closely, with modernized spelling and amending the punctuation only where it is clearly advisable. The Elizabethan poets and dramatists used very little punctuation, as is evident in extant manuscripts. Their playscripts were left to be punctuated by the playhouse scribe, who inserted commas etc., to indicate where a pause or *caesura* in a speech should fall when spoken by the actor, *with emphasis on the flow of the poetry of the spoken words – not* according to strict grammatical syntax. Even a question mark might be omitted where no upward lilt of the voice was required in speaking the line. This approach is also apparent in the *Sonnets* as printed by Thorpe. I am entirely in sympathy with G.B. Harrison's excellent Penguin edition of the *Sonnets* (1938, revised and reprinted 1949, 1955) in which he has the sensitivity to leave Thorpe well alone, except for spelling, or where there is a good reason for amending his punctuation. Some modern editors have introduced rather pedantic, modern syntaxical punctuation, which may be formally correct, but sometimes alters the emphasis, or meaning, of a line, and adds nothing to the poem's beauty, or its sense where this was already clear. It often detracts by chopping up a line in a way that encourages a prosaic reading. The most heavy-handed in this respect is Stanley Wells' edition for Oxford University Press (1987) – beautifully printed, but marred by over-punctuation, disturbing the flow of the verse, at times changing its emphasis and/or its meaning, and even altering words in a determination to improve on Thorpe. A few examples from many will suffice to illustrate the subtle difference this produces.

> Thorpe   (spelling modernized) *Sonnet 57*
> Save where you are, how happy you make those
> Wells: Save, where you are, how happy you make those
> (The comma added checks the flow quite unnecessarily)

> *Sonnet 69*
> Thorpe: Then churls their thoughts (although their eyes were kind)
> Wells: Then, churls, their thoughts – although their eyes were kind
> (The meaning is altered)

Sonnet 93

Thorpe: So shall I live, supposing thou art true,
            Like a deceived husband,

Wells: So shall I live supposing thou art true
            Like a deceived husband;

(In this case the removal of all punctuation lends ambiguity)

Sonnet 123

Thorpe: No! Time, thou shalt not boast that I do change,

Wells: No, time, thou shalt not boast that I do change!

(A complete change of emphasis)

Wells also alters words in the sonnets without any apparent reason, and certainly on no authority except his own:

Sonnet 127

Thorpe: Her *eyes* so suited, and they mourners seem,

Wells: Her *brow* so suited, and they mourners seem

(This removes one of the significant repetitions of 'eyes')

Sonnet 129

Thorpe: A bliss in proof and *proud and* very woe

Wells: A bliss in proof and *proved,* a very woe

(This deliberately alters the sense removing the *double entendre*)

Sonnet 112

Thorpe: In so profound *abysm* I throw all care

Wells: In so profound *abyss* I throw all care

(*abysm* is morebeauiful than the hissing *abyss*)

    . . . .

Thorpe: That all the world besides *me thinks y'are dead.*

Wells: That all the world besides, *methinks, they're dead.*

(If Thorpe's line is unclear Wells' is nonsense)

Sonnet 33

Thorpe: But out alack, he was but one hour mine,

Wells: But out, alas, he was but one hour mine;

(Altering *alack,* a far stronger more emotive word, to *alas* weakens the heart-cry of this poem)

We have to be very sure of our ground before tampering with a poet's work, especially when that poet is Shakespeare, whose thoughts are so subtle and witty.

As introduction to reading this famous collection in a fresh light, I offer this superb passage from C.L. Barber's 'Essay on the Sonnets', prefacing the American Laurel edition, admirably edited by C.J. Sisson and Francis Ferguson. The sonnets are all in the style that has been named the 'Shakespearean sonnet' of three quatrains and an ending couplet, to which he adheres so loyally and distinctively that, as Barber remarks, 'it *does* tell his name!'[1] He writes:

> 'normally the sentences close with the close of each quatrain, or else are balanced symmetrically within the four-line unit. Within sentences, grammar and thought typically pause or turn at the end of the line; where they do run over, enjambment is rarely emphatic. Shakespeare does not exploit the more outward forms of variation because within the pattern he is making astonishingly beautiful designs with sound and syllable and cadence. He is like an accomplished figure skater who sticks to the classical figures because what he cares about is what he can make of each evolution. . . Each sonnet is different, but the difference is achieved not by changing the framework of form but by moving in fresh ways within it.

> 'It seems clear that Shakespeare wrote by quatrains. In coming to know a sonnet by heart, you find yourself recalling it one quatrain at a timej and often getting stuck trying to move to the next, for lack of a tangible link. The imagery does not regularly carry through; what does carry through is the momentum of the discourse. The movement from quatrain to quatrain is usually a shift of some sort, though it can be simply a continuing with fresh impetus. The figure skater starts each evolution by kicking off from an edge, and can move from one evolution to another either by staying on the same edge of the same blade, or changing from inside edge to outside edge, or from left foot inside to right foot outside, and so on – each of these technical moves focusing a whole living gesture of the balancing, moving body. People praise Shakespeare's sonnets because each one is about one thing: one should add that each is *one motion* about one thing, the motion normally being composed of three large sweeps and the shorter couplet.'[2]

GROUP A
THE SONNETS TO 'MR.W.H.' (1587-88)

The Sonnet-sequence opens chronologically with a poem of lyrical inspiration, one of the loveliest and most famous of all, *Sonnet 18*. This introduces us to the Poet's first patron, the youthful 'Mr.W.H.' in the Christmas of 1587-88.

There are fifteen sonnets addressing him with unalloyed praise in this early, broken group which is scattered through the sequence in single sonnets or in small clusters. The first cluster of five, *Sonnets 18, 19, 20, 21, 22*, are to William Hatcliffe as the 'Prince' of the Grayan Court, and perfectly express the Poet's admiration of the beauty of the young man chosen to be Prince of Purpoole. He is hymned by his sonneteer as the embodiment of exemplary young manhood, whom the Poet is presenting to the public eye. The inference is that Marlowe already knew Will Hatcliffe from their Cambridge days, and he is here doing a first-rate public relations job for his youthful patron.

These sonnets beautifully fit the description of the 'sugred Sonnets' referred to by Meres, which were written for general reading by the Grayan courtiers. The use of plurals hints at their public character, whilst the difference in age of Poet and 'Prince' is indicated in *Sonnet 22*.

Sonnet 18

Shall I compare thee to a summer's day?
Thou art more lovely and more temperate:
Rough winds do shake the darling buds of May,
And summer's lease hath all too short a date.
Sometime too hot the eye of heaven shines,
And often is his gold complexion dimm'd,
And every fair from fair sometime declines,
By chance, or Nature's changing course untrimm'd:
But thy eternal summer shall not fade,
Nor lose possession of that fair thou ow'st,
Nor shall Death brag thou wander'st in his shade,
When in eternal lines to time thou grow'st.
   So long as men can breathe or eyes can see,
   So long lives this, and this gives life to thee.

If this is the first sonnet that Shakespeare ever wrote what an exquisite little opus with which to launch his brilliant sonneteering! Nothing more perfect could be imagined than this evocation of a summer's day in mid-winter likening its loveliness to the beauty of the young 'Prince', admired by all.

Marlowe matured early as a poet, before he matured as a dramatist for he had much to learn about stagecraft, whereas he had been encouraged to compose verse in Latin in his childhood.

Sonnet 19

Devouring Time, blunt thou the lion's paws,
And make the earth devour her own sweet brood,
Pluck the keen teeth from the fierce tiger's jaws,
And burn the long-liv'd Phoenix in her blood;
Make glad and sorry season as thou fleet'st,
And do whate'er thou wilt, swift-footed Time,
To the wide world and all her fading sweets:
But I forbid thee one most heinous crime,
O carve not with thy hours my love's fair brow,
Nor draw no lines there with thine antique pen,
Him in thy course untainted do allow
For beauty's pattern to succeeding men.
   Yet do thy worst, old Time; despite thy wrong
   My love shall in my verse ever live young.

Time, as the enemy of youth and beauty, and his 'antique pen' are a recurring theme in this group. The Elizabethan connotation of 'love' towards a patron applies in all these sonnets.

Sonnet 20

A woman's face with Nature's own hand painted
Hast thou, the Master-Mistress of my passion;
A woman's gentle heart, but not acquainted
With shifting change, as is false women's fashion;
An eye more bright than theirs, less false in rolling,
Gilding the object whereupon it gazeth;
A man in hue, all hues in his controlling,
Which steals men's eyes and women's souls amazeth.
And for a woman wert thou first created,
Till Nature as she wrought thee fell a-doting,
And by addition me of thee defeated,
By adding one thing to my purpose nothing.
   But since she prick'd thee out for women's pleasure,
   Mine be thy love, and thy love's use their treasure.

The term 'passion' is used here in its Elizabethan sense meaning a poem or verse. That this young man is in the public eye is clear from the line 'Which steals men's eyes and women's souls amazeth'.

There is recurring sexual innuendo in the extant *Gesta Grayorum* of 1594, which doubtless used the same texts and ceremonies as the 1587/8 Christmas festivities for the Prince of Purpoole. This aspect is wittily slipped into the couplet in the use of the word 'prick'd', which would have delighted the youthful student 'courtiers'! Poetry readings of the sonnets were probably a feature of this 'court' in which the extrovert side of Marlowe's nature would have revelled. He was only just down from the university himself, and had probably already fallen deeply in love with an enchanting dark-eyed courtezan, for the Dark Lady sonnets also date from this time.

Sonnet 21

So is it not with me as with that Muse
Stirr'd by a painted beauty to his verse,
Who heaven itself for ornament doth use,
And every fair with his fair doth rehearse,
Making a couplement of proud compare
With sun and moon, with earth and sea's rich gems,
With April's first-born flowers and all things rare,
That heaven's air in this huge rondure hems.
O let me true in love but truly write,
And then believe me, my love is as fair
As any mother's child, though not so bright
As those gold candles fix'd in heaven's air.
   Let them say more that like of hearsay well;
   I will not praise that purpose not to sell.

He is satirizing the sonneteering convention which indulges in extravagant eulogy of the subject addressed, (usually a patroness —which is implied by his reference to 'a painted beauty') whereas this is in praise of a genuinely beautiful young patron.

Sonnet 22

My glass shall not persuade me I am old,
So long as youth and thou are of one date;
But when in thee time's furrows I behold,
Then look I death my days should expiate.
For all that beauty that doth cover thee
Is but the seemly raiment of my heart,
Which in thy breast doth live, as thine in me;
How can I then be elder than thou art?
O therefore, love, be of thyself so wary
As I, not for myself, but for thee will,
Bearing thy heart, which I will keep so chary

As tender nurse her babe from faring ill.
Presume not on thy heart when mine is slain:
Thou gav'st me thine not to give back again.

Not only the reference to a difference in age of the sonneteer and his 'Prince',
but the slightly admonishing tone of the poem preclude that this is addressed
to Walsingham. This tone of an elder, wiser poet to a youthful and exquisitely
beautiful 'Boy' is subtly present in these sonnets addressing Hatcliffe, whose
beauty deeply moves the Poet's heart, and his eventual disillusionment with
the beautiful young 'Prince' must have been a great disappointment.

Sonnets 53, 54, and 55

This triple group, which belongs to the early Hatcliffe sequence, is inserted
into the large group of the *Sonnets of Exile* to help to break this up.

The use of the plural form 'we' in *Sonnet 53* marks this as a poem in praise
of the 'Prince' whose coat-of-arms was three 'True-love' primroses, which is
lightly touched upon in praising his 'constant heart'. The allusion to 'millions
of strange shadows' that tend on his person is a subtle reflection of the hugely
exaggerated, tongue-in-cheek tribute of astronomically large sums of money
owed to the 'Prince' by his 'homagers and vassals' in the delightful tomfoolery
of this Grayan 'Court' of law students. For instance, 'Mariotto Marquerillo de
Holborn' was to render 'yearly two hundred millions sterling', and this rises to
'one hundred thousand million sterling' to be exacted from 'Baldwine de
Islington'. The number of his 'shadows', the play-acting courtiers of Graya, is
here commensurately multiplied into 'millions' to match this. Surely this is yet
further confirmation of the correctness of Dr Hotson's identification of
'Mr.W.H.' as William Hatcliffe, the Prince of Purpoole, is it not?

Sonnet 53

What is your substance, whereof are you made,
That millions of strange shadows on you tend?
Since every one hath, every one, one shade,
And you but one, can every shadow lend:
Describe Adonis, and the counterfeit
Is poorly imitated after you;
On Helen's cheek all art of beauty set,
And you in Grecian tires are painted new:
Speak of the spring and foizon of the year,
The one doth shadow of your beauty show,
The other as your bounty doth appear,
And you in every blessed shape we know,
In all external grace you have some part,
But you like none, none you for constant heart.

436

Sonnet 53 is a pair with Sonnet 54, in which the plural pronoun 'we' again features. There is some affinity with Sonnet 20 in the lavish praises showered on this young Adonis in both these sonnets. Here his fair exterior is seen as the perfect foil for a perfect nature, in which the sonneteer as yet sees no flaw. The Prince of Purpoole, being 'royal', is seen as absolute perfection, a pattern for all men to follow. It is apparent that the Poet's relationship with this young 'Adonis' is definitely one of patronage for this is indicated in the reference to 'your bounty'.

Sonnet 54

O how much more doth beauty beauteous seem
By that sweet ornament which truth doth give!
The rose looks fair, but fairer we it deem
For that sweet odour which doth in it live.
The canker blooms have full as deep a dye
As the perfumed tincture of the roses,
Hang on such thorns, and play as wantonly
When summer's breath their masked buds discloses;
But for their virtue only is their show,
They live unwoo'd and unrespected fade,
Die to themselves. Sweet roses do not so;
Of their sweet deaths are sweetest odours made:
   And so of you, beauteous and lovely youth,
   When that shall fade, my verse distils your truth.

Thorpe has 'by verse' but most editors alter this to 'my verse', which is perhaps correct and seems preferable. It may be a misprint in the original.

Sonnet 55

Not marble, nor the gilded monuments
Of Princes shall outlive this powerful rhyme,
But you shall shine more bright in these contents
Than unswept stone, besmear'd with sluttish time.
When wasteful war shall statues overturn,
And broils root out the work of masonry,
Nor Mars his sword, nor war's quick fire shall burn
The living record of your memory.
'Gainst death, and all-oblivious enmity
Shall you pace forth, your praise shall still find room
Even in the eyes of all posterity
That wear this world out to the ending doom.
   So till the judgement that yourself arise,
   You live in this, and dwell in lovers' eyes.

In this courtly poem there is again the use of plurality in 'lovers' eyes', and it is a well designed tribute to a young man play-acting the part of the Prince of Purpoole.

Although this sonnet has a suitably martial ring as befits a 'Prince', the critical intelligence of Marlowe shines through in his reference to war as 'wasteful', which is apparent even in such a warlike play as his *Tamburlaine the Great,* which was probably at this time being played by the Lord Admiral's Men. Marlowe's surprisingly modern critical attitude towards war, which derives from his compassion for human suffering, is an aspect of his writings that has not been sufficiently noted by critics.

Sonnets 59 and 62, 63, 64, 65

These five sonnets are also inserted into the *Sonnets of Exile,* but they clearly belong to the Hatcliffe group. In *Sonnet 59* the sonneteer descants on history in his reference to 'some antique book' – a favourite theme in this group. Mention of 'subjects' again glances at kingship.

Sonnet 59

If there be nothing new, but that which is,
Hath been before, how are our brains beguil'd,
Which, labouring for invention, bear amiss
The second burthen of a former child?
Oh that record could with a backward look,
Even of five hundred courses of the sun,
Show me your image in some antique book,
Since mind at first in character was done,
That I might see what the old world could say
To this composed wonder of your frame;
Whether we are mended or whe'er better they,
Or whether revolution be the same.
    Oh sure I am the wits of former days
    To subjects worse have given admiring praise.

In this group of courtly sonnets the Poet's intellectual quality is strikingly evident. These poems are without doubt the works of a young man whose mind has been developed in the discipline of university study. They could not have been written by the provincial half-educated man from Stratford-upon-Avon, whose 'poetic' talent was at the level of doggerel rhyme

In Sonnet 62, in an inward-looking, intellectual, philosophizing mood, he conforms to the sonneteering convention of exaggerating his own age as 'Beated and chopped with tann'd antiquity'. This sonnet is part of the quartet with 63, 64, 65, which all harp on 'Time's injurious hand', and 'Age's cruel knife', and make play with royal imagery in such lines as 'all those beauties whereof now he's king', and the 'hungry Ocean, which is also associated with kingship, which encroaches on 'the kingdom of the shore'. This imagery places these sonnets firmly in the Hatcliffe group. They also have a hint of formality which accords with the notion that they were written for the 'Prince' and his 'Court', and were passed round among his student 'courtiers' to be read aloud and enjoyed. These would undoubtedly have formed a critical and appraising audience for such a delightful poetry reading.

Sonnet 62

Sin of self-love possesseth all mine eye,
And all my soul, and all my every part;
And for this sin there is no remedy,
It is so grounded inward in my heart.
Methinks no face so gracious is as mine,
No shape so true, no truth of such account.
And for myself mine own worth do define,
As I all other in all worths surmount.
But when my glass shows me myself indeed,
Beated and chapp'd with tann'd antiquity,
Mine own self-love quite contrary I read;
Self so self-loving were iniquity.
 'Tis thee (my self) that for myself I praise,
 Painting my age with beauty of thy days.

This is a sophisticated poem in which the sonneteer relishes the use of exaggerated age as a striking contrast to the beauty of the youthful and beautiful 'Prince'. It belongs obviously with *Sonnet 63* which is addressed to the young man who is 'king' and reigns in his beauty.

Sonnet 63

Against my love shall be as I am now,
With Time's injurious hand crush'd and o'erworn,
When hours have drain'd his blood and fill'd his brow
With lines and wrinkles, when his youthful morn
Hath travell'd on to age's steepy night,
And all those beauties whereof now he's king
Are vanishing, or vanish'd out of sight,
Stealing away the treasure of his spring;

For such a time do I now fortify
Against confounding age's cruel knife,
That he shall never cut from memory
My sweet love's beauty, though my lover's life.
 His beauty shall in these black lines be seen,
 And they shall live, and he in them still green.

The sonnets in this group in unalloyed praise of this 'royal' young man were evidently intended for public reading, for several of them are not addressed to the 'Prince' directly but refer to him in the third person.

These are early sonnets when our Poet was developing his sonneteering technique, and in the above pair he enjoys experimenting with the sonneteering conventions contrasting youth with age.

Sonnet 64

When I have seen by Time's fell hand defaced
The rich proud cost of outworn buried age,
When sometime lofty towers I see down razed,
And brass eternal slave to mortal rage;
When I have seen the hungry Ocean gain
Advantage on the kingdom of the shore,
And the firm soil win of the wat'ry main,
Increasing store with loss, and loss with store;
When I have seen such interchange of state,
Or state itself confounded to decay,
Ruin hath taught me thus to ruminate,
That Time will come and take my love away.
 This thought is as a death, which cannot choose
 But weep to have that which it fears to lose.

The theme of Time as the ravager of youth and beauty runs right through this group. *Sonnet 65* carries on the themes of the 'boundless sea' and links this into a quartet of sonnets that were probably all composed together.

Sonnet 65

Since brass, nor stone, nor earth, nor boundless sea,
But sad mortality o'ersways their power,
How with this rage shall beauty hold a plea,
Whose action is no stronger than a flower?
O how shall summer's honey breath hold out
Against the wrackful siege of battering days,
When rocks impregnable are not so stout,
Nor gates of steel so strong, but time decays?

O fearful meditation! Where, alack,
Shall Time's best jewel from Time's chest lie hid?
Or what strong hand can hold his swift foot back,
Or who his spoil of beauty can forbid?
    O none, unless this miracle have might,
    That in black ink my love may still shine bright.

Marlowe was a very politically aware young man, and one wonders whether the rumbling threat of the Armada, which was the backcloth to the fantastic Grayan festivities that Christmas season, had perhaps induced the mood of melancholy that underlies this group of courtly sonnets.

Sonnet 105

Let not my love be call'd idolatry,
Nor my beloved as an idol show,
Since all alike my songs and praises be
To one, of one, still such, and ever so.
Kind is my love today, tomorrow kind,
Still constant in a wondrous excellence;
Therefore my verse, to constancy confin'd,
One thing expressing, leaves out difference.
'Fair, kind, and true', is all my argument,
'Fair, kind, and true', varying to other words;
And in this change is my invention spent,
Three themes in one, which wondrous scope affords.
    Fair, kind, and true have often lived alone,
    Which three till now never kept seat in one.

This sonnet is the heart of the group to 'Prince' Will Hatcliffe, whose coat-of-arms of 'True-Love' primroses (or four-leaf clover) is wittily embodied in its theme and format. This has been more fully explained according to Dr Hotson's identification of the meaning of this emblematic poem in Chapter 12.

Sonnet 106

When in the chronicle of wasted time
I see descriptions of the fairest wights,
And beauty making beautiful old rhyme,
In praise of ladies dead and lovely knights;
Then in the blazon of sweet beauty's best,
Of hand, of foot, of lip, of eye, of brow,
I see their antique pen would have express'd
Even such beauty as you master now.

So all their praises are but prophecies
Of this our time, all you prefiguring,
And for they look'd but with divining eyes,
They had not skill enough your worth to sing:
    For we which now behold these present days,
    Have eyes to wonder, but lack tongues to praise.

The Poet again resorts to history's 'antique pen' for comparison with the present beauty of the 'Prince' who is the admiration of his 'courtiers', whose presence is indicated in the plurals 'we', 'eyes' and 'tongues'.

    These two sonnets conclude the group of the justly famous 'sugred Sonnets' to the Prince of Purpoole. Those that follow take on a very different tone of admonition and disappointment in the young man who was his 'idol'.

❖   ❖   ❖

GROUP B

THE FRIENDSHIP TURNS SOUR (Early 1588)

This group of thirteen scattered sonnets, some deliberately placed to be mis-leading, has bedevilled the understanding of the story behind the *Sonnets* by confusing the identities of 'Mr.W.H.', the 'lascivious' young 'Prince', with the true Patron. Disillusionment with his 'Prince's' perfection has set in, and he writes to him admonishing him for his misdemeanours when he steals the Poet's mistress and reveals his 'lascivious' and faithless nature, wherein we see the Poet's wonderful magnanimity of spirit which suffuses the whole sequence. Pity rather than anger is evoked by his sexual jealousy at this faith-lessness. In these sonnets he is writing out of his system his injured love for the young man whom he had valued so highly as his true friend and patron. All except *Sonnet 94* address him in the second person.

Sonnet 35

No more be griev'd at that which thou hast done;
Roses have thorns, and silver fountains mud,
Clouds and eclipses stain both moon and sun,
And loathsome canker lives in sweetest bud.
All men make faults, and even I in this,
Authorizing thy trespass with compare,
Myself corrupting salving thy amiss,
Excusing thy sins more than thy sins are:
For to thy sensual fault I bring in sense,
Thy adverse party is thy advocate,
And 'gainst myself a lawful plea commence;
Such civil war is in my love and hate,
    That I an accessory needs must be,
    To that sweet thief which sourly robs from me.

The next sonnet plays on Hatcliffe's coat-of-arms – the 'True-Love' emblem – which is contrasted with his faithless nature. The Poet's sincere love for the young man may, indeed, be called 'true love', which is the opposite of the lascivious love affair the faithless 'Prince' is indulging in with the Poet's mis-tress. Thorpe has 'this self' (line 7), but some editors prefer 'thyself'.

Sonnet 40

Take all my loves, my love, yea, take them all;
What hast thou then more than thou hadst before?
No love, my love, that thou mayst true love call,
All mine was thing before thou hadst this more:

Then if for my love, thou my love receivest,
I cannot blame thee for my love thou usest;
But yet be blam'd, if thou this self deceivest
By wilful taste of what thyself refusest.
I do forgive thy robb'ry, gentle thief,
Although thou steal thee all my poverty:
And yet love knows it is a greater grief
To bear love's wrong, than hate's known injury.
   Lascivious grace, in whom all ill well shows,
   Kill me with spites, yet we must not be foes.

Sonnet 41

Those pretty wrongs that liberty commits,
When I am sometime absent from thy heart,
Thy beauty and thy years full well befits,
For still temptation follows where thou art.
Gentle thou art, and therefore to be won,
Beauteous thou art, therefore to be assailed;
And when a woman woos, what woman's son
Will sourly leave her till he have prevailed?
Aye me, but yet thou mightst my seat forbear,
And chide thy beauty, and thy straying youth,
Who lead thee in their riot even there
Where thou art forc'd to break a two-fold truth:
   Hers by thy beauty tempting her to thee,
   Thine by thy beauty being false to me.

Sonnets 40, 41, 42 are a triplet displaced chronologically in the *Sonnets of Exile*. The reference to 'my seat' makes it clear that it is the Poet's mistress whom the 'Prince' has stolen. However, it is not the Dark Lady who is the mistress in this case, for the Poet apparently gives her up to his young friend without a struggle, rationalizing his jealousy in these witty sonnets. The loss of this mistress is not so hard to bear as the discovery of his young patron's faithlessness, in whom he feels he has lost a friend.

Sonnet 42

That thou hast her, it is not all my grief,
And Yet it may be said I lov'd her dearly;
That she hath thee is of my wailing chief,
A loss in love that touches me more nearly.
Loving offenders, thus I will excuse ye:
Thou dost love her, because thou know'st I love her,
And for my sake even so doth she abuse me,

Suff'ring my friend for my sake to approve her.
If I lose thee, my loss is my love's gain,
And losing her, my friend hath found that loss:
Both find each other, and I lose both twain,
And both for my sake lay on me this cross.
    But here's the joy: my friend and I are one.
    Sweet flattery! Then she loves but me alone.

This affair has been the first rift in the lute. The value, in every sense, of the young 'Prince' as the Poet's trusted and well-loved patron has been irrevocably marred – and this represents the Poet's grievous loss. Patronage and the friendship of a patron were vitally important to a young Elizabethan poet who was low-born. He was only a cobbler's son, and men of this class were rated as servants, so that at this early stage in our Poet's career he still had the necessity to establish himself by gaining a patron whose influence would help him to rise in society.

Sonnets 57, 58

With this sonnet-pair the mood becomes decidedly more embittered. There is heavy sarcasm in his description of himself as the 'Prince's' 'slave', who is kept waiting in vain for his 'sovereign' – perhaps while his young friend is with his mistress? The reference to 'Will' (which is capitalized in Thorpe's edition, but not italicized, so that it is a little ambiguous) is probably intended as a play in *double entendre* on the name of Will Hatcliffe and the Elizabethan connotation of 'will' as sexual desire, which is later repeated more pointedly in the Dark Lady sonnets.

Sonnet 57

Being your slave, what should I do but tend
Upon the hours and times of your desire?
I have no precious time at all to spend,
Nor services to do, till you require;
Nor dare I chide the world-without-end hour
Whilst I (my sovereign) watch the clock for you.
Nor think the bitterness of absence sour,
When you have bid your servant once adieu.
Nor dare I question with my jealous thought
Where you may be, or your affairs suppose,
But like a sad slave stay and think of nought
Save where you are, how happy you make those.
    So true a fool is love, that in your Will,
    (Though you do anything) he thinks no ill.

The Poet is learning that being in the patronage of this spoilt young 'Prince' has distinct disadvantages. But his innate loyalty to the beautiful Will Hatcliffe who was (we may assume) at this time still his patron, lends him exceptional forbearance.

Sonnet 58

That god forbid, that made me first your slave,
I should in thought control your time of pleasure,
Or at your hand th' account of hours to crave,
Being your vassal bound to stay your leisure.
Oh let me suffer (being at your beck)
Th' imprison'd absence of your liberty,
And patience, tame to sufferance, bide each check,
Without accusing you of injury.
Be where you list, your charter is so strong,
That you yourself may privilege your time
To what you will; to you it doth belong,
Yourself to pardon of self-doing crime.
   I am to wait, though waiting so be hell,
   Not blame your pleasure, be it ill or well.

Sonnets 69, 70

These two sonnets, although now critical of the young 'Prince', contain obvious references to his 'royal' status, which verifies their placement in the Will Hatcliffe group. Thorpe's edition follows with two sonnets about the Poet's anonymity in exile in the sonnet-sequence demonstrating the deliberate mix-up of themes.

Sonnet 69

Those parts of thee that the world's eye doth view,
Want nothing that the thought of hearts can mend:
All tongues (the voice of souls) give thee that due,
Utt'ring bare truth even so as foes commend.
Thine outward thus with outward praise is crown'd,
But those same tongues that give thee so thine own,
In other accents do this praise confound
By seeing farther than the eye hath shown.
They look into the beauty of thy mind,
And that in guess they measure by thy deeds.
Then churls their thoughts (although their eyes were kind)
To thy fair flower add the rank smell of weeds.
   But why thy odour matcheth not thy show,
   The soil is this: that thou dost common grow.

The references to 'All tongues (the voice of souls)' with which his 'outward praise is crown'd', and 'thou alone kingdoms of hearts shouldst owe', confirm that these sonnets are addressed to the Prince of Purpoole. Whether these sonnets were also circulated amongst his 'courtiers' is, however, doubtful, although it seems that others besides the sonneteer himself had begun to note the flaws in this exquisite young 'Prince's' nature; '(although their eyes were kind)' he tells us. In contradistinction to the 'public' poems of effusive praise to Hatcliffe, these are very private poems from the Poet to his young and erring patron.

Sonnet 70

> That thou are blam'd shall not be thy defect,
> For slander's mark was ever yet the fair;
> The ornament of beauty is suspect,
> A crow that flies in heaven's sweetest air,
> So thou be good, slander doth but approve
> Thy worth the greater, being woo'd of time;
> For canker vice the sweetest buds doth love,
> And thou present'st a pure unstained prime.
> Thou hast pass'd by the ambush of young days,
> Either not assail'd, or victor being charg'd;
> Yet this thy praise cannot be so thy praise,
> To tie up envy evermore enlarg'd.
> > If some suspect of ill mask'd not thy show,
> > Then thou alone kingdoms of hearts shouldst owe.

Sonnets 93, 94, 95 and 96

This quartet of sonnets to Will Hatcliffe are (deliberately) tacked onto the end of the *Sonnets of the Rival Poet,* which gives a subtly confusing twist to the sequence at this point, for the Poet has been expressing his anguished jealousy to his True Patron in the fourteen preceding sonnets. Now he speaks of his deteriorating relationship with Will Hatcliffe — a different set of emotions involving a different young man, with whom he is critically at odds for a totally different reason. By now total disillusionment is fast setting in.

Sonnet 93

> So shall I live, supposing thou art true,
> Like a deceived husband; so love's face
> May still seem love to me, though alter'd new,
> Thy looks with me, thy heart in other place.
> For there can live no hatred in thine eye,
> Therefore in that I cannot know thy change.

In many's looks the false heart's history
Is writ in moods and frowns and wrinkles strange;
But heaven in thy creation did decree
That in thy face sweet love should ever dwell;
Whate'er thy thoughts or thy heart's workings be,
Thy looks should nothing thence but sweetness tell.
  How like Eve's apple doth thy beauty grow
  If thy sweet virtue answer not thy show!

The coldness praised in the next sonnet is chastity, which, being hard, is nevertheless a virtue in Elizabethan eyes, and it rightly graces outward beauty. The final line appears in Marlowe's *Edward the Third,* which was also written in 1588, in celebration of the defeat of the Armada. In the play, Warwick speaks these same words to his daughter, exhorting her to chastity by resisting King Edward's lascivious advances, which she does dramatically by threatening to kill herself rather than submit to his lust.

Sonnet 94

They that have power to hurt, and will do none,
That do not do the thing they most do show,
Who moving others, are themselves as stone,
Unmoved, cold, and to temptation slow:
They rightly do inherit heaven's graces,
And husband nature's riches from expense;
They are the lords and owners of their faces,
Others but stewards of their excellence.
The summer's flower is to the summer sweet,
Though to itself it only live and die,
But if that flower with base infection meet,
The basest weed outbraves his dignity.
  For sweetest things turn sourest by their deeds:
  Lilies that fester smell far worse than weeds.

The youthfulness of 'Mr.W.H.' is declared by the reference to 'the beauty of thy budding name!'.

Sonnet 95

How sweet and lovely dost thou make the shame,
Which like a canker in the fragrant rose,
Doth spot the beauty of thy budding name!
Oh in what sweets dost thou thy sins enclose!
That tongue that tells the story of thy days,
Making lascivious comments on thy sport,

Cannot dispraise, but in a kind of praise;
Naming thy name, blesses an ill report.
Oh what a mansion have those vices got
Which for their habitation chose out thee,
Where beauty's veil doth cover every blot,
And all things turn to fair that eyes can see!
    Take heed (dear heart) of this large privilege:
    The hardest knife ill us'd doth lose its edge.

The admonishing tone in these sonnets is totally different from anything the Poet ever wrote to Walsingham, even in the critical sonnets of the Rival Poet which have just preceded this foursome of chiding sonnets to Hatcliffe. There is also a direct or implicit reference to the youthfulness of the young man being addressed which makes this difference unmistakable that it is to Hatcliffe he is speaking, not to Walsingham.

Sonnet 96

Some say thy fault is youth, some wantonness,
Some say thy grace is youth and gentle sport.
Both grace and faults are lov'd of more and less;
Thou mak'st faults graces that to thee resort.
As on the finger of a throned Queen
The basest jewel will be well esteem'd,
So are those errors that in thee are seen
To truths translated, and for true things deem'd.
How many lambs might the stern wolf betray,
If like a lamb he could his looks translate:
How many gazers mightst thou lead away
If thou wouldst use the strength of all thy state!
    But do not so: I love thee in such sort,
    As thou being mine, mine is thy good report.

Despite the Poet's disillusionment with the exquisite young 'Prince' Will, who does not live up to his beauteous looks, the relationship is evidently still one of patronage as indicated by the words 'thou being mine'.

Sonnet 126 marks the end of his true friendship with the beautiful young William Hatcliffe, his 'Prince' and evidently his first patron, whom he honoured by his dedication (if cryptic) of his *Sonnets* to 'Mr.W.H.', identified and discovered by Dr Hotson. This exquisite young gentleman, wealthy, fêted, well-born, a member of the landed gentry class whose place in the social hierarchy was just a rung below the nobility – it was to this class also that Thomas Walsingham belonged – was a beautiful mirage of friendship and patronage for the Poet.

Here Hatcliffe is addressed as 'my lovely Boy'. The brackets indicating the missing couplet are given in Thorpe's edition, and imply, perhaps, that these two lines were cut. It is highly unlikely that they were never written. Cutting them may have been a last minute decision, because they were too revealing. Leaving the brackets may also have significance – a hint of some kind, to be understood by some who had known the full story.

The late placement of this sonnet *just before the commencement of the large group to the Dark Lady* is surely also deliberate, for 'Prince' Will is the rival 'Will' who features in these sonnets – this time in the context of a passionate love-affair with the black-eyed courtezan whose 'black' beauty completely captivated our Poet, and the rivalry with 'Prince' Will caused him real anguish. He appears in these sonnets only in the third person, and he soon makes his exit, having apparently tired of the Dark Lady before she tired of him! So the Poet wins her back.

In this lovely sonnet, which has an air of sadness, he writes his valediction to his first young patron, the 'lovely Boy' of the *Sonnets.*

Sonnet 126

O thou my lovely Boy, who in thy power
Dost hold Time's fickle glass, his sickle, hour:
Who hast by waning grown, and therein show'st
Thy lovers withering, as thy sweet self grow'st.
If Nature (sovereign mistress over wrack)
As thou goest onwards still will pluck thee back,
She keeps thee to this purpose, that her skill
May Time disgrace, and wretched minute kill.
Yet fear her, O thou minion of her pleasure,
She may detain, but not still keep her treasure!
Her audit (though delay'd answer'd must be,
And her quietus is to render thee.
    (   )
    (   )

FINIS

GROUP C
FIRST LOVE (1587-88)

Sonnets 23 and 24

This sonnet-pair introduces us to the great love-theme of sacred and profane love that is the *leit-motif* of the whole sequence. This, I believe, explains its early placement in Thorpe's edition, which begins with the sonnets to Southampton, which were commissioned, and do not belong to the sequence proper, since they are not autobiographical. The autobiographical story begins with our introduction to the Poet's first patron, the 'beauteous and lovely Youth', 'Prince' Will Hatcliffe, who was, for the Poet, his ideal young friend to whom he gave his heart in Platonic Love, until he proved unworthy. The group of first five sonnets to his 'Mr.W.H.' *Sonnets 18, 19, 20, 21,* and *22,* are all of that 'honeymoon' period when he thought his young friend was as virtuous as he was beautiful.

With *Sonnets 23* and *24* we are introduced to profane love, as personified by the woman with whom he fell so desperately and passionately in love – his Dark Lady, Mistress Luce Morgan. She was also associated with 'Prince' Will, and this episode belongs to that Christmas season which had such a profound effect emotionally on the vulnerable young Poet, then aged 23 years. Perhaps the number chosen for the placement of *Sonnet 23* even describes this, for, as we have seen, the numbering of the sonnets has special significance for the Poet.

These two sonnets express the overwhelming power of intense, sexual love, in which the Poet finds himself tongue-tied by the blind force of his passion. This is how Marlowe reacts typically towards the powerful sensation that falling in love exerts over him, for so he has described it in his plays, *Tamburlaine the Great* and his *Edward the Third.* When King Edward is pierced to the heart on his first encounter with the beautiful Countess of Salisbury and falls hopelessly in love with her on the spot, he immediately begins to talk distractedly, and lapses into rhymed couplets instead of blank verse! [1] His first impulse is to run away from what he recognizes as a dangerous obsession, and he makes excuses for not accepting the invitation to become the Countess's guest at the castle. But then he cannot resist when she importunes him to honour her by staying, and thereafter he can think of nothing but how to seduce her and consummate his conquest.

Similarly Tamburlaine melts at his first sight of the lovely Zenocrate, and he immediately launches into an ecstatic speech promising her the most exaggerated luxuries if she will accept his offer of himself 'to fair Zenocrate'. His friend and companion-at-arms, Techelles, exclaims in utter amazement:

> Techelles: What now! in love?
> Tamburlaine: Techelles, women must be flattered:
> But this is she with whom I am in love. [2]

451

And so it is – a true deep love that the Scythian warrior has conceived for the beautiful Zenocrate, and when she dies (in *The Second Part of Tamburlaine*) he runs mad, like Othello for whom life without Desdemona is darkness. The most famous line in *Hero and Leander* is probably: 'Whoever lov'd, that lov'd not at first sight?'. In *Dido Queen of Carthage* Marlowe portrays the same overpowering reaction when she is smitten with love for Aeneas, and she likewise speaks confusedly, betraying sudden loss of control in the grip of this powerful emotion. Marlowe was ever the great romantic at heart.

In his *Sonnet 23* the Poet is suddenly 'O'ercharg'd with burthen of mine own love's might' and cannot speak. This is the passion engendered in him at his first meeting with the lovely dark-eyed courtezan who is the subject of the twenty-five sonnets that conclude the sequence, but she is introduced here because this is the point at which the Poet falls in love with her. In the Dark Lady sonnets his love affair with her is already established. These sonnets cannot be addressing either 'Mr.W.H.' or Thomas Walsingham, for he was never tongue-tied in their presence. The feelings of love expressed to his two patrons are of altogether a different nature, of ardent admiration, certainly, but not having this wild sexually generated, passionate response as expressed in these two sonnets we are here considering.

That the lady in question is Luce Morgan is established by the recurring use of the words 'eyes' and 'more'. As Dr Hotson has pointed out, her Welsh name, Morgan, means a man of the *sea,* in Welsh 'mor', which is significantly played upon also in *Sonnet 135:* 'Shakespeare compares Luce Morgan with *the sea,* made *more:*

> The sea, all water, yet receives rain still,
> And in abundance addeth to his store;
> So thou, being rich in will, add to thy will
> One will of mine, to make thy large will more.

And he further calls her

> . . . the bay where all men ride'³

The Elizabethans were fond of playing on a name as a form of poetic witticism. Dr Hotson quotes several examples, and he remarks that 'with English versifiers dealing in names embodying *Mor* – the tendency to play upon them appears ingrained.'

As in: When we read in Francis Davison's poem "Pure and Endless" – on sending a ring to his love – the lines

> Shall make *more* precious, when you shall wear it . .
> Doth it the purer grow the *more* 'tis tried? . .
> That whereas gold, the *more* 'tis purified . .
> My love doth grow *more* pure by your more trying . .

it is safe to say that her name was not Cholmondeley.'⁴

He quotes also the doggerel verse on Sir Thomas More:

> 'When More two years had Chancellor been
> No *more* suits did remain;
> The same shall never *more* be seen
> Till More be there again.' [5]

In the *Sonnets* the word 'more' features seventeen times in one hundred and twenty-nine poems (that is, excluding the Dark Lady group and *Sonnet 23*), but in the twenty-five Dark Lady sonnets 'more' is used *fourteen times*. In addition the words 'mourn', 'mourners', 'mourning' and morning' *(Sonnet 132)* are played upon, also 'mortgag'd', adding another seven 'Mor' words, totalling *twenty-one* that may be intended to connote *Morgan*. In *Sonnet 23* 'more' is repeated three times in a single line, where it is emphasised, even exaggerated, so that I think Dr Hotson has a point regarding the use of 'more' as a play on her name, Morgan.

Wherever 'more is used elsewhere in the sonnets it occurs naturally and could scarcely have been replaced by any other word, but in *Sonnet 23* it is somewhat contrived, while the final line brings in 'eyes' which are significantly played upon in *Sonnet 24*. Surely these two poems show us the young twenty-three-year-old Marlowe falling head-over-heels in love with his *femme fatale*, Luce Morgan?

Sonnet 23

As an unperfect actor on the stage,
Who with his fear is put besides his part,
Or some fierce thing replete with too much rage,
Whose strength's abundance weakens his own heart;
So I, for fear of trust, forget to say
The perfect ceremony of love's rite,
And in mine own love's strength seem to decay,
O'ercharg'd with burthen of mine own love's might.
O let my books be then the eloquence
And dumb presagers of my speaking breast,
Who plead for love, and look for recompense,
More than that tongue that more hath more express'd.
 O learn to read what silent love hath writ:
 To hear with eyes belongs to love's fine wit.

Just as in the Dark Lady group where 'eyes' are dwelt on so strikingly, *Sonnet 24* descants on 'eyes' as its main theme, and we know that 'eyes' are symbolic of the name Lucy or Luce, as Dr Hotson's research has elucidated for us. Although eyes feature elsewhere in the *Sonnets* which are so generally concerned with beauty, there is nothing like the specific emphasis that is given to the organs of our sight as in the Dark Lady group *and* in *Sonnet 24.* The notable exceptions are the sonnet-pair expressing his joy at receiving the exquisite *impresa* miniature of his Patron, in *Sonnets 46* and *47.* There the whole theme is the interchange between 'eye and heart' as he gazes at the portrait, which is entirely appropriate to the subject of this sonnet-pair. In *Sonnet 24* the Poet also imagines himself as the painter who is limning the beloved's face and form on his heart.

Sonnet 24

Mine eye hath played the painter, and hath steel'd
Thy beauty's form in table of my heart.
My body is the frame wherein 'tis held,
And perspective it is best painter's art;
For through the painter must you see his skill,
To find where your true image pictured lies,
Which in my bosom's shop is hanging still,
That hath his windows glazed with thine *eyes.*
Now see what good turns *eyes* for *eyes* have done:
Mine eyes have drawn thy shape, and thine for me
Are windows to my breast, where-through the sun
Delights to peep, to gaze therein on thee.
   Yet *eyes* this cunning want to grace their art,
   They draw but what they see, know not the heart.

A characteristic of Marlowe's work that has been remarked upon by his critics, is his tendency to repeat himself, and it must be said this is noticeable in the *Sonnets* as a whole: a characteristic that has made the detection of the various groups into which the poems fit at times extremely difficult. There may be some readers who will disagree with some of the placements of sonnets here suggested, but I think that, all in all, the story that is revealed is a truly autobiographical one that is remarkably consistent and convincing. Certain key sonnets in the sequence (discussed earlier) are undeniably revealing of this autobiographical history and can hardly be queried. But, because of this tendency to repetition of certain favourite, and very beautiful, poetic words, phrases, and thoughts, it has only been by a constant rereading and the most careful evaluation of what the Poet is saying, and to whom he is saying it, together with a knowledge of the background and historical context, that a final revelation of where each sonnet belongs, has been possible.

The sonnet-pair here under consideration is surely correctly interpreted. These two speak with the authentic voice of Marlowe in his depiction of first love in his other works. Comparable instances exist, of course, in Shakespeare – *As You Like* It comes immediately to mind. This view of first love, married to

Dr Hotson's meticulous research on Elizabethan language and its emblematic meanings, has brought the conclusion that these two sonnets can be none other than the celebration of the Poet's falling in love, in which *Sonnet 24* specifically points to Luce as the Christian name of his beloved, while *Sonnet 23* points to her surname, Morgan. This kind of precision, wit, and subtlety is typical of the *Sonnets,* which we have until now only dimly perceived.

The reason for the separate early placement of these two sonnets is, I suggest, both aesthetic and autobiographical. The introduction of the profane love-theme at this early stage in the sequence following our introduction to 'Prince'Will Hatcliffe brings him and Luce Morgan into close proximity chronologically, emotionally, and sexually as the symbols of profane love and fallen virtue. This concept adds another dimension to our understanding of the sonnet-story, and the Poet's evaluation of the essential meaning of Love in all its forms – 'the broken lines of Eros'.

GROUP D
THREE SONNETS BY THE QUEEN'S SECRET AGENT
(1588 and 1589)

Sonnet 107

The 'Armada' sonnet was written in celebration of the English victory in that momentous naval campaign, in which recent research has revealed that Christopher Marlowe himself played an active part.

Experts have claimed him as the sitter in the 'Armada' portrait painted in 1588, which shows a rather wan-looking, much thinner young man than in the Corpus Christi portrait, whose features are nevertheless recognizably the same. The words of *Sonnet 107* echo his sense of relief at having survived the dangers of the sea-battles, which were followed tragically by the onset of an epidemic of ships' fever that carried off more of England's naval mariners than had perished in the whole of the fighting at sea.

Dr Hotson has shown that this sonnet is numbered in association with *Psalm 107*. See pages 191-199 for the Armada background to this sonnet. That he had personally survived danger in this fight is intimated in the line 'and Death to me subscribes'.

Sonnet 107

> Not mine own fears, nor the prophetic soul
> Of the wide world, dreaming on things to come,
> Can yet the lease of my true love control,
> Suppos'd as forfeit to a confin'd doom.
> The mortal Moon hath her eclipse endur'd,
> And the sad augers mock their own presage;
> Incertainties now crown themselves assur'd,
> And peace proclaims olives of endless age.
> Now with the drops of this most balmy time
> My love looks fresh, and Death to me subscribes,
> Since spite of him I'll live in this poor rhyme,
> While he insults o'er dull and speechless tribes.
>   And thou in this shalt find thy monument,
>   When tyrants' crests and tombs of brass are spent.

Sonnets 123 and 124 have been generally declared 'difficult' sonnets, which scholars had puzzled over in vain until Dr Hotson's research revealed their political content. They were undoubtedly inspired by Marlowe's espionage work, in which he travelled abroad and gained first-hand insight into the political turmoil in France, reflected in *Sonnet 124,* and the intrigues between the Catholic and Protestant factions. They fit the hand of Marlowe as sonneteer and secret agent to an uncanny degree. Both these sonnets, intricate in their thought and intellectually challenging to the reader, were distilled out of his political experience gleaned through his professional work as one of Sir Francis Walsingham's and Lord Burghley's most trusted secret agents.

The 'pyramids' referred to in *Sonnet 123* are the great stone obelisks that Caligula had originally brought from Egypt, and which Pope Sixtus V had re-erected in Rome in the years 1586 to 1589, one in each of the four years. His personal viewing of these sixteenth century wonders by the Poet is implied in this contemplative sonnet, in which the last lines reaffirm his commitment to his service to Queen and country.

Sonnet 123

No! Time, thou shalt not boast that I do change.
Thy pyramids built up with newer might
To me are nothing novel, nothing strange,
They are but dressings of a former sight:
Our dates are brief, and therefore we admire
What thou dost foist upon us that is old,
And rather make them born to our desire,
Than think that we before have heard them told.
Thy registers and thee I both defy,
Not wond'ring at the present, nor the past;
For thy records, and what we see doth lie,
Made more or less by thy continual haste.
   This I do vow and this shall ever be,
   I will be true despite thy scythe and thee.

Sonnet 124 is also numbered to link it with *Psalm 124,* as Dr Hotson's research has revealed. Marlowe's involvement in the uncovering of the Babington Plot, aimed at the assassination of Queen Elizabeth, I suggest is reflected in the couplet ending this sonnet.

Sonnet 124

If my dear love were but the child of state,
It might for fortune's bastard be unfathered,
As subject to Time's love, or to Time's hate,
Weeds among weeds, or flowers with flowers gather'd.
No, it was builded far from accident;
It suffers not in smiling pomp, nor falls
Under the blow of thralled discontent,
Whereto th' inviting time our fashion calls.
It fears not policy, that heretic,
Which works on leases of short-number'd hours,
But all alone stands hugely politic,
That it nor grows with heat, nor drowns with showers.
   To this I witness call the fools of Time,
   Which die for goodness, who have liv'd for crime.

For a full discussion of both these politically-inspired sonnets see pages 250-257.

GROUP E

THE COMMISSIONED SONNETS (1590)

Sonnets 1 to 17 form a tightly knit group of seventeen consecutive sonnets all on a single theme, without any interruption or variation, all exhorting a handsome and well-born youth to marry and beget heirs to his line. Such a young man would by inference be a nobleman. Henry Wriothesley, 3rd Earl of Southampton was addressed by Shakespeare as his chosen patron in the dedication of *Venus and Adonis,* and since he had been affianced against his inclinations by his Guardian, Lord Burghley, whose Ward of Court he was, to marry Burghley's granddaughter, the Lady Elizabeth de Vere, but was strenuously resisting the consummation of these nuptials, (to the great annoyance of Lord Burghley) it is entirely natural, reasonable and obvious to conclude that these sonnets are addressing the young Earl of Southampton. This premise is fairly widely accepted, but the problem arises when all the rest of the sonnets addressing a young man are also seen as written to Southampton – for they don't fit him at all.

However, when these seventeen poems are read as Lord Burghley's commissioned sonnets written for him by the poet who was there at his elbow, already in his employ as his trusted government agent, to be presented to his recalcitrant Ward of Court as his Lordship's present on his seventeenth birthday, after his year's grace granted to allow Southampton to get used to the idea of marriage, they make perfect sense and fit Southampton, the circumstances, and Lord Burghley, and the poet identified as his agent Marlowe absolutely precisely. *This* scenario has no flaw.

. This also precisely dates these sonnets as having been completed and written fair in manuscript, and doubtless bound into a handsome little presentation volume, by 6th October 1590 when the young Earl attained his seventeenth birthday – seventeen charming sonnets, one for each year of his young life.

Sonnet 1

From fairest creatures we desire increase,
That thereby beauty's rose might never die,
But as the riper should by time decease,
His tender heir might bear his memory;
But thou, contracted to thine own bright eyes,
Feed'st thy light's flame with self-substantial fuel,
Making a famine where abundance lies,
Thyself thy foe, to thy sweet self too cruel.
Thou that art now the world's fresh ornament,
And only herald to the gaudy spring,
Within thine own bud buriest thy content,

And, tender churl, mak'st waste in niggarding.
  Pity the world, or else this glutton be,
  To eat the world's due, by the grave and thee.

This is the only sonnet outside the group to 'Prince' Will Hatcliffe in which the plural 'we' occurs, implying that here the Poet is not just speaking for himself.

Sonnet 2

When forty winters shall besiege thy brow,
And dig deep trenches in thy beauty's field,
Thy youth's proud livery, so gaz'd on now,
Will be a tatter'd weed of small worth held.
Then being ask'd where all thy beauty lies,
Where all the treasure of thy lusty days,
To say within thine own deep-sunken eyes,
Were an all-eating shame and thriftless praise.
How much more praise deserv'd thy beauty's use
If thou couldst answer, this fair child of mine
Shall sum my count, and make my old excuse,
Proving his beauty by succession thine.
  This were to be new made when thou art old,
  And see thy blood warm when thou feel'st it cold.

Sonnet 3

Look in thy glass, and tell the face thou viewest,
Now is the time that face should form another,
Whose fresh repair, if now thou not renewest,
Thou dost beguile the world, unbless some mother.
For where is she so fair whose unear'd womb
Disdains the tillage of thy husbandry?
Or who is he so fond will be the tomb
Of his self-love to stop posterity?
Thou art thy mother's glass, and she in thee
Calls back the lovely April of her prime;
So thou through windows of thine age shalt see,
Despite of wrinkles, this thy golden time.
  But if thou live remember'd not to be,
  Die single, and thine image dies with thee.

Sonnet 4

Unthrifty loveliness, why dost thou spend
Upon thyself thy beauty's legacy?
Nature's bequest gives nothing, but doth lend,
And being frank, she lends to those are free.
Then, beauteous niggard, why dost thou abuse
The bounteous largess given thee to give?
Profitless usurer, why dost thou use
So great a sum of sums yet canst not live?
For having traffic with thyself alone,
Thou of thyself thy sweet self dost deceive;
Then how when nature calls thee to be gone,
What acceptable audit canst thou leave?
    Thy unus'd beauty must be tomb'd with thee,
    Which used lives th' executor to be.

Sonnet 5

Those hours that with gentle work did frame
The lovely gaze where every eye doth dwell,
Will play the tyrants to the very same,
And that unfair which fairly doth excel;
For never-resting time leads summer on
To hideous winter, and confounds him there,
Sap check'd with frost and lusty leaves quite gone,
Beauty o'er-snow'd and bareness everywhere.
Then were not summer's distillation left
A liquid prisoner pent in walls of glass,
Beauty's effect with beauty were bereft,
Nor it nor no remembrance what it was.
    But flowers distill'd, though they with winter meet,
    Lease but their show, their substance still lives sweet.

Sonnet 6

Then let not winter's ragged hand deface
In thee thy summer ere thou be distill'd.
Make sweet some vial; treasure thou some place
With beauty's treasure ere it be self-kill'd:
That use is not forbidden usury
Which happies those that pay the willing loan;
That's for thyself to breed another thee,
Or ten times happier, be it ten for one,
Ten times thyself were happier than thou art,
If ten of thine ten times refigur'd thee;

Then what could death do if thou shouldst depart,
Leaving thee living in posterity?
   Be not self-will'd, for thou art much too fair
   To be death's conquest and make worms thine heir.

Sonnet 7

Lo, in the orient when the gracious light
Lifts up his burning head, each under eye
Doth homage to his new-appearing sight,
Serving with looks his sacred majesty;
And having climb'd the steep-up heavenly hill,
Resembling strong youth in his middle age,
Yet mortal looks adore his beauty still,
Attending on his golden pilgrimage.
But when from high-most pitch, with weary car,
Like feeble age he reeleth from the day,
The eyes ('fore duteous) now converted are
From his low tract and look another way,
   So thou, thyself out-going in thy noon,
   Unlook'd on diest unless thou get a son.

Sonnet 8

Music to hear, why hear'st thou music sadly?
Sweets with sweets war not, joy delights in joy:
Why lov'st thou that which thou receiv'st not gladly,
Or else receiv'st with pleasure thine annoy?
If the true concord of well-tuned sounds
By unions married do offend thine ear,
They do but sweetly chide thee, who confounds
In singleness the parts that thou shouldst bear.
Mark how one string, sweet husband to another,
Strikes each in each by mutual ordering,
Resembling sire, and child, and happy mother,
Who all in one, one pleasing note do sing;
   Whose speechless song, being many, seeming one,
   Sings this to thee: 'Thou single wilt prove none.'

Sonnet 9

Is it for fear to wet a widow's eye
That thou consum'st thyself in single life?
Ah, if thou issueless shalt hap to die,
The world will wail thee like a makeless wife;
The world will be thy widow, and still weep

That thou no form of thee hast left behind,
When every private widow well may keep
By children's eyes her husband's shape in mind.
Look what an unthrift in the world doth spend,
Shifts but his place, for still the world enjoys it;
But beauty's waste hath in the world an end,
And kept unus'd, the user so destroys it.
   No love toward others in that bosom sits
   That on himself such murd'rous shame commits.

Sonnet 10

For shame, deny that thou bear'st love to any,
Who for thyself art so unprovident.
Grant if thou wilt, thou art belov'd of many,
But that thou none lov'st is most evident;
For thou art so possess'd with murd'rous hate
That 'gainst thyself thou stick'st not to conspire,
Seeking that beauteous roof to ruinate
Which to repair should be thy chief desire.
O, change thy thought, that I may change my mind.
Shall hate be fairer lodg'd than gentle love?
Be as thy presence is, gracious and kind,
Or to thyself at least kind-hearted prove;
   Make thee another self for love of me,
   That beauty still may live in thine or thee.

Sonnet 11

As fast as thou shalt wane, so fast thou grow'st
In one of thine, from that which thou departest;
And that fresh blood which youngly thou bestow'st
Thou mayst call thine, when thou from youth convertest;
Herein lives wisdom, beauty, and increase,
Without this, folly, age, and cold decay.
If all were minded so, the times should cease,
And threescore year would make the world away.
Let those whom Nature hath not made for store,
Harsh, featureless, and rude, barrenly perish.
Look whom she best endow'd, she gave the more,
Which bounteous gift thou shouldst in bounty cherish;
   She carv'd thee for her seal, and meant thereby
   Thou shouldst print more, not let that copy die.

Sonnet 12

When I do count the clock that tells the time,
And see the brave day sunk in hideous night;
When I behold the violet past prime,
And sable curls ensilver'd o'er with white;
When lofty trees I see barren of leaves,
Which erst from heat did canopy the herd,
And summer's green all girded up in sheaves
Borne on the bier with white and bristly beard:
Then of thy beauty do I question make
That thou among the wastes of time must go,
Since sweets and beauties do themselves forsake,
And die as fast as they see others grow;
   And nothing 'gainst Time's scythe can make defence
   Save breed to brave him, when he takes thee hence.

Sonnet 13

O that you were yourself, but, love, you are
No longer yours than you yourself here live;
Against this coming end you should prepare,
And your sweet semblance to some other give.
So should that beauty which you hold in lease
Find no determination: then you were
Yourself again after your self's decease,
When your sweet issue your sweet form should bear.
Who lets so fair a house fall to decay,
Which husbandry in honour might uphold
Against the stormy gusts of winter's day,
And barren rage of death's eternal cold?
   O, none but unthrifts; dear my love, you know
   You had a father, let your son say so.

Sonnet 14

Not from the stars do I my judgement pluck,
And yet methinks I have Astronomy;
But not to tell of good or evil luck,
Of plagues, of dearths, or seasons' quality;
Nor can I fortune to brief minutes tell,
Pointing to each his thunder, rain, and wind,
Or say with Princes if it shall go well
By oft predict that I in heaven find;
But from thine eyes my knowledge I derive,

And, constant stars, in them I read such art
As truth and beauty shall together thrive,
If from thyself to store thou wouldst convert.
   Or else of thee this I prognosticate:
   Thy end is Truth's and Beauty's doom and date.

Sonnet 15

When I consider every thing that grows
Holds in perfection but a little moment,
That this huge stage presenteth nought but shows
Whereon the stars in secret influence comment;
When I perceive that men as plants increase,
Cheered and check'd even by the selfsame sky;
Vaunt in their youthful sap, at height decrease,
And wear their brave state out of memory:
Then the conceit of this inconstant stay
Sets you most rich in youth before my sight,
Where wasteful Time debateth with Decay
To change your day of youth to sullied night;
   And all in war with Time for love of you,
   As he takes from you, I engraft you new.

Sonnet 16

But wherefore do not you a mightier way
Make war upon this bloody tyrant Time?
And fortify yourself in your decay
With means more blessed than my barren rhyme?
Now stand you on the top of happy hours,
And many maiden gardens yet unset,
With virtuous wish would bear your living flowers,
Much liker than your painted counterfeit.
So should the lines of life that life repair
Which this (Time's pencil or my pupil pen)
Neither in inward worth nor outward fair
Can make you live yourself in eyes of men.
   To give away yourself, keeps yourself still,
   And you must live, drawn by your own sweet skill.

Sonnet 17

Who will believe my verse in time to come
If it were fill'd with your most high deserts?
Though yet, heaven knows, it is but as a tomb
Which hides your life, and shows not half your parts.

If I could write the beauty of your eyes
* And in fresh numbers number all your graces,
The age to come would say, this poet lies,
such heavenly touches ne'er touch'd earthly faces.
So should my papers (yellowed with their age)
Be scorn'd, like old men of less truth than tongue,
And your true rights be term'd a poet's rage,
And stretched metre of an antique song.
    But were some child of yours alive that time,
    You should live twice: in it, and in my rhyme.

* The term 'numbers' refers to poems or writings in Elizabethan English.

With the seventeenth sonnet we surely come to certainty that these sonnets are a commissioned group. Not only does the Poet stick to his theme with absolute consistency, but, *if* this were some young poet seeking a patron (as, for instance, would be the case for William Shakespeare from Stratford-upon-Avon) then he would unquestionably be 'selling' himself as a poet whose verse would give his young patron immortality. This idea he slips into the couplet of *Sonnet 15,* but then immediately dismisses it in *Sonnet 16,* as though aware that he was straying from the terms of his commission, perhaps? He returns to it in *Sonnet 17,* but here again is very careful to repudiate it emphatically as of far lesser worth to bestow immortality on the young man's beauty than his own creation of progeny would be.

All this is so contrary to everything else we find in the *Sonnets* that one must come to the conclusion that the Poet is only writing in this manner *because* he has a commission to fulfil.

Where else in the poetic literature of the time do we find a poet dispraising his own works in favour of the begetting of children? Certainly Ovid's disciple Marlowe was not speaking in his own voice, but on behalf of Lord Burghley, the great man who employed him to state this argument in eloquent poetry.

❖ ❖ ❖

GROUP F

THE SONNETS OF EXILE AND ANONYMITY

(1593 – 1600 ?)

This, the largest group of sonnets on one theme, contains poems of great variety, expressing many aspects of the Poet's experience, emotions and thoughts during his exile, veering from moods of despair to joy and relief and, always, gratitude; but running right through them is this undercurrent of absence from his Patron, his friends and his homeland, and the tragic sense of his disgrace and anonymity. Many of them are in the form of verse-letters to his Patron telling him his inmost thoughts and feelings. They invite our closest study for they comprise an autobiographical, historical record of the greatest importance to our understanding of the Poet of the Sonnets and what happened to him.

Although *Sonnet 25* is given below as the first in this group, I have some doubts about this placement, for while the Poet tells us he is out of favour with his stars this may here be used conventionally as this philosophical mood does not quite fit the tragical theme. This poem may, perhaps, date from the time when he first was taken into the blessed patronage of Thomas Walsingham, after his disillusionment with the spoilt young 'Prince' Will Hatcliffe. Thomas Walsingham came into his inheritance at the time when Marlowe and Watson were in trouble over the Bradley affray, in which, even though Marlowe was innocent of slaying that rash fellow, he had needed the exoneration of the law, so that in this sense he was rather down on his luck when Walsingham's new position as the lord of Scadbury fortuitously enabled him to become a patron to a poet. It may be that this is the background to this sonnet, but I have left it here because it serves to introduce us to Thomas Walsingham, who was the author of the Poet's escape from his fate at the hands of the Star Chamber Court, and to him as Marlowe's dear Friend and Patron all the ensuing sonnets are addressed.

Sonnet 25

Let those who are in favour with their stars
Of public honour and proud titles boast,
Whilst I whom fortune of such triumph bars,
Unlook'd for joy in that I honour most.
Great princes' favourites their fair leaves spread
But as the marigold at the sun's eye,
And in themselves their pride lies buried,
For at a frown they in their glory die.
The painful warrior famoused for might,
After a thousand victories once foil'd

Is from the book of honour razed quite,
And all the rest forgot for which he toil'd.
  Then happy I, that love and am beloved
  Where I may not remove, nor be removed.

He had known what it was to be a 'Prince's' favourite!

Sonnet 26 rightly begins the *Sonnets of Exile* addressing Walsingham as the 'Lord of my love' to whom he owes inexpressible gratitude. This, his first verse-letter, was probably written on board ship as he was sailing from England and home.

Sonnet 26

Lord of my love, to whom in vassalage
Thy merit hath my duty strongly knit,
To thee I send this written ambassage
To witness duty, not to show my wit;
Duty so great, which wit so poor as mine
May make seem bare in wanting words to show it,
But that I hope some good conceit of thine
In thy soul's thought (all naked) will bestow it;
Till whatsoever star that guides my moving
Points on me graciously with fair aspect,
And puts apparel on my tatter'd loving,
To show me worthy of thy sweet respect.
    Then may I dare to boast how I do love thee,
    Till then, not show my head where thou mayst prove me.

With this he commences his long journey.

Sonnet 27

Weary with toil, I haste me to my bed,
The dear repose for limbs with travel tired,
But then begins a journey in my head
To work my mind, when body's work's expired;
For then my thoughts (from far where I abide)
Intend a zealous pilgrimage to thee,
And keep my drooping eyelids open wide,
Looking on darkness which the blind do see:
Save that my soul's imaginary sight
Presents thy shadow to my sightless view,
Which like a jewel (hung in ghastly night)

Makes black night beauteous, and her old face new.
  Lo, thus by day my limbs, by night my mind,
  For thee, and for myself, no quiet find.

Thorpe's edition has 'their shaddoe' which, in that case, means his 'thoughts', but modern editors prefer 'thy shadow' in line ten. The deep anxiety that is expressed in this sonnet exactly fits the kind of troubled spirit that Marlowe must have suffered in this early period of his exile, especially as he must have known that Walsingham also stood in some danger in case anything leaked out about the events at Deptford.

  Sonnet 28 is probably a pair to *Sonnet 27*. He seems often to have composed sonnets in pairs, developing the thought further in the second poem.

Sonnet 28

How can I then return in happy plight,
That am debarr'd the benefit of rest?
When day's oppression is not eas'd by night,
But day by night and night by day oppress'd?
And each (though enemies to either's reign)
Do in consent shake hands to torture me,
The one by toil, the other to complain
How far I toil, still farther off from thee.
I tell the day to please him, thou art bright,
And do'st him grace when clouds do blot the heaven;
So flatter I the swart-complexion'd night,
When sparkling stars twire not, thou gild'st the even.
  But day doth daily draw my sorrows longer,
  And night doth nightly make grief's strength seem stronger.

Sonnet 29 is one of the most poignant of this large group, and one of the most impossible for orthodox Shakespeareans to explain. It so exactly reflects the circumstances in which Marlowe would have found himself following his flight from Deptford that it would be hard to put any other interpretation on it.

Sonnet 29

When in disgrace with Fortune and men's eyes,
I all alone beweep my outcast state,
And trouble deaf Heaven with my bootless cries,
And look upon myself and curse my fate,
Wishing me like to one more rich in hope,
Featur'd like him, like him with friends possess'd,
Desiring this man's art, and that man's scope,

With what I most enjoy contented least:
Yet in these thoughts myself almost despising,
Haply I think on thee, and then my state,
Like to the lark at break of day arising
From sullen earth, sings hymns at Heaven's gate,
   For thy sweet love remember'd such wealth brings,
   That then I scorn to change my state with kings.

'With what I most enjoy contented least' is surely a reference to his creative writing, which is the typical response of the self-critical artist of genius. His contact in exile with Italian Renaissance culture was to prove an unforeseen bonus for his development as a dramatist .

Sonnets 30 and 31 are again a sonnet-pair, this time descanting on his homesickness, his friends 'hid in death's dateless night' and the 'vanish'd sights' he misses. The 'death' referred to is his own 'death' at Deptford, not that of his friends, who are doubtless alive and well.

Sonnet 30

When to the sessions of sweet silent thought,
I summon up remembrance of things past,
I sigh the lack of many a thing I sought,
And with old woes new wail my dear time's waste:
Then can I drown an eye (unus'd to flow)
For precious friends hid in death's dateless night,
And weep afresh love's long-since cancell'd woe,
And moan th' expense of many a vanish'd sight.
Then can I grieve at grievances foregone,
And heavily from woe to woe tell o'er
The sad account of fore-bemoaned moan,
Which I new pay, as if not paid before.
   But if the while I think on thee (dear friend)
   All losses are restor'd, and sorrows end.

Sonnet 31

Thy bosom is endeared with all hearts,
Which I by lacking have supposed dead,
And there reigns Love and all Love's loving parts,
And all those friends which I thought buried.
How many a holy and obsequious tear
Hath dear religious love stol'n from mine eye,
As interest of the dead, which now appear
But things remov'd that hidden in thee lie.

Thou art the grave where buried love doth live,
Hung with the trophies of my lovers gone,
Who all their parts of me to thee did give:
That due of many, now is thine alone.
　Their images I lov'd, I view in thee,
　And thou (all they) hast all the all of me.

On ruminating the intricately-woven thought-patterns of this sonnet one wonders whether it was this verse-letter that had prompted Walsingham to adopt the personification of Apollo Loxias for his *impresa* portrait where he symbolizes this very concept of 'things remov'd that hidden in thee lie'.

Descanting on death in application to himself is a feature of the *Sonnets,* especially in this group.

Sonnet 32

If thou survive my well-contented day
When that churl Death my bones with dust shall cover,
And shalt by fortune once more re-survey
These poor rude lines of thy deceased lover,
Compare them with the bett'ring of the time,
And though they be outstripp'd by every pen,
Reserve them for my love, not for their rhyme,
Exceeded by the height of happier men.
Oh then vouchsafe me but this loving thought:
Had my friend's Muse grown with this growing age,
A dearer birth than this his love had brought
To march in ranks of better equipage;
　But since he died, and poets better prove,
　Theirs for their style I'll read, his for his love.

Sonnet 33 suggests that his journey is now taking him through the Alps – those 'mountain tops' and 'pale streams' are very evocative of this scenery – leading him to Italy, the country of his long exile, as is supported by the undeniable influence of Italy in his plays from this time forward. In this sonnet he bewails the eclipse of his bright fame. When Fate struck him down Marlowe was at the peak of his fame, as evidenced by Greene's salutation: 'Thou famous gracer of Tragedians'.

Sonnet 33

Full many a glorious morning have I seen
Flatter the mountain tops with sovereign eye,
Kissing with golden face the meadows green,
Gilding pale streams with heavenly alchemy;

Anon permit the basest clouds to ride
With ugly rack on his celestial face,
And from the forlorn world his visage hide,
Stealing unseen to west with this disgrace.
Even so my sun one early morn did shine
With all triumphant splendour on my brow;
But out alack, he was but one hour mine,
The region cloud hath mask'd him from me now.
 Yet him for this, my love no whit disdaineth:
 Suns of the world may stain, when heaven's sun staineth.

The Sonnets of Exile seem, on the whole, to be chronologically presented. They are interspersed with a scattering from the Hatcliffe group (mainly) which breaks them up, but then the story of exile is again resumed, apparently in sequence, although one can only be sure of this where sonnet-pairs are presented, or some thematic sequence is manifested.

Sonnet 34 is a very revealing sonnet. It is the heart-cry of dismay wrung from the exiled Marlowe when he finally learned the full implication of the events at Deptford. Walsingham's clever ruse had saved him from a fearful fate, but his character and good name had been 'murdered' there! How bitter was his awakening to the realization that a horrible cloud of calumny had descended on him, which he was powerless to refute; and which Walsingham was equally unable to put right.

Walsingham's deep regret and sorrow that the outcome of his device had not been foreseen, was the only consolation he could offer to the Poet, who must bear the cross of his disgrace from this time forward.

Sonnet 34

Why didst thou promise such a beauteous day
And make me travel forth without my cloak,
To let base clouds o'ertake me in my way,
Hiding thy brav'ry in their rotten smoke?
'Tis not enough that through the cloud thou break
To dry the rain on my storm-beaten face,
For no man well of such a salve can speak
That heals the wound, and cures not the disgrace.
Nor can thy shame give physic to my grief;
Though thou repent, yet I have still the loss.
Th'offender's sorrow lends but weak relief
To him that bears the strong offence's cross.
 Ah, but those tears are pearl which thy love sheds,
 And they are rich, and ransom all ill deeds.

Then *Sonnet 35* from the second Hatcliffe group, chiding the young 'Prince' for his 'sensual fault', is cleverly inserted to confuse the reader as to whom, and to what injury, *Sonnet 34* might be referring. This is the extraordinarily subtle mixture of the presentation of the sonnet-sequence that has kept its real story hidden for so long under a deliberate blanket of disinformation worthy of an intelligence agent! The story is then resumed with *Sonnet 36* which may originally have been written as a pair to *Sonnet 34*.

Sonnet 36

Let me confess that we two must be twain,
Although our undivided loves are one,
So shall those blots that do with me remain,
Without thy help, by me be borne alone.
In our two loves there is but one respect,
Though in our lives a separable spite,
Which though it alter not love's sole effect,
Yet doth it steal sweet hours from love's delight.
I may not evermore acknowledge thee,
Lest my bewailed guilt should do thee shame,
Nor thou with public kindness honour me,
Unless thou take that honour from thy name.
    But do not so: I love thee in such sort,
    As thou being mine, mine is thy good report.

With *Sonnet 37* we reach a slight hiccup for this is a doubtful sonnet when seen as a sonnet of the exile group. It apparently employs the terms of the sonneteering convention in its figurative use of 'lameness'. There is no evidence that Marlowe was lame (or Shakespeare, for that matter) but he uses it again in *Sonnet 89* in the *Rival Poet* sequence: 'Speak of my lameness, and I straight will halt'. In his dramatization of the life of Tamburlaine, who was actually lame (his name Timur-lane means this) Marlowe ignores this defect. On the other hand, it was probably known, for the contemporary interest in the great Scythian warrior was avid; and Marlowe was himself nicknamed 'Tamburlaine' in Greene's satifical references to him, and also by Harvey in his poem *Gorgon*. Was this reference to 'lameness' then entirely figurative? Dr Hotson would argue that *Sonnet 37* is definitively in praise of Hatcliffe, since it compares the Poet as a father seeing 'his active child do deeds of youth', and describes him as 'crowned' by his beauty, birth, wealth, and wit; and refers to 'this shadow' in a sense appropriate to the young man playing his part as the 'shadow' Prince of Purpoole. Is this then mere conventional flattery by a 'poor' poet to his rich patron?

Sonnet 37

As a decrepit father takes delight
To see his active child do deeds of youth,
So I, made lame by Fortune's dearest spite,
Take all my comfort of thy worth and truth;
For whether beauty, birth, or wealth, or wit,
Or any of these all, or all, or more,
Entitled in thy parts do crowned sit,
I make my love engrafted to this store.
To then I am not lame, poor, nor despis'd,
Whilst that this shadow doth such substance give
That I in thy abundance am suffic'd
And by a part of all thy glory live.
    Look what is best, that best I wish in thee;
    This wish I have, then ten times happy me.

I confess to agreeing with Dr Hotson at heart, but I have left the sonnet here as a pointer to the degree of confusion of themes from the different sonnet groups that it highlights. It is followed by *Sonnet 38* which speaks in the authentic tone of voice used in praise of his true Patron, Walsingham, and *Sonnet 39* is again a verse-letter to Walsingham about their 'separation'. Then follow *Sonnets 40, 41,* and *42* all from the second Hatcliffe group where he has stolen his sonneteer's mistress. After this interruption we are back in the *Sonnets of Exile* for ten consecutive sonnets, until we reach *Sonnets 53, 54, 55* which are all in praise of Hatcliffe. The single *Sonnet 56* is to Walsingham again and speaks of their sad separation, but with *Sonnets 57, 58, 59* we come to two very bitter sonnets to Hatcliffe, followed by an early one in his praise. It is a fine mix-up.

Having made this point we now continue with the *Sonnets of Exile* as extracted from all this deliberate confusion.

In *Sonnet 39* it is Absence personified which is addressed as 'thou', in lines nine onwards in this subtle, witty sonnet, whereas the first 'thou' addresses Walsingham.

Sonnet 39

O, how thy worth with manners may I sing
When thou art all the better part of me?
What can mine own praise to mine own self bring,
And what is't but mine own when I praise thee?
Even for this, let us divided live,
And our dear love lose name of single one,
That by this separation I may give
That due to thee which thou deserv'st alone.

O absence, what a torment wouldst thou prove
Were it not thy sour leisure gave sweet leave
To entertain the time with thoughts of love,
Which time and thoughts so sweetly doth deceive,
    And that thou teachest how to make one twain,
    By praising him here who doth hence remain.

In *Sonnet 43*, after a break addressing Hatcliffe, the repetition of 'shadows' is not to be construed as referring to the 'shadow' play-acting Prince of Purpoole, for this sonnet is surely written from his exile, and is reminiscent of *Sonnet 27* in its theme of sleeplessness in which he also refers to the 'imaginary sight' of his Patron as a 'shadow'.

Sonnet 43

When most I wink, then do mine eyes best see,
For all the day they view things unrespected,
But when I sleep, in dreams they look on thee,
And darkly bright, are bright in dark directed.
Then thou, whose shadow shadows doth make bright,
How would thy shadow's form, form happy show
To the clear day with thy much clearer light,
When to unseeing eyes thy shade shines so?
How would (I say) mine eyes be blessed made
By looking on thee in the living day,
When in dead night thy fair imperfect shade
Through heavy sleep on sightless eyes doth stay?
    All days are nights to see till I see thee,
    And nights bright days when dreams do show thee me.

Sleeplessness engendered by anxiety in his outcast state is a recurring theme in the sonnets of this group.

Thorpe has 'their fair imperfect shade' in line 11. But this is surely a misprint, and editors have all preferred 'thy' which alone makes sense.

In *Sonnets 44 and 45*, which are a true sonnet-pair, the Renaissance concept of the four elements of earth, water, fire and air are played with. These sonnets were written, not only to convey his feelings, but to delight his Patron, who was a discriminating man of cultured tastes. The subtlety and wit of his poetry was greatly valued, and in these remarkably finely-crafted sonnets we see why Marlowe was so greatly admired by his friend Thorpe as 'that pure elementall wit, Chr. Marlow'.

Sonnet 44

If the dull substance of my flesh were thought,
Injurious distance should not stop my way,
For then, despite of space, I would be brought
From limits far remote where thou dost stay.
No matter then although my foot did stand
Upon the farthest earth remov'd from thee,
For nimble thought can jump both sea and land
As soon as think the place where he would be.
But ah, thought kills me that I am not thought,
To leap large lengths of miles when thou art gone,
But that so much of earth and water wrought,
I must attend time's leisure with my moan,
    Receiving nought by elements so slow,
    But heavy tears, badges of either's woe.

Sonnet 45

The other two, slight air, and purging fire,
Are both with thee wherever I abide,
The first my thought, the other my desire,
These present absent with swift motion slide;
For when these quicker elements are gone
In tender embassy of love to thee,
My life, being made of four, with two alone
Sinks down to death, oppress'd with melancholy,
Until life's composition be recured
By those swift messengers return'd from thee,
Who even but now come back again assured
Of thy fair health, recounting it to me.
    This told, I joy; but then no longer glad,
    I send them back again and straight grow sad.

Here we have not only the four elements, but a glancing reference to the Renaissance theory of the four humours of Man's composition. People were said to be either predominantly sanguine, choleric, phlegmatic or melancholic. Melancholy in its most elevated form, when properly 'tempered', was the humour of genius, of poets, thinkers, philosophers. The young Earl of Northumberland affected to have himself painted in melancholy humour in his *impresa* portrait. It was very fashionable. We have to remember that these sonnets are written by an Elizabethan poet to his Elizabethan patron, and their whole style reflects the times. Beautiful, immortal poetry though they are, the Elizabethan period is their true climate.

Sonnets 46 and 47 are again a true sonnet-pair, which are, in a sense, the Poet's 'thank you' letters in delightfully witty verse to Walsingham for the exquisite, miniature *impresa* portrait he had received, doubtless brought to him by one of 'those swift messengers' mentioned in *Sonnet 45*. These, while representing here symbolically, the 'quicker elements' of air and fire, would also have been real messengers, for the network of espionage built up under Sir Francis Walsingham would have provided ready channels of communication between the exiled Poet and his Patron, if not from Walsingham's own servants.

Sonnet 46

Mine eye and heart are at a mortal war
How to divide the conquest of thy sight;
Mine eye, my heart thy picture's sight would bar,
My heart, mine eye the freedom of that right;
My heart doth plead that thou in him dost lie,
(A closet never pierc'd with crystal eyes),
But the defendant doth that plea deny,
And says in him thy fair appearance lies.
To 'cide this title is empannelled
A quest of thoughts, all tenants to the heart,
And by their verdict is determined
The clear eye's moiety, and the dear heart's part,
   As thus: mine eye's due is thine outward part,
   And my heart's right, thine inward love of heart.

Sonnet 47

Betwixt mine eye and heart a league is took,
And each doth good turns now unto the other;
When that mine eye is famish'd for a look,
Or heart in love with sighs himself doth smother,
With my love's picture then my eye doth feast,
And to the painted banquet bids my heart.
Another time mine eye is my heart's guest,
And in his thoughts of love doth share a part.
So either by thy picture of my love,
Thyself away, art present still with me,
For thou no farther than my thoughts canst move,
And I am still with them, and they with thee;
   Or if they sleep, thy picture in my sight
   Awakes my heart to heart's and eye's delight.

It would be hard to imagine a more movingly sincere, appropriate and witty response than this grateful poetic tribute devised as a legal argument between heart and eye. Can we doubt that this perfect pair were inspired by Hilliard's exquisite miniature of his Patron?

Sonnet 48

How careful was I when I took my way
Each trifle under truest bars to thrust,
That to my use it might unused stay
From hands of falsehood, in sure wards of trust.
But thou, to whom my jewels trifles are,
Most worthy comfort, now my greatest grief,
Thou best of dearest, and mine only care,
Art left the prey of every vulgar thief.
Thee have I not lock'd up in any chest,
Save where thou art not, though I feel thou art,
Within the gentle closure of my breast,
From whence at pleasure thou mayst come and part;
    And even thence thou wilt be stol'n, I fear,
    For truth proves thievish for a prize so dear.

The Elizabethan term 'trifle' is played upon, denoting a work of poetry or romantic writing as distinct from an academic work. These 'trifles' are probably *Venus and Adonis* and *Hero and Leander,* left unfinished at Scadbury. *Venus and Adonis* was already with Richard Field, perhaps set up in print when the dedication and pseudonym were added on its title page before it appeared on the bookstalls and a copy was bought on 12th June by one, Richard Stonley for 12d. and noted in his Account Book.[1] So someone, we do not know who, moved swiftly to get it into print very soon after the murder at Deptford.

Sonnet 49

Against that time (if ever that time come)
When I shall see thee frown on my defects,
Whenas thy love hath cast his utmost sum,
Called to that audit by advis'd respects;
Against that time when thou shalt strangely pass
And scarcely greet me with that sun, thine eye,
When love converted from the thing it was
Shall reasons find of settled gravity:
Against that time do I ensconce me here
Within the knowledge of mine own desert,
And this my hand against myself uprear,
To guard the lawful reasons on thy part.
    To leave poor me thou hast the strength of laws,
    Since why to love I can allege no cause.

Marlowe was on bail, technically under arrest, hence he was still a wanted man. This is alluded to in his reference to 'the strength of laws'. The Poet's dependence on his Patron and his anxiety not to lose him are very marked in these sonnets.

Sonnet 50 and its pair Sonnet 51 may not be sequentially in order, or else his journeying was resumed. The indications are that he made a prolonged and distant journey, one undertaken in great sorrow, and that his absence was expected to be of some years' duration.

Sonnet 50

How heavy do I journey on the way,
When what I seek (my weary travel's end)
Doth teach that ease and that repose to say:
Thus far the miles are measur'd from thy friend.
The beast that bears me, tired with my woe,
Plods dully on, to bear that weight in me,
As if by some instinct the wretch did know
His rider lov'd not speed, being made from thee.
The bloody spur cannot provoke him on,
That sometimes anger thrusts into his hide,
Which heavily he answers with a groan
More sharp to me than spurring to his side;
    For that same groan doth put this in my mind,
    My grief lies onward and my joy behind.

Sonnet 51

Thus can my love excuse the slow offence
Of my dull bearer, when from thee I speed:
From where thou art why should I haste me thence?
Till I return, of posting is no need.
O what excuse will my poor beast then find,
When swift extremity can seem but slow?
Then should I spur, though mounted on the wind,
In winged speed no motion shall I know.
Then can no horse with my desire keep pace;
Therefore desire (of perfect'st love being made)
Shall neigh, no dull flesh in his fiery race.
But love, for love, thus shall excuse my jade:
    Since from thee going he went wilful slow,
    Towards thee I'll run, and give him leave to go.

The archaic term 'posting' is used meaning making haste.

It was seemingly envisaged that he would one day be able to return to his homeland. Possibly these two sonnets describing his sad journey from his Patron are part of a quartet with the next two, Sonnets 52 and 53, which speak of a reunion, and his grief is sharpened by the sense of recent separation in which he is once again travelling into his exile.

Sonnets 52 and 56 show that there were occasional re-unions between the Poet and his Patron, but the indication is that the absence endured was a very long one.

These two sonnets, although so intimate, are essentially poems in the tradition of Elizabethan patronage so well understood by Raleigh in his 'lofty, insolent and passionate' poems to Queen Elizabeth as 'the dear Empress of my heart'. The intimate imagery of his extravagant endearments has been most carefully devised to praise his patron.

Sonnet 52

So am I as the rich, whose blessed key
Can bring him to his sweet up-locked treasure,
The which he will not ev'ry hour survey,
For blunting the fine point of seldom pleasure.
Therefore are feasts so solemn and so rare,
Since, seldom coming, in the long year set,
Like stones of worth, they thinly placed are,
Or captain jewels in the carcanet.
So is the time that keeps you as my chest,
Or as the wardrobe which the robe doth hide,
To make some special instant special blest,
By new unfolding of his imprison'd pride.
   Blessed are you whose worthiness gives scope,
   Being had, to triumph, being lack'd, to hope.

Sonnet 56

Sweet love, renew thy force, be it not said
Thy edge should blunter be than appetite,
Which but today by feeding is allay'd,
Tomorrow sharpen'd in his former might.
So love be thou, although today thou fill
Thy hungry eyes, even till they wink with fullness,
Tomorrow see again, and do not kill
The spirit of love with a perpetual dullness.
Let this sad interim like the ocean be
Which parts the shore, where two contracted new
Come daily to the banks, that when they see
Return of love, more blest may be the view;
   Or call it winter, which being full of care,
   Makes summer's welcome, thrice more wish'd, more rare.

From Dover where his grandparents lived, Marlowe would have been able to see Calais on a fine, clear day. Perhaps the recollection of this boyhood memory inspired this poem imbued with nostalgia for things lost. The imagery invoking the ocean and the shore is suggestive of exile in a foreign land, and perhaps he may have been in France at this time, having met his Patron there.

The sea imagery is continued in *Sonnet 60* with a sense of Time's inexorable march. In philosophic mood he reflects on his own fate, when he was eclipsed in his maturity, and the gifts Time gave were confounded. The weaving of the thoughts in this sonnet is most skilful and beautiful.

Sonnet 60

Like as the waves make towards the pebbled shore,
So do our minutes hasten to their end,
Each changing place with that which goes before:
In sequent toil all forwards do contend.
Nativity, once in the main of light,
Crawls to maturity, wherewith being crown'd,
Crooked eclipses 'gainst his glory fight,
And Time that gave doth now his gift confound.
Time doth transfix the flourish set on youth,
And delves the parallels in beauty's brow,
Feeds on the rarities of nature's truth,
And nothing stands but for his scythe to mow.
    And yet to times in hope my verse shall stand,
    Praising thy worth, despite his cruel hand.

Sonnet 61 is fraught with anxiety engendered by their long separation, and he harps on sleepless nights.

Sonnet 61

Is it thy will, thy image should keep open
My heavy eyelids to the weary night?
Dost thou desire my slumbers should be broken
While shadows like to thee do mock my sight?
Is it thy spirit that thou send'st from thee
So far from home into my deeds to pry,
To find out shames and idle hours in me,
The scope and tenor of thy jealousy?
O no, thy love, though much, is not so great:
It is my love that keeps mine eye awake,
Mine own true love that doth my rest defeat,
To play the watchman ever for thy sake.

For thee watch I, whilst thou dost wake elsewhere,
From me far off, with others all too near.

The exiled Poet's dependence on his Patron and his fear of losing him is evident in this sonnet, which echoes the trauma we find so strongly expressed in the *Sonnets of the Rival Poet*.

After nine sonnets, mainly from the Hatcliffe group, we are presented with two on the theme of his anonymity.

Sonnet 71

No longer mourn for me when I am dead,
Than you shall hear the surly sullen bell
Give warning to the world that I am fled
From this vile world with vilest worms to dwell;
Nay, if you read this line, remember not
The hand that writ it, for I love you so,
That I in your sweet thoughts would be forgot,
If thinking on me then should make you woe.
O if (I say) you look upon this verse,
When I (perhaps) compounded am with clay,
Do not so much as my poor name rehearse,
But let your love even with my life decay,
    Lest the wise world should look into your moan,
    And mock you with me after I am gone.

Sonnet 72

O lest the world should task you to recite
What merit liv'd in me, that you should love,
After my death (dear love) forget me quite;
For you in me can nothing worthy prove,
Unless you would devise some virtuous lie,
To do more for me than mine own desert,
And hang more praise upon deceased I
Than niggard truth would willingly impart.
O lest your true love may seem false in this,
That you for love speak well of me untrue,
My name be buried where my body is,
And live no more to shame nor me, nor you;
    For I am sham'd by that which I bring forth,
    And so should you, to love things nothing worth.

A sudden twist of meaning in the final couplet is a dexterous trick giving ambiguity to veil the too obvious detection of the true situation.

482

In many of the sonnets we see a Renaissance poet searching for new imagery with which to please and praise his patron.

Sonnet 75

So are you to my thoughts as food to life,
Or as sweet-season'd showers are to the ground;
And for the peace of you I hold such strife
As 'twixt a miser and his wealth is found.
Now proud as an enjoyer, and anon
Doubting the filching age will steal his treasure,
Now counting best to be with you alone,
Then better'd that the world may see my pleasure.
Sometime all full with feasting on your sight,
And by and by clean starved for a look,
Possessing or pursuing no delight
Save what is had or must from you be took.
 Thus do I pine and surfeit day by day,
 Or gluttoning on all, or all away.

The Poet's utter dependence on his Patron is a product of his tragic circumstances of anonymity. One wonders whether he was here on a brief visit to England staying at Scadbury, perhaps, in hiding?

In *Sonnet 76* he is anxious that his famous style – that identity of Marlowe's and Shakespeare's works that has puzzled scholars – may be detected.

Sonnet 76

Why is my verse so barren of new pride,
So far from variation or quick change?
Why with the time do I not glance aside
To new-found methods and to compounds strange?
Why write I still all one, ever the same,
And keep invention in a noted weed,
That every word doth almost tell my name,
Showing their birth, and where they did proceed?
O know sweet love, I always write of you,
And you and love are still my argument.
So all my best is dressing old words new,
Spending again what is already spent;
 For as the sun is daily new and old,
 So is my love still telling what is told.

Sonnet 81 is surely a product of that harvest of bitter suffering that Stephen Spender speaks of which yielded 'an extraordinary blossoming'.

Sonnet 81

Or I shall live your epitaph to make,
Or you survive when I in earth am rotten.
From hence your memory death cannot take,
Although in me each part will be forgotten.
Your name from hence immortal life shall have.
Though I, once gone, to all the world must die.
The earth can yield me but a common grave
When you entombed in men's eyes shall lie.
Your monument shall be my gentle verse,
Which eyes not yet created shall o'er-read,
And tongues to be your being shall rehearse
When all the breathers of this world are dead,
    You still shall live (such virtue hath my pen)
    Where breath most breathes, even in the mouths of men.

Sonnet 97 is a sonnet of absence indicating the passing of seasons. It is imbued with the lyrical melancholy of much Elizabethan music in a minor key, and is surely one of the loveliest of them all.

Sonnet 97

How like a winter hath my absence been
From thee, the pleasure of the fleeting year!
What freezings have I felt, what dark days seen,
What old December's bareness everywhere!
And yet this time remov'd was summer's time,
The teeming autumn big with rich increase,
Bearing the wanton burthen of the prime,
Like widow'd wombs after their lords' decease.
Yet this abundant issue seem'd to me
But hope of orphans, and unfather'd fruit,
For summer and his pleasures wait on thee,
And thou away, the very birds are mute;
    Or if they sing, 'tis with so dull a cheer
    That leaves look pale, dreading the winter's near.

Sonnet 98 continues the theme of absence in the passing of seasons of the year, and may be a pair with *Sonnet 97*, though it is not possible to calculate how many years are indicated if indeed they were written at the same time, which is doubtful as there is a leap from December to April in the imagery invoked. It is rather more likely that the Poet has returned to a favourite theme later, than at one sitting.

Sonnet 98

From you have I been absent in the spring
When proud-pied April, dress'd in all his trim,
Hath put a spirit of youth in everything.
That heavy Saturn laugh'd and leap'd with him.
Yet nor the lays of birds, nor the sweet smell
Of different flowers in odour and in hue
Could make me any summer's story tell,
Or from their proud lap pluck them where they grew.
Nor did I wonder at the lily's white,
Nor praise the deep vermilion in the rose;
They were but sweet, but figures of delight,
Drawn after you, you pattern of all those.
 Yet seem'd it winter still, and you away,
 As with your shadow I with these did play.

Sonnet 99 does not mention absence, but it continues the theme of nature and recollection of his Patron's beauty that suggest contemplation of one dear to him whose presence is missed. I have, therefore, placed it here, but it is not counted in the *Sonnets of Exile;* it is the thirty-seventh sonnet of this thirty-six sonnet group.

Sonnet 99

The forward violet thus did I chide:
Sweet thief, whence didst thou steal thy sweet that smells,
If not from my love's breath? The purple pride
Which on thy soft cheek for complexion dwells
In my love's veins thou hast too grossly dyed.
The lily I condemned for thy hand,
And buds of marjoram had stol'n thy hair;
The roses fearfully on thorns did stand,
One blushing shame, another white despair;
A third, nor red, nor white, had stol'n of both,
And to his robb'ry had annex'd thy breath;
But for this theft, in pride of all his growth
A vengeful canker ate him up to death.
 More flowers I noted, yet I none could see,
 But sweet or colour it had stol'n from thee.

In presenting the large group of the *Sonnets of Exile* I have assumed that they are chronologically printed in Thorpe's edition, with the interspersed sonnets from the early group to 'Mr.W.H.' and a few others unrelated to his exile dividing up this large collection. To rearrange the *Sonnets of Exile* would be arbitrary and irrelevant to this thesis.

Sonnet 109 offers apologies, not for his 'absence' which is offered rather as his excuse, but probably for a period of silence when he had not been able to communicate, or had been chided for failing to do so. The reason for his apologetic poem is obscure. One can imagine anything.

Sonnet 109

O never say that I was false of heart,
Though absence seem'd my flame to qualify.
As easy might I from myself depart,
As from my soul, which in thy breast doth lie.
That is my home of love; if I have rang'd,
Like him that travels, I return again,
Just to the time, not with the time exchang'd,
So that myself bring water for my stain.
Never believe, though in my nature reign'd
All frailties that besiege all kinds of blood,
That it could so preposterously be stain'd
To leave for nothing all thy sum of good:
    For nothing this wide universe I call,
    Save thou my Rose, in it thou art my all.

I would give a lot to know what prompted this poem. Research on his period of exile and his activities and movements is a most intriguing area beckoning the best brains and skills to concentrate on those clues that have been suggested in the foregoing pages.

Some may say that this sonnet does not belong to the *Sonnets of Exile,* but I believe it does for 'absence' and reference to himself as one who 'travels' are evoked as background to his life; they are not brief excursions in the normal run of daily living. They are part of his exile, for there is heartache in this poem.

The theme of praise for his Patron's beauty continues in *Sonnets 113 and 114* in what is evidently a context of absence and loneliness in which his mind plays him false.

Sonnet 113

Since I left you mine eye is in my mind,
And that which governs me to go about
Doth part his function, and is partly blind,
Seems seeing, but effectually is out;

For it no form delivers to the heart
Of bird, of flower, or shape, which it doth latch:
Of his quick objects hath the mind no part,
Nor his own vision holds what it doth catch;
For if it see the rud'st or gentlest sight,
The most sweet favour or deformed'st creature,
The mountain, or the sea, the day, or night,
The crow, or dove, it shapes them to your feature.
    Incapable of more, replete with you,
    My most true mind thus maketh mine untrue.

Sonnet 114

Or whether doth my mind, being crown'd with you,
Drink up the monarch's plague, this flattery?
Or whether shall I say mine eye saith true,
And that your love taught it this alchemy
To make of monsters, and things indigest,
Such cherubins as your sweet self resemble,
Creating every bad a perfect best
As fast as objects to his beams assemble?
O 'tis the first, 'tis flatt'ry in my seeing,
And my great mind most kingly drinks it up.
Mine eye well knows what with his gust is 'greeing,
And to his palate doth prepare the cup.
    If it be poison'd, 'tis the lesser sin
    That mine eye loves it and doth first begin.

Here we have the Ovidian concept of the poet as 'king'.

Finally *Sonnet 125* is a sonnet of anonymity. This obscure sonnet has completely foxed even the wide-ranging intelligence of Dr Hotson, who exclaims in despair: 'Who was this base informer? Who suborned him? And of what crime did he impeach or accuse Shakespeare to his Prince? Anyone who can throw light here will earn our gratitude.'² I will do my best. This poem has no application in the context of the Stratford actor, but when we hear the voice of the exiled, anonymous Marlowe we begin to understand the temptation with which the Poet is wrestling – to reveal himself! The Patron to whom the Poet is offering his 'oblation' is not the false 'lovely Boy' but his true Patron, Thomas Walsingham. The reference to bearing 'the canopy' is symbolic, for this is the public honour accorded to courtiers of the Queen who were chosen to hold the royal canopy over her in important public processions. This coveted honour is figuratively denied him.

Sonnet 125

Were't aught to me I bore the canopy,
With my extern the outward honouring,
Or laid great bases for eternity,
Which proves more short than waste or ruining?
Have I not seen dwellers on form and favour
Lose all, and more by paying too much rent,
For compound sweet forgoing simple savour,
Pitiful thrivers in their gazing spent?
No, let me be obsequious in thy heart,
And take thou my oblation, poor but free,
Which is not mix'd with seconds, knows no art,
But mutual render only me for thee.
    Hence, thou suborn'd informer! A true soul
    When most impeach'd, stands least in thy control.

Sonnet 125 may be deemed a test of this thesis. I submit it is destined to remain intractable unless seen in the circumstances of Marlowe's tragedy – his enforced anonymity. The Poet begins by modestly disclaiming that it is of any importance to him that he is debarred from the acknowledgement of his works, and the public acclaim for his poetic and dramatic art – the symbolic canopy of honour borne in the public eye.

> Were't aught to me I bore the canopy,
> With my extern the outward honouring,
> Or laid great bases for eternity,

Ah, but there's the rub. Our Poet was in his heart an ambitious young man, who indeed aspired to lay 'great bases for eternity'! At Cambridge he had translated Ovid whose Elegy XV promises immortality to poets, and this had a special significance for Marlowe for he chose two lines from it as his motto (defined as a word or phrase used to express a *principle, goal or ideal*) when launching his pseudonym 'William Shakespeare' with *Venus and Adonis* :

> *Vilia miretur vulgus; mihi flavus Apollo*
> *Pocula Castalia plena ministret aqua*

This Elegy in Marlowe's translation reads :

ELEGY XV
To those who envy Poets their Eternity of Fame

Envy, why carp'st thou my time is spent so ill,
And term'st my works fruits of an idle quill?

488

Or that unlike the line from whence I come
War's dusty honours are refus'd being young?
Nor that I study not the brawling laws,
Nor set my voice to sale in every cause?
Thy scope is mortal, mine eternal fame,
That all the world may ever chant my name.

 . . .

Verse is immortal, and shall ne'er decay.
To verse let kings give place, and kingly shows,
And banks o'er which gold-bearing *Tagus* flows.
Let base-conceited wits admire vile things,
Fair Phoebus lead me to the Muses' springs.
About my head be quivering myrtle wound,
And in sad lovers' heads let me be found.
The living, not the dead, can envy bite,
For after death all men receive their right.
Then though death rakes my bones in funeral fire,
I'll live, and as he pulls me down mount higher.

The italicized lines are those he chose for his motto, and they are the start of a passage which is almost prophetic for Marlowe. He had just written his *Hero and Leander*, which although unfinished was yet left with the publisher John Wolfe, if not by Marlowe himself, then by Walsingham, and registered in September 1593. In it Marlowe's immortal name is found in 'sad lovers' heads', and his challenge to death in the final lines is strikingly apt. When we recall that it was this promise of immortality in his poetic works made by Ovid whose words he had translated in his youth, and which he had taken to his heart as the inspiration of his life, we begin to understand how bitterly he must have felt over his enforced anonymity. The 'suborn'd informer' of *Sonnet 125* is his own treacherous heart prompting him to declare his true identity to the world, which he is here silencing, although the longing to claim that immortality which was rightly his remained always with him.

Scholars have noted that Ovid's influence is ever present in the works of Marlowe and Shakespeare, though where Shakespeare drank so deep at those Ovidian springs we do not know, it is only there unmistakably present in his works. Ovid pictured a poet as a 'king' among men, and this imagery pervades the *Sonnets*. The Poet *does* see himself as a king in his poetic art, and the temptation to declare himself must at times have been overwhelming. It is significant that he finally succumbed to the extent of offering Thorpe his *Sonnets* for publication as 'SHAKE-SPEARES SONNETS' after having taken extraordinary care to obscure their autobiographical story-line, as we have seen, by his skilful presentation of the poems in a-chronological and partial thematic confusion. Yet perhaps hoping that one day his true story would be understood by posterity.

It is his own ambition that he addresses in the exhortation:

> Hence, thou suborn'd informer! A true soul
> When most impeach'd, stands least in thy control.

And impeached he was. His own time accused him of criminal Atheism and blasphemy, and his name was tainted with an ignoble end in a violent brawl over the payment of 'le recknynge' – a paltry matter – at Dame Elinor Bull's house. All this he had to bear with patience, mercifully not knowing that posterity would further distort his image. Most regrettably there has been a marked escalation in the twists added to this impeached image in recent books on him. William Urry's *Christopher Marlowe and Canterbury* was reviewed by Douglas Dunn for the Glasgow Herald under the heading *'Ruffian Brawler'* claiming that 'He kept the company of hotheads, ruffians, and underworld men, and might even have been by nature one of their true number'. [3.]

This distorted image has been further developed in Charles Nicholl's book *The Reckoning: The Murder of Christopher Marlowe* (1992) presenting the ultimate defamation of Marlowe's character as a 'swindler' and a predatory 'poet-spy' who allegedly insinuated himself into the circle of Raleigh and Northumberland as a spy for his own gain, concocting this false hypothesis, not from evidence, but from mere prejudice and malicious insinuation. The widely acclaimed publication of Nicholl's book was carefully timed to herald the quatercentenary of Marlowe's death in 1993, which was marked by a spate of pseudo 'historical' novels from writers jumping on this bandwagon to sell their pretentious fictions, all of them variants of the distorted image ranging from the merely shocking to lurid pornography! Thus the quatercentenary shamefully brought the calumny of Marlowe to its basest level, out-doing and up-dating Baines for modern consumption.

The final answer to these malignant voices has been preserved for posterity in his beautiful *Sonnets* which tell the true story of the man and his tragic life. The decision to publish them must have involved an inner struggle. This is what is reflected in *Sonnet 125.*

Sonnet 125 is closely associated with the *Sonnets of Vilification,* a small but immensely important group, which follows. They constitute a kind of addendum to the *Sonnets of Exile,* for the theme of this group is the cause of his banishment and anonymity.

GROUP G

THE SONNETS OF VILIFICATION (After 1593)

This small group of four sonnets is vitally important to this thesis, for in these anguished poems we have the verification of Marlowe's downfall. The strength of feeling expressed cannot be interpreted as Shakespeare's lament for his lowly status as an actor. He was an affluent, propertied man within four years of his first documented appearance as an actor with the Lord Chamberlain's Men. The Shakespeares applied for and were granted a coat-of-arms, so that clearly the family fortunes were rising rapidly. Edward Alleyn rose to become the honoured guest of the Archbishop of Canterbury and members of the nobility, and he was never despised as an actor, rather he was the object of envy in the eyes of Robert Greene! Ben Jonson never complained about his status as an actor-dramatist. Such arguments applied to William Shakespeare are futile attempts to fit him into the picture of the *Sonnets,* not borne out by the records of history.

The use of theatrical imagery in *Sonnet 110* was common to people of all walks of life, even members of the Privy Council used this colourful language. It does not imply that the Poet is an actor, but he was certainly a dramatist. That he had 'look'd on truth /Askance and strangely' is an admission that aptly fits Marlowe's questioning of the Holy Trinity when he may have come, for a time, under the spell of Bruno's Deist philosophy, and that he discussed his religious ideas with those who were not of his own open, questioning turn of mind, and made the fatal error of trusting them.

Sonnet 110

Alas, 'tis true, I have gone here and there,
And made myself a motley to the view,
Gor'd mine own thoughts, sold cheap what is most dear,
Made old offences of affections new.
Most true it is, that I have look'd on truth
Askance and strangely: but by all above,
These blenches gave my heart another youth,
And worse essays prov'd thee my best of love.
Now all is done, have what shall have no end;
Mine appetite I never more will grind
On newer proof to try an older friend,
A God in love, to whom I am confin'd.
    Then give me welcome, next my heaven the best,
    Even to thy pure and most, most loving breast.

This moving confession and tribute say it all, and confirm that this is indeed Christopher Marlowe writing to his dear Patron, who did not abandon him but saved his life.

Sonnet *111* is again a confessional of his past indiscretion in proselytizing and talking with those outside their esoteric circle, which exposed him to danger.

Sonnet 111

O for my sake do you with Fortune chide,
The guilty goddess of my harmful deeds,
That did not better for my life provide
Than public means, which public manners breeds.
Thence comes it that my name receives a brand,
And almost thence my nature is subdued
To what it works in, like the dyer's hand.
Pity me then, and wish I were renew'd,
Whilst like a willing patient I will drink
*Potions of eysell 'gainst my strong infection;
No bitterness that I will bitter think,
Nor double penance to correct correction.
    Pity me then, dear friend, and I assure ye,
    Even that your pity is enough to cure me.

Sonnet 112

Your love and pity doth th'impression fill
Which vulgar scandal stamp'd upon my brow,
For what care I who calls me well or ill,
So you o'er-green my bad, my good allow?
You are my All the world, and I must strive
To know my shames and praises from your tongue;
None else to me, nor I to none alive,
That my steel'd sense or changes right or wrong.
In so profound abysm I throw all care
Of others' voices, that my adder's sense
To critic and flatterer stopped are.
Mark how with my neglect I do dispense:
    You are so strongly in my purpose bred,
    That all the world besides me thinks y'are dead.

I follow Thorpe's edition in the last line, for he was surely working from the Poet's manuscript which leaves this slightly obscure for obvious reasons – a teazer for the reader to ponder.

---

* Gloss: 'Potions of eysell' in *Sonnet 111* refers to the vinegar made from the juice of the crab apple. *The English Dialect Dictionary* (ed. Joseph Wright, 1900) cites Lancashire dialect: 'as sour as eysell' and 'bed him galle and eysel to dryncke' (c. 1300) considered a sovereign cure for many ailments.

Sonnet 121 is the bitterest sonnet of them all. This noted free-thinker is making a spirited defence of his right to free thought and free action, to pursue what his aspiring mind aims to discover without the scandalizing, the persecution and the opprobrium of his ignorant, bigoted critics.

Sonnet 121

'Tis better to be vile than vile esteemed,
When not to be, receives reproach of being,
And the just pleasure lost, which is so deemed,
Not by our feeling, but by others' seeing.
For why should others' false adulterate eyes
Give salutation to my sportive blood?
Or on my frailties why are frailer spies,
Which in their wills count bad what I think good?
No, I am that I am, and they that level
At my abuses, reckon up their own.
I may be straight though they themselves be bevel;
By their rank thoughts my deeds must not be shown.
   Unless this general evil they maintain,
   All men are bad and in their badness reign.

GROUP H
TO THE TRUE PATRON

The nine sonnets in this segregated group are, of course, not the only ones addressed to the true Patron, Thomas Walsingham. Almost the entire sequence apart from those to Will Hatcliffe, and to Southampton, and to the Dark Lady, was written to Walsingham, many of them in the form of verse-letters. There is also a small group of introspective and miscellaneous sonnets which do not refer to him.

The total sonnets which directly address Thomas Walsingham number seventy-one. Those to Hatcliffe total twenty-eight. This discrepancy highlights that the real purpose of the dedication of the Sonnets to `Mr.W.H.', accepting that Hotson's solution of the conundrum is correct in his identification of 'the onlie Begetter' as 'Mr.W. HATLIV', was a ruse to mislead readers from recognizing the true Patron, and a very clever one, to judge by its effectiveness.

Not only the weight of numbers, but the impressive testimony of genuine, mutual loving friendship and deep respect expressed in the sonnets to Walsingham leave us in no doubt about the vital importance of their relationship, which nurtured Marlowe's spirit and sustained his art, his divine Muse. Repeatedly he tells his beloved Patron 'my spirit is thine'.

In *Sonnet 38* the Poet invocates Walsingham as the 'tenth Muse', a role he marvellously fulfilled in inspiring the persecuted genius and thus giving to posterity his superb canon of works. There is a subtle difference in tone in the sonnets to his true Patron, which the discerning reader will not fail to appreciate when comparing them critically with those to Hatcliffe, or those to Southampton.

Sonnet 38

How can my Muse want subject to invent
While thou dost breathe, that pour'st into my verse
Thine own sweet argument, too excellent
For every vulgar paper to rehearse:
O give thyself the thanks if aught in me
Worthy perusal stand against thy sight,
For who's so dumb that cannot write to thee,
When thou thyself dost give invention light?
Be thou the tenth Muse, ten times more in worth
Than those old nine which rhymers invocate,
And he that calls on thee, let him bring forth
Eternal numbers to outlive long date.
　　If my slight Muse do please these curious days,
　　The pain be mine, but thine shall be the praise.

This poem perfectly expresses the relationship between a Renaissance patron and his poet, deriving from the Platonist teaching that divine inspiration is only truly engendered by contemplation of his patron's virtues.

Sonnet 100 and *Sonnet 101* are both poems of apology to his Patron, suggesting that the Poet is leading a very busy life, perhaps active on assignments for the government at this time, in which he finds insufficient leisure for his creative writing. The term 'numbers' is an Elizabethanism meaning poems, or literary works. The implication is that he had spent time writing plays, not sonnets.

Sonnet 100

Where art thou Muse, that thou forgett'st so long
To speak of that which gives thee all thy might?
Spend'st thou thy fury on some worthless song,
Dark'ning thy power to lend base subject light?
Return, forgetful Muse, and straight redeem
In gentle numbers time so idly spent,
Sing to the ear that doth thy lays esteem,
And gives thy pen both skill and argument.
Rise, resty Muse, my love's sweet face survey,
If Time have any wrinkle graven there;
If any, be a satire to decay,
And make Time's spoils despised everywhere.
   Give my love fame faster than Time wastes life:
   So, thou prevent'st his scythe and crooked knife.

Sonnet 101

O truant Muse, what shall be thy amends
For thy neglect of truth in beauty dyed?
Both truth and beauty on my love depends;
So dost thou too, and therein dignified.
Make answer, Muse, wilt thou not haply say,
Truth needs no colour with his colour fix'd,
Beauty no pencil, beauty's truth to lay,
But best is best, if never intermix'd;
Because he needs no praise, wilt thou be dumb?
Excuse not silence so, for 't lies in thee
To make him much outlive a gilded tomb,
And to be prais'd of ages yet to be.
   Then do thy office Muse, I teach thee how
   To make him seem long hence as he shows now.

The line in *Sonnet 29,* in the *Sonnets of Exile,* 'With what I most enjoy contented least' suggests that his favourite writing is the making of plays, for Marlowe, as has been remarked, was a born dramatist; and becoming absorbed in some new dramatic work he had been neglecting to give his Patron those delightful sonnets due to him.

Sonnets 102 and 103 continue this apologetic and self-recriminatory theme, so that it is possible that these are a quartet of sonnets written on the same occasion of neglect of his Patron. The line, 'Our love was new, and then but in the spring' suggests a date before the events of 1593. If we take 1589 as the year when Walsingham became his Patron, this brings us to the year 1592, a year in which he seems to have been exceptionally busy if we may judge from the haste with which he wrote a new play for Alleyn at the Rose, recorded by Henslowe in his *Diary* as *'harey the vj'* – later to become *1 Henry VI* – performed on 3rd March 1591/2 for the re-opening of the newly refurbished Rose theatre, with its striking addition of a novel turret which this play specifically features, the subject of a brilliant thesis by Dr Allison Gaw. [1]

Sonnet 102

My love is strengthen'd, though more weak in seeming,
I love not less, though less the show appear.
That love is merchandized whose rich esteeming
The owner's tongue doth publish everywhere.
Our love was new, and then but in the spring
When I was wont to greet it with my lays,
As Philomel in summer's front doth sing,
And stops her pipe in growth of riper days:
Not that the summer is less pleasant now
Than when her mournful hymns did hush the night,
But that wild music burthens every bough,
And sweets grown common lose their dear delight.
   Therefore, like her, I sometime hold my tongue,
   Because I would not dull you with my song.

Sonnet 103

Alack, what poverty my Muse brings forth,
That having such a scope to show her pride,
The argument all bare is of more worth
Than when it hath my added praise beside.
O blame me not if I no more can write!
Look in your glass, and there appears a face
That overgoes my blunt invention quite,
Dulling my lines, and doing me disgrace.

Were it not sinful then, striving to mend,
To mar the subject that before was well?
For to no other pass my verses tend,
Than of your graces and your gifts to tell;
And more, much more than in my verse can sit,
Your own glass shows you, when you look in it.

This sonnet affords an example of how we need to be sensitive to the Poet's use of words – either in their common English sense, or as wittily playing on their connotations in *double entendre*. Here the repetition of 'more' obviously has no association with the name of his mistress, Morgan. Nor is 'pride' used in its alternative Elizabethan sense connoting a courtezan as used in the sonnets to the Dark Lady. Both pride and more recur frequently.

We may hazard a guess that Marlowe's friendship with Thomas Walsingham developed during the latter part of 1588, when perhaps they faced the dangers of the Armada together, of which there is a hint in *Sonnet 107*, and he then became his patron at his inheritance in November 1589 when Walsingham was twenty-six 'and more', still a young man, so that the passing of the years indicated in *Sonnet 104* suggests 1591, if the first of 'Three winters cold' is that of 1588-89. The third summer, in that case, gives Walsingham's age as twenty-eight and Marlowe as twenty-seven when both were still 'fresh' and 'green'. These sonnets are not in an ascertainable chronological order, but they seem to date from the last years before the events at Deptford, 1591 and 1592, a period of fairly prolific writing of dramatic works for Marlowe.

Sonnet 104

To me, fair friend, you never can be old,
For as you were when first your eye I eyed,
Such seems your beauty still. Three winters cold
Have from the forests shook three summers' pride,
Three beauteous springs to yellow autumn turn'd
In process of the seasons have I seen,
Three April perfumes in three hot Junes burn'd,
Since first I saw you fresh, which yet are green.
Ah yet doth beauty, like a dial hand,
Steal from his figure, and no pace perceiv'd;
So your sweet hue, which methinks still doth stand,
Hath motion, and mine eye may be deceiv'd.
For fear of which, hear this, thou age unbred,
Ere you were born was beauty's summer dead.

In *Sonnet 108,* which seems to be of a later date, the term 'sweet boy' is used agelessly, as we call a friend 'old boy' irrespective of his age. Even a father will call his son, who may be a mere 'old boy' of six years, by this typically English term of affection.

Sonnet 108

What's in the brain that ink may character,
Which hath not figur'd to thee my true spirit?
What's new to speak, what now to register,
That may express my love, or thy dear merit?
Nothing, sweet boy, but yet, like prayers divine,
I must each day say o'er the very same,
Counting no old thing old, thou mine, I thine,
Even as when first I hallowed thy fair name.
So that eternal love in love's fresh case
Weighs not the dust and injury of age,
Nor gives to necessary wrinkles place,
But makes antiquity for aye his page,
 Finding the first conceit of love there bred,
 Where time and outward form would show it dead.

Sonnets 115 and *116.* This most beautiful sonnet-pair suggests a date probably long after 1593 when their great friendship had withstood its supreme test.

Sonnet 115

Those lines that I before have writ do lie,
Even those that said I could not love you dearer;
Yet then my judgement knew no reason why
My most full flame should afterwards burn clearer.
But reckoning Time, whose million'd accidents
Creep in 'twixt vows, and change decrees of kings,
Tan sacred beauty, blunt the sharp'st intents,
Divert strong minds to th'course of alt'ring things:
Alas, why fearing of Time's tyranny,
Might I not then say, now I love you best,
When I was certain o'er incertainty,
Crowning the present, doubting of the rest?
 Love is a babe, then might I not say so,
 To give full growth to that which still doth grow.

Sonnet 116

Let me not to the marriage of true minds
Admit impediments. Love is not love
Which alters when it alteration finds,
Or bends with the remover to remove.
O no, it is an ever fixed mark
That looks on tempests and is never shaken;
It is the star to every wand'ring barque,
Whose worth's unknown although his height be taken.
Love's not Time's fool, though rosy lips and cheeks
Within his bending sickle's compass come;
Love alters not with his brief hours and weeks,
But bears it out even to the edge of doom.
   If this be error and upon me proved,
   I never writ, nor no man ever loved.

❖ ❖ ❖

GROUP I

THE POET IDENTIFIED (AFTER 1593)

In these two remarkable sonnets the Poet unmistakably identifies himself. Their all but central placement at the very heart of the sonnet-sequence as numbers *73* and *74* cannot be accidental, for we have seen with what extreme care the sonnet order has been put together. This significant placement has been most carefully thought out, and when one ponders the implication of this, the irresistible conclusion is borne in upon the mind that our hidden Poet published his autobiographical *Sonnets* in hope that one day we would read his message aright and know him as he truly is.

Both poems are addressed to Walsingham. In *Sonnet 73* he pictures himself, now balding, contemplating his life in retrospect, from his choirboy days in Canterbury when he played among the ruins of St Augustine's Abbey near his home, to his emergence as a secret agent and dramatist when, at twenty-one, he had his portrait painted with his chosen motto QUOD ME NUTRIT ME DESTRUIT, the consuming fire of his genius.

Sonnet 73

> That time of year thou mayst in me behold
> When yellow leaves, or none, or few do hang
> Upon those boughs which shake against the cold,
> Bare ruin'd choirs, where late the sweet birds sang.
> In me thou seest the twilight of such day
> As after sunset fadeth in the West,
> Which by and by black night doth take away,
> Death's second self that seals up all in rest.
> In me thou seest the glowing of such fire
> That on the ashes of his youth doth lie,
> As the death-bed, whereon it must expire,
> Consum'd with that which it was nourish'd by.
> > This thou perceiv'st, which makes thy love more strong
> > To love that well, which thou must leave ere long.

His evocation of 'Death's second self' is surely also pregnant wityh meaning. The contemplation of death is continued in the next sonnet where he actually makes a deliberate revelation of his 'death' by 'a wretch's knife'.

500

In *Sonnet 74* the words *'arrest'* and *'bail'* with *'my body being dead, The coward conquest of a wretch's knife'* are undeniable details of the 'murder' of 30th May, 1593.

Sonnet 74

But be contented: when that fell arrest
Without all bail shall carry me away,
My life hath in this line some interest,
Which for memorial still with thee shall stay.
When thou reviewest this, thou dost review
The very part was consecrate to thee.
The earth can have but earth, which is his due;
My spirit is thine, the better part of me.
So then thou hast but lost the dregs of life,
The prey of worms, my body being dead,
The coward conquest of a wretch's knife,
Too base of thee to be remembered.
    The worth of that, is that which it contains,
    And that is this, and this with thee remains.

When was William Shakespeare ever arrested and on bail? Marlowe was both, and according to official record he was stabbed with a dagger.

GROUP J

THE RIVAL POET: JEALOUSY (1598)

This group of fourteen sonnets expresses a storm of passionate jealousy concerning the Rival Poet who was also in Walsingham's patronage. Only singular circumstances could have engendered such turbulent feelings of anguished bitterness and apprehension in this gentle Poet. As suggested in Chapter 12, I believe that it was Walsingham himself who had made the *faux pas* of proposing to Marlowe's good old friend, George Chapman, that he should complete Marlowe's unfinished *Hero and Leander,* assuring him that Marlowe would have wished him to do this, in order to present the completed work to the world; dedicating his part to his Patron's bride, the Lady Audrey Walsingham, as an epithalamium for their marriage, thus bringing her into the patronage of his two poets. Walsingham's well-meaning and typically generous gesture became a bitter source of jealousy to the absent, and pathetically dependent Poet.

Chapman's noted learning is referred to in *Sonnet 78* which opens this group.

Sonnet 78

So oft have I invok'd thee for my Muse,
And found such fair assistance in my verse,
As every alien pen hath got my use,
And under thee their poesy disperse.
Thine eyes, that taught the dumb on high to sing
And heavy ignorance aloft to fly,
Have added feathers to the learned's wing,
And given grace a double majesty.
Yet be most proud of that which I compile,
Whose influence is thine, and born of thee,
In others' works thou dost but mend the style,
And arts with thy sweet graces graced be.
　　But thou art all my art, and dost advance
　　As high as learning my rude ignorance.

Sonnet 79

Whilst I alone did call upon thy aid
My verse alone had all thy gentle grace,
But now my gracious numbers are decay'd,
And my sick Muse doth give another place.
I grant (sweet love) thy lovely argument
Deserves the travail of a worthier pen,
Yet what of thee thy Poet doth invent
He robs thee of, and pays it thee again.

He lends thee virtue, and he stole that word
From thy behaviour; beauty doth he give,
And found it in thy cheek: he can afford
No praise to thee but what in thee doth live.
    Then thank him not for that which he doth say,
    Since what he owes thee, thou thyself dost pay.

Only one sonnet to Sir Thomas Walsingham (as he was then) by Chapman is extant, dating from 1605 when his comedy *All Fools* was published. It seems there may have been others.

Sonnet 80 is one of those in this group which clearly points to George Chapman as the Poet's rival for his Patron's patronage.

In 1598, the same year as the appearance of *Hero and Leander*, Chapman also published the first seven books of his translation of the *Iliad*, which he dedicated to the Earl of Essex. This work was highly acclaimed and still rates as one of the great achievements of the Elizabethan age, so that to the exiled Marlowe he appeared as a formidable rival. This fear is voiced in his sonnet.

Sonnet 80

O how I faint when I of you do write,
Knowing a better spirit doth use your name,
And in the praise thereof spends all his might,
To make me tongue-tied speaking of your fame.
But since your worth, wide as the ocean is,
The humble as the proudest sail doth bear,
My saucy bark (inferior far to his)
On your broad main doth wilfully appear.
Your shallowest help will hold me up afloat,
Whilst he upon your soundless deep doth ride;
Or, being wreck'd, I am a worthless boat,
He of tall building and of goodly pride.
    Then if he thrive, and I be cast away,
    The worse was this: my love was my decay.

His Patron's 'knowledge' which is praised in *Sonnet 82*, manifests Walsingham's interest in learning which was typical of all the members of Raleigh's circle, and which Walsingham's patronage of two poets of the intellectual quality of Marlowe and Chapman reflects. Chapman was especially revered among his contemporaries for his great learning.

Sonnet 82

I grant thou wert not married to my Muse,
And therefore mayst without attaint o'erlook
The dedicated words which writers use
Of their fair subject, blessing every book,
Thou art as fair in knowledge as in hue,
Finding thy worth a limit past my praise,
And therefore art enforc'd to seek anew
Some fresher stamp of these time-bettering days.
And do so, love; yet when they have devis'd
What strained touches rhetoric can lend,
Thou, truly fair, wert truly sympathiz'd
In true plain words by thy true-telling friend;
   And their gross painting might be better us'd
   Where cheeks need blood: in thee it is abus'd.

In *Sonnet 83* there is an indication that Marlowe's criticism expressed in his recent verse-letters had begun to bite somewhat. It seems that a perhaps slightly worried rebuke had been received from Walsingham that his Poet had not been sending any news of himself. It is clear that our Poet is by now nursing a grievance, and his reference to 'both your Poets' is somewhat bitter.

Sonnet 83

I never saw that you did painting need,
And therefore to your fair no painting set.
I found (or thought I found) you did exceed
The barren tender of a Poet's debt:
And therefore have I slept in your report,
That you yourself, being extant, well might show
How far a modern quill doth come too short,
Speaking of worth, what worth in you doth grow.
This silence for my sin you did impute,
Which shall be most my glory, being dumb,
For I impair not beauty, being mute,
When others would give life, and bring a tomb.
   There lives more life in one of your fair eyes,
   Than both your Poets can in praise devise.

Sonnet 84

Who is it that says most, which can say more
Than this rich praise: that you alone are you,
In whose confine immured is the store
Which should example where your equal grew?
Lean penury within that pen doth dwell
That to his subject lends not some small glory,
But he that writes of you, if he can tell
That you are you, so dignifies his story.
Let him but copy what in you is writ,
Not making worse what nature made so clear,
And such a counterpart shall fame his wit,
Making his style admired everywhere.
    You to your beauteous blessings add a curse,
    Being fond on praise, which makes your praises worse.

This hurt has gone very deep. There is even a sting in the tail of this sonnet.

Sonnets 85 and 86 identify George Chapman precisely. The reference to his poetic work as a 'hymn' is an accurate description of what has been called his 'Neoplatonic' poem, entitled 'The Shadow of Night', which is composed of 'hymns' on the subject of night and day.

Sonnet 85

My tongue-tied Muse in manners holds her still,
While comments of your praise, richly compil'd,
Reserve their character with golden quill,
And precious phrase by all the Muses fil'd.
I think good thoughts, whilst others write good words,
And like unlettered clerk still cry, Amen,
To every hymn that able spirit affords
In polish'd form of well-refined pen.
Hearing you prais'd I say, 'Tis so, 'tis true,
And to the most of praise add something more;
But that is in my thought, whose love to you,
Though words come hindmost, holds his rank before.
    Then others for the breath of words respect,
    Me for my dumb thoughts, speaking in effect.

Sonnet 86 has been cited by many authoritative critics as pointing clearly to George Chapman as the Rival Poet. It is hardly possible to deny this positive identification, and in the context of this thesis it makes perfect sense for the first time. Even the words 'that struck me dead' are significant.

Sonnet 86

Was it the proud full sail of his great verse,
Bound for the prize of all-too-precious you,
That did my ripe thoughts in my brain inhearse,
Making their tomb the womb wherein they grew?
Was it his spirit, by spirits taught to write
Above a mortal pitch, that struck me dead?
No, neither he, nor his compeers by night
Giving him aid, my verse astonished.
He, nor that affable familiar ghost
Which nightly gulls him with intelligence,
As victors of my silence cannot boast;
I was not sick of any fear from thence.
    But when your countenance fill'd up his line,
    Then lack'd I matter that enfeebled mine.

The deep hurt expressed in *Sonnet 87* is very bitter indeed. Perhaps it was Marlowe's sight of a copy of the completed *Hero and Leander*, which must have upset him the more, that prompted this bitter outpouring.

Sonnet 87

Farewell, thou art too dear for my possessing,
And like enough thou know'st thy estimate.
The charter of thy worth gives thee releasing:
My bonds in thee are all determinate,
For how do I hold thee but by thy granting,
And for that riches where is my deserving?
The cause of this fair gift in me is wanting,
And so my patent back again is swerving.
Thyself thou gav'st, thy own worth then not knowing,
Or me, to whom thou gav'st it, else mistaking;
So thy great gift, upon misprision growing,
Comes home again, on better judgement making.
    Thus have I had thee, as a dream doth flatter,
    In sleep a king, but waking no such matter.

Having sent this bitter shaft he relents somewhat in the next sonnet, where the consciousness of what he owes Walsingham is recollected in his reference to 'faults conceal'd wherein I am attainted', the awful tragedy of his falling foul of the state that culminated in the events at Deptford, which must forever bind these two together.

Sonnet 88

When thou shalt be dispos'd to set me light,
And place my merit in the eye of scorn,
Upon thy side against myself I'll fight,
And prove thee virtuous, though thou art forsworn,
With mine own weakness being best acquainted,
Upon thy part I can set down a story
Of faults conceal'd wherein I am attainted,
That thou in losing me shalt win much glory.
And I by this will be a gainer too,
For bending all my loving thoughts on thee,
The injuries that to myself I do,
Doing thee vantage, double vantage me.
 Such is my love, to thee I so belong,
 That for thy right myself will bear all wrong.

In *Sonnet 89* the Poet makes a second reference to his 'lameness' as applicable to himself, which gives some cause to wonder whether he was, in fact, lame, perhaps through some accident during the Armada campaign? The other reference to his lameness is in *Sonnet 37* in the *Sonnets of Exile.* J.P. Collier claimed that he had discovered a contemporary ballad entitled 'The Atheist's Tragedy' about Marlowe which tells of his lameness. I have seen the manuscript which is obviously in Collier's forged 'Elizabethan' hand, a clumsy attempt at forgery which is easily detected. This is, however, a curious coincidence because Collier in no way linked the ballad with Shakespeare's *Sonnets*.

Sonnet 89

Say that thou didst forsake me for some fault,
And I will comment upon that offence;
Speak of my lameness, and I straight will halt,
Against thy reasons making no defence.
Thou canst not (love) disgrace me half so ill,
To set a form upon desired change,
As I'll myself disgrace; knowing thy will,
I will acquaintance strangle, and look strange,
Be absent from thy walks, and in my tongue
Thy sweet beloved name no more shall dwell,
Lest I, too much profane, should do it wrong,
And haply of our old acquaintance tell.

For thee, against myself I'll vow debate,
For I must ne'er love him whom thou dost hate.

Sonnet 90

Then hate me when thou wilt, if ever, now,
Now while the world is bent my deeds to cross,
Join with the spite of fortune, make me bow,
And do not drop in for an after-loss:
Ah do not, when my heart hath 'scap'd this sorrow,
Come in the rearward of a conquer'd woe,
Give not a windy night a rainy morrow,
To linger out a purpos'd overthrow.
If thou wilt leave me, do not leave me last,
When other petty griefs have done their spite,
But in the onset come; so shall I taste
At first the very worst of fortune's might.
    And other strains of woe, which now seem woe,
    Compar'd with loss of thee, will not seem so.

In reading these anguished sonnets the impression gained is that they would not have been written or sent singly, but in pairs, or more likely in a quartet of poems, when their impact on the recipient would have been considerable.

Sonnets 91 and 92 conclude the traumatic episode of the Rival Poet, which was followed by a heart-warming and very lovely reconciliation, but the sonnets telling of this (*Sonnets 117* to *120*) are separated from those of his searing jealousy over the Rival Poet by a miscellany having nothing to do with this subject. Immediately in the sequence there follow four sonnets about Hatcliffe's lascivious faults, which clever placing sows confusion as to the cause of the disaffection between the Poet and his Patron in a manner that deliberately obscures the identities of Walsingham and Hatcliffe. A subtle and effective device. So subtle that even now I am not certain about the placement of these two sonnets.

Sonnet 9

Some glory in their birth, some in their skill,
Some in their wealth, some in their body's force,
Some in their garments, though new-fangled ill:
Some in their hawks and hounds, some in their horse,
And every humour hath his adjunct pleasure,
Wherein it finds a joy above the rest,
But these particulars are not my measure.

508

All these I better in one general best:
Thy love is better than high birth to me,
Richer than wealth, prouder than garments' cost,
Of more delight than hawks or horses be,
And having thee, of all men's pride I boast,
    Wretched in this alone: that thou mayst take
    All this away, and me most wretched make.

Sonnet 92

But do thy worst to steal thyself away,
For term of life thou art assured mine,
And life no longer than thy love will stay,
For it depends upon that love of thine.
Then need I not to fear the worst of wrongs
When in the least of them my life hath end.
I see a better state to me belongs
Than that which on thy humour doth depend.
Thou canst not vex me with inconstant mind,
Since that my life on thy revolt doth lie.
O, what a happy title do I find,
Happy to have thy love, happy to die!
    But what's so blessed fair that fears no blot,
    Thou mayst be false, and yet I know it not.

Marlowe's first youthful patron played him false with his mistress, and he
suspected Walsingham had deserted him for Chapman. It is the bitterness and
passion expressed in these two sonnets that tipped the scales and seemed to
say they belong to the *Sonnets of the Rival Poet*. His beloved Patron is
accused of 'inconstant mind' but not of the lasciviousness associated with
Hatcliffe. The latter did not transfer his patronage to another – it was Marlowe
who finally *rejected him* as his patron.

GROUP K

THE RIVAL POET: RECONCILIATION (1600 ?)

The reconciliation that followed the episode triggered off by the completion of *Hero and Leander* by George Chapman, which in Marlowe's eyes was a betrayal of his work, resulted from what must have been a full explanation offered about how and why George Chapman came to complete this poem. Evidence presented in the sequel to this book suggests that when Marlowe returned from his exile he lived in England under the protection of the Brotherhood of the Freemasons.

The indications in *Sonnet 117* are that Marlowe had been preoccupied with others: 'I have frequent been with unknown minds'. One of these was very likely the stimulating mind of Francis Bacon. We also know that Walsingham was not a Freemason, but kept himself carefully aloof from them. It may be that Walsingham had expected that Marlowe would live cloistered at Scadbury upon his return to England, but this did not happen. Instead he had 'hoisted sail to all the winds'. This, I suggest is the background to this sonnet.

Such a scenario is not a wild hypothesis without foundation of evidence, as will be seen in due course, and it makes complete sense of this sonnet, which it is feasible to date tentatively to 1600-1.

Sonnet 117

Accuse me thus: that I have scanted all
Wherein I should your great deserts repay,
Forgot upon your dearest love to call,
Whereto all bonds do tie me day by day;
That I have frequent been with unknown minds,
And given to time your own dear-purchas'd right;
That I have hoisted sail to all the winds
Which should transport me farthest from your sight.
Book both my wilfulness and errors down,
And on just proof surmise accumulate;
Bring me within the level of your frown,
But shoot not at me in your wakened hate,
　　Since my appeal says I did strive to prove
　　The constancy and virtue of your love.

Sonnet 118

Like as to make our appetites more keen
With eager compounds we our palate urge,
As to prevent our maladies unseen,
We sicken to shun sickness when we purge:
Even so, being full of your ne'er-cloying sweetness,
To bitter sauces did I frame my feeding,
And, sick of welfare, found a kind of meetness
To be diseas'd ere that there was true needing.
True policy in love, t'anticipate
The ills that were not, grew to faults assured,
And brought to medicine a healthful state
Which, rank of goodness, would by ill be cured.
 But thence I learn, and find the lesson true,
 Drugs poison him that so fell sick of you.

Sonnets 119 and 120 tell us that it had been an ill-starred misunderstanding. Walsingham had never intended to hurt his Poet, and was finally able to explain, and the full realisation brought this very beautiful and typically generous reconciliation. This is foreshadowed by the reference in the previous Sonnet 118 to 'The ills that were not grew to faults assured', which tells us that the cause for complaint was illusory.

Sonnet 119

What potions have I drunk of siren tears
Distilled from limbecks foul as hell within,
Applying fears to hopes, and hopes to fears,
Still losing when I saw myself to win!
What wretched errors hath my heart committed
Whilst it hath thought itself so blessed never!
How have mine eyes out of their spheres been fitted
In the distraction of this madding fever!
O benefit of ill! Now I find true
That better is by evil still made better,
And ruin'd love when it is built anew
Grows fairer than at first, more strong, far greater.
 So I return rebuk'd to my content,
 And gain by ills thrice more than I have spent.

The word 'crime' in *Sonnet 120* seems strong to us, but in Elizabethan usage passes for a trespass. The recollection of 'our night of woe' is surely a reference to their shared experience of the traumatic events that culminated at Deptford.

Sonnet 120

That you were once unkind befriends me now,
And for that sorrow which I then did feel
Needs must I under my transgression bow,
Unless my nerves were brass or hammered steel.
For if you were by my unkindness shaken
As I by yours, you've pass'd a hell of time,
And I, a tyrant, have no leisure taken
To weigh how once I suffered in your crime.
O that our night of woe might have remembered
My deepest sense, how hard true sorrow hits,
And soon to you, as you to me then tendered
The humble salve which wounded bosoms fits!
    But that your trespass now becomes a fee,
    Mine ransom yours, and yours must ransom me.

This sonnet is a moving tribute to their true friendship and to Walsingham's magnanimous nature.

GROUP L
FOUR PROBLEM SONNETS

Sonnet 66 in the sequence follows a quartet, *Sonnets 62 to 65,* which extoll 'Prince' Will Hatcliffe's youthful perfections in contrast to exaggerated depiction of his own age as 'Beated and chapp'd with tann'd antiquity', and descanting on 'Time's fell hand'. These are tinged with a sense of melancholy, but there is nothing like the bitter disillusionment of *Sonnet 66,* which does not appear to belong to the Hatcliffe group, or any other group.

There is some affinity with Raleigh's famous poem 'The Lie'. Was it, perhaps, written as Marlowe's riposte to Raleigh's poem, as Raleigh wrote his 'Reply' to Marlowe's 'Come Live with Me'? Or is the wickedness of the world in all its cynicism depicted here as the contrasted backdrop to the perfection of his 'Prince'?

But all this is hypothesis. I have no real clues to offer.

Sonnet 66

Tir'd with all these, for restful Death I cry:
As to behold Desert a beggar born,
And needy Nothing trimm'd in jollity,
And purest Faith unhappily forsworn,
And gilded Honour shamefully misplac'd,
And maiden Virtue rudely strumpeted,
And right Perfection wrongfully disgrac'd,
And Strength by limping sway disabled,
And Art made tongue-tied by Authority,
And Folly (doctor-like) controlling Skill,
And simple Truth miscalled Simplicity,
And captive Good attending Captain Ill.
   Tir'd with all these, from these would I be gone,
   Save that to die, I leave my love alone.

Sonnets 67 and 68 carry forward the mood of disillusionment with the world, but this sonnet-pair possibly does not belong with Sonnet 66. They are unusual because the subject is in the third person, an as yet unidentified 'he', who may be 'Prince True-Love', perhaps when doubts are creeping in? I am not sure.

Sonnet 67

Ah wherefore with infection should he live,
And with his presence grace impiety,
That sin by him advantage should achieve,
And lace itself with his society?
Why should false painting imitate his cheek,
And steal dead seeing of his living hue?
Why should poor beauty indirectly seek
Roses of shadow, since his rose is true?
Why should he live, now Nature bankrout is,
Beggar'd of blood to blush through lively veins?
For she hath no exchequer now but his,
And proud of many, lives upon his gains.
   O him she stores, to show what wealth she had,
   In days long since, before these last so bad.

The reference to 'holy antique hours' seems to conjure 'Prince' Will. In that case it should join Group A. The question is, are Sonnet 67 and 68 a pair, or not?

Sonnet 68

Thus in his cheek the map of days outworn,
When beauty liv'd and died as flowers do now,
Before these bastard signs of fair were borne,
Or durst inhabit on a living brow:
Before the golden tresses of the dead,
The right of sepulchres, were shorn away,
To live a second life on second head,
Ere beauty's dead fleece made another gay:
In him those holy antique hours are seen,
Without all ornament, itself and true,
Making no summer of another's green,
Robbing no old to dress his beauty new;
   And him as for a map doth Nature store,
   To show false Art what beauty was of yore.

514

The introspective *Sonnet 146* comes from the Dark Lady group. It has no obvious, direct application to her, although the mood expressed may have been engendered by his love-affair with her. The word 'more' appears twice in this sonnet. Is this intended to conjure up the Poet's association with Luce Morgan? The second line repeats the words 'My sinful earth', which some editors choose to alter assuming that Thorpe's edition is in error, but their improvements have little to commend them. The following is Thorpe's version in which admittedly the line does not scan.

Sonnet 146

Poor soul, the centre of my sinful earth,
My sinful earth, these rebel powers that thee array,
Why dost thou pine within and suffer dearth
Painting thy outward walls so costly gay?
Why so large cost, having so short a lease,
Dost thou upon thy fading mansion spend?
Shall worms, inheritors of this excess,
Eat up thy charge? Is this thy body's end?
Then soul, live thou upon thy servant's loss,
And let that pine to aggravate thy store;
Buy terms divine in selling hours of dross:
Within be fed, without be rich no more.
   So shalt thou feed on Death, that feeds on men,
   And Death once dead, there's no more dying then.

❖ ❖ ❖

GROUP M
TWO SONNETS OF GIFTS

These two sonnets both refer to gifts, given or received. The first is a book with blank pages, which the Poet apparently presented to Will Hatcliffe, as may be surmised from the somewhat admonishing tone of his poem – perhaps as a parting gift on leaving his patronage?

Sonnet 77

Thy glass will show thee how thy beauties wear,
Thy dial how thy precious minutes waste,
The vacant leaves thy mind's imprint will bear,
And of this book, this learning mayst thou taste.
The wrinkles which thy glass will truly show,
Of mouthed graves will give thee memory;
Thou by thy dial's shady stealth mayst know
Time's thievish progress to eternity.
Look what thy memory cannot contain,
Commit to these waste blanks, and thou shalt find
Those children nurs'd, deliver'd from thy brain,
To take a new acquaintance of thy mind.
   These offices, so oft as thou wilt look,
   Shall profit thee, and much enrich thy book.

In *Sonnet 122* the gift of 'tables' received was presumably from Walsingham. The contrast in tone clearly exemplifies the difference in the relationship between the Poet and his first patron, the wealthy, spoilt young Hatcliffe, and his true Patron, Walsingham.

Sonnet 122

Thy gift, thy tables, are within my brain
Full character'd with lasting memory,
Which shall above that idle rank remain
Beyond all date, even to eternity.
Or at the least, so long as brain and heart
Have faculty by nature to subsist;
Till each to raz'd oblivion yield his part
Of thee, thy record never can be miss'd:
That poor retention could not so much hold,
Nor need I tallies thy dear love to score;
Therefore to give them from me was I bold,
To trust those tables that receive thee more.
   To keep an adjunct to remember thee
   Were to import forgetfulness in me.

GROUP N
THE DARK LADY (1587-88 to 1593?)

This group of twenty-five sonnets to the Dark Lady are placed last in Thorpe's edition, and I have left them there, although they were undoubtedly written early in the sequence, since 'Prince' Will features in them as the Poet's rival for the love of this black-eyed beauty. They rightly belong, I suggest, with *Sonnet 23 and 24*, which record the heart-stopping experience of the young Poet's first falling in love with her. Here his love-affair is already well established.

Sonnet 127

In the old age black was not counted fair,
Or if it were it bore not beauty's name:
But now is black Beauty's successive heir,
And Beauty slander'd with a bastard shame;
For since each hand hath put on Nature's power,
Fairing the foul with Art's false borrow'd face,
Sweet Beauty hath no name, no holy bower,
But is profan'd, if not lives in disgrace.
Therefore my Mistress' eyes are raven black,
Her eyes so suited, and they mourners seem
At such who, not born fair, no beauty lack,
Sland'ring Creation with a false esteem.
    Yet so they mourn becoming of their woe,
    That every tongue says Beauty should look so.

Sonnet 128

How oft, when thou, my Music, music play'st
Upon that blessed wood whose motion sounds
With thy sweet fingers when thou gently sway'st
The wiry concord that mine ear confounds,
Do I envy those jacks that nimble leap
To kiss the tender inward of thy hand,
Whilst my poor lips, which should that harvest reap,
At the wood's boldness by thee blushing stand.
To be so tickled they would change their state
And situation with those dancing chips
O'er whom thy fingers walk with gentle gait,
Making dead wood more bless'd than living lips.
    Since saucy jacks so happy are in this,
    Give them thy fingers, me thy lips to kiss.

Since *Sonnet 129* is placed in this group the intense revulsion to sex as a 'waste of shame' here expressed is doubtless associated with his shame at having fallen in love with a harlot, to whose 'black' beauty he finds himself fatally attracted.

Sonnet 129

Th' expense of Spirit in a waste of shame
Is lust in action, and till action lust
Is perjur'd, murd'rous, bloody, full of blame,
Savage, extreme, rude, cruel, not to trust,
Enjoy'd no sooner but despised straight,
Past reason hunted, and no sooner had,
Past reason hated as a swallowed bait
On purpose laid to make the taker mad:
Mad in pursuit, and in possession so,
Had, having, and in quest to have, extreme,
A bliss in proof and proud and very woe;
Before, a joy propos'd, behind, a dream.
    All this the world well knows, yet none knows well
    To shun the heaven that leads men to this hell.

Sonnet 130 is a clever satire on the sonneteering convention which indulges in hyperbole, eulogizing the beloved lady of the sonneteer in extravagant terms. In this witty antidote the Poet brings his fellow poets back to earth with a bump.

Sonnet 130

My Mistress' eyes are nothing like the sun,
Coral is far more red than her lips' red.
If snow be white, why then her breasts are dun;
If hairs be wires, black wires grow on her head.
I have seen roses damask'd, red and white,
But no such roses see I in her cheeks;
And in some perfumes is there more delight
Than in the breath that from my Mistress reeks.
I love to hear her speak, yet well I know
That music hath a far more pleasing sound.
I grant I never saw a goddess go:
My Mistress when she walks treads on the ground.
    And yet, by heaven, I think my love as rare
    As any she belied with false compare.

In *Sonnet 131* the use of 'proudly' and his declaration, 'In nothing art thou black save in thy deeds' clearly indicate that his Mistress' profession is that of a courtezan.

Sonnet 131

Thou art as tyrranous, so as thou art,
As those whose beauties proudly make them cruel,
For well thou know'st to my dear doting heart
Thou art the fairest and most precious jewel.
Yet, in good faith, some say that thee behold,
Thy face hath not the power to make love groan;
To say they err, I dare not be so bold,
Although I swear it to myself alone.
And to be sure that is not false I swear,
A thousand groans but thinking on thy face,
One on another's neck do witness bear
Thy black is fairest in my judgement's place.
    In nothing art thou black save in thy deeds,
    And thence this slander, as I think, proceeds.

In *Sonnet 132* there is much play with the words 'mourners', 'morning', 'mourning', which Dr Hotson suggests is evoking her name Morgan, as well as recurring reference to her profession in the use of 'black', which in association with 'eyes' connotes her name Luce. One might call this sonnet a portrait of Luce Morgan.

Sonnet 132

Thine eyes I love, and they, as pitying me,
Knowing thy heart torment me with disdain,
Have put on black, and loving mourners be,
Looking with pretty ruth upon my pain.
And truly, not the morning Sun of Heaven
Better becomes the grey cheeks of th' East,
Nor that full Star that ushers in the Even
Doth half that glory to the sober West
As those two mourning eyes become thy face:
O let it then as well beseem thy heart
To mourn for me since mourning doth thee grace,
And suit thy pity like in every part.
    Then will I swear Beauty herself is black,
    And all they foul that thy complexion lack.

Sonnets 133, 134, 135, 136, are a quartet in which 'Prince' Will makes his entry in the story of the Poet's love-affair with the beautiful, dark-eyed courtezan, Luce Morgan. Six years later we have documentary evidence of her appearance at the 'court' of the next Prince of Purpoole, Henry Helmes in the Christmas season of 1594. It may be assumed that this was a repeat performance by Mistress Morgan of her success at the Grayan celebrations of 1587-88, when she first played her part as 'Abbess de Clerkenwell' and paid homage to the young 'Prince' Will Hatcliffe, as required 'by night service in *Cauda'* and supplied 'a choir of nuns, with burning lamps, to chant *Placebo* to the gentlemen of the Prince's privy-chamber'. An affair with the 'Prince' was hardly avoidable after such an introduction! Luce Morgan was a rather high class courtezan, for she had been one of Queen Elizabeth's favourite gentlewomen at one time. In every way she is ideally suited to be the Dark Lady of the *Sonnets,* and her identification by Dr Hotson, which forms such a perfect conjunction with 'Prince' Will, is one of the most felicitous finds of his inspired research.

Sonnet 133

Beshrew that heart that makes my heart to groan
For that deep wound it gives my friend and me;
Is't not enough to torture me alone,
But slave to slavery my sweet'st friend must be?
Me from myself thy cruel eye hath taken,
And my next self thou harder hast engrossed;
Of him, myself, and thee I am forsaken,
A torment thrice threefold thus to be crossed.
Prison my heart in thy steel bosom's ward,
But then my friend's heart let my poor heart bail;
Who'er keeps me, let my heart be his guard,
Thou canst not then use rigour in my jail.
   And yet thou wilt, for I being pent in thee,
   Perforce am thine, and all that is in me.

Sonnet 134

So now I have confess'd that he is thine,
And I myself am mortgag'd to thy will;
Myself I'll forfeit, so that other mine
Thou wilt restore to be my comfort still.
But thou wilt not, nor he will not be free,
For thou art covetous, and he is kind;
He learn'd but surety-like to write for me,
Under that bond that him as fast doth bind.
The statute of thy beauty thou wilt take,
Thou usurer that putt'st forth all to use,

And sue a friend came debtor for my sake,
So him I lose through my unkind abuse.
   Him have I lost, thou hast both him and me:
   He pays the whole, and yet am I not free.

The *double entendre* in these sonnets playing on the sexual connotation of
'will' and the name of his rival 'Will' is clearly intentional. Thorpe's edition
has been followed in capitalizing and italicizing the word, so that there can be
no doubt that this was the Poet's presentation of how he intended that these
poems should be read. In this witty poem the use of 'more', the Welsh word
for sea (mor) connoting Morgan (sea-man) is also surely intended.

Sonnet 135

Whoever hath her wish, thou hast thy *Will*,
And *Will* to boot, and *Will* in over-plus,
More than enough am I that vex thee still,
To thy sweet will making addition thus.
Wilt thou, whose will is large and spacious,
Not once vouchsafe to hide my will in thine?
Shall will in others seem right gracious,
And in my will no fair acceptance shine?
The sea, all water, yet receives rain still,
And in abundance addeth to his store,
So thou being rich in *Will*, add to thy *Will*
One will of mine to make thy large *Will* more.
   Let no unkind, no fair beseechers kill;
   Think all but one, and me in that one *Will*.

Sonnet 136

If thy soul check thee that I come so near,
Swear to thy blind soul that I was thy *Will*,
And will, thy soul knows, is admitted there;
Thus far for love, my love-suit sweet fulfil.
Will, will fulfil the treasure of thy love,
Ay, fill it full with wills, and my will one.
In things of great receipt with ease we prove,
Among a number one is reckon'd none.
Then in the number let me pass untold,
Though in thy store's account I one must be;
For nothing hold me, so it please thee hold,
That nothing me, a something sweet to thee.
   Make but my name thy love, and love that still,
   And then thou lov'st me for my name is *Will*.

Before publishing the *Sonnets* in 1609 there would obviously have been some careful editing, as there was careful arrangement in the matter of how to present the sequence. The final couplet of *Sonnet 136* may, I suggest, have been revised so as to bring in his pseudonymous name Will (Shakespeare) for the publication of Thorpe's cryptic edition of 1609, as a sensible precaution. It will be argued by orthodox Shakespearean scholars that this is evidence of William Shakespeare's authorship. If this were the conclusive evidence one would accept it, but unfortunately for the Stratfordian case it is the only sonnet which can be argued as supporting this. All the rest overwhelmingly contradict it. Will Hatcliffe is a strong contender in these 'Will' sonnets. By 1609, of course, Marlowe was 'Will Shakespeare'.

Dr Hotson's research discovering Luce Morgan as the Dark Lady of the *Sonnets* has established something that other scholars have not fully appreciated, that the beloved woman was not merely some court lady with rather loose morals, but actually a harlot by profession. Probably she became this after her seduction by one of the courtiers who made it their sport to prey with 'fox-like subtlety on the tame beasts' who were the Queen's ladies-in-waiting.

Sonnet 137 presents Luce Morgan as 'the bay where all men ride', using sea imagery again. The fact that the Poet contracted a venereal disease also confirms the identification of her as a harlot.

Sonnet 137

Thou blind fool Love, what dost thou to mine eyes
That they behold, and see not what they see?
They know what beauty is, see where it lies,
Yet what the best is, take the worst to be.
If eyes corrupt by over-partial looks
Be anchored in the bay where all men ride,
Why of eyes' falsehood hast thou forged hooks
Whereto the judgement of my heart is tied?
Why should my heart think that a several plot,
Which my heart knows the wide world's common place?
Or mine eyes, seeing this, say this is not,
To put fair truth upon so foul a face?
    In things right true my heart and eyes have erred,
    And to this false plague are they now transferred.

Sonnet 138 is one of two that first appeared in Jaggard's collection *The Passionate Pilgrim*, who possibly acquired it because it had been handed round and often recopied in manuscript by the Grayan students. This recopying would account for the variations in Jaggard's version, which is an inferior poem. The sonneteer is here deliberately exaggerrating his age in the sonneteering convention. Luce Morgan would have been older than her Poet-lover by some four years.

Sonnet 138

When my love swears that she is made of truth,
I do believe her though I know she lies,
That she might think me some untutor'd youth,
Unlearned in the world's false subtleties.
Thus vainly thinking that she thinks me young,
Although she knows my days are past the best,
Simply I credit her false-speaking tongue,
On both sides thus is simple truth suppress'd.
But wherefore says she not she is unjust?
And wherefore say not I that I am old?
O, love's best habit is in seeming trust,
And age in love, loves not t' have years told.
    Therefore I lie with her, and she with me,
    And in our faults by lies we flattered be.

Sonnet 139

O call not me to justify the wrong
That thy unkindness lays upon my heart.
Wound me not with thine eye, but with thy tongue;
Use power with power, and slay me not by art.
Tell me thou lov'st elsewhere, but in my sight,
Dear heart, forbear to glance thine eye aside.
What need'st thou wound with cunning when thy might
Is more than my o'erpress'd defence can bide?
Let me excuse thee: ah, my love well knows
Her pretty looks have been mine enemies,
And therefore from my face she turns my foes
That they elsewhere might dart their injuries.
    Yet do not so, but since I am near slain,
    Kill me outright with looks, and rid my pain.

Sonnet 140

Be wise as thou art cruel, do not press
My tongue-tied patience with too much disdain,
Lest sorrow lend me words, and words express
The manner of my pity-wanting pain.
If I might teach thee wit, better it were,
Though not to love, yet love, to tell me so,
As testy sick men when their deaths be near
No news but health from their physicians know.
For if I should despair I should grow mad,
And in my madness might speak ill of thee.
Now this ill-wresting world is grown so bad,
Mad slanderers by mad ears believed be.
    That I may not be so, nor thou belied,
     Bear thine eyes straight, though thy proud heart go wide.

Sonnet 141

In faith, I do not love thee with mine eyes,
For they in thee a thousand errors note;
But 'tis my heart that loves what they despise,
Who in despite of view is pleas'd to dote.
Nor are mine ears with thy tongue's tune delighted,
Nor tender feeling to base touches prone;
Nor taste, nor smell, desire to be invited
To any sensual feast with thee alone;
But my five wits, nor my five senses can
Dissuade one foolish heart from serving thee,
Who leaves unsway'd the likeness of a man,
Thy proud heart's slave and vassal-wretch to be.
    Only my plague thus far I count my gain,
     That she that makes me sin awards me pain.

A complexity of feelings is displayed in these sonnets. His ardent, profane sexual love for this fallen woman torments him.

Sonnet 142

Love is my sin, and thy dear virtue hate,
Hate of my sin grounded on sinful loving.
O, but with mine compare thou thine own state,
And thou shalt find it merits not reproving,
Or if it do, not from those lips of thine
That have profan'd their scarlet ornaments,
And seal'd false bonds of love as oft as mine,
Robb'd others' beds' revenues of their rents.

Be it lawful I love thee as thou lov'st those
Whom thine eyes woo as mine importune thee.
Root pity in thy heart, that when it grows,
Thy pity may deserve to pitied be.
    If thou dost seek to have what thou dost hide,
    By self-example mayst thou be denied.

In *Sonnet 143* his rival 'Will' is again mentioned, but in his absence, for it seems he had tired of Mistress Morgan's charms before she tired of him. She longs to have him back, while her Poet-lover pleads in turn for her love to be restored to him.

Sonnet 143

Lo, as a careful housewife runs to catch
One of her feathered creatures broke away,
Sets down her babe and makes all swift dispatch
In pursuit of the thing she would have stay,
Whilst her neglected child holds her in chase,
Cries to catch her whose busy care is bent
To follow that which flies before her face,
Not prizing her poor infant's discontent;
So runn'st thou after that which flies from thee,
Whilst I, thy babe, chase thee afar behind.
But if thou catch thy hope, turn back to me
And play the mother's part: kiss me, be kind.
    So will I pray that thou may'st have thy *Will*,
    If thou turn back and my loud crying still.

Sonnet 144 was also published in a slightly variant form in Jaggard's piratical miscellany of 1599. Its theme recalls *Sonnet 42*, but we cannot doubt that in this case the 'man right fair' is 'Prince' Will, and the 'woman colour'd ill' is Luce Morgan.,

Sonnet 144

Two loves I have of comfort and despair,
Which like two spirits do suggest me still:
The better angel is a man right fair,
The worser spirit a woman colour'd ill.
To win me soon to hell my female evil
Tempteth my better angel from my side,
And would corrupt my saint to be a devil,
Wooing his purity with her foul pride;

525

And whether that my angel be turn'd fiend,
Suspect I may, yet not directly tell;
But being both from me, both to each friend,
I guess one angel in another's hell.
    Yet this shall I ne'er know, but live in doubt,
    Till my bad angel fire my good one out.

Sonnet 145

Those lips that Love's own hand did make
Breath'd forth the sound that said, I hate,
To me that languish'd for her sake.
But when she saw my woeful state,
Straight in her heart did mercy come,
Chiding that tongue that ever sweet
Was us'd in giving gentle doom;
And taught it thus anew to greet:
I hate, she alter'd with an end,
That follow'd it as gentle day
Doth follow night, who like a fiend
From heaven to hell is flown away.
    I hate, from hate away she threw,
    And sav'd my life saying, not you.

It is clear that our love-sick Poet did win Luce Morgan back, and their love-affair may have continued over the years, perhaps until his exile.

Sonnet 147

My love is as a fever, longing still
For that which longer nurseth the disease.
Feeding on that which doth preserve the ill,
Th' uncertain sickly appetite to please.
My reason, the physician to my love,
Angry that his prescriptions are not kept,
Hath left me, and I desperate now approve.
Desire is death, which physic did except.
Past cure I am, now reason is past care,
And frantic mad with evermore unrest,
My thoughts and my discourse as mad men's are,
At random from the truth vainly express'd.
    For I have sworn thee fair, and thought thee bright,
    Who art as black as hell, as dark as night.

Sonnet 148

O me! what eyes hath love put in my head,
Which have no correspondence with true sight,
Or if they have, where is my judgement fled,
That censures falsely what they see aright?
If that be fair whereon my false eyes dote,
What means the world to say it is not so?
If it be not, then love doth well denote
Love's eye is not so true as all men's: no,
How can it? O how can love's eye be true,
That is so vex'd with watching and with tears?
No marvel then though I mistake my view,
The sun itself sees not till heaven clears.
    O cunning love, with tears thou keep'st me blind,
    Lest eyes well seeing thy foul faults should find.

It will be noted that there is frequent emphasis on 'eyes', 'looks', 'blind' and also 'bright' in all the foregoing sonnets, combining with historical evidence, delineating a pen-portrait of Luce Morgan as the Dark Lady of Hotson's detection.

The intimations of a lovers' quarrel are present in many of these sonnets, and this surfaces in the following and concluding sonnets in the sequence.

Sonnet 149

Canst thou, O cruel, say I love thee not,
When I against myself with thee partake?
Do I not think on thee when I forgot
Am of myself, all tyrant for thy sake?
Who hateth thee that I do call my friend?
On whom frown'st thou that I do fawn upon?
Nay, if thou lour'st on me, do I not spend
Revenge upon myself with present moan?
What merit do I in myself respect,
That is so proud thy service to despise,
When all my best doth worship thy defect,
commanded by the motion of thine eyes?
    But love, hate on, for now I know thy mind;
    Those that can see thou lov'st, and I am blind.

The love he bears his black-eyed mistress is a torment because of her constant unfaithfulness, and there were probably some stormy scenes between them!

527

Although the Poet's beloved woman is clearly described by him as a harlot, albeit evidently of somewhat superior class for she is a delightful musician, this is more than a mere professional sexual relationship in which she is selling her body to him for money. This, in fact, is never mentioned in these sonnets, which implies that their relationship is, perhaps, not that of courtezan and client in the conventional vulgar sense, but rather as lovers. The Poet really does love this seductive siren passionately, and it would be a hard woman who did not respond to his ardour also with some love. The fact that Love and Hate are juxtaposed in a way that includes her emotional response indicates a deeper relationship than that of superficial sex.

These sonnets are a celebration of human sexual love in a stormy, passionate relationship fraught with problems arising from Luce Morgan's profession. We have to remember also that she was apparently married to a man named Parker, whose name, however, she did not use. Her professional name was Morgan. It is their emotional content that has given SHAKE-SPEARES SONNETS their pre-eminent place in the love poetry of our language.

The last three sonnets to the Dark Lady again emphasize her name, Morgan, in the thrice-repeated use of 'more' and her profession, 'proud of this pride' and 'eyes', 'blindness', and 'brightness', all picturing Luce Morgan.

Sonnet 150

O from what power hast thou this powerful might
With insufficiency my heart to sway,
To make me give the lie to my true sight,
And swear that brightness doth not grace the day?
Whence hast thou this becoming of things ill,
That in the very refuse of thy deeds
There is such strength and warrantise of skill
That in my mind thy worst all best exceeds?
Who taught thee how to make me love thee more,
The more I hear and see just cause of hate?
Oh, though I love what others do abhor,
With others thou shouldst not abhor my state.
   If thy unworthiness rais'd love in me,
   More worthy I to be belov'd of thee.

Sonnet 151

Love is too young to know what conscience is,
Yet who knows not conscience is born of love?
Then, gentle cheater, urge not my amiss,
Lest guilty of my faults thy sweet self prove.
For, thou betraying me, I do betray
My nobler part to my gross body's treason:

My soul doth tell my body that he may
Triumph in love; flesh stays no farther reason,
But rising at thy name doth point out thee
As his triumphant prize. Proud of this pride,
He is contented thy poor drudge to be,
To stand in thy affairs, fall by thy side.
    No want of conscience hold it that I call
    Her 'love', for whose dear love I rise and fall.

Sonnet 152

In loving thee thou know'st I am forsworn,
But thou art twice forsworn to me love swearing,
In act thy bed-vow broke and new faith torn,
In vowing new hate after new love bearing:
But why of two oaths' breach do I accuse thee,
When I break twenty? I am perjur'd most,
For all my vows are oaths but to misuse thee,
And all my honest faith in thee is lost.
For I have sworn deep oaths of thy deep kindness,
Oaths of thy love, thy truth, thy constancy,
And to enlighten thee gave eyes to blindness,
Or made them swear against the thing they see.
    For I have sworn thee fair: more perjur'd eye
    To swear against the truth so foul a lie.

❖   ❖   ❖

GROUP O

L'ENVOY (possibly written in 1609 for Thorpe's publication)

The final sonnet-pair is a summation of the Poet's sonnet-sequence in which the theme that underlies this personal story is sacred and profane Love, concluding with profane Love, personified by Eros, or Cupid, the little Love-god, who exerts a powerful and sometimes devastating force over human lives. In these last two sonnets the Poet ruefully describes the price of Love that he had to pay.

Sonnet 153

Cupid laid by his brand and fell asleep.
A maid of Dian's this advantage found,
And his love-kindling fire did quickly steep
In a cold valley-fountain of that ground,
Which borrow'd from this holy fire of love
A dateless lively heat, still to endure,
And grew a seething bath, which yet men prove
Against strange maladies a sovereign cure.
But at my mistress' eye Love's brand new-fired,
The boy for trial needs would touch my breast.
I sick withal the help of bath desired,
And thither hied, a sad distemper'd guest.
   But found no cure; the bath for my help lies
   Where Cupid got new fire: my mistress' eyes.

Sonnet 154

The little Love-god lying once asleep,
Laid by his side his heart-inflaming brand,
Whilst many nymphs that vow'd chaste life to keep,
Came tripping by; but in her maiden hand
The fairest votary took up that fire,
Which many legions of true hearts had warm'd,
And so the General of hot desire
Was sleeping by a virgin hand disarm'd.
This brand she quenched in a cool well by,
Which from Love's fire took heat perpetual,
Growing a bath and healthful remedy
For men diseas'd: but I, my Mistress' thrall,
   Came there for cure, and this by that I prove:
   Love's fire heats water, water cools not love.

FINIS

THE EPILOGUE

Epilogue

Touchstone: *When a man's verses cannot be understood, nor a man's good wit seconded with the forward child understanding, it strikes a man more dead than a great reckoning in a little room.* [1]

SHAKE-SPEARES SONNETS have now been submitted in their theme-groups and, where possible, in identifiable chronological contexts for critical scrutiny. It is time to assess these findings, and to ask the question: Have they passed the test to show that the story that the *Sonnets* tell is peculiarly and precisely applicable to Christopher Marlowe, the cobbler's son of Canterbury, who was marked from childhood as a genius? Briefly to summarize the evidence, we begin with the inception of the sonnet-sequence in the twenty-three year old Marlowe's first flush of fame with *Tamburlaine the Great*, when he acquired 'princely' patronage.

- the 'sugred Sonnets' to William Hatcliffe, Prince of Purpoole, at the Christmas festivities of Gray's Inn in 1587-88:

  'You live in this, and dwell in lovers' eyes'   *Sonnet 55*

- the 'beauteous and lovely youth' begins to reveal his true nature as flawed:

  'The hardest knife ill'us'd doth lose his edge.'   *Sonnet 95*

- enter the Dark Lady, the beautiful harlot with whom both Poet and 'Prince' become entangled identified by Dr Hotson as Luce Morgan – a perfect photo-fit:

  'Thou blind fool Love, what dost thou to mine eyes'   *Sonnet 137*
  'Whoever hath her wish, thou hast thy *Will*,'   *Sonnet 135*

- two political sonnets written out of his espionage experience, *Sonnets 123 and 124*, and his celebration of survival of the Armada's 'mortal moon':

  'and Death to me subscribes,
  Since spite of him I'll live in this poor rhyme.'   *Sonnet 107*

- Lord Burghley commissions 17 sonnets for the Earl of Southampton's seventeenth birthday cajoling him to marry, and finds his ideal sonneteer in his employ:

  'You had a father, let your son say so.'   *Sonnet 13*

- his sudden eclipse as London's unrivalled poet-dramatist ' ien he was apparently murdered during the witch-hunt of 1593:

> 'Even so my sun one early morn did shine,
> With all triumphant splendour on my brow,
> But out, alack, he was but one hour mine,' *Sonnet 33*

– the 'murder' at Deptford that saved his lefe but destroyed his reputation:

> 'my body being dead,
> The coward conquest of a wretch's knife,' *Sonnet 74*

– his flight into exile:

> 'I all alone beweep my outcast state' *Sonnet 29*

– his debt of gratitude to Thomas Walsingham, the true friend and Patron, who saved his life and never deserted him:

> 'A god in love, to whom I am confin'd *Sonnet 110*

– his anonymity and loss of identity:

> 'My name be buried where my body is,
> And live no more to shame nor me, nor you.' *Sonnet 72*

– his vilification and disgrace, which he is powerless to refute:

> 'Your love and pity doth th'impression fill,
> Which vulgar scandal stamp'd upon my brow,' *Sonnet 112*

– the Rival Poet, identified as George Chapman, who so perfectly fits the scenario of the Patron with his 'two poets' and completed Marlowe's *Hero and Leander:*

> 'Was it his spirit, by spirits taught to write
> Above a mortal pitch, that struck me dead?' *Sonnet 86*

– the Poet's self-identification in his contemplative sonnet recollecting his childhood as a chorister, and his youth when he had his portrait painted at the age of twenty-one with his motto, QUOD ME NUTRIT ME DESTRUIT, rendered in English in this sonnet in which he speaks about Death:

> 'As the death-bed whereon it must expire,
> Consum'd with that which it was nourish'd by.' *Sonnet 73*

Gathering the sonnets into their theme-groups has revealed something that was hitherto obscured, namely that the dominant group is that of the *Sonnets of Exile*. If these are the Poet's autobiographical poems this can only reflect Marlowe's predicament.

Surely the verdict must be: Passed with Distinction.

Without forcing the sense of a single word or phrase these autobiographical poems fall naturally into place in the story that has been unfolded, giving the whole that intrinsic quality of an autobiographical tale which has the ring of truth, even the 'bitter, frustrating, unrewarding truth' of a life not unacquainted with suffering.

In serving their author, it is gratifying that the *Sonnets* have proved such trusty guides, vindicating the method followed – listening intently to the Poet's Word – as valid for historical research in this case as in Homer's, and not some will-o'-the-wisp leading us into that dread 'Serbonian Sonnet-bog in which whole armies have been sunk'! We have not been drowned in mud, but bathed in light, often unexpectedly, knowing only that this must be the right road because every new piece of evidence slotted into the jigsaw to fill out the picture. And what a wonderful picture! A portrait of Shake-speare and his friends.

Those former nonentities, 'Mr.W.H.' and the Dark Lady, have emerged as real people, historical personalities of flesh and blood as recognizable as the Poet of the *Sonnets* himself. His true Patron, Thomas Walsingham, stands forth as a man to whom we owe a debt of gratitude for saving his Poet; and the traumatic experience concerning George Chapman and *Hero and Leander* is revealed as that authentic historical episode, long sought by the literary sleuths, which was the cause of the searing jealousy expressed in the *Sonnets of the Rival Poet* – unique in literary history.

This voyage of discovery, plotted for a distant posterity to stumble upon, has led us unerringly *via* his *Sonnets* to their hidden author, whose character, human relationships and experiences are revealed in the light of a truly remarkable life. We perceive him at last in his true colours; no longer besmirched by the base libels and misunderstandings of centuries that have obscured Christopher Marlowe. Cloaked in the mundane person of William Shakespeare of Stratford-upon-Avon he had escaped our recognition as *both* the 'Morning Star' and the noon-day 'Sun' of the greatest period of English drama; one superbly gifted poet-playwright whose dramatic output, placed end to end, reveals a momentous sweep of development from *Dido Queen of Carthage* to *The Tempest;* from *Tamburlaine the Great* to *King Lear;* from his 'Armada' play in 1588, *Edward the Third* which launched the great English history cycle, to its conclusion in the flaming destruction of the Globe during a performance of his last play in 1613, *Henry VIII* – a feast to which the critics are invited with the compliments of the Poet. A life of dramatic achievement with drama enough to enthrall all lovers of Shakespeare.

534

The honour of having led us to the real Shakespeare belongs to our 'Sherlock Holmes' of the Elizabethan age, Leslie Hotson. From his first coup in tracking down the coroner's inquisition on the death of Christopher Marlowe in 1925, following by his brilliant and highly original research in *Shakespeare's Sonnets Dated, Mr.W.H.* and *The First Night of Twelfth Night,* his has been the hand on the helm that has steered this ship safely home. Fellow academics, who have tended to view him as a maverick, will have to concede that Leslie Hotson's inspired research has indeed 'laid great bases for eternity'. Justice posthumously accords him the honour he has deserved.

This thesis, based on his work, is offered as a blue-print inviting others to follow up the exciting clues indicated that may trace the Poet's life after 1593 in greater detail. Predictably, their research will substantiate its validity, but cannot disprove it, for it is firmly anchored on the rock of the *Sonnets,* the Poet's own testimony.

> It fears not policy, that heretic,
> Which works on leases of short-numbered hours,
> But all alone stands hugely politic,
> That it nor grows with heat, nor drowns with showers.

Sonnet 124

The extraordinary events surrounding the plot for his faked murder at Deptford, and the interplay of the characters in this human drama are unfolded in his poetic diary to give us a portrait of the Poet that pulsates with life. At last we begin to *know* Shakespeare as a man of distinctive personal qualities within a historical context, and not just a nebulous genius. He suffered 'the slings and arrows of outrageous fortune', and lived a real life drama that exceeds the invention of fantasy and makes William Shakespeare, the burgher of Stratford, a figure of dull indifference. On the other hand, he is wholly credible as that solid citizen who faithfully fulfilled his protective role as one born to the part that Destiny had allocated him, as much as the Muse's Darling was born to greatness.

Cries of dismay and disbelief will doubtless greet this thesis. Shakespeare of Stratford has reigned secure for four centuries, his native town groomed and nurtured as the charmed and myth-bound centre of Shakespearean drama, and my plea is that it should ever so remain. The revelation that his role was that of front man covering the identity of the persecuted genius Christopher Marlowe will prove a severe shock to many, but, eventually, inevitably, they will come to terms with it, for the alternative is to relegate the *Sonnets* to the level of beautiful, meaningless nonsense –

> a tale
> Told by an idiot, full of sound and fury,
> Signifying nothing. [2]

The sincerity and integrity of this lovely sonnet-sequence argue eloquently against such a pusillanimous conclusion, and the consensus of informed and authoritative criticism upholds their essentially autobiographical testimony.

Academic ranks will doubtless close and powerful voices will try to dismiss this work. In reply I will concede this much. If this thesis can be proved to be flawed, I would relinquish all contention. It is for those who would dispute these findings to produce evidence that the *Sonnets* apply as precisely throughout the sequence to the life of William Shakespeare of Stratford-upon-Avon as author.

It may be feared also that Stratford-upon-Avon is threatened. Such fears are groundless. I confess to dearly loving Stratford-upon-Avon. Recently, as I sat on the banks of the Avon, I pondered its future: looking west past the Royal Shakespeare Theatre to the distant spire of Holy Trinity Church silhouetted against the setting sun, the sound of the honking geese and comfortable quacking of ducks and the regal swans adding their special grace to this supremely beautiful scene. Stratford-upon-Avon is a delightful dream celebrating the dainty plays. To disturb it would be a sacrilege. No matter if it is based on myth. That is Stratford's strength, not its weakness. Our culture thrives on myths. What is there more powerful and enduring in western culture than the rich heritage of Greek mythology? Nordic mythology inspired Wagner's immortal 'Ring'. It is the element of myth and fairy tale in the plays of Shakespeare mixed with the drama of human lives of his characters that has captivated a world-wide audience, for the marvellous plays are in many instances spun out of myth. It is entirely appropriate that the man we have revered for these 400 years since he burst upon the scene with *Venus and Adonis* should have been in essence a myth.

One might say that Stratford is itself testimony to man's infinite capacity for creating and perpetuating myth, for it is idle to pretend that doubts about William Shakespeare's authorship have never, even if dimly, assailed intelligent Stratfordians, and been assiduously concealed, dismissed, subverted in statements and books about him to maintain the myth intact. The protector of the hidden author has in turn been most carefully protected with intense loyalty and devotion. The myth-spirit has created the Royal Shakespeare Theatre built on its superb site, lapped by the rippling Avon with its cargo of swans and waterfowl, the movement of the ever-flowing river giving a sensation of being on board a ship as one sits in the Waterside Restaurant of the theatre – a charming illusion that complements the catharsis offered by the plays. A visit to Stratford-upon-Avon refreshes the soul. It fulfils a human need for us all. It is a part of our national heritage, shared by visitors from all over the world.

Nevertheless, all this beauty providing the perfect setting for the plays and homage to the genius of Shakespeare must not blind us to the historic truth, stifling our quest for discovery and knowledge, or stultifying historic research. Truth cannot hurt us. It will enhance what has been created here in myth-worship by bringing a deeper and truer understanding of the man who wrote the

536

plays, with insight into their content and message not possible before. Stratford-upon-Avon will experience a Shakespearean renaissance!

Nor is there anything to fear from Canterbury as a rival, if this is handled with vision and understanding. The ancient city of his birth will be wise to remain true to its historic tradition, as a place of pilgrimage to the beautiful Cathedral where he sang as a choirboy, leaving Stratford-upon-Avon to build yet further on its glorious dramatic heritage as the guardian of the myth. Shakespeare's theme or message in play after play is reconciliation. It is the message of Marlowe, the Canterbury shoemaker's son, who was educated for the church. His aspiration to sow seeds in the hearts of his audiences for a better world through human understanding in which reconciliation is possible, for his own world was being cruelly torn apart by warring religious-political factions, is as relevant for us today. For him the only sin was ignorance. Let us therefore also fear only ignorance, and welcome the Shakespearean renaissance.

The inexorable wheel of fortune turns despite our desire to halt it, and the dawn of a new day for Shakespeare has finally arrived. My plea is that we may greet it in a spirit of blessed Shakespearean reconciliation. My hope is that an exciting revolution concerning the image of Shakespeare will be achieved without rancour or prejudice, to accept honestly what is the historical truth about this greatest of poet-dramatists, cradled in Canterbury, Marlowe the Muse's Darling.

> Like as the waves make towards the pebbled shore,
> So do our minutes hasten to their end,
> Each changing place with that which goes before:
> In sequent toil all forwards do contend.
> Nativity, once in the main of light,
> Crawls to maturity, wherewith being crown'd,
> Crooked eclipses 'gainst his glory fight,
> And Time that gave doth now his gift confound.
> Time doth transfix the flourish set on youth,
> And delves the parallels in beauty's brow,
> Feeds on the rarities of nature's truth,
> And nothing stands but for his scythe to mow.
>   And yet to times in hope my verse shall stand,
>   Praising thy worth, despite his cruel hand.

Sonnet 60

NOTES AND REFERENCES

NOTES AND REFERENCES

PROLOGUE

Page   *Ref.*

(i)   1.   G.B. Harrison: 'Introduction': *The Sonnets and A Lover's Complaint.* Penguin Books Ltd (1938 reprinted 1949, 1955) pp.13-14

CHAPTER 1   SHAKESPEARES SONNETS: Neuer Before Imprinted

1   1.   Edward Hubler: 'Shakespeare and the Commentators', *The Riddle of the Sonnets* (1962) N.Y. p.3

2   2.   Edward Alleyn's letter d. 19th June1609. G.F. Warner: *Catalogue of MSS and Muniments of Dulwich College* (1881) MS 2, fol. 44v

     3.   Thomas Heywood: 'Epistle to the Printer', *Apology for Actors* (1612)

3   4.   Samuel Schoenbaum: *William Shakespeare: A Compact Documentary Life* (1977) OUP, Oxford and N.Y. p.268

4   5.   Francis Meres: *Palladis Tamia or The Second Part of Wits Common Wealth* (1598) Sig. Oo2v

5   6.   *Poems: Written by Wil. Shakespeare Gent.* (1640) Preface: 'To the Reader', ed. J. Benson

     7.   Logan Pearsall Smith: *On Reading Shakespeare* (1933) p. 29

     8.   C.L. Barber: 'An Essay on the Sonnets', *The Laurel Shakespeare* ed. Francis Fergusson: *The Sonnets of Shakespeare* (1960) N.Y. p. 10

6   9.   J. Leslie Hotson: *Mr.W.H.* (1964) London, pp.9-10

     10.   W.H. Auden: 'Introduction': *Shakespeare's Sonnets* ed. William Burto, Signet Classic Shakespeare (1964) p.xxxiv

     11.   Stephen Spender: 'The Alike and the Other', *The Riddle of the Sonnets* (1962) p. 93

     12.   Leslie A. Fielder: 'Some Contexts of Shakespeare's Sonnets', *Ibid:* p.82

7   13.   C.L. Barber: *op. cit.* p. 7

     14.   G.B. Harrison: *op.cit.* pp. 13-14

     15.   G.P.V. Akrigg: *Shakespeare & the Earl of Southampton* (1968) p.228

     16.   F.J. Furnivall: 'Introduction': *The Leopold Shakespeare* (1877) p.lxvi

     17.   F.S. Boas: *Shakespeare and His Predecessors.* (1896) Oxford, p.ll5

     18.   Walter Raleigh: *Shakespeare,* (1907) Oxford, p. 87f.

     19.   A.C. Bradley: *Oxford Lectures,* (1909) London. p. 330

8   20.   A.W. Schlegel: *A Course of Lectures,* trans. Black & Morrison (1846) London. p. 352

     21.   James Winny: *The Master-Mistress: A Study of Shakespeare's Sonnets* (1968) London. p. 1

Page	Ref.	
8	22.	E.K. Chambers: *Shakespearean Gleanings* (1944) London. p. 120 Winny: *op. cit.* p.4
	23.	J. Dover Wilson: *The Sonnets* (1966) Cambridge. pp.xl-xli Winny: *op. cit.* p. 7
	24.	C.L. Barber: *op. cit.* p. 10

CHAPTER 2   THE POET'S WORD

14	1.	Donald W. Foster: 'Master W.H., R.I.P.': *PMLA Vol. 102, No. 1* Jan. 1987. p.51
15	2.	*Ibid.* p. 51
	3.	*Ibid.* p. 52
	4.	*Ibid.* p. 52

CHAPTER 3   DR. HOTSON'S 'MR.W.H.'

17	1.	Donald W. Foster: *op. cit* pp. 42-52
	2.	J.L. Hotson: *Mr. W.H.* (1964) pp.150-156
18	3.	*Ibid.* pp.154-56. Hotson's decipherment is the only valid solution of this 16th century puzzle which is a classic example of an Elizabethan cryptogram. Reproduced by kind permission of Mrs Mary Peabody Hotson.
19	4.	Ibid. pp.159-61. Whilst I wholly accept Hotson's brilliant decipherment identifying 'Mr.W.H.' as Master William Hatcliffe, I part company with his attempts to persuade us that the *Sonnets* reveal the name of Hatcliffe in such verbal links as HAT...LIFE, HAT...LEAVE, or LEF ..HAT. This is clutching at straws by textual manipulations to bolster his hypothesis that 'Mr.W.H.' is the sole patron – which is Thorpe's clever 'red herring' leading us into the 'Serbonian Sonnet-bog'! This has lost him credibility and tragically obscured the validity of his research.
20	5.	*Ovid's Amores* trans., Christopher Marlowe and entitled *Elegies. Marlowe's Plays and Poems*, ed. M.R. Ridley: Everyman's Library No. 383 (1909, reprinted 1958) pp. 439-40
21	6.	Thorpe's Letter to Blount in 1600 throws a remarkable light. (See Chapter 24)

CHAPTER 4   THE BROKEN LINK

23	1.	Ralph Waldo Emerson: *Shakespeare: Essays on Representative Men*, ed. De la More (1904) pp. 27-28
	2.	Goethe: *Zu Shakespeares Namenstag* trans. J.A.C. Hildner, *Götz von Berlichingen*, 'Introduction', p. xxxiii
	3.	T. Carlyle: *'The Hero as Poet'*, ed. De la More (1904) pp. 9 and 17
	4.	S. Taylor Coleridge: *Lectures on Shakespeare and Other English Poets* (1888) p. 179
	5.	Robert Ingersoll: *Lectures and Essays (Second Series)* (1904-5) London. p. 101

Page	Ref.	
25	6.	Emerson: *op. cit.* pp. 36-7
	7.	Schoenbaum: *op. cit.* pp. 221-222
	8.	*Ibid.* pp. 232, 236, 245-247
26	9.	*Ibid.* p. 241
27	10.	J. Dover Wilson: *The Essential Shakespeare* (1967) Cambridge Univ. Press, p. 7
	11.	*Ibid.* p. 39
	12.	*Ibid.* pp. 41-2
28	13.	George Greenwood: *The Shakespeare Problem Restated* (1908) p. 18
29	14.	Schoenbaum: *op. cit.* pp. 39-40
	15.	Douglas Hamer: 'Was William Shakespeare, William Shakeshafte?' *R.E.S.* 1970. XXI, 41-8
30	16.	Anthony à Wood: *Athenae Oxonienses &c.* (1692)
	17.	E.A.J. Honigmann: *Shakespeare: the 'lost years'* (1985) Manchester Univ. Press. p.3
	18.	*Brief Lives, chiefly of Contemporaries, set down by John Aubrey between the years* 1669 & 1696. Edited from the Author's MSS by Andrew Clark. (1898) Oxford. Vol. I, pp. 96-7
31	19.	Honigmann: *op. cit.*
32	20.	J.S. Smart: *Shakespeare, Truth and Tradition* (1928) p. 196
	21.	D. Allen Carroll: 'Greene's "Vpstart Crow" Passage: A Survey of Commentary' (1985) *Research Opportunities in Renaissance Drama, XVIII.* Univ. of Kansas
33	22.	Warner: *Catalogue of MSS cit. MS I. Article 67.* Dulwich College Library. W.W. Greg ed. *Henslowe Papers* (1907) pp. 64-5
	23.	*The True Tragedy of Richard Duke of York,* Praetorius reprint of 1595 Quarto. p. 20
	24.	Ivor Brown: *Shakespeare* (1940, 2nd ed. 1951) London, p. 172
35	25.	A.D. Wraight: *Christopher Marlowe and Edward Alleyn* (1993) Presents evidence revealing Edward Alleyn as the authentic original of Greene's 'Shake-scene' diatribe, with a detailed refutation of the spurious case for William Shakespeare as Greene's hated great actor.

CHAPTER 5   THE SHAKESPEARE MYTHOS

Page	Ref.	
37	1.	Nicholas Rowe: *Life* prefacing his edition of *The Works of Mr William Shakespear: in Six Volumes* (1709) Vol. l, p.XXXIV
	2.	*Ibid.* Vol. I, p. II-III
38	3.	*Ibid.* Vol. I p. V
39	4.	*Ibid.* Vol. I, p.VIII
	5.	See Wraight: *Christopher Marlowe and Edward Alleyn,* pp.211-218
	6.	Rowe: *op. cit.* Vo. I, p.X
	7.	F.E. Halliday: *A Shakespeare Companion 1550-1950* (1952) p.155 This story emanates from Richard Davies (d.1708) a local cleric who first recorded the deer-stealing incident.

Page	Ref.	
	8.	Aubrey: *Lives of Eminent Men* (1813) Vol.II, pp.537-39
40	9.	Halliday: *op. cit.* p. 169. Dowdall's letter reporting his visit to Stratford-upon-Avon is in the Folger Shakespeare Library.
	10.	Rowe: *op. cit.* Vol. I. p.II
	11.	Schoenbaum: *op. cit.* p. 42
	12.	Halliday: *op. cit.* p. 688
41	13.	F. Schelling ed. *Ben Jonson: Timber or Discoveries made upon Men and Matter* (1892) 'Introduction' p. xii, quoting A.W. Ward
42	14.	Thomas Fuller: *Worthies of England* (1662) Warwickshire, p.126
43	15.	Schoenbaum: *op. cit.* p. 305
	16.	Thomas Heywood: *op. cit.* Epistle to the Printer.
44	17.	Ben Jonson: *op. cit.* ed. Schelling. *'De Shakespeare Nostrati'* p.23
46	18.	John Webster: *The White Devil* (1612)
47	19.	Thomas Heywood: *The Hierarchie of the Blessed Angels* (1631)
	20.	*The Hectors; or the False Challenge* (1656) p. 50 *Ben Jonson's Allusion Book* ed. J.F. Bradley & J.L. Adams (1922) p. 309
	21.	Schoenbaum: *op. cit.* p.254
48	22.	Sir George Greenwood: *Ben Jonson and Shakespeare* (1921) p. 38 Schoenbaum omits to mention this piece of documentary evidence.
	23.	*Ibid.* p. 39-40 P.R.O. *LC. 5/133.* pp. 41-51 Document 20. Answer to Cuthbert Burbage, William Burbage, Winifred Burbage to petition by Robert Benfield, Heliard Swanston and Thomas Pollard to the Lord Chamberlain, 1635.
	24.	Schoenbaum: *op. cit.* p. 231
49	25.	Henry James: *Letters*, Vol. I. p.432 (1920) Letter to Miss Violet Hunt, August 1903.
50	26.	Greenwood: *The Shakespeare Problem Restated*, (1908. Athenaeum Press London ed. 1937) pp. 50-51
	27.	Greenwood: *Ben Jonson and Shakespeare* (1921) pp. 26-27
51	28.	Greenwood: *The Shakespeare Problem Restated*, p. 63

CHAPTER 6   THE RIDDLE OF THE SONNETS ANSWERED

63	1.	Calvin Hoffman: *The Murder of the Man Who Was Shakespeare* (1955) p. viii and p. vii
65	2.	See A.D. Wraight: *The Real Christopher Marlowe: For All Those To Whom Historical Truth is of Concern.* (1992, 3rd ed. 1993) This 36-page pamphlet challenges Nicholl's book with his deliberate distortions by concealment and omission of documentary evidence to draw his defamatory picture of Marlowe as a 'poet-spy' who is 'devious', 'predatory', 'a swindler', a man given to violence, a blaspheming atheist and (of course) a homosexual. This prejudiced portrait is cunningly drawn by insinuation in a text peppered with pejorative terms (all espionage is termed 'snooping') and embellished by titillating pieces of Elizabethan gossip. The style and content are aimed at the general reader rather than the

historian who is less easily taken in by his clever thesis, for which he finally admits he has no evidence to explain the Deptford murder. Unfortunately the journalist-critics and media have fallen for the 'shocking' and sensationalist element in Nicholl's book and given him unanimous high praise,in a stupendous launch of media 'hype' and financial backing.

CHAPTER 7   THE POET IDENTIFIES HIMSELF

68   1.   John Bakeless: *The Tragicall History of Christopher Marlowe* (1942) Connecticut, USA. Vol. II, p. 208
      2.   *Ibid.* Vol. II, p. 213
      3.   *Ibid.* Vol. II, pp. 214-216
69   4.   *Ibid.* Vol. II, Chap. X, pp. 3-4
70   5.   Harry Levin: *The Overreacher* (1934) p. 24
      6.   Michel Poirier: *Christopher Marlowe* (1951) pp. 208-9
      7.   A.H. Bullen: Introduction: ed. *The English Dramatists*, Vol. I,'The Works of Christopher Marlowe', p. lxxxiv
      8.   A.C. Swinburne: *Letters on the Elizabethan Dramatists* (1910) 'Greene, Peele and Marlowe', pp. 16-17
      9.   F.S. Boas: *Marlowe and His Circle* (1929) p. 135
      10.   Edward Dowden: Introduction: *The Tragedies of William Shakespeare* (1912)
      11.   T.M. Parrott: *William Shakespeare: A Handbook* (1934) p. 121

CHAPTER 8   THE SONNET-STORY TESTED

79   1.   Discovered by R.B. Wernham: 'Christopher Marlowe at Flushing in 1592': *Historical Review*, vol. XCI (1976) pp. 344-5. Letter from Sir Robert Sidney to Lord Burghley, 26 Jan. 1592: *P.R.O. SP 84/44, f.60* (calendared in *LASP Foreign 3, No. 81*)
80   2.   Stephen Spender: *op. cit.* p. 93

CHAPTER 9   THE MUSE'S DARLING

81   1.   William Urry: *Christopher Marlowe and Canterbury*, posthumously ed. by Andrew Butcher (1988) p. 2
83   2.   *Statutes* 1541, Chapter XXVII A.F. Leach: *Educational Charters and Documents* (1911) pp. 452-469
      3.   C.E. Woodruff and H.J. Cape: *Schola Regia Cantuariensis* (1908) p. 51
      4.   Urry: *op. cit.* Appendix I, pp. 99-107
      5.   *Ibid.* pp. 42-43 The Latin funerary inscription to Sir Roger Manwood is signed 'C.M.' (Christopher Marlowe). Manwood also built almshouses at Hackington (or Hawe) near Canterbury, indicating a desire to acquire a reputation as a local philanthropist. See Wraight and Stern: *op. cit.* p. 127
      6.   For instance, the young Anthony Rushe was sent to Oxford at the

Page	Ref.	
		charge of Dean Wotton from King's, to return later as headmaster, followed by a brilliant career in the church.
		D.L. Edwards: *A History of the King's School* (1957) p. 74
84	7.	Urry: *op. cit.* pp. 47-48 and Appendix II. 'The Inventory of John Gresshop, 1580', pp. 108-122. The inventory contains a copy of *The fall of the late Arrian*, valued at 2d. A manuscript copy of this treatise belonging to Marlowe led to his arrest as a heretic and 'Atheist' in 1593.
85	8.	See Wraight and Stern: *op. cit.* p. 24 citing *The Massacre at Paris*, 11. 1209-1215, and *Edward II*, 11. 393-397 in almost identical speeches on iconoclasm.
	9.	*The Jew of Malta*, IV, 319-321
86	10.	John Nichols' *Progresses of Queen Elizabeth*, (edition 1823) Vol. I, p. 339 and f-n. From the correspondence of Bishop Parkhurst with Gualter of Zuric. The French ambassador at the time was Comte de Retz.
	11.	*Ibid.* p. 345
	12.	Michel Poirier: *op. cit.* p. 209
87	13.	Bakeless: *op. cit.* Vol. I, p. 64. John Strype: *Life and Acts of Matthew Parker, Vol. III, bk. IV, Appendix* pp. 336-337. Dr. John Parker, the Archbishop's son, administered these scholarships according to Matthew Parker's will, dated 1575, reserving the nomination of candidates to himself. *Corpus Christi Statutes &c. fols.* 56-57 and 35.
	14.	*Corpus Christi College Audit Books*, transcribed by G.C. Moore Smith: 'Marlowe at Cambridge': *M.L.R.* 4 January 1909. See Bakeless: *op. cit.* Vol. I, pp. 72-75
	15.	John Shute: *Two Very Notable Commentaries* (1562) This is dealt with further in Chapter 14.
88	16.	F.S. Boas: *Christopher Marlowe* (1940) pp. 13-15. Bakeless: *Christopher Marlowe, the Man in His Time*, pp. 334-5 gives a reprint of the Buttery Book.
	17.	The fact that Marlowe's absences coincide precisely with the period when Gilbert Gifford, the double agent in the Babington conspiracy, was resident at Rheims as sub-deacon of the church of St. Remigius is strongly suggestive that Marlowe's visit to Rheims was connected with this plot. I believe Marlowe was assigned to act as Gifford's go-between liaising with Walsingham, a task in which his youth and innocence would have been a most effective cloak.
89	18.	*MS. Acts of the Privy Council, VI*, 29 June 1587, (spelling modernized)
90	19.	PRO. *Cal State Papers relating to Scotland and Mary Queen of Scots, VIII*, 602.
	20.	Bakeless: *op. cit.* Vol. I. pp. 83-4. Bakeless names other Cambridge scholars who were similarly recruited into the government's espionage service.
	21.	Gabriel Harvey's letter to Edmund Spenser, dated 1579, the year

before Marlowe arrived at Cambridge, reports the illicit reading that was going on: 'I warrant you some good fellows amongst us begin now to be pretty well acquainted with a certain parlous book called, as I remember me, Il Principo di Nicolo Machiavelli, and I can peradventure name you an odd crew or two that are cunning in his Discorsi, in his Historia Fiorentina, and in certain Turkish discourses . . '

The Works of Gabriel Harvey, ed. A.B. Grosart, Vol. I, pp. 137-8

91   22.   Correspondence of Thomas Cely to Lord Burghley transcribed by J.K. Laughton: *State Papers relating to the Defeat of the Spanish Armada* (1894) Vol. I, pp. 262-267. *Letter ccxii, 57,* dated 17 July 1588

23.   Garrett Mattingly: *The Defeat of the Spanish Armada* (1959, reprinted ed. 1983) Jonathan Cape, London, pp. 126-7

24.   My search for a reference to Marlowe in the Chamber Accounts has drawn a blank.

25.   See Wraight: *The Real Christopher Marlowe,* pamphlet written as riposte to Charles Nicholl, pp. 9-12. Nicholl's attempt to demote Marlowe to a lowly position in government's espionage service is unsupported by any evidence, indeed is contradicted by the Privy Council's letter of commendation.

93   26.   I have revised my previous view that Marlowe probably presented his portrait to Dr Norgate's successor, Dr Copcott. Norgate was still Master at the time of Marlowe's M.A. and Marlowe had known him for six and a half years by then. He would have been the natural recipient of this gift.

27.   Wraight and Stern: *op. cit.* pp. 66-8 and 214 ff.

94   28.   Bakeless and Fleay have expressed their conviction that Marlowe must have written more plays than the seven extant works of his accredited canon.
Bakeless: *op. cit.* Vol. II, p. 207

29.   *The True History of George Scanderbeg,* was entered in the Stationers' Register, 3 July 1601, but no extant copy has surfaced to date.

30.   Wraight: *Christopher Marlowe and Edward Alleyn,* (1993) Chapter III, presents a resume of the research attributing *Edward the Third* unequivocally to Marlowe's hand, which is the subject of my forthcoming book: *Christopher Marlowe and the Armada.* (publication Spring 1995).

31.   *Arden of Faversham* is undoubtedly an early play by Marlowe. The evidence is presented in my forthcoming *Scanderbeg, the Young Marlowe.* (publication scheduled for 1995)

95   32.   Wraight: *Christopher Marlowe and Edward Alleyn,* Chap. VIII. Allison Gaw: *The Origin and Development of 1 Henry VI; In Relation to Shakespeare, Marlowe, Peele and Greene,* (1926) Univ. of Southern California.

33.   C.F. Tucker Brooke: *The Authorship of the Second and Third*

Page	Ref.	
		Parts of 'King Henry VI' (1921)
		Bakeless: *op. cit.* Vol. II, pp. 221-241
		Gaw: *op. cit.* There has never been a more thorough critical examination of the *First Part of Henry VI*. Gaw's attribution of the play mainly to Marlowe, but in a hasty collaboration with Greene and Peele cannot be faulted. Which is doubtless why it was studiously ignored by the 'new orthodoxy' of Prof. Peter Alexander.
	34.	Michael Drayton: *Epistles of Poets and Poesy* (1635)
96	35.	Wraight and Stern: *op. cit.* pp. 124-125
97	36.	Mark Eccles: *Christopher Marlowe in London* (1934) pp. 57-64 A letter from William Reynolds to Cecil describes Orrell as a follower of Essex in the 1601 rebellion where he gave full vent to his bellicose nature: 'he did run and leap in the forefront with Sir Christopher Blunt and Mr. Bushell, their weapons drawn, crying, "Saw, saw, saw, saw, saw, tray, tray." ' It was observed that Orrell held 'his neck awry'. *Historical MSS, Commission, Calendar of the MSS, at Hatfield House, XI (1906) no. 46 cf. 44 and XIV (1923) 171*
	37.	*Ibid.* p. 10. Bradley's words are quoted verbatim in the inquisition.
	38.	*Ibid.* pp. 8-9 *Chancery Miscellanea Bundle 68, file 12, no. 362* for the writ and return into Chancery of the Gaol Delivery at Newgate, quotes the coroner's inquisition on William Bradley.
98	39.	Aubrey: *Eminent Lives,* Vol. II, p. 368
	40.	Eleanor Grace Clark: *Ralegh and Marlowe* (1941) N.Y. p. 265
100	41.	George Chapman: Preface to *The Whole Works of Homer* (1598) translated by Chapman
	42.	Bakeless: *op. cit.* Vol. I, p. 135 Addit. MS. 6786 fol. 491r
102	43.	Greene's *Groatsworth of Wit:* (1592). Letter to his Quondam Acquaintance.
	44.	Nashe: 'A Private Epistle of the Author to the Printer': *Pierce Penilesse His Supplication to the Divell* (second ed. 1592) Sig. 2v. See McKerrow; Works I, p. 154
103	45.	*B.L. Harl. MS 7368* See *The Booke of Sir Thomas More,* Malone Society Reprint (1911) Sig.A
	46.	*B.L. Harl. MS 6848 ff. 188-9*
	47.	Kyd's first letter to Sir John Puckering. *B.L. Harl. MS 6849, ff.218-219ᵛ*
	48.	P.R.O. *PC 2/20 Acts of the Privy Council,* ed. J.R. Dasent, *XXIV*, p. 244
104	49.	*Ibid.* (spelling modernized)
105	50.	Charles Norman: *The Muse's Darling* (1960) p. 175)

CHAPTER 10   THE DEATH OF MARLOWE

| 106 | 1. | PRO. *Cal. State Papers relating to Scotland and Mary Queen of Scots, VIII,* 602 and 627 |

Page	Ref.	
	2.	Bakeless: *op. cit.* Vol. I, pp. 181-2, see also p. 161
	3.	Urry: *op. cit.* pp. 84-6
	4.	Eugenie de Kalb: 'Robert Poley's Movements as a Messenger of the Court, 1558 to 1601'. *R.E.S.* January 1933, pp. 13-18
		F.S. Boas: *Christopher Marlowe* (1940) pp. 268-9 and 275.
	5.	*Ibid.*
107	6.	Urry: *op.cit.* p. 86
		Boas: *op. cit.* pp. 265-6
		Bakeless: *op. cit.* Vol. I, p.157 and f-n.48 'Frizer's pardon states that the Queen was then at Kewe. Presumably she was also there at the time of the murder, but E.K.Chambers (Elizabethan Stage, IV, 108) does not give the location of the court at this time'. Urry quotes Boas as placing the Queen at Nonsuch on 8 June. Some authorities place the court at Greenwich, near to Deptford, at this crucial period. Both Nonsuch and Kewe would fall just 'within the verge'.
	7.	Wraight and Stern: *op. cit.* p. 279
109	8.	P.R.O. *Chancery Miscellanea 64.8.241b.* The coroner's inquisition trans. by J.L. Hotson: *The Death of Christopher Marlowe* (1925) Cambridge, Harvard Univ. Press.
110	9.	P.R.O. *LC 4/192.* P. 267. Hotson: *op. cit.* p. 48
	10.	Bakeless: *op. cit.* Vol. I. p. 168
111	11.	*Ibid.* p. 168
	12.	*Ibid.* p. 182
	13.	*Ibid.* p. 157 John Cory Jefferson: *Middlesex Records* I, xlv-xlvi. Original documents in the Middlesex Guildhall.
	14.	S. Tannenbaum: *The Assassination of Christopher Marlowe* (1928) N.Y. pp. 41-42 and Appendix A, 'Opinions of Medical Experts'.
112	15.	Baines' *Note:* B.L. Harl. MS 6848 fol. 185-6 (spelling modernized)
	16.	Eleanor Grace Clark: *op. cit.* p. 242
113	17.	*Ibid.* p. 280
	18.	No evidence to support a government involvement has ever been discovered. It remains mere hypothesis.
116	19.	B.L. *Harl. MS 6853, fols. 307-308* (formerly *fols. 320-321).* This note appears only on this copy for the Queen.
	20.	Urry: *op. cit.* p. 85
	21.	*Ibid.* p. 172 n. 22. The important discovery of the draft will was made by Miss Jane Apple. For the will and pedigree of Blanche Parry. See PCC *Drury 16:* BL *Lansdowne MS.62, fol. 123*
	22.	*Ibid:* P. 83. Urry gives an interesting description of 16th century Deptford.
117	23.	Charles Nicholl: *The Reckoning: The Murder of Christopher Marlowe* (1992) p. 263
	24.	Elizabeth Jenkins: *Elizabeth the Great* (1958) p. 263
118	25.	*Ibid:* p. 264

Page	Ref.	
118	26.	*Calendar of the MSS of the Marquis of Salisbury, Hatfield. Reports of Historical MSS Part II, Vol. 9 (1888) p.509; no.1171, 149/37*
	27.	Letter from the Privy Council to Cambridge Authorities: *MS Acts of the Privy Council, VI,* 29 June 1587
119	28.	G.F. Warner: *Catalogue of MSS and Muniments of Dulwich College* (1881) MS I, 27 and 29. Warrant from Charles Howard, Earl of Nottingham.
121	29.	Hotson: *The Death of Christopher Marlowe* (1925) p.27 PRO.*Chancery Miscellanea Bundle 64, File 8, No. 241a* Dr. Hotson's English Trans.
	30.	*Ibid:* pp. 37-8
122	31.	Poley's assignment to The Hague for which he was paid 30 shillings: 'To Robert Poley, upon warrant signed by Mr Vice-Chamberlain, dated at the Court the 22 day of June 1593, for carrying of letters in post for Her Majesty's special and secret affairs of great importance from the Court at Croydon, the 8th of May 1593 into the Low Countries to the town of The Hague in Holland, and for the returning back again with letters of answer to the Court at Nonsuch the 8th of June 1593, *being in Her Majesty's service all the aforesaid time:* '(Spelling modernised) Discovered by Eugenie de Kalb: *op.cit.* There is an implication here that whatever else he was up to in the period covered had the sanction of royal authority.
123	32.	C. Kuriyama's identification of Richard Baines as the man granted the rectorship of Waltham is doubtful.
	33.	The *Jew of Malta,* III F.S. Boas: 'Informer against Marlowe', T.L.S. 16: Sept. 1949
125	34.	*A Midsummer Night's Dream, III,* sc.ii,.115

CHAPTER 11   GORGON, OR THE WONDERFULL YEARE

Page	Ref.	
130	1.	Nashe: *Have with You to Saffron-Walden* (1596) *Works,* ed. McKerrow, Vol.III, p. 85
131	2.	Gabriel Harvey: *A New Letter of Notable Contents with a Strau̧ ̧e Sonet, intituled Gorgon or the wonderfull yeare* (1593) Sig. B2
132	3.	Chas. Nicholl: *op.cit:* p.64
133	4.	*Transcripts of the Stationers' Register,* ed. E.Arber, Vol.III p. 677, 1 June 1599
	5.	Nashe: *op.cit:* Works, ed. McKerrow, Vol. III, p.133
135	6.	I am indebted to Michael Rowett for his research on Harvey's Latin quotations, and for the translations.
138	7.	*Gloss* – as defined in *Reader's Digest Great Illustrated Dictionary Vol. I*

CHAPTER 12   THE PATRON: A TRIPLE PORTRAIT

141   1.   Akrigg: *op.cit:* p.28
       2.   Akrigg concedes that these first sonnets were probably a commissioned group. All the evidence points to this. Stephen Spender supports this view: 'The first seventeen sonnets are usually regarded as being outside the main series. They are so, [but then follows the fallacy which assumes they are all addressing the one patron]but they are also a kind of prelude, and throw light on the character   of the friend.' Spender: *op.cit:* p.120
       3.   Hotson: *Mr.W.H.* pp. 29-30 and pp. 136-140
142   4.   Hotson: *Shakespeare's Sonnets Dated* (1949) p. 34
144   5.   Akrigg: *op.cit.* p. 39
             Stonyhurst MSS. Angl. Vol. I, n.82 The English Jesuit Father Garnet's letter endorsed 19 Nov. 1594 contains the comment: 'The young Erle of Southampton refusing the Lady Veere payeth 5000^{li} of present payment.'
147   6.   Stephen Spender: *op. cit.* p. 112
148   7.   Hotson: *Mr. W.H.* pp. 117-8
       8.   *Ibid.* pp. 57-8
151   9.   *Ibid.* pp. 165-6
       10.   *Ibid.*
152   11.   *Ibid.* pp. 175
153   12.   *Ibid.* p. 127. Gerard Legh: *The Accedens of Armoury* (1576) p. 95
       13.   *Ibid.* p. 169
       14.   *Ibid.* pp. 182-193. Hotson cites Nichols' account of the 'Gesta Grayorum' at length.
154   15.   Dasent: *Acts of the Privy Council, New Ser. XIII* contains numerous letters signed in this style. In the Alleyn Papers there is a letter to Edward Alleyn from the Earl of Arundel, with whom Alleyn sometimes dined, which is signed: 'Yor loving frend, T. Arundel', dated 'xvijth of Septemb. 1616. Such endearments were common courtesy.
157   16.   T. Thorpe's letter to Edward Blount, prefacing his publication of Marlowe's translation of the *First Book of Lucan*, (1600)
160   17.   Hotson: *Mr.W.H.* pp. 290-291 and 295-300
161   18.   *Ibid. p.* 291
       19.   *Ibid.* p. 300
162   20.   Bakeless: *op.cit.* Vol.I. pp. 161-2 He gives an interesting account of the intelligence service of the Walsingham brothers of this generation, of whom Thomas was the youngest.
163   21.   P.R.O. *Cal. State Papers Elizabeth, 351/542, fols. 19^v, 20, 21, 23^r, 45^r* record Thomas Walsingham's employment as government courier to France; *Cal. State Papers, Foreign, 1579-80, p. 491* records payment to Thomas Walsingham of 100s. See also *Ibid. 1581-1582, p. 365; Ibid. 1583, Addenda, p. 142* de Kalb: *op.cit.* pp. 53 ff.

Page	Ref.	
163	22.	Queen Elizabeth's Letter to the Duke of Anjou is in a clerk's copy only in *Reports of the Historical Commission, Hatfield MSS Part II, 1888, Vol. 9 p. 509, 1171 dated 25 July 1582*.
	23.	F.S. Boas: *Sir Philip Sidney: Representative Elizabethan* (1955) pp. 31-33
164	24.	P.R.O. *Chancery Inq. PM. Ser. 2. Vol. 226, no. 181*
	25.	See Wraight and Stern: *op.cit.* pp. 281-2 My research has established Thomas Walsingham's age, which had long been mistakenly accepted as making him four years Marlowe's junior.
	26.	Wraight: *Christopher Marlowe & the Armada* (publication scheduled for early 1995)
166	27.	Watson's memorial eclogue *Meliboeus* (1590) was dedicated to Thomas Walsingham as the chief mourner on the death of Sir Francis Walsingham; his English translation of the poem was dedicated to Frances Walsingham, Sir Francis's only daughter, so that these two appear as son and daughter of the deceased testifying to the close family feeling that existed between Thomas and his much older cousin. In the poem Thomas is represented by the character Tityrus, whose 'words have wings at will', which outshine Watson's 'humble style', implying that Thomas was also a gifted poet.
	28.	Wraight and Stern: *op.cit.* pp. 257-8.
	29.	*Ibid.* pp. 249-282. This photographic record of the ruins of Scadbury Manor, the moat and the grounds in all their natural lush beauty was taken in 1962. These remains are no longer at Scadbury, and the grounds are administered by Bromley Council, who purchased Scadbury Park after the death of the last co-lateral descendant to own it, Major John Marsham-Townshend, in 1975.
167	30.	*Antony and Cleopatra*, II.ii. 239
	31.	Nichol's *Progresses* &c. Vol. III, p. 591. *Abstract of the present state of his Majesties Revenew, p. 35 Cal. State Papers, Domestic, 1611-1618*, p. 380, and *1619-1623*. p. 472 Wraight and Stern: *op.cit.* pp. 259-263 gives the fullest account to date on Lady Audrey Walsingham.
	32.	*Ibid.* p. 251
168	33.	The identification of George Chapman as the Rival Poet was first made by William Minto: *Characteristics of the English Poets from Chaucer to Shirley* (1885, 2nd edition 1885) pp. 221-223
170	34.	See Chapman's dedication of his play *All Fools* (1605) in which he speaks of himself as 'drown'd in dark death-ushering malancholy'. This was the temper of the man.
	35.	This passage does not occur until the 183rd line of the Third Sestiad which begins Chapman's part of *Hero and Leander*, where it is inserted incongruously, literally interrupting the narrative to express Chapman's consciousness of the fact that he is completing another's work, and he suddenly speaks in his own person addressing the original author.

Page	Ref.	
171	36.	Chapman's highly acclaimed translation of *Homer* appeared in 1598, the same year as his completion of *Hero and Leander,* giving added fuel for Marlowe's intense jealousy.
	37.	Phyllis Bartlett, ed.: *The Poems of George Chapman* (1941) Oxford. Introduction, p. 1
173	38.	*Ibid.* p. 5
	39.	Millar Maclure: *George Chapman: A Critical Study* (1966) Univ. of Toronto. p. 31
	40.	Arthur Acheson: *Shakespeare and the Rival Poet* (1903) p. 70
176	41.	D.N.B. Vol.10 p. 49 *George Chapman*
	42.	William Lyon Phelps, ed. *The Best Plays of the Old Dramatists,* (1895) London. Introduction, pp. 28-29
176	43.	J.M. Robertson: *Shakespeare and Chapman* (1917) pp.14, 18.
	44.	Maclure: *op.cit.* p.11
177	45.	D.N.B. Vol. 10, p.47. Citing Anthony à Wood: *Athenae Oxonienses* ed. P. Bliss (1813-20)
	46.	George Chapman: *The Shadow of Night* (1594) Dedicatory Epistle to Matthew Roydon

HERO AND LEANDER

183	1.	I follow Singer's edition of 1821 in his re-sequencing of lines 279-300, which on close rereading appear to have been displaced in the original printing. His editorial correction makes much better sense of these lines. Modern editors do not all follow this sequencing. (Spelling modernized).

CHAPTER 13   THE SONNETS OF EXILE

190	1.	Hotson: *Mr. W.H.* Chapter VIII, 'The Portrait of Mr.W.H.'
191	2.	*Ibid.* p. 208 Wm. Camden: *Remains &c.* (ed. 1674) pp. 366-67
	3.	*Ibid.* pp. 208-9
	4.	*Ibid.* p. 209. Allot: *Wits Theater of the Little World* (1599) p. 66
192	5.	*Ibid.* p. 211. Cesare Ripa: *Iconologie* (ed. J. Baudoin) 1698, p. 10
	6.	*Ibid.* p. 211 Harrison: *Description of Britaine* (1577) I. xx Sylvanus Morgan: *The Sphere of the Gentry* (1667) p. 3
	7.	*Ibid.* p. 211. Lyly: *Endimion.* 3.4, pp. 114-116
	8.	*Ibid.* p. 211. Bodenham: *Politeuphuia* (1597) p. 10
	9.	*Ibid.* pp. 211-12. Tilley: *Dictionary of Proverbs.* B.673
	10.	*Ibid.* p. 212. W.C. Wade: *The Symbolism of Heraldry* (1898) p. 133
	11.	Hotson: *Shakespeare by Hilliard* (1977) p. 96 Martianus Capella, I. 56
193	12.	*Ibid. p.* 96 and f-n.
	13.	*Ibid.* p. 96
	14.	*Ibid.* p. 97
	15.	*Ibid.* p. 94

Page	Ref.	
193	16.	*Ibid.* p. 94. Robert Tofte: *Laura* (1597) 3. p.22
194	17.	*Ibid.* p. 98
		Algarotti: *Saggio sopra la Pittura* (1762) p. 44

The immense value of Hotson's research in his two related theses, *Mr. W.H.* and *Shakespeare by Hilliard* has been obscured by the fact that he allowed himself to be carried away by his desire to fit William Shakespeare into the picture. He was convinced that another famous miniature by Hilliard, 'Unknown Man Clasping a Hand issuing from a Cloud', must be a portrait of Shakespeare, as a companion piece to 'Young Man among Roses'. This is a fallacy. This second *impresa* is identifiable in all aspects of its detail and likeness with the young Ferdinando Stanley, Lord Strange, briefly Earl of Derby until his tragic early death, of whom other portraits exist confirming the likeness. He was widely acclaimed as an accomplished poet (e.g. by Spenser) and was a notable *maecenas* of poets, hence his personification as Mercury. *A Pair of Hands Clasped* was the heraldic emblem of the Stanleys.

	18.	Hotson: *Mr.W.H.* p. 213
		Lucan: *De Bello Civili VIII*, pp. 485-86
	19.	*Ibid.* pp. 212-213
	20.	*Ibid.* p. 213
	21.	Lucan: *op.cit.*
	22.	Hotson: *op.cit.* p. 213
195	23.	See Chapter 10, *The Death of Marlowe.*
196	24.	Roy Strong: *The English Renaissance Miniature* (1983) p. 102
198	25.	Hotson: *Mr.W.H.* p. 214

CHAPTER 14   POET, PRINCE AND PATRON

Page	Ref.	
201	1.	A.W. Ward: *History of English Dramatic Literature* (1875, 1899) Vol. I, pp. 362-63
	2.	C.L. Barber: *op.cit.* p. 30
202	3.	*Ibid.* p. 27
204	4.	J.C. Jordan: *Robert Greene* (1915) p. 138
	5.	George Puttenham: *The Arte of English Poesie* (1589) Bk. I. Chap. XXXI
	6.	BL. *MS Addit. 22602*
	7.	Sir Robert Naunton: *Fragmenta Regalia* (1641) p. 30
206	8.	*Stationers' Registers* ed. Arber, Vol. III. pp. 316-317
208	9.	This play was registered at the *Stationers' Register* on 3 July 1601 to Edward Alde, but no extant copy is known.
	10.	John Shute: *Two Very Notable Commentaries* (1562) in which are bound the three books of Cambine's *Turkish affares* and *A Commentarie of the Warres of the Turcks made against George Scanderbeg, prince of Epirro, Sig.* U.iiii
211	11.	Wraight: *Christopher Marlowe and Edward Alleyn*, (1993) Chapter III, 'An "Armada" English History Play' gives a resumé

Page	Ref.	
		of this research to be published in my *Christopher Marlowe & the Armada* in 1995.
214	12.	*Julius Caesar*, III.ii.45
217	13.	W.H. Auden: *op. cit.* pp. xxx-xxxi
	14.	Leslie Fielder: *op. cit.* p. 88

CHAPTER 15   BEAUTY HERSELF IS BLACK

Page	Ref.	
221	1.	Hotson: *Mr.W.H.* p. 241
	2.	*Ibid.* p. 243
224	3.	*Ibid.* p. 243
	4.	*Ibid.* p. 241
	5.	*Ibid.* p. 241
	6.	*Ibid.* p. 241
	7.	*Ibid.* p. 245
225	8.	*Ibid.* p. 245
	9.	*Ibid.* pp. 244-45
226	10.	*Ibid.* p. 246
	11.	*Ibid.* p. 241
	12.	*Ibid.* p. 246
227	13.	*Ibid.* pp. 248-9
	14.	Greene's *Groatsworth of Wit*, Sig. D4. Roberto's song.
229	15.	Nichols: *Progresses*, Vol. II, 'Gesta Grayorum'. See Hotson: *Mr.W.H.* pp. 188-193
230	16.	Nichols: *op. cit.* p. 809
231	17.	*Ibid.* pp. 9-10
232	18.	John Aubrey, cited by Hotson: *op.cit.* p.250
	19.	Hotson: *op.cit.* p. 250
	20.	*Ibid.* p. 250
	21.	*Ibid.* p. 253 *K.B. 27/1336/Crown 15, Michaelmas 1595*
	22.	*Ibid.* p. 253 *Middlesex Session Rolls*, ed. J.C. Jeafferson, I. 234
	23.	*Ibid.* p. 254 *Aldermen's Court Repertories, No. 25*, p. 24
233	24.	*Ibid.* pp. 254-55 BL. *MS Egerton 2804. fol. 133ᵛ* (spelling modernized)
	25.	*Ibid.* p. 255
	26.	*Ibid.* pp. 251-2

CHAPTER 16   THREE SONNETS BY THE QUEEN'S SECRET AGENT

Page	Ref.	
237	1.	Hotson: *Mr.W.H.* p. 269
	2.	Hotson: *Shakespeare's Sonnets Dated*, pp. 4-20 This research is re-worked by Hotson in his *Mr.W.H.* to good effect, pp. 73-84 for the dating of Sonnet *107*.
238	3.	Hotson: *Mr. W.H.* p. 272

Page	Ref.	
238	4.	*Ibid.* p. 275 and f-n: 'See "November 17th" in Sir John Neale's absorbing study in his *Essays in Elizabethan History*, 1958.'
239	5.	The Geneva Bible, MDLXII, Printed at Geneva, Psalm CVII, p. 229v. Marlowe's reference would be either the Geneva or the Bishops' Bible. The Vulgate has a different numbering of the psalms.
240	6.	Hotson was unaware of this, but his extraordinary intuitive perception that informs his Elizabethan research leads him to discoveries that are valid in the light of new data discovered by others. His evidence amassed in the works cited bearing on *Sonnet 107* has fully (and unexpectedly) been endorsed by this latest discovery of Marlowe's involvement in the Armada campaign, giving the personal experience which inspired his 'Armada' sonnet.
241	7.	J.L.: *The Birth, Purpose and mortall Wound of the Romish holie League* (1589) Sig. A3^r
	8.	Hotson: *Mr. W.H.* pp. 76-8 Garrett Mattingly: *The Defeat of the Spanish Armada* (1959, 2nd. ed. 1983) pp. 166-167
242	9.	John Harvey: *A Discoursive Probleme concerning Prophesies* (1588) From the title page.
	10.	Hotson: *Shakespeare's Sonnets Dated*, pp. 12-14 *Mr. W.H.* pp. 76-83
	11.	Hotson: *Mr. W.H.* pp. 82-3 and n.
243	12.	*Ibid.* p. 77
	13.	*Ibid.* pp. 74-83
246	14.	See Wraight: *Christopher Marlowe and Edward Alleyn*, Chapter III.
250	15.	Hotson: *Shakespeare's Sonnets Dated*, pp. 21-24 and *Mr. W.H.* pp. 85-92
251	16.	Hotson: *Mr. W.H.* pp. 87-89
	17.	Bakeless: *op.cit.* Vol. I, pp.286-290
252	18.	Hotson: *Shakespeare's Sonnets Dated*, pp. 29-31 *Mr. W.H.* pp. 93-98
253	19.	Hotson: *Shakespeare's Sonnets Dated*, p. 28 *Mr. W.H.*, p. 93
254	20.	*Ibid.* p. 93
255	21.	*The Massacre at Paris.* ll. 640-654
	22.	*Ibid.* ll. 902-908
	23.	*Ibid.* l. 1040
256	24.	The Geneva Bible, Psalm XXIIII, p. 233^v

CHAPTER 17   THE POET VILIFIED AND VINDICATED

| 260 | 1. | Bakeless: *op.cit.* Vol. I. p. 124 |
| 261 | 2. | Thomas Beard: *Theatre of God's Judgement* (1597) (spelling modernized) See Wraight and Stern: *op.cit.* pp.306-7 for contemporary texts defaming Marlowe's reputation. |

Page	Ref.	
261	3.	Charles Norman: *op.cit.* p. 243
262	4.	B.L. *Harleian MS. 6848, fols. 187-189 (formerly fols. 172-174*
	5.	*'Rembraunces of wordes & matter against Ric. Cholmeley'* B.L. *Harl. MS 6848, fols 190 recto and verso. Unsigned.*
		It is not in Richard Baines's handwriting, but was obviously written by an informer doing similar work. See Wraight and Stern: *op.cit.* pp. 354-55 for facsimile and transcript.
	6.	Bakeless: *op. cit.* Vol. I, p. 133.
		Henry Foley: *Jesuits, III*, pp. 461-62
	7.	F.S. Boas: 'New Light on Sir Walter Raleigh': *Literature, 7:113*, 18 August 1900
	8.	Baines *Note:* B.L. *Harl. MS 6848, fols. 185/186.*
		See Wraight and Stern: *op.cit.* pp. 308-9 for facsimile and transcript.
263	9.	*Ibid.* Item 1.
	10.	Paul H. Kocher: *Christopher Marlowe: A Study of His Thought, Learning and Character* (1962) N.Y. Univ. of N. Carolina, p. 56, reiterated on p. 57 although this is pure hypothesis.
	11.	*Ibid.* p. 68
264	12.	*Ibid.* pp. 51-2
	13.	This is a typical attitude of Marlowe re-echoed in plays in the First Folio. See especially *Henry VI*, but also many later works.
	14.	Kocher: *op.cit.* p. 68
265	15.	These items echo the blasphemous statements against Christ found in the contemporary writings of the Jews, or cited against the Jews, Muslims and free-thinkers – anyone who was considered an enemy of the established ecclesiastical authorities – as supposedly representing their views.
	16.	Kocher: *op. cit.* p. 59
	17.	*Ibid.* pp. 52-3
266	18.	*Ibid.* p. 56
	19.	*Ibid. p.* 56
267	20.	Chas. Nicholl: *op.cit.* p. 128
	21.	*Ibid.* p. 128
	22.	*Ibid.* pp. 128-9
	23.	Thomas Lodge: *Wits Miserie and the Worlds Madnesse* cited by Kocher: *op.cit.* pp. 53-4 and f-n.
269	24.	'Rembraunces of wordes & matter against Ric. Cholmeley' B.L. *Harl. MS 6484 f. 190 recto & verso, f. 191.* See Wraight and Stern, *op.cit.* Appendix, pp. 354-5
	25.	B.L. *Harl. MS 6848 f. 188*
	26.	Kocher: *op.cit.* p. 53
270	27.	Annotations are in a copy of *Hero and Leander* owned by Henry Oxinden (1609-1670) and repeated in his Commonplace Book citing Aldrich and Fineux. See Bakeless: *op. cit.* vol. I, pp. 116-123 for an account of these records of contemporary gossip.
	28.	Kocher: *op.cit.* p. 57

Page	Ref.	
271	29.	*Ibid:* p. 33
272	30.	John Bossy: *Giordano Bruno and the Embassy Affair* (1991) p. 155
273	31.	Watson spoke fluent Italian and was a great admirer of Bruno. See Wraight and Stern: *op.cit.* pp. 123-128
274	32.	Frances A. Yates: *Giordano Bruno and the Hermetic Tradition* (1966) London, p. 249
	33.	*Ibid.* p. 254
	34.	*Ibid.* p. 290
275	35.	*Ibid.* p. 254
	36.	*Ibid.* p. 206
	37.	*Ibid.* p. 249.

Compare Yates's translation from the *Corpus Hermeticum XI* of the optimist gnosis which Bruno accepted as his own: 'All beings are in God but not placed in a place, for it is not thus that they are placed in the incorporeal faculty of representation.' Yates: *op. cit.* p. 32.

| 276 | 38. | Kocher: *op.cit.* p. 52. |

See Yates: *op.cit.* p. 197.

She shows Mornay as a preacher of reconciliation between Christian factions, who is tinged with Hermetic philosophy, but evidently he did not extend his tolerance to followers of Allah. Marlowe is remarkable for the breadth of his tolerance.

| | 39. | *Ibid.* p. 52. |

Philippe Du Plessis Mornay: *Trewnesse of the Christian Religion* (1581) Chap. XXXIII, p. 624

277	40.	Sears Reynolds Jayne: trans., ed. *Marsilio Ficino's Commentary on Plato's Symposium* (1944) Univ. of Missouri, *Studies No. 1. Vol. XIX.* p. 18. f-n cites Shorey: *Platonism*, p. 121
	41.	*Ibid.* p. 27
278	42.	*Ibid.* pp. 22-3
279	43.	Kocher: *op.cit.* p. 77
280	44.	*Ibid.* p. 101
	45.	*Ibid.* p. 137
281	46.	*Ibid.* p. 68

CHAPTER 18   A MURDERED REPUTATION

| 283 | 1. | Baines' *Note:* Item 9. Some critics have inferred from this that Marlowe was a secret Catholic. How little they have understood him! |
| | 2. | B.L. *Harl. MS 6848. fol. 154.* |

Kyd's second Letter, unsigned. (spelling modernized)

| 284 | 3. | B.L. *Harl. MS 6853, fols. 307-308* |
| 285 | 4. | This puzzle has never been satisfactorily resolved heretofore. Constance Kuriyama's study of Baines completely misreads his devious character. |

Page	Ref.	
286	5.	P.R.O. *SP 84/44, f.60. LASP Foreign 3. No. 81.*

Letter from Sir Robert Sidney, Governor of Flushing, to Lord Burghley, dated 26 Jan. 1592, reporting the apprehension of Marlowe on a charge of coining. Discovered by R.B. Wernham: 'Christopher Marlowe at Flushing in 1592' in *English Historical Review, VOL. XCI* (1976) pp. 344-5.

See Nicholl: *op.cit.* pp. 235-239 reviewing this episode. He draws the wrong conclusion regarding Marlowe's involvement at Flushing and leaves the matter hanging in the air, unresolved. Marlowe was undoubtedly working for Burghley to trace the source of the illicit coining that was going on. This is supported by the otherwise inexplicable fact that no criminal charges were brought against Marlowe for what was a capital crime, and Burghley subsequently expressed his displeasure with Sidney for troubling him by sending him further prisoners for examination. Clearly the old man was irritated by Sidney's over-zealous officiousness which had probably spoilt the plan to which Marlowe was assigned.

286	6.	Baines *Note.* Item 15.
287	7.	Tucker Brooke: *Life and 'Dido'.* (1930).
		Bakeless: *op.cit.* Vol. I. p. 84
	8.	Urry: *op.cit.* pp. 84-6. The will and pedigree of Blanche Parry revealing her relationship with Elinor Bull were discovered by Jane Apple and given to Urry.
		PCC *Drury 16:* B.L. *Lansdowne MS 62, fol. 123*
288	9.	William Hudson: *A Treatise of the Court of Star Chamber* (1792) in *Collectanea Indica, Vol. 2,* p. 19
290	10.	*Ibid.* p. 16
	11.	*Encyclopaedia Britannica:* Article 'The Court of Star Chamber' Vol. XXV, p. 795
	12.	Hudson, *op.cit.* p. 3
291	13.	*Ibid.* p. 19
	14.	*D.N.B.* Vol. 57. p.52. *Richard Topcliffe*
		citing Dodd: *Church History,* ed. Tierney, Vol. III, Appendix p. 197
	15.	*Ibid.* citing Dr. Jessopp: *One Generation of a Norfolk House.*
	16.	Sir Thomas Smith: *The Common Wealth of England* (1633) Chap. III. p.223
292	17.	P.R.O. *PC. 2/20,* p. 374
	18.	Harry Levin: *The Overreacher: A Study of Christopher Marlowe* (1953) p. 14
294	19.	Cited by Bakeless: *op.cit.* Vol. I. p. 115. Boas followed Tucker Brooke in seeing Kyd's hand in the copy of the Arrian Treatise found in his chamber. If Kyd had indeed copied this paper for Marlowe in his profession as a noverint, this would have fuelled his baneful accusations against Marlowe (now dead and unable to testify) in a desperate attempt to extricate himself from any involvement with Atheism.

Page	Ref.	
295	20.	Kyd dedicated his last work *Cornelie* (1594) to the Countess of Sussex, seeking her influence with the Earl of Sussex to take him back in his patronage, is the obvious implication, for it was the Sussex's Men who first performed *Titus Andronicus* at the Rose on 23rd January 1594, which I believe was that work on which Kyd was collaborating when they were 'writing in one chamber twoe years synce'. Kyd had no connection with Lord Strange whom critics have been assiduously promoting as Kyd's 'lord' who was so offended with Marlowe's alleged 'Atheism' that he threw him out. This is illogical, for Lord Strange himself was a member of Raleigh's free-thinking circle! Sussex, on the other hand, perfectly fits the description Kyd gives of a nobleman who was incensed at the idea of anyone espousing 'Atheism'.

	21.	B.L. *Harl. MS 6849, fols. 218-218^v* (spelling modernized). Kyd's Latin tags are here rendered in an English translation. See Wraight and Stern: *op.cit.* pp. 324-316 for facsimiles of Kyd's letters.
296	22.	*Ibid.* The Latin citation is *'Quia mortui non mordent.'*
	23.	*Ibid.*
297	24.	*Ibid.*
	25.	B.L. *Harl. MS 6848. fol. 154*
	26.	*Ibid.*

CHAPTER 19   THE DISTORTED IMAGE

Page	Ref.	
300	1.	Charles Norman: *op. cit.* Foreword, p. xiv
	2.	Bakeless: *op. cit.* vol.I. p.113
301	3.	This episode was recorded by Henslowe in his letter to Edward Alleyn dated 26 Sept. 1593. See Wraight: *Christopher Marlowe and Edward Alleyn*, p. 347
	4.	Ben Jonson: *Conversations with Drummond of Hawthornden* ed. David Laing (1842) Published for the Shakespeare Society.
	5.	Akrigg: *op.cit.* pp. 104-5
	6.	Eccles: op. cit. p. 105. *Middlesex Session Roll. 309. no. 13*
	7.	Schoenbaum: *op. cit.* pp. 198-200. Halliday: *A Shakespeare Companion 1550-1950* (1952) p. 691. Discovered by Hotson.
302	8.	Urry: *op.cit.* p. 67 and Appendix IV, pp. 130-1. Discovered by William Urry in the archives of the Library of the Dean and Chapter of Canterbury.
	9.	*Ibid.* p. 66 and Appendix IV.
	10.	*Ibid.*
303	11.	*Ibid.* pp. 66-67
	12.	*Ibid.* p. 66
304	13.	*The Massacre at Paris*, ll. 626-630
	14.	Urry: *op.cit.* pp. 67-8. See Ref. 16 in 'Notes and References', p. 169 *CCAL BAC J/b/392.* 'Nower'
305	15.	*Ibid.* p. 68

Page	Ref.	
305	16.	*Ibid.* p. 68
306	17.	*Ibid. p.* 98
	18.	*Ibid.* p. 90
307	19.	George Peele: *Honour of the Garter* (1593)
	20.	Thomas Thorpe: Dedicatory Letter to Edward Blount, prefacing Marlowe's translation: *First Book of Lucan* (1600)
	21.	J.M.: *The New Metamorphosis* (c. 1600-15). B.L. *Addit. MS 14824, Vol. I. Pt. I. fol. 39*
	22.	Michael Drayton: *Epistles of Poets and Poesy* (1635)
	23.	Tucker Brooke: *Life &c.* p. 51
	24.	J.H. Ingram: *Christopher Marlowe & His Associates* (1904). Preface, p. vii and p. ix
308	25.	Boas: *Marlowe and His Circle* (1929) pp. 70-1
	26.	*Ibid.* p. 76
	27.	*Leycesters Commonwealth*, ed. 1641. p. 86
309	28.	Bakeless: *op.cit.* Vol. I. p. 158
	29.	S.A. Tannenbaum: *The Assassination of Christopher Marlowe* (1942) pp. 41-43
310	30.	*Sonnet 115.* To Walsingham, the true friend and Patron.

CHAPTER 21		CANTERBURY TALES
321	1.	Urry: The 'Foreword'to Wraight and Stern: *op.cit.* p. vii
	2.	Boas: 'Informer against Marlowe' in *T.L.S.* 16 Sept. 1949
322	3.	Urry: *op. cit.* Introduction by Andrew Butcher, pp. xxxii-xxxiv. Discovered by Wm. Urry in the archives of the Library of the Dean and Chapter of Canterbury Cathedral, given in Dr Urry's transcript and translation.
	4.	*Ibid.* 'Introduction' ed. Andrew Butcher, p. xxxii-xxxiii
323	5.	*Ibid.* p. xxxiii
	6.	*Ibid.* p. xxxii
	7.	The late Mr Thomas Bushell, Vice-president of the Men of Kent and Kentish Men and Chairman of The Marlowe Society which he was instrumental in founding in 1955, told me of this Kentish legend, but I have not been able to trace it.
325	8.	Bakeless; *op.cit.* Vol. I, pp. 24-25. *MS Accounts 1502-1602. vol. XVI, fol. 11; Roll of the Freemen of Canterbury.* Discovered by Bakeless.
	9.	E.H.C. Oliphant: *Shakespeare and His Fellow Dramatists* (1924) comments on this prejudiced view: 'We are told that Marlowe was destitute of humour. Was he? No one can say. Had a comedy from him come down to us, we might be able to express a definite opinion.' Vol. I. p.33
326	10.	Urry: *op. cit.* 'Introduction' ed. Andrew Butcher. pp. xxxiv-xxxv
329	11.	The First Folio; Histories: fol. 138, 1.2401. *The Norton Facsimile* ed. Charlton Hinton (1968) p. 493. The misreading by editors of Shakespeare's works of Chartam, clearly so printed in the First

Page	Ref.	

Folio, as Chatham, reflects a suggestive evasion of a close association with Canterbury.

334   12.   Urry: op. cit. p. 2

13.   Garrett Mattingly: *op.cit.* p. 137

14.   'Mr Morley' was Burghley's messenger mentioned in a letter to Burghley from Utrecht, October 1587. Was this Marlowe?
Cal. State Papers, Domestic, Elizabeth, Addit 1580-1625, p. 217.
Original in *Vol. XXX, no. 43, fol. 100, 2 Oct. 1587 SP. 15/30.*
Nicholl: *op.cit.* pp. 339-340 dismisses this as being inconclusive, but is unable to provide evidence to negate it.
A 'Mr Marlin' was messenger for Sir Henry Unton, English ambassador accompanying Henry of Navarre in 1591-2, which is a far more interesting association in which to find Marlowe, but Nicholl does not mention it, probably because he would find it hard to dismiss.
See Joseph Stevenson: *Correspondence of Sir Henry Unton, Knt.* Roxburgh Club, no. 64, p. 388.
Ethel Seaton: 'Robert Poley's Ciphers'. R.E.S. 7: 146 (1931)
P.R.O. *Declared Accounts, E 351/342, fol. 125^v*

337   15.   Urry: *op.cit.* pp. 65-66

342   16.   *Stationers' Register, Vol. III*, p. 57

343   17.   The relationship of *The Taming of the Shrew* to the old play of the Pembroke's Men called *The Taming of A Shrew* presents a challenge calling for further research in the light of the present thesis. The latter is a shorter, inferior play which is chiefly remarkable for the lengthy passages of blank verse which are brazenly plagiarizing *Tamburlaine* and *Faustus*. Is this why Marlowe decided to rewrite it and make it authentically his own play?

CHAPTER 22   ENTER WILLIAM SHAKESPEARE

350   1.   *D.N.B.* Vol. 58, p. 189

2.   *Stationers' Register, Vol. II*, p. 511. 24 Dec. 1588

351   3.   Frances Yates: *The Rosicrucian Enlightenment* (1972, paperback ed. 1986) p. 216

4.   Wraight and Stern: *op.cit.* pp. 257-8

354   5.   Akrigg: *op.cit.* gives a very full account of this incident.

358   6.   Henslowe's Letter to Edward Alleyn, dated 28 Sept. 1593. Warner: *Catalogue, MSS I. 14.*
Wraight: *Christopher Marlowe and Edward Alleyn*, p. 347

7.   Nicholas Rowe: *op.cit.* vol. I, p.VI

8.   *Chamber Accounts, 1595. P.R.O. E.351/542. m.207d*

359   9.   Halliday: *op.cit.* pp. 162-3

360   10.   *Henslowe's Diary* ed. E.A. Foakes and R.T. Rickert (1981) Cambridge, p. 21, fol. 8v

362   11.   *Ibid.* pp. 21-22, fol. 9

12.   *Ibid.* pp. 21-22, fols. 9 and 9v

Page   Ref.

CHAPTER 23   THE ITALIAN YEARS

365   1.   Edward Dowden, ed. *The Warwick Shakespeare:* The Comedies (1893) London. Introduction to *The Two Gentlemen of Verona*, p. 80

2.   Henry of Navarre, at whose court *Love's Labour's Lost* is imaginatively set, represented the chivalric hero of the Protestant cause on whom was fixed the hope that he would make possible a religious conciliation under a liberal French monarchy. Frances Yates in her *Astraea: The Imperial Theme in the Sixteenth Century* (1975) develops a wonderful insight into the symbolic themes of Shakespeare's plays, in which he was 'deeply concerned with monarchy' and with the 'imperial theme' of the good monarch who would bring justice to the people. She poses the question:'Was the imperial theme, for Shakespeare, not only national but also religious, in a Dantesque sense?' Then makes the comment, 'Shakespeare's treatment of the Astraea image . . leaves him with the eternal question mark against his name.' *op.cit.* p. 76

366   3.   Boas: *Christopher Marlowe*, p. 235

4.   Sir Sidney Lee: *Shakespeare and the Italian Renaissance*, The British Academy: The Annual Shakespeare Lecture (1915) p. 21

367   5.   *Ibid.* p. 22

6.   Ernesto Grillo: *Shakespeare and Italy* (1949) p. 144

7.   *Ibid:* p. 141

8.   *Ibid:* p. 136

9.   *Ibid:* pp. 97-98

10.   *Ibid:* p. 126

368   11.   *Ibid:* p. 135

12.   *Ibid:* p. 137

13.   *Ibid.*

369   14.   *Ibid:* pp. 125, 126-7

15.   *The Winter's Tale*, V.ii. 93-98

16.   Sidney Lee: op.cit. p. 23

370   17.   Hotson: *The First Night of Twelfth Night* (1954) pp. 44-45 *Bibl. Vat. Cod. Ottobon. lat. 2694*, as printed by J.A.F. Orboan, 'Un viaggio di Clemente VIII nel Viterbese' in *Archivi della R. Societa romana di storia patria, XXXVI (1913)*, 143-4

371   18.   Hotson: *op.cit.* p. 39

372   19.   *Ibid.* The Orsini Archives, formerly in Rome in the Archivio Storico Capitolino, have since been moved and split up, some to the University of California, Los Angeles (UCLA)

375   20.   Thomas Birch: *Memoirs of the Reign of Queen Elizabeth*, (1754) Vol. I 95 ff. Standen eventually returned to England and was given a knighthood.

376   21.   *Ibid.* p. 443. Birch gives this reference as *Vol. IX, fol. 139* but I have not been able to trace it in the Bacon Papers in Lambeth Palace Library.

Page	Ref.	
	22.	*Ibid. Vol. X. fol. 123.* The same applies.
377	23.	Ibid. pp. 443-444
CHAPTER 24		THORPE WRITES A LETTER
378	1.	Hotson: *The First Night of Twelfth Night* (1954) is the brilliant result of Hotson's discovery of the misdating by one year of the documents recording the visit of Don Virginio Orsino, Duke of Bracciano to the court of Queen Elizabeth on 6th January 1601.
	2.	Eleanor Grace Clark: *Ralegh and Marlowe* (1941)
381	3.	*Stationers' Register*, Vol. V, p. 200
	4.	*Ibid.* Vol. III. pp. 164-65
	5.	*Ibid.* Vol. III, p. 37
	6.	*Ibid.* Vol. III, pp. 169-70
	7.	*Ibid.* Vol. III. p. 37
	8.	See the Quartos of *Henry V* (1600) and *Much Ado* (1600)
382	9.	Hotson: *Mr. W.H.* p. 149
	10.	*Ibid.* 149
	11.	*Ibid.* p. 149
	12.	*Ibid.* p. 149
383	13.	*As You Like It*, III.iii. 9-13
CHAPTER 25		A GRAND FLORENTINE WEDDING
385	1.	Hotson: *The First Night of Twelfth Night*, p.38
386	2.	*Ibid.* p. 49. See pp. 54-55 for a description of this *dramma per musica* according to Bentivoglio.
	3.	*Ibid.* p. 48
	4.	*Ibid.* p. 55
387	5.	*Ibid.* p. 61. P.R.O. *Newsletters SP. 101/9/264*
	6.	*Ibid.* p. 51. The whole of Hotson's absorbing Chap. II, 'Orsino' is exemplary historical reportage.
388	7.	*Ibid.* pp. 52-2
	8.	*Ibid.* pp. 61-2 *SP. 78/44/352.* Winwood's letter, dated 20 Nov. from Lyons to 'his chief, Sir Henry Neville, on leave in London.'
389	9.	*Historical MSS Comm.,Third Report, app. 51b.* Hotson: *op. cit.* pp. 14-16 and Chapter I, 'On the Track'.
	10.	Hotson: *op.cit.* p. 49
	11.	*Ibid.* p. 208. Orsino's letter to his Contessa dated 18 (8) January 1600(1601): 'This morning I am invited to the house of the Cecils.'
	12.	*Ibid.* p. 54. The Contessa was present at the wedding festivities and lavish entertainments in Florence, where Don Virginio 'cut a brilliant and central figure with his Duchess Flavia'.
	13.	*Ibid.* pp. 58 and 64 Don Virginio wrote twice to the Grand Duke appraising him of his plan to visit Elizabeth, to no avail.
	14.	Sir Ralph Winwood's letter cited, dated 20 November 1600.
390	15.	Hotson: *op. cit.* p. 63

Page	Ref.	
390	16.	*Ibid.* p. 184. Orsino's letters are printed in Italian in the Appendix of 'Original Documents'.
	17.	*Ibid.* p. 184

CHAPTER 26   'THE FIRST NIGHT OF TWELFTH NIGHT' BY LESLIE HOTSON

391	1.	*Ibid.* p. 21
		H.M.C. Report, Appendix 244, Marquis of Ripon MSS.
392	2.	*Ibid.* p. 22
	3.	Mikulin's report to his Tsar is careful to colour the events to obscure anything that might be interpreted as a slight to his dignity. When the Queen walked with Orsino she sent Mikulin ahead to lead the procession with Garter King-of-Arms. Hotson: *op.cit.* pp. 191 and 199.
	4.	Orsino reported to his Contessa: 'it being the custom in Muscovy that if he [Mikulin] had not been seen eating in the Queen's presence, his Great Duke would have had him beheaded.' Hotson: *op.cit.* p. 200
	5.	*Ibid.* pp. 184-5
	6.	*Ibid.* p. 191
	7.	*Ibid.* p. 194
	8.	*Ibid.* p. 201. Orsino must have observed the Queen's handwashing before she commenced eating, as was her wont, for later he retired to eat his own meal next door. Mikulin reports on her handwashing after the meal, which was again performed with great ritual.
393	9.	*Ibid.* pp. 19-20
	10.	*Ibid.* pp. 185-6
	11.	*Ibid.* p. 134
	12.	*Ibid.* p. 135.
	13.	*Ibid.* p. 135
	14.	*Ibid.* p. 67
	15.	*Ibid.* p. 202. Orsino wrote to his Duchess: 'I stood ever near Her Majesty, who bade me cover, and withal caused a stool to be fetched for me; and although she willed me a thousand times to sit, I would however never obey her. She conversed continually with me.'
	16.	Other sources have been proposed, but these all go back to Bandello's *Novella*, which in turn is based on the popular Siennese comedy, *Gl' Ingannati*.
	17.	*Twelfth Night*, I.ii. 24-34
395	18.	*Ibid.* I.ii. 45-46
	19.	*Ibid.* V.i. 215-216
	20.	Hotson: *op.cit.* p. 42
	21.	*Ibid.* pp. 151-2

Page	Ref.	
395	22.	*Ibid.* pp. 151-2.
		Nashe: 'Bargalus, the strong Illyrian pirate' and 'Their riotous neighbours, the Illyrians'. Nashe's *Works* ed. McKerrow, 3. p. 367. In *Twelfth Night,* Antonio is described as that 'notable pirate' and 'salt-water thief'. (V.ii. 62)
396	23.	*Twelfth Night,* I.iii. 36-40
	24.	*Ibid.* line 18.
	25.	Hotson: *op.cit.* p. 115
	26.	*Twelfth Night,* I.iii. 39
	27.	The First Folio has 'castigliano vulgo' which I have followed. Hotson renders this as 'volgo' giving a slightly different interpretation: 'I'm thinking of the castilian'. *(op.cit.* p. 115)
	28.	Hotson: *op.cit.* 115
	29.	*Ibid.* pp. 115-116
397	30.	*Twelfth Night,* I.iii. 120-125
	31.	*Ibid.* III.ii. 58-61
	32.	Hotson: *op.cit.* p. 115
	33.	*Twelfth Night,* I.iii. 79-81
	34.	Hotson: *op.cit.* pp. 149-150
	35.	*Ibid.* p. 150
	36.	*Ibid.* p. 150, f-n.
398	37.	*Ibid.* pp.99-100
	38.	*Ibid.* p. 103.
		Letters printed by Lady Newdegate-Newdigate: *Gossip from the Mumiment Room* (1877).
	39.	The text of *Twelfth Night* so precisely confirms Hotson's identification of Lord Knollys as the eminent original who is lampooned that it can hardly be doubted. Other identifications have been suggested, but the name Malvolio in derivation from these has no relation to the text of the play and is by comparison superficial.
399	40.	*Twelfth Night,* II.iii. 109-110
	41.	Hotson: *op.cit.* p. 109.
		L'Estrange's *Jest Book* (1650)
	42.	*Twelfth Night,* II.iii. 84-85
	43.	*Ibid.* line 113
	44.	*Ibid.* II.v. 102-103
	45.	*Ibid.* II.v. 126-127
	46.	Hotson: *op.cit.* p. 166
400	47.	*Ibid.* p. 166.
		Citing R.C.: *The Time's Whistle* (E.E.T.S. 1871) p. 117
	48.	*Ibid.* p. 166 and f-n.
	49.	*Ibid.* p. 167
	50.	*Ibid.* p. 108
	51.	*Ibid.* p. 108
401	52.	*Ibid.* p. 106 and f-n
	53.	*Twelfth Night,* II.v. 180
	54.	Hotson: *op.cit.* p. 113

Page	Ref.	
402	55.	*Ibid.* p. 155
	56.	*Ibid.* p. 155
	57.	*Ibid.* p. 153
	58.	*Ibid.* p. 154.
		George Chapman: *Alphonsus, Emperor of Germany.*
		T.M. Parrott ed. *The Tragedies of George Chapman* (1910) p. 699
	59.	*Twelfth Night,* I.iv. 25-26
	60.	Hotson: *op.cit.* pp. 129-130
403	61.	*Ibid.* pp. 136-140.
		Hotson sets the scene in superbly satisfying detail.
	62.	*Ibid.* p. 139.
		Twelfth Night, III.i. 131
	63.	*Ibid.* line 25
404	64.	*Ibid.* IV.ii. 20-41
	65.	Hotson: *op.cit.* p. 145
	66.	*Ibid.* p. 145
	67.	*Ibid.* pp. 189-190
	68.	*Ibid.* p. 147
405	69.	*Twelfth Night,* I.v. 201-214
	70.	Hotson: *op.cit.* p. 180
406	71.	*Twelfth Night,* II.iv. 1-2
	72.	Hotson: *op.cit.* p. 181
	73.	*Ibid.* pp. 167-172
407	74.	*Ibid.* p. 168
	75.	*Ibid.* p. 168.
		King Lear, III.ii. 74-77

CHAPTER 27		THE ELIZABETHAN ENCHANTMENT
409	1.	Hotson: *op.cit.* 'Original Documents', pp. 229-230
	2.	*Ibid.* p. 199
410	3.	*Ibid.* p. 201
	4.	*Ibid.* p. 201
	5.	*Ibid.* pp. 201-202
	6.	*Ibid.* p. 202
	7.	*Ibid.* p. 181
	8.	*Ibid.* p. 201.
		Orsino's letters give an intensely alive view of the brilliance of Queen Elizabeth's court, noting every detail. He wrote to his Duchess: 'there was a music of some instruments to my belief never heard in Italy, but miraculous.' His love of music is reflected in the character of Orsino in the play.
	9.	The felicitous opening lines of *Twelfth Night.*
411	10.	Hotson: *op.cit.* p. 203
	11.	*Ibid.* p. 204
	12.	*Ibid.* p. 210
412	13.	*Ibid.* p. 210

Page	Ref.	
412	14.	*Ibid.* pp. 210-211
	15.	*Ibid.* p. 212.
		John Chamberlain's letter to Dudley Carlton.
		P.R.O. *State Papers, Domestic. SP. 12/278/223*
	16.	*Ibid.* p. 218
	17.	*Ibid.* p. 217
413	18.	*Ibid.* p. 218
	19.	J.E. Neale: *Queen Elizabeth I* (1934) p. 377
	20.	*Ibid.* p. 376
	21.	Hotson: *op.cit.* p. 219.
		Elizabeth's letter to Tsar Boris Godunov.
		P.R.O. *State Papers, Russia SP. 91/3/160*
	22.	*Ibid.* p. 220

CHAPTER 28   RETURN FROM EXILE

414	1.	Hotson: *op.cit.* p. 180
	2.	*Ibid.* p. 179
	3.	*Ibid.* p. 179
	4.	*Ibid.* p. 179
	5.	*Ibid.* p. 180
	6.	*Ibid.* p. 180
415	7.	*Ibid.* p. 179
	8.	*Ibid.* p. 62.
		SP. 78/44/352
	9.	*Ibid.* p. 63.
		SP. 78/44/354
	10.	*Ibid.* p. 180
416	11.	*Ibid.* pp. 182-83
	12.	*Ibid.* pp. 95-97
417	13.	*Ibid.* p. 98
	14.	*Twelfth Night,* I.v. 242-246
	15.	Hotson: *op.cit.* pp. 124-125.
		Twelfth Night, V.i. 91
419	16.	*Ibid.* pp. 217-218
420	17.	Nichols: *Progresses &c.* Vol. II.
		Under the heading 'Ambassador from the Emperor of Russia, 1600'.
	18.	Hotson: *op.cit.* pp. 19-20
	19.	*Ibid.* p. 185
	20.	*Ibid.* pp. 185-86
		Mikulin's costume described
421	21.	Nichols: *op.cit.* Vol. III, pp. 453-454.
		In July 1600 the Queen gave Lady Audrey Walsingham a purse of gold. This was no doubt as christening gift on the birth of her son, little Thomas.
	22.	*Ibid.* p. 454
423	23.	*Twelfth Night,* II.v. 141-142

Page   Ref.

THE THEMES OF THE SONNETS ANALYSED

432   1.   C.L. Barber: *op.cit.* p. 13
        2.   *Ibid.* pp. 13-14

GROUP C   FIRST LOVE (1587-88)

451   1.   *Edward III*, I.ii. 125-166
        2.   *Tamburlaine, Part One*, I.ii. 106-108
452   3.   In *Edward III* when the besotted King is describing to his courtier
                Lodowick how he must write his poem to the Countess, with whom
                Edward is so desperately in love, he also repeats the word 'more'
                four times in four consecutive lines that build a mounting crescendo
                in passionate praise of her beauty. This play was written at the time
                when he had just fallen in love with Luce Morgan, and had been
                writing his love sonnets to her. Is the repetition of 'more' in
                Edward III more than mere coincidence?
                See Hotson: *Mr. W.H.* p. 252
        4.   *Ibid.* p. 250
453   5.   *Ibid.* p. 250.
                Verses to Thomas Morley's *Madrigalls.* . 1594.

GROUP F   THE SONNETS OF EXILE (1593-1600 ?)

478   1.   Schoenbaum: *op.cit:* pp.275-6 with facsimile entry from Stonley's
                Diary Account Book, 1593.
                Folger Shakespeare Library *MS V a.460. f.9*
487   2.   Hotson: *Mr.W.H.* p. 142
490   3.   *The Glasgow Herald,* 28 May 1988, 'Weekender' p. 10

GROUP H   TO THE TRUE PATRON

496   1.   Allison Gaw: *The Origin and Development of 1 Henry VI: In
                Relation to Shakespeare, Marlowe, Peele and Greene* (1926)
                Univ. of S. California

        EPILOGUE

531   1.   *As You Like It, III. iii. 9-13*
534   2.   *Macbeth,* V.v. 26-28

INDEX

Davenant, Sir William, 37, 38, 39
Davies, John, 233
Davies, Rev. Richard, 39
Davison, Francis, 452
De Bry, 351
Dekker, Thomas, 35, 46
Deptford, 64, 74, 104; assignation at Dame Bull's house, 106-9; 111, 114, 115; its singular situation, 116; mentioned in writ of *certiorari* 120-1, 124, 125, 131; departure by ship from, 184; Marlowe's death at, 260-1; Baines' Note, 284; Bradley affray linked with, 301; Deptford inquisition credited, 305; cf. *Measure for Measure*, 340; private performance of Jew, 345; disgrace of Deptford, 472; 352, 374, 383, 348
Derby, Earl of, (Lord Strange), 79, 285, 361
De Vere, Elizabeth, 39, 142-5, 465
Devereux, Lady Penelope, 3
Dido,-Queen of Carthage, 88, 94, 210, 534
Digges, Leonard, 4
Dionysius the Aeropagite, 278
Dorset, Countess of, 40
Dorset, Richard, Earl of, 232
Dowden, Edward, *The Tragedies of William Shakespeare*, (1912), 67, 70, 365
Dowland, John, 410
Doux, Monsieur le,375-7
Drake, Sir Francis, Vice-Admiral, 240, 287, 410
Drayton, Michael, 40, 79, 95, 200, 307
Droeshout, Martin, 4, 26
Dunn, Douglas, 490
Du Plessis Mornay, 276
Durrell, Canon William, 330
Dyce, Alexander, 67

Earl of Derby's Men, 359, 361
Earl of Oxford's Men, 94, 20
Earl of Pembroke's Men, 3
Earl of Sussex's Men, 359, 360-1
Earl of Worcester's Men, 30
Edmondes, Richard, 322, 324
Edward the Second, 31, 95, 139, 209-10, 289
Edward the Third, 94, 211-3, 218, 246-8, 246-8; cited in *Sonnet 94*, 448, 534

Eggenberg (Eckenberg), Prince of Austria, 135
Eliot, George, 50
Elizabeth I, 44-5; progress to Canterbury, 86; the Babington plot*, 88-90, 164-5, 256; and Raleigh, 101, 119, 204, 289, 486; her Court, 105, 153-4; at Nonsuch, 106, 116; her religious views, 102-3, 117; her pardon of Watson, 110; her character and attitudes, 117-20; Elinor Bull's connexion, her 'family' at Court, 116, 127; her diplomacy with her suitor Alençon, 118, 163-4, 253; *writ of certiorari*, 120-2; stigmatized as heretic, atheist, bastard, 122; the 'Phoenix', 135; and Essex*, 144, 243, 418; her childhood, 151, 413; Thomas Walsingham* her envoy, 96, 163-4; her visit to Scadbury, 166-7; and Lady Walsingham, 167; her personal colours, 192, 401; her appreciation of humour, 200; her music, 226, 238, 406, 410; her Ladies, 226, 526; at Gesta Grayorum, 230; the Armada*, 242-3, 243, 238, 287; her 'Armada' portrait, 238; Baines' Note delivered to her, 285; Orsino's visit, 390, 392, 394, 402-3, 405-6, 409-11, 412; Pope Sixtus V's admiration for her, 371; Essex's rebellion, 413
Emerson, Ralph Waldo, 23-4, 138
Essex, Robert Devereux, 2nd Earl of, 3; friend to Spenser, 41; friend to Southampton, 144; Chapman's patron, 170, 173; recited psalms at his execution, 237; and the Star Chamber, 290; his marriage to Frances Walsingham, 243, 353; Bacon in his service, 374-6; his rebellion and treachery, 413
Eusebius, *Ecclesiastical History*, 265
Every Man in his Humour, 381
Falconer, Prof. A.F., *Shakespeare at Sea* (1964), *A Glossary of Shakespeare's Sea and Naval Terms, including Gunnery* (1965), 249
Farmer, Richard, 67
Faustus, Doctor, 94, 102, 251, 274, 279, 363
Feake, James, 111
Fei, Emilio, 390
Ferguson, Francis, 432

Ficino, Marsilio, 216, 277-8; *Theologia Platonia de Immortalitae Animae* (1482), 277; *Liber de Vita* (1489), 278; *Apologia*, 278; *Dialogues*, 278; *Enneads*, 278; *Commentary on the Symposium*, 278; his Careggian Academy, 278-9; his influence, 279-80

Field, Henry, 35

Field, Richard (son), 350-2, 354, 364, 478

Fielder, Leslie A., 6, 21

Fitton, Mary, 140, 398, 416, 420

Flasket, J., 387

Fleay, F.G., 67

Fleet Prison, 140

Fletcher, John, 41, 46

Folger Shakespeare Library, 168, 248

Fontana, Domenico, 250

Ford, John, 47

Fortune Theatre, 35

Foster, Donald W., Acknowledgements (v), 14, 15, 17

Freemasons, The, 72, 140, 288, 361, 374, 510; First Folio published by, 352

Frisius, Gemma, 100

Frizer, Ingram, Thomas Walsingham's servant, 74; his part in Marlowe's death, 88, 106-11, 113-5, 123-4, 130, 195; 295, 298, 309, 372; the coroner's inquisition, 109, 300, 309

Frobisher, Sir Martin, 240

Frye, Northrop, 20

Fulbecke, William, 195

Fuller, Thomas, *Worthies of England* (1662), 42

Furnival, F.J., 7

Galileo, 113

Gaw, Dr. Allison, *Origin and Development of I Henry VI:In Relation to Shakespeare, Marlowe, Peele and Greene* (1926), 31, 67, 96, 359

Gawdy, Philip, 233

Gesta Grayorum, 153, 229, 231

Gibbons, Orlando, 410

Gifford, Gilbert, 89

Gilbert, Gifford, 289

Globe Theatre, 48

Goethe, 24, 138

Gorge, Edward, 415

Gorgon, or the wonderfull yeare, (see Harvey*, Gabriel), 129-138

Grant White, Richard, 67

Gray's Inn, 17, 146-8, 153

Greene, Robert, 24, 32; his *Groatsworth of Wit* (1592) and "Shake-scene", 32-6, 102; his Letter, 35; his envy of Marlowe, 78, 95, 102; his dying confession, 102; lampoons Harvey, 130; *Never Too Late* (1590), 203 and J.C. Jordan's comments on it, 203-4; lampoons and attacks Marlowe and Alleyn, 246, 293, 359; his charge of Atheism against Marlowe, 260, 346

Greenwood, George (Sir Granville), *The Shakespeare Problem Restated* (1908), 49; *Is there a Shakespeare Problem?* (1916), 49; *Ben Jonson and Shakespeare* (1921), 49; 49-51

Gregory XIII, Pope, 193

Gresshop, Dr. John, 84

Greville, Fulke, 274

Grey, Lady Jane, 237

Grey, Lord, 301

Griffin, James, Acknowledgements (v)

Grillo, Professor Ernesto, 367-9

Groatsworth of Wit (1592) (see Greene*, Robert), 32-6, 102, 260

Guise, Duke of, 135, 241, 254-5

Hakluyt, Richard, *The Principal Navigations, Voyages and Discoveries of the English Nation* (1589), 96

Hales, Robert, 406

Hall, Dr. John, 4

Hallam, Henry, 67

Halliday, F.E., 359

Hamer, Douglas, "Was William Shakespeare, William Shakeshafte?" (1970), 30, 31

Hariot, Thomas, mathematician and astronomer, 79, 98, 100; Chapman's dedication, 176; Marlowe's friend, 263, 270, 296, 307-8; his love of tobacco, 289; *The New Found Land of Virginia* (1590), 351; a free-thinker, 361

Harrington, tr: *Orlando Furioso,* 350

Harrison, G.B., Prologue (i), 6, 436

Harvey, Gabriel, dramatist, 87; the Cambridge Don, subject of envy, 129; *Gorgon or the wonderfull yeare* (1593), its cryptic style and his *A New Letter of Notable Contents* (1593),

his, to Anne Hathaway, 27;
*Mattingley, Garrett, on the Armada,
334; Mendenhall, Dr., 312; monument
and grave, his, 41; Muse's Darling,
The, identified as Shakespeare, 310;
name, his, on various publications, 2-
5; name as playbroker, 350, 352, 355-
63; doubts about his authorship, 49-51;
Ovid, his knowledge of, 20, 88, 495;
poet of the Sonnets, he fails to qualify
as, 12-13, 23, 60, 80, 143; portraits,
his, 26; the Droeshout engraving, 26;
Schoenbaum, on his life, 25-26; scholarly opinion, 23-5, 67-9, 308; 'Shake-
scene' re-identified, 32-6; Sonnets,
the, writers' comments, also as record
of his life, 6-8, 25-26; *Southampton,
Earl of, 141-4, 243, 356-7; Stratford-
upon-Avon, 22, 24,28, 29-30, 37, 40-
3, 48, 60, 62, 337, 350, 352, 354-5,
359; *Twelfth Night*, the evidence of its
composition, 414, 421-3; *Venus and
Adonis*, 26-7, 28, 47, 48, 54, 62, 124,
133, 356-7; Victorian fantasies about
him, 44-5; Wilson, Dover, comments
and conjectures about his life, 8, 26-7
Shelton, Lady Audrey (later Lady
Walsingham), 76, 114, 166-7
Shelton, Sir John, 166
Shirley, Sir Robert, 408
Shute, John, *Two Very Notable
Commentaries* (1562) 208
Sidney, Mary, Countess of Pembroke,
139
Sidney, Sir Philip, *Astrophel and Stella*,
3, 5, 156; *Arcadia*, 140, 156, 166, 204,
220; patron of Bruno, 274; founder of
the Areopagus, 140, 278; notable free-
thinker, 288, 289, 353
Sidney, Sir Robert, 286
Sisson, C.J., 432
Sixtus V, Pope, 250-2, 371, 388
Skeres, Nicholas, 74, 106-10, 113, 123,
195, 308-9, 372
Sluys, Battle of (1340), 248; (1587), 334
Smart, J.S., 32
Smith, Rev. Henry, 263-4
Socrates, 202, 216, 265, 270
Soer, Dorothy, 301
Sonnets: consensus on autobiographical
content, 6-8, 12-13; Sonnets quoted in
Text on Themes of:- Anonimity: 16,

54-5, 189, 481, 484; Commissioned:
144, 459 ff., 466; written to communicate: 13; to Dark Lady: 205, 222-3,
225-6, 227, 228, 229, 188, 234-5, 452,
517-27; on Disgrace and sudden
eclipse: 11, 59-60, 78, 188, 471-2; on
Exile: 11, 55, 56-7, 127, 184-8, 189,
364, 372-4, 468-71, 472-82, 483-5,
486; on First Love: 453-4, 455;
Identifying himself: 58-9, 67, 77, 88,
108, 500-1; Introspection: 511, 515;
Lameness: 26, 473, 507; Ovidian
influence: 19-20, 488-9; portrait
received from his Patron: 196-7, 477;
religious apostasy, 159, 283-4, 491-2;
Rival Poet: 175-6, 179-80, 502-9; and
remorse over his jealousy: 178, 179,
510-12; Royalty reflected: 155, 437,
445, 447, 449; on Time: 155-6, 434,
439-41, 450, 457, 458, 464, 465, 495,
498, 499; to the True Patron in praise
and gratitude: 73, 216, 219, 486-7,
494-99; his Secret Service: 251-2, 253,
457-8; service in the Armada campaign: 242, 246, 456; satire: 164, 204,
513, 518; on Sex: 165, 202, 205, 218,
518; on venereal infection: 234, 526,
530; on Vilification of his character:
57-8, 66, 198, 497-8, 282-4; to
'Mr.W.H.' in praise of his beauty and
virtue: 150, 152, 154-6, 165, 205, 433-
42; to 'Mr.W.H.' in criticism of his
lasciviousness and faithlessness: 146,
156-7, 158, 159-60, 161, 443-50;
'Will' Hatcliffe his rival in love: 159-
60, 521. See 'The Book of the
Sonnets', Part Three, for all 154 sonnets presented in their Theme Groups,
433-530. Thorpe's edition, its a-
chronological confusion, 146-7; the
mix-up, 438, 444, 447, 482, 486
Southampton, Henry Wriothesley, 3rd
Earl of, 27; doubtful connexion with
Shakespeare, 39, 41, 76; dedication to,
47, 62, 356-7; his secret marriage, 120,
144; his early history, 141-4; sonnets
to him: friendship with Essex,353;
convicted of high treason, 243; his
duel with Lord Grey, 301; his aid to
Danvers brothers to escape the law,
353-4
Southwell, Robert, 29

Warner, Walter, 79, 98, 296, 297, 308
Warren, John, 5
Watson, Thomas, 46, 79, 96; the Bradley affray, 97, 110, 122, 302-3, 301, 306; *Aminta Gaudia*, 139; *Passionate Century of Love* (1582) as sonneteer, 220, 273, 297; *Meliboeus*, 166
Wayte, William, 303
Webster, Archibald, 'Was Marlowe the Man?', 64
Webster, John, *The White Devil* (1612), 46, 176, 371
Weelkes, Thomas, 410
Wells, Stanley, 430-1
'W.H., Mr.', in first edition of the Sonnets, its cryptic dedication to him, 2, 4, 18; Benson's edition erases him, 5; Hotson's trail, 14, 17-18, 19-21, 139-44; Foster's theory, 14-17; the riddle that has baffled scholars, 1-2, 6-9, 10-13; 'Mr.W.H.' is Will Hatcliffe! Hotson's identification, 18-20, 145-62, 190-7, 229-31; his 'royalty' as Prince of Purpoole, 436, 439, 440; his inception as patron of his sonneteer, 149-50; his Poet's valediction to his first young patron whose virtue was flawed, 450; not the sole patron of the Sonnets, 139, 145-7
White, John, 351
Whitgift, Archbishop, Privy Councillor, his witch-hunt against free-thinkers, 65, 103, 112, 120, 123, 291-2; his signature on Privy Council letter about Marlowe, 88, 103; censor of literature, 133, 207, 388; reference to him in the Gloss on *Gorgon?* 135, 137; a Puritan preacher, 340; his death, 346, 383; present at performance of *Twelfth Night*, 404
Whitney, Blanche, 116
Wilkens, Iman, Prologue (ii) (iii), *Where Troy Once Stood* (1990)
Williams, Dr. C.B., Acknowledgements (v) and Chapter 20
Williams, George Hunston, *The Radical Reformation* (1962), 352
Williams, Sir Roger, 334
Wilson, J. Dover, *The Essential Shakespeare*, 8, 26, 27, 28
Wilson, Thomas, 251
Winny, James, *The Master-Mistress: A Study of Shakespeare's Sonnets* (1968), 8
Winston, Giles, 303
Winter's Tale, The, 344, 368
Winwood, Sir Ralph, 388, 389, 415
Wolfe, John, 131-3, 135, 172
Wolsey, Cardinal, 290, 402
Wood, Anthony à, *Athenae Oxoniensis*, 30, 38
Woodleff, Drew, 110
Woodward, John, 357
Worcester, Earl of, 415
Wordsworth, William, 1, 8; *Ode to Immortality*, 217
Wraight, A.D., *Christopher Marlowe and Edward Alleyn* (1993), 31, 364; *Christopher Marlowe and the Armada*, 95, 239, 246, 359n; with Virginis F. Stern, *In Search of Christopher Marlowe* (1965, 1993) 360n
Wychegerde, Jan, 91
Wyse, 307

Yates, Frances, *Giordano Bruno and the Hermetic Tradition* (1964), 274; *The Rosicrucian Enlightenment* (1972), 351; *Astraea: The Imperial Theme of the Sixteenth Century*, 363

Zutphen, Battle of, 140
Zonares, 264

585